Fodor's
see it™

germany

WITHDRAWN

FODOR'S TRAVEL PUBLICATIONS
NEW YORK • TORONTO • LONDON • SYDNEY • AUCKLAND

WWW.FODORS.COM

Contents

KEY TO SYMBOLS

- ✚ Map reference
- ✉ Address
- ☎ Telephone number
- 🕐 Opening times
- ✋ Admission prices
- Ⓤ U-Bahn/S-Bahn station
- 🚌 Bus number
- 🚉 Train station
- ⛴ Ferry/boat
- 🚗 Driving directions
- ℹ Tourist office
- 🎫 Tours
- 📖 Guidebook
- 🍽 Restaurant
- ☕ Café
- 🍷 Bar
- 🛍 Shop
- 🚻 Toilets
- ① Number of rooms
- 🅿 Parking
- 🚭 No smoking
- ❄ Air conditioning
- 🏊 Swimming pool
- 🏋 Gym
- ❓ Other useful information
- 🛍 Shopping
- 🎭 Entertainment
- 🍸 Nightlife
- ⚽ Sports
- ★ Activities
- ♥ Health and Beauty
- 👶 For Children
- ▷ Cross reference
- ★ Walk/drive start point

2

HOW TO USE THIS BOOK

Understanding Germany is an introduction to the country, its geography, economy and people. **Living Germany** gives an insight into Germany today, while **The Story of Germany** takes you through the country's past.

For detailed advice on getting to Germany—and getting around once you are there—turn to **On the Move**. For useful practical information, from weather forecasts to emergency services, turn to **Planning**.

Out and About gives you the chance to explore Germany through walks, drives and organized tours.

The **Sights**, **What to Do**, **Eating** and **Staying** sections are divided geographically into six regions, which are shown on the map on the inside front cover. These regions always appear in the same order. Towns and places of interest are listed alphabetically within each region.

Map references for the **Sights** refer to the atlas section at the end of this book or to the individual town plans. For example, Hamburg has the reference ✚ 429 F4, indicating the page on which the map is found (429) and the grid square in which Hamburg sits (F4).

UNDERSTANDING GERMANY

Germany is not only blessed with varied and beautiful scenery, but also
has a multifaceted past that has endowed it with a rich tapestry of
historic buildings, art collections and fascinating towns and cities.
Perhaps the most misrepresented country in western Europe, the new
Germany has much to offer curious and open-minded visitors, from a
bracing dip in the Baltic Sea off its northern shores to culture of every
kind in Berlin, label-hunting in Munich's boutiques, and skiing and
hiking in the Alps. Germany is divided into 16 administrative regions,
known as *Länder*. Some of these *Länder*, like Berlin and Bremen, are
city states, while others, like Bavaria, cover hundreds of square kilometres. Some 130 years after Chancellor Otto von Bismarck brought the
disparate German states together, regional identities remain strong, and
visitors will still discover distinctive local traditions and accents today.

Germany is now unified under one flag

LANDSCAPE

With an area of 356,978sq
km (137,829sq miles),
Germany is one of west-
ern Europe's biggest
nations. It is about 450km
(280 miles) at its widest
and some 853km (530
miles) long, and it has
907km (564 miles) of
coastline along the North and Baltic seas. The
internal border separating the former German
Democratic Republic (GDR) and Federal
Republic of Germany (FDR) cut off 107,680sq
km (41,575sq miles) to the east and ran for
1,393km (866 miles). Germany shares a border
with nine other European countries: France, the
Netherlands, Belgium, Luxembourg, Switzerland,
Austria, the Czech Republic, Poland and Denmark.

North-flowing rivers delimit large stretches of
both Germany's western and eastern borders,
while the Bavarian Alps mark the country's
southern edges and contain the Zugspitze, its
highest peak at 2,962m (9,718ft). Along the
western border is the Rhine valley, whose steep
castle-topped banks are the quintessence of
Romantic Germany. The Schwarzwald (Black
Forest), and Swabian, Harz and Bohemian
ranges are all lower than the Alps, but are still
high enough for winter sports. Elsewhere, the
landscape is characterized by fertile valleys, hills
cloaked in deciduous and spruce trees, and, to
the north, low-lying plains.

POLITICS

Since reunification in 1989,
political life has largely followed the relatively stable
model established in post-war
West Germany. The head of
state is the president, elected
for a renewable five-year term
of office by an equal number
of national and regional
deputies. Day-to-day decision-making power,
however, lies with the chancellor, who is elected
by the 669 members of the Bundestag (lower
house) on a proposal from the president. Willy
Brandt, former mayor of Berlin and the first
leader to begin negotiations with the GDR, and
Helmut Kohl, who presided over German reunification, are the best-known chancellors.

The Bundestag's members are voted for in
parliamentary elections, while the upper house,
the Bundesrat, is made up of representatives
from the 16 *Länder*. The two main post-war parties have been the Christian Democrats (CDU)
and the Social Democrats (SDU), but the Green
Party, one of Europe's strongest, has now taken
over the Free Democrats' former role as king-
maker. At the regional level, each of the 16
Länder has its own *Landrat*, or parliament, and
these exert considerable influence through the
Bundesrat. Built on consensus, the German federal system does not easily lend itself to swift or
radical change, and has been criticized in recent
years for holding back much-needed reform.

ECONOMY

The first years of the 21st century have seen Germany's economy stumble as the 'miracle' of post-war reconstruction gives way to the harsh realities of globalization, an ageing workforce and increased labour unrest. Politicians are reluctant to administer an overdue but painful revamp of the generous state welfare system, while the banks and management press for urgent structural changes, lower taxation and greater flexibility in employment legislation.

Growth has been slower than predicted in recent years, unemployment has remained high, especially in the east, and the European Union has expressed dissatisfaction at a budget deficit that exceeds 3 per cent. Despite this, the general standard of living remains higher than in many other European countries, and Germany continues to play a leading role in the motor vehicle, electronic goods, electrical machinery and metal industries, as well as in the chemical and pharmaceutical industries. Former industrial areas such as the Ruhr have suffered badly following the decline of heavy industry and mining, and regional authorities are making efforts to develop a strong tertiary sector—although competition from eastern European countries with cheaper workforces poses challenges.

The Zugspitze (left) is Germany's highest peak; the Brocken (middle) in the Harz Mountains is popular with hikers; and the Rhine (right), Germany's principal river

GERMANY'S REGIONS

NORTHERN GERMANY

Bremen is a city state that was formerly a member of the Hanseatic League, an alliance of trade ports that stretched across northern Europe and the Baltics. The region consists of Bremen itself and the smaller town of Bremerhaven, an important port 65km (40 miles) downstream on the Weser. Bremen's riverside location made it an important hub for shipping and trade, both of which continue to play dominant roles in the state's modern economy.

Hamburg is another city state and is Germany's second-largest metropolitan area, with a long history that reflects its strategic maritime role. Liberal, lively and full of parks (40 per cent of the city's area is made up of gardens, parks, woodland and arable land), it's a cosmopolitan place with plenty of culture.

Niedersachsen (Lower Saxony) is second only to Bavaria in size, and stretches from the North Sea to the Harz mountains. It is one of the least densely populated regions in Germany, making it a wonderful place for visitors who want to get away from it all and take part in outdoor activities. Destinations such as the Harz Mountains, the Ostfriesische Inseln (East Friesian Islands) and the orchard-covered lowlands provide a varied natural setting, and make a pleasant contrast to Hannover, the state capital. Although the automobile firm Volkswagen is the area's largest employer, agriculture continues to play an important economic role.

Mecklenburg-Vorpommern (Mecklenburg-Lower Pomeriana) remains a largely agricultural state, with thousands of lakes and a diverse coastline edging the Baltic Sea. The region attracts both German and foreign visitors, who come to explore the white cliffs of Rügen, the dozens of nature reserves and the state's superb architectural heritage. Rapidly developing towns such as Rostock are helping to change the region's economic climate.

Schleswig-Holstein lies between the North and the Baltic seas, and as the most northerly of Germany's states has complex linguistic and historical traditions (Danish and Friesian minorities here both speak their own languages). Lübeck's red-brick architecture is a major draw, as are the long beaches and opportunities for sailing.

WESTERN GERMANY

Hessen (Hesse) is a prosperous region that lies at the heart of modern German life: Frankfurt am Main is a major financial and commercial hub, while Kassel draws the international art world to its Documenta exhibitions. The wooded hills and waterways of Waldecker *Land*, meanwhile, provide a pleasant contrast to settlements such as Wiesbaden (the state capital) and Marburg, a romantic university town. Vineyards play an important role in the state's economy: Riesling from the Eltville area is the most appreciated of the local wines.

Nordrhein-Westfalen (North Rhine-Westphalia) has the highest population of all of Germany's *Länder*. Once dependent on heavy industry, particularly along the Ruhr valley, it has experienced considerable change over recent decades, so that service industries now employ more than 60 per cent of the workforce. Agricultural land covers more than half the territory, however, and there is a good balance of outdoor pursuits in areas such as the northern Eifel mountains and Teutoburger Wald (Teutoburg Forest), and fascinating cities such as Köln (Cologne) and Aachen.

Rheinland-Pfalz (Rhineland-Palatinate) is a wonderfully scenic region, where vine-covered slopes rise from the winding Rhine and tributaries such as the Mosel. Picturesque castles, wine routes and historic towns such as Trier are dotted around the state.

Saarland, the country's smallest region, nestles in the hilly triangle where Germany shares its

Schloss Sanssouci (left) at Potsdam is one of Eastern Germany's highlights; try the local brew in one of Munich's beer gardens (middle); and the Alpine peaks soar in Berchtesgaden Land (right)

borders with Luxembourg and France. Its ownership was disputed for centuries, but it finally became part of the German Federal Republic in 1957. Saarland's location is ideal for trade fairs, and the capital, Saarbrücken, attracts students from across Europe. The state's industrial heritage is best seen at the Völklingen ironworks.

BERLIN

As the country's political hub, Berlin is at the heart of the new Germany's transformation. Wonderful museums, extensive parks and vibrant streets make it a fascinating place to visit, while its proximity to eastern Europe adds further interest.

EASTERN GERMANY

Brandenburg is a largely rural region, although its capital, Potsdam, contains some of Germany's most attractive palaces and formal gardens. The area's landscape is harmonious rather than dramatic, with lowland plains, the Spree and Havel rivers, and several nature reserves, including the Nationalpark Unteres Odertal (Lower Oder National Park), which extends into Poland and is jointly managed by the two countries.

Sachsen (Saxony) has as its biggest draw the beautiful city of Dresden, while Leipzig is another town of considerable historical and cultural interest. The population density is high here, and some places have been heavily and unattractively industrialized. That said, the Erzgebirge Mountains, the highest range in eastern Germany, along with the imposing rock formations of Sächsische Schweiz (Saxon Switzerland), lure visitors away from the urban areas.

Sachsen-Anhalt (Saxony-Anhalt) has a varied landscape, with the splendid Harz Mountains to the southwest, flat land to the north (the Altmark) and heavily industrialized areas to the east near Dessau and Halle. It is home to the historic town of Wittenberg, where Martin Luther launched the Reformation in 1517, and Madgeburg, the capital, which was rebuilt after heavy wartime bombing. The region is crisscrossed by the Salle, Elbe and Wipper rivers.

Thüringen (Thuringia) is sometimes called the 'green heart' of Germany and is a region that preserves many aspects of its traditional lifestyles. It is largely rural, with the mountainous Thüringer Wald (Thuringian Forest) to the south, yet its medieval castles and abbeys speak of a varied and rich history. Weimar, home to the writers Johann von Goethe and Friedrich von Schiller, and,

The winged figure of Victory on top of Berlin's Siegesäule

Germany is divided into 12 Lander and three city states: Berlin, Bremen and Hamburg

more generally, to the German Enlightenment movement, is one of the country's cultural treasures. Erfurt is the well-preserved capital of this fairly compact *Land*, which also contains several winter sports resorts.

MUNICH

While not, strictly speaking, a separate region, München (Munich) has a vibrant urban atmosphere that distinguishes it from the rest of Bavaria. As an artistic and media hub, it contains superb galleries and museums, while its baroque and rococo churches attest to a long tradition of religious patronage.

SOUTHERN GERMANY

Baden-Württemburg is both a prosperous and picturesque region of southern Germany. The Schwarzwald (Black Forest) and Bodensee (Lake Constance) are just two of its many attractive natural areas, while the towns of Stuttgart, Heidelberg and Freiburg also repay exploration.

Bayern (Bavaria) is Germany's largest state, and has some of its loveliest scenery. Once inhabited by Celts and Romans, the area was formerly divided into dozens of smaller territories. The modern region still has a strong regional identity, but there's more than lederhosen and beer on offer here. Stunning Alpine scenery forms the backdrop for fairy-tale castles and some exceptionally rich ecclesiastical architecture.

THE BEST OF GERMANY

NORTHERN GERMANY

Bremen (▷ 72–73) Wander round the Kunsthalle's impressive art collection, explore the quirky historic district of Schnoorviertel, or just count the ships in one of Germany's busiest ports.

Kiel (▷ 75) Try to visit during the *Kieler Woche*, the glamorous annual regatta held in June, when sailing ships compete with ferries for a place in the harbour.

Hamburg (▷ 76–81) A bustling city with great architecture, a cosmopolitan feel and a strong maritime tradition.

Lübeck (▷ 86–87) This historically important town is famous for its unique brickwork architecture.

Nordfriesische Inseln and Ostfriesische Inseln (▷ 89 and 91) The low-lying North Friesian and East Friesian islands are two different archipelagos, but they share the same natural beauty and a reputation for summer fun.

The quayside at Hamburg (left)

Life in Kiel is focused around its harbour

WESTERN GERMANY

Aachen (▷ 94) Enjoy a Wednesday evening concert under the dome of Charlemagne's cathedral, or have a flutter in the neo-classical casino.

Köln (▷ 100–105) Worth seeing just for its skyline, Cologne is best visited during the pre-Lenten *Karneval*; if the revellers get too much, explore the Dom, one of Europe's most splendid Gothic buildings.

Koblenz (▷ 106) The Mosel flows into the Rhine at Deutsches Eck, literally the 'German corner', and this attractive town has grown up at the confluence.

Saarland (▷ 111) This region's UNESCO-listed Völklingen steel mill commemorates a bygone industrial heritage, while the interior of the Ludwigskirche in Saarbrücken is a white baroque dream.

Rheintal (▷ 112–113) The Rhine flows north along its valley past fortresses and steep vine-covered slopes. While the legendary singing siren may no longer be spotted near Lorelei rock, this remains an enticing and dramatic region.

Ruhrgebiet (▷ 114–115) The Ruhr area has a fascinating industrial legacy, important design museums and art galleries, and, in the city of Dortmund, a long beer-making tradition.

Trier (▷ 116–117) Wonderful and extensive Roman ruins and the oldest cathedral in Germany are the main attractions of Trier, which was the birthplace of Karl Marx.

The formal gardens at Herrenhäuser, Hannover

Köln's towering cathedral dominates the skyline

BERLIN

Fernsehturm (▷ 125) Take in a 360-degree view of Berlin from the top of the television tower.

Brandenburg Tor (▷ 128) A symbol of historical and contemporary upheaval, the Brandenburg Gate is one of Berlin's most recognizable landmarks.

Gemäldegalerie (▷ 130–135) All the major European schools of painting are represented in this masterpiece-studded collection.

Jüdisches Museum (▷ 136) A museum with a disorientating and disturbing exterior, and an intelligently designed and thought-provoking interior.

Pergamonmuseum (▷ 138–143) The enormous Pergamon Altar and the stunning Ishtar Gate from Babylon are among this museum's highlights.

Reichstag (▷ 145) Weighted with historical significance and now topped with a symbol of transparent government, Germany's parliament building is a must-see.

Tiergarten (▷ 148–149) The green lung in the heart of Berlin is the ideal spot for a stroll or a Sunday afternoon picnic.

Take a trip along the Mosel, starting at Koblenz

The Pergamonmuseum, Berlin

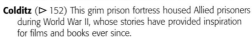

THE BEST OF GERMANY

EASTERN GERMANY

The Quadriga on top of the Brandenburg Gate, Berlin

Colditz (▷ 152) This grim prison fortress housed Allied prisoners during World War II, whose stories have provided inspiration for films and books ever since.

Dessau (▷ 153) This key location for Bauhaus architecture is surrounded by acres of landscaped park.

Dresden (▷ 154–158) Having overcome wartime bombing, flooding and neglect, Dresden is once again a visually stunning city with a renowned cultural heritage.

Potsdam (▷ 168–173) Brandenburg's capital is best known for its palaces and its magnificent Sanssouci park. It makes an excellent day trip from Berlin, although it is really best explored at greater leisure.

Sächsische Schweiz (▷ 174) Visit the untamed region of Saxon Switzerland to explore its bizarre rock formations, good hiking territory and attractive spa towns.

Spreewald (▷ 175) Take a punt around this UNESCO Biosphere Reserve and try some of the local pickled gherkins.

Weimar (▷ 176) This town is the historic heart of German literary and intellectual life.

The Zwinger in Dresden

MUNICH

Asamkirche (▷ 184) No other church in Germany can match this over-the-top feast of rococo architecture.

Hofbräuhaus (▷ 185) Come to this huge beerhall and shaded beer garden for the archetypal Bavarian experience.

Deutsches Museum (▷ 186–191) 'How does it work?' This vast and fascinating museum, full of interest for adults and children alike, provides the answers.

Englischer Garten (▷ 192) Surf, paddle, stroll or sunbathe in Munich's own central park, a natural haven for busy city-dwellers.

Marienplatz (▷ 193) Sit over a beer or coffee in the summer, or hunt for presents in the Christmas market—this is the city's real heart.

Schloss Nymphenburg (▷ 200–201) Relax in the grounds of this vast baroque palace, or admire the models portrayed in the Schönheitengalerie (Gallery of Beauties).

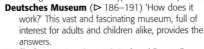

Surf's up in Munich's Englisher Garten

Raising a stein (right)

SOUTHERN GERMANY

Baden-Baden (▷ 206) Take the waters in the outdoor pools used by Roman Emperor Caracalla, or test your luck in the classy casino.

Berchtesgadener Land (▷ 208–209) Alpine lakes, snow-covered peaks and scenic villages make this a spectacular place to explore.

Garmisch-Partenkirchen (▷ 216) Germany's winter sports capital has a well-deserved reputation: Come here for skiing, snowboarding or après-ski.

Heidelberg (▷ 214–215) Stroll along the Philosopher's Way, cross the Neckar on the old stone bridge or catch an open-air performance in the grounds of the imposing Schloss.

Nürnberg (▷ 218–219) Medieval and modern history combine in the busy town of Nuremberg. Its Christmas market is atmospheric and very popular.

Schloss Neuschwanstein (▷ 224–227) Ignore the crowds and soak up the atmosphere of the original fairy-tale castle and its beautiful setting.

Stuttgart (▷ 228–229) Pay homage to the German motor car industry at the Mercedes Benz Museum—even if you don't drive, you'll admire these beautiful cars.

Looking over Heidelberg

The Porsche Museum, Stuttgart

TOP 15 EXPERIENCES

Indulge in *Kaffe und Küchen* (coffee and cakes) at a Konditorei, where you can choose from huge slices of mouthwatering cheesecake, rich Black Forest gateau or tangy fruit tart.

Hunt for presents at an atmospheric Christmas market, or simply chase away the end-of-year chill with a glass of warm *Glühwein* (mulled wine) and spicy *Lebküchen* (gingerbread).

Relax in ornate 19th-century thermal baths, or plump for a more modern spa experience; both are on offer at Baden-Baden and other classic resorts.

Take a boat trip on one of Germany's many rivers and lakes. You can opt for anything from a one-hour round trip on Bodensee (Lake Constance) to a week-long cruise down the Rhine or the Danube.

Examine artistic masterpieces from every era in Germany's excellent collections. Every region has at least one fine museum or art gallery, while art lovers are spoiled for choice in the main cities.

Join in the pre-Lenten carnival atmosphere in towns and villages along the Rhine. Centuries-old traditions are revived each year as people dress up and entire communities look forward to the arrival of spring.

Wander around a castle or palace, choosing from among the dozens of historical monuments that are open to visitors—from stern fortresses and romantic ruins to the elegant homes of former rulers.

Hike or cross-country ski along mountain paths that have been marked out for sporting enthusiasts from the Schwarzwald (Black Forest) to the Harz Mountains.

Learn to distinguish between the hundreds of local beers, starting in Bamberg, with its dozens of breweries, and then joining thousands of drinking buddies at Munich's *Oktoberfest*.

Party all night to the latest techno rhythms in Berlin (its nightlife is one of the liveliest in Europe), or relax to the more traditional sounds of a world-class orchestra at one of the countless concert venues.

Escape to the mountains to climb a summit under your own steam, race downhill on a challenging ski run or simply enjoy the après-ski.

Take the easy way up on one of the funiculars or cable cars that provide access to hilltop walks and stunning views. The narrow-gauge railway through the Harz Mountains adds another dimension to mountain climbing.

Island-hop in the North and Baltic seas. From car-less Helgoland to rugged Rügen, Germany's islands have a unique maritime history and a relaxing get-away-from-it-all atmosphere.

Window-shop for German fashion, as every city has a chic retail district as well as more affordable outlets. Düsseldorf is the fashion capital, while leading designers such as Jil Sanders are based in Hamburg.

Partake in a wine-tasting at a local vineyard to see why Germany's wine-makers are now winning a greater share of the international market.

Sample one of Germany's many different beers (below left)

Taking a break from shopping on Berlin's busy Ku'damm

Cruising on Berlin's canals makes a great day trip

Dressing up for Karneval

Visit the Alps on the Bayrische Zugspitzbahn

Ludwig II's Schloss Linderhof

Shopping for souvenirs in Munich (left)

Living Germany

A moment of reflection for Formula 1's Michael Schumacher (below)

Snowboarding is popular in Germany's mountainous South (below left)

In 1985, German tennis player Boris Becker became the youngest ever winner of Wimbledon (left)

Sports and Leisure

Whether as enthusiastic spectators or hands-on participants, many Germans love sports. Good facilities exist for most activities, and organized sports clubs are very popular. The country's natural diversity allows for a full range of outdoor sporting activities, from bracing beach holidays by the North Sea to water sports in Alpine lakes and skiing and snow-boarding in the mountain regions.

The whole family takes to the water at Heilbronn

The most keenly watched professional sport is soccer, with fans focusing their hopes on young stars such as Michael Ballack and dreaming of a fourth World Cup victory (the most recent was in 1990). Tennis fans are hoping that a new generation of *wunderkinds* such as Thomas Haas will replace the superstars Boris Becker and Steffi Graf. Motor-racing's Michael Schumacher is a sporting legend, but Formula 1 races in Hockenheim are watched as much for the cars as the drivers. Leisure time is also used by all generations for domestic and foreign travel, and for shopping, albeit to a lesser extent than in other countries such as the UK and US.

Successful Steering

Behind every motor-racing champion is a team of technicians and design experts—not to mention a manager. Michael Schumacher, one of the world's highest-paid sportsmen, races for the Italian firm Ferrari but has been managed since 1983 by Bavarian Willi Weber. Weber recognized the young Schumacher's talent and took him into his Formula 3 WTS team in 1989, paying Schumacher's considerable costs for his first few seasons; in return, 'Schumi' agreed to hand over 20 per cent of his winnings. Since Schumacher moved to Formula 1 in 1991, Weber has continued to manage his career (as he does for Schumacher's younger brother Ralf).

Germans love to keep fit, and inline skating (right) is great exercise

Frankfurt's cyclists hit the streets *en masse* (left)

Berlin's Olympic Stadium (below), home to the 1936 Games

Germans on Holiday

Post-war prosperity opened up leisure travel to West Germans, and the industry is now huge. Foreign travel declined after the terrorist attacks of September 2001, but Germans are once again returning to foreign destinations for their annual *Urlaub* (vacation). Spain, Italy and Greece are their preferred European destinations, but the number of Germans holidaying within their own country has risen in recent years. Almost a third now take their main holiday in Germany (Mecklenburg-Vorpommern and Bavaria are the top domestic destinations). Reflecting ongoing economic differences, only half of East Germans go abroad, compared with 65 per cent of West Germans. Habits are changing: People are taking shorter and less frequent breaks, and tend to organize their own trips with low-cost airlines, last-minute deals or discounted advance bookings.

Health and Wealth

Baden-Baden might be the country's best-known spa, but many other towns have built their economy around the 'wellness' industry, which employs more than 600,000 people nationwide. After World War II, a generous medical insurance system enabled West Germans to take two- or three-week thermal 'cures' at the state's expense. The official Register of Health Spas identified those health resorts to which doctors could send patients to 'take the waters', and entitlement to visit a health spa was an integral part of employment conditions. Although the state has stopped paying for 'preventative' visits to health resorts since 2003, Germans are even entitled to go abroad if the specific treatment they need isn't available nationally— an option confirmed in March 2004 by the European Court of Justice.

Day of Rest

Germany's strict legislation on opening hours has long been a source of frustration. Until recently, most shops would close at lunchtime on Saturday, and while a few stores were allowed to remain open until 4pm, further consumer spending had to wait until Monday. In June 2003, the Bundestag (parliament) passed legislation enabling shops to remain open until 8pm on Saturdays, but Sunday trading still remains out of the question. Trade unions have so far resisted any calls for seven-day opening. Fuel stations are exempt from this rule, and make handsome profits from Sunday sales of bread and beer. In addition, retailers can now hold discount sales at any time, rather than during the traditionally designated end-of-season periods. As the country struggles to avoid recession, bargain-happy customers may be one way to keep the economy moving.

A Place to Dream

Munich's 1972 Olympic village was heralded as the most technologically and architecturally innovative design of its type: A high transparent roof swept over a 62,000-seat stadium, ice-rink, swimming complex and vast hall, and tall steel girders created a tent-like effect. After the ill-fated games (▷ 43), the city faced the challenge of ensuring that these purpose-built facilities benefited the Bavarian community and sporting enthusiasts. Two soccer teams came to the rescue: FC Bayern Munich, German and European cup winners; and TSV 1860 Munich, their lesser-known local rivals. For over two decades the teams shared the stadium, entertaining fans and attracting big-name visitors. The arrangement ended in 2004, when the city authorities decided that the entire Olympic complex needed major facelift: The refurbished stadium will be used for other sports.

A giant illuminated Ferris wheel (left)

National costume is often worn for festivals (above)

A street entertainer poses as a statue (left)

Fun and Festivals

Germans like to enjoy themselves. Of all the stereotypes about Germany, the image of a serious and *angst*-ridden nation is farthest from the mark. Although a deeply conventional streak certainly runs through society, this is more than balanced by an equally strong interest in creativity, counter-culture and sheer fun. In Berlin, cabaret was developed into an art form, techno music first had its own city-wide parade and entire districts are known for their 'alternative' lifestyles. Throughout the country, the year is punctuated by great popular festivals that are as lively today as they ever were. These annual bouts of revelry and merry-making see thousands of ordinary people putting on fancy dress and letting their hair down in events that frequently tap into fairy-tales and pagan legends.

Whether clubbing with Europe's trendiest DJs or waltzing to a small-town brass band, Germans believe in making the most of life. Reality shows, game shows and comedies litter the TV schedules, and the national sense of humour is alive and well (if sometimes impenetrable to non-German speakers).

Women Rule the Rhine

Cologne's pre-Lenten *Karneval* is one of Germany's oldest and most boisterous festivals. It begins on the Thursday before Ash Wednesday, and the first day's festivities are always the same: The day is called *Weiberfasnacht* and, for once, women are in charge of proceedings. It's not clear when women began to enjoy this prerogative, but they have (almost) free rein to break everyday conventions. Sensible men take precautions and don fancy dress in sympathy—anyone caught in business clothing is likely to have the end of his tie snipped off by trophy-collectors. Along the Rhine valley, singing groups of women 'storm' their local government premises, where mayors symbolically hand over the keys to the city.

Traditional brass bands (left) still perform at Bavarian weddings

Cabaret is alive and kicking at La Vie en Rose, Berlin (left)

We're Only Here for the Beer

It's the Big Daddy of beer festivals: 16 days of frothing beer mugs, fairground rides and concerts. Munich's *Oktoberfest* began as a celebration of the future King Ludwig's wedding in 1810, and has grown into the world's largest annual party, with 7 million visitors descending on 14 beer tents in the Bavarian capital. The festivities open in mid-September with the arrival of horse-drawn brewery wagons, much pomp and the ceremonial tapping of a beer keg. Over the next two weeks, a folklore concert, a spectacular costume parade (with lots of *lederhosen*) and brass-band concerts provide an ongoing excuse for downing even more beer—5.5 million litres (1.5 million US gallons) are drunk by the first Sunday in October, when city life returns to normal and the seven Munich breweries count their profits.

The Camera Never Sleeps

In recent years, 'reality' television shows have had a big impact on Germany's screens. The German version of *Big Brother*, the series in which contestants live together and are gradually voted out by viewers, has been as controversial here as in other countries—the leader of the Hesse region attempted to have it taken off the air in March 2000, arguing that it violated the constitutional provisions on human dignity. The series is filmed in a house outside Cologne, and has attracted celebrity visitors (such as Chancellor Schröder's half-brother) and fame-hungry competitors. At least one marriage has taken place (after the second series), but producers must continually come up with new challenges, especially as each run now lasts 12 months.

One for All

In the ideological 1960s, anarchist and hippie communes were created in Berlin and Hamburg as a reaction against 'middle-class' values of individualism and consumerism. Today, increasing numbers of young urban professionals are opting to join a *Wohngemeinschaft* (flat-sharing community), but for different reasons. Berlin's 19th-century apartment blocks have numerous rooms leading off long hallways; and renting one of these rooms, splitting bills and sharing a kitchen and bathroom facilities may be cheaper than finding a one-person flat. Commitments usually include a weekly meeting and may involve socializing, but the counter-culture has long disappeared: The magazine *Der Spiegel* even ran a competition in 2003 to identify the country's best *Wohngemeinschaft*.

Raising the Spirits

In Germany, Schnapps is a general term for any kind of spirit that warms you up on the inside. A sixth of all Germany's schnapps distilleries are in the Freiburg region of Germany, most of them on Black Forest farms. An ancient church edict gave Black Forest farmers the right to distil their own schnapps, and the ruling still applies today. Farms with distillery rights are allowed to produce and sell locally 350 litres (80 gallons) a year. If a distillery falls into disuse, it cannot be revived and no further concessions are given. The best Black Forest schnapps is made from cherries (the famous Kirsch), but you can also find excellent ones produced from damsons (Pfümli) and Williams pears (Williams).

Schnapps is served in small measures (2cl/ 0.65fl oz), but once a bottle has been opened, it gradually loses its taste, so it's best shared with friends.

Street sculpture in Berlin (left)

Frankfurt is home to modern ballet (right)

German Culture

Modern art with a serious message: This memorial to those killed while fleeing to the West is made from armoured cars

Contemporary German artists and musicians are following in the footsteps of a wealth of illustrious predecessors: In the fields of the visual arts, classical music and literature, Germany has been at the forefront of European artistic life for centuries. Ecclesiastical and aristocratic patronage enabled artists such as Albrecht Dürer (1471–1528) and Matthias Grünewald (c1470–1528) to flourish, and Caspar David Friedrich (1774–1840) and Emil Nolde (1867–1956), to name but two, played important roles in the Romantic and Expressionist movements respectively. The country's role as a leader in the modern art world is confirmed by the Kassel Documenta, the Art Forum Berlin and the Kunstmesse Köln, which attract international artists.

Composers such as Ludwig van Beethoven, Johann Sebastian Bach and Richard Wagner need no introduction, and the great orchestras of Berlin, Munich and Leipzig still generate controversy and enthusiasm. Music festivals, often concentrating on the work of a single composer, are held throughout the summer—the Wagner festival in Bayreuth is the best known.

Cannes in the Cold

After Cannes and Venice, the Berlinale film festival is the third biggest in Europe. The location isn't as chic as the French Riviera (and in any case, the festival is held in February, so there's little chance of would-be starlets stripping down to their bikinis for the cameras), but according to the festival's organizers, 16,000 industry professionals from more than 100 countries come here to do serious business away from the awards ceremony. This makes sense, since Germany is Europe's largest market for films and is where big-money deals can be reached. On the artistic front, the Golden and Silver Bear awards are much prized, and recognition in Berlin often means further commerical and artistic success.

The world-famous Passion Play, performed by the citizens of Oberammergau every 10 years (left)

The Documenta modern art exhibition (above) is held in Kassel every five years—the next is in 2007

Installation art at Frankfurt's Schirn Kunsthalle (left)

Hollywood on the Iser

Das Boot (The Boat), Wolfgang Petersen's claustrophobic submarine drama, has been one of German cinema's most successful exports since it first gripped cinema-goers and television audiences in 1981. Based on an autobiographical bestseller by Lothar-Günther Buchheim (1918–), the six-hour production was the most expensive German film ever made at the time, at a cost of US$14 million. Shot at the Bavarian Filmstadt near Munich (▷ 278), home of German cinema since 1919, *Das Boot* rekindled discussion of U-boat crews' forgotten wartime role. Much of the set is still preserved at the studios, including the reconstructed submarine, which was composed of three separate sections to facilitate shooting. The submarine subsequently appeared briefly at the end of Steven Spielberg's *Raiders of the Lost Ark* (1981).

Schmaltzing Along

A frequent source of amusement and irony inside Germany and abroad is *Schlager*, a form of popular music that continues to draw crowds and sell CDs. Characterized by overly sentimental lyrics and uncomplicated, easily remembered tunes, the ballads are derived from 19th-century operetta, but are perhaps best described as a blend of pop and country-and-western music. The lyrics generally incorporate a 'boy-meets-girl, girl-leaves-boy' scenario, and express feelings of loneliness, disillusionment or, conversely, hope. Widely regarded as kitsch and musically unsophisticated, *Schlager*'s catchy tunes nonetheless appeal to a sizeable audience, and are a staple of German airwaves and restaurant sing-alongs. One of *Schlager*'s most famous performers is Heino, best known for 'Schwarz-braun ist die Haselnuss' ('Dark-brown is the Hazelnut').

Bringing Art to the Masses?

In 2003, the Aldi discount supermarket chain commissioned seven contemporary artists to create 140,000 limited-edition etchings and graphic prints, each of which was to be signed and numbered by its creator. These original artworks and limited-edition prints went on sale for €10–15 each in 1,500 of the chain's branches across southern Germany. Artists interested in this new 'retail outlet' included the controversial Felix Droese, who is particularly known for his 1981 installation *I Bumped Off Anne Frank*, which sparked strong criticism. Of the supermarket's idea, Droese told one journalist, 'I have the art and Aldi has the customers'. As a method of removing pictures from the sometimes élitist world of galleries and fairs, such 'off-the-shelf' originals typify the best of Germany's iconoclastic approach to affordable art.

Trees as Art?

At first sight, the planting of *7000 Oaks* in and around Kassel in 1982 didn't have much to do with art. But when each tree was accompanied by a 1.2m (4ft) column of basalt stone, it became clear that this was no ordinary forestry scheme, but a sculpture project created to coincide with that year's Kassel Documenta. The man behind the idea was Joseph Beuys (1921–86), one of post-war Germany's best-known and most controversial artists, who represented his country at the Venice Biennale art exhibitions in 1976 and 1980. Intent on breaking down the barriers between ordinary life and the arts, Beuys argued that artists could help promote environmental change and urban renewal. As his ideas on art's social role developed, he became involved in political activism and was closely connected with the founding of the German Green Party in 1979.

Detail of the intricate brickwork (right) on Germany's *fachwerkhäuser* (timbered buildings)

Munich's glass and aluminium Hypobank headquarters (below)

The new alongside the old—Berlin's Gedachniskirche (above)

Traditional and Modern
Architecture

Germany's regional diversity and plethora of independent states, all with leaders who wished to impress rivals or leave memorials to their piety, have resulted in a multitude of wonderful buildings in a variety of styles. Even small towns find themselves with a Romanesque, Gothic or baroque place of worship, while the Renaissance and neoclassicism are also well represented. In addition, German artists and architects played important roles in developing art nouveau (called *Jugendstil* here) and Modernism. Many fine churches, palaces and castles survived the 20th century's ravages, while others have been carefully reconstructed; one felicitous effect of this was a revival of interest in traditional building crafts.

Modern German homes are generally built with great care, and environmentally friendly materials and designs are commonly used. On a grander scale, showcase buildings such as James Stirling's Staatsgalerie in Stuttgart demonstrate public investment in innovative design, and reunification provided a powerful impetus for rebuilding in Berlin, particularly Sir Norman Foster's glass dome on the Reichstag.

Form follows function, at the Bauhaus, Dessau

Inner-city Industry

In December 2001, Volkswagen opened the Gläserne Manufaktur (literally 'glass factory') amid Dresden's baroque churches and palaces. Designed by the Munich architect Günter Henn, the new assembly plant (for VW's luxury Phaeton model) is an ultra-modern set of buildings, filled with light. A circular 40m (131ft) glass tower, in which completed cars are stored, rises from the main structure, while smaller pods emerge from the sides. The complex is in parkland in the Strassburger Platz, and components are delivered on environmentally friendly freight trams. The futuristic VW factory marks a new departure in design. Here, industry is enhancing Dresden's heritage rather than detracting from the city's resurrected beauty.

The Reichstag's glass dome (right)

Decoration from Munich's first Jugendstil house (right)

The clocktower on Count Lennart Bernadotte's Mainau Island (right)

Painted houses (left) are popular in Southern Germany

The Washing Machine

Post-reunification Berlin was both a giant construction site and an architect's dream. However, not all the new buildings have met with unanimous approval. The new Federal Chancellery, designed by Axel Schultes and Charlotte Frank and opened in May 2001 at a cost of €263 million, was described as 'too monumental' by Chancellor Schröder, who feared that the building's vast proportions would send out the wrong message about German ambitions. The newspaper Die Welt labelled it a 'concrete monster', and Berlin residents have given it their own name: the washing machine. Yet the design is highly symbolic: A ribbon of government buildings brings together West and East, crossing the former borderline twice, and the spacious arches are intended to create an impression of governmental transparency.

Preserved Heritage

After World War II, the GDR set to work redeveloping bombed cities such as Berlin and Leipzig, although frequently with unattractive results. Fortunately, the former Hanseatic port of Wismar (▷ 92) was only slightly damaged by bombing and was neglected by authorities. Inadvertently, they preserved the town: Restoration work was left undone, but the buildings themselves remained. Wismar's circular street layout has stayed unchanged for centuries, and about a quarter of the building façades in the middle of town are listed for their historical importance. Since reunification and an injection of European Union funds, Wismar and nearby Stralsund have been spruced up (without destruction) and designated as a Unesco World Heritage Site, bringing in cultural and historical visitors—and reassuring locals who felt that the money would have been better spent on direct job creation.

Living in a Glass House

One of the most innovative and radical buildings erected in Germany in recent years is a family home: House R 128 (alias Römerstrasse 128), on a hillside overlooking Stuttgart, was designed by the engineer Werner Sobek in 2000. The minimalist four-floored house was intended to be recyclable, emission-free and self-sufficient in its use of energy. Built around a steel frame, it has no brick walls, merely glass panels. Except for the sanitary facilities, everything is open plan. Triple glazing (rarely used in European housing) prevents overheating in the summer, and electricity is generated by 48 solar-power modules on the roof. As a home, Römerstrasse 128 has little intimacy and even less furniture. As a contribution to environmentally sustainable futuristic lifestyles, however, it's a daring experiment—and, in its own way, a beautiful building.

Bauhaus

Disillusioned with traditional 'academic' approaches to training, Walter Gropius (1883–1969) opened the Bauhaus school of architecture and applied arts in Weimar in 1919. With its emphasis on functionalism and the search for Neue Sachlichkeit (new objectivity), Bauhaus's impact on modern architecture was immense, both inside and outside Germany. In 1927, some 16 architects—including Le Corbusier, Mies van der Rohe, Peter Behrens and Gropius himself—came together to design the Weissenhof Estate in Stuttgart. The 21-house project exemplified the movement's approach: clean lines, flat roofs, large windows and a daring use of new materials. The Nazis condemned the architects as 'decadent', and the school closed its doors in 1933. Wartime bombing destroyed several of the Weissenhof houses, but 11 can still be seen today (▷ 153).

Engineers at Siemens check the large steam turbines (right)

A Junghaus radio-controlled watch (left)

The Mercedes-Benz S Coupe

Bosch is a top name in kitchen appliances, like this built-in oven (above) and high-speed washing machine (below)

Science and Technology

Germany has been a leading industrial nation since the 19th century, when it exported steel and coal to the world. However, it really came into its own as Europe's pre-eminent scientific and technological nation in the second half of the 20th century. While engineering and the chemical industry have formed the backbone of industrial progress, the IT industry, pharmaceutical and biomedical laboratories now attract international scientists, and the European Patent Office's location in Munich reflects Germany's standing as a heartland for innovative and applied research. Much of Germany's manufacturing output is destined for export, whether medical drugs and equipment, aircraft components or electronic goods. The port of Hamburg is the main focus of cargo transportation. Food processing, textiles and environmental technology are also important employers.

But progress has brought moral dilemmas—pharmaceutical companies, for example, have been criticized for not sharing information about AIDS medication with poorer nations. Globalization is also raising challenges for both industrial giants and for the government, with jobs being outsourced to Eastern Europe or Asia.

Beetling Along

The classic Beetle (or *Käfer* in German) was the best-selling car of all time, and although the last model rolled off VW's Mexican production line in summer 2003, its status as a collector's item is assured. Vehicle design and technology, not to mention the automobile market, have moved on since Volkswagen sold the first *Käfer* in 1947 as a low-price model that would bring car ownership to the masses. In 1988, VW brought out the New Beetle (also known as the 'Newbie'). This model has retained elements of the original iconic design, but has been updated with a contemporary twist and more sophisticated features, such as airbags.

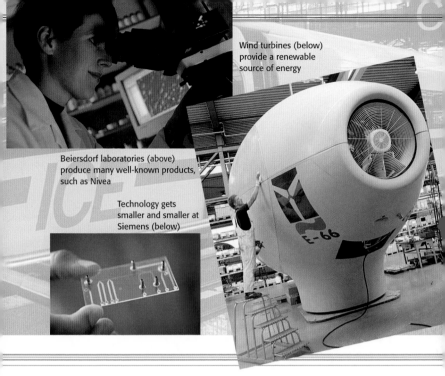

Wind turbines (below) provide a renewable source of energy

Beiersdorf laboratories (above) produce many well-known products, such as Nivea

Technology gets smaller and smaller at Siemens (below)

Ruhr Valley Fortunes

In its prime, the Ruhr Valley was the most developed industrial region in the world. While trade and service industries have partially replaced mines and furnaces, the human cost of deindustrialization has been high, and towns have been forced to find new uses for the steelworks and coal mines. Factories have been converted into nightclubs or housing, while other premises—including mines, model housing developments and pitheads—have been conserved as monuments to a proud industrial past. Opened in 1898, the Zeche Zollern II/IV colliery just outside Dortmund (▷ 115) has an art nouveau machine hall and neo-Gothic façades, showing the change from historicism to art nouveau. It is now the headquarters of the Westphalia Industrial Museum, preserving the past and providing a new kind of employment.

You Are What You Drive

The automobile industry may be built on engineering excellence, but it is driven by the Germans' love of cars and the pride and social prestige they associate with them. Germans bought 3.2 million cars in 2003, more than any other country in Europe—a figure that works out at 39.2 new cars for every 1,000 people. Germans in the former East might, understandably, be gradually replacing their Trabants, but where other countries have a class system, German professionals are judged by their cars. In this intensely competitive market, manufacturers such as Mercedes-Benz, BMW and VW are increasingly aware of the importance of image as well as technological superiority, and regularly issue next-generation models of their flagship vehicles in a bid to achieve and maintain brand loyalty.

Nuclear Reaction

Nuclear power has always divided Germany's citizens. The Green Party's emergence was closely linked to anti-nuclear protests, and the transportation of nuclear waste from France in 2001 mobilized hundreds of demonstrators. Yet Germany has 19 nuclear power stations of its own at 14 sites, accounting for about a third of the country's electricity production. Under the Green Party's influence, legislation was adopted in 2002 on the phasing out of nuclear energy as a power source: No new nuclear plants are to be built, the operational life of existing plants has been restricted and there are caps on the amount of electricity each plant may produce. However, as alternative energy sources are not yet sufficiently developed to make up the shortfall, and as oil prices remain unstable, some politicians have called for a rethinking of the policy.

Puffing Round the Mountain

Saxony's Harz Mountains are home to the Harzer Schmalspurbahnen, a network of narrow-gauge railways that extends for over 130km (80 miles). The most spectacular stretch is the Brockenbahn, which winds around northern Germany's highest mountain near the former East–West border. After decades of closure (the line had been deemed too close to a Soviet listening post), passenger services resumed in 1992. It is now very popular with visitors. Most of the trains are pulled by steam locomotives introduced in the 1950s (when steam was already being phased out elsewhere). In a country that prides itself on high-speed inter-city links, they are a throwback to another era.

Being part of Europe is an important part of German politics (right)

Berlin is an ethnically diverse city, with many Turkish people living and working in the Kreuzberg district

Economy, Politics and
Europe

The Pension Pot

Germany's pensioners are among the youngest and most prosperous in Europe, but a declining birth rate is raising the thorny issue of who will pay for generous state pensions in the future. The official retirement age might be 65, but the average German retires just after 62, and pensions account for more than 10 per cent of GDP. According to the Federal Statistics Office, there will soon be more Germans aged over 65 than under 15, so to maintain demographic stability and pension levels, Germany will have to accept large numbers of immigrants. One centre-right politician has called for 'Kinder statt Inder' (children, not Indians), but such sentiments have been widely criticized, and few young people are willing to have large families.

For 45 years, West Germany experienced *Wirtschaftswunder* (rapid economic growth), which made it the most prosperous and stable country in Europe. The post-war Marshall plan injected millions of dollars into the economy, and bolstered by technological innovation and harmonious industrial relations, the country boomed, but the cost of integrating 16.1 million people following reunification has been high. Unemployment and taxes have both risen as millions of euros have been pumped into regenerating the eastern regions. A global economic slump and political unwillingness to tackle reform have resulted in low economic growth, and Germany is under increasing pressure to modernize its labour regulations, immigration policy and welfare and taxation systems.

The Communist legacy is gradually being overcome in the east, but more than two million first- and second-generation Turkish immigrants have still to be fully integrated into German society, where the issue of national identity remains fraught with tension. Meanwhile, the European Union is expanding eastward, opening up new markets and creating foreign policy challenges for Germany as it seeks to maintain its pivotal role in European development while renegotiating vital relationships with France and the United States.

Trabant cars (left) are a symbol of the former East Germany

The German government is based in Berlin's Reichstag (right)

Germans believe in their right to protest (below)

Senat soll einpacken!
Solidarität statt Ausgrenzung

SoPo

East Berlin from the Inside

In the years immediately after the 1990 *Wende* (change), *Ossis* (Easterners) had very mixed feelings about their past. Some of this changed in 2003, when Wolfgang Becker's bittersweet comedy *Good Bye Lenin!* was an unexpected critical and popular success throughout the new Germany. The story tells of Alex's staunchly Communist mother, who falls into a coma just before the collapse of the Berlin Wall, remaining unaware of reunification and the subsequent social transformations. When she comes round, Alex goes to extraordinary lengths to spare her any sudden shocks. *Good Bye Lenin!* swept the boards at the 2003 German film awards, and gave West Germans an insight into ordinary life in the former German Democratic Republic, helping to break down divisive stereotypes.

Outsiders or Citizens?

Germany's complex and ambiguous citizenship policies are seen most starkly in the situation of the Turkish *Gastarbeiter* (guest workers). Following an agreement in the early 1960s between West Germany and Turkey, hundreds of thousands of Turks were invited to make up Germany's manpower shortage and rebuild the economy. Most intended to stay for only a few years, but ended up settling down, opening businesses and having children. Critics of Germany's *jus sanguinis* policy (by which nationality is conferred by blood rather than place of birth) point to the low educational achievements and poor employment figures typical of this second-generation group which has no German status but nonetheless makes a huge and distinctive contribution to the country.

Rebuilding Bridges

When the Oder–Neisse line was chosen as the new Polish–German border in 1945, it drove a wedge between people who lived only a few hundred metres from each other. At Germany's easternmost point, the Saxon town of Görlitz found itself divided: The historical heart lay on the west bank (and therefore in the GDR), while the residential districts on the opposite bank became the Polish town of Zgorzelec. The enlargement of the European Union has brought new challenges to the towns' respective mayors. The political culture and language may be different, but inter-municipal cooperation is both desirable and logical. Having seen a sharp rise in unemployment since 1990, Germans are suspicious of less expensive Polish manpower. Poles, on the other hand, tend to be more optimistic about the opportunities of an open market and visa-less travel.

Who is German?

For decades the small Black Forest town of Lahr was home to Canadian troops. Since they withdrew in 1993, some 9,000 'Russian Germans' have moved into town, and now account for 22 per cent of the population. They are descended from German farmers who settled along the Volga in 1763, and were exiled to Siberia or Kazakhstan in 1941. Many gradually assimilated and married Russians, and the younger generations often hid their German origins. Since the collapse of the Soviet Union, 2.4 million 'ethnic Germans' have taken advantage of an article in the German Constitution that enables them to claim citizenship, and they now constitute the country's biggest minority. The German authorities introduced a language test in 1997 to control the influx, and a quota system is now also in place.

Wind turbines in Sauerland (left)

Protesting against nuclear waste (below)

Germans sort out all their waste for recycling, even in public places (below)

Green
Germany

The majority of Germans share a genuine concern about the environment. Partly a legacy of the 19th-century Romantic Movement, this consensus has found expression in the public's reaction to industrial pollution along the Rhine, tree disease in the 1970s and nuclear power. In 1994, a provision (Article 20a) was inserted into the constitution emphasizing the state's duty to preserve the country's natural resources, and Germans continue to be among Europe's most enthusiastic recyclers and exponents of alternative energy. Green Party leaders such as Petra Kelly (1947–92) and Joschka Fischer (1948–) have become household names, and no other Green Party in the world has had such a direct impact on national policy. Effort and expense has gone into landscaping rail lines, abandoned industrial sites have been turned into parks or leisure areas, and images of toxic waste from the eastern regions have prompted substantial clean-up efforts since reunification.

Here to Stay
Many of Germany's native animal species, such as the beaver and wild cat, are threatened with extinction. Yet the numbers of one imported species have increased so rapidly that it is now regarded as an urban menace. A single pair of North American racoons was released into the wild in 1934, and more escaped from a fur farm during a World War II bombing raid. With no natural predators, their numbers grew rapidly, and a million of these carnivores are now at large, foraging through bins and occasionally entering houses in search of food. Kassel is particularly badly affected, and has even appointed an official whose sole task is to deal with the pests.

Doing Your Bit
Environmental action in Germany goes much further than lip-service. German homes have a series of containers for household waste, which is separated into bio or organic, plastics, glass, paper and other waste, and disposed of accordingly. Most people cooperate, and children are encouraged to conserve water and energy resources. Public waste bins also have separate sections, and plastic grocery bags are not generally available in supermarkets. Although transportation firms grumbled at the imposition of an 'ecology tax' on fossil fuels in 1999, individual drivers accepted the increase and the Constitutional Court backed the government, which claims that carbon dioxide emissions have fallen as a direct result.

The Story of Germany

Germans and *Romans*

The remains of one of the very first inhabitants of the land now known as Germany were discovered at Neanderthal near Düsseldorf in 1856, and the place gave its name to an early species of man, *Homo Neanderthalensis*.

From around the fifth century BC onwards, the Celts, widespread throughout western Europe, had to contend with Germanic tribespeople moving in from the north and east. By the first century BC, nearby Celtic Gaul—today's France—had been incorporated into the Roman Empire. Seeking to extend their domain eastward, the Romans were soon in contact with the Germanic tribes, although their ideas of the lands beyond the Rhine were fanciful in the extreme: Lurking in their dark forests, the hairy, bearskin-clad Germans were thought to keep company with unicorns and other exotic beasts. On more than one occasion, the legions marched east, but for the most part Roman civilization was confined to the lands west of the Rhine and south of the Danube. The end of the Roman Empire came in the fifth century AD, when, in the 'Migration of the Peoples', the Roman defences were overwhelmed. But even today, traces of the long Roman presence can be discerned: As well as relics like the Porta Nigra in Trier (▷ 116), some say there are subtle differences in culture and behaviour between the Romanized inhabitants of the Rhineland and their relatives to the east, where Rome's influence was never felt.

The skull of Neanderthal Man (right), who took his name from the valley where he was found

The Roman Wall

As they did at other extremities of their empire, the Romans attempted to hold their barbarian foes at bay by building formidable frontier defences. In Germany, the gap of several hundred kilometres between the natural boundaries of the Rhine and Danube was filled in the second century AD by an extraordinary earthwork called the Limes. Reinforced by a palisade and a wide dry moat, the Limes was guarded by more than a thousand timber watchtowers and fortlets sited within hailing distance of one another. Some way to the rear of the frontier, around a hundred stone castles were built to house the troops of the border garrisons.

Carving of a German cavalry man (right)

Before

The Romans introduced vines to western Germany (above)

The German Celts would have worn torques like this around their necks

Vines Along the Rhine

As the Romans transformed the area protected by the Limes, they made sure their taste for wine was met, not just by importing it from Gaul and Italy, but by planting vines along the sunnier slopes of the Rhine and Mosel. The fourth-century AD politician and poet Decimus Magnus Ausonius was so taken by the sight of the vineyards lining the Mosel that he composed the long poem *Mosella*, comparing this northern landscape positively with his native Bordeaux. Archaeologists continue to turn up implements associated with the wine trade of Roman times, and perhaps the most poignant are inscriptions on tombstones attributing a long and happy life to judicious consumption of the fruit of the vine.

Formidable Foes

The Romans were inclined to dismiss the Germans as idle, quarrelsome savages, at their happiest when eating and drinking to excess and fighting among themselves. Perhaps exposure to Roman ways might civilize them, they thought. Among selected German leaders invited to serve in the Roman army and even given citizenship was Arminius (c. 17BC– AD21; Hermann in German). But Arminius returned to his roots, raising the flag of revolt and defeating an army sent to teach him a lesson. At the Battle of the Teutoburger Wald in AD9, a force of 20,000 legionaries was led into a swamp and cut to pieces by Arminius' men. In the 19th century, nationalists promoted Hermann as the first great German hero, and erected a huge monument to him on what was thought to be the site of his victory.

A replica Roman ship (below) from the Römisch-Germanische Museum in Mainz

Attila the Hun

The fiercest of the warrior folk who swarmed westwards across the Rhine as the Roman Empire crumbled were the nomadic Huns. Living, sleeping and fighting on horseback, they were led by the semi-legendary Attila (c.AD406–453). In AD451 he led his horde in a great rampage across northern France as far as the modern-day city of Orléans. Hearing that an army composed mostly of Germanic tribesmen was on his trail, Attila retraced his steps eastward. The adversaries met on 20 September in one of the greatest massacres of ancient times, the Battle of the Catalaunian Fields. Attila survived the slaughter, but two years later he was dead, overcome in the arms of his bride by the effects of an over-sumptuous wedding banquet.

Julius Caesar (c. 100–44BC)

Franks

The most powerful of the Germanic peoples inheriting the remains of the Roman Empire were the Franks. Originally just a group of tribes given to squabbling among themselves, they were eventually united under chieftain Clovis (c.AD466–511), who slaughtered his rivals, routed the last Roman ruler of Gaul and was proclaimed king by being raised upon the shields of his redoubtable red-headed warriors. Clovis accepted Christianity, but many pagan beliefs persisted. He and his successors were thought to have magical powers, and could make crops flourish by walking over the fields. From their power base in what is today's Belgium, the Franks extended their sway both east and west. They gave modern France its name (Frankreich in German) and settled in what is now Franken (Franconia). A fight with the heathen Saxons was settled when the Frankish army was able to ford the River Main at what is now Frankfurt.

AD 700

Trier's Porta Nigra (above) was a second-century gate in the fortified Roman walls

Kings, Emperors and Popes

The memory of Rome's glory persisted long after its downfall, and in turbulent times the rulers of Germany were anxious to identify themselves with the empire's stability, culture and prosperity. The greatest of the Frankish kings was Charlemagne (AD742–814; Karl der Grosse in German), who united much of Europe, promoted learning and the arts and on Christmas Day AD800 was crowned Holy Roman Emperor by the pope. But Germany was still too vast and diverse a land to be held together easily. After Charlemagne's death, the Frankish realm was split into three: an eastern part ruled by Louis the German; a western part—forerunner of modern France—in the hands of Charles the Bald; and a middle kingdom under Lothar (whose name survives in Lotharingen, the German name for the French province of Lorraine). Central power became ever weaker, and the responsibility for warding off attacks from Vikings and marauding Magyars (from modern-day Hungary) often fell to local leaders, whose domains eventually became powerful dukedoms such as Saxony, Franconia and Bavaria. These leaders were well able to resist the re-establishment of imperial power and prestige, not least because the Holy Roman Emperor's attention was often focused on his possessions outside Germany, notably in Italy.

AD701

Evangelizing the Germans

After the fall of Rome, Christianity continued to flourish on the edge of Europe, in Britain and Ireland, and it was from here that St. Boniface set out to convert the mostly heathen Germans. His first mission was to the Friesian coastlands of northern Germany, whose inhabitants were unreceptive to his teachings. Boniface had better luck in Hessen, where he demonstrated the impotence of the ancient gods by cutting down a sacred oak. When this awesome outrage was not avenged, the Hessians converted *en masse*. But Boniface's career came to an abrupt end. When he tried once more to exercise his persuasive powers on the Friesians in around AD754, they lost patience and put him to the sword.

Emperor Otto the Great is commemorated in Magdeburg (left)

Charlemagne's throne in Aachen Cathedral (above) has seen the coronation of 30 kings

Charlemagne

Charlemagne's rule as king of the Franks lasted from AD768 to 814. A great warrior-king, he fought dozens of battles, the bloodiest of which were against the Saxons, whose stubborn resistance was finally brought to an end in AD782 by the execution of more than 4,000 of their fighters. Charlemagne exercised control over his vast territories by means of a mobile court, which settled periodically in one of his many estates. But his home base was the cathedral city of Aachen, to which he summoned wise men and scholars to create a great seat of learning, law-giving, art and architecture. The glorious octagonal chapel he ordered to be built here has miraculously survived (▷ 94).

Charlemagne (747–814AD)

Canossa

Throughout the Middle Ages, popes, princes and emperors squabbled constantly about the extent of their respective powers. In the winter of 1073, faced with excommunication by Pope Gregory VII (c.1020–85) and with rebellious dukes in Germany, King Heinrich IV (1050–1106) made his way to the castle at Canossa where Pope Gregory had sought refuge. In an astonishing ploy, Heinrich huddled in a hair shirt in the snow-packed courtyard for three days and nights until the puzzled pope ordered him to be let in. The monarch prostrated himself before the pope, begging for readmission to the Church. Moved, Pope Gregory granted the supplicant's wish. Ever since, *Canossa* has been a German byword for abject submission to a superior power (even though Heinrich subsequently succeeded in deposing Pope Gregory and replacing him with another pope).

The Hansa

Germany prospered in the high Middle Ages, and German settlers and merchants moved throughout Europe, founding towns and trading hubs. Control of commerce around the Baltic was exercised by the Hanseatic League, originally an association of harbour cities formed to secure the sea lanes and protect its shipping from the depredations of pirates. The most notorious of these buccaneers was Klaus Störtebecker, a kind of Robin Hood of the waves who in the 15th century operated from his base on the Swedish island of Gotland. Störtebecker and his fellow freebooters were eventually overcome by a fleet sent by the Hanseatic League, and he was brought in triumph to Hamburg, where he was publicly put to death. Hamburg is still proud of its Hanseatic traditions; cars licensed here carry plates labelled HH (Hansestadt Hamburg), and other old Hansa towns do likewise (HB is used in Bremen and HRO in Rostock).

Barbarossa

The most illustrious of medieval German rulers was the handsome and energetic Friedrich I (1152–90), known to his Italian subjects as 'Barbarossa' for his flowing red beard. The splendour of Friedrich's court, his constant forays into Italy, his fearlessness in battle and his revival of the glories of Charlemagne's rule, together with his tragic death on his way to deliver Jerusalem from the Saracens, made him a legendary figure even in his own lifetime. The legend was later added to, when the great emperor was thought not to be dead, but asleep, waiting for the moment when a German empire should rise once more.

Barbarossa and his sons (below)

The Stralsund Seal of 1329 (above), showing a Kogge ship

The Holstentor in Hanseatic Lübeck (left)

Romanesque Michaeliskirche in Hildesheim (right)

Reformation, Rebellion and War

Before the terrible devastation of the Thirty Years War (1618–48), Germany was showing many signs of national progress, with an increasingly vibrant cultural, intellectual and commercial life based around cities such as Nuremberg. The Habsburg Holy Roman Emperors still saw themselves as the successors to Charlemagne, but unlike him they had only limited power over the myriad states into which Germany was still divided. Nevertheless, the Holy Roman Empire remained an important player in the game of European power politics.

As the Continent emerged from the Middle Ages, discontent with the Church grew and took a particularly radical form in Germany, the home of Martin Luther. The Reformation brought increasing political as well as religious tension, as many but by no means all territories converted to Protestantism, leaving Germany with a gaping confessional divide. The real catastrophe, however, was the Thirty Years War, which devastated the country in a way not to be seen again until the 20th century, leaving cities in ruins and the population barely able to feed itself. Germans fought against Germans in alliance with foreign powers such as Sweden and France. In 1648, the Peace of Westphalia brought an end to this conflict, but this pattern of internal strife would go on to be repeated.

Wallenstein

As the Thirty Years War wore on, the religious passions that had inspired it were replaced by the lust for power and plunder. Many soldiers were brutal and unprincipled mercenaries—the notorious *Landsknechte*—drawn from the dregs of half of Europe. Some of their commanders were little different, notably Albrecht von Wallenstein (1583–1634), the war's most successful general. Having wormed his way into the good will of Holy Roman Emperor Ferdinand II (1578–1637), this minor nobleman from Bohemia used every opportunity to enrich himself. When Wallenstein's troops showed more loyalty to their commander than to the emperor, Ferdinand ordered his elimination.

A coin commemorating the Peace of Westphalia (left)

1401

A page from the Gutenberg Bible (right)

Gutenberg

Originally endowed with the name of Gensfleisch ('Gooseflesh'), Johann Gutenberg of Mainz (c.1399–1468) was the man responsible for what has been called 'Germany's greatest single contribution to civilization'. His invention of modern printing and all the technology to go with it—presses, inks and, above all, moveable type cast in metal—revolutionized the production of books, which hitherto had been laboriously copied out by hand or printed from wooden blocks incapable of reuse. Basically unchanged until the 19th century, Gutenberg's technology made possible the rapid diffusion of the radical ideas leading to the Reformation; his magnificent Bible dating from around 1455 is his greatest monument. But poor Gutenberg failed to profit from his genius. Greedy creditors reduced him to financial ruin, and he ended his days in the Mainz poorhouse.

Johann Gutenberg
(1400–68)

Thomas Müntzer

Originally a follower of Luther, the charismatic Thomas Müntzer (c.1489–1525) later diverged from his master's teachings, propagating an apocalyptic version of Christianity and denouncing the worldly rule of princes and potentates. This made him a natural leader of the impoverished peasantry, many of whom had been reduced to the status of serfs. Under Müntzer they rose up against their lords in the Peasants' War of 1524–25, which although vicious was short. The peasant army was massacred at the Battle of Frankenhausen on 15 May 1525; Müntzer was taken to Mühlhausen, where, after expert torturers had persuaded him to recant, he was beheaded. Luther denounced him as a fanatic and tarnished his own reputation by condemnation of the peasants. Müntzer enjoyed a brief after-life of glory when he entered the GDR's pantheon of proto-Communist heroes.

Luther

As a professor of theology at the University of Wittenberg, Martin Luther (1483–1546), like many other Germans, had become increasingly concerned with the serious failings and corrupt practices of the Catholic Church. The Reformation is said to have begun when he famously nailed his '95 Theses' to the door of the church in Wittenberg. Such an overt provocation soon saw him excommunicated and branded an outlaw, and his books ordered to be burned. He might easily have suffered the fate of so many other heretics had not Friedrich III, Elector of Saxony, given him a safe haven in Wartburg castle. Like other German princes, Friedrich had seen that a religious struggle could help him gain a greater degree of independence. Luther's pamphlets and his translation of the Bible into German were printed in quantity by Gutenberg's press.

Martin Luther
(1483–1546)

The Sack of Magdeburg

In April 1630, the prosperous Protestant city of Magdeburg was besieged by the Catholic Count of Tilly (1559–1632). General Tilly was a pious man of great personal rectitude, but his largely mercenary army was more interested in plunder than the rightness of their cause. When Tilly offered the Magdeburgers his personal protection if they opened their gates, they were inclined to submit, but they were overruled by the city's fanatical Protestant pastor, who preached resistance to the bitter end. Tilly reluctantly gave the order to attack, and the defences were duly stormed. But his men then ran amok, killing, raping, pillaging and destroying everything they could not steal. Carrying an infant that he had found in the arms of its murdered mother, the general rode through the burning city, powerless to halt the destruction. Magdeburg was reduced to ashes, and of its population of 30,000, only 5,000 survived.

1700

The Thirty Years War (far left) was a bloody conflict, pitting German against German

Luther's study at Schloss Wartburg (left)

The Fuggerei (below) was an early form of welfare housing

Enlightenment and Absolutism

Under the absolute rule of King Louis XIV (1638–1715), France was Europe's undisputed super-power, and the style of his court at Versailles was imitated all over the Continent. However petty their realm, 18th-century German rulers also saw themselves as the heart of the state, answerable only to God. They competed with one another in the splendour of their palaces and formal gardens and in their promotion of the arts. Some became patrons of the Enlightenment, the philosophical movement based on reason rather than traditional belief, and surrounded themselves with the foremost thinkers and writers of the day, most notably at Friedrich the Great's Potsdam and the Weimar of Goethe, Herder and Schiller. Music, too, owed much to princely patronage, though Bach's greatest days were spent in the service of the city of Leipzig rather than as a court musician.

Throughout the century, Germany remained divided by political entities of every conceivable size and character. However, Prussia began a process that was to lead to its dominance over German affairs in the next century. In a series of internal reforms and successful wars, Prussia's Hohenzollern kings transformed their realm into a highly efficient, centralized state with a mighty army. Even so, by the end of the 18th century, no power in Germany proved able to resist the might of revolutionary Napoleonic France.

1701

The Sergeant-King

King Friedrich Wilhelm I of Prussia (1688–1740) was given the derisive name 'the Sergeant-King' by his fellow monarchs because of his obsession with all things military. A man of thuggish manners, Friedrich Wilhelm was at his happiest drilling his soldiers. His best-loved troopers were his *lange Kerle* (literally 'tall fellows'), recruited at great expense from all over Europe. Behind the comic façade, the king built the hitherto insignificant Prussian army up into a formidable fighting force.

Friedrich the Great and Voltaire at Potsdam (left)

Friedrich II (1712–86)

The Bachhaus in Eisenach (above)

Augustus the Strong

Known as 'the Strong' not least for the hundreds of children he fathered with an array of mistresses, Friedrich August I of Saxony (1670–1733) was the most flamboyant of the absolute rulers in 18th-century Germany. Under his extravagant sway, his capital, Dresden, became one of the most beautiful cities of the baroque age—although his subjects groaned under the burden of taxation. Augustus succeeded in his candidature for the throne of Poland by converting to Roman Catholicism, a step that caused offence in solidly Lutheran Saxony and proved the final straw for his pious wife Christiane, who left him. Augustus' body is buried in his Polish capital of Kraków, but his heart was brought to Dresden, where it is kept in the Court Church vaults.

Bach & Co.

The greatest musical genius of the German baroque, Johann Sebastian Bach (1685–1750), was far from being the first musician in the family. Four generations of his forefathers had worked as organists, municipal bandsmen or court musicians, and one of his most influential teachers was his composer cousin Johann Christoph. The devout Bach not only mastered the craft of musicianship but took it to increasingly sublime heights. He declared the purpose of music to be not only 'recreation of the spirit' but also 'praise of the Lord'. After his death, his music fell into neglect, and some of his numerous offspring were more highly regarded than their father. Revived in the mid-19th century by composer Felix Mendelssohn, Bach's music has remained supreme ever since.

Goethe in Weimar

The giant of German literature, Johann Wolfgang von Goethe (1749–1832), was a master of poetry, the novel, drama, the essay and even autobiography. His questioning mind led him into every field of thought, and his scientific achievements included a famous treatise on colour. At the same time, Goethe's position as a high official in the ducal court at Weimar satisfied a parallel taste for practical action; he even managed to be present when a German army was defeated by the French at Valmy in 1792. Still regarded as the greatest play in the German language, his *Faust* ends with the lines 'Whoever strives shall be redeemed'. Goethe saw his life as a work of art in which he strove to experience all the possibilities open to humankind.

A Much-loved Princess

Prussian monarchy generally presented a martial, ultra-masculine face to the world, but the pretty Princess Luise von Mecklenburg-Strelitz (1776–1810) made a pleasing exception. Married at the age of 16 to the future King Friedrich Wilhelm III in what was self-evidently a romantic love match, she soon won all hearts with her kindly nature and complete lack of pretension. Luise had brains as well as beauty; as Prussia strove to modernize its creaking administration in the face of the Napoleonic onslaught, she stood firmly on the side of the reformers. Forced to flee from Potsdam by French invasion, in 1807 Luise bravely sought an audience with Napoleon and pleaded with him not to impose over-onerous terms on the defeated Prussia. The emperor responded to her charm but not to her plea; Prussia lost all its possessions west of the Elbe.

Johann Wolfgang von Goethe
(1749–1832)

Augustus the Strong
(1670–1733)

Johann Sebastian Bach
(1685–1750)

Princess Luise von
Mecklenburg-Strelitz

1806

Johann Gottfried Schadow's Quadriga (left) of 1794 tops the Brandenburg Gate

A statue of Goethe in his home town of Frankfurt (above)

ENLIGHTENMENT AND ABSOLUTISM 33

Restoration, Revolution and Reaction

Napoleon's retreat from Moscow in 1812 was the signal for an extraordinary outburst of patriotism among Germans. Anti-French riots broke out all over Germany, and volunteers flocked to join the army in what became a struggle for national liberation. Napoleon's fate was sealed at a series of battles, of which the greatest and deadliest on German soil was the so-called 'Battle of the Nations' at Leipzig in 1813.

There were fervent hopes, particularly among patriotic students, that the post-Napoleonic order would not only mean an end to French domination but the establishment of a united and democratic Germany. But at the Congress of Vienna in 1815, representatives of the old regimes gathered with an agenda of restoration and reaction. Germany remained divided, though Prussia acquired territory that extended it westward as far as Aachen.

The reinstalled regimes, still terrified of the ideas of the French Revolution, went to great lengths to nip opposition in the bud, with strict censorship and control of education. Incongruously, these crypto-feudal regimes presided over a Germany that was entering the modern world; the country's first railway train steamed out of Nuremberg in 1835, heralding the arrival of the industrial age. The reimposed old order was bound to be challenged sooner or later but a liberal revolution failed in 1848, and German unity was eventually imposed by Prussian military might, an ominous portent for the country's later development.

Friedrich the Great on horseback

Romantic Genius

Nowhere more so than in Germany did the Europe-wide Romantic movement find such intense expression and popular acclaim. Poets excelled one another in exploring the deeper recesses of the human soul, while among artists the reclusive painter Caspar David Friedrich (1774–1840) was perhaps most in tune with the spirit of the age. His canvases show human-ity—frequently in the form of a single lonely figure—lost in contemplation of the vastness and mystery of nature. As the artist aged, his scenes became more melan-choly, and Friedrich fell into a deep depression, eventually dying in a Dresden asylum.

Friedrich's *Wanderer Above a Sea of Fog* (c.1818)

1807

Towards 1848

The outbreak of revolution in 1848 was heralded by large-scale unrest among working people, their poverty made all the more unbearable by the prosperity and complacency of the middle class. In 1844, the decline of their industry in the face of British competition caused such desperation among the linen weavers of Silesia that they revolted, storming the factories. In the years following the revolt, a series of poor harvests meant near-starvation for tens of thousands. There were food riots in a number of cities, including the Berlin 'Potato Revolution' of 1847. In that same year, the undernourished poor of Silesia were visited by a terrible typhus outbreak, which killed 16,000.

Robert Alexander Schumann (1810–56)

The Austro-Prussian War of 1866 (below)

The Frankfurt Talking Shop

For a whole year, from May 1848 to May 1849, some 600 delegates from all over Germany met in St. Paul's Church, Frankfurt, as members of the National Assembly, which all present hoped would result in the proclamation of a united Germany. Although joined in their opposition to the reactionary regimes that had ruled since 1815, they soon fell out among themselves. Should the new Germany include Austria or just Prussia and the southern German states? Should it be a monarchy or a republic? Most of the delegates were lawyers, professors and bureaucrats, and the discussions were interminable. By the time a constitution of sorts had been hammered out, conservative forces had regained their confidence. Those members of the National Assembly who had not had the good sense to return home were dispersed by Prussian troops.

Auf Wiedersehen, Deutschland!

Many of the leaders of the abortive 1848 revolution fled the country when the old regimes were re-established. In numerical terms, however, they made up only a tiny fraction of the total number of German emigrants who quit their homeland in their millions throughout the 19th century. Driven by rural overpopulation, poverty and unemployment, a total of 6 million Germans had left by 1913, most of them heading for the United States, though significant numbers went to Canada, South America, South Africa and Australia. Their departure was seen as a loss by patriotic fellow countrymen, who agitated for Germany to acquire colonies that could absorb surplus population. However, the rapid expansion of German industry in the latter part of the century provided employment at home, and by the 1880s the exodus had peaked.

Sedan

In the centuries-old struggle between France and Germany, the name of Sedan became synonymous with French despair and German elation. It was at this small town on the banks of the Meuse in September 1870 that the outcome of the Franco-Prussian War of 1870–71 was decided. Surrounded by a superior Prussian force, their ranks raked by artillery firing, their commander wounded and Emperor Napoleon III in a state of utter exhaustion, the French fought desperately but without hope. The defeat cost France 120,000 men and Napoleon III his throne. Some 80 years later, in May 1940, fear struck Frenchmen's souls once again, as German Panzers swarmed across the Meuse at Sedan in the Battle of France.

First German emperor Wilhelm I (1797–1888)

1870

The Meissen manufactory moved from its secure citadel site in 1863

The Leipzig's memorial to the Battle of Nations in 1813

The Second Reich

Most Germans rejoiced when the Franco-Prussian War led to the unification of the country. Many saw the new Germany as the successor to the old Holy Roman Empire, justifying its title of 'Second Reich'. But Austria was excluded, and not everyone was happy with the overwhelmingly Prussian character of the new empire. Formally, the Second Reich was a federation of states, still ruled nominally by dukes, princes and kings (Ludwig of Bavaria only gave his assent to the new arrangements on receipt of a substantial bribe from Chancellor Bismarck). Holding the federation together was the Kaiser (emperor), who was also king of Prussia and commander of the armed forces.

The first Kaiser, Wilhelm I (ruled 1871–88), considered his new title a 'cheap decoration' and would have preferred to remain a mere king. But his grandson, Wilhelm II (ruled 1888–1918), relished the ostentation of his office; it was he who presided over an increasingly nationalistic and expansionist Germany, which flaunted its industrial and military muscle in the face of the old imperial powers of Britain and France. However, instead of achieving its 'Place in the Sun', with colonies to match, Germany's ambitions led to the Great War (1914–18), defeat and the replacement of the short-lived empire in 1918 by a democratic republic.

1871

Wilhelm Konrad von Röntgen discovered x-rays (left) in 1895

A cartoon of Wilhelm I and Otto von Bismarck (right) from the 1870s

The Prussian infantry marches on St-Denis, near Paris, in 1871 (above)

Karl Marx (1818–83) and Friedrich Engels (1820–95)

The Kaiser…

Emperor Wilhelm II embodied much of the flamboyant spirit of the Second Reich. A grandson of Queen Victoria, he conducted a love-hate relationship with Britain, which he both admired (for its world empire and great navy) and detested (for the same reasons). The archaic ruler of a rapidly industrializing country, with a democratically elected parliament and active trade unions, he hankered for the power and glory of absolute monarchy. Going along with the game of great power brinkmanship in the years before 1914, he was nevertheless dismayed as war finally broke out: 'If grandma were alive, she would never have allowed it!' he cried.

…and the Captain

The Second Reich promoted discipline and obedience to orders. That this could have comic consequences was demonstrated in 1906 by the unemployed cobbler and former jailbird Wilhelm Vogt, who had acquired a discarded army captain's uniform. He donned it, and set off on an adventure that had all Germany laughing. Encountering some soldiers, Vogt ordered them to fall in and follow him. They instantly obeyed. Policemen were added to the troop, which he marched to the town hall at Köpenick just outside Berlin. Here, the 'captain' arrested the mayor and his staff, and confiscated Köpenick's cash reserves (DM3,577). Eventually arrested, Vogt spent a term in jail, then lived off the proceeds of a successful autobiography.

The *Lusitania*

Few passengers boarding the Cunard Line's mighty *Lusitania* in New York on 1 May 1915 had taken much notice of the ominous announcement by the 'Imperial German Embassy' that all vessels entering British waters were 'liable to destruction'. But as the *Lusitania* approached the Irish coast, she was struck by two torpedoes fired by a U-boat lurking beneath the surface. The great liner soon sank, taking almost 1,200 of the passengers with her. Of the dead, 129 were citizens of the still-neutral United States; Americans were outraged, and there were frenzied calls for war to be declared on Germany. For a while, U-boat skippers were instructed to choose their victims with greater care, but in spring 1917 Germany once more declared open season on all shipping approaching Britain. President Wilson called the German submarine campaign a 'war against all nations' and the United States entered World War I on the Allied side.

Types of Trench

In spring 1918, after three-and-a-half years of stalemate on the Western Front, the German army embarked on its last attempt at victory. The trenches from which the troops emerged to attack the British lines were testimony to Teutonic thoroughness. Penetrating far beneath the surface , they could even seem homey, with planked floors and panelled walls hung with pictures. But by 1918, Germany was running out of food and raw materials, and every soldier was aware of the sufferings and near-starvation of the civilians back home. As the soldiers overran the less solidly built British entrenchments, they found such evidence of plenty—coffee, whisky and tinned goods—that they were soon demoralized. The offensive petered out in looting and drunkenness, and the remorseless Allied counterattack that was to end the war soon began.

1918

Life in the German trenches (left)

A propaganda postcard marking the sinking of the *Lusitania* in 1915 (below)

Between the Wars

The constitution of the post-war republic was drawn up in Weimar, to where the parliamentary delegates had fled from chaos in Berlin. Almost miraculously, the democratic Weimar Republic survived catastrophes such as the hyper-inflation of 1923 and attempted *coups d'état* from both left and right (including one in Munich, led by an obscure agitator named Adolf Hitler). In the second half of the 1920s, the country enjoyed a brief golden age of relative prosperity and outward social calm. But society remained deeply divided. After the Wall Street Crash in 1929, Germany was the country worst affected by the Great Depression. With industry crippled and 6 million unemployed on the streets, democracy was discredited.

For many, Adolf Hitler (1889–1945) offered an alternative to renewed chaos and the prospect of Communist revolution. An unholy alliance of conservatives and Nazis made him chancellor in January 1933. Within months, a totalitarian dictatorship was in place. The defeat of unemployment through rearmament and a massive schedule of public works, combined with a stunning series of foreign policy triumphs, left most Germans in a state resembling euphoria, willing to follow the Führer wherever he went.

Peace for a Time
The treaty ending World War I, signed in the Palace of Versailles in 1918, was a painful humiliation for a Germany whose unity had been proclaimed there half a century earlier. The terms of the treaty were humiliating, too. Germany lost about 20 per cent of its territory, including Alsace-Lorraine and industrial Upper Silesia. A wedge—the so-called 'Polish Corridor'—was driven between east Prussia and the rest of the country in order to provide Poland with access to the Baltic. Germany's pride, its great army, was reduced to a fraction of its former size and forbidden to garrison the Rhineland. A crippling indemnity of billions of dollars was to be paid to compensate the Allies for war damage. Here were the seeds of a future war.

Airships designed by Count Zeppelin (left) were in regular use until the Hindenberg disaster in 1937

Hitler Youth poster (below)

1919

Marlene Dietrich (1904–92)

GRAF ZEPPELIN
DEM SOHNE DER
STADT KONSTANZ
ZUM GEDACHTNIS

Adolf Hitler (above) was a passionate public speaker

Trillion-mark Tragedy

In early 1923, struggling to keep up reparations payments to the Allies and maintain public services, Germany resorted to printing money. Inflation, already rampant, now spiralled out of control. In January 1923, a loaf of bread cost DM250, compared with DM2 in 1920; by September 1923 its price had risen to DM1.5 million, and by December to nearly DM400 billion. People rushed from work to spend their wages before the passage of a few hours made them worthless. Barter became the norm, while middle-class folk were ruined when their investments evaporated. The disaster wrecked confidence in the new Weimar Republic and helped open the door to political extremism.

Inflation in the 1920s saw the Mark become almost valueless

Goodbye to Weimar

The most acute observer of the doomed world of Weimar society was the English-born writer Christopher Isherwood (1904–86), who lived in Berlin as Germany slid into the Great Depression and the embrace of the Nazis. His cast of barely fiction-alized characters thronging the capital's seedy nightlife includes gigolos, rent boys, stage lesbians, Communist toughs in tight shorts, and Nazi thugs baying for blood. The most memorable creature among this nocturnal fauna is his friend Sally Bowles, throaty-voiced singer in the Lady Windermere nightclub. With her green finger-nails, champagne habit and utter unreliability, Sally was fated never to find the millionaire who would finance her break-through into cinematic stardom. However, she achieved immortality not only in the pages of Isherwood's *Goodbye to Berlin*, but also in the play *I am a Camera* and the musical *Cabaret*.

Extremism on the Streets

The Nazis understood better than anyone the appeal—and effective-ness—of political violence. In addition to fighting for control of the streets against their rivals, their private militia, the Sturmabteilung (SA), impressed the German public with its smart uniforms, brass bands, catchy marching songs and apparent discipline. Some of its members were idealists, others came straight from the underworld, well versed in the use of the black-jack and knuckleduster. Many were drawn from the same social strata as their opponents in the equivalent Communist militia, the Red Front, and 6 million unem-ployed proved willing recruits to movements offering comradeship and some purpose in life. Such similarities failed to diminish the ferocity of the fighting on the streets, however, which the police seemed powerless to control.

The Nuremberg rallies (below left) were the annual meetings of the Nazi party

Olympics '36

But for the outbreak of World War I, Berlin would have hosted the Olympic games in 1916, although it's doubtful that the Kaiser's regime could have matched the Nazis' efforts when Germany's turn came round again in 1936. The Berlin games were a propaganda triumph, stage-managed with the consummate showmanship developed for the Nazi Party's Nuremberg rallies. As at Nuremberg, the specta-cle was recorded in a documentary by the Führer's best-loved film-maker, Leni Riefenstahl (1902–2003). Careful concentration on key sports meant that the Third Reich carried off the greatest number of medals, while its Axis allies Italy and Japan also excelled. However, to Hitler's intense annoy-ance, the real hero of the games was the black American athlete Jesse Owens (1913–80), who because of his race was considered in Nazi terms an *Untermensch* (subhuman); he won three gold medals.

The 1936 Olympics (left) were a triumph for Nazi propaganda

1938

Karl Marx's quote 'Religion is opium for the people' is taken up by anti-religious protesters

Defeat and Division

In contrast to 1914, when crowds had cheered the troops on their way to the front, the mood on Berlin's streets in early September 1939 was sombre. Nearly all Germans had rejoiced at Hitler's achievements abroad and were glad that they had been accomplished without war. *Blitzkrieg* tactics led to easy victories over Poland, the Low Countries and France, and many assumed that Germany could now rest on her laurels. Hitler, however, had other plans: The subjugation of the East, the enslavement of Russia and the destruction of European Jewry remained his fundamental aims. For him, the Battle of Britain in 1940 was a sideshow; the real struggle began on 21 June 1941 when his armies marched into the Soviet Union. It was a fatal miscalculation. The Red Army proved more than a match for the *Wehrmacht* (armed forces), and with the Western Allies' invasion of Normandy in June 1944, the fate of the Third Reich was sealed.

After the war, fearful of a revival of German militarism, Germany's opponents thought of dismantling the country's industry and returning it to what it had once been, a collection of largely agricultural, semi-independent statelets. In the end, Germany lost much of its eastern territory while the remainder of the country was divided into four occupation zones, Soviet, American, British and French. Living in the ruins of their towns and cities, a demoralized German population cared more about immediate survival than the political status of their country.

German troops invaded Moscow in 1941 (right)

1939

How to Start a War

A grisly pretext for the attack on Poland that precipitated World War II was provided by SS chiefs Heinrich Himmler and Reinhard Heydrich, aided and abetted by secret police chief Heinrich Müller. Fitted out in Polish uniforms and sworn to secrecy, a squad of SS soldiers stormed a German radio station close to the border with Poland, locking the startled staff in the basement. A short broadcast was made in Polish, then the pseudo-Poles withdrew, leaving behind a number of 'Germans' apparently killed while defending the transmitter. Nazi propaganda made the most of this outrage, putting the blame for the subsequent outbreak of hostilities fairly and squarely on Poland. In reality, the 'German' corpses were concentration camp inmates, drugged and shot by Müller's minions before being dumped outside the radio station. The cynical code name for the gruesome episode was 'Canned Goods'.

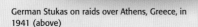

German Stukas on raids over Athens, Greece, in 1941 (above)

Decision at Wannsee

A palatial lakeside residence in the exclusive Berlin suburb of Wannsee was the setting for the most monstrous single decision of the war. America's entry into the conflict in December 1941 had confirmed Hitler's fantasy that an international Jewish conspiracy was bent on Germany's destruction. On 20 January 1942, the SS convened a conference at Wannsee villa to make arrangements for the 'Final Solution' to the imagined 'Jewish Problem'. With Adolf Eichmann taking heavily censored minutes that glossed over the real purpose of the meeting, Reinhard Heydrich outlined his frightful plans, expecting opposition from some delegates. But all concurred in setting up the administrative machinery for what was to be the murder of millions. Relieved, Heydrich and Eichmann retired to a side room to drink a self-congratulatory toast of cognac.

Count Claus von Stauffenberg (1907–44)

A German PZIV tank (below)

Count Stauffenberg

Behind its façade of unity, the Third Reich was opposed by individuals and groups, among them brave students and principled clergymen. But the only force capable of overturning the Nazi regime was the army, elements of which had plotted against Hitler since the 1930s. After several abortive attempts to assassinate the dictator, on 20 July 1944 Colonel Count Claus von Stauffenberg seemed to have succeeded. The bomb he had placed beneath Hitler's conference table at the 'Wolf's Lair' in east Prussia exploded, apparently killing everyone around it. Stauffenberg hastened to Berlin hoping to place the country under military control. But Hitler had survived. Stauffenberg was arrested and shot, his accomplices hunted down and put to death.

Hamsters

'Enjoy the war, the peace is going to be terrible' was a common wisecrack as Germany's enemies closed in on her. And so it was. Cities and towns lay in ruins, released slave workers took their revenge on the population and there was no fuel for heating during the cold winters. Food was rationed, but supplies were erratic. City-dwellers swarmed into the countryside, on foot or clinging to the outside of infrequent and overcrowded trains. Dubbed 'hamsters', they carried rucksacks stuffed with precious possessions that they bartered for food from farmers ready to cut a deal. The lucky ones came back with butter, sides of ham or perhaps a sack of potatoes. Tales were told of cow byres carpeted with precious Persian rugs and of farmers' wives flouncing around the fields in furs.

The Berlin Airlift

At the end of the war in May 1945, not only Germany but its erstwhile capital had been divided into four sectors, Soviet, American, British and French. As relations between Russia and the West deteriorated, the city became the principal theatre of the Cold War. In June 1948, in a test of the Western Allies' resolve, the Soviet authorities cut off power supplies and closed the land routes connecting the western sectors of Berlin with West Germany, knowing that only a few days' supply of essential provisions remained in the city. In a miracle of improvisation, the Americans and British organized hundreds of aircraft to fly in not only medicines and foodstuffs, but also heavy loads like coal; at one stage a plane was landing every 48 seconds. Berliners responded with enthusiasm to what they called *Die Luftbrücke* (the air bridge) and its *Rosinenbomber* (cookie bombers), and after a year the Russians lifted the blockade.

The Berlin Airlift memorial (left), outside Tempelhof airport

1948

Cities, such as Cologne (below), suffered severe bomb damage

German troops invaded Moscow in 1941 (left), but were ill-equipped to cope with Russian winters

41

Two Germanys

The most important front line of the Cold War ran down the middle of Germany and through divided Berlin. As antagonism worsened between the Soviet Union and the West, each bloc sought to integrate 'its' Germany. West Germany rearmed and became a member of NATO, while East Germany, already highly militarized, became a formidable member of the Soviet-dominated Warsaw Pact. The ancient antagonism between France and Germany evaporated, replaced by genuine friendship and by cooperation as the leading partners in the Common Market, subsequently the European Union.

Professions of eternal friendship between the Soviet Union and the German Democratic Republic, the so-called 'First German Workers' and Peasants' State', were less convincing. Throughout the 1950s, East Germans voted against Communism with their feet, crossing the still open boundary between East and West Berlin. Many of them were highly qualified, an irreplaceable loss to the ailing East German economy. The building of the Berlin Wall in 1961 staunched the flow, and within a few years the GDR was claiming to have created one of the world's strongest economies. Its population knew better, not least because nearly everyone could watch Western television and see the realities of life in the West. When the USSR's President Mikhail Gorbachev loosened the reins of Soviet control in the late 1980s, pressure for change grew irresistible, though few expected the regime to collapse as quickly as it did.

1948

'Too Ugly, Too Noisy'

With these words, the British motor magnate William (later Lord) Rootes threw away Britain's chance of taking over production of what was to become the world's most successful automobile, the Volkswagen. The 'Beetle' had been conceived under the Nazi regime as the car to motorize the Master Race, but only a handful had been produced by the time the war broke out. In 1945, Rootes' reluctance was ignored by the British officer in charge of the run-down works in Wolfsburg. Scraping together a workforce and getting hold of materials, Major Ivan Hirst managed to restart production. By the 1950s, with German management once more in charge, the Volkswagen was selling hundreds of thousands of Beetles worldwide.

Crossing the border in Berlin (right)

Memorials in Berlin to those who died trying to cross to the west

Strike on the Stalinallee

While their Western counterparts were beginning to enjoy the fruits of prosperity, East German workers suffered shortages and were exhorted to work harder for less pay. Matters came to a head on 17 June 1953. Builders working on the Stalinallee, a prestigious Soviet-style boulevard in East Berlin, downed tools and marched *en masse* through the streets. Their example was followed throughout East Germany, with strikes and demonstrations occurring in some 200 cities and towns. The Communist leadership panicked, and called for Russian help. Hurled cobblestones were no match for Soviet tanks, and the rebellion was soon crushed, though not before an unknown number of demonstrators had been killed. West German outrage was intense, and 17 June was declared a national day of commemoration, the 'Day of German Unity'.

The Wall

In the early morning of 13 August 1961, not long after the East German leader Walter Ulbricht had proclaimed 'We have no intention of building a wall', workmen began constructing a barrier between East and West Berlin. At first it consisted of crudely laid blockwork and barbed wire, and wasn't much of a deterrent to determined escapers. But later the barrier became a very formidable obstacle indeed. Called the 'Anti-Fascist Defence Rampart' by its creators, it consisted of a virtually unclimbable smooth concrete wall 4m (13ft) high, backed by a 'death strip', tank and vehicle traps, tripwires and a further fence. Guards and their dogs patrolled constantly. During its three decades of existence, the Wall claimed the lives of more than 100 would-be escapees.

Interrupted Olympics

Germany's turn to host the Olympic games came round again in 1972. This time the venue was not Berlin, divided since 1961 by the Communists' Wall, but the southern city of Munich. All seemed set for what were to be the biggest games yet, with more than 7,000 athletes from 121 countries. Munich turned itself inside out in a frenzy of construction, building a glittering new U-Bahn to take visitors to the sensational stadium in the north of the city, spectacularly set among swelling landforms and lakes and overlooked by a tall tower that afforded an astonishing view of the distant Alps. But the exploits of the athletes were overshadowed by tragedy, when Palestinian gunmen stormed the Olympic village, killing 11 Israelis. This was an especially bitter blow to a Germany that had strived to build a positive relationship with the new state of Israel.

From Street-fighter to Foreign Minister

Germany's 'Generation of 1968' was as radical as that of any other country and frequently more violent, with some of its members—including the Baader-Meinhof Gang—turning to actual terrorism. Others abandoned protest in preference to working within the 'system', none more successfully than the charismatic, chameleon-like Joschka Fischer. He was in the front line of protest in the 1960s and 1970s, but later eschewed action on the street for politics. Fischer became a prominent member of Germany's influential Green Party, taking it into government in 1998 in coalition with the Social Democrats. As Foreign Minister, Fischer made a huge impact, encouraging reluctant fellow Greens into military action in Kosovo while rowing in public over Iraq with hard-line US hawks such as Donald Rumsfeld.

Walter Ulbricht
(1893–1973)

Germany's unification flag (far left), and the Soviet insignia (left)

WIR RUFEN DIE JUGEND DER WELT

MÜNCHEN 1972

1989

An anti-Olympics poster (above left) from 1972

Konrad Adenauer
(1876–1967)

DER SPIEGEL

One of the *Rosinenbombers* (above) used in the Berlin Airlift

Germany Reunited

Euphoria at the fall of the Berlin Wall in 1989 and reunification in 1990 soon turned into disillusionment. On the one hand, West Germans resented paying extra taxes to support the shaky economy of the East; on the other, many East Germans were bitter about the loss of the comprehensive social security the Communist regime had provided, and some felt lost in the individualistic and competitive world of Western consumerism. The physical reality of the Wall might be gone, but a wall of sorts continued to exist in the minds of West Germans (*Wessis*) and Easterners (*Ossis*). Nevertheless, the peaceful reunification of the divided country remained a huge achievement, a tribute to a Germany that seemed at last to have overcome the tribulations of its often tormented history.

Fall of the Wall

As demands for total reform of the GDR intensified in the autumn of 1989, the Communist leadership twisted and turned in its attempts to remain in power. The long-serving leader, Erich Honecker, was forced to resign, but his successor, Egon Krenz, was equally out of touch. At a press conference on the 9 November, a minister mumbled something about easing travel to the West. This was the signal for thousands of East Berliners to flock to the Wall, where confused guards had no option but to let them through. In the following days and weeks, a carnival atmosphere gripped Berlin as its long-separated populations mixed joyously.

The Stasi

As the East German regime crumbled, its 'sword and shield', the secret police known as the Stasi (short for STAastSIcherheit, or State Security) worked frantically to destroy evidence of its all-pervasive presence, shredding, pulping and burning files. Citizens' groups halted this activity, with records subsequently administered by appointed commissions that have revealed the extent of Stasi surveillance and control. Some 100,000 uniformed and armed officials were backed by 500,000 'unofficial collaborators', members of the public who informed regularly on fellow workers, friends and even spouses. A further 2 million informers provided occasional information.

Chancellor Kohl

The towering figure of Helmut Kohl dominated German politics for most of the 1980s and 1990s. He was driven by a deep determination to draw the nations of Europe together to make future war between them unthinkable. Kohl's greatest achievement was the unification of his country, which he steamrollered through when more cautious spirits advocated a long period of transition.

A remaining section of the Berlin Wall (left)

Helmut Kohl (1930–)

1989 to today

Dismantling the Stasi's weapons room (above)

Erich Honecker and Leonid Brezhnev depicted on the western side of the Berlin Wall (right)

On the Move

ARRIVING

BY AIR

Although Berlin has regained its status as Germany's capital city, the country's largest and most important airport is not here but in Frankfurt. As West Germany's financial hub, centrally located Frankfurt was the logical place to develop a major international airport, and its vast range of facilities and excellent accessibility have kept it ahead in the post-reunification period. It is here that the national airline, Lufthansa, has its base, and it is here that the majority of international flights arrive and depart, connecting with services to and from all major German cities.

Berlin is served not by a single airport, but by three, a reflection of the city's divided past. A pre-war, inner-city airport, Tempelhof, is used mostly by smaller airlines and charter flights. Schönefeld was built by the Communist regime to serve East Berlin and much of the GDR, and is some distance away from the middle of the city on its southeastern outskirts. It is used by a number of international carriers, including budget airlines and charter flights. Most international carriers land at Tegel, the modern airport built in the western suburbs to serve West Berlin.

Elsewhere in Germany, a number of regional capitals and other cities are served by international airlines, notably Munich and Düsseldorf, but also Cologne/Bonn, Hannover, Hamburg, Leipzig/Halle and Dresden. Budget airlines have exploited the low charges of smaller airports such as Erfurt, Friedrichshafen (for Lake Constance), Hahn (for Frankfurt), Niederrrhein and Lübeck (for Hamburg).

GETTING INTO TOWN FROM THE AIRPORT

AIRPORT	FRANKFURT	BERLIN: TEGEL	BERLIN: TEMPELHOF	BERLIN: SCHÖNEFELD
DISTANCE TO CITY	12km (7 miles)	8km (5 miles) to Zoologischer Garten	5km (3 miles) to Zoologischer Garten	18km (11 miles) to Friedrichstrasse
TAXI	Price: €20–25 Journey time: 20 min	Price: about €15 to Zoologischer Garten Journey time: 20–30 min	Price: about €12 to Zoologischer Garten Journey time: 10–15 min	Price: about €23 to Friedrichstrasse or Zoologischer Garten Journey time: 30–40 min
TRAIN	**From Regionalbahnhof:** S-Bahn S8 or S9 to Hauptbahnhof (main train station), Offenbach or Hanau Frequency: 15 min Price: €3.25 Journey time: 15 min **From Fernbahnhof:** frequent (two-hourly, one-hourly, half-hourly) intercity trains to major cities	n/a	U-Bahn station Platz der Luftbrücke; line 6 direct to Friedrichstrasse	**Airport Express** to Alexanderplatz, Friedrichstrasse, Zoologischer Garten Journey time: about 35 min **S-Bahn line 9** to same destinations. Mainline rail connections
BUS	Services to towns in the region, e.g. Heidelberg, Mannheim	**Express bus X9** (or local bus 109) to Zoologischer Garten or Jakob-Kaiser-Platz, with connections to U-Bahn, S-Bahn and DB (mainline railway). **Express bus TXL** to Unter den Linden and Alexanderplatz. **Local bus 128** to Kurt-Schumacher-Platz U-Bahn station, then onward by U-Bahn to any city destination. Price €2 for a single ticket to anywhere in central Berlin	Local buses 119 (to Kurfürstendamm and Grunewald), 184, 341	Local bus 191 to U-Bahn station Rudow, with onward connections to any city destination
CAR	Direct access to Autobahns A3 (Cologne–Munich) and A5 (Hannover–Basel), and to expressway B43	Direct access to A111 expressway, linking to national autobahn network and city streets	Direct access to A100 expressway	Direct access to Autobahn A113 (expressway towards middle of city is under construction)

The major airports have generally good access and facilities for visitors with a disability. Let your travel agent or airline know your requirements before your trip and allow some extra time for check-in. See page 68 for more information.

Signs in airports are normally in English as well as German, although on approach roads note that *Abflug* means 'departure', *Ankunft* means 'arrival', and *Rückgabe Mietwagen* means 'rental vehicle return'.

Frankfurt-Rhein-Main is Germany's busiest airport and is home to Lufthansa, the national airline

GETTING INTO TOWN FROM THE AIRPORT

MUNICH	DÜSSELDORF-RHEIN-RUHR	HAMBURG	LEIPZIG-HALLE
32km (20 miles)	10km (6 miles)	13km (8miles)	15km (9 miles)
Price: €45–50 Journey time: 45 min	Price: €16 Journey time: 20 min	Price: €17–18 Journey time: 30 min	Price: €30 Journey time: 30 min
To city's Ostbahnhof (East Station): S-Bahn line 1 Frequency: 20 min Price: €8 Journey time: 30 min **To city's Ostbahnhof, Marienplatz and Hauptbahnhof:** S-Bahn line 8 Frequency: 20 min Journey time: 30–40 min Price: €8	**To Düsseldorf Hauptbahnhof (main train station):** S-Bahn line 7 from S-Bahnhof Düsseldorf Flughafen Terminal Frequency: 20–30 min Journey time: 13 min Price: €1.85 **To cities in region and beyond from Düsseldorf Flughafen mainline rail station:** 350 local, regional and intercity trains daily	S-Bahn and U-Bahn links from 2007	**Airport Express** to Leipzig Hauptbahnhof (main train station) and Halle Hauptbahnhof (main train station) Frequency: 30 min (less at night) Journey time: 14 min (Leipzig), 16 min (Halle) Price: €3.30. Mainline train services from airport station to cities in region and beyond
Autobus Oberbayern to Schwabing and Hauptbahnhof Frequency: 20 min 6.20am–9.40pm Journey time: 45 min. Price: €9. Buses to several cities in region and Austria	Local services. Express bus to Aachen	**To Hauptbahnhof (main train station):** Airport Express Frequency: 15–20 min daily 5am–9pm Journey time: 30 min. Price: €4.35 **To U-Bahn/S-Bahn station Ohlsdorf, with U-Bahn and S-Bahn connections with all destinations in Hamburg:** City bus 110 Journey time: Airport to U-Bahn Ohlsdorf 11 min. Price: €2.20 Local bus services (e.g. 39 to Wandsbek Markt) and regional bus services to Kiel and Lübeck Expressway B433n south then	Bus services to cities in region, including Havag Bus every hour into Halle
Direct access to Autobahn A92 (Deggendorf–Munich), leading south into city	Direct access to Autobahn A44, then expressway B8 into city	B433 into city. Hannover–Kiel Autobahn A7 (interchange 23) 4km (2.5 miles) west	Autobahn A14 east, then south at interchange 17a on B2 to Leipzig. Autobahn A14 north-west, then west at interchange 11 on B100 to Halle

MAIN PORTS AND AIRPORTS

This map shows Germany's main ports and international airports. See pages 64–65 for details of other airports in Germany.

DK

Cuxhaven
Hamburg
Fühlsbüttel
Lübeck
Rostock

Wilhelmshaven

Bremerhaven

Hamburg

PL

Bremen

NL

Hannover
Tegel
BERLIN
Tempelhof

Münster
Schönefeld

Düsseldorf-
Rhein-Ruhr

Düsseldorf
Leipzig
Halle

Köln
Leipzig
Dresden

B
Bonn
Köln/Bonn
Erfurt

Frankfurt
am Main

Mainz

Frankfurt-Rhein-
Main
Würzburg
CZ

Heidelberg
Nürnberg

F
Regensburg

Stuttgart

Freiburg
im Breisgau
München
A

CH

Frankfurt (tel 01805 372 46 36, www.frankfurt-airport.de) is 12km (7 miles) from downtown Frankfurt and officially known as Frankfurt-Rhein-Main. This gigantic international airport is not only the largest in Germany but also the busiest on mainland Europe, handling more than 40 million passengers annually. It has two terminals and a third is on the drawing board. The sheer size of the airport means you should leave plenty of time to find your check-in desk and for connections. The terminals are linked by a driverless overhead train called the Sky Line.

The range of facilities at the airport is impressive, and Frankfurt's public transportation connections are among the best in Europe. There are two train stations: beneath Terminal 1 is the Regionalbahnhof, which is served by local and regional trains, including the Frankfurt S-Bahn; some distance away, but accessible by covered pedestrian walkway, is the Fernbahnhof, used by intercity trains. From the Fernbahnhof you can travel swiftly to every major town in Germany (and to several in other countries), either directly or at most with just one change.

Berlin Tegel is the city's busiest airport and was originally built during the Berlin Airlift of 1948–49. It's a modern complex in the northwestern suburbs, with easy access into the city, albeit without a direct rail link. It is promoted locally as Berlin's 'frequent flyer airport'. Tegel has a full range of services, including a tourist information desk (daily 5am–11pm), car rental desks, shops, banks and restaurants. This is the Berlin airport at which visitors from abroad are most likely to arrive, certainly if they are coming on a scheduled flight by a national carrier.

Munich's airy, modern airport has good transportation links to the city

Berlin Tempelhof inner-city airport is almost within walking distance of the attractions of central Berlin, but it is relatively little used nowadays and has limited facilities. Together with Tegel, it is likely to be phased out altogether when the controversial expansion of Schönefeld as Berlin's single international airport goes ahead.

Berlin Schönefeld is on the southeastern outskirts of the city and is sometimes referred to as 'Berlin's holiday airport'. It was built in GDR times as the international airport to serve East Berlin and much of East Germany. It now specializes in flights to and from holiday destinations in southern Europe and the Middle East, and is home to charter airlines and budget carriers. It has been brought up to date in a number of ways and now has most of the usual facilities. There are ambitious plans to redevelop it completely as Berlin's sole international airport—Berlin Brandenburg International—with world-class facilities worthy of a capital city. The expansion is controversial, and a date is yet to be agreed. A shuttle takes visitors

to the train station (mainline and local services), which is also within walking distance.

For more information on any of the Berlin airports, contact 0180 500 01 86 or check online at www.berlin-airport.de.

Munich: Franz-Josef-Strauss-Flughafen (tel 089 975 00, www.munich-airport.de) was named after Bavaria's most famous post-war politician. This ultra-modern airport stands in open countryside well to the northeast of the city, to which it is linked by S-Bahn and autobahn. Its lavish facilities and glittering architecture are in complete contrast to the old inner-city airport it has replaced, and it is the country's second-busiest airport. To cope with the additional traffic, a second terminal was opened in 2003.

Düsseldorf Rhein-Ruhr (tel 0211 42 10, www.duesseldorf-international.de) is a modern airport, just on the northern edge of Düsseldorf's built-up area, and well placed to serve the vast Ruhr conurbation and its 6 million inhabitants. The airport is linked by the fully automatic

overhead Skytrain (ticket necessary) to its own mainline railway station, which is served by regional and intercity trains, making it easy to travel swiftly and conveniently to most towns in the region. Local trains depart from their own station right in the terminal. The airport has a full range of facilities, including a stylish shopping arcade and a choice of places to eat and drink.

Hamburg-Fuhlsbüttel (tel 040 507 50, www.ham-airport.de) is the fifth-busiest airport in Germany and only 13km (8 miles) from the downtown area. There are flights to and from most large German cities and other mostly European destinations. There is also a good range of facilities. Planned extensions of the underground and S-Bahn networks will improve access into the city; in the meantime, a bus service runs frequently and rapidly.

Leipzig-Halle (tel 0341 224 11 55, www.leipzig-halle-airport.de), on the northern edge of the city, has been comprehensively modernized, and is still being extended to serve the cities of

MAJOR CAR RENTAL COMPANIES		
COMPANY	**TELEPHONE**	**WEBSITE**
Avis	0180 0230 48 98	www.avis.com
Europcar	0180 580 00	www.europcar.de
Hertz	0800 654 30 01	www.hertz.com
Sixt	0180 525 44 44	www.e-sixt.de

Major international car rental companies have offices at all the main airports, in city downtown areas and at railway stations. Airport desks usually have extended opening hours and you can normally return a car at any time.

It may pay to reserve a rental car in advance, and you should certainly investigate any special deals that are being offered, perhaps through your airline. Otherwise, rates are somewhat higher than the European average. The German firm Sixt (linked to Budget) may offer slightly better rates. Check whether there is an additional fee for picking up a car at one point and returning it to another.

Insurance is compulsory, and drivers must have a current licence and be older than 21 (sometimes 25) years old. An international driving licence is theoretically necessary, but it is unlikely you will be asked for one except possibly by a small rental firm. Additional drivers must be noted on any documentation.

Make sure you are certain about what fuel your car requires before you drive off, and familiarize yourself with the controls, particularly if you are used to a right-hand drive. The car should be equipped with a warning triangle and first-aid kit. Check also that there is no damage to the car's bodywork that has not already been noted in the contract. There are likely to be restrictions on which countries the car may be driven in; even countries in the European Union such as Poland may be excluded.

Rental cars are normally supplied with a tankful of fuel. You should fill up before returning the vehicle; if you leave this to the rental firm, they will charge you an additional amount, possibly double the cost of whatever topping-up is required.

east-central Germany. It handles flights to and from major German cities and a number of European destinations. Facilities are excellent, and there are mainline train connections as well as a fast link into Leipzig and to the new trade fair grounds.

BY FERRY

The only direct car and passenger ferry service from Britain to Germany is operated by DFDS Seaways (tel 0870 5333 000 from the UK; www.dfdsseaways.co.uk) between Harwich and the port town of Cuxhaven at the mouth of the River Elbe. The well-equipped boat sails on alternate days and the crossing takes 20 hours. Cuxhaven has a direct connection to the autobahn network and is 120km (75 miles) by main road from Hamburg. A bus to and from Hamburg connects with the ferry's arrival and departure.

Scandlines (tel 0381 54 350 from Germany; www.scandlines.de) run services linking the Baltic coast towns of Kiel with Klaipeda in Lithuania; Rostock with Gedser in Denmark, Liepaja in Latvia and Trelleborg in Sweden; Puttgarden with Rødby; and Sassnitz with Rønne, both in Denmark and Trelleborg in Sweden.

BY TRAIN

International trains connect most European countries to the German rail network. There is no direct link from Britain, but Eurostar services (tel 08705 186

Signposting in Germany is very clear, often using symbols for places of interest

Gute Fahrt— *have a good journey*

186 from the UK; www.eurostar .com) through the Channel Tunnel connect in Brussels with the high-speed Brussels–Aachen–Cologne line, making this route an attractive alternative to air travel. From Cologne there are good connections to all major German cities. An early evening train from London connects at Brussels with a DB Nachtzug sleeper train to a number of German cities, including Berlin and Hamburg. Eurostar trains currently depart from London Waterloo; from 2007 most trains will use the new terminal at London St. Pancras, further reducing journey times. Check-in at Waterloo is 30 minutes before departure, and you are allowed two suitcases and one item of hand luggage, all of which must be labelled with your name, address and seat number. You should not change your seat during the journey. Passports are required. Return ticket prices London–Cologne are from around £95, and the journey time is 4.5 hours.

BY CAR

To bring your own car to Germany you will need a valid driving licence. Your home licence is normally sufficient if

Munich's busy railway station, Hauptbahnhof

you are from other European countries or the US, but bring an international permit if you have one. Residents of countries other than these will need an international permit and the car registration document. Vehicles must be insured and display a sign at the rear indicating the country of origin.

Germany is connected to its neighbours by a dense network of motorways and main and minor roads. Frontier installations with EU countries have been progressively dismantled and controls relaxed, so border hold-

ups are few. The most popular route for motorists driving from Britain begins with the Channel Tunnel or the short sea crossing from Dover to Calais. At Calais, you join the European motorway network. E40 leads through Belgium to Aachen, Cologne and beyond, while E42 and E25 lead through Belgium and Luxembourg to the central Rhineland and the southwest of the country.

High-speed trains link major German cities with other European destinations

GETTING AROUND

City Transportation: Berlin

ON THE MOVE

Comprising underground (U-Bahn) and overhead (S-Bahn) trains, plus buses, trams and ferries, Berlin's fully integrated public transportation network makes it possible to explore the whole city without ever needing a car. The system is run by BVG (Berliner Verkehrs-Betriebe, or Berlin Traffic Enterprises).

INFORMATION

There is a BVG information pavilion (tel 030 29 71 29 71; www.bvg.de; Mon–Fri 6.30–8.30, Sat, Sun 9–3.30) at the entrance to the Hardenbergplatz bus station in front of Bahnhof Zoologischer Garten (Zoo Station) where the staff can provide you with tickets and travel information, including a basic public transportation map. There is also a public transportation information desk at Tegel airport.

Public transportation maps are also available at all stations, and tourist information offices dispense travel information.

THE NETWORK

Berlin's public transportation system is fully integrated, and many journeys will be made using a ticket or pass that allows you to change from one mode of travel to another.

● The S-Bahn (*Stadt-Bahn*, or City Rail), identified by a large letter 'S', runs through the middle of the city, linking it to the suburbs and beyond.
It runs mostly on overhead tracks, although some sections are underground. The elevated section from Savignyplatz and Zoologischer Garten in the west to Friedrichstrasse, Alexanderplatz and Ostbahnhof in the east is particularly useful for visitors and offers a glimpse of key parts of the city. Trains run at approximately 10-minute intervals between 4am and 1am. An hourly night service is provided on lines 3 to 10.

You can take your bicycle on the U-Bahn, but you will need to buy a special ticket

● The U-Bahn (*Untergrundbahn*, or Underground) comprises nine lines and 163 stations, the latter identified by a prominent letter 'U'. The network is densest in the central parts of the city, though some lines penetrate far into the suburbs, where they may run at ground level. There is even a curious elevated section between Nollendorfplatz and Warschauerplatz, which gives an interesting view of the Landwehr canal and the attractions of Kreuzberg. Trains run at approximately 10-minute intervals between 4am and 1am. Lines 1, 9 and 15 provide an all-night service at 15-minute intervals.

● Berlin's extensive fleet of yellow-painted double-decker buses run from 4.30am–1am, as well as a number of night services. Bus stops (as everywhere in Germany) are identified by a green 'H' on a yellow background. Always enter the bus by the front doors and leave by the middle or rear doors.

● Before 1989, trams were confined to East Berlin. There are 30 tram lines, some of which have been extended into western Berlin.

TICKETS

Tickets come in various forms, including short-distance, single-journey, day and week tickets, ranging from €1.20 to €24.50, and it is worth considering carefully what trips you are likely to make during your stay before any purchase is made. All tickets except the short-distance ticket allow you to make as many transfers as you need between lines or from one mode of travel to another. Berlin is divided into three travel zones, A, B and C; most visitor trips will be within the two inner zones (A and B). The outer zone (C) includes Potsdam.

You can buy tickets that are valid for up to one day from the orange and yellow vending machines at the entrances to the stations. Instructions are in English as well as German. Coins and sometimes notes are accepted and change is given. Tickets must be validated before travel by being stamped in one of the red machines on the platform or aboard buses and trams. Single-journey and day tickets may also be purchased from bus drivers and on board trams.

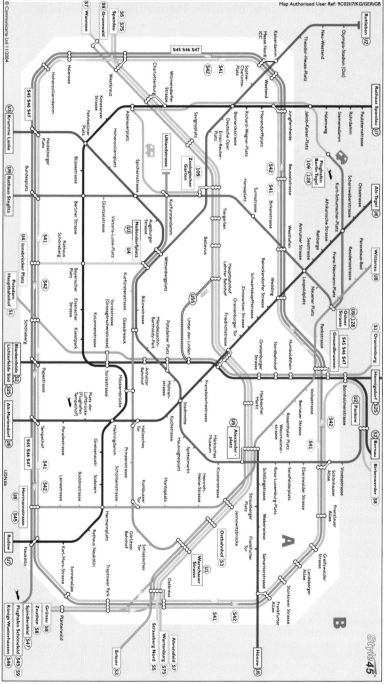

Map Authorised User Ref: 9C02II7/KG/GER/GB

© Communicarta Ltd 11/2004

Style45

City Transportation: Munich, Hamburg and Frankfurt

Public transportation makes getting around Munich easy

Most German cities have integrated public transportation systems based on buses and trams, while the larger cities and conurbations also have S-Bahn local trains and U-Bahn underground trains. Through ticketing means that you can transfer between lines or change from one mode of travel to another on a single ticket.

Fare systems are usually based on zones, with tickets increasing in price the more zones are crossed. Ticket vending machines usually display a clear map of the network showing the different zones. The majority of visitor destinations in cities are likely to be within a single, central zone. Many vending machines have instructions in English, and they often accept notes as well as coins (and in some cases credit cards as well), and they give change. Before starting your journey, you must validate your ticket by inserting it into a stamping machine on the platform or on board the vehicle.

Single-journey tickets are available, but it will often be worth purchasing a *Tageskarte* (day ticket), *Familienkarte* (family ticket) or *Wochenkarte* (weekly ticket). A *Streifenkarte*

(strip ticket) consists of a strip of usually 10 single-journey tickets at a reduced price. The real bargain in many cities is the Welcome Card, valid for between one and seven days, and giving concessions on entry to museums, galleries and other visitor attractions as well as unlimited use of public transportation. See individual entries for details.

Tickets are not checked before boarding, but non-uniformed inspectors are active, and on-the-spot fines are levied if you do not have a ticket or if the one you have is incorrect. Claiming that you are an ignorant tourist is unacceptable as an excuse.

MUNICH

MVV (Münchener Verkehrs- und Tarifverbund), Hauptbahnhof (main train station)
Tel 089 210 330
www.mvv-muenchen.de
🕐 Daily 7am–8pm
Also at Marienplatz (below ground)
🕐 Mon–Fri 9am–8pm, Sat 9am–4pm
The MVV (Munich Transport Authority) runs a comprehensive public transportation network comprising eight S-Bahn lines and six U-Bahn lines, plus trams and buses. Several S-Bahn lines run underground through the middle of the city, linking the Hauptbahnhof with Karlsplatz and the important hub of Marienplatz.

A single-journey ticket costs €2.10, a strip of 10 is €9.50, day tickets from €4.50 (depending on the number of zones) and a three-day ticket is €11.

The bus-stop symbol is the same throughout the country

HAMBURG

HVV (Hamburger Verkehrsverbund), Steinstrasse 27, 20095 Hamburg
Tel 040 194 49
www.hvv.de
🕐 Daily 7am–8pm
Also at the Hauptbahnhof (main train station) 🕐 Mon–Fri 7am–8pm, Sat 8.30–5, Sun 11–8
The HVV (Hamburg Transport Authority) is responsible for a public transportation network comprising 15 S-Bahn and U-Bahn lines, more than 200 bus routes and several river and ferry services. Important hubs include Hauptbahnhof (the main train station), serving north and south sections, Jungfernstieg (S-Bahn station, close to Alster and Rathausplatz) and Landungsbrücken (for harbour trips and the promenade).

A single-journey ticket for travel in the central zone costs €1.05.

FRANKFURT

Information
RMV (Rhein-Main Verkehrsverbund), Am Kreishaus 1–5, 65719 Hofheim
Tel 0180 235 14 51, 01805 768 46 36 (hotline)
🕐 Mon–Thu 7–3, Fri 7–1.30
www.rmv.de
The RMV (Rhine-Main Transport Authority) administers public transportation in a vast area that is focused on Frankfurt and takes in the cities of the whole region around the confluence of the Rhine and Main rivers, among them Wiesbaden, Bad Homburg and Darmstadt. In addition to trams and 100 bus routes, there are several S-Bahn and U-Bahn lines. Important interchange stations in central Frankfurt include the Hauptbahnhof and there is also a direct S-Bahn link to the citiy's airport.

Domplatz

Altstadtbus

CityTour

StadtRundfahrt Altstadtbahn CityTour

ON THE MOVE

Driving

The quality of the German road network makes driving an excellent way to explore the country. Although constant driving at high speed can be tiring, the autobahn makes it possible to cover long distances in a short time, enabling you to move easily from one area of interest to another. A car is the best way of getting around if you aim to explore smaller towns and villages and the countryside. If your interest is confined to a city or group of cities, public transportation will almost certainly be your better option.

The best-known feature of Germany's extensive and well-maintained road system is the autobahn, the network of toll-free motorways covering the whole country, but other roads like Bundesstrassen (national roads) and Landstrassen (main roads) are generally engineered to a high standard, with good surfaces and helpful signposting. Autobahns are identified by a white letter 'A' and a number on a blue background (e.g. A1, A2), and national roads by a black letter 'B' and a number (e.g. B1, B2) on a yellow background. The previously inadequate road network of eastern Germany has been transformed beyond recognition through the construction of motorways like the Ostseeautobahn, linking the Baltic coast to the rest of the country, and through the improvement of other roads. The downside to all this is the density of traffic; congestion can be acute in built-up areas like the Rhine–Ruhr and Rhine–Main conurbations, and anywhere at holiday times.

More than 100 named tourist routes crisscross the country.

Some, such as stretches of the Deutsche Alpenstrasse (German Alpine Road), were purpose-built as scenic highways, although most are ordinary roads linking places of similar interest. The

Signposting in Germany is usually very clear

best known is probably the Romantische Strasse (Romantic Road), which runs from Würzburg in northern Bavaria to Füssen at the foot of the Alps, passing through picturesque, historic towns on the way. Even if they are not designated as such, many of the roads through the country's well-wooded uplands

qualify as scenic routes, and extensive sections of the autobahn network (for example, Cologne–Limburg–Frankfurt, Munich–Salzburg and the Thuringian Forest autobahn) offer spectacular visual experiences.

Germans are fast drivers, and determined popular resistance among motorists has prevented the adoption of a compulsory speed limit on the autobahn. It can be unnerving when overtaking at the suggested maximum speed of 130kph (80mph), only to glance in your mirror and spot a powerful vehicle coming up behind you at 200kph (125mph) or more. Most drivers are aware of what they are doing and respect the rules of the road, having passed the country's particularly rigorous driving test. Once you have become used to conditions, you will find the behaviour of fellow road-users fairly predictable.

BRINGING YOUR OWN CAR
Before You Leave
● If you have a right-hand drive car, adjust your headlights for driving on the right.

SPEED LIMITS			
AREA	**BUILT-UP AREAS**	**OUTSIDE BUILT-UP AREAS**	**AUTOBAHNS**
SPEED LIMIT	50kph (31mph) 30kph (18mph) in some residential and central areas	100kph (62mph)	Advisory limit is 130kph (80mph), otherwise there is no limit (though many heavily trafficked or curving stretches have speed limits of between 90kph (56mph) and 120kph (75mph))
SIGN	Indicated by the name of the town or village in black lettering on a yellow background (end of limit is shown by an identical sign with a diagonal red band through the place-name)		Minimum speed is indicated by a number on a blue circular sign

MAIN ROAD NETWORK

This map shows only the main routes between major cities. For more detailed information, see the Atlas section, beginning on page 427

● Contact your motor insurer or broker at least one month beforehand to make sure you will be covered to drive abroad.
● Have your car serviced.
● Fit a wing mirror on the left if you don't already have one.
● Ensure you have adequate breakdown assistance cover, such as the Automobile Association's Five Star (tel 0800 444500; www.theaa.com).

You Will Need
● A valid national driving licence (a translation may be required if you are from a non-EU country or the US; check with your local Germany tourist bureau—
▷ 419—before setting off) or

Speed limits vary, depending on what type of road you are on

international driver's licence.
● The vehicle registration document if you are from a non-EU country.
● A vehicle insurance certificate; third-party cover is the minimum required.
● A red breakdown triangle, spare bulb kit and first-aid kit (including surgical gloves).
● A nationality sticker unless you have EU plates.
● Winter tyres or snow chains if you intend to drive in mountain areas during winter.

RULES OF THE ROAD
● Drive on the right.
● On roads without yellow diamond priority signs, give way

56 GETTING AROUND

to traffic from the right.

- Seat belts must be worn by all occupants of a vehicle.
- Children under 12 must use an appropriate safety seat.
- Halt at tram stops where there is no central reservation and allow passengers to cross the road to board and disembark.
- Give way to trams and buses as they leave stops.
- Use dipped headlights in poor visibility and in tunnels.
- Do not use side lights when driving.
- Give way to pedestrians when turning right or left at uncontrolled junctions (intersections).

- Do not drink and drive. The penalties are severe.
- Traffic lights are supplemented by priority signs, which must be obeyed when the lights are not functioning (e.g. at night or during weekends).
- A flashing light may indicate that a right turn is permitted when traffic lights are red, but you must give way to traffic coming from the other direction.
- Insulting behaviour to other drivers or police is an offence.
- Fines can be imposed on the spot by police and vehicles may be confiscated.

THE AUTOBAHN

With a total length approaching 12,000km (7,500 miles), the autobahn network connects all major cities and towns. Many places are linked to the system by more than one interchange, and it is sensible to check the map to see which exit suits you best. Interchanges are numbered. Signs show the distance between service areas, which are generally closely spaced. In addition, there are rest areas with basic facilities, plus picnic areas, particularly on scenic stretches. Service areas vary in their provision of facilities; some have hotels, and all have

DISTANCES BETWEEN MAJOR CITIES

City	Berlin	Bonn	Bremen	Dresden	Düsseldorf	Erfurt	Frankfurt-am-Main	Freiburg	Hamburg	Hannover	Heidelberg	Köln	Leipzig	Mainz	München	Münster	Nürnberg	Regensburg	Rostock	Stuttgart	Würzburg
Berlin	—	552	400	216	530	310	535	741	254	306	615	543	211	545	552	441	426	453	219	617	453
Bonn	593	—	333	542	050	349	156	401	433	315	223	031	517	143	531	149	348	441	631	337	248
Bremen	391	342	—	432	309	441	441	658	128	134	521	323	344	451	725	153	549	626	326	629	453
Dresden	191	570	473	—	549	210	435	617	449	335	455	534	120	445	428	510	302	326	414	453	329
Düsseldorf	549	67	298	599	—	356	224	429	410	253	252	037	511	211	600	125	417	509	608	406	317
Erfurt	299	366	469	215	395	—	243	500	500	343	322	341	145	253	408	343	241	309	445	420	244
Frankfurt-am-Main	547	177	448	463	223	259	—	248	511	353	110	209	410	043	406	258	223	316	709	224	123
Freiburg	805	426	715	677	472	526	276	—	728	610	152	414	617	246	414	515	340	425	917	210	303
Hamburg	282	452	118	503	408	499	496	762	—	153	550	423	403	521	744	255	608	645	220	648	512
Hannover	285	312	122	371	268	356	353	619	152	—	433	306	247	403	628	204	450	529	351	531	354
Heidelberg	629	242	530	520	288	341	91	189	578	435	—	237	450	108	335	337	218	304	748	128	142
Köln	566	26	316	568	35	364	191	441	425	286	256	—	509	156	545	140	402	454	621	351	302
Leipzig	184	511	370	117	532	156	404	662	400	268	486	508	—	420	427	422	301	328	347	452	328
Mainz	571	164	472	487	210	283	39	280	519	376	95	178	427	—	419	308	236	328	719	222	136
München	588	572	775	460	618	419	410	416	805	673	336	586	445	434	—	634	155	128	729	241	256
Münster	474	175	173	561	130	388	281	547	280	194	363	148	458	304	678	—	451	543	453	451	355
Nürnberg	438	395	583	310	441	269	234	383	613	470	226	410	294	258	173	502	—	111	602	216	113
Regensburg	481	501	667	345	547	312	339	474	697	565	317	515	337	363	132	607	112	—	629	302	206
Rostock	226	640	306	447	596	500	684	1006	197	340	766	614	384	708	789	468	638	681	—	753	628
Stuttgart	628	356	639	500	402	433	206	206	669	526	119	371	485	210	226	477	206	297	829	—	140
Würzburg	497	288	485	369	334	279	127	321	515	372	164	303	353	151	285	404	109	214	697	144	—

To plan your car journey, use the blue top part of the chart above to work out the estimated journey time between major towns (hours in larger type and minutes in smaller); the lower, green chart shows distances in kilometres

GLOSSARY OF ROAD SIGNS

GERMAN	ENGLISH
Abblenden	dip headlights
Alle Richtungen	all directions
Anfang	start
Anlieger frei	except residents
Ausfahrt	exit
Baustelle	works
Einbahnstrasse	one-way street
Einfahrt	entrance
Ende	end
Gefahr	danger
Links	left
Radweg	bicycle path
Raststätte	service area
Rechts	right
Rollsplitt	loose chippings
Stau	hold-up, traffic jam
Steinschlag	falling rocks
Umleitung	diversion
Unfall	accident
Vorrang/Vorfahrt	priority
Vorsicht	careful
Zentrum	central city

refreshments and well-maintained lavatories. Vehicles joining the autobahn must give way to traffic already on it. Keep to the right-hand lane except when overtaking, and indicate your intention before you change lanes. Emergency telephones are placed at regular intervals, their location indicated by arrows.

PROBLEMS

If your car breaks down or you are involved in an accident, turn your hazard warning lights on and place your warning triangle at a safe distance behind the vehicle (200m/220 yards on the autobahn, less on other roads). You can obtain assistance by calling national German motoring organizations on one of the following numbers:

- ACE tel 01802 34 35 36
- ADAC tel 01802 22 22 22
- AvD tel 0800 9 90 99 09

If an accident has occurred, exchange details with anyone involved (name, address, car details, insurance company's name and address). If anyone is injured, the police must be called (tel 110). Call an ambulance (tel 110) or the fire brigade if required (tel 112). Do not admit liability even if you know you were in the wrong.

PARKING

There are strict rules for when and where you may not park. Parking is forbidden in many, fairly obvious places, for example within 5m (5.5 yards) of a pedestrian crossing or road junction, or within 15m (16.5 yards) of a bus or tram stop. Less obviously, do not park on a main road in the countryside, or where parking restrictions may be indicated solely by the standard sign (which you may have to look for).

Competition for parking spaces can be acute in densely built-up residential areas as well as in the middle of cities. In the former, many spaces will be reserved for residents, while in the latter you will usually have to pay a fee, and the time you may park on the street is likely to be limited to two hours or less. Payment for on-street parking is usually made by using a ticket machine (some of which accept credit cards), or less frequently by inserting coins in a parking meter. Where parking is free but limited in time, you may need to obtain a parking disc (from newspaper kiosks or filling stations) and set it to the correct time.

Rather than waste time driving

MITFAHRERZENTRALE

This is the name given to offices in major cities that arrange car sharing for intercity trips. Drivers planning to undertake such a journey and who have a seat or seats to spare register with the office and are put in touch with others wishing to travel to the same destination. The fee is arranged between driver and passenger(s), and a fee is charged by the *Mitfahrerzentrale*, which also arranges insurance.

around in an attempt to find an on-street space, it may be better to park off-street. Purpose-built parking (*Parkhäuser*) is well signposted, often with an indication of how many spaces are still available. The system usually involves taking a time-stamped ticket on arrival, then inserting it into the pay station just before departing, paying the sum indicated and retaining the ticket for use to raise the exit barrier. Parking areas may be closed at night.

Vehicles parked on the street must be clearly visible at night; leave side lights on in poorly lit areas.

FUEL

Germany pioneered the introduction of lead-free fuel, and

Scenic routes, such as the Alpenstrasse (Alpine Road, above) often have rest areas where you can admire the view

leaded fuel is now unobtainable. On sale are super (*Benzine bleifrei*—95 octane), super-plus (*Super bleifrei*—98 octane) and diesel (*Diesel*). Most filling stations are self-service and often also function as mini-markets. Many are open 24 hours. When purchasing fuel, check the number of the pump and pay the cashier. Credit cards are normally accepted, but you need to check this before purchase, particularly in country areas. Prices vary slightly according to the degree of competition; the cheapest fuel comes from supermarket filling stations, the most expensive on the autobahn or in remote areas. Avoid running out of fuel on the autobahn; you will incur a fine if you do. Depending on exchange rates, fuel prices are slightly cheaper than those in Britain (€1.26 per litre for super unleaded, €0.99 per litre for diesel) but much more expensive than in the US.

SELECTED ROAD SIGNS

Bus or tram stop	**One-way street** (*Einbahnstrasse*)	**Snow chains compulsory**	**Compulsory minimum speed**

Maximum speed limit	**Intersection with priority from right**

Level crossing	**Level crossing without gate or barrier**	**Parking half on pavement permitted**	**Autobahn number**

Bundesstrasse (national road) number	**Euro Route number**

Start of built-up area	**Priority road**	 **Autobahn direction sign**	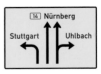 **Bundesstrasse** (national road) direction sign

End of built-up area and 50kph (31mph) speed limit	**End of priority road area**

Trains

Germany has a comprehensive rail network totalling some 42,000km (27,000 miles) of track linking all places of any size. Overall control is exercised by Deutsche Bahn (German Rail), which has several operating arms. There has been heavy public investment in the rail system over many years and services generally are of a very high standard. The efficiency and near-complete cover of the system, combined with the availability of a range of special tickets, make travel by rail a very attractive option for a holiday in Germany. Nearly all trains have smoking coaches or compartments, and first- and second-class accommodation, and many also have lavatories for people with a disability.

TYPES OF TRAIN

● InterCityExpress (ICE) are state-of-the-art trains that run at speeds up to 319kph (198mph). The latest has a first-class lounge giving passengers a spectacular driver's-eye view of the track.
● Metropolitan (MET) is a prestige train linking Hamburg with Essen, Düsseldorf and Cologne. There is a choice of three seating zones: 'Office', with fax, etc.; 'Silence', which is mobile- and computer-free; and 'Club', with DVD facilities, etc.
● InterCity (IC) trains are only marginally less luxurious and swift than ICE trains, and link major cities and towns across the country. They are air-conditioned and have a restaurant or bistro.
● InterRegio (IR) fast trains connect regional hubs with the national network. They have buffet or bistro facilities or a refreshment trolley.
● RegionalExpress (RE) and StädteExpress (SE) are fast, limited-stop local trains, often with double-decker coaches.
● RegionalBahn (RB) local trains are usually diesel-powered and stop at all stations.

MAIN RAIL NETWORK

These are the main rail routes through Germany, but the network is extensive and covers many minor towns.

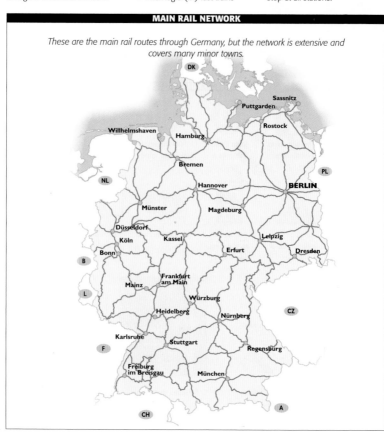

• S-Bahn trains are the suburban trains in large cities and the Ruhr conurbation.

OVERNIGHT SERVICES
• DB Nachtzug (NZ) are domestic and international night trains with modern sleepers, couchettes or reclining seats.
• CityNightLine (CNL) has luxury cabin, standard and couchette accommodation on services between German cities and to Austria and Switzerland.
• DB AutoZug carries cars on double-decker wagons while passengers sit in coaches or stay overnight in sleeping accommodation. These trains link major German cities with popular summer and winter destinations in Germany and abroad.

The high-speed InterCityExpress prepares to leave Cologne

RAIL JOURNEY TIMINGS

The chart below shows the journey time by rail between major cities. The hours are in larger type and the minutes in smaller.

Code	Berlin	Bonn Hbf	Bremen Hbf	Dresden Hbf	Düsseldorf Hbf	Erfurt Hbf	Frankfurt (Main) Hbf	Freiburg (Breisgau) Hbf	Hamburg Hbf	Hannover Hbf	Heidelberg Hbf	Köln Hbf	Leipzig Hbf	Mainz Hbf	München Hbf	Münster (West) Hbf	Nürnberg Hbf	Regensburg Hbf	Rostock Hbf	Stuttgart Hbf	Würzburg Hbf
A437																					
A245	328																				
B158	613	534																			
A408	044	237	620																		
B253	356	405	214	404																	
A329	137	321	426	137	210																
A549	328	553	651	336	435	203															
A210	359	054	441	305	415	319	600														
A131	304	058	412	235	244	207	429	110													
A431	210	423	537	218	321	052	134	421	308												
A417	019	259	555	021	339	110	310	326	243	148											
B132	500	414	107	508	102	313	538	400	252	424	440										
A405	125	411	504	149	248	029	216	409	256	050	117	353									
A618	450	546	649	458	430	323	418	558	434	304	431	458	338								
A325	207	117	606	117	348	300	458	216	144	336	143	454	311	619							
A439	348	413	505	358	246	205	421	413	254	301	328	314	239	139	443						
A543	450	517	618	458	401	305	528	517	358	409	431	414	344	126	547	057					
C243	709	331	508	615	610	550	901	213	340	707	636	443	642	901	458	716	821				
A455	234	459	557	242	341	118	153	459	346	039	214	446	122	212	404	211	320	747			
A345	251	315	418	259	202	108	329	319	200	215	231	307	142	228	345	050	153	622	212		

Germany's rail network links all its major towns

TICKETS AND FARES
Travel by rail in Germany using standard tickets is not cheap, but you can significantly reduce the cost by choosing from the range of discount tickets. You can buy your tickets at train stations (from the booking office, travel office or a ticket machine), from some travel agents (who may charge a fee) or online (www.bahn.de). You can buy tickets on board some trains (but not on local services, where you will be fined if you are without a ticket), although only standard tickets are available and you will be charged a fee. Seats can be reserved on long-distance trains for a small fee, which is a good idea at peak times, such as weekends and during national holidays.

● Standard tickets vary in cost depending on the length of journey—the longer the trip, the lower the price per kilometre. Fares on ICE trains are more expensive. Tickets are fully refundable. Accompanied children under 14 travel free. Groups of six or more people can save at least 50 per cent if they buy tickets seven days in advance and 70 per cent if they buy them 14 days in advance.

● Sparprice tickets allow you to make savings if you purchase your ticket in advance and limit yourself to a particular day and train—you can save 25 per cent (Sparprice 25) or 50 per cent (Sparprice 50) of the cost of a standard return ticket. There are weekend restrictions on the use of Sparprice 50. Up to two companions can travel with you at a 50 per cent discount. There are some restrictions on refunds.

● The €29 Schönes-Wochenende-Ticket ('Lovely Weekend' ticket) gives unlimited second-class travel on local trains for up to five people on Saturdays or Sundays. It is not valid on ICE and similar long-distance trains.

● The Länder-Ticket costs €21–25, and gives unlimited second-class travel on local trains within a particular region for 24 hours between Monday and Friday. Like the Schönes-Wochenende-Ticket, it can be used by up to five people.

RAIL PASSES
● The Euro Domino Pass is valid for travel on between three and eight days in any one month on services within Germany (including ICE and IC). The three-day pass costs €274 first class and €186 second class, while an eight-day pass costs €404 first class and €286 second class. This pass is worth buying if you intend to cover long distances during your stay.

● The German Rail Pass is similar to the Euro Domino Pass but is intended only for visitors from outside Europe and is available for 5 or 10 days.

INFORMATION
There are several ways to obtain train information:

● Larger stations have a travel office (*Reisezentrum*) with English-speaking staff and a range of facilities.

● Timetables give information about departure times and platform numbers (yellow sheet) and arrivals (white).

● Train composition diagrams on the platform show the make-up of long-distance trains. Coaches are identified by a letter corresponding to a section of the platform, enabling you to position yourself at the exact spot where your coach will stop.

● Loudspeaker announcements in stations and on board trains give information in German and sometimes in English.

● The website www.bahn.de /international (in English) gives rail information and allows you to purchase tickets online.

OTHER POINTS
● In larger stations, the travel office (*Reisezentrum*) provides left luggage facilities (lockers as well as a manned office) and currency exchange.

● Up to 30kg (66lb) of personal luggage is carried free. The trolleys provided in larger stations take a coin (usually €1), which is returned when you replace the trolley at a collection point.

● Bicycles are carried on most but not all trains. Tickets for bicycles are inexpensive.

● Most long-distance trains run at regular intervals and the timetable is coordinated to make changing trains as straightforward as possible. Many changes can be made simply by crossing from one side of the platform to the other.

Germany's transport system is fully integrated

Long-distance Buses, Taxis and Bicycles

LONG-DISTANCE BUSES

The comprehensive extent of the German rail system means that the country has an under-developed long-distance bus network, certainly compared with other countries. Local and regional bus services are operated by municipalities, an array of private companies and by Deutsche Bahn. Many bus routes make connections with rail services, and through ticketing may be available. Tickets can be obtained from bus offices and from the driver.

Berlin Linien Bus GmbH
Mannheimer Strasse 33/34, 10713 Berlin
Tel 030 861 93 31
www.berlinlinienbus.de
Buses run by Berlin Linien Bus connect the capital with 350 destinations in Germany, including all major cities.

Zentraler Omnibusbahnhof (ZOB)
Masurenallee 4–6, 14057 Berlin (Charlottenburg)
Tel 030 302 53 61
Berlin's central bus station.

Deutsche Touring GmbH
Am Römerhof 17, 60486 Frankfurt
Tel 069 79 03 50
www.touring.de
As well as running guided tours of varying duration, this company operates a limited number of long-distance luxury coach routes of interest to tourists (for example, along the Romantic Road from Frankfurt and from Würzburg to Füssen), with the possibility of unlimited stopovers.

TAXIS
Universally identifiable by their cream paintwork, German taxis are available at stands in all towns and cities or can be ordered by phone. There are stands at rail stations, public transportation interchanges, airports and key downtown

locations. It may not be easy to hail a taxi on the street. Licensing is carefully administered, and most taxis are vehicles of a high standard (Mercedes or similar) and are well maintained. Fares are shown on a meter and consist of a minimum fee of around €3.50 plus a charge per kilometre of around €1.30. Evening and weekend rates may be higher and there is a small extra charge for each item of luggage. It is customary to round up the fare as a tip. Public transportation operators in some larger cities can arrange for a taxi to meet passengers at a particular stop or station, particularly in the evening or at night.

BICYCLES
Bicyclists are well provided for in Germany. The network of long-distance bicycling trails is well maintained and signposted, and a bicycling holiday in Germany is

Travel in style, but don't forget the meter is still running while you are caught in traffic

an attractive proposition. Many Germans take their bicycles with them on vacation, particularly when camping, and use them for excursions from their holiday base. Bicyclists can be just as territorial as other vehicle users about their allotted space, and pedestrians are advised not to loiter on cycleways!

Bicycles can be taken on most local and long-distance trains and on the Berlin U-Bahn, although you will usually need to buy a special ticket. They can be rented in most places, and Deutsche Bahn operates a Call-A-Bike rental service in Berlin, Cologne, Frankfurt and Munich (tel 01805 15 14 15).

Bicycling holidays in Germany allow you to see the country at a leisurely pace

Domestic Flights

There are regular internal flights between the major German cities. The majority of services are run by the national airline, Lufthansa, and many are designed to connect with its international hubs at Frankfurt and Munich. These flights are supplemented by services run by other airlines, which also serve a number of minor airports. Many flights are timetabled with business people in mind, and have early morning departures and late-afternoon/early evening return flights. An impact on previously expensive fares has been made by the entry into the market of a number of budget operators, and some lower fares are available through advance and online booking; this makes an internal flight an alternative to the otherwise excellent rail services.

DOMESTIC AIRLINES				
AIRLINE	**BASE**	**WEBSITE**	**TELEPHONE**	**AIRPORTS SERVED**
Air Berlin	Berlin	www.airberlin.com	01805 737800	Berlin-Tegel, Bremen, Cologne, Dortmund, Dresden, Düsseldorf, Erfurt, Frankfurt, Hamburg, Hannover, Karlsruhe-Baden-Baden, Leipzig, Munich, Münster/Osnabrück, Nürnberg, Paderborn, Rostock-Laage, Saarbrücken, Stuttgart
Cirrus (Lufthansa partner)	Saarbrücken	www.cirrus-airlines.de	06893 800440	Berlin-Tempelhof, Dresden, Frankfurt, Hamburg, Heringsdorf-Usedom, Leipzig-Halle, Mannheim, Rostock-Laage, Munich, Westerland-Sylt
dba (formerly Deutsche BA)	Munich	www.flydba.com	01805 359322	Berlin-Tegel, Cologne-Bonn, Düsseldorf, Hamburg, Munich, Stuttgart
German Wings	Cologne-Bonn	www.germanwings.com	01805 95 58 55	Berlin-Schönefeld, Cologne-Bonn, Dresden, Munich
Germania Express	Hannover	www.gexx.de	01805 737100	Berlin–Tegel, Bremen, Cologne-Bonn, Düsseldorf, Frankfurt, Hamburg, Hannover, Munich, Stuttgart
Lufthansa	Frankfurt	www.lufthansa.com	0180 583 8426	Augsburg, Berlin, Bremen, Dortmund, Düsseldorf, Dresden, Frankfurt, Friedrichshafen, Hamburg, Hannover, Hof-Plauen, Cologne-Bonn, Leipzig-Halle, Kiel, Munich, Nürnberg, Stuttgart
Luftverkehrsgesellschaft Walter	Dortmund	www.lgw.de	0231 21980	Berlin-Tempelhof, Cologne-Bonn, Dortmund, Dresden, Düsseldorf, Erfurt, Hamburg, Nürnberg, Stuttgart, Westerland-Sylt
Ostfriesische Lufttransport	Bremen	www.olt.de	04921 8992-0	Berlin-Tempelhof, Dresden, Erfurt, Leipzig-Halle, Nürnberg, Paderborn. Seasonal services to the East and North Friesian Island
Sylt Air	Westerland	www.syltair.de	01900 55677	Berlin-Tempelhof, Hamburg, Westerland
VBird	Niederrhein	www.vbird.com	0190 172500	Berlin-Schönefeld, Munich

AIRPORTS
Major Airports

In addition to the international airports described on pages 46–50, Germany has a number of well-equipped and well-located airports linked to other major cities, most with several daily domestic flights as well as some international services.

Bremen
Tel 0421 55950
www.airport-bremen.de

Dresden
Tel 0351 881 3360
www.dresden-airport.de

Hannover (Hanover)
Tel 0511 977 1899
www.hannover-airport.de

Köln-Bonn (Cologne-Bonn)
Tel 02203 404001, 02203 404002
www.airport-cgn.de

Nürnberg (Nuremberg)
Tel 0911 93700
www.airport-nuernberg.de

Stuttgart
Tel 0711 9480
www.flughafen-stuttgart.de

Local Airports

With a limited number of flights and a more restricted range of facilities, these airports serve smaller cities and in some cases are located conveniently close to popular holiday areas.

Augsburg
Tel 0821 270810
www.augsburg-airport.de
Limited number of flights to Berlin and Düsseldorf.

Dortmund
Tel 0231 921301
www.flughafen-dortmund.de
Daily flights to Berlin, Dresden, Erfurt, Leipzig-Halle, Munich, Nuremberg and Stuttgart.

Erfurt
Tel 0361 6560, 0361 656 2200
www.flughafen-erfurt.de
Limited number of flights to Berlin, Düsseldorf, Hamburg, Cologne and Munich.

Friedrichshafen
Tel 07541 28401

Franz-Josef-Strauss Flughafen, Munich (far left); Lufthansa (left), the national airline

www.fly-away.de
Virtually in the lakeside town of Friedrichshafen, this airport serves the holiday towns and villages around the Bodensee (Lake Constance) and the western section of the German Alps. Daily flights to major cities.

Heringsdorf
Tel 038376 2500
www.flughafen-heringsdorf.de
This is the small airport for the Baltic holiday island of Usedom. It has infrequent flights to Berlin.

Staff at airport information desks (above) can advise you on all aspects of your journey. In major towns and cities, there will often be English-speaking staff

Hof-Plauen
Tel 09292 9550, 09292 95518
www.airport-hof.de
On the outskirts of the northern Bavarian town of Hof. Limited number of daily flights to Frankfurt.

Kiel
Tel 0431 329190
www.airport-kiel.de
The airport of this city on the Baltic coast of Schleswig-Holstein has a limited number of flights to Frankfurt and Cologne.

Münster-Osnabrück
Tel 02571 943360
www.fmo.de
Just off the A1 Ruhr-Hamburg autobahn, midway between the cities of Münster and Osnabrück. Limited number of daily flights to Berlin, Frankfurt, Munich and Stuttgart.

Niederrhein
Tel 02837 666111
www.airportniederrhein.de
Just off the Düsseldorf–Netherlands autobahn, close to the old city of Kleve, the Lower Rhine airport is being developed for budget flights. Limited services to Berlin and Munich.

Saarbrücken
Tel 06893 83272
www.flughafen-saarbruecken.de
Limited number of flights to Berlin, Hamburg, Leipzig–Halle and Munich.

Westerland-Sylt
Tel 04651 920612
www.flughafen-sylt.de
The airport serving the holiday island of Sylt offers mostly seasonal flights to major cities.

North Sea and Baltic Islands

A number of local companies operate small aircraft over short distances between the German mainland and holiday islands in the North Sea and Baltic.

LFH (Luftverkehr Friesland Harle)
Tel 04464 94810
www.inselflieger.de
Flights to Helgoland and to Wangerode, Langeoog, Baltrum, Juist and Borkum in the Ostfriesische Inseln (East Friesian Islands) from Harlesiel.

Reederei Frisia
Tel 04932 9130
www.reederei-frisia.de
To Juist and Nordeney in the Ostfriesische Inseln (East Friesian Islands) from Norddeich.

Domestic Ferries and Riverboats

FERRIES

Ferries are the most popular and economical way of reaching Germany's holiday islands in the North Sea and Baltic. There are regular services all year round, though frequency is less out of season. Timetables may be affected by tides and adverse weather.

Germany's great rivers are plied by a variety of craft, among them century-old paddle-steamers taking day-visitors to nearby destinations and modern vessels providing luxurious accommodation for cruises of several days' duration. Most river trips are in the nature of excursions, with a return to the starting point, but steamers can be used as an alternative to rail in order to reach a particular destination, especially along the Rhine and Mosel.

ISLAND FERRY SERVICES				
DESTINATION	FERRY COMPANY	MAINLAND PORT	JOURNEY	FARE
Ostfriesische Inseln (East Friesian Islands)				
Baltrum	Reederei Baltrum-Linie, Haus No. 278, 26579 Insel Baltrum (tel 04939 91300; www.baltrum-linie.de)	Nessmersiel	20 min	€21 round-trip
Borkum	AG Ems, Postfach 11 54, 26691 Emden-Aussenhafen (tel 04921 89070; www.ag.ems.de)	Emden	2.25 hr	€26.50 round-trip
Langeoog	Schiffahrt Langeoog, Kurverwaltung Langeoog, Hauptstrasse 28, 26465 Langeoog (tel 04972 6930; www.langeoog.de/schiffahrt)	Bensersiel	1 hr	€17 round-trip
Norderney	Reederei Frisia, Postfach 1262, 26534 Nordeney (tel 04932 9130; www.reederei-frisia.de)	Norddeich	55 min	€13.50
Spiekeroog	Spiekeroog Schiffahrt und Kurverwaltung, Postfach 1160, 26466 Spiekeroog (tel 04976 919 3101; www.spiekeroog.de)	Neuharlingersiel	45 min	€17 round-trip
Wangerooge	Schiffahrt und Inselbahn Wangerooge, Kurverwaltung Wangerooge, Postfach 1620, 26480 Wangerooge (tel 04469 990)	Harlesiel	1.25 hr	€15.50 round-trip
Nordfriesische Inseln (North Friesian Islands)				
Föhr and Amrum	Wyker Dampfschiffs-Reederei, Hafendeich 20, 25938 Wyk auf Föhr (tel 04681 800; www.wdr-wyk.de)	Dagebüll	Wyk (Föhr) 1 hr, Wittdün (Amrum) 1.5–2 hr	Dagebüll–Wyk €10.10 round-, trip Dagebüll–Wittdün €14.70 round-trip
Pellworm	Fähre Pellworm, Postfach 69, 25849 Pellworm (tel 04844 753755; www.faehre-pellworm.de)	Nordstrand	35 min	€9 return
Hiddensee (Baltic coast)	Reederei Hiddensee, Fährstrasse 16, 18439 Stralsund (tel 03831 268116; www.reederei-hiddensee.de)	Stralsund, Schaprode (Rügen Island)	Stralsund 1 hr 30 min Schaprode 30 min	Stralsund €16.40 Schaprode €14.40

Sightseeing by boat isn't restricted to the rivers; this tour boat (far left) is on Berlin's Landwehrkanal, while passengers with bicycles (above) explore the area around one of many inland lakes and ferries (left) connect the islands off the Baltic Coast

RIVERBOAT SERVICES					
RIVER	**FERRY COMPANY**	**MAIN TOWN**	**ROUTES**	**JOURNEY**	**FARE**
Danube	Donauschiffahrt Wurm & Köck, Höllgasse 26, 94032 Passau (tel 0851 92 92 92; www.donauschiffahrt.de)	Passau (also Deggendorf)	Passau–Engelhartszell–Passau, Schlögen meanders, Passau–Linz –Vienna (Austria)	Passau–Linz: about 6 hr (return possible by train)	from €7.50
Elbe	Sächsische Dampfschiffahrt GmbH, Hertha-Lindner-Strasse 10, 01067 Dresden (tel 0351 86 60 90; www.saechsische-dampf schiffahrt.de)	Dresden	All towns between Seusslitz, Meissen, Dresden, Pirna, Bad Schandau and Decin (Czech Republic)	Dresden–Bad Schandau: 5.25 hr (single journey)	Dresden–Bad Schandau: €18 round-trip
Mosel	Personenschiffahrt Kolb, Georg-Schmitt-Platz 2, 54292 Trier (tel 0651 26 666; www.kolb-mosel.com)	Trier	Local excursions on Mosel and Saar rivers	varies	round-trip from €7; day trip €25
Neckar	Rhein-Neckar-Fahrgast-gesellschaft, Untere Neckarstrasse 17, 69117 Heidelberg (tel 06221 201 81; www.rnf-gmbh.de)	Heidelberg	Heidelberg–Neckarsteinach–Heidelberg	3-hr round-trip	€9.50 round-trip
Neckar	Berta Epple GmbH und Co. KG, Anlegestelle Wilhelma, 70376 Stuttgart (tel 0711 54 99 70 60; www.neckar-kaeptn.de)	Stuttgart	Local excursions on the Neckar from Bad Cannstatt near Stuttgart	daily from 10.30am 6-hr trip	from €20
Rhine, Main and Neckar	Frankfurter Personenschiffahrt Anton Nauheimer GmbH, Mainkai 36, 60311 Frankfurt (tel 069 133 83 70; www.primus-linie.de)	Frankfurt	Frankfurt–Rhine Gorge, Frankfurt–Aschaffenburg, Frankfurt–Heidelberg	Frankfurt–Heidelberg–Frankfurt: 10.5 hr (9am–7.35pm)	Frankfurt–Heidelberg–Frankfurt: €27
Rhine and Mosel	Köln-Düsseldorfer Deutsche Rheinschiffahrt AG, Frankenwerft 35, 50667 Köln (tel 0221 208 83 18; www.k-d.com)	Köln (Cologne)	All riverside towns between Cologne, Bonn, Koblenz and Mainz, and between Koblenz and Cochem on the Mosel	Cologne–Koblenz: 5 hr	Cologne–Koblenz: €33.60 (one way)
Weser	Flotte Weser GmbH und Co. KG, Deisterallee 1, 31785 Hameln (tel 05151 93 99 99; www.flotte-weser.de)	Hameln (Hamelin)	Most riverside towns between Bad Karlshafen, Hameln, Minden and Bremen	Hamelin–Bodenwerder–Hamelin: day (10am –7pm), 4.5 hr on board	Hamelin–Bodenwerder–Hamelin: excursion €21 round-trip

VISITORS WITH A DISABILITY

Compared with many other countries, Germany is well equipped to receive visitors with a disability, particularly in terms of public transportation and access to buildings. All modern facilities are designed to allow wheelchair access and many (but not all) older buildings have been suitably adapted. In addition, a wealth of information is available from a variety of sources to help visitors plan their trip and move easily around the country.

GENERAL ADVICE

● Think about where you are going to go and what you want to do well in advance, and make the necessary contacts. Specialist tour operators can help with this.

● If you are flying to Germany, let the airline know in good time about your requirements. They will inform the airport about what help and facilities you will need. Allow plenty of time to check in.

● Deutsche Bahn (German Railways) aims to make the use of its trains and stations as easy as possible for people with limited mobility. Some intercity trains have wheelchair access, and Nachtzug sleeping-car trains (▷ 61) have couchette compartments designed for wheelchair users. Help with boarding and luggage is available if requested in advance

● In Berlin, S-Bahn and U-Bahn stations with good wheelchair access are indicated on the plan of the network, and some trams and buses have retractable ramps.

● Berlin's Telebus services are available for people with limited mobility. Advance contact is necessary: Telebus-Zentrale, Esplanade 17, 13187 Pankow (tel: 030 410200); Lazarus-Telebus, Wendenschlossstrasse 129, 12557 Köpenick (tel: 030 651 6642; www.lazarus.de/berlin).

● Most other cities can provide comprehensive access information, including city plans showing wheelchair-accessible buildings and public lavatories, and lists of wheelchair-accessible restaurants, hotels, museums and public buildings. Contact tourist information offices or use the relevant city website—see individual city entries for details. Most have information in English.

● Most of the German *Länder* have travel information on their websites for visitors with a disability (sometimes only in German).

● The blue badge currently being issued to drivers with a disability in Britain is valid throughout the EU. The accompanying leaflet explains how to use it.

USEFUL ORGANIZATIONS
In Britain and the US
Disabled Travels.com
www.disabledtravels.com
Provides information about worldwide accommodation for visitors with disabilities.

Mobility International USA
P.O. Box 10767, Eugene, or 97440, USA
Tel 541/343-1284
www.miusa.org
Information on travel and international exchange schemes for people with disabilities.

Many U-Bahn stations have access for wheelchair users

Holiday Care
7th Floor, Sunley House, 4 Bedford Park, Croydon, Surrey CR0 2AP
Tel 0845 124 9971
www.holidaycare.org.uk
Information about the level of facilities and accessibility available at various destinations.

In Germany
Bundesarbeitsgemeinschaft der Clubs Behinderter und ihrer Freunde e.V. (National Association of Clubs for the Disabled and their Friends)
Eupener Strasse 5, 55131 Mainz
Tel 06131 225514
www.bagcbf.de
Dispenses information about all aspects of travel for visitors with a disability. Stocks lists of specialized travel operators and publications, including city access guides.

Bundesverband Selbsthilfe Körperbehinderte e.V. (National Association Disabled Self-Help)
Postfach 20, 74238 Krautheim/Jagst
Tel 06294 68110
www.bsk-ev.de
Provides advice and organizes travel for people with limited mobility, including provision of accompanying helpers.

Touristik Union International
Karl-Wiechert-Allee 4, 30625 Hannover
Tel 0511 56600
www.tui.de
This large travel operator, with offices in many cities, has a comprehensive range of information about accessible travel and accommodation facilities, and can organize group and individual travel.

This chapter is divided into six regions (see pages 5–7). Places of interest are listed alphabetically in each region, and the key sights are listed at the beginning of each section. All places of interest are shown on the Atlas on pages 428–443.

The Sights

NORTHERN GERMANY

Consisting of the *Länder* of Niedersachsen, Schleswig-Holstein and Mecklenburg-Vorpommern, and the city-states of Hamburg and Bremen, North Germany's countryside is mainly flat, sometimes rolling, and encompasses the country's entire maritime coastline. Its many bustling harbour towns, once members of the Hanseatic League, are complemented by the agricultural hinterland.

MAJOR SIGHTS

Katharinenkirche in the Hagenmarkt, Braunschweig

Celle's half-timbered houses, known as Fachwerkhäuser

Goslar's eye-catching Rathaus (town hall)

THE SIGHTS

BRAUNSCHWEIG

➕ 434 F6 ℹ Vor der Burg 1, 38100 Braunschweig, tel 0531 273550
🚆 Braunschweig
www.braunschweig.de

Heinrich der Löwe, ruler of the short-lived Duchy of Saxony and Bavaria, gave Braunschweig (or Brunswick in English) an early political boost by making it his residence in 1166. It was 1753 before this town on the River Oker again experienced political power, when the Duchy of Brunswick was established here.

Braunschweig's response to the destruction of its Altstadt in World War II was to rebuild in modern style, interspersed with *Traditionsinseln*—islands of traditional architecture—a combination that gives the town a patchwork feel while maintaining some of its former character. The Gewandhaus (Cloth Hall) on Altstadtmarkt, originally built in 1303, was redesigned and decorated in an intricate Renaissance style in 1591. It faces two fine Gothic monuments across Altstadtmarkt: the 14th-century, two-floor Altes Rathaus and the 12th- to 14th-century Martinikirche. To the east, on Burgplatz, stands the Gothic and Romanesque Dom, begun in 1173, containing the side-by-side tombs of Heinrich der Löwe and his wife Mathilde. A replica lion sculpture on the square commemorates Heinrich.

BREMEN

See pages 72–73.

CELLE

➕ 433 F6 ℹ Markt 14–16, 29221 Celle, tel 05141 1212 🚆 Celle
www.region-celle.de

This town, 45km (28 miles) northeast of Hannover, at the southern extremity of the Lüneburger Heide (▷ 88), has a well-preserved roster of 16th- to 18th-century *Fachwerkhäuser* (half-timbered houses) The Altstadt is a virtual open-air museum of 480 of these houses, many ornately decorated and inscribed. Those on Zöllnerstrasse are among the finest in Germany; a superb example is Hoppener-Haus (1532) at Poststrasse 8.

For more than three centuries to 1705, Celle was a residence of the dukes of Braunschweig and Lüneburg, and their graceful, many-gabled Schloss (guided tours hourly Apr–end Oct Tue–Sun 11–3; Nov–end Mar Tue–Sun 11 and 3), west of the Altstadt, survives. Dating from the late 14th century, on a 13th-century foundation, it was rebuilt in Renaissance style and contains a beautiful baroque theatre.

FLENSBURG

➕ 429 E2 ℹ Rathausstrasse 1, 24937 Flensburg, tel 0461 909 0920
🚆 Flensburg
www.flensburg-tourist.de

Germany's northernmost town has belonged off and on to Denmark, and Danish character still shines through. Always an important harbour town, Flensburg is still orientated towards the sea, though now mostly as a base for pleasure craft. Past maritime trading glories are recalled in the Museumswerft, a wharf lined with old ships, and in the neatly restored 17th- to 19th-century merchants' courtyards and warehouses, many of them converted to apartments, offices and artists' studios. In one such warehouse at Schiffbrücke 39, the Schiffahrtsmuseum (Apr–end Oct Tue–Sun 10–5; Nov–end Mar 10–4) celebrates the town's nautical traditions, while the Rum-Museum in its cellar does the same for rum-making.

Try to leave time to visit 16th-century Schloss Glücksburg (May–end Sep daily 10–6; Oct Tue–Sun 10–6; Nov–end Apr Sat–Sun 10–5), 9km (6 miles) northeast of Flensburg, along the sheltered waters of the Flensburger Förde. Inside the brilliantly white, moated castle, which is said to have been inspired by a Loire Valley château, are 18th-century Flemish tapestries.

GOSLAR

➕ 433 F7 ℹ Markt 7, 38640 Goslar, tel 05321 78060 🚆 Goslar
www.goslar.de

On the northwestern foothills of the Harz Mountains (▷ 300–302), Goslar, a former residence of Germany's Holy Roman Emperors, has both fresh air and historical significance in abundance. Begin your stroll through the handsome Altstadt, a UNESCO World Heritage Site, at the Marktplatz. In the gable of the Kämmereigebäude (treasury) across the square, a glockenspiel is accompanied by a parade of mechanical figures representing an emperor, knights and miners. The streets leading from here are full of *Fachwerkhäuser*, 16th-century half-timbered houses with ornate carvings.

On the southern edge of the old town, on a broad stretch of grass, the stone-built Kaiserpfalz (daily 10–4 or 5) is an imposing but overly-pristine 19th-century reconstruction of the 11th-century Romanesque imperial palace. Its 12th-century chapel is more authentic-looking and contains the heart of Kaiser Heinrich III (1017–56). Just out of town, the Bergbaumuseum Rammelsberg (hourly guided tours 9–6), also a UNESCO site, has mines that have been worked for a thousand years for silver, tin, zinc, copper, lead and even gold.

Bremen

Bustling Bremen retains reminders of its past trade-based glories and wealth; the Rathaus is a masterpiece of Weser Renaissance architecture. The international harbour downriver at Bremerhaven is worth a visit by boat.

Bremerhaven's Schiffahrtsmuseum has exhibits both outside (above left) and in (above right). The Gothic Rathaus in Bremen (above middle) hides behind its Renaissance façade

RATINGS	
Historic interest	● ● ●
Cultural interest	● ● ●
Photo stops	● ●
Walkability	● ●

A statue of a musician, Bremen

SEEING BREMEN

The city-state of Bremen, 94km (58 miles) southwest of Hamburg, is on the River Wesen. Most sightseeing attractions are in the Altstadt (old town), on the north bank of the Weser, between the river and a line of angular ponds that once formed a moat, and particularly around the central Marktplatz, where you find the Rathaus, the Dom and other monumental, historic buildings. Just east of this core, but still within the line traced by the old moat, is the Schnoorviertel, a district of 15th- to 18th-century higgledy-piggledy houses that were once inhabited by the town's fisherfolk but have been gentrified and partly given over to trendy shops, cafés and restaurants.

HIGHLIGHTS

FOCKE-MUSEUM

Schwachhauser Heerstrasse 240 ☎ 0421 361 3575 🕓 Tue 10–9, Wed–Sun 10–5 💰 Adult €4, child €2

You have to travel a bit to get to this museum—also known as the Bremer Landesmuseum für Kunst und Kulturgeschichte—on the eastern edge of the city, but the trip out there is well worth it. The museum holds a varied and fascinating collection of regional art, history, archaeology, decorative art from the homes of the rich and powerful, ecclesiastical art, folk art and more. By way of a bonus it's set in an attractive park. The diverse collection reaches back across more than a thousand years of Bremen history, and is clearly and interestingly presented. Maritime history, from the city's rich Hanseatic period up to the days of the great ocean liners taking German emigrants to the US, is given plenty of space.

KUNSTHALLE BREMEN

Am Wall 207 ☎ 0421 329080 🕓 Tue 10–9, Wed–Sun 10–5 💰 Adult €5, child €2.50

One of Germany's most important art collections is housed in this museum in the eastern reaches of a park area known as the Wallanlagen, just outside what used to be the city walls. There's a fine collection of 19th- and 20th-century paintings, including Camille Pissarro's *Girl Lying on a Grassy Slope* (1882), Eugène Delacroix's *King Rodrigo* (1833), and Claude Monet's *Camille* (1866). There are also works by artists of the local 19th-century Worpswede School.

In 2001, artworks belonging to the museum that had been looted by Russian troops from a storage depot elsewhere in Germany during World War II were returned after turning up on the black market in New York. They include etchings by Rembrandt and watercolours by Albrecht Dürer, and are now on display once again.

MARKTPLATZ

Photographers trying to capture the essence of this beautiful old square do their best to exclude the architecturally challenged 1966 state parliament building, the Haus der Bürgerschaft. That proviso noted, the rest of the square, which is dominated by the Rathaus and the St. Petri Dom (see below), rewards closer study. Out on the cobblestones is a monumental sculpture (1404) of Roland, a nephew of Charlemagne (Karl der Grosse), who is seen as the protector of the city. A less portentous sculpture, from 1953 in bronze, of four animals—a donkey, a dog, a cat and a cockerel—standing one atop the other, is that of the Bremer Stadtmusikanten, characters in a Brothers Grimm fairy-tale who set out to become town musicians in Bremen.

RATHAUS

Marktplatz ☎ 01805 101030 ⏰ Tours Mon–Sat 11, 12, 3, 4, Sun 11, 12 💶 Adult €4, child €2

Behind the Town Hall's Weser Renaissance façade from 1612 lurks an original Gothic building from 1410, but it's no surprise that the magnificent façade is what people notice, along with the great bronze roof and the decorative gables. The sculptures of Charlemagne and seven Electors of the Holy Roman Empire are, however, copies (the originals are in the Focke-Museum; see above).

ST. PETRI DOM

Marktplatz ☎ 0421 365040 ⏰ Mon–Fri 10–5, Sat 10–2, Sun 2–5 💶 Free

On the eastern edge of Marktplatz rise the twin towers (98m/321ft) of the imposing Dom, dedicated to St. Peter. The present building was begun in 1219, but there has been a church on this site since 789. Bremen's restored cathedral has been altered and added to over the centuries so that today it presents a mix of styles. Once frequented by the emperor and the archbishop, the church acquired decorative elements appropriate to its status, including a fine pulpit and organ. If you are of a somewhat morbid disposition, you can visit the *Bleikeller*, a lead-lined cellar in which the mummified bodies of workers said to have been killed in accidents during the building's construction, were entombed.

BACKGROUND

Founded near the end of the eighth century during Charlemagne's campaigns to subdue the Saxons, Bremen soon became an important port and later a powerful member of the Hanseatic League, which it joined in 1358. The city was hard hit by Allied bombs during World War II and most monumental buildings have had to be rebuilt. For many of the finest parts of the handsome pre-war Altstadt, however, there could be no rebirth and they have vanished for good. But Bremen has been coming back up in the world since then, and has a character that combines old and new in a way that's attractive to the eye.

BASICS

🗺 433 D5 ℹ Findorffstrasse 105, tel 01805 101030; Mon–Fri 8.30–6, Sat 9.30–1
🚆 Bremen
www.bremen-tourism.de

In addition to German, the website has information in English (and several other languages), on history, attractions, dining, hotels, nightlife and more, and though the text is brief, it's informative as far as it goes. Webcams provide a real-time picture of some of Bremen's interesting places, like the bustling riverside Schlachte promenade.

The flag of the city-state of Bremen

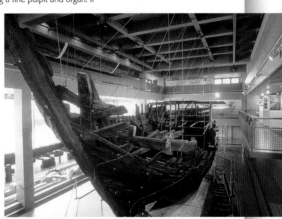

Hanseatic Kogge ship in Bremerhaven's Schiffahrtsmuseum, which charts Germany's maritime history

Göttingen's famous Goosegirl statue, outside the Rathaus

Greifswald: a port town, seen from the air

Hameln's Pied Piper in biscuit form

GÖTTINGEN

✠ 433 E8 ℹ Altes Rathaus, Markt 9, 37073 Göttingen, tel 0551 499800
🚉 Göttingen
www.goettingen-tourismus.de

A prominent university town, Göttingen is notable for the all-hours activity a big student population creates. On the River Leine, the town has a handsome setting, fine medieval and neoclassical architecture and traditional *Fachwerkhäuser* (half-timbered houses). The Georg-August-Universität was founded in 1734 by the Hanoverian King of Britain (and Elector of Hannover) George II, but the town was founded in 953 as the Saxon village of Gutingi.

In the trim Markt, in front of the arcaded Altes Rathaus, begun around 1270 as a trading hall and completed as the town hall in 1443, stands the famous Gänseliesel-Brunnen. This bronze fountain (1901) is in the shape of a girl carrying geese and a basket—male students tradition-ally kiss the girl when they receive their doctorates.

GREIFSWALD

✠ 431 J4 ℹ Rathaus, Am Markt, 17461 Greifswald, tel 03834 521380
🚉 Greifswald
www.greifswald.de

Close to the Baltic, on the banks of the River Ryck, this old Hanseatic League town has a neatly restored Altstadt. In the central zone around the Markt, the towers of a cathedral and two churches—the 15th-century *Backsteingotik* (brick Gothic) Dom Sankt-Nikolai, 14th-century Marienkirche and 13th-century Jacobikirche—form a distinctive triptych. The Romantic landscape painter Caspar David Friedrich (1774–1840) was born in Greifswald, and you can see a few of his works, including *The Ruins of Eldena Abbey in the Riesengebirge* (1815), in the Gemäldegalerie of the Pommersches Landesmuseum (May–end Oct Tue–Sun 10–6; Nov–end Apr Tue–Sun 10–5), which occupies a cluster of restored buildings in Mühlen-strasse, close to the Markt.

GÜSTROW

✠ 430 H4 ℹ Domstrasse 9, 18273 Güstrow, tel 01805 681068 🚉 Güstrow
www.guestrow-tourismus.de

Memories of Güstrow's former wealth and status as the seat of the Duchy of Mecklenburg-Güstrow abound in the Altstadt's elegant patrician houses. The town, 60km (37 miles) north-east of Schwerin, avoided damage from World War II bombs and East Germany's Communist planners alike, and its buildings have been spruced up to something like their former distinction. Their highlight is the fine Schloss Güstrow (Tue–Sun 9–5), built in a variety of styles by Italian and Dutch architects between 1558 and 1588, and set in ornamental French gar-dens. A tour of the graceful interior reveals many pieces of furniture that have always been in the castle, along with decorative art elements from the collection of Schwerin's State Museum. Nearby, the 13th- to 14th-century *Backstein-gotik* (brick-built Gothic) Dom distinctive triptych. The Romantic (May–end Oct daily 10–5; Nov–end Apr Tue–Sun 9–12, 2–4) towers over the town. Inside, look for the figures of the Apostles from around 1530, carved in oak, and a replica (the original was destroyed) of Ernst Barlach's striking bronze *Hovering Angel* (1927).

HAMBURG

See pages 76–81.

HAMELN

✠ 433 E7 ℹ Deisterallee 1 (Am Bürgergarten), 31785 Hameln, tel 05151 957819 🚉 Hameln
www.hameln.de

Although attractive enough, and dotted with buildings in the flamboyant 16th- to 17th-century *Weser Renaissance* style, Hameln doesn't have many superlatives—apart from the fairy-tale of its *Rattenfänger*, the infamous Pied Piper of Hamelin. For many chil-dren, this will be ample. The story goes that in 1284 Hameln was infested by rats, which the Pied Piper agreed to get rid of in return for a generous payment. Playing his magic pipe, he drew the rats after him to the River Weser, where they drowned. When the townsfolk went back on their financial agreement, he played his pipe once more, this time luring 130 of the town's children into a cave, never to be seen again. Robert Browning's poem, *The Pied Piper of Hamelin* (1842), popularized the legend.

Every Sunday at noon (May–end Sep), you can watch a free costumed Pied Piper play per-formed on the terrace of the Hochzeitshaus on Osterstrasse, and at 4.30pm on Wednesdays, there's a short musical entitled *Rats*. Three times every after-noon, the Hochzeitshaus's glockenspiel plays and mechani-cal figures emerge from the upper façade to re-enact the tale.

The interior of one of Hildesheim's Fachwerkhäuser, now converted to a restaurant

Kiel's harbour is popular with pleasure craft

HANNOVER

See pages 82–83.

HILDESHEIM

🔲 433 E7 🛈 Rathausstrasse 18–20, 31134 Hildesheim, tel 05121 17980
🚏 Hildesheim
www.hildesheim.de

Until 22 March 1945, Hildesheim, 30km (19 miles) southeast of Hannover, was the pride of North German Renaissance architecture, with thousands of beautiful ornamented *Fachwerkhäuser* (half-timbered houses). On that day, near the end of World War II, Allied aircraft dropped bombs on the town, igniting a firestorm that reduced 95 per cent of the Altstadt into rubble. A few postwar reconstructions give an idea of what was lost. On the central Marktplatz, the famed Knochenhaueramtshaus, the Butchers' Guildhouse, was rebuilt in the 1980s along the lines of the 1529 original, all of wood. It looks a little too pristine, but is an impressive reconstruction. Next door is the Bäckeramtshaus, the Bakers' Guildhouse, from 1451, but restored to its 1800 form.

Hildesheim's role as a key ecclesiastical town, which began in AD815 when Emperor of the Franks, Louis the Pious, founded the bishopric, is recalled in a quartet of imposing churches in the Altstadt. These are the Romanesque Michaeliskirche, a UNESCO World Heritage Site, founded by St. Bernward in the 11th century and containing the tomb of the saint and a mostly original painted ceiling; the Romanesque Dom, begun in the 11th century, also a UNESCO site, with sculpted bronze doors and an illustrated bronze column; the 14th- to 16th-century Gothic Andreaskirche; and the 12th-century Godehardikirche.

The town has one of Germany's most notable museums, the Roemer-Pelizaeus-Museum (daily 10–6), at Am Steine 1, in a modern building on the edge of the Altstadt. It contains a fine collection of ancient Egyptian relics, including several mummies, Inca finds and Chinese porcelain. The museum is best known, though, for its temporary exhibitions.

HUSUM

🔲 429 E3 🛈 Historisches Rathaus, Grossstrasse 27, 25813 Husum, tel 04841 89870 🚏 Husum
www.husum.de

A busy fishing port at the point where the River Mühlenau flows into the Heverstrom fjord, Husum is a sailing and holiday destination on the Schleswig-Holstein coast. Watching the harbour is a popular activity, but a stroll through town reveals other charms. Around the central Markt and nearby streets, elegant 16th- to 17th-century patrician houses testify to the wealth seafaring brought to the town. Ferries depart from Husum for the Nordfriesisches Inseln (▷ 89) and Helgoland.

An interesting excursion is to Friedrichstadt, 12km (7 miles) south on the River Eider. It was founded in 1621 by Dutch religious refugees, at the invitation of Duke Friedrich III, who had visions of creating a trading powerhouse like Amsterdam. That didn't work out, but with its canals and gabled houses, the town remains a transplanted piece of Golden Age Holland.

INSEL RÜGEN

See pages 84–85.

JEVER

🔲 428 D4 🛈 Alter Markt 18, 26441 Jever, tel 04461 71010 🚏 Jever
www.stadt-jever.de

This pretty Frisian town—best known in Germany for its herby Jever beer—makes a good, if brief, stopping point on the road from Oldenburg or Bremen to the Ostfriesische Inseln (▷ 91). Along with taking a stroll through the central area around the Neuer Markt, you should visit Schloss Jever (Tue–Sun 10–6, plus Mon in Jul and Aug). This magnificent rose-and-white palace, was begun as part of a 14th-century fortification (since demolished). In the 16th century, local ruler Maria von Jever transformed it into a Renaissance-style palace. It has an imposing tower with an onion-shaped dome and is set in fine gardens. A tour of the rooms gives a good idea of aristocratic lifestyles from the 16th to the 19th centuries.

KIEL

🔲 430 F3 🛈 Andreas-Gayk-Strasse 31 24103 Kiel, tel 0180 565 6700 🚏 Kiel
www.kiel-tourist.de

Founded in the 10th century, Kiel received its town charter in 1242 and later became a member of the Hanseatic League (▷ 29). It might have remained a minor port town, except that in 1865 it was the main base of Germany's fast-expanding navy. The Nord-Ostsee-Kanal (Kiel Canal) opened in 1895, affording both the fleet and commercial shipping a secure passage between the North Sea and the Baltic, and it is still a busy trading artery today. Kiel's naval installations brought about its destruction by Allied air raids in World War II, and today, it has little of historical interest, though it's worth exploring the *Jugendstil* (art nouveau) Rathaus from 1911 and the Gothic Nikolaikirche. It is Germany's busiest ferry port, and popular with sailboats, particularly during the annual June *Kieler Woche*, the world's largest regatta.

DOLLHOUSE

DOLLHOUSE DINER

Hamburg

Cosmopolitan Hamburg is a trend-setting example to the rest of Germany. A great extent of parks, lakes and other waterways give much of Hamburg an open, green aspect that belies its status as Germany's second largest city.

An environmentally friendly way of getting around Hamburg

Hamburg's famous skyline, seen across the Binnenalster

The city's history as a port can still be seen at St.-Pauli's ferry terminal

SEEING HAMBURG

Germany's second most populous city after Berlin, Hamburg covers a spread-out area on the north bank of the Elbe River, straddling its confluence with the River Alster. But most places of interest lie within, or just outside, the old walled city, marked by a semicircle of boulevards that still trace the curve of the former city walls. Although it stands 120km (74 miles) from the North Sea, Hamburg is Germany's busiest port. A considerable part of its waterfront is occupied by docks, harbour installations and warehouses. Vessels ranging in size from ocean-going cargo ships to barges that ply the inland waterways come and go constantly. This maritime tradition gives Hamburg a rakish air that extends from the old salts who sing the praises of harbour tours at the Elbe Landungsbrücken to the notorious red-light haunts of the Reeperbahn. But behind this rough and ready façade, Hamburg is wealthy, sophisticated and cosmopolitan. The old walled city is divided into the Altstadt, a tiny kernel whose origins date from Hamburg's earliest days in 1189, and the outer Neustadt, which was first settled a mere 300 years later.

RATINGS

Historic interest	●●●
Cultural interest	●●●
Chainstore shopping	●●●●
Walkability	●●●

BASICS

✚ 429 F4

🏠 Hauptbahnhof (Kirchenallee), tel 040 3005 1201; daily 7am–10pm

🏠 Landungsbrücken (Harbour), tel 040 3344220; Mon, Wed, Sun 8–6, Tue, Thu, Fri, Sat 8–7

🚉 Hamburg

www.hamburg-tourismus.de

HIGHLIGHTS

BINNENALSTER & AUSSENALSTER

✚ 79 C1 and 79 D1

The Binnenalster is the smallest of these two connected lakes, which stretch from the middle of the city out to the northeast. Its shores are lined by elaborate houses, hotels (including the famed Vier Jahreszeiten) and offices and its surface peppered by tour boats and small pleasure craft (and in winter by ice skaters if the water freezes). Next to the bustling street called the Jungfernstieg on the south shore is a pier from which tour boats leave on cruises through the two lakes and along the River Alster. The lakeside Alsterpavillon café-restaurant here is invariably crowded with people enjoying both the good things on offer inside and the view over the water. A stroll around the lake is a popular pastime.

Larger than the Binnenalster, the outer lake, the Aussenalster, has a number of jetties dotted around its shores, where the tour boats from

The vibrant signs for the clubs and bars of the St.Pauli district (opposite)

JACOBKIRCHE

➕ 79 D2 • Jacobikirchhof 22 ☎ 040 303 7370 🕐 Mon–Sat 10–5

Constructed between the 14th and 15th centuries and all but destroyed during World War II, St. James's Church, in the east of the Altstadt, has a recreated exterior, and a plain interior that's been done mostly in a modern style rather than restored. Some medieval altars and decorative elements like sculptures remain in place.

PETRIKIRCHE

➕ 79 C2 • Mönckebergstrasse ☎ 040 325 7400 🕐 Mon, Tue, Thu, Fri 10–6.30, Wed 10–7, Sat 10–5, Sun 9–9

Although missing its superb medieval altarpiece (now in the Kunsthalle, see this page), the central St. Peter's Church—originally Gothic on a Romanesque foundation but rebuilt after the 1842 fire and again after World War II—is still worth visiting. Artworks in the church include a 14th-century bronze doorknocker and a 15th-century Madonna.

The modern Chilehaus office building blends well with Hamburg's historic architecture

the Jungfernstieg stop to take on and disembark passengers. A particularly good place to stop for a while in good weather is the Alstervorland, a large park on the northwest shore, close to a district of fine 19th-century villas.

KUNSTHALLE

➕ 79 D1 • Glockengiesserwall ☎ 040 4281 31200 🕐 Tue–Wed and Fri–Sun 10–6, Thu 10–9 💰 Adult €8.50, child €5 (includes Galerie de Gegenwart)

Between the Hauptbahnhof and the northeastern corner of the Binnenalster, this vast art gallery, which opened in 1869, is the most important in North Germany. There are 144 exhibition rooms, so even if you spend no more than a minute in each one, allowing for walking between them, you're looking at a minimum visit of 3 hours. Be selective and use the museum's floor plan to identify the areas you want to concentrate on. The museum's elegant Café Liebermann is worth visiting in its own right, either for a light meal or just coffee and cake.

While there are masterpieces by many international artists—such as Anthony van Dyck's *The Adoration of the Shepherds* (*c.*1632), Rembrandt's early *Simeon and Hanna in the Temple* (*c.*1627), one of Edvard Munch's 20th-century series, *Girls on a Bridge*, and Edouard Manet's *Nana* (1877)—there are many stellar paintings by German artists. Look for the superb altarpiece (1379) from Hamburg's Petrikirche by Master Bertram of Minden, its multiple panels depicting scenes from the Creation and early Jewish history. A strong collection of work by Caspar David Friedrich includes the striking *Polar Sea* (1824), showing the flotsam of a wooden ship's collision with an iceberg, and the foreboding *Winter* (1834), a fine example of his North German landscapes. Among a few works by the short-lived Hamburg painter Phillip Otto Runge (1777–1810) is *Morning* (1809), the only completed piece of a planned series, the *Phases of the Day*.

Connected to the older gallery by an underground passage, the Galerie der Gegenwart, opened in 1997, focuses on modern art from 1960s pop art onwards.

LANDUNGSBRÜCKEN

➕ 78 A3

On the Elbe waterfront of the St.-Pauli district, west of the Neustadt, this long pier connected to the shore by a series of bridges affords a marvellous view of the busy river and is the home base of fleets of boats that offer *Hafenrundfahrten* (harbour tours). There are plenty of variations in these tours, but the primary division is established by the kind of boat you take. The small, old-fashioned and grubby boats moored on the landward side of the pier, and generally piloted by an idiosyncratic Hamburg riverman with sardonic wit to match, putter their

way into the nooks and crannies of the harbour on a typically one-hour jaunt. These tours have more character than those operated by the sleek, powerful cruisers moored on the river side of the pier, some of which have fancy restaurants and bars onboard, and power their way up and down on the often choppy waters of the Elbe.

On the shore, close to the western end of the Landungsbrücken, is a handsome bronze-domed building that is the north-bank entrance to the Alter Elbtunnel. From here, people and cars descend on elevators before taking the tunnel under the river.

MICHAELISKIRCHE

✚ 78 A3 • Englische Planke ☎ 040 3767 8100 ◎ Church and platform May–end Oct Mon–Sat 9–6, Sun 11.30–5.30; Nov–end Apr Mon–Sat 10–4.30, Sun 11.30–4.30. Vaults May–end Oct Mon–Sat 11–5, Sun 11.30–5; Nov–end Apr Sat, Sun 11–4.30. Multivision Thu, Sat, Sun 12.30–3.30, every 30 mins 🚋 Church: free; observation platform and vaults: Adult €3, child €1.50

The copper-sheathed spire of the originally 17th-century baroque St. Michael's Church, dubbed the 'Michel', in the southwestern reaches of the Neustadt soars 132m (433ft) and is a distinctive symbol of Hamburg. From an observation

The modern buildings in Hamburg's harbour belie its long, sea-going history

THE SIGHTS

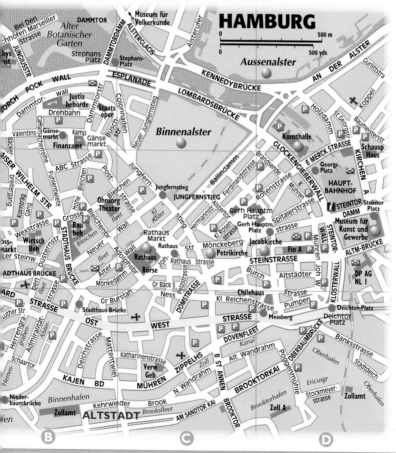

This central axis of the St.-Pauli red-light district and the streets leading off it, where the sex industry is exposed in all its garishness, might not appeal to everyone. Hamburg is a port city and such places have traditionally had their district of low-life haunts for sailors on shore leave. So the Reeperbahn and the streets diverging off it, with their bordellos, strip clubs, sex shows and video parlours, are merely following in a long if not exactly noble local tradition. Some of the sex clubs are quite tame, while others are pornographic in the extreme, but you don't need to partake of the sexual services for sale to get something out of a visit here: It's become the latest meeting place for young Hamburgers and tourist crowds, and there's plenty of nightlife in the bars, dance clubs, theatres and restaurants that intersect with the flesh trade only by way of their proximity.

platform two-thirds of the way up there are great views across the city and along the Elbe. The church was destroyed in World War II, but has been beautifully rebuilt and its bright and elegant interior restored to period perfection. The extravagant pulpit made from tropical hardwood is particularly worth noting. In addition to ascending the tower, you can descend into the vaults for a sound-and-slide show, and to see where the composer Carl Philipp Emanuel Bach (1714–88) is buried.

Across the street from the church, in Krayenkamp, you find the Krameramtswohnungen, a closed alley of half-timbered cottages that together formed an almshouse and are now occupied by boutiques, galleries and cafés.

MUSEUM FÜR HAMBURGISCHE GESCHICHTE

✛ 79 A2 • Holstenwall 24 ☎ 040/4281 3223-80 🕐 Tue–Sat 10–5, Sun 10–6 🎟 Adult €7.50, child €1.50

A clear focus on Hamburg's history gives this museum, in the Grosse Wallanlagen park between the Michaeliskirche and the St.-Pauli district, its special character. A visit here lends context to what can be a bewilderingly large and complex city, even though much of what the exhibits show has vanished into the mists—or fires—of time. The most instructive displays are the models of Hamburg at various periods of time, and particularly those that show the changing face of the port, which has always driven the city's development. It's interesting to compare the model waterfront scene from 1497, for instance, with its gabled houses and warehouses, small wooden ships, cranes and horse-drawn carts, with the full-scale industrial reality of today. And you can enter the lifestyles of the past, by visiting living quarters that range from an elegant 17th-century merchant's home to a World War II air-raid shelter. The model railway display should have special appeal for children.

MUSEUM FÜR KUNST UND GEWERBE

✛ 79 D2 • Steintorplatz 1 ☎ 040 4285 4273-2 🕐 Tue–Wed and Fri–Sun 10–6, Thu 10–9 🎟 Adult €7.50, child €5

Just south of the Hauptbahnhof, this large museum houses a wide

Bustling St.-Pauli ferry terminal—the modern face of Hamburg

range of art and applied art from a variety of periods and cultures, beginning with ancient Greece and Rome and including the Orient, though there's an inevitable focus on Germany. The medieval section has superb religious reliquaries in bronze and silver, along with sculptures and embroideries. Gold objects and jewellery, textiles, furnishings and some of the finest works of German porcelain grace the collections that cover the Renaissance and baroque periods, and into the 19th century. A memorable highlight is the separate exhibit on antique keyboard instruments. Art nouveau (or *Jugendstil*, as the genre was known in Germany) objects and design, and an extensive section on photography, which brings this eclectic experience up to the present time.

MUSEUM FÜR VOLKERKUNDE
✚ Off 79 C1 • Rothenbaumchaussee 64 ☎ 01805 308888 🕔 Tue–Wed and Fri–Sun 10–6, Thu 10–9 💲 Adult €6, child €2

The ethnography collections at this museum are wide ranging, stretching as far as the South Pacific, where Germany once had colonies. Their traditional exhibits, such as those of ceremonial masks from the South Seas islands, are complemented by others that treat the communities in a modern context and examine some of the problems they face. The same thing applies to the sections on Europe, Africa, the Arab World, Asia and North and South America.

RATHAUS
✚ 79 C2 • Rathausmarkt ☎ 040 428310 🕔 Guided tours hourly Mon–Thu 10.15–3.15, Fri–Sun 10,15–1.15 💲 €1.50

Standing on an inverted forest of 3,780 pinewood piles sunk into the marshy soil, the imposing but somewhat overdone neo-Renaissance structure dates from 1897 and stands in a large square at the heart of the Altstadt. This is the fifth in a succession of Hamburg town halls, its predecessors over the centuries having been destroyed by war, fire or both, as indeed this one was in World War II. On guided tours (when parliament is not in session) you can visit some of its 600 rooms, including the council chamber. On the north side is the Alsterfleet canal, and adjoining the southwest face is Hamburg's stock exchange, the Borse.

BACKGROUND

Hamburg traces its origins to the fortress of Hammaburg, built at the confluence of the Elbe and the Alster rivers early in the ninth century by Charlemagne during his military campaigns against the Saxons. A settlement grew up around the fort, and its history as a port began in 1189, when the Holy Roman Emperor Friedrich I Barbarossa granted it certain trading privileges and fishing rights on the Elbe. This role received a major boost in the 14th century, when Hamburg joined the Hanseatic League (▷ 29), eventually growing to rival and surpass that medieval trade federation's powerbase, Lübeck (▷ 86–87). Proclaimed a free imperial city in 1618, Hamburg continued to grow in importance, aided by a shift in trade patterns towards the west and across the Atlantic. In 1842, it was devastated by fire, a destruction that was repeated 101 years later during World War II, when Allied aircraft dropped thousands of bombs that created a devastating firestorm. Still one of the world's major ports today, and a German federal state in its own right, it recalls its proud history by calling itself the Free and Hanseatic City of Hamburg.

The Planten und Blomen, Hamburg's green lung

THE FAB FOUR
Hamburg revels in its association with the early days of The Beatles. It was in the clubs on the St.-Pauli red-light area between 1960 and 1962 that the group first began to make a musical impact. At that time there were five members: John Lennon, Paul McCartney, George Harrison, Stuart Sutcliffe and Pete Best. Sutcliffe and Best later left (the former died in Hamburg). Ringo Starr, who joined at the end of the Hamburg period, completed the 'Fab Four' lineup. None of the clubs where the group played remain open.

Carl Borrner's 1903 statue of Christopher Columbus

Hannover (Hanover)

**Hannover's large and attractive artificial lake, the Maschsee, is the setting for a broad range of leisure activities.
The city is famous for the extent and quality of its parks and gardens.**

The Neues Rathaus (new town hall) has a lakeside view

Hannover's famous Herrenhäuser Gärten has ponds, statues and ornamental gardens

THE SIGHTS

RATINGS	
Historic interest	● ●
Cultural interest	● ●
Chainstore shopping	● ● ●
Walkability	● ●

BASICS

✠ 433 E6 ❢ Ernst-August-Platz 2, tel 0511 1234 5111; Mon–Fri 9–6, Sat 9–2
🚻 Hannover
www.hannover-tourismus.de

One of Herrenhäuser Gärten's numerous statues

SEEING HANNOVER

Close to the middle of Niedersachsen, Hannover is one of North Germany's principal cities. Trade fairs at the congress and exhibitions complex on the city's southern edge have long brought foreign visitors to town; this was given a huge boost by the successful Expo 2000. It's a spread-out city, with relatively few stellar sights for the large area it covers. Two other places to visit are the superb Herrenhäuser Gärten to the northwest, and the Maschsee, a large lake in the south.

HIGHLIGHTS

HERRENHÄUSER GÄRTEN

Herrenhäuser Strasse 4, 30419 Hannover ☎ 0511 1684 7576 ◎ Grosser Garten and Berggarten: daily Nov–end Jan 9–4.30; Feb 9–5.30; Mar and Oct 9–6; Apr and Sep 9–7, May–end Aug 9–8 (Grotto in Grosser Garten closes 30 min earlier Sep–end Apr; one hour earlier May–end Aug) 💰 Apr–end Sep Adult €4, child (under 15) free; Oct–end Mar Grosser Garten free, Berggarten and Grotto Adult €2, child (under 15) free

Hannover's reputation as a green city owes much to the extensive ornamental gardens and parkland of the Herrenhausen district in the northwest. These cover 135ha (334 acres) and are connected by an avenue, the Herrenhäuser Allee, lined with lime trees. The huge baroque French-style Grosser Garten, begun in 1666, was extended and embellished during the next 50 years. Its harmonious array of flower beds, lawns, paths, statuary and hedges is enlivened by fountains—one of which, the Grosse Fontäne, spurts 80m (260ft) high. The adjacent, English-style Georgengarten was laid out in the mid-19th century as a 'natural' lansdscaped park.

LEINESCHLOSS

Hinrich-Wilhelm-Kopf-Platz 1

The seat of the present-day state government of Lower Saxony, the Leineschloss dates from the 17th century, but was largely remodelled in neoclassical style in the mid-19th century, and rebuilt after World War II. It is not open to the public.

82 NORTHERN GERMANY HANNOVER

MASCHSEE

Created between 1934 and 1936 by diverting the waters of the River Leine, this artificial lake, 2.4km (1.5 miles) long and about 500m (1,620ft) wide, begins just south of the Neues Rathaus. Appropriately, it's a great place of diversion for the people of Hannover. In summer, the banks are invariably humming with activity, and they're popular for weekend and evening strolls at any time of the year. Restaurants and cafés line the shores and there's a casino on the north bank. All kinds of small pleasure craft use the waters, and tour boats sail between several landing stages around the shore.

NEUES RATHAUS

Trammplatz 2 ☎ 0511 1684 2292 🕐 Daily by appointment only 🎫 Tour: Adult €2.50, child €2. Tour and tower: Adult €3.50, child €2.50

The 'New' Town Hall is an extravagantly ornate neo-baroque structure begun in 1901 and completed in 1913. The original was an expressive representation of the high point of Germany's wealth and self-confidence in the period just before World War I, but this is a reconstruction following the original's destruction in World War II. You can tour the elegant interior to admire its rich decorative detail, and ride to the top of the bronze-domed cupola on an inclined elevator. In the domed entrance hall are four large and fascinating models of Hannover at different periods in its history: the walled town in 1689; the pleasant regional capital in 1939; the war-devastated city in 1945; and the modern commercial city today.

NIEDERSÄCHSISCHES LANDESMUSEUM

Willy-Brandt-Allee 5 ☎ 0511 980 7666 🕐 Tue–Wed and Fri–Sun 10–5, Thu 10–7 🎫 Adult €4, child €1.50

The Lower Saxony State Museum's multifaceted collection—which covers geology, natural history, marine biology, art and more—gives you a broad insight into a considerable swathe of north Germany. A fine aquarium is a reminder that the land has an extensive North Sea coastline, though it covers the world's oceans more generally. Among some fascinating prehistoric exhibits are several preserved corpses recovered from the region's peat bogs. The museum's art gallery has paintings by Low Countries masters like Rembrandt, Peter Paul Rubens, Salomon van Ruysdael (or Jacob van Ruisdael) and Anthony van Dyck, and Italian painters Sandro Botticelli and Giovanni Battista Tiepolo.

BACKGROUND

Although it gained its town charter in 1241, Hannover was for a long time a minor market town on the trade route from the Netherlands through Braunschweig and Magdeburg to Berlin. That changed in 1636, when members of the Calenberg family, who were dukes of Braunschweig and Lüneburg, made it their seat. The Calenberg ruler Ernest Augustus I was made an imperial elector in 1692, and in 1714 his successor mounted the British throne as George I. In the 19th and early 20th centuries, Hannover grew to be an important industrial city. Heavily damaged by World War II bombing, it was rebuilt mostly along modern lines.

Water, water everywhere at the Herrenhäuser Gärten

VON LEIBNIZ

In the Neustadter Kirche is the tomb of the philosopher, jurist and mathematician Gottfried Wilhelm von Leibniz (1646–1716), who lived and worked in the city for a considerable part of his career. Leibniz developed calculus independently of Isaac Newton and engaged in a dispute with Britain's Royal Society over who had precedence. This eclectic forerunner of the Enlightenment published works on metaphysics and educational reform.

Insel Rügen

This island has a variety of landscapes, some of which have earned national park status. It is popular in summer but has enough open space to handle the crowds. Its own getaway island, beautiful Hiddensee, is just off the west coast.

The clock tower on the seafront at Binz, on the western coast

This column marks the middle of the circus at Putbus

Putbus is an example of 19th-century town planning

RATINGS	
Good for kids	●●●○
Outdoor pursuits	●●●○
Photo stops	●●○
Walkability	●○

BASICS

➕ 431 K3 ℹ️ Bahnhofstrasse 15, Bergen, tel 03838 80770; Mon–Fri 10–6
🚉 Bergen
www.ruegen.de

TIP

● Take a trip on the steam train of the narrow-gauge railway that runs from Putbus in the southeast to the nearby Ostseebäder resorts of Binz, Sellin, Baabe and Göhren.

SEEING INSEL RÜGEN

Germany's largest island, Rügen lies in the Baltic Sea, close enough to the Mecklenburg-Vorpommern mainland to be connected by road and rail via a chain of islets, a causeway and bridges from Stralsund (▷ 92). On such a large island, getting around by car affords the most flexibility, but you can also go by bus, train (including narrow-gauge railway), taxi and, if you are up to the long distances, by bicycle. The varied scenery includes sea cliffs, coastal plains, forested and agricultural land, low hills, moors, and beaches. National parks and nature reserves protect several sites of scenic and wildlife importance. Rügen is very nearly cut in two by a long jagged inlet, the Grosser Jasmunder Bodden, and by the smaller nearby Kleiner Jasmunder Bodden, on the other side of a land bridge—both stretches of water are good places for birdwatching.

HIGHLIGHTS

KAP ARKONA

Beyond Putgarten, the scenic, cliff-fringed northern tip of the island sports a brick lighthouse from 1829, and a more functional-looking, striped model from the turn of the 20th century. About 1km (0.5 miles) southeast of Putgarten, and accessible on foot or by horse and carriage, is the handsome little fishing village of Vitt, its thatched cottages seemingly suspended in time.

NATIONALPARK JASMUND

Dense forests of beech and oak cover the Jasmund peninsula north of Sassnitz and reach right to the edge of the sea. They end at a line of white chalk sea cliffs called the Stubbenkammer, which is marked by a series of lofty viewpoints connected by a clifftop path. The finest and most frequented by tourists—of these is the Königsstuhl, a cliff at the midpoint, 119m (390ft) above the sea. As the peninsula curves away to the west, the cliffs give way to sands around the resort of Glowe. From the port at Sassnitz, ferries sail to various points around the Baltic.

OSTSEEBÄDER

From the early 19th century until well into the 20th, a cluster of four bathing resorts in the southeast of the island were popular watering holes among well-to-do German society, primarily because of their excellent sand beaches. The resorts are Binz, Sellin, Baabe and Göhren, and although their popularity declined somewhat during the post-World War II period, they have been making a comeback in recent years, although the fancy, restored *fin-de-siècle* mansions that line their streets are now more likely to hold hotels, apartments or restaurants than to be privately owned. In keeping with the island's modern tradition of caring for its natural treasures, the resorts lie within the Biosphärenreservat Südost Rügen, a reserve that protects the forests and wildlife of the area.

Binz is the most popular resort town and has the longest beaches. On the southern edge of the town you'll find the

Jagdschloss Granitz (May–end Sep daily 9–6; Oct–end Apr Tue–Sun 10–4), a hunting lodge from 1836 in the shape of a neo-Gothic Tudor fantasy castle. You get a fine view of the surrounding land- and seascapes from a high viewing platform in the courtyard.

PUTBUS

On the way to the Ostseebäder (see above), you may pass through this town, which was built in the early 19th century by Prince Wilhelm Malte. The prince's castle is no more, but the planned neoclassical town that was created around it survives, though many of its flamboyant villas have been turned into hotels and apartments. On the coast 3km (2 miles) to the southeast, the fishing village of Lauterbach retains traces of the grandeur Malte gave it as Putbus's bathing resort.

HIDDENSEE

By German standards, this island just off of Rügen's west coast is respectably sized at 17km (11 miles) long by a maximum of 2km (1.25 miles) wide, but by comparison with nearby Rügen it seems like no more than an islet. The reality is far different on the ground, where you have to get around on foot, by bicycle or by horse and cart (the island is car-free). Dubbed the 'pearl of the Baltic' for its isolation, tranquillity and variety of beautiful landscapes. Hiddensee can be reached by boat from Stralsund and Zingst on the mainland and from Schaprode and Wiek on Rügen. Boats sail between 1 and 3 times per day. The island is an outpost of the Nationalpark Vorpommersche Boddenlandschaft, which extends across to the ancient forests of the Zingst peninsula on the mainland, and is a prime zone for observing migrating birds. A lighthouse from 1888 stands on the Dornbusch hill, 72m (236ft) high, on the north coast, and a number of resorts that get busy in summer and are built around fishing and farming villages—Grieben, Kloster, Vitte and Neuendorf—are strung along the island's spine.

BACKGROUND

Shaped by the advance and retreat of Ice Age glaciers, Rügen was occupied by the Huns as they pressed westwards during the early part of the fifth century AD. It was in Slavic hands until the 12th century, and later shuttled back and forth between Danish and Swedish rule before falling to Prussia at the end of the Napoleonic Wars. Members of polite German society liked to see and be seen at its bathing resorts right up to the start of World War II, but in 1936, Rügen's truly insular status was lost when the causeway across the straits from Stralsund was completed.

A ROMANTIC VISTA

The Romantic landscape painter Caspar David Friedrich (1774–1840) was a frequent visitor to Rügen. Among his best-loved subjects here were the chalk cliffs of the Jasmund peninsula. Today's painters, both amateur and professional, continue this tradition.

THE SIGHTS

Seeing Rügen by bicycle (above) is popular with both Germans and foreign visitors Rügen's west coast towns, such as Jasmund, are a great place to watch the sun set (below)

Lübeck
●

**Once the seat of the powerful Hanseatic League, historic Lübeck
is among the most handsome of German cities. It has more than 1,000
medieval buildings, from the monumental to the domestic.**

*Lübeck life still revolves around
the water*

*Near by Travemünde continues Lübeck's
sea-going heritage*

*The Holstentor
guards the Altstadt*

RATINGS	
Historic interest	●●●○
Cultural interest	●●●○
Photo stops	●●●○
Walkability	●●●●

BASICS

✚ 430 F4 🛈 Breite Strasse 62,
tel 01805 882233; Mon–Fri 9.30–9,
Sat 10–3
🚉 Lübeck
www.luebeck-tourismus.de

TIPS

● Take advantage of Lübeck's
proximity to the Baltic coast
by visiting the beaches and
seafood restaurants at nearby
Travemünde, and the sea cliffs
of the Brodtener Steilufer
(▷ 289).
● Lübeck has been famous for
its marzipan since the 16th
century. The Niederegger
Marzipan Salon has a fantastic
selection of this confection and
has been at Breite Strasse 98,
across from the Rathaus, since
1806.

SEEING LÜBECK

Just 66km (41 miles) east of Hamburg, and with good road and
rail connections from around north Germany, Lübeck is easy to
get to. Thanks to its compact Altstadt—a UNESCO World Heritage
Site—and a relaxed urban pace that together make walking a
pleasure, it's also easy to get to know and to appreciate.
Radiating from the central Marktplatz, a network of main streets
reaches out to a moat formed by the River Trave and its connecting canals. All of the city's principal attractions lie within, or just
beyond, the central island created by this oval of water.

HIGHLIGHTS

BUDDENBROOKHAUS

Mengstrasse 4 ☎ 0451 122 4100 ◷ Daily 10–5 💶 Adult €4, child free
This is a place of pilgrimage for lovers of *Buddenbrooks*, the 1901
novel by Lübeck native Thomas Mann (1875–1955), which tells
the story of the rise and fall of a Lübeck merchant family. The 16th-
century townhouse, rebuilt in gabled baroque style in 1758, was
owned by the grandparents of Thomas Mann.

HAUS DER SCHIFFERGESELLSCHAFT

Breite Strasse 2 ☎ 0451 76776 ◷ 10am–1am
You might easily think you've strayed back in time to Hanseatic
Lübeck when you enter the late-Gothic Seafarers' Guild House from
1535, now an excellent, if touristy, restaurant (▷ 345). Behind the
red-brick, stepped-gable façade, a veritable fleet of incredibly detailed
model sailing ships hangs from the beamed ceiling in the gloomy
interior, and medieval furnishings complete the picture.

HOLSTENTOR

Holstentorplatz ☎ 0451 122 4129 ◷ Tue–Fri 10–5 (winter until 4), Sat, Sun 11–5
(winter until 4) 💶 Adult €4, child 50c
Guarding the western entrance to the Altstadt, the twin-towered
city gate, built between 1466 and 1477 was influenced by Flemish
models like those of Bruges, fostered by Hanseatic trade connections.

It seems to have been as much a monumental statement of civic wealth and pride as a practical means of controlling entrance to the city. Traffic now passes around instead of through it, but the gate continues its symbolic function. Its twin towers and central step gable form an enduring image of Lübeck, and it stands in a green space that sets it off nicely for photographers. Inside the squat brick walls, which on the city side are elaborately decorated with terracotta friezes, is the Museum Holstentor. This skips through a thousand years of municipal history, focusing strongly on the Hanseatic period, and displays a superb model of 17th-century Lübeck.

MARIENKIRCHE

Marienkirchhof ◎ Daily 10–6. Tour of vault Sat 3.15 ⓖ Free

A masterpiece—perhaps *the* masterpiece—of the *Backsteingotik* (Brick Gothic) style, the Church of Our Lady was built between 1200 and 1350 on the town's highest point, just north of the Rathaus. Very nearly brought to the ground by World War II bombing, the vast church was largely restored after the war. Its twin towers, each 125m (410ft) high, are Lübeck's loftiest. In the south tower, two giant bells that came crashing down during the war have been left where they fell, in what is now a memorial chapel. The central nave is a vast space, supported on great columns and suffused with light during the day. Danish-born composer Dietrich (born Diderik) Buxtehude (1637–1707), who lived for a considerable part of his life in Lübeck, and influenced both Bach and Händel, was appointed church organist in 1668. His tradition of Advent organ recitals is continued to this day.

Travemünde, farther out along the estuary, is best reached by boat

RATHAUS

Rathausplatz ☎ 0451 122 1005 ◎ Tours: Mon–Fri 11, 12, 3 ⓖ Adult €3, child €1.50

Dating from 1230, but extended and rebuilt several times over the centuries, the multi-turreted, red-and-black-brick Town Hall is mostly Gothic, but has earlier Romanesque elements and a later Renaissance sandstone loggia. It's a fantastical, rambling building that was not completed until 1571. From the Marktplatz you can take in the L-shaped ensemble as a whole, before moving in for a close-up look at some of its ornamental details: graceful pillars and arcades, intricate carved decorations, sculptures and coats-of-arms, medallions on the façade, and an external stone staircase in Breite Strasse. Inside there's rococo decoration from 1756 to 1760, including graceful chandeliers, in the Audienzsaal. A superbly atmospheric, traditional German restaurant occupies the cellar (▷ 344).

Haus de Schiffergesellschaft: now a popular restaurant

BACKGROUND

Lübeck was founded in 1143 by the Graf Adolf von Schauenburg on the site of an earlier Slavic settlement, Liubice, which had been razed in 1138. Almost immediately, the new town near the mouth of the River Trave began to develop as a trading hub, attracting merchants from as far away as Westphalia, the Rhineland and Holland, but its growth was cut short for a time by a disastrous fire in 1157. By 1226, Lübeck had been made a free imperial city. In the same century it rose to leadership of the powerful Hanseatic League (▷ 29). Vast wealth flowed into Lübeck and its civic pride was expressed in great Gothic churches filled with art and topped with mighty gilded spires, and in elaborate civic and mercantile buildings. A significant part of the Altstadt was destroyed by Allied air raids in 1942 but enough survived, or was rebuilt and restored after the war, to lead UNESCO in 1987 to declare it a World Heritage Site.

Lüneberg is famous for its brick-and-timber houses

Lüneberger Heide's natural-looking heathland is manmade

The reedbeds of Müritz-Nationalpark's 'small lake'

THE SIGHTS

LUDWIGSLUST

✚ 430 G5 ℹ Schlossstrasse 38, tel 03874 526252 🚉 Ludwigslust
www.stadtludwigslust.de

Duke Friedrich von Mecklenburg-Schwerin moved in 1764 from his ancestral palace in Schwerin (▷ 91) to this purpose-built town 34km (21 miles) to the south. He later set up house at Schloss Ludwigslust (Apr–end Sep Mon–Fri 9–5, Sat, Sun 10–5; Oct–end Mar daily 10–5), built between 1772 and 1776. The castle's stately late-baroque sandstone exterior is complemented by its setting in a 19th-century English-style landscaped garden, where water in fountains, ponds and canals is the main focus.

Money got tight before Duke Friedrich's dream castle was finished. In a brilliant solution, much of the castle's interior ornamentation was produced from a specially formulated papier mâché. You might think that the results would be shoddy, but the hard-wearing substance is indistinguishable from marble, filigreed carved wood and other noble materials, and is in near perfect condition.

LÜNEBURG

✚ 430 F5 ℹ Rathaus Am Markt 7, tel 04131 207 6620 🚉 Lüneburg
www.lueneburg.de

Just east of the Lüneburger Heide (see below), Lüneburg received its town charter in 1247 and was a member of the Hanseatic League (▷ 29). Untouched by World War II, and isolated from the main currents of the post-war economic miracle,

Detail of a carving from a house in Lüneburg

Lüneburg has kept many of its past graces. Construction of the Rathaus (one-hour guided tours daily at 10, 11.30, 1, 2.30 and 3.30, €4.50), on Am Markt in the north of the town, was begun in the 13th century, and work continued until the 18th century.

A tour of the surrounding district, with its traditional brick houses, can be complemented by a stroll among the warehouses and mills of the atmospheric Wasserviertel, the old harbour along the River Ilmenau. Look for the *Abtswasserturm* from 1531, which employed a water wheel to collect river water for Lüneburg's breweries. Salt has been mined here since the 11th century and was the principal source of the town's prosperity during the Hanseatic period. The Deutsches Salzmuseum (Sülfmeisterstrasse 1; Apr–end Sep daily 9–5; Oct–end Mar daily 10–5), in the southwest of the town, takes you through the local history and economic importance of salt extraction.

LÜNEBURGER HEIDE

✚ 430 F5 ℹ Tourismusverband Lüneburger Heide, Barckhausenstrasse 35, Lüneburg tel 01805 200705
www.lueneburger-heide.de

The Lüneburger Heide's heaths, glades and forests cover 775sq km (299sq miles) west and southwest of Lüneburg. What seems the epitome of a natural north German landscape was, in fact, manmade. Before the Middle Ages, the entire area was covered by forest, but the trees were cut down, creating grazing land for sheep and cattle.

A local strain of moorland sheep, known as *Heidschnucken* still keep the heather down and the forests away.

The Bergen-Belsen Konzentrationslager (Concentration Camp) stood on the southern reaches of the Heide, and is recalled in the Gedenkstätte (daily 9–6), where documentation illustrates the history of the camp and its prisoners. Among the many thousands of victims of this Nazi death camp was a young Jewish diarist: Anne Frank.

MÜRITZ-NATIONALPARK

✚ 431 J5 ℹ Nationalpark-amt Mürtiz, Schlossplatz 3, Hohenzieritz, tel 039824 2520
www.mueritz-nationalpark.de

The central part of Mecklenburg-Vorpommern, south of Schwerin, known as the Mecklenburgische Seenplatte, is thickly speckled with lakes—around 1,000 of them—created by glaciation during the last Ice Age. They range in size from little more than ponds to the 117sq km (45sq miles) of the Müritzsee, southeast of Güstrow. Ironically, this lake, Germany's second largest, after Bavaria's Bodensee, takes its name from the Slav for 'small lake'.

East of the lake and focused around Neustrelitz, the national park's 322sq km (124sq miles) encompass a still largely unspoiled—and often hard to access—landscape of lakes, forests, heathland, marshes and traditional villages. This is a paradise for birdwatchers, particularly during the migration and breeding seasons for waterbirds. For anyone who wishes to get away from it all in north Germany, there are few better ways to do so than on a guided nature tour from one of the park's visitor centres.

Neubrandenburg's Treptower Tor, at the western end of the Altstadt, is one of four city gates

Satirical sculpture outside Johanniskirche, Osnabrück

NEUBRANDENBURG

✚ 431 J4 ℹ Stargarder Strasse 17, tel 0395 19433 ⊠ Neubrandenburg www.neubrandenburg.de

Founded in 1248, few towns present such a startling contrast between the old and the new. The *Stadtbefestigung*, a circuit of medieval town walls, 2.3km (1.4 miles) long, is one of the finest surviving in Germany. Sadly, little of the once character-rich Altstadt that nestled inside the walls survived World War II, and the East German authorities replaced surviving structures with character-free buildings. But the walls themselves are worth seeing, and there are some reconstructed points of interest in the town.

You can stroll around the circuit on Ringstrasse, just inside the walls, and in a park area on the outside. The four original 14th- to 15th-century gates—clockwise from the northeast, the Friedländer Tor, Neues Tor, Stargarder Tor and Treptower Tor—are its most impressive features. Both the Friedländer Tor and the Neues Tor are decorated on their interior faces with terracotta sculptures. Built into the walls as further defensive strongpoints were 57 half-timbered *Wiekhäuser*, of which 26 have been rebuilt. Inside the walls, the 13th-century Gothic Marienkirche, near the middle of the city, and the 14th-century Johanniskirche, beside the walls to the north, have been partly restored.

NORDFRIESISCHE INSELN

✚ 429 D2

A group of barrier islands, each with a different character, the North Frisian islands form the above-water segment of the Nationalpark Schleswig-Holsteinisches Wattenmeer. The remainder is a zone of inter-tidal mudflats bathed by a shallow sea, a haven for seabirds and wading birds stretching the length of Schleswig-Holstein's west coast. The islands are, from south to north, Nordstrand, Pellworm, Hooge, Langeness, Amrum, Föhr and Sylt.

Sylt, the largest and most northerly island, has long had the reputation of being a party island, an anything-goes kind of place, a paradise for gay people, naturists and fashion demons. It is also a place of great natural beauty, with long beaches of white sand, dune landscapes and red cliffs along the shore and an interior of sandy moorland. One reason for the frenetic summer partying in the main resort of Westerland and the chic village of Kampen might be the fear that Sylt won't always be around. It's held in place against eroding North Sea winds and tides by wiry salt grasses, but these are slowly losing their defensive battle. Sylt is connected to the mainland by the Hindenburgdamm railway causeway.

OLDENBURG

✚ 433 D5 ℹ Wallstrasse 14, Oldenburg, tel 0441 361 6130 ⊠ Oldenburg www.oldenburg-tourist.de

At the southeastern gateway to the East Friesian peninsula, this former capital of the Grand Duchy of Oldenburg-Holstein-Gottorp belonged to Denmark for a period until 1773. Today it's a pleasant-looking and lively university town with several interesting museums. South of the central Markt, over which towers the late-Gothic Lambertikirche, the old grand-ducal Schloss is an attractive but sober mix of Renaissance, baroque and neo-classical styles. It houses the Landesmuseum für Kunst und Kulturgeschichte (Tue–Wed, Fri 9–5, Thu 9–8, Sat, Sun 10–5), which contains a collection of classical-revival paintings by the local artist Johann Heinrich Wilhelm Tischbein (1751–1829), along with works by Dutch and Italian Old Masters. Across from the castle is the Schlossgarten, an English-style landscaped garden.

The Landesmuseum für Natur und Mensch Oldenburg (Tue–Thu 9–5, Fri 9–3, Sat, Sun 10–5), at Damm 38–44, focuses on the natural history of Niedersachsen. Its collection includes a number of preserved pre-historic corpses recovered from the region's once ubiquitous peat bogs.

OSNABRÜCK

✚ 432 C6 ℹ Bierstrasse 22/23, tel 0541 323 2202 ⊠ Osnabrück www.osnabrueck.de

Osnabrück played a valuable role in the history of peacemaking when it hosted part of the 6-year negotiations that led to the 1648 Peace of Westphalia and brought the Thirty Years War to an end. It was the home town of author Erich Maria Remarque (1898–1970), whose novel *All Quiet on the Western Front* (1929) is an anti-war classic. In World War II, the town was heavily damaged by Allied air raids. In the Markt, a triangular 'square' in the middle, are rebuilt gabled mansions and guildhouses, the 16th-century Rathaus (where the Peace of Westphalia was announced) and the Gothic Marienkirche. In nearby streets are most of Osnabrück's surviving half-timbered houses, and the 12th- to16th-century Dom St. Petrus, which is notable for having one Romanesque and one Gothic tower.

THE SIGHTS

Historic interest	● ● ●
Cultural Interest	● ●
Photo stops	● ●
Walkability	● ● ●

BASICS

✚ 430 H3 ℹ Neuer Markt 3, tel
0381 19433; Jan–end Apr, Oct Mon–Fri
10–6, Sat 10–3; May–end Sep Mon–Fri
10–6. Sat, Sun 10–4; Jun–end Aug
Mon–Fri 10–7, Sat, Sun 10–4
🚉 Rostock
www.rostock.de

TIP

● Boat tours of Rostock
harbour and as far north as the
port, fishing harbour and busy
seaside resort of Warnemunde,
10km (6 miles) to the north
on the Baltic Sea, leave from
jetties at Stadthaven on the
River Warnow (known as the
Unterwarnow at this point).

*Modern sculpture in the
Universitätsplatz (top)*

*This intricate carving (below)
decorates the wall of a
Rostock home*

ROSTOCK

**Rostock's bustling waterfront along the River Warnow is a
reminder of its past maritime trading glories.**

Rostock, 90km (56 miles) northeast of Lübeck, stands on the south
bank of the River Warnow at the point where it opens into a broad
estuary. It has been a flourishing maritime city since the 13th century
when it joined the Hanseatic League (▷ 29) and has retained that
distinction to the present day. That the town has an attractive character at all today owes much to the extensive rebuilding undertaken by
the former East German government to repair heavy damage inflicted
by Allied air raids during World War II.

THROUGH THE ALTSTADT

The primary places of interest are in the Altstadt, within the city walls,
a section of which survives in the southwest of the old town. The
Rathaus, a rambling affair consisting of three 13th- to 14th-century
gabled houses and seven towers, behind an 18th-century baroque
façade, is in the central Neuer Markt. Across the way, the Marienkirche
(Oct–end Apr Mon–Sat 10–12.15, 2–4, Sun, hols 11.15–12.15;
May–end Sep Mon–Sat 10–6, Sun, hols 11.15–5), built between
1300 and 1550 is mostly original, having escaped serious damage in
the war—though it was damaged badly enough during construction
when the nave collapsed.

Pedestrianized Kröpeliner Strasse, leading west from Neuer Markt, is
the town's main street, and its parade of gabled 16th- to 19th-century
houses has been beautifully restored. It passes by a fountain in
Universitätsplatz that is a popular meeting point for the town's students (the university dates from 1419). Note also on the triangular
'square' a sculpture of local hero Marshal Blücher, who commanded
the Prussian army at Waterloo.

MAKING HISTORY

The Schiffahrtsmuseum (Tue–Sun 10–6), at August-Bebel-Strasse 1,
celebrates Rostock's maritime traditions from its earliest days but
focuses on the 19th and 20th centuries. Among many model ships
on display are *Hansekoggen* sailing ships and battleships from World
War I's High Seas Fleet. The Kulturhistorisches Museum (late Jun to
early Aug Tue–Sun 1.30–6), off Universitätsplatz, is housed in the
Gothic Kloster zum Heiligen Kreuz, a former Cistercian convent and
church founded in 1270. Its collection covers religious art, folk art and
works by local artists. Among its finest pieces is the 15th-century
Three Kings Altarpiece.

The picturesque town of Schleswig

Schweriner Schloss—a home fit for a grand duke

Hanseatic Stade's restored riverside houses

OSTFRIESISCHE INSELN

✚ 428 C4 ℹ 01805 202096
www.die-nordsee.de

Seven low-lying islands, havens of natural beauty, are connected by ferry across the shallow Wattenmeer from harbours on the Ostfriesland peninsula. In a line from west to east, they are: Borkum, Juist, Norderney, Baltrum, Langeoog, Spiekeroog and Wangerooge, plus a few others that are uninhabited sand banks. The entire archipelago, the Wattenmeer and the adjacent coastline belong to the Nationalpark Niedersächsisches Wattenmeer. Considerable areas have been set aside as protected zones for birds and other wildlife and for plants. Enough remains outside these domains to ensure that the islands are a holiday zone *par excellence*, as are the mainland fishing ports and ferry harbours. Their long sandy beaches are the islands' most popular assets, but hiking in the dunes, birdwatching, seal-watching and sailing have plenty of devotees.

Borkum is the busiest and most developed of the islands, with casinos, a marina and hotels ranging from 19th century to the most modern. Second in size is Norderney, where handsome villas, grand hotels and a casino recall the island's 19th-century heyday as a watering hole for Germany's rich and powerful. All the other islands are car-free; you get about on foot or by horse-drawn cart. Borkum, Langeoog and Wangerooge have little railways.

SCHLESWIG

✚ 429 E2 ℹ Plessenstrasse 7, tel 01805 880007 🚉 Schleswig
www.schleswig.de

Schleswig, 40km (25 miles) northwest of Kiel, was founded by the Vikings in the ninth century on the Schlei, a long Baltic fjord. The Dom (May–end Sep Mon–Sat 9–5, Sun 1.30–5; Oct–end Apr Mon–Sat 10–4, Sun 1.30–4), begun in the 12th century and completed in the 15th, contains the oak triptych Bordesholm Altarpiece by Hans Brüggemann from 1521, a masterpiece of Gothic sculpture, and has a spire 112m (367ft) high.

Schloss Gottorf, the rambling 16th–18th-century seat of the dukes of Schleswig-Holstein-Gottorf (Apr–end Oct daily 10–6; Nov–end Mar Tue–Fri 10–4, Sat, Sun 10–5), on a tiny islet in the Bergsee on the western edge of town, houses two fine museums: the Schleswig-Holsteinisches Landesmuseum, with a collection of local art and applied art, and the Archäologisches Landesmuseum, which has a small boat from around AD350 and a gruesome collection of preserved corpses recovered from peat bogs.

SCHWERIN

✚ 430 G4 ℹ Am Markt 14, tel 0385 592520 🚉 Schwerin
www.schwerin-tourist.de

The capital of Mecklenburg-Vorpommern is 54km (33 miles) southeast of Lübeck, on the shore of the Schweriner See. Its undoubted highlight is the Schweriner Schloss (mid-Apr to mid-Oct Tue–Sun 10–6; mid-Oct to mid-Apr 10–5), on an island in the Burgsee, an inner arm of the lake. Built in 1843, this former seat of the grand dukes of Mecklenburg-Schwerin, who ruled from Schwerin for most of the period 1318–1918, is a vast and fantastical conglomeration of 'neo' architectural styles—primarily neo-Renaissance but with a dab of neo-Gothic and a touch of neo-baroque—enlivened by spires, gables and domes. The island has its own garden, but an even finer one, the Schlossgarten, lies across the south bridge.

If you take a stroll through the streets of the town, you should look for the 19th-century mock-Tudor Rathaus and the 13th- to 15th-century Gothic Dom, both in the heart of the town. The Galeriegebäude (mid-Apr to mid-Oct Tue 10–8, Wed–Sun 10–6; mid-Oct to mid-Apr Tue 10–8. Wed–Sun 10–5), at Alter Garten 3 across the north bridge from the Schloss, has a notable collection, including *Die Schildwache (The Sentinel,* 1654) by Rembrandt's pupil Carel Fabritius, and Lucas Cranach the Elder's *Venus and Cupid with a Honeycomb* (1527).

STADE

✚ 429 E4 ℹ Hansestrasse 16, tel 04141 409170 🚉 Stade
www.stade.de

On the banks of the River Schwinge close to where it flows into the Elbe, Stade, 36km (22 miles) northwest of Hamburg, is an old Hanseatic town (▷ 29) that has retained much of its historical character. It has few outstanding sights, but shines rather as an ensemble and an almost perfect example of a traditional north German town—even if it has been a bit too pristinely renovated. Half-timbered houses line the streets of the Altstadt, particularly along riverside Alter Hafen, the old harbour, many of them converted to restaurants and trendy shops and galleries. The Schwedenspeicher-Museum (Tue–Fri 10–5, Sat, Sun 10–6), at Wasser West 39, in a warehouse from 1705 whose name recalls Stade's period of Swedish occupation during the Thirty Years War, has displays of local history.

Gothic Stralsund was once an important member of the Hanseatic League

Wismar's gabled houses reflect its Scandanavian past

THE SIGHTS

STRALSUND

✚ 431 J3 ℹ Alter Markt 9, tel 03831/24690 🚇 Stralsund
www.stralsund.de

Gateway to the Baltic holiday island of Rügen (▷ 84–85), Hanseatic Stralsund maintains the maritime bustle resulting from its fantastic natural harbour, though these days the water contains primarily fishing boats and pleasure craft. In the Altstadt, ringed by lakes and the sea, are many Gothic buildings that are fully the equal of those in Lübeck (▷ 86–87) and Rostock (▷ 90), and have been restored to their earlier grandeur. A former abbey, the Katherinenkloster at Mönchstrasse 25, hosts the Deutsches Museum für Meereskunde und Fischerei (Jul, Aug daily 9–6/7, Sep–end Jun 10–5). This fine oceanographic museum has sections on the fish and plant life of the Baltic, but also covers the seven seas. The large tropical aquarium is particularly fine, and the turtle pool is the latest addtion.

West of here, and stretching northwards, are the finest surviving sections of Stralsund's medieval walls. These protected, among other things, two superb Gothic buildings: the 13th- to 14th-century Rathaus in Alter Markt, near the middle of town, and the 13th-century Nikolaikirche.

USEDOM

✚ 431 K4
www.usedom.de

This developing Baltic holiday island, 60km (37 miles) east of Greifswald, has two distinguishing characteristics: a strip of land in the east belongs to Poland, and it was the birthplace of rocketry. At the Peenemünde research base on the island's west coast, Wernher von Braun,

the engineer whose expertise would later help to put Americans on the moon, developed the World War II V2 rocket that bombarded London. A Historisch-Technisches Informazionszentrum (Apr, May, Oct Tue–Sun 9–6; Jun–end Sep daily 9–6; Nov–end Mar 10–4) details the history of Peenemünde's rocket projects and their role in the history of space exploration.

Elsewhere, the island has a variety of landscapes: moors, dunes, forests and extensive beaches along the Baltic shore. The sands are edged by a string of resorts with elegant architecture and a popularity that extended from the 19th century to just before World War II, and is being revived in particular at the Kaiserbäder (Imperial Resorts) of Bansin, Heringsdorf and Ahlbeck.

WISMAR

✚ 430 G4 ℹ Am Markt 11, tel 03841 251 3025 🚇 Wismar
www.wismar.de

Founded in 1229 and later a wealthy member of the Hanseatic League (▷ 29), this Baltic harbour town went into decline and became little more than a fortified Swedish outpost from 1648 until 1803. A new form of decline was instituted under the neglectful rule of the East German government, but since 1989 the beautiful Altstadt has been undergoing a revival, with renovation and restoration giving it back its historic shine.

The wide open space of the large, central Markt is surrounded by an array of gabled guildhouses and mansions in a variety of styles that spans the centuries. But your attention is likely to be drawn first to the domed, Dutch Renaissance Wasserkunst pavilion from 1602 that contains a spring outlet. From there, explore

the white stone of the neoclassical Rathaus from 1819, and the red-brick Gothic Alter Schwede mansion (now a traditional restaurant) from around 1380.

Restoration of the war-damaged Gothic Georgenkirche, dating from 1295, west of the Markt is a work in progress. But the vast 14th- to 15th-century Nilolaikirche at Hinter dem Chor, just north of an artificial water course called the Grube, is c omplete. It contains the fine Krämergilde altarpiece from 1430. A stroll around the old town and its harbour is a good way to complete the picture of Wismar.

WOLFENBÜTTEL

✚ 434 F7 ℹ Stadtmarkt 7, tel 01801 934636 🚇 Wolfenbüttel
www.wolfenbuettel-tourismus.de

Wolfenbüttel is notable for its Weser Renaissance *Fachwerkhäuser*. More than 500 examples of these decorated half-timbered houses survive, many of them from the 16th century. Between 1432 and1753 the town was the seat of the Duchy of Brunswick and Lüneburg. This period saw the building of some fine monumental buildings. First among them is the Renaissance and baroque ducal Schloss (Tue–Sun 10–5), which stands in extensive grounds on the western edge of the Altstadt, and is now a museum retaining the 18th-century appearance of the state apartments.

Just north of the Schloss stands the Herzog-August Bibliothek (Mon–Fri 8–8, Sat 9–1), founded in 1572 by Duke Augustus and added to over the centuries. The library holds 860,000 volumes, many of them rare and valuable editions, including the 12th-century illuminated Evangelistary (Gospel) that belonged to Heinrich der Löwe.

WESTERN GERMANY

There's much more to western Germany than the economic powerhouses of Düsseldorf, Bonn, Frankfurt and Köln—spectacular though they are. Once you've seen Köln's cathedral, Düsseldorf's K20 museum and Beethoven's birthplace in Bonn, retreat to the wine-producing valleys of the Mosel and the Rhine, and explore their castles. For cultural highlights, look also to the attractive towns of Münster, Trier, Aachen and Mainz.

MAJOR SIGHTS

Aachen Cathedral is famous for its connection with Charlemagne

AACHEN

One of the oldest established spa towns in western Germany, dating back to AD60, with a superb domed cathedral that was the country's first ever UNESCO World Heritage Site.

RATINGS

Historic interest	●●●○
Cultural interest	●●●○
Walkability	●●●○

BASICS

✚ 436 A8 ℹ️ Information Office Elisenbrunnen, Friedrich-Wilhelm-Platz, 52062 Aachen, tel 0241 180 2960; Mon–Fri 9–6, Sat 9–2 year-round, plus Apr–end Sep Sun, public hols 10–2
🖼️ A museum card (covering entry to five museums) costs €5 and is valid for three months: It's available from participating museums or from the tourist information office
🚇 Aachen

www.aachen.de
Published in German, English and French, Aachen's official tourism website is a joy to use and has comprehensive information on everything from museums and festivals to restaurants and accommodation. The on-line booking service is only available in German, although it's not all that hard to make out what's required.

TIP

● To fully appreciate the cathedral's serenity, time your visit to coincide with one of its Wednesday evening concerts (details from the tourist information office, or from the notice board in the cathedral's main entrance hallway).

It was the Romans who first realized the therapeutic potential of Aachen's foul-smelling springs (local tribes thought that the water came directly from hell), founding the spa town of Aquis Granum here in the middle of the first century AD (Grannus was the Celtic god of healing and water). After the fall of the Romans, Aachen gradually fell into ruin, until Charlemagne revived the city's fortunes by establishing his capital here in AD794; 11 years later, he consecrated the city's cathedral, which became an important pilgrimage site following his death in AD814. In 1165, Aachen was granted market rights and became an important city for copper production. In the 19th century, Princess Elisabeth, wife of Wilhelm IV, made bathing in Aachen fashionable again, and it has been a thriving resort town ever since. Like many cities in western Germany, Aachen was all but destroyed during World War II. However, much of the Altstadt has since been restored, and these days it is a thriving commercial town.

AACHENER DOM

At the heart of Aachen Cathedral (daily 7–7) is Charlemagne's magnificent octagonal chapel, which at the time of its consecration in AD805 was the largest domed structure north of the Alps. It consists of a two-level arcaded gallery, embellished throughout with Italian marble and gilt trim. Almost as important as the building itself, however, are its relics: Mary's robe, Christ's swaddling clothes and the decapitation cloth of John the Baptist are all said to have been brought here by Charlemagne. In the 13th century, his remains were interred in the elaborately gilded Karlschrein, commissioned by Friedrich I. Charlemagne's white marble throne, which between 936 and 1531 was ascended by no fewer than 30 German kings, also survives, but can only be seen on a guided tour.

Further highlights include the huge 12th-century chandelier (also commissioned by Friedrich I) and the intricately decorated choir, which was added in the 15th century to commemorate the 400th anniversary of Charlemagne's death (and to accommodate the sheer numbers of pilgrims flocking through the church). With its striking tracery windows (at 27m/89ft high, they were then the tallest north of the Alps), it became known as 'The Glass House of Aachen.' The Dom was granted World Heritage status in 1978.

BONN

Bonn was the capital of the former West Germany, and the birthplace of 18th-century composer Ludwig van Beethoven.

It's thought that Bonn was first settled more than 6,000 years ago, but it wasn't until the Romans rode into town in the 2nd century BC that it became a major player in the region's history. The town's patron saints, Cassius and Florentius, were both Roman soldiers executed in Bonn for refusing to participate in the persecution of Christians. The 11th-century cathedral is built on the site where they are said to have been buried.

Bonn is also famous for being made the capital of the newly formed West German state in 1949, a distinction it retained until East and West Germany were reunified in 1990. Following reunification, six of the government's fifteen ministries opted to remain in Bonn, and as a result the city still plays an important part in German political life.

BONNER MÜNSTER
Bonn's Altstadt is dominated by the five spires of its lofty basilica, begun in the 11th century and not completed until two centuries later (daily 7–7). It has a Romanesque (round-arched), nave, three floors high, flanked by single-storey aisles. Many of the more flamboyant decorative elements, such as the high altar and the splendid apse mosaic, were added in the 19th century. The highlight, though, is the crypt, which is said to house the remains of Cassius and Florentius, contained in a wooden shrine encased in decorative lead plating (if the latter looks a little modern to be found in a Romanesque cathedral, that's because it is: It was designed in 1971).

BEETHOVEN HAUS
Ludwig van Beethoven was born in Bonn on 17 December 1770, and today it's hard to escape the great man's influence, what with the imposing Beethoven Memorial in the middle of Münsterplatz, the ultra-modern Beethoven Concert Hall just to the north of the city, and the annual Beethoven Festival (founded by fellow composer Franz Liszt in 1845). But the first port of call for any music-lover has to be the Beethoven House (Apr–end Oct Mon–Sat 10–6, Sun, public holidays 11–6; Nov–end Mar Mon–Sat 10–5; Sun, public holidays 11–5), where the composer was born and spent the first few years of his life. Part museum, part restored family home, it chronicles Beethoven's life in a series of numbered rooms, complete with portraits, instruments and original scores. Captions are in German only, but the museum can provide a comprehensive leaflet in English.

Bonn: Not just Beethoven and bubblecars

RATINGS
Historic interest	● ● ●
Cultural interest	● ● ●
Walkability	● ● ● ●

BASICS
✚ 436 B9 🛈 Bonn Information, Windeckstrasse 1, 53103 Bonn, tel 0228 775000; Mon–Fri 9–6.30, Sat 9–4, Sun, holidays 10–2

💳 BonnCard €9 for 24 hours, €14 for 48 and €18 for 72

🚉 Bonn

www.bonn.de
This is a German-only site, although it does provide extensive information on everything from sporting facilities to concert listings if your language skills are up to it. The on-line hotel booking facility is, however, available in English.

TIP
● Bonn's Museum of Contemporary History (Tue–Sun 9–7) brings to life the last 50 years of Germany's history with interactive exhibits. Information panels are in German, but you can buy a translation of the main ones for €2. Particularly memorable is a film about the fall of the Berlin Wall—you won't have to speak German to appreciate the emotions involved.

Fortified Burg Eltz was attacked only once, in the 14th century

Fulda's 18th-century Orangery now houses the Martim Hotel, hiding a modern interior behind its baroque façade

BURG ELTZ

🕇 436 B10 • Gräflich Eltz'sche Kastellanei, Burg Eltz, 56294 Münstermaifeld 📞 02672 950500; Apr–end Oct daily 9.30–5.30 🎫 Tours: Adult €6, child/student €4.50; Treasure Vault: Adult €2.50, child/student €1.50 🚊 From Koblenz or Trier to Moselkern; from here, it's a strenuous but rewarding one-hour walk to the castle (signed) 🅿 St. Antonius Chapel, a 15-minute walk from the castle; there's a shuttle bus (€1.50 each way) 🚌 In German, English, French and Dutch 🕰 Every 15 minutes, in German, English, French and Dutch 🎁 Amazing range of keepsakes, from postcards to suits of armour 🍴 Two self-service restaurants www.burgeltz.de

Perched high in a forested valley overlooking the banks of the Mosel River, Burg Eltz is one of Germany's most romantic-looking castles, its sheer walls supporting a series of slate-roofed towers. The castle consists of several closely packed towers grouped around a diminutive inner courtyard. Guided tours take you through wonderfully preserved halls and rooms. Highlights include the Rübenach Lower Hall, with an impressive 15th-century wooden ceiling; the Rübenach Bedroom with its filigreed frescoes from 1470; the Knights' Hall, with its weapons and armour; and the elegantly vaulted, 15th-century ceiling of the Banner Hall.

COLOGNE

See Köln, pages 100–105.

DARMSTADT

🕇 437 D10 🛈 Info Darmstadt, Luisenplatz 5, 64283 Darmstadt, tel 06151 951 5013 🚊 Darmstadt www.darmstadt.de

Darmstadt's bustling pedestrian precinct is focused around the vast, cobbled Luisenplatz and the 39m (128ft) Ludwigsmonument,

built in 1844 to commemorate the reign of local duke Ludwig I, who—among other things—was responsible for the baroque façade of the palace that still dominates the 14th-century Marktplatz. But the city's highlight, and the reason for its continued renown, lies about 1km (0.6 miles) to the east, at Mathildenhöhe. Here, in 1899, Grand Duke Ernst Ludwig founded an artists' colony, which went on to become the heart of the *Jugendstil* (art nouveau) movement. Today, it is home to a superb museum (Tue–Sun, 10–6) with posters, paintings and designs by the likes of Joseph Olbrich, Peter Behrens and Hans Christiansen; captions are in German and English, as are detailed biographies of all the artists. Fans of art nouveau, or anyone interested in design and architecture, will love this intimate and superbly presented museum. Also worth exploring are the grounds and nearby streets, to see sculptures and buildings designed by the artists-in-residence.

EIFEL

🕇 436 A10 🛈 Tourismus Ahr Rhein Eifel, Felix-Rütten-Strasse 2, 53474 Bad Neuenahr-Ahrweiler, tel 02641 97730 🚊 Bad Neuenahr-Ahrweiler www.bad-neuenahr-ahrweiler.de

Hemmed in by the Mosel, the Rhine and the Belgian border, the Eifel is the westernmost of Germany's upland massifs. Its swathes of forests and deep valleys provide the perfect opportunity for escaping the crowds of the Rhine and the Mosel, and offer some excellent hiking, particularly around Hohe Acht, the region's highest point at 747m (2,450ft). But the Eifel is perhaps best known for its Spätburgunder wine, considered by many connoisseurs to be the finest of

Germany's otherwise undistinguished reds. An ideal place to sample a bottle is Altenahr, an attractive little town on the banks of the Ahr River. Altenahr is also the starting point for the Rotweinwanderweg, or Red Wine Hiking Trail, which follows the Ahr as far as Bad Bodendorf—about 35km (22 miles). You can get maps from local tourist information offices.

FRANKFURT AM MAIN

See pages 98–99.

FULDA

🕇 437 E9 🛈 Tourism Fulda, Bonifatiusplatz 1, 36037 Fulda, tel 0661 102 1814; Mon–Fri 8.30–6, Sat 9.30–4, Sun 10–2 🚊 Fulda www.tourismus-fulda.de

A small city with a fascinating history, Fulda is within an hour's drive of Frankfurt, making it an ideal destination for a day trip. It was founded as a Benedictine monastery in AD744 by St. Boniface, an English missionary who was later martyred in Frisia, northern Germany (▷ 28). His remains were returned to Fulda, which soon became an important pilgrimage site. A rather gruesome-looking object that is purported to be his skull can still be seen in the Cathedral Museum (Apr–end Oct Tue–Sat 10–5, Sun 12.30–5.30; Nov–end Mar Tue–Sat 10–12.30, 1.30–4, Sun 12.30–4); you can also catch a glimpse of the foundations of the original basilica, built at the end of the eighth century to house the saint's remains. The basilica itself was torn down in 1704 and rebuilt in the baroque style by Johann Dientzenhofer, who is said to have worked from a model of St. Peter's in Rome (Apr–end Oct Mon–Fri 10–6, Sat 10–3, Sun 1–6; Nov–end Mar Mon–Fri 10–5, Sat 10–3, Sun 1–6).

DÜSSELDORF

Düsseldorf is one of Germany's richest cities and a serious rival to nearby Cologne in terms of its thriving artistic and cultural life.

The Rheinhafen Centre, designed by Frank O. Gehry

First mentioned in historical archives in 1135, Düsseldorf has long been the capital of the northern Rhine region, but it was Johann Wilhelm II (1679–1716), affectionately known as Jan Wellem, who really put the city on the map with his ambitious building schemes and his enthusiastic patronage of the arts (today, he's commemorated by a statue outside the Renaissance Rathaus). Of course, much of Wellem's diligent town planning—in fact 80 per cent of it—was laid to waste during the Allied bombing raids of 1944, but Düsseldorf has risen resplendently from the ashes to become one of the most affluent cities in Germany. Today, this wealth is reflected in the über-trendy boutiques and malls that line the renowned Königsallee, while the sensitively restored Altstadt is the heart of the city's cultural and culinary scenes. The Altstadt is also very compact and largely traffic-free, making it easy to explore on foot.

K20 MUSEUM

The sinuously curved Kunstsammlung Nordrhein-Westfahlen, or K20 for short, is home to one of the most important collections of 20th-century art in Germany (Tue–Fri 10–6, Sat, Sun 11–6). Particularly well represented are pop protagonists Andy Warhol and Jackson Pollock, German expressionists Ernst Kirchner and Max Beckmann, and abstract artist Paul Klee, not to mention all of the usual suspects like Henri Matisse, Piet Mondrian and Pablo Picasso. Top billing, though, goes to Joseph Beuys, a native of Düsseldorf whose numerous works include the intriguing *7000 Oaks* (▷ 17) or *End of the 20th century* (1963): a number of natural basalt columns with small, cone-shaped holes drilled into their sides, which have then been roughly repaired by wrapping the removed cones in cloth and replacing them. 'Too little,' Beuys seems to be saying, 'too late'. If all of these abstracts ideas start to hurt your head, you can always seek out the sublime works of Pierre Bonnard and André Derain on the top floor. Major works have captions in English, but most don't, so it's well worth paying the extra €1 for an audioguide.

If you like your art even more cutting edge, K21 (same opening times), right next door to its older brother, focuses on international contemporary art and presents a growing permanent collection alongside its temporary exhibitions. Its trendy bar, on the ground floor, is a great place to grab a coffee between museums.

RATINGS

Cultural interest	●●●●
Specialist shopping	●●●●●
Walkability	●●●●●
Good for food	●●●●

BASICS

⊞ 432 B8 🛈 Tourist Information Hauptbahnhof, Immermannstrasse 65b, 40210 Düsseldorf, tel 0211 172020; Mon–Fri 9.30–6.30, Sat 9.30–6

🛈 Tourist Information Burgplatz, Burgplatz 2, 40123 Düsseldorf, tel 0211 602 5753; daily 11–6

🎟 Welcome Card (free public transport and admission to many museums, plus other reductions): €9 for 24 hrs, €14 for 48 hrs, €19 for 72 hrs

🚃 Düsseldorf

www.duesseldorf-tourismus.de
Slick and accessible site, with up-to-the-minute information on events, sightseeing, arts and culture, fashion and shopping, and of course eating and drinking. A wide range of accommodation, from budget pensions to luxurious hotels, can be booked online.

TIP

● Get a great view of the city from the viewing gallery at the top of the Rheinturm (daily 10am–11.30pm), a 20-minute walk south of the Altstadt. A café serves snacks and hot drinks, but if you want to splash out, there's a restaurant on the top floor, some 180m (590ft) above the Rhine.

Frankfurt am Main

A city rich in culinary traditions, including *Handkäse mit Music* and *Apfelwein*, and home to a plethora of world-class museums, Frankfurt is the economic heart of Germany and one of its most cosmopolitan cities.

Frankfurt's skyline at night

A brightly painted tram travels past the Messe tower

A modern building for the Museum of Applied Arts

RATINGS

Good for kids	● ● ●
Cultural interest	● ● ● ● ●
Chainstore shopping	● ● ● ●
Walkability	● ● ● ●

BASICS

🚩 437 D10 🛈 Tourist Information Hauptbahnhof, 60329 Frankfurt am Main, tel 069 2123 8800; Mon–Fri 8am–9pm, Sat, Sun, holidays 9–6
🛈 Tourist Information Römer, Römerberg 27, 60311 Frankfurt am Main, tel 069 2123 8800; Mon–Fri 9.30–5.30, Sat, Sun, holidays 10–4
🎫 Frankfurt Card (free public transport, 50 per cent discount at 21 museums, plus other discounts): €7.80 for one day or €11.50 for two days
🔲 Frankfurt

www.frankfurt-tourismus.de
Fast and functional, this website provides information on tours and attractions, events and trade shows, and sporting attractions and facilities. It also has extensive restaurant and hotel listings, the latter with a facility for online booking; hotels and pensions can be searched either alphabetically, by region, or by room rate.

The Goethe statue (top)

SEEING FRANKFURT

Known locally as Mainhattan, Frankfurt am Main (pronounced 'Mine') is the closest thing western Germany has to a high-rise metropolis. Its striking skyline includes the 299m (981ft) Commerzbank, designed by renowned British architect Sir Norman Foster, and the Main Tower (200m/656ft), the new headquarters of the European Central Bank. The city is also home to the Bundesbank (Germany's central bank) and the German stock exchange, and is renowned for its numerous trade fairs. Not surprisingly, this world of commerce is reflected at street level in the designer stores that line the city's streets (▷ 253). But beyond the *wolkenkratzer* (literally 'cloud-scrapers') and bright lights of the financial district lies a city with an attractive medieval core, and plenty to interest visitors.

HIGHLIGHTS

RÖMERBERG

The focus of Frankfurt's compact Altstadt is the beautifully restored Römerberg, a cobbled, octagonal square that's known locally as the Gut Stubb, or Great Parlour. Market fairs were held here as early as the ninth century, and the striking Town Hall (daily 10–12 and 2–5), made up of three buildings united by a Gothic gable, was originally built in the 15th century. It was here that coronations were celebrated in the days of the Holy Roman Empire (see Background). Although there's not actually much more to see here, it's a perfect starting point for exploring the rest of the city.

STÄDEL-MUSEUM

Schaumainkai 63, 60596 Frankfurt am Main ☎ 069 605 0980 🕒 Tue, Fri–Sun 10–5, Wed, Thu 10–9 🎫 Adult €6, child €5, under 12 free
www.staedelmuseum.de
At the heart of Frankfurt's Museum Embankment, just a few minutes' walk from the Römerberg, is the Städel Art Institute, one of Germany's leading fine art museums. The permanent collection contains more than 600 masterpieces of European art from the 14th to the 20th

centuries, including works by Albrecht Dürer, Lucas Cranach, Jan van Eyck, Sandro Botticelli, Andrea Mantegna and Canaletto, to name just a few. Highlights include a pair of small but exquisite Goyas, and Hans Holbein's famous *Meyer Madonna* (c.1526). Captions are in German only, but audioguides (in various languages, including English) cost €2.

MUSEUM FÜR MODERNE KUNST

Domstrasse 10, 60311 Frankfurt am Main ☎ 069 2123 0447 🕐 Tue, Thu–Sun 10–5, Wed 10–8 🎟 Adults €6, child €3, under 6 free
www.mmk-frankfurt.de

The Museum of Modern Art is in a striking triangular building, designed by Viennese architect Hans Hollein. The core of the museum's collection consists of American and European art from the 1960s and '70s, with works by Andy Warhol, Roy Lichtenstein and

Joseph Beuys among the highlights. Alongside these well-known names are also works by contemporary artists. Look out for a piece by Nedko Solakov: 14 tiny, scribbled captions throughout the museum, each chatting about the 14 stages of Christ's crucifixion, with the odd amusing aside about the museum's overzealous attendants, referred to as 'guards.'

DEUTSCHES ARCHITEKTURMUSEUM

Schaumainkai 43, 60596 Frankfurt am Main ☎ 069 2123 8844 🕐 Tue, Thu–Sun 10–5, Wed 10–8 🎟 Adult €6, child €3
www.dam-online.de

Most of the gallery space in this splendid museum is set aside for temporary shows, but the permanent exhibition is worth the entry price alone. Twenty five brilliant models of some of the world's most famous buildings offer you a complete guided tour of architectural history, from mud huts to skyscrapers. Highlights include Speyer Cathedral (▷ 118), the Royal Cresent in Bath, England and New York's Chrysler building. Accompanying information is beautifully presented, and all captions are in English as well as German.

BACKGROUND

The first official mention of Frankfurt was made in AD794, but it wasn't until 1240 that it was declared a market city by Friedrich II. Barely a hundred years later, in a charter dated 1356, Frankfurt was named as the electoral site of all German kings, a privilege it retained right up until the dissolution of the German Holy Roman Empire in 1806. (The King's Room, or Kaisersaal, in Frankfurt's medieval Town Hall contains 52 life-size portraits of past monarchs.) In 1848, Germany's first democratically elected parliament convened at St. Paul's Church, which is now considered to be the birthplace of democracy in Germany. More than three quarters of the city was destroyed by the bombing raids of World War II, and despite the rapid reconstruction of commercial institutions, the meticulous restoration of the Römerberg wasn't completed until 1983.

TIPS

● For a great view of the city, head up to the observation platform at the top of Main Tower (Apr–end Sep Sun–Thu 10–9, Fri, Sat 10–11; Oct–end Mar Mon–Sun 10–7), or have dinner or drinks at the ever-so-elegant Main Tower Restaurant and Bar (▷ 348).

● Many of the museums are free one Wednesday each month. Check with the tourist office for details.

MORE TO SEE

KAISERDOM

Domplatz, 1 60311 Frankfurt ☎ 069 1337 6186 🕐 Mon–Thu, Sat 9–12, 2.30–6, Fri 2.30–6, Sun 3–6 🎟 Free

Frankfurt's 13th-century cathedral served as the electoral site for German kings from 1356, and as the coronation site of emperors from 1562 to 1792 (hence the name). The striking late Gothic tower (currently closed for restoration) was added following a fire in 1867; it is 95m (312ft) tall, a climb of 324 steps, and was one of the few buildings left standing after World War II.

Modern architecture in the city (left)

HISTORISCHES MUSEUM

Saalgasse 19 (Römerberg), 60311 Frankfurt am Main ☎ 069 2123 5599 🕐 Tue, Thu, Fri, Sun 10–5, Wed 10–8, Sat 1–5 🎟 Adult €4, child €2
www.historisches-museum.frankfurt.de

Although this museum is worth visiting in its own right, it's possible to pay just €1 to see the splendid model of Frankfurt in the 1930s, which is exhibited alongside a second model of the city as it looked at the end of the war, when 80 per cent of the city had been destroyed and 120,000 people had been left homeless. Just off to one side is the tiny, 12th-century Saalhof Chapel, Frankfurt's oldest building, and in a separate room visitors can admire the city's stunning collection of silverware.

The late Gothic tower of Frankfurt's cathedral

THE SIGHTS

Köln (Cologne)

The mighty Dom, with its delicately filigreed twin spires and its forest of flying buttresses, is one of the most magnificent cathedrals in Europe. Cologne has stylish shops, fabulous restaurants and a thriving cultural scene.

Cologne's famous skyline

Reliquary busts from the church of St. Ursula

One of the cathedral's highlights, the Gero Cross

SEEING COLOGNE

The skyline of Cologne is dominated by the twin towers, 157m (515ft) tall, of its massive cathedral, which is without doubt one of the architectural highlights of the entire country. Nearby is the Roman-Germanic Museum—home to one of the most important Roman collections in Europe—and the ultra-modern Ludwig Museum and Concert Hall.

To the south of the cathedral, strung out along the riverfront and surrounding the medieval Altermarkt, is the immaculately restored Altstadt, which is crammed with intimate cafés, welcoming bars and superb traditional restaurants. Culinary highlights are also thick on the ground either side of the Hohenzollernring, about a kilometre (0.6 miles) to the west of the city, while on the other side of the river are the wide open spaces of the Rheinpark, and the warm, soporific waters of the Claudius Thermal Baths. Finally, to the south of the Altstadt, on the banks of the Rhine just a short walk beyond Deutzer Brücke, is Cologne's famous Chocolate Museum, right next door to the equally fascinating Museum of German Sport.

HIGHLIGHTS

KÖLNER DOM

✚ 103 B1 • Domforum, Domkloster 3, 50667 Köln ☎ 0221 9258 4730
🕐 Mon–Fri 10–6.30, Sat 10–5, Sun 1–5 🎫 Cathedral: free; tower: Adult €2, child €1; guided tours (Mon–Sat 11, 12.30, 2, 3.30, Sun 2, 3.30): Adult €4, child €2 (in English); Multivision multi-media show, various languages (Mon–Sat 10.30, 2.30, Sun 2.30): Adult €1.50, child €1
www.domforum.de (mainly German, a little English)
Cologne Cathedral was begun in the 13th century, but because of funding problems it wasn't actually completed until the end of the 19th century. Throughout this time, however, far-sighted architects remained faithful to the original drawings, which miraculously survived. (The original drawing of the west façade still hangs in the ambulatory, but is kept behind a curtain to protect it from the light.) The resulting harmony of structure and decoration, achieved on such

RATINGS	
Historic interest	●●●●●
Cultural interest	●●●●●
Walkability	●●●●
Good for food	●●●●

BASICS

✚ 436 B8 ℹ Unter Fettenhennen 19, 50667 Köln (Dom), tel 0221 2213 0400; Jul–end Sep Mon–Sat 9am–10pm, Sun 10–6; Oct–end Jun Mon–Sat 9–9, Sun 10–6 🎫 Welcome Card (free public transport and cut-price tours, plus reductions in many museums, music venues and churches): €9 for 24 hrs and €14 for 48 hrs
🚉 Köln

www.koeln.de
This superb website is a one-stop shop for all things Cologne. There's comprehensive information on walking tours, exhibitions and events, museums, the cathedral and other attractions, spectator sports and facilities, and of course eateries and hotels (although the online hotel reservation service is available only in German).

A street artist puts the finishing touches to his picture of Beethoven outside the cathedral (opposite)

KÖLSCH

As well as being the name of the intractable dialect spoken by natives of Cologne, Kölsch is also the name of the city's traditional beer, which is served in every single bar, bistro and restaurant in town. A light, refreshing brew, it is invariably served in small, narrow glasses. Since 1986, the name Kölsch has been protected by law, and can only be given to beer brewed in or near Cologne.

a massive scale, made it one of the most awe-inspiring and audacious Gothic structures ever built, and at the time of its completion in 1880, it was the tallest structure in the world (although it was superseded just 10 years later by the Eiffel Tower).

Externally, its sheer mass is relieved by the miraculous delicacy of its flying buttresses and its lace-like masonry, while internally it seems hard to believe that the towering nave is barely a quarter of the height of the soaring spires. Indeed, the best way to appreciate just how tall these spires are is to climb the 519 steps to the platform at the base of the southern steeple. On the way, you'll pass St. Peter, the largest working bell in the world. Sadly, the platform itself is badly graffitied, but this doesn't detract from its magnificent views.

The cathedral's other highlights include its vast expanses of priceless stained glass, which if laid flat would cover the floor of the

Riverside buildings near the heart of the city

At least part of the cathedral will be covered by scaffolding when you visit

The cathedral has an incomparable collection of stained glass, some of which dates from the 13th century

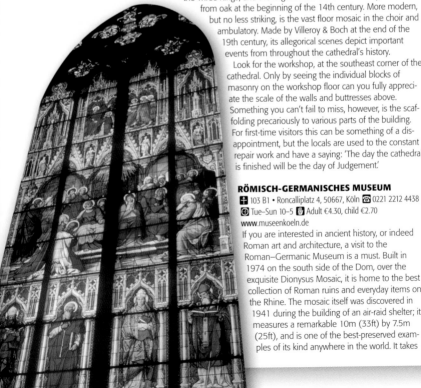

cathedral twice over; the Gerokreuz (Gero Cross), a wooden crucifix dating from AD970, which is unusual for showing Christ with his eyes closed, not as a resplendent Messiah, but as a dying man; the Shrine of the Three Magi, an unimaginably ornate, jewel-encrusted sarcophagus built between 1180 and 1225 and said to contain the bones of the Three Kings; and the largest choir stalls in Germany, carved from oak at the beginning of the 14th century. More modern, but no less striking, is the vast floor mosaic in the choir and ambulatory. Made by Villeroy & Boch at the end of the 19th century, its allegorical scenes depict important events from throughout the cathedral's history.

Look for the workshop, at the southeast corner of the cathedral. Only by seeing the individual blocks of masonry on the workshop floor can you fully appreciate the scale of the walls and buttresses above. Something you can't fail to miss, however, is the scaffolding precariously to various parts of the building. For first-time visitors this can be something of a disappointment, but the locals are used to the constant repair work and have a saying: 'The day the cathedral is finished will be the day of Judgement.'

RÖMISCH-GERMANISCHES MUSEUM

✚ 103 B1 • Roncalliplatz 4, 50667, Köln ☎ 0221 2212 4438
🕐 Tue–Sun 10–5 💶 Adult €4.30, child €2.70
www.museenkoeln.de

If you are interested in ancient history, or indeed Roman art and architecture, a visit to the Roman–Germanic Museum is a must. Built in 1974 on the south side of the Dom, over the exquisite Dionysus Mosaic, it is home to the best collection of Roman ruins and everyday items on the Rhine. The mosaic itself was discovered in 1941 during the building of an air-raid shelter; it measures a remarkable 10m (33ft) by 7.5m (25ft), and is one of the best-preserved examples of its kind anywhere in the world. It takes

KÖLN

0   200 m

0   200 yds

its name from the images of Dionysus, the Greek god of wine, who is also known as Bacchus. It is thought to have been the dining-room floor of a merchant's villa in 220–230AD.

Under the Romans, Cologne was an important area of glass production, so the museum also has a collection of glassware. The most famous items on display are the Serpentine Thread Glasses dating from the 2nd century AD, and the 4th-century Cage Cup, with its astonishingly intricate surface decoration. Equally beguiling are everyday items like jewellery and toys, which help to give everything a more human context. Exhibit captions are in English as well as German.

Nearby are the ruins of the Roman gateway at Domplatz, and the foundations of the old city walls that have been preserved in a parking area beneath the main square.

Tall, pastel houses near the church of Gross St. Martin

The Wallraf-Richardz-Museum: An old collection in a modern building

WALLRAF-RICHARTZ-MUSEUM FONDATION CORBOUD

✚ 103 B2 • Martinstrasse 39, 50667 Köln
☎ 0221 2212 1119 ⏰ Tue 10–8, Wed–Fri
10–6, Sat, Sun 11–6 💶 Adult €5.80, child
€3.30
www.museenkoeln.de/wallraf-richartz-museum

Founded in 1861, the Wallraf-Richartz-Museum is the oldest museum in Cologne, but its original home was destroyed in World War II. It wasn't until 2001 that it finally found a permanent home, in a purpose-built, post-modern building designed by Cologne's architect of the moment Oswald Mathias Ungers. His simple design, with its clean lines and wide, open spaces, has been a hit with architects and gallery-goers alike. The building was deliberately positioned at the heart of the Altstadt, which during the Middle Ages would have housed the workshops of the Cologne Masters, whose works form an important part of the museum's collection. Rubens and Rembrandt are also well represented, as are early 19th-century romantics like Caspar David Friedrich.

Enjoy the views from Köln's Rhineside promenade

EAU DE COLOGNE

The world's most famous fragrance was first manufactured by an Italian immigrant early in the 18th century and was originally sold for medicinal purposes, to treat everything from gout to gangrene. In 1810, however, Napoleon decreed that the formula of all medicines must be revealed for the good of the people, something which the manufacturers of the Eau Admirable were understandably keen to avoid. Their simple but ingenious solution was to re-classify it as a product 'for the care of the body.' Overnight, miracle water became toilet water, and Eau de Cologne was born.

MUSEUM LUDWIG

✚ 103 B1 • Bischofsgartenstrasse 1, 50667 Köln ☎ 0221 2212 6165 ⏰ Tue–Thu 10–6, Fri 11–6 (1st Fri of each month 11–11), Sat, Sun 10–6 💶 Adult €7.50, child €5.50, audioguide €2
www.museenkoeln.de.museum-ludwig

The Ludwig Museum, with its vast underground concert hall and industrial-looking roofline, houses one of the best collections of 20th-century art in Germany. The ubiquitous Andy Warhol is much in evidence, as are German expressionists George Baselitz and Max Beckmann. There's also plenty on offer for those who prefer the early years of modern art, with the likes of Marc Chagall, Pablo Picasso and Paul Klee all getting a look in. There's little information provided about the paintings or artists, so unless you're an expert, you'd be well advised to get an audioguide. Its intimate café is popular (▷ 349).

SCHOKOLADEN MUSEUM

✚ 103 C3 ✉ Rheinauhafen 1a, 50678 Köln ☎ 0221 931 8880 ⏰ Tue–Fri 10–6, Sat, Sun, holidays 11–7 💶 Adult €6, child €3.50
www.schokoladenmuseum.de

Officially known as the Imhoff-Stollwerck-Museum, Cologne's fabulous Chocolate Museum, on the banks of the Rhine just south of the Altstadt, is a must for children of all ages. In a well-ordered sequence of exhibits, it tells the fascinating story of chocolate production, from the harvesting of cocoa beans to the making of Easter eggs, and all of the information is presented in English as well as German. To start with there's just too much information to take in, but once you get to the working production line, all you have to do is look on in wonder as ingredients are mixed, heated, rolled and churned, before being moulded, cooled, wrapped and bagged. Many of the machines have perspex-protected cutaways so you can see what's going on inside them, and it's also possible to sample rationed amounts of liquid chocolate from a chocolate fountain.

DEUTSCHES SPORT UND OLYMPIA MUSEUM

✚ 103 C3 • Rheinauhafen 1, 50678 Köln ☎ 0221 336090 ⏰ Tue–Fri 10–6, Sat, Sun 11–7 💶 Adult €5, child €2.50
www.sportmuseum-koeln.de

Right next door to the Chocolate Museum, this enthralling sports museum is the perfect opportunity to work off any calories—both real and imagined—that might have been gained gazing at tumbling truffles. You are guided through a series of exhibition areas that follow a time-line from ancient Greece to the present day. Many of the captions are in English as well as German, and there's not so much

Everything about the cathedral is massive, including this arched doorway

TIPS

• It's often a good idea to take a quick guided tour of a city just to get your bearings, and nowhere is this more true than in Cologne. The city is so full of history, and so rich in significant sites, that only a local expert can really do it justice. The same goes for the cathedral, which is crammed from top to bottom with fascinating little details. Ask at the tourist office for details.

• The best time to see the outside of the cathedral is at night, when the whole thing gives off a green, ethereal glow. It perhaps looks most striking from the footpath that crosses the railway bridge (or Hohenzollernbrücke) at the east end of the cathedral, or from the far side of the Rhine, from where you can really appreciate the intricacies of the flying buttresses that surround the ambulatory.

THE SIGHTS

information that you feel overwhelmed. Obviously, the focus is on German sport, but this only serves to make it all the more interesting, particularly when it comes to the role sport played in the rise of the Third Reich. The Berlin Olympics of 1936 are well covered, and there is a section on Jesse Owens, all but hidden behind another display. But the highlights are the interactive exhibits: the triple-jump runway showing how far Britain's Jonathan Edwards jumped when he set a world record of 18.29m (60ft) at the 1995 Gothenburg World Championships; the wind tunnel, where you can cycle until your legs scream; and the multi-media screen, where you can watch a selection of the best goals ever scored by German soccer players (and there are some real corkers). Just don't try the standing jump too many times, or you might not be able to walk properly the next day.

BACKGROUND

Founded by the Romans in 38BC, Cologne was granted city status less than a hundred years later by Julia Agrippina, the wife of Emperor Claudius, who was born and raised here. Its importance as a Roman outpost is reflected in exquisite workmanship of the vast Dionysus Mosaic, which today forms the focus of the Römisch-Germanisches Museum, opposite the Dom (laid out well below street level, the mosaic can be glimpsed through display windows at the northwest corner of the museum). By the Middle Ages, Cologne had become the largest city in Germany, an accolade it held well into the 19th century. In 1942, the city was the target of the first Allied 1000-bomber raid, and over the next three years 90 per cent of the buildings in the Altstadt were destroyed; remarkably, the 700-year-old cathedral seemed to withstand the worst of the blasts, but it suffered structural damage that continues to plague it to this day. Following the war, the Altstadt was sympathetically restored, although the rest of Cologne seems to have been rebuilt with varying degrees of sensitivity (and success). However, its former street pattern has been preserved, a measure which has helped it to retain some of its historic feel.

The baroque Golden Chamber (above) in the church of St. Ursula

Hohe Strasse (below) is great for shopping

Wilhelmshöhe Palace in Kassel houses the State Art Collection

Koblenz's Liebfrauenkirche is built in a mixture of styles

Limburg's cathedral dominates the Lahn Valley landscape

KASSEL

➕ 433 E8 ℹ️ Tourism Kassel, Obere Königsstrasse 15, 34117 Kassel, tel 0561 707707 🚉 Kassel
www.kassel.de

Just 130km (80 miles) north of Frankfurt, workaday Kassel was badly damaged during World War II and has since been subjected to some pretty unflattering reconstruction. Its saving grace is its stunning setting, best appreciated at Park Wilhemshöhe, 6km (4 miles) west of the city. A sweeping, romantic landscape created for Willhelmshöhe Palace in the 18th century, it has a statue of Hercules on top of an enormous octagonal amphitheatre, which can be reached by climbing a seemingly endless series of steps (or by road if you prefer). The views alone are worth the €1.80 fee (mid-Mar to mid-Nov daily 10–5). The palace was once the home of Wilhelm II (▷ 37), and now houses an impressive exhibition of paintings by northern Renaissance masters such as Albrecht Dürer, Titian, van Dyck and Peter Paul Rubens, not to mention the largest Rembrandt collection in Germany (Tue–Sun 10–5).

KOBLENZ

➕ 436 C9 ℹ️ Koblenz Tourist Information, Bahnhofplatz 7, 56068 Koblenz, tel 0261 31304; Tourist Information Rathaus, Jesuitenplatz 2, 56068 Koblenz, tel 0261 129610 🚉 Koblenz

Historic Koblenz, at the confluence of the Rhine and the Mosel, can trace its origins back to 9BC, when the Romans first built a fortress here. In subsequent years, it was captured by the Franks, became an important commercial district under Germany's prince electors, and was overrun by the French, a history that reflects the changing

fortunes of much of the region. It's perhaps fitting, then, that Koblenz is home to the Middle Rhine Museum (Tue–Sat 10.30–5, Sun 11–6; leaflet available in English), which houses a superb collection of paintings relating to the river's history, including a number of works by English artists such as George Clarkson Stanfield, whose much-vaunted Koblenzer Moselfront mit Balduinbrücke (bridge, c.1858) epitomises the 19th-century notion of the Romantic Rhine. From here, a short walk along the Mosel leads you to its confluence with the Rhine at the so-called Deutsches Eck, or German Corner, dominated by the monumental equestrian statue of Emperor Wilhelm I (c.1897). The statue itself was destroyed in 1945, but the pedestal remained as a 'Memorial to German Unity' until a replica of the original statue was erected in 1993.

KÖLN

See pages 100–105.

LAHN VALLEY

➕ 437 C9 ℹ️ Limburg Tourism, Hospitalstrasse 2, 65549 Limburg an der Lahn, tel 06431 6166 🚉 Limburg
www.limburg.de

Rising high in the Rothaargebirge Hills, the River Lahn flows for much of its length through a pretty wooded gorge, and is much less commercialized than the Rhine or the Mosel. In addition to Marburg (▷ 111), two towns along the river are worthy of exploration: Heading downstream from Marburg, you come first to Weilburg, which is dominated by a 16th-century, early Renaissance Schloss. Although the palace's interior is impressive enough, the real draw here is its gardens, which march down to the river in a series of

sweeping terraces. Boat traffic can bypass the promontory on which the palace is built by taking a shortcut through a 235m (771ft) tunnel, the longest of its kind in Germany.

Limburg, a few kilometres downstream, is in a more open part of the valley, and is best known for its striking orange and white St. Georg's Dom (Apr–end Sep daily 8–7; Oct–end Mar daily 9–5. Guided tours Mon–Fri 11, 3, Sat 11, Sun 11.15), which is perched on a rocky spur overlooking the river. Built during the transition from Romanesque round arches to Gothic pointed ones, it is a fine example of its type and houses a collection of 12th-century paintings.

LEMGO

➕ 433 D7 ℹ️ Lemgo Tourism, Kramerstrasse 1, 32657 Lemgo, tel 05261 98870 🚉 Lemgo
www.lemgo.de

One of the best-preserved medieval towns in northern Germany, lively Lemgo was once a member of the Hanseatic League (▷ 29). Not surprisingly, this brought considerable wealth to Lemgo throughout the Middle Ages, and because the town escaped damage during World War II, many of its medieval merchants' houses and administrative buildings can still be seen. The most famous of these is the Hexenbürgermeisterhaus, or House of the Witches' Mayor (Tue–Sun 10–5).

The house takes its name from one Hermann Cothmann, who during his stint as Mayor of Lemgo (from 1667 to 1683) sentenced no fewer than 90 women to death for witchcraft. Until 1999, it housed a small local history museum, with a collection of items and exhibits that included a macabre section on medieval torture devices.

MAINZ

**Johannes Gutenburg, father of the modern printing press, was born in Mainz.
The stunning stained-glass windows by Marc Chagall are an unexpected highlight.**

Mainz has long been a city of economic importance, thanks in part to its strategic position at the confluence of the Rhine and Main rivers. The Romans founded a military garrison here in the first century BC, and since the Middle Ages it has been the seat of a succession of archbishops, many of whom are entombed in the city's vast cathedral. Much of the city was destroyed during World War II, but has since been meticulously rebuilt. Today, Mainz is a thriving university town with pleasant, pedestrianized areas and an exceptionally mild climate.

GUTENBURG MUSEUM
The city's most famous son is undoubtedly Johannes Gutenberg (1397–1468), who around 1438 became the first European to print books using moveable type. The Gutenburg Museum (Tue–Sat 9–5, Sun 11–3) in Liebrauenflatz has a series of exhibits outlining his work and the evolution of modern printing. Captions are in German only, but some sections have laminated explanation sheets in English hanging from nearby pillars. The museum also publishes a detailed guide in a number of different languages, including English (€4).

DOM MAINZ
Dominating the city's Altstadt is its cathedral (Mar–end Oct Mon–Fri 9–6.30, Sat 9–4, Sun 12.45–3, 4–6.30; Nov–end Feb Mon–Fri 9–5, Sat 9–4, Sun 12.45–3, 4–5), a mountain of red sandstone that was begun in AD975, but which burned down a day before its consecration in 1009. Most of what survives was built in the 12th and 13th centuries, and today, only the vast bronze doors of the south entrance remain from the original. Apart from its sheer size, the most impressive thing about it is its collection of archbishops' tombs, which document the gradually evolving styles of memorial design between the 13th and 19th centuries, from Gothic to baroque and rococo.

CHAGALL'S STAINED GLASS
If it's serenity you're after, head for St. Stephen's Church (Mon–Sat 10–12, 2–5, Sun 2–5), about 10 minutes' walk to the southwest of the Dom. The church itself is pleasant enough, but the sublime blues of Chagall's stained glass (above), made between 1978 and 1984, when the artist was in his 90s, are simply breathtaking.

One of the sublime Chagall-designed windows (above) in St. Stephen's church

A replica ship (top left) at the Römisch-Germanische museum

RATINGS	
Historic interest	●●●●
Cultural interest	●●●
Walkability	●●●

BASICS
✚ 437 C10 ℹ Mainz Tourist Information Office, Brückenturm am Rathaus, 55116 Mainz, tel 06131 286210; Mon–Fri 9–6, Sat 10–3
🎫 Mainzcard (free entry to many museums, free public transport, free guided city tour, plus a free hotel drink): €6 per day or €10 for a family ticket (2 adults and 2 children under 16)
🚆 Mainz

www.mainz.de
Plenty of information about what's on offer in terms of attractions and festivals, but doesn't have much on hotel accommodation or food and drink.

Mosel Valley

**The Mosel is a romantic river, best seen by boat.
The magnificent imperial castle dominates the picturesque riverside
town of Cochem.**

*Visitors to Cochem watching a
giant chess game*

*The raw ingredients of the
Mosel's most famous export*

*The castle at Krov watches over the
valley's ubiquitous vineyards*

RATINGS	
Good for Wine	●●●●
Historic interest	●●●
Photo stops	●●●●

BASICS

➕ 436 B10 ℹ️ Tourist Information
Ferienland Cochem, Endertplatz 1,
56812 Cochem, tel 02671 60040;
May–mid-Jul 9–5, Sat 9–3; mid-Jul to
end Oct Mon–Fri 9–5, Sat 10–noon;
Oct–end Apr Mon–Fri 9–5
🚉 Cochem
🚢 Boat trip between Koblenz and
Cochem: Adult €21 one way, €25
return, child (4–13) €3.20. Boats depart
Koblenz 9.45, arrive Cochem 3, depart
Cochem 3.40, arrive Koblenz 8
www.cochem.de

SEEING THE MOSEL VALLEY

One of the best ways to reach the towns and villages along the
banks of the Mosel is by boat. The two main departure points are
Koblenz (▷ 106) and Trier (▷ 116–117): from either city it's possible to take a cruise either up- or downriver before returning by
boat or train to where you started. If you want to avoid the worst
of the summer crowds but still make the most of the sunny
weather, plan your trip for late May to early June or late
September to early October. One of the nicest excursions is from
Koblenz to Cochem, operated by KD Cruises (www.k-d.com).
Boats depart between April and the end of October, from near
Deutsches Eck; the exact location may change from year to year,
so you'll need to contact the tourist information office in Koblenz
for up-to-date information. The trip from Koblenz to Cochem
takes 5 hours 15 minutes; the return journey is about an hour
shorter because the boat is going downstream.

HIGHLIGHTS

BOAT TRIP TO COCHEM

Unless you want to spend only 40 minutes in Cochem (the time
available if you're going back to Koblenz by boat the same day), you
have three options: staying overnight and taking the boat back to
Koblenz the following afternoon; catching a train back to Koblenz later
that day or the next morning; or catching an early train from Koblenz
to Cochem and then returning by river that afternoon. If you've only
got a day to spare, the last is arguably the best option, as it allows
time to explore the town and have lunch at one of Cochem's riverside
restaurants, before putting your feet up on the boat as it bears you
gently back to Koblenz. Trains between Cochem and Koblenz (and
vice-versa) run at least once an hour between 7am and 10pm, with
the journey taking a little less than an hour. If you are staying in
Cochem, the friendly, family-run Hotel Am Hafen (www.hotel-am-
hafen.de) has rooms with balconies overlooking the river and the
castle. More modern, but without the views, is the Hotel Café
Germania (www.mosel-hotel-germania.de) on Moselpromenade.

COCHEM'S SIGHTS

Approaching Cochem from downstream, it's impossible to miss the town's magnificent castle, perched on a steep-sided, vine-clad hill high above the right bank. Originally built in around 1000, it became an imperial castle in 1151 under the Hohenstaufen dynasty. It was later destroyed by marauding French forces in 1689, and wasn't rebuilt until 1868. Today it houses a fine museum (daily 9–5: guided tours in German only, but translation sheets available. Adult €4, child €2). The walk up from the river takes about 15 minutes, and although it's quite steep, the views from the hilltop are worth the effort, even when the castle's closed.

Another, less strenuous, way to get great views of the town and valley is to take the chairlift (Easter–mid Nov daily 9.30–6.30. Adult €4 one way, €5.50 return, child (under 14) €1.80 one way, €2.50 round trip) up to Pinnerkreuz, a memorial cross on a high knoll just downstream of the castle. The bottom of the chairlift is on Endertstrasse (which eventually becomes Moselbrücke, the town bridge).

THE WINE TRAIL

It's possible to walk back down to Cochem through the vineyards—detailed maps can be obtained from the local tourist information office. A wine tasting is an essential part of any visit to the Mosel and there are half-a-dozen cellars to choose from. One of the most inviting is Beim Weinbauer (Easter–Dec daily 10–late), a *Weinstube* and restaurant on the Moselpromenade, between the bridge and the castle. If you have any time (or energy) to spare, you could also visit the 19th-century Historisches Senfmühle (mustard mill: daily 10–6) on the east bank of the river.

A leisurely boat trip on the Mosel is a welcome change of pace

BACKGROUND

Rising high in the Vosges Mountains of eastern France, the River Mosel follows the border between Luxembourg and Germany before flowing through the ancient city of Trier. From here, it cuts through the Hunsrück and Eifel mountains in a series of dramatic loops until it merges with the Rhine at Koblenz. The whole stretch of 200km (125 miles) is lined with vineyards, which cling to the steep southern slopes of the valley, and these vineyards produce the region's famous Mosel wines.

Burg Vischering (left) and the Gothic Rathaus (right)

RATINGS

Historic interest	● ● ● ○
Cultural interest	● ● ● ○
Walkability	● ● ● ○

BASICS

✚ 432 C7 ℹ️ Münster Information, Heinrich Brüning Strasse 9, 48143 Münster, tel 0251 492 2710; Mon–Fri 9.30–6, Sat 9.30–1

🚉 Münster

www.marketing.muenster.de
A German-only site, although it's very informative if you can read the language.

MORE TO SEE

RATHAUS

🕐 Tue–Fri 10–5, Sat, Sun and hols 10–4

Don't miss the impressively gabled Town Hall, which in 1648 bore witness to the signing of the Peace of Westphalia, which brought the Thirty Years War to an end. Badly damaged during Allied air raids, it was restored in the 1950s. Today, it's one of the finest examples of secular Gothic architecture in Germany. The Hall of Peace, where the treaty was signed contains the original carved panels, which were removed during World War II to protect them.

MÜNSTER

This attractive, beautifully restored university town is home to Dom St. Paul, which has a working astronomical clock that's almost 500 years old.

Founded as a monastery in AD793 by one of Charlemagne's cohorts (the name comes from the Latin word *monasterium*), Münster became a bishopric just 12 years later, and it wasn't long before a cathedral was built to mark the city's importance. A second cathedral replaced the first in 1090, but was burnt down some 30 years later. A third cathedral wasn't begun until 1225, and it is this structure that has survived to the present day. Today, Münster is a lively and attractive university town, where immaculately renovated baroque buildings jostle for attention on spacious, cobbled streets, while high overhead false gables hide steeply pitched slate rooftops.

DOM ST. PAUL

Münster's massive cathedral (Mon–Fri 6.30–6, Sun 6.30am–7.30pm) was built mostly in the 13th century, and as such is a mixture of Romanesque round arches and blind arcading and Gothic pointed arches and windows. Inside, visitors are greeted by a huge (5m/16ft) baroque statue of St. Christopher (c.1627) by Johann von Bocholt, but even more impressive is the vast and intricate astronomical clock (c.1542) on the south side of the ambulatory. The inscription in its gable explains that the clock shows the time, the position of the sun and the planets and the phases of the moon, and has a calendar calibrated until the year 2071. Remarkably, it's still clunking away almost 500 years after it was built, and chimes every 15 minutes.

GRAPHIKMUSEUM PABLO PICASSO

The only museum in the world dedicated solely to Picasso's graphic works, the Pablo Picasso Graphics Museum (Tue–Fri 11–6, Sat, Sun, and hols 10–6) was established in 2000 to exhibit a permanent collection of some 780 lithographs bequeathed by Westphalian native and graphic artist Gert Huizinga. Titles, captions and background information are given in English and German. This is an absolute must for those who can't seem to get to grips with modern art: Picasso's famous series sketches lead you on a journey through the various stages of pictorial representation, from a detailed drawing of a realistic-looking bull (for example) to the four or five lines that are needed to depict the bull's basic essence. In addition to its light and airy gallery spaces, the museum also has a small bookshop dedicated to the father of modernism, and a relaxing, designer café.

Exquisite detail on the church of St. Elisabeth, Marburg

The courtyard of the Schloss at Saarbrücken

The wooded Naturparks in Sauerland are good for walking

MARBURG

➕ 437 D9 ℹ️ Tourism Marburg, Pilgrimstein 26, 35037 Marburg, tel 06421 99120 🚉 Marburg
www.marburg.de

Medieval Marburg, an hour's drive north of Frankfurt, has more than its share of historic highlights, including Germany's earliest Gothic church and Europe's first Protestant university. The latter was founded in 1527 and is now in buildings scattered throughout the town. The Church of St. Elisabeth (Apr–end Sep Mon–Sat 9–6, Sun and hols 11.15–6; Oct Mon–Sat 9–5, Sun and hols 11.15–6; Nov–end Mar Mon–Sat 10–4, Sun and hols 11.15–6), was built between 1235 and 1283 on the tomb of St. Elisabeth (1207–31) who founded a hospice in Marburg. Such was the impact of her short life that she was canonized just four years after her death, and the church was begun a year later. Its exterior is dominated by lofty twin towers, bolstered by massive buttresses. Much of the town, including the beautifully preserved, half-timbered Altstadt, is built on a hillside, with steep steps leading to the 13th-century castle (now a local history museum), with fantastic views.

RHEINTAL

See pages 112–113.

RUHRGEBIET

See pages 114–115.

SAARLAND

➕ 436 A11 ℹ️ Tourism Saarland, Franz-Josef-Röder-Strasse 9, 66119 Saarbrücken, tel 0681 927200; Tourism Saarbrücken, Reichsstrasse 1, 66111 Saarbrücken, tel 0681 938090
🚉 Saarbrücken
www.saarland.de, www.saarbruecken.de

While the Rhine and Mosel regions are more popular, Saarland isn't without its charms, and in the high season it offers a nice change of pace from the tourist stampede of the nearby towns. The region's capital is Saarbrücken, an unprepossessing, industrialized city that offers little in the way of cultural highlights. If you're passing through, however, it's worth stopping at the Schloss to visit the city's excellent Historical Museum (Tue–Sun 10–6), which charts the changing fortunes of the region from 1914 to 1959.

Beyond Saarbrücken, other attractions worth seeking out include the superb museum of industrial heritage at the former Völklinger Ironworks (Apr–end Oct daily 10–7; guided tours or audioguides are available), which is a UNESCO World Heritage Site; the Ceramic Museum at Mettlach (Mon–Fri 9–6, Sat, Sun 9.30–4), a stone's throw from the headquarters of Germany's leading ceramics manufacturer, Villeroy & Boch (for those who want to take a small piece of V&B home with them, there are four factory outlets in Mettlach); and, last but not least, the panorama at nearby Cloef, overlooking a spectacular hairpin bend in the Saar River.

SAUERLAND

➕ 437 C8 ℹ️ Sauerland Tourism, Johannes-Hummel-Weg 1, 57392 Schmallenberg, tel 0297496980
🚉 Schmallenberg, Bad Fredeburg
www.sauerland-touristik.de

A gently rolling range of forested hills to the southeast of the Ruhrgebiet, Sauerland is made up of five nature parks, the most scenic of which is the Naturpark Rothaargebirge. At the heart of this region is Winterberg, which has the best winter sports facilities north of the Alps, including a 1,600m (5,248ft) bobsleigh run (▷ 258). In the winter, the whole place has a lively, après-ski feel, while in the summer it makes a great base for trekking and mountain biking. One of the most accessible (but also one of the busiest) trails leads to the top of Kahler Asten, the second highest point in Sauerland at 841m (2,762ft). The plateau summit, which takes about an hour to reach on foot, is swathed in trees, which restrict your view, but for €1 you can climb to the top of the weather station for a more expansive vista. The weather station has a couple of cafés and a small regional museum (information in German only), and there's parking for those who'd prefer to drive up.

SOEST

➕ 432 C7 ℹ️ Tourist Information Soest, Teichmühlengasse 3, 59494 Soest, tel 02921 6635 0050 🚉 Soest
www.soest.de

Historic Soest, with its half-timbered Altstadt and its narrow, cobbled lanes, was once the most important market town in northern Westphalia, and today it is home to architectural and cultural treasures. Chief among these are its churches, which dominate the skyline for miles around. The twin Romanesque cathedrals of St. Petri and St. Patrokli face each other across Rathausstrasse, but neither are as interesting as the 14th-century Church of St. Maria zur Wiese, known locally as Wiesenkirche (Mon–Sat 10–4, Sun 12–4, but times can vary). As well as being one of the most exquisitely decorated Gothic churches in Germany, it's also home to the *Westphalian Last Supper*, a 14th-century stained-glass window that shows Jesus and his disciples tucking into a meal of beer, ham and pumpernickel.

SPEYER

See page 118.

Rheintal (The Rhine Valley)

As well as being one of the biggest wine-producing regions in the country, the Rhine Valley is packed with charming, half-timbered houses and romantic, crag-top castles.

Burg Rheinfels affords great views of the river

The two towers of St. Kastor Church, Koblenz

Deutsches Eck in Koblenz, where the Mosel merges into the Rhine

RATINGS			
Good for kids	●	●	●
Historic interest	●	●	● ●
Cultural interest	●	●	● ●
Photo stops	●	●	● ●

BASICS

✚ 436 B9

TIP

● For the ultimate castle-going experience, book on a night-time tour of Rheinfels castle (Fridays, Apr–end Oct). Tours can be arranged in English for groups of ten or more.

Redundant wine presses are put to alternative uses

SEEING THE RHINE

The mighty Rhine begins its life high in the Swiss Alps, following first the Swiss-German border and then the French-German border before delving into Germany proper near Karlsruhe (▷ 217). From here, it flows north before spilling into the North Sea at Rotterdam. But it is between Bingen and Bonn where the river is at its most scenic, and it is here that the notion of the 'Romantic Rhine,' with its dramatic, castle-clad crags and its impossibly steep vineyards, first flourished. These days, of course, it's busy with visitors in the summer, but if you travel out of season, or head even a little way off the beaten track, you'll find a region that's every bit as picturesque as it was when British and French artists first started visiting in the 18th and 19th centuries.

HIGHLIGHTS

LORELEY BESUCHERZENTRUM

Auf der Loreley, 56346 St. Goarshausen ☎ 06771 599093 ◉ Apr–end Oct Tue–Sun 10–5 ▨ Adult €1, child 50c
www.loreley-touristik.de
The first major landmark along the Rhine gorge as you travel north from Bingen is the famous Lorelei Rock, an unremarkable slab of granite presiding over a particularly tight bend in the river. According to legend, a flaxen-haired siren once lured sailors to their deaths here with her seductive singing. The best views of it are from the west bank, but even from there it's nothing to write home about. More impressive is the state-of-the-art visitor centre on the east bank, which has a multi-media myth room, plus other displays on navigation, wine, and flora and fauna in the region. (There are regular ferries across the river at St. Goar if you find yourself on the opposite bank.)

BURG RHEINFELS

Schlossberg, 56329 St. Goar ☎ 06741 7753 ◉ Mar–end Sep daily 9–6; Oct daily 9–5; Nov–end Feb Sat, Sun 11–5 ▨ Adult €4, child €2, family €10
www.burg-rheinfels.com

Perched high above the village of St. Goar are the ruins of spectacular Burg Rheinfels, once the biggest and most impressive castle on the Rhine. Begun in 1245 as a customs house, it went on to be an important administrative town throughout the Middle Ages. In 1692, it was the only fortress on the west bank not to fall to Louis XIV's troops, but less than a hundred years later it was handed over to Napoleon's forces without a struggle, and much of it was blown up. Apart from its sheer size, its most impressive feature is its labyrinth of tunnels and trenches, which you can still visit.

BOPPARD

🔲 436 C10 ℹ️ Tourist Information Boppard, Marktplatz (Altes Rathaus), 56154 Boppard, tel 06742 3888; May–end Sep Mon–Fri 8–6, Sat 9–1; Oct–end Apr Mon–Fri 8–4
www.boppard.de

Boppard is an attractive medieval town, complete with half-timbered houses and a lovingly preserved late-Romanesque church—don't miss the 13th-century Triumphal Crucifix hanging above the altar, which is unusual for showing Christ as a suffering man rather than a resilient king. But the highlights of Boppard lie beyond the town. For great views of the Rhine, take the chairlift at the west end of town to the top of the Vierseenblick (Apr–end Oct daily 10–5). Another worthwhile excursion is by train to Buchholz (€1.90). The scenic, ten-minute journey takes you across two viaducts and through no fewer than five tunnels during its 330m (1,083ft) ascent. The walk back through woodland is all downhill, and brings you out at a great viewpoint overlooking the town (it's well signed, but good maps can be obtained from the tourist information office if required). After this, the path gets quite narrow, and traverses some steep slopes, so be sure to wear shoes with good grip in wet weather.

FRIEDENSMUSEUM BRÜCKE VON REMAGEN

Brücke von Remagen, 53424 Remagen am Main, tel 02642 20159; May–end Oct daily 10–6; Mar–end Apr, Nov daily 10–5 🎟️ Adult €3.50, child €1
www.bruecke-remagen.de

The narrow, cobbled streets of Rüdesheim, once popular with Romantic artists, is a great place to buy your Rhine souvenirs

Remagen is a must for history buffs. In 1945, retreating German troops tried desperately to blow up every bridge across the Rhine, but the bridge at Remagen was secured by American troops and survived shelling, bombing and frogmen for ten days before finally falling into the river. By this time Allied forces had managed to establish a bridgehead on the west bank. Hitler suspected sabotage, and had five of his officers court-martialled and shot. The bridge was never rebuilt, but one of its towers now houses a Peace Museum, with displays on the bridge's dramatic final days (captions are in English and German, and a leaflet in English is available free of charge).

BACKGROUND

The Rhine has long provided an important trade route between the Alps and the North Sea, and most of the towns and castles along its banks owe their existence to commerce. Throughout the Middle Ages, wealthy barons added to their coffers by extorting taxes from those transporting goods along the river; at one time there were as many as 15 customs stations between Koblenz and Bingen alone.

It was the Romans who first brought wine to the region, although it wasn't until the 6th century that people began to cultivate vines here. The steep, man-made terraces that are so typical of the Rhine have dominated the landscape since the 12th century. The most famous grape grown in the region is Riesling, which typically produces white wine with a lively, fruity bouquet, and can range in taste from very dry to very sweet.

The Pfalz, on an island near Kaub, once a toll station

Ruhrgebiet (The Ruhr Area)

**The area around the Ruhr is densely-populated, modern and commercial,
with a thriving cultural scene and a rich industrial heritage.
Essen's Zollverein coal mine is now a UNESCO World Heritage Site.**

Industry as Art, from the National Mining Museum at Bochum

Zeche Zollverein—Essen's mining heritage

The monorail is a modern transport solution, linking local towns

RATINGS	
Cultural interest	● ● ●
Historic interest	● ● ● ●
Chainstore shopping	● ● ● ●

BASICS

Essen
✚ 432 B7 ℹ Touristikzentrale Essen,
Hauptbahnhof 2, 45127 Essen, tel 0201
887 2041; Mon–Fri 9–5.30, Sat 10–1
🔲 RuhrCard (free public transport and
free or reduced price entry to 120
attractions throughout the Rhur area):
adult €39.80, child (under 14) €24.80
for three days, plus other offers and
reductions for a year
🚇 Essen
www.essen.de
Information in English on visitor
attractions and a facility for booking
hotel accommodation online.

Dortmund
✚ 432 C7 ℹ Dortmund Tourist
Information, Königswall 18a, 44137
Dortmund, tel 0231 1899 9222;
Mon–Fri 9–6, Sat 9–1
🔲 TouristCard (free transport and free
or reduced-price entry to numerous
attractions): €8.90 for two days
🚇 Dortmund
www.dortmund-tourismus.de
Dortmund's website offers the same
sort of information as Essen's, but in a
bit more detail; its hotel search facility
is in German only.

SEEING THE RUHR AREA

Named after the river running along its southern boundary, the
Ruhr Area comprises a narrow corridor of industrialized cities
between Dortmund in the east and Duisburg in the west. Though
coal and steel are no longer as important as they once were, this
corridor is still referred to as Germany's Kohlenpott, or Black
Country, and industry still characterizes much of the landscape.
Having said that, however, the region is making a real effort to
overcome its reputation as a cultural wasteland, not by denying
or destroying its industrial heritage, but by embracing and celebrating it. The Industrial Heritage Trail, linking a series of
manufacturing museums, preserved pitheads and technological
curiosities, is just one way to explore the area's legacy. Attempts
have also been made to consolidate the area's green spaces and
to make them more accessible, with a series of footpaths and
cycle-ways linking them to cities throughout the region.

HIGHLIGHTS

ESSEN

Essen is a heaving, industrial city in the heart of the Ruhrgebiet, 20km
(12 miles) to the northeast of Düsseldorf. Essen enjoys a lively cultural scene, thanks to its plethora of world-class venues, and is a great
shopping district. But the best way to appreciate the city's—and the
region's—heritage is to pay a visit to Zeche Zollverein. This massive
mining complex was first opened in 1847, although it wasn't until
Shaft XII opened in 1932 that it became the largest coal-mining oper-
ation in the world. The mine workings and its buildings were designed
in the Bauhaus style, and is considered to be a landmark of industrial
architecture. It remained open until 1986, and, just 15 years later, it
was designated a UNESCO World Heritage Site. Today it's home to
the fantastic Red Dot Design Museum at the Design Centre
Nordrhein-Westfalen (Tue–Thu 11–6, Fri–Sun and hols 11–8).

In the Design Centre, conceived by British architect Sir Norman
Foster, are masterpieces of modern design, from bicycle frames to
bath-tubs, exhibited alongside rusting girders, red-brick walls and

massive industrial piping. It's not obvious which route you're supposed to take, but it's still impressive, and is a must for anyone
interested in design.

Zollverein's Shaft XII has its own visitor centre (daily Apr–end Oct
10–7; Nov–end Mar Sat–Thu 10–5, Fri 10–7), which leads guided
tours of the colliery itself (Apr–end Oct Mon–Fri 2, 4, Sat, Sun 11, 1,
2, 3, 4; Nov–end Mar Mon–Fri 2, Sat, Sun and hols 11, 1, 2, 3, 4)—if
you miss a tour, or if you can't get enough people together to arrange
one in English, it's still worth exploring the site on your own, along
designated footpaths, to marvel at the scale of the complex.

The excellent Museum Folkwang (Goethestrasse 41, Tue–Sun
10–8) has a collection of paintings, prints and sculptures from the
19th and 20th centuries. The museum also has a rare collection of
early photographic prints.

DORTMUND

*The headframe of one
of the mines*

Dortmund is one of Germany's biggest
beer-producers, with six breweries producing well over 500 million litres (132 million
gallons) of beer a year. The brewers of
Dortmund and their predecessors have
quenched the thirst of generations of
miners, whose lives form the focus of the
Westfälisches Industrial Museum (Tue–Sun
10–6; leaflet available in English). No less
fascinating, but much more harrowing, is
the Steinwache Memorial Site (Tue–Sun
10–5), a former Gestapo prison where
some 30,000 people were tortured and
executed during World War II; the cell
blocks survived Allied air raids and can still
be seen (again, an information leaflet is available in English).

Other historic highlights of Dortmund include a trio of medieval
churches: near the station is the 14th-century Petrikirche (Tue–Fri
12–5, Sat 11–4), whose magnificent 16th-century altar is adorned
with more than 500 gilded figures and 50 relief images carved into
the wood. Nearby is the Romanesque Reinoldikirche (daily 10–7),
dominated by its steeple (100m/328ft); it's named after the city's
patron saint, who is depicted in a life-size statue inside the church,
opposite a statue of Charlemagne. Finally, the 12th-century
Marienkirche (Tue–Fri 10–12, 2–4, Sat 10–1) is thought to be the
oldest vaulted church in Westphalia, and has an altarpiece triptych
(c.1420) by local artist Conrad von Soest. Although the original was
cropped in 1720 to fit its existing baroque frame, it remains one of
the finest altarpiece paintings in western Germany, thanks to its
unusual composition and its rich blue and gold hues.

*Villa Hugel in Essen (above and
below): Home to Alfred Krupp, a
19th-century arms manufacturer*

BACKGROUND

Many of the cities along the Ruhr were on an important
medieval trade route, but it wasn't until the 19th century that
the region's rich deposits of coal propelled it to the forefront of
the nation's economy. With the extraction of coal came the
production of steel, and it wasn't long before the mines and factories of Germany's Black Country became the most productive
in the world. This made them a prime target
for allied bombing raids, and most of the
region's cities were all but obliterated during
World War II. The rapid rebuilding that followed left little room for architectural
sensitivity, and for decades the Ruhrgebiet was
seen as a wasteland of mills and belching
smoke stacks. Today, technology and banking
have all but replaced coal and steel as the
mainstays of the region's economy, and cities
like Dortmund and Essen are enjoying an
economic and cultural revival that's well
worth experiencing.

Trier

Trier is Germany's oldest town, and one of the finest medieval cities in the country. It's the birthplace of Karl Marx, and home to some of the most imposing and best-preserved Roman ruins in the country.

Trier's ancient heritage: the Roman amphitheatre

The mismatched towers of the Dom

Porta Nigra's black staining is caused by pollution

RATINGS

Good for kids	● ● ● ○
Historic interest	● ● ● ● ●
Cultural interest	● ● ● ●
Walkability	● ● ● ●

BASICS

✚ 436 A10 ℹ Tourist-Information Trier, An der Porta Nigra, 54290 Trier, tel 0651 978080; May–end Oct Mon–Sat 9–7, Sun 10–5; Mar, Apr, Nov, Dec Mon–Sat 9–6, Sun 10–3; Jan, Feb Mon–Sat 10–5, Sun 10–1; Dec 24 and 31, 10–1

🎫 Trier Card (free public transport, 50 per cent reduction on Roman monuments, 25 per cent reduction on museums, plus other discounts): €9 per person, €15 per family, valid for 3 days

🚉 Trier

www.trier.de/tourismus
The usual information on attractions, plus up-to-the-minute details of guided tours and package deals offered by the local tourist office. Restaurant and hotel listings can be browsed by budget or location—the latter can be booked online.

SEEING TRIER

Trier is a compact city with an extensive pedestrian precinct that's easy to explore on foot. At the heart of the beautifully preserved Altstadt is the Markt, dominated by the Market Cross (erected in AD958) and St. Petrusbrunnen (St. Peter's Fountain *c.*1595), the latter surrounded by sculptures of the four cardinal virtues: Justice, Temperance, Prudence and Fortitude (be sure not to miss the impish monkeys behind these maidens, signifying their opposites). The square itself is hemmed in by restored Renaissance and baroque buildings, the most important of which is the Steipe. But Trier's highlight is undoubtedly its superb collection of Roman ruins, which are worth at least a day's exploration on their own.

HIGHLIGHTS

PORTA NIGRA

Porta Nigra Platz, 54290 Trier ☎ 0651 75424 🕐 Apr–end Sep daily 9–6; Oct, Nov, Feb, Mar daily 9–5; Dec, Jan daily 9–4.30 💰 Adult €2.10, child (under 18) €1; combination ticket to all the Roman monuments (valid indefinitely): Adult €6.20, child (under 18) €2.50

Built at the end of the 2nd century AD, the monumental Porta Nigra, or Black Gate, is one of four gates that once defined the axes of ancient Augusta Treverorum (see Background). Remarkably, no mortar was used, the massive sandstone blocks instead being held together by small iron clamps. Many of the city's Roman monuments were plundered for building materials in the Middle Ages, but the Porta Nigra survived thanks to St. Simeon, who in 1028 incarcerated himself inside the gate for seven years as an act of penance. After his death, it was transformed into a church in his memory (only its Romanesque apse now remains), and as such it was saved from looting by local builders. It even survived the heavy hand of Napoleon, who was told it was a building of Gallic origin and therefore worthy of preservation. The black staining, caused by a combination of weather and pollution, is at its worst at the southwest corner, the direction of the prevailing wind.

BASILIKA

Konstantinplatz, 54290 Trier ☎ 0651 72468 ⏰ Apr–end Oct Mon–Sat 10–6, Sun and hols 12–6; Nov–end Mar Tue–Sat 11–12, 3–4. Sun 12–1 🎟 Free

Trier's remarkable Roman basilica was probably built at the end of the 3rd century AD as Constantine's throne room, and was once part of a much larger complex. It is the second-largest enclosed Roman building in existence, after the Pantheon in Rome. Unusually, it was made entirely of brick. The arched sections of brickwork at ground level are remnants of a highly efficient under-floor heating system. Inside, it looks even bigger than it does from the outside, thanks largely to the fact that there are no aisles or other obstructions to limit the sense of space. The windows at the east end are also slightly smaller than those at the sides, to make it look even longer than its 72m (236ft). It was badly damaged during World War II, but was painstakingly restored. Today it is a Protestant church, a function that is very much in keeping with its spare, Spartan feel.

KAISERTHERMEN

Im Palastgarten, 54290 Trier ☎ 0651 44262 ⏰ Apr–end Sep daily 9–6; Oct, Nov, Feb, Mar daily 9–5; Dec, Jan daily 9–4.30 🎟 €2.10

The Imperial Baths are impressive not for what remains above ground, but for what lies below. Originally intended as a massive spa complex and later relegated to serve as a military garrison, the vast courtyard area is criss-crossed with a maze of catacombs. Many of these labyrinthine corridors are almost perfectly preserved, and some sections are over 100m (328ft) long.

KARL MARX HAUS

Brückenstrasse 10, 54290 Trier ☎ 0651 970680 ⏰ Apr–end Oct Tue–Sun 10–6, Mon 1–6; Nov–end Mar Tue–Sun 10–1, 2–5, Mon 2–5 🎟 Adult €2, child €1

The Karl Marx House is a must for anyone interested in history. A numbered sequence of rooms guides you through the life and times of both Marx (1818–83) and Engels (1820–95), and although captions are in German only, a detailed leaflet is available in English. You can also see a 20-minute documentary on Marx's work in German, English or French. Highlights include a comprehensive collection of the Communist Manifesto in various languages, a first edition of his most famous work, *Das Kapital*, which was to prove so influential to Lenin, and letters and articles in the great man's erratic, spidery hand.

BACKGROUND

Reputed to be Germany's oldest town, the area around Trier is known to have been settled as long ago as the third century BC. Founded as Augusta Treverorum under Emporer Augustus in 16BC (Treveri was the name of the local tribe), it later became the capital of the entire West Roman Empire. In the fourth century AD, Constantine the Great, Rome's first Christian emperor, made it Germany's first bishopric and indeed, after centuries of stagnation following the fall of the Roman Empire, it was the bishops of Trier who re-established the city's political power in the 13th century. Much of the city was destroyed in World War II, although remarkably the Porta Nigra survived almost intact.

TIPS

● If you've got time, take a guided tour—the city is so rich in history, and so packed full of fascinating buildings and details, that it's simply impossible to do it justice here. Ask the tourist office for details.

● If you're in Trier on a Friday, Saturday or Sunday in summer (Apr–end Oct), head to the Roman amphitheatre (a short walk to the east of the Imperial Baths) at 6pm (4.30 in Oct) to see a re-enactment of a gladiatorial contest. Full details can be found at www.valerius-trier.de (in German only).

● A nice spot for a picnic is the Palace Gardens, which are presided over by the striking, pink and cream façade of the magnificently kitsch Electoral Palace (c.1768).

MORE TO SEE

DOM

Dom Information Trier, Liebfrauenstrasse 12, 54290 Trier ☎ 0651 9790790 ⏰ Apr–end Oct daily 6.30–6; Nov–end Mar daily 6.30–5.30 🎟 Free admission; hourlong tours (German only) daily in summer at 2pm: adult €3, child (4–16) €1. Tours in other languages can be booked through Dom Information www.dominformation.de

Trier's Romanesque Dom, with its curiously mismatched towers (a result of religious one-upmanship directed at nearby St. Gangolf Church in the 15th century), contains a curious mix of architectural styles, from its fabulous Romanesque tympanum in the south aisle to its gigantic art deco organ (1974) hanging from the ceiling. But once again the highlight is Roman: The foundations of a third-century church, beneath the visitor centre, make this the oldest cathedral site north of the Alps. These foundations can only be seen on guided tours, and numbers are strictly limited.

The Kaiserthermen, or the Imperial Baths, an early German spa complex

THE SIGHTS

The impressive Kurhaus, at Wiesbaden

This tower is a remnant of the old city walls at Worms

SPEYER

437 C11 Tourism Speyer, Maximilianstrasse 13, 67346 Speyer, tel 06232 142392 Speyer
www.speyer.de

Ancient Speyer, founded around 2,000 years ago, is rightly renowned for its magnificent Kaiserdom, the largest surviving Romanesque cathedral in Europe (Apr–end Oct Mon–Sat 9–7, Sun 1.30–6; Nov–end Mar Mon–Sat 9–5, Sun 1.30–5). Founded in 1030, it was redesigned at the end of the 11th century to include four towers and two domes, and later became one of Germany's three Imperial cathedrals (the other two being at Worms and Mainz). It is an astonishing 134m (440ft) long (a distance best appreciated from the top of the steps leading up to the transept), with a nave height of 33m (108ft), but its deceptively plain design somehow manages to make it look more massive still. Even the crypt, with its simple walls, banded arches and solid cylindrical columns, is bigger than many parish churches. The ante-crypt, accessed via a gloomy set of steps from the main crypt, houses the modest tombs of eight Salian emperors.

Beyond the cathedral's west façade stretches Maximilianstrasse, a wide, cobbled avenue, lined with shops and cafés, that terminates at the 13th-century Altpörtel, Speyer's only remaining medieval gateway. Just to the south of the cathedral is the town's Historical Museum, which charts the history of Speyer from Roman times to the present day (Tue–Sun 10–6). Highlights include the remarkably ornate Golden Hat of Schifferstadt, which dates back to the 14th century BC, and a third-century bottle of wine, with its contents intact.

WIESBADEN

437 C10 Tourist Information Wiesbaden, Marktstrasse 6, 65183 Wiesbaden, tel 0611 17290 Wiesbaden
www.wiesbaden.de

The ancient spa town of Wiesbaden was first settled by the Romans in AD40 and it has provided a welcome retreat for the old and infirm ever since. These days, most of the city's thermal baths are housed in hotels, but two can be visited by the public: the traditional Kaiser Friedrich Thermae in the city (Sat–Thu 10–10, Fri 10–midnight), and the renovated Thermalbad Aukammtal, about 1km (0.6 miles) to the northeast (Fri, Sat 8am–midnight, Mon, Wed, Thu, Sun 8am–10pm, Tue 6am–10pm). The former is decked out like a Roman bathhouse and encourages 'textile-free bathing,' while the latter has a more modern feel and welcomes those who prefer to keep their textiles on!

The town is dominated by the lofty Market Church, a Gothic-revival monstrosity built by Karl Boos in the middle of the 19th century (Tue–Sun 10.30–12.30); unusually for a cathedral, it is made entirely of brick, which makes it look even higher than its 92m (300ft). Even more striking, and of far more artistic integrity, is the splendid Kurhaus, a neoclassical masterpiece built at the beginning of the 20th century and now housing a convention venue and casino (▷ 258). A short walk south of the Kurhaus on Wilhelm Strasse is the Museum Wiesbaden (Tue 10–8, Wed–Fri 10–4, Sat, Sun 10–3), which has a superb collection of vibrant paintings by Russian expressionist Alexej von Jawlensky (1864–1941), who lived in Wiesbaden for the last 20 years of his life.

WORMS

437 C11 Tourist Info Worms, Neumarkt 14, 67547 Worms, tel 06241 25045 Worms
www.worms.de

Over the centuries, the unassuming city of Worms has probably born witness to more history than any other town in western Germany. Originally settled by the Celts and then the Romans, in the fifth century AD it became the home of the Nibelungen, a tribe whose demise was immortalized in the epic poem *Nibelungenlied* (c.1200), which in turn inspired Wagner's equally epic opera cycle *Der Ring des Nibelungen* (1854–76). As one of three imperial cities on the Rhine (along with Mainz and Speyer), Worms hosted over a hundred imperial diets, or assemblies, the most famous of which took place in 1521, when Martin Luther was banned from the Empire for refusing to renounce his beliefs. Worms is also the home of Liebfraumilch (literally 'milk of our lady'), the white wine that takes its name from the 14th-century Liebfrauenkirche.

Sight-seeing highlights include the city's magnificent 12th-century cathedral (Apr–end Oct daily 9–6; Nov–end Mar daily 9–5), and in particular the imposing Romanesque Kaiserportal on the north side; the Gothic frieze of the south porch, displaying dozens of astonishingly detailed biblical scenes; and, inside, the unashamedly extravagant altarpiece, designed and built by baroque master Johann Balthasar Neumann in 1742.

Don't miss The Luther Memorial in Lutherplatz (c.1868) shows the great reformer addressing his detractors. The pedestal is inscribed with what are thought to be his closing words: 'Here I stand. I have no choice. May God help me. Amen.'

BERLIN

Once-divided Berlin is one of Europe's most dynamic cities. Amid the exciting modern architecture, places that resonate with history—the Brandenburg Tor, the Reichstag—still top sightseers' itineraries. Districts, such as bohemian Kreuzberg, have their own distinct identities. And, as a walk past the sunbathers on a summer's day in the Tiergarten will confirm, the city has recovered its open-minded tolerance.

MAJOR SIGHTS

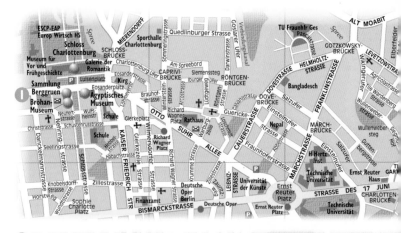

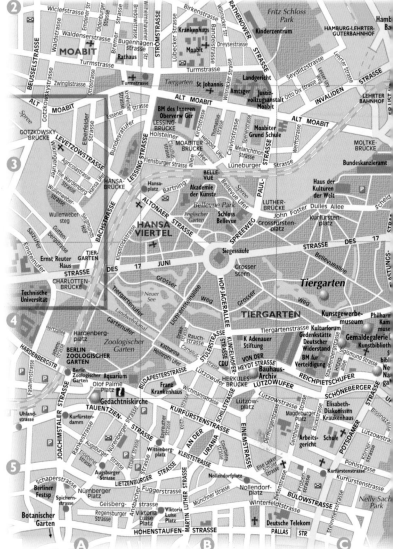

THE SIGHTS

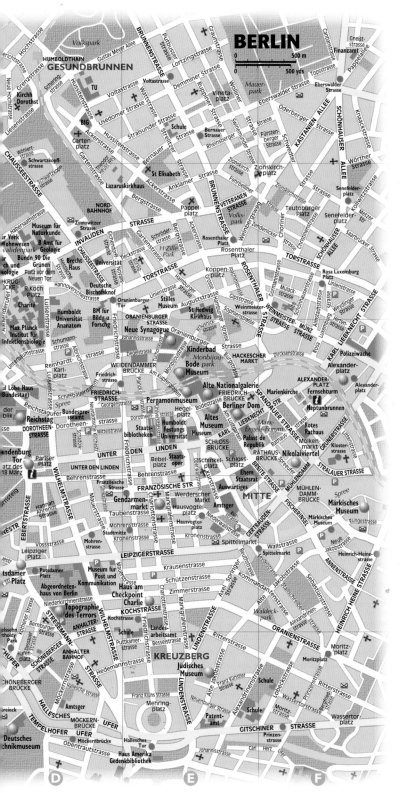

BERLIN

0   500 m

0   500 yds

Berlin

ℹ 124 A4 • Tourist Info Center Europa-Center, Budapester Strasse 45, tel 030 250025 Ⓤ Zoologischer Garten
ℹ 125 D3 • Tourist Info Center Brandenburger Tor (side wing), tel 030 250025 Ⓤ Unter den Linden
ℹ 125 F3 • Tourist Info Café unter dem Fernsehturm, am Alexanderplatz, tel 030 250025 Ⓤ Alexanderplatz
www.berlin-tourist-information.de

The west tower of the Gedächtniskirche

Sir Norman Foster's Reichstag

A boat passes through the grounds of Schloss Charlottenburg

THE SIGHTS

TIP

• For a less costly alternative to sightseeing tours, catch the No. 100 or 200 bus from Zoologischer Garten station in the west to the Prenzlauer Berg district in the east.

WELCOME CARD

The €21 Welcome Card, available from tourist offices, BVG and S-Bahn ticket offices and many hotels, allows one adult and up to three children (under 14) three days' travel on buses and trains in zones A, B and C. It comes with discount vouchers for tourist attractions.

A gate detail, Schloss Charlottenburg

SEEING BERLIN

Berlin is a great mix of old and new and is constantly redefining itself. Your first port of call should be the top of the Fernsehturm (Television Tower) in Alexanderplatz (▷ 125), where you can get a 360-degree view over the city. Another great way to get your bearings is to take a guided tour or hop on a sightseeing bus. Alternatively, try the walk on pages 298–299.

Most cities have one heart, but Berlin has two, the western heart revolving around the Kurfürstendamm and the Kaiser Wilhelm Gedächtniskirche (▷ 129) and the eastern heart extending from Pariser Platz and the Brandenburger Tor (▷ 128) to Alexanderplatz and the Fernsehturm (▷ 125). A regenerated commercial and entertainment hub is also emerging around Potsdamer Platz (▷ 144). There are many ways to get to know the city—on foot, by bus, on a boat, by bicycle or by tram. The S- and U-Bahn are fast and efficient, but sometimes a bus, tram or bicycle ride is a better way to appreciate Berlin's various parts. A Museums Pass costs €12 and provides entry to more than 50 museums, including all the Berlin State Museums, over a period of 3 consecutive days.

BACKGROUND

Berlin was founded in 1237, when a treaty was signed between the margraves of Brandenburg and the Bishop to settle a dispute about the right to levy taxes. The Thirty Years' War (1618–48) hit the city hard and it was left to Friedrich Wilhelm I, the Great Elector, to reconstruct it. By 1701, Berlin had been built up enough to be named the capital of Prussia under King Friedrich I. Things were fairly stable for a century, but during the Franco-Prussian war in 1806, Napoleon entered the city through the Brandenburg Gate, starting a French occupation that was to last for two years. When Berlin was liberated, Berliners elected their first municipal assembly, but it took another half century before the city became the capital of the newly created German Reich in 1871.

At the end of World War I, food shortages, currency devaluation and rationing prompted strikes. Adolf Hitler took power in 1933

and Berliners felt the consequences almost immediately. The Nazis destroyed the Reichstag and set up the headquarters of their secret police (Gestapo) in the capital. On 9 November 1938, Berlin was the scene of the Reichskristallnacht, a pogrom in which synagogues and Jewish shops and businesses were destroyed: Before the Nazi regime, there were 160,000 Jewish people living in the capital—today there are only 10,000.

During World War II, Allied bombing destroyed many historic buildings. At the end of the war, Berlin was divided into four zones, administered by American, British, French and Soviet forces. In 1949, when Germany was divided in two, the border ran through the heart of the city. The GDR (East Germany) built the notorious Berlin Wall in 1961, dividing East and West Berlin. The border was heavily guarded, and in the 28 years the Wall stood, 152 people died trying to escape East Germany.

In 1989, the Berlin Wall came down, followed in 1990 by elections for the newly unified Germany. Today, Berliners have moved on from the division, but rebuilding has bankrupted the city and there is still much to do. Yet despite its troubled past, Berlin now looks forward to the future.

The vast Ishtar Gate, in the Pergamonmuseum (left)

TV Tower (right)

The famous bust of Queen Nefertiti (above). Subdued lighting lends a temple-like air to the museum (top)

RATINGS

Historic interest	●●●●●
Good for kids	●●●
Value for money	●●●●

BASICS

✚ 120 A1 (inset) • Schlossstrasse, 14059 Berlin (Charlottenburg)
☎ 030 3435 7 11
🕐 Daily 10–6
🎟 Adult €6, child €3
🚇 Sophie-Charlotte-Platz, Richard-Wagner-Platz
🚌 145, 210, X21
🎧 Guided tours tel 030 2090 5566; free audioguide
🛍 🎫 Gift shop selling souvenirs and books on Ancient Egyptian history and archaeology ♿

www.smb.spk-berlin.de/amp/s.html

TIP

● As this is a little way out of town, it is worth making a day of it and combining a visit here with a tour of the nearby Sammlung Berggruen (▷ 150), Bröhan-Museum (▷ 128) or Schloss Charlottenburg (▷ 146–147).

ÄGYPTISCHES MUSEUM

This collection of 2,000 ancient masterpieces spans three millenia.
Come here to admire the bust of Queen Nefertiti.

The Egyptian Museum is due to move to Museum Island in 2009. Until it does, key exhibits are being displayed at the Schloss Charlottenburg complex in the Stülerbau (▷ 146–147). The current exhibition focuses predominantly on excavations in the Tell of Amarna and ranges from finds from Metjen's burial chamber, dating from around 2600BC, to Roman mummy masks from the first and second centuries AD. Illuminated by a spotlight in the dark room on the right of the foyer is the undisputed highlight of the museum: the famous bust of Nefertiti.

NEFERTITI

The wife of Pharaoh Akhenaton, Queen Nefertiti was given more rights and responsibility than any other royal Egyptian consort before or after her. Her bust portrait was discovered in 1912, along with other royal portraits, in what had been the house of Thutmose, a sculptor. Made from limestone and plaster, the bust dates from around 1340BC and is almost perfectly preserved. The symmetrical model is thought to have functioned as a teaching tool for sculptors, hence the empty socket revealing the artist's techniques. Although precise, the bags under the eyes and the soft, warm skin lend vitality to the expression. The life-like portrayal appears to embody the contemporary western ideal of femininity and timeless beauty, and she has been a hit with visitors since the day she was first put on display in the 1920s.

THE TEMPLE GATE OF KALABSHA

The Temple Gate was a gift from the Egyptian government to the German Federal Republic, thanking them for their assistance during an international archaeological rescue mission, when the monuments of the Nubian Nile Valley were threatened by the construction of the Aswan High Dam. The Roman Emperor Augustus built the Temple Gate in 20BC, ten years after he had taken control of Egypt following Queen Cleopatra's suicide. The gate is covered in reliefs, depicting the Roman Emperor as an Egyptian Pharaoh.

Don't miss The Hippopotamus figurines on display were placed inside burial tombs to guarantee eternal life (1800BC)—the ones with open mouths were thought to ward off evil spirits and banish curses.

ALEXANDERPLATZ

**Modern architects have transformed this historic square into a bustling meeting place and transport hub.
Enjoy a panoramic view from the top of the Fernsehturm.**

Alexanderplatz was named after the Russian Tsar Alexander I in 1805. In the 1920s and '30s it became a bustling crossroads for Berlin's traffic and a popular meeting place. Destroyed during World War II, it was transformed into a pedestrianized square during the 1960s, but today it is generally visited for the sights around it.

FERNSEHTURM

At 368m (1,207ft), the Television Tower, affectionately known to locals as the Tele Asparagus, is the tallest building in Berlin (Mar–end Oct daily 9am–1am; Nov–end Feb daily 10am–midnight). Inside, elevators whisk you up to the viewing platform in the silver sphere, 203m (666ft) above the ground, at an ear-popping 5m per second (16.5ft per second) for a 360-degree view of the city. Above the viewing gallery is the Telecafé (Mar–end Oct daily 10–1am; Nov–end Feb daily 10–midnight), where you can sit in the revolving restaurant and enjoy the panoramic view over *caffee und kuchen* or a light meal.

MARIENKIRCHE

The Marienkirche (Apr–Oct Mon–Sat 10–6, Sun 10.30–6; Nov–end March Mon–Sat 10–4, Sun 10.30–4) is the second-oldest parish church in Berlin, after Nikolaikirche (▷ 150). It was first mentioned in records as early as 1294, but burned down in 1380 and was later rebuilt. Highlights include the alabaster baroque pulpit (1703) by Andreas Schlüter, decorated with reliefs of John the Baptist and personifications of the Virtues, and the *Dance of Death* (1490) fresco in the vestibule, rediscovered by August Stüler in 1860 behind the whitewash walls.

ROTES RATHAUS

The Rotes Rathaus (Mon–Fri 9–6; closed during official events) is the official seat of the Mayor of Berlin and contains the magistrates' offices and state rooms. The frieze known as the 'stone chronicle' was added in 1879 and depicts historical figures and economic and scientific events that shaped the city. The building suffered extensive damage during World War II and was rebuilt in the 1950s when it was the seat of the East Berlin authorities. After reunification the Rotes Rathaus became the base for the city's officials. Inside, climb the red-carpeted staircase to admire the modern stained-glass windows.

The Fernsehturm and Rotes Rathaus (above). A mural on the side of a house (top)

RATINGS				
Photo stops	●	●	●	●	●
Historic interest	●	●	●	
Walkability	●	●	●	●	

BASICS

🔲 121 F3 • 10178 Berlin (Mitte)

🚇 Alexanderplatz

🚌 100, 157, 200, 348; Tram 2, 3, 4, 5, 6, N54, N92

🚻 Public toilets in the Alexanderplatz U-Bahn station, around the kiosks near the Rotes Rathaus and in the Fernsehturm

TIPS

● The entrance to the Fernsehturm is on the eastern side of the tower, opposite the station at Alexanderplatz.
● If you are going to the Telecafé you will need to check your coats and bags in at the cloakroom near the toilets in the viewing gallery. You may have to wait to be shown to a table during busy times.
● There are regular classical music recitals in the Marienkirche—pick up a leaflet, call 030 2345 7461 or check online (www.marienkirche-berlin.de) for the latest details.

Come to the Old National Gallery for some of the best examples of modern painting and sculpture in Berlin

ALTE NATIONALGALERIE

A comprehensive collection of 19th-century German painting. There are French Impressionist works by Monet, Manet and Renoir.

RATINGS	
Cultural interest	● ● ● ● ●
Historic interest	● ● ● ●
Value for money	● ● ● ●

BASICS

✚ 121 E3 • Bodestrasse 1–3, 10178 Berlin (Mitte)
☎ 030 2090 5801
🕐 Tue–Sun 10–6, Thu 10–10
💶 Adult €8, child €4
Ⓢ Friedrichstrasse
🚌 100, 200, 348
Guided tours tel 030 2090 5566
📖 🛍 🍴 Small bookshop where they also serve coffee
🍴

www.alte-nationalgalerie.de
This is part of the official state museums website. You can find out more about the collection and the history behind it, and there is up-to-date information on temporary exhibitions. English and German.

In 1861, the Berlin banker Joachin Heinrich Wilhelm Wagener left his collection of 262 paintings to Prince Wilhelm (later King and Emperor Wilhelm I). The gallery first opened its doors to the public on the King's birthday, 21 March 1876.

THIRD LEVEL

Begin at the top of the red-carpeted marble staircase on the third level. At the top of the stairs, lean on the balustrade and look across to Anselm Feverbach's huge painting *The Symposium* (1871–73). It illustrates an episode in Plato's *Symposium* when the poet Alcibiades makes a drunken entrance. The philosopher Socrates stands on the right, the poet is in the middle and the figure of Desire is depicted on the left. The elaborate frame is painted and incorporated into the picture, prompting the viewer to question the nature of reality and illusion. Room 3.06 is dedicated to the painter Casper David Friedrich. The artist is famous for his nighttime landscapes and depictions of moonlight reflected over water. *Moonrise over the Sea* (1822) shows two women and a man sitting on a rock, looking out to the sea and waiting for the returning ships. The group symbolizes companionship and safety, while the moonlight backdrop hints at the vast expanse of the universe. Return to room 3.04 and continue your tour clockwise round the third floor.

SECOND LEVEL

Room 2.03, the large room in the middle at the far end of the second level, is dedicated to the French impressionists. Auguste Rodin's statue *The Thinker* (1881–83) is also in this room. A larger-than-life version stands on his grave, but this smaller version is the original. Look closely and you can detect Rodin's fingerprints and tool marks, left behind in the clay model before it was forged in bronze.

FIRST LEVEL

The first level focuses predominantly on realist painting, including works by John Constable, Gustav Courbet and Adolph Menzel. The main attraction is the neoclassical sculpture in the first long room you come to on the first floor, room 1.01. The *Double Statue of Crown Princess Luise and Friederike of Prussia* (1795–97) by Schadow is the first life-size neoclassical double statue made.

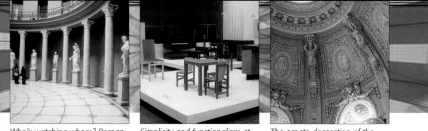

Who's watching whom? Roman gods in the Altes Museum

Simplicity and functionalism at the Bauhaus-Archiv

The ornate decoration of the Berliner Dom

ALTES MUSEUM

🔲 121 E3 • Museumsinsel, Lustgarten, 10178 Berlin (Mitte) ☎ 030 2090 5244 🕐 Tue–Sun 10–6 💶 Adult €6, child €3 🚇 Friedrichstrasse 🚌 100, 147, 200, 348; tram 1, 2, 3, 4, 5, 6, 7, 13, 52, 53 📻 Free audioguide 🏪 🎁 Small shop selling guide books, history books and gift items 🛈
www.smb.spk-berlin.de

The Altes Museum is the oldest museum in Berlin. Built between 1824 and 1830 by Karl Friedrich Schinkel, it was destroyed in World War II and rebuilt in the 1960s. Following reunification, its divided collection was reunited and put on display in the newly restored Altes Museum in 2001.

The focal point is the Rotunda, a perfect setting for the classical, white marble statues of Roman gods, such as Jupiter, Juno and Venus standing regally on plinths between Corinthian columns.

The first compartment is dedicated to Greek Prehistory, and contains sculpture and pottery from the Cycladic, Minoan and Mycenaean cultures (3000–2000BC). There is a large collection of Attic vases and ceramics dating from the early sixth and fifth century BC, decorated with illustrations that reflect Greek life at the time, from sport and war to dancing and mythology.

Don't miss A perfectly preserved mosaic from the Villa Adriana in Tivoli, Italy, (AD118–138) is in compartment 30, illustrating the ambush of a pair of centaurs by lions.

BAUHAUS-ARCHIV

🔲 120 B4 • Klingelhöferstrasse 14, 10785 Berlin (Tiergarten) ☎ 030 254 0020 🕐 Wed–Mon 10–5 💶 Adult €4, child €2 🚇 Nollendorfplatz 🚌 100, 129, 187, 341 ☕ Café serving hot drinks, cakes, soups and sandwiches 🎁 Bauhaus design books, posters, gifts and household items 🛈
www.bauhaus.de

The Bauhaus-Archiv celebrates the origins, techniques and work of the Bauhaus school of design, which ran from 1919 to 1933. The school was open for only 14 years before the Nazi regime closed it down, but the founders and pupils have been extremely influential.

This small museum is packed full of ground-breaking work by the masters and students of the Bauhaus, including Paul Klee (1879–1940), Vassily Kandinsky (1866–1944) and Oskar Schlemmer (1888–1943). The permanent exhibition traces the development of the Bauhaus style as expressed through all aspects of design and art from architecture, household items and furniture to paintings, sculpture, graphic design and photography. The mysterious Light-Space modulator by László Moholy-Nagy, has a prominent position at the heart of the collection. Moholy, who taught at the Bauhaus from 1923 to 1928, described this sculpture as 'an experimental apparatus for painting with light', which he captured in his film *Motion Picture Black-White-Grey*. The reconstructed kinetic sculpture is fully functional—press the red button to see it in action.

BERLINER DOM

🔲 121 E3 • Am Lustgarten, 10178 Berlin (Mitte) ☎ 030 2026 9119 🕐 Mon–Sat 9–7 (until 8 in summer), Sun 12–7 💶 Adult €5, child €3 🚇 Alexanderplatz, Hackescher Markt 🚌 100, 200, 157, 348; tram 2, 3, 4, 5, 6 🎁 Concert tickets, history books, guides to the cathedral, souvenirs
www.berliner-dom.de

On the eastern edge of the Lustgarten (the pleasure garden) is the Berliner Dom, the largest Protestant cathedral in Germany. Johann Bumann built the first cathedral on this site between 1747 and 1750 as a church for the Hohenzollern family.

The cross on top of its copper dome stands 114m (375ft) above the ground. Climb up the 270 steps to the outside viewing platform to enjoy the 360-degree view, with Museum Island to the west and the Fernsehturm (▷ 125) to the east. The Sauer Organ, by Messrs Wilhelm Sauer, dominates the Sermon Church, the soaring congregational area. Its 113 registers and more than 7,200 pipes fill one of the huge Romanesque arches of the rotunda. The crypt was heavily damaged in 1945. After restoration it was reopened in 1999, and now contains around 100 sarcophagi and gravestones, including the tombs of the first king of Prussia, Friedrich Wilhelm I, and Queen Sophie Charlotte.

Don't miss Look out for the dove in the stained-glass skylight of the Sermon Church.

BODE-MUSEUM

🔲 121 E3 • Museumsinsel, Monbijoubrücke, Am Kupfergraben, 10178 Berlin (Mitte) 🚇 Hackescher Markt 🚌 100, 157, 348, tram 1, 50

The Bode-Museum, at the north end of Museum Island, was built by Ernst von Ihne between 1898 and 1904 and is named after its founder Wilhelm Von Bode (1845–1929), art critic, writer and director of the royal Prussian museums. It is currently closed for renovation and is due to reopen in October 2006, when it will contain the Museum für Spätantike und Byzantinische Kunst (Museum of the Late Antiquity and Byzantine Art), the Münzkabinett (The Coin Cabinet), the state sculpture collection, paintings from the early Middle Ages to the late 18th century and a children's gallery.

The greenhouses at the Botanischer Garten are beautiful examples of early 20th-century architecture

The Quadriga: the crowning glory of the Brandenburg Tor

BOTANISCHER GARTEN

✚ Off 120 A5 • Königin-Luise-Strasse 6–8, 14191 Berlin (Dahlem) ☎ 030 8385 0100 🕐 May–Jul daily 9–9, Apr, Aug 9–8, Sep 9–7, Mar, Oct 9–6, Feb 9–5, Nov–Jan 9–4 💶 Adult €5, child €2.50, under 6 free 🚊 Rathaus Steglitz, Dahlem Dorf, Botanischer Garten 🚌 101, 148, 183, X83 ☂ Sun (free; in German only) 🍴 Restaurant Landhaus (closed winter). The Bistro serves snacks and drinks 🏪 Two shops; one selling botanical books and gifts and the other plants and local produce 🛈 www.bgbm.org/bgbm www.botanischer-garten-berlin.de

Berlin's Botanical Garden has over 18,000 species of plant life growing in its glasshouses and 43.3ha (107 acres) of gardens.

Its history can be traced back to a 17th-century kitchen and herb garden of the former Berlin palace. The Kurfürst's garden, on your right as you pass through the south entrance near Unter den Eichen, is a reconstruction of this original garden. Farther along, the art nouveau Dahlem Greenhouses were erected between 1900 and 1909. The Mediterranean greenhouse, Greenhouse P, is recognizably turn-of-the-20th-century in design. Look for the tropical waterfall in the large, domed Greenhouse A, the huge spiky cacti in Greenhouse H and I, and the giant Amazonian water lilies (*Victoria amazonica*) in Greenhouse O.

BRANDENBURG TOR

✚ 121 D3 • Ebert Strasse/Unter den Linden, Berlin (Mitte) 🚊 Unter den Linden, Friedrichstrasse 🚌 100, 248

Berlin's last remaining city gate is the city's most symbolic and recognizable landmark. Carl Gotthard Langhans built the neo-classical arch for King Friedrich Wilhelm II between 1788 and 1791. In 1794, Johann Gottfried

Schadow topped off the gate by adding the Quadriga, the statue of the four-horse chariot driven by Irene, the goddess of peace, which faces east down Unter den Linden.

The gate's symbolic significance made it the backdrop for many victory parades, the scene of uprisings and a target during conflict. The gate barely survived World War II, and the Quadriga was destroyed except for one horse's head, which is now in the Märkisches Museum (▷ 136). The gate underwent repairs in the early 1950s, and a copy of the Quadriga was placed on top of the gate in 1958.

When the GDR closed the border to West Berlin in 1961, the Brandenburg Gate stood in no man's land just behind the Berlin Wall. When it was finally reopened on 22 December 1989, it became the venue for celebrations of freedom.

BRÖHAN-MUSEUM

✚ 120 A1 (inset) • Schlossstrasse 1a, 14059 Berlin (Charlottenburg) ☎ 030 3269 0600 🕐 Tue–Sun 10–6; closed 24 Dec and 31 Dec 💶 Adult €8, free on the first Wed of the month 🚊 Sophie-Charlotte-Platz, Richard-Wagner-Platz, Westend 🚌 109, 145, 210, X21 🏪 Small shop selling postcards and exhibition books 🛈 www.broehan-museum.de

This intimate museum focuses on the art nouveau, art deco and functionalism movements from 1889 to 1939, and has some of the finest examples of porcelain, sculpture and art produced during this time.

On the ground floor is an array of decorative arts. There are several pieces by the French designer and artist Jean Lambert-Rucki (1888–1967). The cubist movement heavily influenced his work, evident in his painting *Profiles d'Ombres* (Profiles in

Shade, 1919) and the sculpture *Le Baiser* (The Kiss, 1928), a refined piece that captures the emotional essence of the moment. The top floor is dedicated to art nouveau glass. The highlight is *Vase mit Irisblüten* (1899), designed by Albert Klein. The large, green porcelain vase is inspired by the curling leaves and delicate flowers of an iris.

DEUTSCHES TECHNIKMUSEUM

✚ 121 D5 • Trebbiner Strasse 9, 10963 Berlin (Kreuzberg) ☎ 030 254840 🕐 Tue–Fri 9–5.30, Sat, Sun and hols 10–6 💶 Adult €3, child €1.50 🚊 Gleisdreieck, Möckernbrücke, Anhalter Bahnhof 🚌 129, 248 ☂ Guided tours and group visits must be booked in advance (tel 30 90 254 284) 🍴 Sarah Werner Café serving meals, snacks and drinks 🏪 Small shop selling transport and automotive books, postcards, prints and gift items 🛈 www.dtmb.de

This large museum complex, dedicated to the history of technology, covers over 50,000sq m (560,000sq ft) of exhibition space. The first thing you will see as you approach along the Landwehrkanal is the shiny, silver C47 Skytrain, or Rosinenbomber (raisin bomber), suspended on the roof. The plane was used during the Berlin Airlift (▷ 41).

Before you begin exploring the museum, check one of the information boards or ask at the front desk of the main building if there are any demonstrations scheduled. The main building has exhibits on the development of textile technology, communication engineering and photography on the first floor and papermaking and printing technology on the second. There is also an extension dedicated to the history of shipping and aviation. Outside you can stroll

Automotive power at the Deutsches Technikmuseum

The Gendarmenmarkt takes its name from the Gen d'Armes *(police) who were once based here*

around the museum park and look into the engine sheds, windmills and a historical brewery. **Don't miss** Spectrum, the science museum next door, is geared towards children, with plenty of interactive exhibits and hands-on areas.

GEDÄCHTNISKIRCHE

🔢 120 A5 • Breitscheidplatz, 10789 Berlin (Charlottenburg) ☎ 030 218 5023 ⊕ Church: daily 9–7; Gedenkhalle (Memorial Hall): Mon–Sat 10–4 🚇 Zoologischer Garten, Kurfürstendamm 🚌 119, 129, 146 🎫 Small kiosk inside the Gedenkhalle selling souvenirs and guide books

The Kaiser Wilhelm Memorial Church is an mix of old and new architectural styles, which embodies the tension between past and present that has come to define modern Berlin.

Built at the end of the 19th century, the old church was destroyed by bombs in 1943. With insufficient funds to rebuild, the ruined tower became a war memorial. In 1961, the new church designed by Prof. Dr. Egon Eiermann was opened.

Unlike the old church, the new buildings are dominated by straight lines and constructed from concrete and steel, covered with a honeycomb of deep blue stained glass. The walls of the hall of worship and the new tower are filled with 21,292 handmade panes of stained glass, and inside, the rich blue light envelops you, creating a tranquil haven for contemplation away from the traffic outside. By contrast, the entrance hall of the late 19th-century tower is covered in original mosaics from floor to ceiling. Most striking is the floor mosaic of the Archangel Michael slaying a dragon.

GEMÄLDEGALERIE

See pages 130–135.

GENDARMENMARKT

🔢 121 E4 • Gendarmenmarkt, 10117 Berlin (Mitte) 🚇 Stadtmitte, Französische Strasse, Hausvogteiplatz 🚌 100, 147, 200, 257, 348 www.franzoesischer-dom-berlin.de

Friedrich Wilhelm's Gendarmenmarkt is a perfect piece of 18th-century town planning.

The Deutscher Dom (Tue 10–10, Wed–Sun 10–6, summer 10–7), to the south of the square, was built in 1708. The Französische Dom (Tue–Sat 12–5), in the north of the square, was erected around the same time and now also houses the Huguenot Museum (Tue–Sat 12–5, Sun 11–5). You can get a good overall view of the square from the Balustrade viewing platform (daily 9–7).

Johann Bouman the Elder built the original Schauspielhaus (playhouse) in 1774 in the middle of the square. It burned down, and a subsequent theatre (designed by Gotthard Langhams, who also designed the Brandenburg Gate) was also destroyed by fire in 1817. Karl Friedrich Schinkel was commissioned to build a replacement. The new theatre opened in 1821, and today is known as the Konzerthaus. It regularly plays host to the Berlin Symphony Orchestra.

In front of the Konzerthaus is the Schiller

Monument (1869) by Reinhold Begas. Removed by the Nazis in the 1930s, it was reinstated in 1988. Schiller is mounted on a pedestal, surrounded by allegorical figures of Poetry, Drama (with a dagger and cloak), Philosophy (with a covered head) and History (sitting on stone tablets).

HAMBURGER BAHNHOF

🔢 120 C2 • Invalidenstrasse 50–51, 10557 Berlin (Tiergarten) ☎ 030 3978 3412 ⊕ Tue–Fri 10–6, Sat, Sun 11–6 🎟 Adult €9, child €4 🚌 245, 248, 340 🚇 Hauptbahnhof/Lehrter Bahnhof, Zinnowitzer Strasse 📷 Guided tours, tel 030 20 90 55 66 🍽 Sarah Werner Café serving meals, snacks and drinks 🎫 Excellent bookshop selling books on art, philosophy and culture in German and English 🌐 www.smpk.de

The Hamburger Bahnhof was designed and built by Friedrich Neuhaus in 1846 and is the last remaining example of a station of this period in Berlin. Following wartime damage, Joseph Paul Kleihues converted it into an art gallery, and in 1996 the Museum für Gegenwart Berlin (Museum of the Present) opened in the restored Hamburger Bahnhof.

The high-ceilinged rooms are filled with natural light, perfect for displaying large canvases and installations. The long gallery, with its curved glass ceiling, leads you along a tunnel of light to the back wall, dominated by Andy Warhol's huge screen print of *Mao* (1973).

Look out, too, for Anselm Kiefer's three-dimensional paintings/collages in the main hall. His larger-than-life sculpture, *Leviathan,* appears to be a bookcase filled with burned books, an impressive illusion considering they are made out of sheet metal spattered with gravel.

The Gedächtniskirche

Gemäldegalerie

This gallery holds some 2,700 European paintings dating from the 13th to 18th centuries.
Come here to see ground-breaking works by Rembrandt, Caravaggio and Bruegel.

Visitors admire the art   *A poster advertises an exhibition*   The Dance *or* Iris (1719–20) *by Jean Antoine Watteau*

SEEING THE GEMÄLDEGALERIE

This large gallery is rather maze-like and, to add to the confusion, there are two room-numbering systems: Roman numerals for the larger inner rooms and standard numbers for the smaller rooms, called cabinets, on the outside. Pick up a map to help you get around and if you do get lost, return to the central hall to get your bearings. The eleven cabinets that make up the Studiengalerie (Study Gallery), where the displays change regularly, are in the basement in rooms 43–54. If time is short, start your visit with the computers in the Digital Gallery (cabinets 27, 33, 42) to explore the collection on screen and decide what you want to see.

HIGHLIGHTS

THE FLEMISH PROVERBS BY PIETER BRUEGEL, IN ROOM 7

Bruegel brings together 100 proverbs in an absurd, slightly surreal village scene, reminiscent of the work of his predecessor Bosch. Look out for the egg with legs on the right-hand side of the painting, an image that often appears in Bosch's work. Painted in 1559, the painting was originally called *The Upside-Down World*, in reference to the inverted globe on the side of the house, reflecting the topsy-turvy scene. The devil occupies the chapel and takes confession, while Jesus sits outside on the right in front of a hut. A servant covers his face with a flax beard, the mask of a hypocrite. Chaos is the guiding principle, as money is thrown into the water and roses are cast before swine. Bruegel was constantly exploring the spiritual and moral questions of his time and this piece is no exception. The supposedly wise old sayings are used to illustrate man's foolishness and sinfulness in a world without the guidance of God.

CHILD WITH BIRD BY RUBENS, IN ROOM 9

Rubens painted this portrait of his nephew Philip in 1624. Philip was born in 1611 and was the son of Rubens' brother, who died at a young age. Rubens captures the intuitive character of children through the boy's interaction with the bird and reflects his innocence with his white clothes, pale complexion and angelic features.

RATINGS

Cultural interest	●●●●●
Historic interest	●●●●○
Value for money	●●●●●
Specialist shopping	●●●●○

BASICS

✚ 120 C4 • Kulturforum, Mattäikirchplatz, 10785 Berlin (Tiergarten)
☎ 030 2090 5555
🕐 Tue–Sun 10–6, Thu 10–10
💶 Adult €6, child €3
🚇 Potsdamer Platz
🚌 129, 148, 200, 248, 341, 348
📷 Guided tours tel 030 2090 5566; free audioguide
🛍 Shop selling a wide range of art books, postcards and posters 🚻 🅿

www.smb.spk-berlin.de/gg
Part of the official state museums website. There are pictures of some of the famous pieces in the gallery and you can find out more about the history of the collection. English and German.

TIP

● The air in the gallery is kept very dry to preserve the art, but you can take a break every so often by the water sculpture *5–7–9 Series* by Walter de Maria in the central hall.

Outside the Kulturforum (top)

Rooms I–III and 1–4: German painting of the 13th to 16th centuries. *Die Madonna mit dem Zeisig* (The Madonna and Child) by Dürer in room 2, *Die Geburt Christi* (The Birth of Christ) by Schongauer in room 1, *Der Kaufmann Georg Gisze* (The Merchant Georg Gisze) by Hans Holbein the Younger in room 4, *Die Königin von Saba vor Salomon* (The Queen of Sheba before Solomon) by

Malle Babbe *by Frans Hals*

Konrad Witz in room I, *Der Jungbrunnen* (The Fountain of Youth) by Cranach the Elder in room III.

Rooms IV–VI and 5–7: Dutch and French painting of the 14th to 16th centuries. *Die Madonna in der Kirche* (The Madonna in the Church) by Jan Van Eyck in room 5, *Johannes auf Patmos* (Johannes on Patmos) by Bosch in room 6, *Die Niederländischen Sprichwörter* (The Dutch Proverbs) in room 7.

Rooms VII–XI and 8–19: Flemish and Dutch painting of the 17th century. *Der Blumenstrauss* (Bouquet of Flowers) by J. Brueghel the Elder in room 9, *Das Kind mit Vogel* (Child with Bird) by Rubens in room 9, *Der Mann mit dem Goldhelm* (The Man with the Golden Helmet) by Rembrandt (Harmensz van Rijn) in room 16, *Junge Dame mit Perlenhalsband* (Young woman with a Pearl Necklace) by Vermeer in room 18, *Moses mit den Gesetzestafeln* (Moses with the Ten Commandments) by Rembrandt in room X.

LOVE VICTORIOUS BY CARAVAGGIO, IN ROOM XIV

Caravaggio's earthly figure of Love, painted between 1601 and 1602, shows him triumphing over the classical, intellectual love championed by the arts and sciences. Caravaggio's revolutionary portrayal was very controversial at the time: The down-to-earth, naked boy was kept behind a curtain and could only be viewed by men. A laurel wreath, the symbol of eternal fame and lyric poetry, is lying on the floor, while a sceptre and crown, emblems of worldly power, have been pushed to the right. The grubby, cheeky boy even has dirt under his toenails. The figure stands out bright against the dark background and appears to be bathed under a spotlight, illustrating the chiaroscuro technique seen throughout Caravaggio's work. The painting offended his rival Giovanni Baglione, who was commissioned by a cardinal to communicate the established view. His critical response is on display in the same room, to the right of the door, while Caravaggio's interpretation is on the left. Baglione's painting, entitled *The Divine Eros* (1602–03), shows the angel-like eternal Eros dressed in armour, standing over Caravaggio's pale and beaten earthly love and preparing to finish him off with a bolt of lightning. The arrows belonging to earthly love lie broken on the floor and on the left in the background a demon, a symbol of base debauchery, is chained to the ground. Baglione's piece borrows some of Caravaggio's techniques, but remains faithful to the traditional over-stylized and formulaic portrayal of the ideal human form, which sets it apart from Caravaggio's emotional, natural interpretation.

LEDA AND THE SWAN BY CORREGGIO, IN ROOM XV

This piece was painted for the Duke of Mantua, Frederico Gonzago II, in 1531. It is one of four classical amorous adventures painted by the artist. In this piece, Jupiter, in the form of a swan, is shown seducing Leda . Cupid is on the left holding a lyre. After Frederico's death, the painting made its way to Spain and was then passed around various

Moses, painted by Rembrandt

THE SIGHTS

Head of Christ (c1648)
by Rembrandt (above)

Portrait of a Young Woman in a
Pinned Hat (c1435) by Rogier
van der Weyden (left)

European collections for the next 200 years. Philippe of Orléans, the Regent of France, acquired it in 1721. His son, Louis, found the portrait extremely distasteful. In a fit of religious rage he cut it up, completely destroying the head of Leda. The painter Coypel resurrected the painting by piecing it back together and filling in the missing sections, but he left the head of Leda blank. Frederick the Great purchased the traumatized painting for his gallery in Sanssouci in 1755. Leda's head was finally repainted by the artist Jacob Sleschinger in 1830 before it was moved to the Museum am Lustgarten. Look very carefully and you will see some of the joins from where the painting was restored.

THE MAN WITH THE GOLDEN HELMET BY REMBRANDT, IN ROOM 16

The Man With the Golden Helmet (1650–55) is one of the most popular paintings in the gallery, but there is now evidence to suggest that it was not actually the work of Rembrandt. During restoration in the 1980s, the painting was examined in detail and tests revealed that many of the brush strokes were inconsistent with the style of painting seen in Rembrandt's other works. The thickly applied paint on the helmet and the bright, reflected light demonstrate an exaggerated interpretation of Rembrandt's signature technique.

VENUS WITH THE ORGAN PLAYER BY TITIAN, IN ROOM XVI

In this painting, Venus, accompanied by Cupid, is shown lying on a ceremonial couch against a red velvet curtain. A cavalier is sitting in front of the organ on the left-hand side with his hands on the keys and his eyes fixed on the goddess. Painted between 1550 and 1552, this is an extremely early example of Impressionism. Way ahead of its time, it is possible to detect the artist's brush strokes in the painting. The piece moves away from the strict realistic or polished idealistic portrayal of the subject that was popular at the time. You will have to look carefully to detect Titian's experimental handiwork—he cleverly disguised it so as not to be shunned by the rest of the artistic community, who were staunchly committed to the style of realistic portrayal dominant at the time.

THE SIGHTS

GALLERY GUIDE

Rooms 20–22: French, English and German painting of the 18th century. *Der Tanz* (The Dance) by Watteau in room 21, *Die Marsham-Kinder* (The Marsham Children) by Gainsborough in room 20, *Der Zeichner* (The Draughtsman) by Chardin in room 21.

Rooms XII–XIV and 23–27, 28: Italian, German, French and Spanish painting of the 17th and 18th centuries. *Der Campo di Rialto* (Rialto Square) by Canaletto in room XII, *Bildnis einer Dame* (Portrait of a Lady) by Velázquez in room XIII, *Amor als Sieger* (Love Victorious) by Caravaggio in room XIV, *Landschaft mit dem Evangelisten Matthäus* (Landscape with Matthew the Evangelist) in room 25.

Rooms XV–XVII and 29–32, 35–41: Italian painting of the 13th and 16th century. *Madonna Terranuova* by Raphael in room 29, *Vertumnus and Pomona* by Francesco Melzi and *Der hl. Sebastian* (St. Sebastian) by Botticelli in room XVIII, *Venus mit dem Orgelspieler* (Venus with the Organ Player) by Titian in room XVI.

Rooms 43–54: European painting of the 13th to 18th centuries. *Die Auffindung des hl. Sebastian* (The Retrieval of St. Sebastian) by De La Tour in room 43, *Venus* by Botticelli in room 50.

Room 34: Miniaturmalerei (Miniature Painting)

Rooms 27, 33, 42: Digitale Galerie (Digital Gallery)

ARCHITECTURAL VIEW BY FRANCESCO DI GIORGIO MARTINI, IN ROOM XVIII

Set in a panel, this mysterious, idealized townscape appears to be inspired by the courts of Urbino in Italy. The painting has been attributed to Francesco di Giorgio Martini, who lived in Siena between 1439 and 1502, but critics are uncertain about the purpose of the painting and whether he is the artist. The theoretical piece plays with perspective and the three different viewpoints give the painting a sense of depth. Walk from the left to the right of the painting to fully appreciate the effect.

ST. SEBASTIAN BY SANDRO BOTTICELLI, IN ROOM XVIII

Botticelli painted his dedication to the martyr St. Sebastian in 1474 for the church of San Francesco Maggiore in Florence. The figure is shown in the contrapposto position, with his head and upper body twisted in the opposite direction to his hips and legs. Gazing into the middle distance with his head to one side and his eyebrows slightly raised, he appears to be calmly meditating his fate. His elongated legs and the low horizon bring him forward, making him look larger than life.

VERTUMNUS AND POMONA BY FRANCESCO MELZI, IN ROOM XVIII

Melzi painted this episode from Ovid's *Metamorphosis* between 1517 and 1520. Vertumnus, the god of vegetation, has changed his form to woo Pomona, the goddess of fruit and gardens. Pomona has retreated away from society and is living in an all-female community, so Vertumnus assumes the form of an old woman in order to get close to his love and talk to her. In the middle is an elm tree with a vine wrapped around, a powerful symbol of union and co-existence at the heart of the painting. The artist, Melzi, was a student of Leonardo da Vinci, and you can clearly see the teacher's influence in Vertumnus' hands and Pomona's expression, reminiscent of Mona Lisa's famous smile. The male neck and the young feet and hands of Vertumnus hint at the true identity behind the disguise, illustrating the transformation in a single image.

Portrait of the Merchant George Gisze *(1532)* by Hans Holbein the Younger *(above)*

Portrait of Cornelius Anslo and Wife *(detail; 1641)* by Rembrandt *(right)*

The Gemäldegalerie is just one of the cultural venues in the Kulturforum *(below)*

THE PRELIMINARY WORKS, IN ROOMS 19 AND 10

The small circular rooms at the end of the hall contain preliminary works and drafts by famous artists. Many of the Italian masters, such as Michelangelo, made small preliminary works to show to their clients before embarking on the larger canvases, which were often completed by their students. These originals of the originals should not be overlooked.

THE VIRGIN AND CHILD WITH THE INFANT ST. JOHN THE BAPTIST AND A HOLY BOY BY RAPHAEL, IN ROOM 29

This circular painting was Raphael's first tondo, which he created in 1505, shortly after his arrival in Florence, where this style of composition was very popular. It is actually two paintings in one—Raphael completed the background scene first, then added the Madonna and Child and the Holy children on top afterwards.

THE SIGHTS

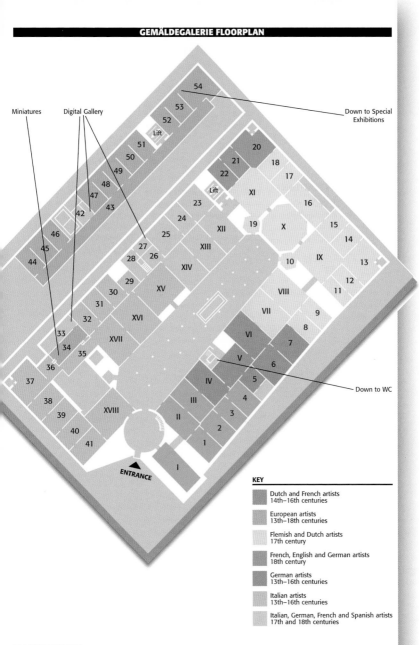

GEMÄLDEGALERIE FLOORPLAN

Miniatures

Digital Gallery

Lift

Lift

Down to Special Exhibitions

Down to WC

ENTRANCE

KEY

Dutch and French artists
14th–16th centuries

European artists
13th–18th centuries

Flemish and Dutch artists
17th century

French, English and German artists
18th century

German artists
13th–16th centuries

Italian artists
13th–16th centuries

Italian, German, French and Spanish artists
17th and 18th centuries

BACKGROUND

The Gemäldegalerie collection began with various European private collections, brought together and then supplemented by others from the royal palaces. In 1815, after Germany's victory over France, King Friedrich Wilhelm III purchased a further 157 paintings for the gallery, from Vincenzo Giustiniani's private collection of Italian paintings, owned at that time by the Parisian art dealer Bonnemaison. Following World War II, the paintings were divided between East and West Berlin, half in the Bode-Museum (▷ 127), and the other half in the former Asian Museum in Dahlem. In 1965, a competition was held to design a complex for the museums of European art, which would stand opposite the Philharmonic Hall. The architect Rolf Gutbrod won the competition and submitted his final designs in 1966, but political and financial debate plagued the project, and it wasn't until 1985 that building work could go ahead. Gutbrod's original drawings were reworked into what is now known as the Kulturforum. After years of discussions and planning, the collection was moved to the Kulturforum and opened to the public in 1998.

A homemade microlight at Haus am Checkpoint Charlie

Liebkind's emotionally charged Jüdisches Museum

The Kunstgewerbe Museum is spread over four floors

HAUS AM CHECKPOINT CHARLIE

🔲 121 E4 • Friedrichstrasse 43–44, 10969 Berlin (Kreuzberg) ☎ 030 253 7250 🕐 Daily 9am–10pm 💷 Adult €9.50, child €5.50, under 10 free 🚇 Kochstrasse, Stadtmitte 🚌 129 🎧 Audioguide €3 🛍 Large shop on the ground floor selling history books, postcards, prints, Berlin wall souvenirs and pieces of the wall 🔁 www.mauermuseum.de

For over 28 years, Checkpoint 'C', or 'Charlie' in the phonetic alphabet, was a major crossing point through the Berlin Wall for diplomats, embassy staff and Allied forces. It marked the main border between the Soviet sector in East Berlin and the American sector in the West. Little is left today of the 155km (96 miles) of barricades that divided the city, and the Mauer Museum (Wall Museum) now occupies the creaky house that once sheltered the border guards. The rooms are small, but every inch of wall space is covered in newspaper articles, photographs and personal accounts of those affected by the Berlin wall.

JÜDISCHES MUSEUM

🔲 121 E5 • Lindenstrasse 9–14, 10969 Berlin (Kreuzberg) ☎ 030 2599 3300 🕐 Daily 10–8 (Mon 10–10); closed on Jewish holidays and 24 Dec 💷 Adult €5, child €2.50, under 6 free 🚇 Hallesches Tor, Kochstrasse 🚌 143, 240 🎧 Guided tour Mon at 7pm, Sat and Sun 11am, 2pm and 3pm; tel 030 25 99 33 05 🍴 Restaurant serving Jewish cuisine, and a kiosk selling cakes, snacks and hot drinks 🛍 Large shop selling books and gifts 🔁 www.jmberlin.de

The Jewish Museum was designed by the American, Polish-born architect Daniel Libeskind in 1989 for the exhibits on Jewish history from the Berlin Museum. Apart from being a museum space, the postmodern structure stands as a monument to the plight of the Jews, with every space and aesthetic aspect designed with an emotional response in mind. From the outside, its zigzag shape resembles a bolt of lighting and the windows cut through the smooth, shiny exterior like cracks.

The Memory Void on the 2nd level is the largest of the closed spaces that cuts through the building. The narrowing empty space represents the expelled and murdered European Jews. The floor is covered with the installation *Shalechet* (Fallen Leaves, 1997–2001) by the artist Menashe Kadishman, made up of more than 10,000 faces cut out of sheet steel.

Although the subject matter is disturbing, the building and museum are intensely thought provoking and designed with children in mind. The historical information is communicated interactively throughout, with photo light boxes, telephones that play historical recordings, and drawers and doors that beg to be opened and the contents explored.

KUNSTGEWERBE MUSEUM

🔲 120 C4 • Kulturforum am Potsdamer Platz, Matthäikirchplatz, 10785 Berlin (Tiergarten) ☎ 030 266 2951 🕐 Tue–Fri 10–6, Sat and Sun 11–6 💷 Adult €6, child €3 🚇 Potsdamer Platz 🚌 129, 148, 200, 248, 348 🛍 Small shop selling books in German and postcards 🍴 Expensive cafeteria serving lunches, snacks and hot drinks 🔁 www.smpk.de

This museum displays European arts and crafts and interior design from the Middle Ages to the present day. The collection is spread over four floors in the Kulturforum museum complex.

Delicate Renaissance and baroque pieces are in room IV, including a collection of intricate navigational instruments such as pocket sundials, watches and compasses. On the ground floor, 20th-century design comes full circle, as postmodern retro furniture sits happily side-by-side with 1950s and '60s style icons.

MÄRKISCHES MUSEUM

🔲 121 F4 • Am Köllnischen Park 5, 10179 Berlin (Mitte) ☎ 030 308660 🕐 Tue–Sun 10–6 💷 Adult €4, child €2, Wed free 🚇 Märkisches Museum 🚌 143, 147, 240, 265 🎧 Guided tour of the Automatophones on Sundays at 3pm, adult €2, child €1 🍴 Small, friendly café serving coffee and cake 🛍 Small shop selling postcards, guide books and history books in German and English 🔁 www.stadtmuseum.de

The museum's permanent exhibition, *Look at this city!*, traces the history and cultural development of Berlin from the Middle Ages to the present day.

The museum takes you on a thematic journey through the city's history, exploring a variety of subjects including medieval sculpture, the development of the press, World War I, immigration, Berlin under the Swastika, the Cold War, and the destruction and reconstruction of Potsdamer Platz (▷ 144).

The one remaining original horse's head from the Brandenburg Tor quadriga, designed by Johan Gotfried Schadow, is in the first room on the left at the top of the stairs (▷ 128). Another unusual piece is the Kaiserpanorama (c.1900), a circular cabinet with 24 individual viewing stations used for watching stereoscopic images. You can sit down and watch a sequence of photos documenting the final stages of the fall of the Berlin Wall.

NEUE NATIONALGALERIE

An outstanding collection of 20th-century painting and sculpture, with works by famous artists, such as Salvador Dalí, Paul Klee and Pablo Picasso.

At the edge of the Tiergarten near the Kulturforum, the New National Gallery was designed by Bauhaus architect Ludwig Mies van der Rohe and built between 1965 and 1968. The square steel structure and glazed walls sit on a raised terrace, creating a spacious and versatile exhibition space for this collection, ranging from early modernism to art of the 1960s and 1970s. Contemporary exhibitions are also held on the upper floor.

SCULPTURE

The Dancer (1911–12) made Georg Kolbe famous and established his reputation as a sensitive sculptor of the human form. It was first shown at the Berlin Seccession in 1912 and was snapped up by the Nationalgalerie. Kolbe was inspired by the work of Rodin, particularly the way in which he conveyed energy and the impression of fluid movement in his sculpture. You can also see one of Alexander Calder's mobiles, *Dancing Star* (1940), a carefully balanced and delicate sculpture made from thin wire and painted metal shapes that dance around with the slightest movement of air. Artist Käthe Kollwitz lost her son Peter, who was a soldier, in 1914. She confronts her loss in the sculpture *Pietá* (1937–38) by reworking the famous religious image into a universal expression of maternal grief. *Woman on a Bench* (1957) is one of Henry Moore's series of seated figures, which all refer to the struggle of life, and the pregnant woman is a comment on the natural process of birth, growth and decay.

PAINTING

Max Liebermann painted many self-portraits. *Self-Portrait* (1925) shows the 78-year-old artist, who was then president of the Prussian Academy of Arts, seated facing the viewer in his studio before a canvas with a brush and palette in his hand. There are two examples of Picasso's analytic cubism on display, *Woman Seated in an Armchair* (1909) and *Woman Playing a Violin* (1911). *Potsdamer Platz* (1914), by Ernst Ludwig Kirchner, shows the famous square at night in autumn 1914. The building with the arcaded loggia in the middle is Potsdam Station. Two life-size female figures, intended to be prostitutes, stand on a traffic island in the foreground with the dark figures of potential clients in the background. These women contrast with the pink figures of the 'respectable' women in the distance.

The sculpture garden (above). A bronze sculpture (top) at the entrance to Neue Nationalgalerie

RATINGS

Cultural interest	● ● ● ● ●
Historic interest	● ● ●
Value for money	● ● ●

BASICS

✚ 120 C4 • Kulturforum am Potsdamer Platz, Potsdamer Strasse 50, 10785 Berlin (Tiergarten)

☎ 030 266 29 51

🕐 Tue–Fri 10–6, Sat and Sun 11–6, Thu 10–10

🎫 Adult €6, child €3

Ⓜ Potsdamer Platz

🚌 129, 148, 200, 248, 348

🎧 Guided tours tel 030 2090 5566

▢

📚 Small art bookshop

🚻

🅿 Kulturforum

www.smb.spk-berlin.de/nng/e/s.html
This is part of the official state museums website. Find out about the collection and about visiting exhibitions. English and German.

Pergamonmuseum

This houses the city's most impressive collection of archaeological discoveries. Walk through and around huge pieces of reconstructed architecture, including the monumental Pergamon Altar, Ishtar Gate and Mshatta Palace Façade.

It needed a vast building to house the Pergamon Altar

Looking down from the Pergamon Altar, one of the museum's star attractions: Its sheer size dwarfs the visitors

RATINGS	
Cultural interest	● ● ● ● ○
Historic interest	● ● ● ● ○
Value for money	● ● ● ● ○

BASICS

✚ 121 E3 • Museuminsel, Am Kupfergraben, 10178 Berlin (Mitte)
☎ 030 2090 5577
🕐 Tue–Sun 10–6, Thu 10–10
💶 Adult €8, child €4
🚉 Hackescher Markt, Friedrichstrasse
🚌 100, 200, 348; tram 1, 2, 3, 4, 5, 6, 13, 15, 50, 53
🎧 Guided tours tel 030 2090 5566; free audioguide
🏪 Two shops sell souvenirs and books
🚻

www.smb.spk-berlin.de
Find out more about the history of the museum; there are links from here to pages dedicated to the three individual collections; English and German.

TIP

• Your day ticket to the Pergamonmuseum also covers entrance to all of the Berlin State Museums, so you could pop into some of the other museums on Museum Island if you have time.

Glazed tiles depicting a lion from the Processional Way (right)

SEEING THE PERGAMONMUSEUM

The Pergamonmuseum is at the heart of the Museum Island complex. It is actually three museums in one: the Collection of Classical Antiquities, the Museum of Ancient Near-Eastern Art and the Museum of Islamic Art. Your ticket covers admission to all of the museum collections, and you can wander freely between them. From the lobby, begin by exploring the Pergamon Altar and Telephus Frieze in the Pergamon room. From here, go into the rooms in the north wing (to the left as you face the altar) containing the rest of the Collection of Classical Antiquities. Return to the Pergamon room and move into the south wing, passing through the Market Gate of Miletus and the Ishtar Gate into the Museum of Ancient Near-Eastern Art. Continue to the end of the Processional Way, then explore the rest of the collection in the rooms that run down either side. Head back toward the Ishtar gate and go up the stairs to the Museum of Islamic Art.

HIGHLIGHTS

THE PERGAMON ALTAR

In 1876, Carl Humann began uncovering the remains of this ancient altar on the Acropolis of Pergamon in the Aegean area of Turkey. The Altar was built by King Eumenes II (197–158BC) and stood on the Acropolis in the Roman capital of the Asian province of Pergamon. The Altar was encircled by a relief frieze, over 2m (6.5ft) high and 120m (394ft) long, which illustrated the war between gods and giants that was finally settled by the heroic Hercules. Known as the Great Frieze, it captures the climax of the battle. Zeus' winged horses, driven by Hera, clear a path through the giants in the middle of the eastern frieze. From here the action moves to the central group, Zeus and his daughter Athena. To the left of Zeus you can just make out the huge figure of his son, Hercules, and to Athena's right is the war god Ares, preparing to charge into battle.

Another smaller frieze ran round the inner walls of the court of the Altar. In contrast to the Great Frieze, which captures the dramatic conclusion of a war, the Telephus Frieze tells the epic story of

THE HEPHAISTON MOSAIC

This second century BC mosaic in the Museum of Classical Antiquities is a rare example of a signed work—look for the inscription on what appears to be a peeling label, which reads 'Hephaiston Eppoie', meaning 'Hephaiston made this'. Unfortunately, the central area of the mosaic has not survived, but the ornamental bands that frame it are in excellent condition. Wave patterns border a black saw-tooth design, followed by a three-dimensional meander band and creepers filled with butterflies and winged cupids.

THE XANTEN BOY

Named after the German town of Xanten in Westphalia where it was found, this is an extremely rare example of a bronze statue from the first century AD. Many other bronze pieces made around this time were melted down during preparations for war when metal was in short supply. The Hellenistic tradition of child portrayal was popular with the Romans and it is likely that this statue stood in a Roman villa and performed the service of a dumb waiter, where he would hold a tray during banquets.

THE MEDEA SARCOPHAGUS

Made in Rome between AD140 and 150, the carving on the surface of the sarcophagus tells the grisly story of the princess and sorceress Medea. Medea fell in love with Jason (of Argonauts fame), but he left her to marry Creusa. Spurned, Medea sought revenge by lacing Creusa's dress with poison. The carving shows Creusa with her hair in flames, burning alive from the effects of the poison. Medea, meanwhile, is leaving the scene in a winged chariot, taking the bodies of her and Jason's two dead children with her. Look closely and you can see their tiny limbs sticking out of the side of the carriage.

Telephus, Hercules' son, using trees or curtains to divide each episode. Telephus is the product of a clandestine affair between Hercules and Auge, the daughter of King Aleos. King Aleos disowns his daughter and she is set adrift in the sea in a boat. The frieze begins with the building of Auge's boat and concludes with Telephus leading the Greeks into battle with Troy and returning victorious to found the city of Pergamon.

THE MARKET GATE OF MILETUS

The Market Gate of Miletus is currently being restored and is covered in scaffolding and netting. It is due to be uncovered in 2008. The ruined city and excavations of the ancient city of Miletus are 120km (75 miles) south of Izmir on the western coast of Turkey, at the mouth of the Meander River. Constructed around AD120, the gate

The carving on the dome from the Alhambra is exquisite

provided access to the city's market, and when Emperor Justinian strengthened the fortifications of the city in AD538, he incorporated the gateway into the city walls. These walls, including the market gate, were destroyed during an earthquake in 1100. The buried fragments of the gate were uncovered between 1903 and 1905 by a team of archaeologists under the direction of Theodor Wiegand and Hubert Knackfuss. The main sections of the gate were brought back to Berlin and reconstructed in the Pergamonmuseum using much of the original material.

THE ISHTAR GATE

As early as 1851, French archaeologists found pieces of glazed bricks around the El-Kasr hill ruin that they believed formed part of a frieze. The Ishtar Gate is just one of at least eight double gates that led into the city of Babylon and formed the northern entrance into King Nebuchadnezzar II's capital. Because of its size, only the smaller outer gate could be reconstructed in the museum.

Ishtar was the Mesopotamian goddess of love and war and one of the protectors of Babylon, along with the city god Marduk and the weather god Adad. The fertile and passionate Adad is depicted on the gate in the form of a bull. The other god who appears on the gate, Marduk, was associated with the dragon Mushhushshu, who possessed the head of a viper, the paws of a lion, the claws of an eagle and the tail of a scorpion, signifying speed, strength, cunning and lethal danger.

THE FAÇADE OF THE THRONE ROOM

On the narrow walls on either side of the Ishtar gate are two sections of the reconstructed façade of the Throne Room from the southern palace of Nebuchadnezzar II. The Babylonian craftsmen who built the royal palace of Babylon in the sixth century BC coded each individual brick, which allowed Walter Andrae to reconstruct the façade of the throne room here between 1899 and 1901. The palace façade was 56m (184ft) wide, but its true height remains uncertain—its present height is determined by the dimensions of the gallery space. Glazed tiles cover the wall, as they do on the Ishtar gate, and the lower section is decorated with a band of lions, reflecting the design of the Processional Way.

THE PROCESSIONAL WAY

The walled Processional Way ran north from the Ishtar Gate, and although only 8m wide in the gallery, it was originally between 20 and 24m (65 to 82ft) wide. The ceremonial road stretched for 250m (820ft) from the Ishtar Gate to a temple on the northern outskirts of the city. In Babylon, the New Year began in early spring and was welcomed with a huge festival, during which the king would be re-enthroned. The festival revolved around the worship of the statues of the city gods, who enjoyed a rapturous reception, as it was believed that the fortunes of the king and the people depended on their welfare. The statues were given pride of place during the festivities and then carefully carried back to the temple on highly decorative thrones, along the Processional Way and through the Ishtar gate, accompanied by musicians and crowds.

THE MSHATTA FAÇADE

The Mshatta façade first came to the world's attention in 1873. The ruin was threatened by the construction of a railway that was planned to pass right through the site, linking Damascus with the holy cites of the Arabian Peninsula. German archaeologists appealed to King Wilhelm II and the Berlin museums to finance a rescue mission, for most of the façade. The rest of the palace remains in its original

THE DOMED ROOF FROM THE ALHAMBRA

This intricately carved cedar and poplar dome, dating from the early 14th century, covered one of the towers in the Moorish palace of Alhambra, overlooking Granada in Spain. The dome has a repeated motif, which reads 'There is no victor but God'. Sixteen panels radiate from a star set in a 16-sided polygon at the top of the dome.

THE PRAYER NICHE

This turquoise blue prayer niche comes from the Beyhekim mosque in Konya, built in the mid- to late 13th century, and is covered in geometric motifs and script capturing the words of the Prophet Mohammad. The technique, known as faience mosaic, is the combined work of calligraphers and expert tile cutters.

The Great Frieze (above) on the Pergamon Altar. Intricate relief carving (below) from the Classical Antiquities collection

THE SIGHTS

Upper Floor
The Museum of Islamic Art
Gallery 1: Lobby. Introduction
Gallery 2: Umayyad Art
Gallery 3: Abbasid and
Fatimid Art
Gallery 4: Selijuk Art (Iran)
Gallery 5: Selijuk Art (Asia
Minor), Ayyubid and Mamluk Art
Gallery 6: Alhambra Dome
Gallery 7: Il-Khanid and
Timurid Art
Gallery 8: Spanish Carpets
Gallery 9: Mshatta Room and
Sassanian Art. Mshatta façade
Gallery 10–11: Temporary
exhibitions
Gallery 12: Early Ottoman Art
Gallery 13: Safavid and
Mughal Art
Gallery 14: High Ottoman Art
Gallery 15–16: Aleppo Room

*The view down processional way
from the Ishtar Gate*

Lower Floor
The Collection of Classical
Antiquities
Gallery 1 and 5: The Lobby.
History of Excavations
Gallery 2–4: The Pergamon
Room, the Telephus Room and
The Pergamon Altar
Gallery 6: Roman Architecture,
the Market Gate of Miletus
Gallery 7: The Hall in the
Trajaneum
Gallery 8: Hellenistic
Architecture
Gallery 9–10: Archaic Sculpture
Gallery 11–12: Classical
Greek Art
Gallery 13: Late Classical
Sculpture
Gallery 14: Ancient Copies of
Greek Masterpieces
Gallery 15: Ancient Copies,
Portraits
Gallery 16: Hellenistic Sculpture
Gallery 17: Ancient Coins
Gallery 18: Roman Art

location. Mshatta Palace was built for the Caliph al-Walid II (AD743–744) 25km (15 miles) from Amman in what is now the Jordanian desert. It was never finished as the Caliph died unexpectedly. The outer wall and some of the interior structures were incomplete, and an earthquake in AD746 reduced most of the building to rubble.

The elaborate decoration on the façade was designed to demonstrate the wealth of the Caliph, and the zigzag band, with rosettes in each triangle, is typical of the decoration seen on early Islamic palaces. Various animals drink out of the basins in the middle of the rosettes, from cattle and lions to mythical beasts such as centaurs, griffins and peacock dragons, creatures seen in pre-Islamic Iranian art. The section of the façade that was closest to the palace prayer niche is more restrained, as it was forbidden to show depictions of animals or people on sacred monuments or religious buildings.

PERGAMONMUSEUM FLOORPLAN

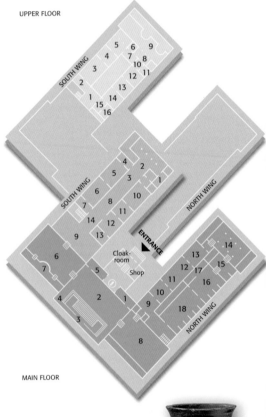

UPPER FLOOR

MAIN FLOOR

KEY

Collection of Classical Antiquities

Museum of Islamic Art

Museum of Ancient Near-Eastern Art

Sea God painting on an Etruscan vase

THE SIGHTS

THE ALEPPO ROOM

The wall panelling, 35m (115ft) in length, once covered the lower part of a function room in a house of a Christian broker working for merchants in Aleppo, in northwest Syria, at the beginning of the 17th century. The inscription to the left of the entrance in the right wing reveals his name, 'Isa ibn Butrus', Jesus Son of Peter. Sections are dated as being painted in 1600, 1601 and 1603, making it the oldest and best preserved painted wall panelling from a Syrian house.

The right-hand section of the panelling is decorated with scenes from the Old and New Testaments. They are very similar to illustrations found in Islamic books at the time and, although the style of painting is Ottoman, the figures depicted resemble those seen in Persian art. The left-hand panels focus on aristocratic life and are decorated with depictions of rulers and hunting scenes. There are

various inscriptions on the panels, including Psalms 1, 2 and 117 and proverbs. In the ante room there is a video installation showing a reconstruction of the entire house, so you can get a sense of what the room was like in its original context.

There are Persian influences in the decoration of the Aleppo Rooms (above)

BACKGROUND

It wasn't until the completion of the first phase of excavations at the Acropolis of Pergamon in 1886 that the question of where to keep these huge architectural discoveries was raised. At this time, the Collection of Greek and Roman Antiquities was on display in the Altes and Neues museums, but there was no way they could accommodate the Pergamon Altar. A provisional home for the collection was opened to the public in 1901 but was only just big enough for the reconstructed altar: Visitors could view it from just 8m (26ft) away, which meant it was difficult to get an overall impression. In 1908, the building had to be demolished when the foundations were found to be unstable, and it was another 22 years before the Pergamon Altar went on view to the public again. Ludwig Hoffmann built the new and much bigger Pergamonmuseum between 1910 and 1930 according to Alfred Messel's designs. Between 1926 and 1930, the Market Gate of Miletus and the Ishtar Gate were also pieced together and integrated into the museum's interior design. The Berlin museums were closed during World War II. Sandbags protected the altar and many of the moveable valuables were put in storage in underground vaults. The Market Gate of Miletus could not be removed and was seriously damaged by the bombing. The Pergamon room was also badly hit, and a bomb destroyed its staircase. Luckily the protective walls sheltered the Ishtar Gate and the Processional Way. The large skylights in the roof of the building were shattered throughout the museum and the rain damaged many of the exhibits.

The Pergamonmuseum, along with the rest of the museums on Museum Island, is a Unesco World Heritage site and, since the reunification of the museums of the former West and East Berlin in 1990, the exhibits and museum itself have undergone extensive restoration. The refurbishment of the Market Gate of Miletus is an ongoing project and the work is due to be completed around 2008.

GALLERY GUIDE

The Museum of Ancient Near-Eastern Art

Gallery 1: Rock Reliefs from Yazilikaya

Gallery 2: Finds from Syria, Asia Minor and Mesopotamia

Gallery 3: Esarhaddon-Stela from Sam'al

Gallery 4: Assyrian Royal Tombs

Gallery 5: Finds from Uruk and Habuba Kabira

Gallery 6: Babylonian Monuments

Gallery 7: Ancient Iranian Monuments

Gallery 8: Processional Way of Babylon

Gallery 9: Ishtar Gate of Babylon

Gallery 10: Finds from Assyria

Gallery 10a: Assyrian Tombs

Gallery 11: Assyrian Palace Room

Gallery 12: Finds from Assyria

Gallery 13: Urartian Monuments

Gallery 14: Stelae from Assur

THE SIGHTS

A section of the Berlin Wall
(above) and the dome of
the Sony Centre (top)

RATINGS

Photo stops	● ● ● ● ●
Cultural interest	● ● ● ●
Historic interest	● ●

BASICS

✚ 121 D4 • 10785 Berlin (Tiergarten)
⬚ Potsdamer Platz
⬚ 142, 148, 248, 348
www.potsdamer-platz.net

TIPS

● The cafés and restaurants on
Potsdamer Platz are a short
walk from the Kulturforum,
making it the ideal place to
wind down after time spent
in the museums.
● If you want to change from
the U-Bahn to the S-Bahn or
vice versa you will need to
come up to street level and
walk between stations.
● Throughout December
there is a Christmas market
here, with an outdoor ice-
skating rink and stalls selling
decorations, gifts, *Glühwein*
and *Wurst*.

POTSDAMER PLATZ

**This redeveloped area is constantly expanding, and is rapidly
growing into a cultural hot spot and sleek business district.**

Potsdamer Platz was once the heart of the city, a major crossroads for
the traffic of Berlin. The 'Stammbahn' rail route, which passed through
the newly built Potsdamer Station towards Potsdam (▷ 168–173),
was opened in 1838, and brought the first signs of hustle and bustle
to the square. Potsdamer Platz marked the point where five major
roads intersected and provided a link between the middle of the city
and the developing West. Famous hotels, department stores and
restaurants lined the streets, and the area became popular with artists
and the politicians and diplomats who were based nearby.

REBUILDING

Most of the buildings in Potsdamer Platz were destroyed by bombing
raids during World War II and the wall between East and West Berlin
ran right through the middle of the square, so that the few buildings
that remained standing fell into disrepair. Shiny skyscrapers of big
corporations such as Daimler Benz now dominate the skyline, and
the square has become a key financial and business district.

THE SONY CENTER

Designed by Helmut Jahn and built between 1996 and 2000, the
Sony Center is one of Berlin's greatest architectural attractions.
The steel and glass dome measures 4,013sq m (43,195sq ft) and
shelters the light, spacious piazza beneath. The fountains and trees
at its heart are surrounded by gleaming office buildings, alfresco
dining establishments and the glass fronted Sony Style Store,
packed with the latest home entertainment gadgets.

FILM

Movie buffs will find plenty here to keep them occupied. There is a
plethora of cinemas to choose from, including two 3D Imax theatres in
the Sony Center and an art house cinema on the ground floor of the
Filmhaus, underneath the Berlin Film Museum (Tue–Sun 10–6, Thu
10–8). The museum, too, is an audiovisual feast; catch the film *Asphalt*
by Joe May (1929) in room 4, which re-creates Potsdamer Platz at its
prime in the late 1920s, before the World War II bombing. At the heart
of the museum is a shrine to the German film star Marlene Dietrich.

Don't miss A line of metal plaques imbedded in the street paving
marks where the Berlin Wall once stood.

REICHSTAG

Walk up Sir Norman Foster's Dome, an impressive architectural statement, to get an inside look at the seat of the German Parliament.

The original Reichstag was built in 1894 by Paul Wallot as the seat of the German Parliament. An inscription above the wide staircase, cast in bronze in 1916, reads '*Dem Deutschen Volke*', meaning 'The German People'. The building was damaged by fire on 27 February 1933 and was completely devastated as a result of heavy fighting around the building during World War II. After extensive restoration, the building was handed to the Federal Administration in 1973, and the first session of the reunified German Parliament was held here on 4 October 1990.

SIR NORMAN FOSTER
In June 1993, the British architect Sir Norman Foster was awarded the commission to restore the Reichstag. Foster preserved the original features and functions of the building, while adding glass walls, a symbol of the transparency of democracy, and a glass roof and chamber that bring light to the heart of the structure. Sections marked by bullet holes and Red Army graffiti have been left exposed in the lobbies and corridors as a reminder of the building's turbulent history.

The new building is self-sustaining and nothing is wasted. The water supply, heating and electricity for the parliament complex is powered by two engines fired by rapeseed oil, a clean and renewable energy source. Any excess heat generated in the summer is stored for the winter in a brine lake 300m (985ft) below ground.

THE DOME
Foster's dome is visible for miles around and has a powerful presence on Berlin's skyline. It has also become a symbol of popular rule, and every day thousands of people climb to the top. Visitors are reflected in the central mirrored funnel as they walk up the gently sloping spiral walkway. From the top you can look down into the chamber, representing open democratic rule. There are information panels around the base of the funnel documenting the history of the Reichstag, and you can walk out of the dome onto the roof terrace to appreciate the view over the city.

Don't miss The 21m (69ft) flag-like panel in the western hall, called *Black, Red and Gold* (1999), by German artist Gerhard Richter is made from recycled glass.

Sir Norman Foster's glass dome is a popular attraction

RATINGS
Cultural interest	●●●●●
Historic interest	●●●●
Value for money	●●●●●
Photo stops	●●●

BASICS

🞣 121 D3 • Deutscher Bundestag, Plenarbereich, Reichstagsgebäude, Platz der Republik, 11011 Berlin (Tiergarten)

☎ 030 2273 2152

🕐 Daily 8am–midnight, last admission 10pm 🎟 Free

Ⓤ Unter den Linden

🚌 100, 248, 257, 348; tram 100

📢 Lectures by prior arrangement

♿

www.reichstag.de
This German website provides links to sites related to the Reichstag and the government, including historical resources, tourist information and state run services.

TIPS
● All visitors have to pass through security checks before entering the building, so be prepared to wait.
● An elevator takes you up to the public roof terrace and the base of the dome, but you have to walk up the sloping spiral path to reach the top.
● The Reichstag is open until midnight (last entry at 10), and there are some great night-time views of the city from the viewing gallery.

Schloss Charlottenburg

Explore the largest palace owned by the Hohenzollern family. Wander around the private apartments of kings and queens, where fine furniture and art from the 17th to the 20th centuries fill every room.

The façade of Schloss Charlottenburg

Part of the Belvedere's porcelain collection

The Palace Gardens are a public park

RATINGS

Photo stops	●●●○
Historic interest	●●●●●
Value for money	●●●●●
Walkability	●●●○

MORE TO SEE

Grosse Orangerie (Large Orangery): Museum für Vor- und Frühgeschiche (Museum of Pre- and Early History).

Neuer Pavilion (Schinkel-Pavilion): Kunst der Schinkelzeit (Art of the Schinkel period): Arts and Crafts, pieces from the Royal Porcelain Manufactory (KPM), busts, sculptures by Schadow and Rauch, fine painting, water-colours, engravings and designs for Schinkel's stage-sets.

Mausoleum: The Hohenzollern family vault.

Belvedere: Former tea house now the Berlin Porcelain Museum, containing 18th-century pieces from the Royal Porcelain Manufactory (KPM).

SEEING SCHLOSS CHARLOTTENBURG

It takes at least a day to see everything in the palace and grounds—you will need to be selective if you have a limited amount of time. You can only visit the royal apartments with a guide, but it is worth paying extra to see the lavish private rooms of King Friedrich I and Queen Sophie Charlotte. Round off your sightseeing with a relaxing stroll around the gardens.

HIGHLIGHTS

THE STATE ROOMS AND APARTMENTS

After passing through the guest suite, you come to the Glass Bedchamber of Queen Sophie Charlotte, decorated with alternating strips of mirror and green damask. From the intimate surroundings of the Queen's Apartments you pass into the more formal chambers of King Frederick I. The tour of the intersecting rooms on the ground floor, from east to west, ends with the Porcelain Cabinet. It once contained 3,000 examples of Chinese and Japanese porcelain dating from the second half of the 17th century, but the room was badly damaged in 1943, and the collection is now made up of pieces acquired after the war, a project that was finally completed in 1993. Thankfully, the lavishness of this room has been preserved.

THE WHITE HALL

The White Hall on the top floor of the Neuer Flügel (New Wing) was Friedrich the Great's banqueting hall and throne room. The room suffered extensive damage during World War II and was reconstructed using the paintings of Friedrich Wilhelm Höder as a guide. The light-filled hall is lined with arched windows and Corinthian pilasters topped with gold stucco capitals. Originally bright pink, the room has faded to white, and the austere Classicism contrasts with the elaborate flourishes of the Golden Gallery next door.

THE GOLDEN GALLERY

Next to the White Hall is the Golden Gallery, the venue for dancing and musical recitals during Friedrich the Great's banquets and parties. The gallery is one of the best examples of a rococo banqueting hall in Germany, its long, bright hall lined with floor-to-ceiling windows and console mirrors increasing the sense of space and reflecting the baroque gardens outside. Look for Flora and her entourage above the entablature over the chimney on the west wall and the cheeky cherubs climbing trees along the cornice.

THE WINTER ROOMS

In 1796, King Friedrich William II converted the former First Apartments of Friedrich the Great into his winter quarters: They all face south, so benefit from the sunshine in the winter months, and are one of the few examples of early Prussian Classicism in existence.

The rooms were damaged during World War II but the furnishings survived, and in 1983 the interior was re-created from archived documents. The small rooms all have marble heating stoves and patterned inlaid parquet floors made from maple, elm and mahogany. Every room is filled with paintings, furniture, fabrics and tapestries, and all still have their original crystal chandeliers.

The Haute-Lisse rooms, to the right of the staircase, are covered with four tapestries illustrating the life of Don Quixote. Made in Paris, they were presented to Prince Henry, the brother of Friedrich the Great, as a gift from Louis XVI of France.

THE GARDENS

The palace grounds were originally laid out in 1697 in the French baroque formal style, with swirling paths and neatly trimmed hedges. In 1819, Friedrich Wilhelm III employed the services of the landscape architect Peter Joseph Lenné, who had previously designed the gardens of Sanssouci (▷ 169) and Potsdam (▷ 168–173). The parallel avenues and the large pool flanked with baroque statues near the Altes Schloss have been preserved, but the network of geometric paths beyond the palace was replaced with wider curving footpaths running around the edge of the park. Broad lawns and forest areas, akin to those seen in English romantic gardens, replaced the topiary and circular flowerbeds. Today, the palace garden is a peaceful public park, popular with runners and dog walkers.

BACKGROUND

Charlottenburg started out in 1695 as a summer residence, then called Lietzenburg Country House. The palace became the official royal residence of King Friedrich I (1688–1705), which he shared with his wife Queen Sophie Charlotte. In 1705, the palace was renamed Charlottenburg, following the death of the Queen. Over the next 100 years, the complex was extended: Eosander added the Orangerie, Georg Wenceslaus von Knobelsdorff designed the Neuer Flügel (the New Wing), while K. G. Langhans was responsible for adding the Belvedere tea rooms. The palace sustained heavy damage during the air raids of 22 and 23 November 1943 and the massive task of rebuilding began after 1945 under the direction of Dr. Margarete Kühn, the director of the State Palace Gardens.

BASICS

✚ 120 A1 (inset) • Spandauer Damm 20–24, 14059 Berlin (Charlottenburg)

☎ 030 3209 1440

🕐 Altes Schloss Tue–Fri 9–5, Sat, Sun 10–5 (the State rooms on the ground floor can only be visited by guided tour, see below); Neuer Flügel Tue–Fri 10–6, Sat, Sun 11–6; Neuer Pavilion Tue–Sun 10–5; Mausoleum Tue–Sun 10–5, Apr–end Oct; Belvedere Tue–Sun 10–5, Apr–end Oct, Tue–Fri 12–4, Sat, Sun 12–5, Nov–end Mar; Grosse Orangerie closed to visitors 💷 Altes Schloss: Adult €8, child €5; Neuer Flügel: Adult €5, child €4; Neuer Pavilion: Adult €2, child €1.50; Mausoleum: €1; Belvedere: Adult €2, child €1.50

Ⓢ Sophie-Charlotte-Platz, Richard-Wagner-Platz, Westend

🚌 109, 145, 210, X21

🎫 Guided tours of the royal apartments in German (information sheets available in other languages, including English): Adult €8, child €5; Neuer Flügel free audioguide

🍴 Restaurant in the Kleine Orangerie

🛍 Posters, postcards, porcelain, souvenirs, books on Prussian history and the Hohenzollerns

🚻 Neuer Flügel (New Wing) 30c; Kleine Orangerie

www.spsg.de

This is the official website of the Foundation of Prussian Palaces and Gardens. There are links to Schloss Charlottenburg, other royal residences in Berlin, Potsdam and the palaces of Brandenburg. There are also pages outlining the history of the palaces and giving details of events being held in the grounds, such as musical recitals and theatrical performances.

Johann Eosander von Göthe added the copper dome (above) in 1702

One of the statues that guard the entrance to the palace (far left)

Tiergarten

A peaceful green haven at the heart of the city, with an abundance of ornamental gardens, lakes and wooded areas to explore. An ideal place to stroll, take a boat or bicycle tour or simply relax with a picnic.

The Strasse des 17 Juni cuts a swathe through the Tiergarten

A mosaic from the first viewing platform of the Siegessäule

The guilded statue of Viktoria looks over the Tiergarten

RATINGS	
Photo stops	●●●●●
Historic interest	●●●○○
Walkability	●●●○○
Value for money	●●●○○

BASICS

✚ 120 C4 • 10785 Berlin (Tiergarten)
Ⓢ Zoologischer Garten, Tiergarten
🚌 100, 109, 119, 129, 145, 146, 149, 187, 245, 249, 341, X9, X34
🚻 Public toilets near the Siegessäule and in the Zoo and Aquarium
🅿 Am ZooBogen, €2.30 an hour
www.zoo-berlin.de

SEEING THE TIERGARTEN

At 202ha (500 acres), the Tiergarten is the city's biggest park, bordered by the River Spree in the north and Potsdamer Platz, the Kulturforum and the Bauhaus Archiv in the south. A network of footpaths and bicycle routes criss-crosses the park, connecting Unter den Linden in the east with the sights around the Kürfurstendamm and Zoologischer Garten in the west. The Grosser Stern and the towering Siegessäule are useful navigational landmarks at the heart of the park, which is intersected by the wide avenue of the Strasse des 17 Juni.

HIGHLIGHTS

SIEGESSÄULE

✚ 120 B3 • Grosser Stern, 10785 Berlin (Tiergarten) ☎ 030 391 29 61
🕐 Apr–end Oct daily 9.30–7; Nov–end Mar daily 9.30–6.30 💶 Adult €2.20, child €1.50, under 12 free

This tower, in the middle of the Tiergarten, is at the heart of Berlin. King Wilhelm I ordered the construction of the monument, which originally stood in Platz der Republik, in 1864, following the victory of Prussia and Austria over Denmark. In 1938, it was moved to the Grosser Stern in the Tiergarten to make room for the rebuilding of the city under the Third Reich. The monument survived World War II, and, more recently, has become a popular meeting place during the Berlin Love Parade (▷ 265). The Siegessäule, designed to convey German strength and dominance, is now a symbol of peace and acceptance.

The four sides of the base of the tower are decorated with bas-reliefs cast from captured bronze cannons, and illustrate scenes from the Danish–German War (1864), the Austro–Prussian conflict (1866) and the Franco–Prussian War (1870–1871). At the base of the tower is a sparse museum dedicated to European national monuments. The interior walls of the spiralling staircase are covered in graffiti left behind by summer revellers, which will keep you entertained during the strenuous climb to the top. The walls of the column on the first viewing platform are covered in a detailed mosaic showing key events in the creation of the German Empire.

Continue climbing to the top and you will reach the final viewing platform, beneath the gilded angel of Victory, designed by Friedrich Drake in 1870. The main attraction is the 360-degree view. If you look down Strasse des 17 Juni towards Brandenburger Tor, you can see all the way down Unter den Linden, with the Reichstag on the left and the Fernsehturm in the distance.

To the north, in a wooded area, is the Schloss Bellevue (not open to the public). Built for Prince Ferdinand of Prussia in 1786, it is now the official residence of the President of the Federal Republic of Germany.

ZOOLOGISCHER GARTEN

⊞ 120 A4• Hardenbergplatz 8 and Budapester Strasse 34, 10787 Berlin (Tiergarten) ☎ 030 254 010 🕓 Daily 9–6.30 (seasonal variations) 💶 Zoo: Adult €10, child €5; Zoo and Aquarium: Adult €15, child €7.50 🛍 Selling postcards, posters and educational toys 🍴 Self-service restaurant with a good selection of snacks, drinks and hot meals 🚻 Near the Elefanten (Elephants), Vogelhaus (Bird house), the souvenir shop and in the Zoo and Summer restaurant

The Tiergarten is a great place to relax in the sunshine

The zoo dates back to 1841, when Friedrich Wilhelm IV, the King of Prussia, donated his pheasant gardens and exotic animal collection to the citizens of Berlin. It suffered serious damage during World War II: Only 91 animals survived and many of the enclosures and buildings were beyond repair. The new director, Dr. Katharina Heinroth, began the lengthy process of rebuilding the zoo and reintroducing animals. Today it has developed into one of the most important zoos in the world, with over 14,000 animals and 1,500 species represented.

Moats and trenches rather than bars and cages define the outdoor enclosures, creating a sense of openness and giving visitors a good view of the animals. The hippopotamus house is the most modern in Europe. Completed in 1997, the two glass domes cover the steamy, climate-controlled home of the Common and Pygmy hippopotamuses. A glass wall in the viewing gallery allows you to watch them swimming under water. The polar bears and seals are also free to swim around in their homes, and the seals even have their own wave machine. The stars of the zoo are the two giant pandas, Bao Bao the male and Yan Yan the female.

AQUARIUM

⊞ 120 A4• Budapester Strasse 32, 10787 Berlin (Tiergarten) ☎ 030 254 010 🕓 Daily 9–6 💶 Aquarium: Adult €10, child €5; Aquarium and Zoo: Adult €15, child €7.50 🚻

A huge statue of an Iguanodon, which became extinct 90 million years ago, guards the entrance here. The aquarium is occupied by a huge variety of fish, frogs, lizards, snakes, crocodiles and turtles from all over the world. The Komodo Dragons dominate the reptile area on the second floor. Measuring 3m (10ft) in length, they are the largest lizards in the world and capable of eating prey as large as deer.

BACKGROUND

Peter Joseph Lenné transformed the former royal game enclosure into a public park at the heart of the city in the 19th century. After World War II, many of the trees were chopped down by Berliners to provide much needed firewood, but reforestation began again in 1949. Today it is a popular refuge for people who want to relax, exercise and picnic. In July, the park is filled with partygoers enjoying the festival atmosphere of the Berlin Love Parade.

TIPS

● The climb up to the top of the Siegessäule is quite challenging, but there are seats to rest on at regular intervals and it is worth it for the panoramic view of the park at the top.

● The zoo covers a large area, so if you want to see the animals being fed, plan your visit around those times. From April to September the feeding times are: seals 11, 1.30, 3.15; penguins 1.30; polar bears 10.30; apes 3.30; monkey house 11, 2, 3.30; carnivore house 2.30; pandas 11.30, 3; hippos 2; pelicans 3.30; cormorants 2; crocodiles 3.30 every Mon. Alterations and winter feeding times are posted on notice boards just inside the gates.

● Smoking is forbidden in the animal houses in the zoo.

The Siegessäule (Victory Tower) is the park's main landmark

The gilded dome of the Neue Synagoge

Picture perfect: a bronze statue in the Nikolaiviertel

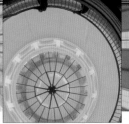
The spiral staircase in the Sammlung Berggruen

THE SIGHTS

NEUE SYNAGOGE

➕ 121 E3 • Oranienburger Strasse 28/30, 10117 Berlin (Mitte) ☎ 030 8802 8300 🕐 Sun–Thu 10–5.30, Fri 10–1.30; closed Sat and on Jewish holidays 🎫 Adult €3, child €2 Ⓢ Hackescher Markt, Oranienburger Strasse, Oranienburger Tor 🚊 Tram 1, 13 🎧 Guided tours in German Wed 4, Sun 2 and 4 and on request (tel 030 88 02 83 16); Adult €1.50, child €1 www.cjudaicum.de

The Neue Synagogue, opened in 1866, was once the place of worship for the largest Jewish community in Germany.

The National Socialists set fire to the building in 1938, although it was saved from total destruction. Services resumed until 1940, when the building was taken over and used as a Military Clothing Office. The rest of the building burned down after a bomb attack in 1943, and today, the reconstructed front section of the building and dome stand as a memorial to Berlin's persecuted Jewish community.

The famous, glistening dome, a key landmark on Berlin's skyline, has been restored according to original plans, but the rest of the building has been only partially reconstructed and now contains the Centrum Judaicum. On the ground floor, the permanent exhibition, *Open Ye the Gates*, explores the history of the synagogue and Jewish life in Berlin. One of the most remarkable exhibits is the Ner Tamid, the eternal lamp, which was rediscovered in 1989 in the protective concrete ceiling when construction workers were removing rubble from the marriage chamber (men's vestibule).

NIKOLAIVIERTEL

➕ 121 F3 • 10178 Berlin (Mitte) Ⓢ Alexanderplatz, Klosterstrasse 🚌 100, 142, 143, 148, 200, 348; tram 2, 3, 4

On an island in the Mitte, this faux old quarter of Berlin was rebuilt between 1981 and 1986 and is a mixture of refurbished old buildings, modern apartments, and arcades filled with craft and gift shops. The quarter's quiet streets and pristine buildings are a little too perfect for their reputed age, making the area feel a little like a film set.

At the heart of the quarter is the reconstructed Nikolaikirche (tel 030 24 72 45 29, Mon–Thu 8–4, Sat, Sun 12–4), the oldest parish church in Berlin. Inside, the Museum der Nikolaikirche (Tue–Sun 10–6; €1.50) explores the history of the church and its links to Berlin's famous personalities. The Knoblauchhaus (Tue–Sun 10–6; adult €2, child €1), at Poststrasse 23, is the oldest surviving house in the Nikolaiviertel and the oldest building still standing in Berlin. Built between 1759 and 1761, it was reconstructed in the early 19th century and now displays a collection of household items and furniture owned by the aristocratic Knoblauch family, along with exhibits documenting the history of Berlin from the 18th to the 20th century.

SAMMLUNG BERGGRUEN

➕ 120 A1 (inset) • Schlossstrasse 1, 14059 Berlin (Charlottenburg) ☎ 030 3269 5815 🕐 Tue–Sun 10–6 🎫 Adult €6, child €3 Ⓢ Richard-Wagner-Platz, Westend 🚌 109, 145, 210, X21, X9 🎧 Free audioguide 🈂 👪 www.sammlung-berggruen.de, or www.smb.spk-berlin.de/shb/i.html

The Berggruen collection, also known as 'Picasso and his Time', is an intimate collection of early modern art by Pablo Picasso and his contemporaries. Heinz Berggruen was a close friend of Picasso and his collection was amassed over 50 years.

The rooms radiate out from the central spiral staircase. On the ground floor, in the middle of the rotunda, is a sculpture by Giacometti entitled *Femme Debout III* (1960), a tall, elongated bronze figure that brilliantly reflects his distinctive style. Upstairs, you will find Giacometti's long and lean sculpture, *Le Chat* (1951), simultaneously abstract and realistic. It was based on his brother's cat and is one of only two animal sculptures by the artist.

TOPOGRAPHIE DES TERRORS

➕ 121 D4 • Niederkirchnerstrasse 8, 10963 Berlin (Kreuzberg) ☎ 030 2548 6703 🕐 Oct–Apr daily 10–dusk; May–Sep daily 10–8 🎫 Free Ⓢ Potsdamer Platz, Kochstrasse 🚌 129, 248, 341 🎧 Audioguide in English www.topographie.de

The Topography of Terror is an open-air exhibition in the excavations of the former National Socialist government district and reveals the development and activities of the National Socialist SS and police state.

Between 1933 and 1945, the genocide of the Jews and the persecution and murder of political opponents to Germany were planned here, and there was a Gestapo prison, used to detain and interrogate suspects. Towards the end of World War II, the buildings were damaged or completely destroyed. Following excavation of the site, the Topography of Terror exhibition was opened in 1987 in a pavilion. In 1995, the cornerstone was laid for a new building that will house the Topography of Terror Foundation's International Documentation and Study Center. It is scheduled to open on the 60th anniversary of the end of World War II on 8 May 2005.

EASTERN GERMANY

The former East Germany states now eagerly welcome visitors, in contrast to the situation during decades of Communist control. The region has caught up and cleaned up quickly. The most famous destinations in Eastern Germany—Colditz and Dresden—carry potent wartime associations. Other key attractions include Leipzig, popular with classical music lovers, and Weimar, once the hub of Germany's artistic Golden Age.

MAJOR SIGHTS

Statues on the façade of Katherinenkirche, Brandenburg

The imposing towers and fortified walls of Schloss Colditz

Cottbus's Jugendstil (art nouveau) Stadt Theater

THE SIGHTS

BAUTZEN

➕ 435 K9 ℹ️ Tourist-Information, Hauptmarkt 1, 02625 Bautzen, tel 035 91/42016; 19433; Mar–end Oct Mon–Fri 9–6, Sat, Sun 10–4; Nov–end Feb Mon–Fri 9–6, Sat, Sun 10–2
🚆 Bautzen
www.bautzen.de

High above a bend in the River Spree, this picturesque thousand-year-old town has substantial remains of the medieval fortifications necessary in this much-contested border region. Within the many towered walls are romantic streets and cobbled alleyways lined with baroque mansions and red-roofed houses, as well as a late-Gothic cathedral, shared, unusually, between Catholics and Protestants. The castle is home to the Sorbski Musej, museum of the local Slav minority, the Sorbs; a look at its attractive displays will give you a good idea of the culture of this ethnic group. Bautzen has its very own leaning tower, the tall Reichenturm (daily Apr–end Oct 10–5); the reward for climbing its 135 steps is a fine view of the city and the surrounding area.

Grim aspects of the more recent past are revealed at the Gedenkstätte Bautzen, the prison where, successively, opponents of Nazis, Soviets and Stasi were held, often in horrible conditions (Tue–Sun 10–4).

BRANDENBURG

➕ 434 H6 ℹ️ Tourist Information, Steinstrasse 66/67, 14776 Brandenburg, tel 03381 585858; May–end Sep Mon–Fri 10–7, Sat, Sun 10–3; Oct–end Apr Mon–Fri 10–7, Sat, Sun 10–2
🚆 Brandenburg
www.stadt-brandenburg.de

Lakes, rivers and woodlands combine to give this millennium-old city one of the most inviting settings in Germany.

Brandenburg was built on a series of islands, first by Slavs, then by Germanic rulers such as 12th-century Albert the Bear, who made it the base for farther eastward colonization and conversion to Christianity. Despite intense industrialization, severe pollution and neglect during GDR times, Brandenburg's medieval street pattern remains intact. Its islands are linked by bridges over the channels of the River Havel and graced by splendid brick-built Gothic churches and other historic buildings. Restoration has proceeded apace, and more and more visitors make the trip here. It's an easy day excursion from Berlin, just over half an hour away by express train, but more fun, if rather longer, by boat. Fun on the water is one of Brandenburg's great attractions; as well as pleasure cruises, there's canoeing, sailing, water-skiing, festivals and regattas on the glorious network of waterways that link to the Oder in the east and the Elbe to the west.

COLDITZ

➕ 434 H9 ℹ️ Tourist Information, Johann-David-Köhler-Haus, An der Kirche 1, 04680 Colditz, tel 034381 4351-9; Apr–end Oct Mon–Fri 9–5, Sat, Sun 10–4; Nov–end Mar Mon–Fri 9–4
www.fremdenverkehrsamt-colditz.de

This little old town stands on a bend in the Mulde, a picturesque stream winding through the attractive countryside of central Saxony. The river passes countless castles along the way, including Thalwitz, Wolkenburg, Rochlitz and Podelwitz. All of them are worth a visit, but none of them have quite the resonance of Colditz itself. The fortress, high above the town, won notoriety in World War II, when it served as a supposedly 100 per cent secure prison for

Allied officers identified by their captors as incorrigible would-be escapers. Perhaps inevitably, it became a university of escape, the exploits of its inmates subsequently celebrated in dozens of books and a famous TV series. The guided tour through court-yards and claustrophobic interiors reveals the astonishing ingenuity exercised by the prisoners in their attempts—10 per cent of them successful—to extricate themselves from the confines of the castle's grim walls. (Tours start from Colditz Town Museum, Tiergartenstrasse 1, Tue–Sun 10.30, 1, 3.)

COTTBUS

➕ 435 K8 ℹ️ Cottbus-Service, Berliner Platz 6/Stadthalle, 03046 Cottbus, tel 0355 754 2455; Mon–Fri 9–6, Sat 9–1 🚆 Cottbus
www.cottbus.de

Cottbus has a reputation for taking nature seriously, perhaps dating from when industrious Huguenot weavers settled here in the 17th century. The lovely woods and waterways of the Spreewald are nearby and Cottbus is one of Germany's greenest cities, with a chain of parks and open spaces along the River Spree. There's the Goethepark, the Spreeauenpark (lavishly laid out for the 1995 National Garden Festival) and the sublime landscape created in the mid-19th century by the eccentric Prince Pückler-Muskau as a setting for his ancestral home, Schloss Branitz (Apr–end Oct daily 10–6; Nov–end Mar daily 11–5). The castle's exotic interiors evoke the prince's travels in Africa and the Orient, while the romantic park reflects his admiration for all things English. At the western end of this landscape, rising from the lake, is a great earthen pyramid, which is the Prince's mausoleum.

DESSAU AND WÖRLITZ

Dessau was home to the Bauhaus movement, and many buildings from this period are dotted around the town.

In the 14th century, the princes of Anhalt built their castle at a point where the River Mulde could be bridged just before it flows into the mighty Elbe. Four hundred years later, their descendant, Prince Leopold, inspired by the spirit of the European Enlightenment and by travels in England and Italy, landscaped great tracts of his lands, creating a garden realm, at the time the most fabulous in Europe. His parks, lakes, garden buildings and statuary remain, and have justifiably become one of the great visitor attractions of eastern Germany. Together with the ecologically rich biosphere reserve of the river floodplains, they are now protected as a UNESCO World Heritage Site.

AVANT-GARDE CITY

Leopold was a most progressive ruler, assembling an array of professional and artistic talent in his little court, giving the public free access to his parks and gardens and promoting education and welfare. His example was followed in the early 20th century, when Dessau became home to the Bauhaus movement. Headed by Walter Gropius (1883–1969), this influential institution in the development of Modernism in design and architecture flourished until it was closed by the Nazis in the early 1930s. Its coolly contemporary buildings, designed by Gropius himself using steel, concrete and glass, still stand, and, well restored, are once more a design education facility that attracts architectural pilgrims from all over the world (guided tour daily, mid-Feb to late Oct).

GARDEN PARADISE

The sheer number of parks and palaces in and around Dessau can be daunting, so if time is short, you shouldn't miss Wörlitz, perhaps Germany's supreme achievement in landscape design. No fence separates the little town from the well-tree'd Schlossgarten, the setting for Leopold's summer residence, built for him by court architect Friedrich Wilhelm von Knobelsdorff between 1769 and 1773. Beyond stretches the park's main lake, the Wörlitzer See, on its banks a further series of delightful landscapes and garden features, among them a temple, a pantheon, a synagogue and the extraordinary Gotisches Haus, one façade Venetian, the other a version of English Tudor. Equally extraordinary is the variety of bridges, which include a mildly perilous-seeming suspension bridge. Experience the ever-changing vistas on foot, ferry or aboard a gondola.

Martin Gropius' Meisterhaus (main picture)
Spending time on the river (inset) at Wörlitz

RATINGS

Historic interest	●●●●
Cultural interest	●●●●●
Photo stops	●●●

BASICS

Dessau
⊞ 434 H7
🛈 Tourist Information Dessau, Zerbster Strasse 2c, 06844 Dessau, tel 0340 204 1442; Apr–end Oct Mon–Fri 9–6, Sat 9–1; Nov–end Mar Mon–Fri 9–5, Sat 10–1
🚉 Dessau
www.dessau.de

Wörlitz
🛈 Wörlitz Information, Förstergasse 26, 06786 Wörlitz, tel 034905 20216; Mar–end Oct daily 9–6; Nov–end Feb Mon–Fri 9–4, plus Sat, Sun 11–3 in Feb
www.woerlitz-information.de

TIPS

● In summer, the best way to arrive in Wörlitz is by train from Dessau. There's also a 40km (25-mile) circular bicycle tour—Fürst Franz Weg—taking in many of Prince Leopold's landscapes.
● If the gondolas are crowded, leave them behind and discover the park at your own pace on foot.

Dresden

A handsome city, rebuilt after its wartime destruction and home to some of Germany's best art and architecture. On Saxony's Wine Road, and close to the state's finest scenery, Dresden makes a great base for touring.

The moated outside wall of Dresden's Zwinger

You will still see Trabants on Dresden's streets

Ornate façades on Dresden's houses

SEEING DRESDEN

Opinion surveys regularly show Dresden heading the list of Germany's most beautiful cities. The capital of Saxony is on a broad bend of the Elbe, and its famous silhouette of baroque towers, spires and domes is once more intact, the result of decades of devoted reconstruction following the bombing raid of 13 to14 February 1945. Few places in Germany are so well endowed with galleries and museums, their paintings, sculptures and other objets d'art accumulated by extravagant rulers over the years. Most of the museums are within easy walking distance of each other. Cultural life flourishes, and ranges from performances in the superlative setting of Gottfried Semper's great opera house to the cabarets of the Neustadt on the far bank of the Elbe. The 18th-century Neustadt largely escaped the effects of the bombing, and it is here that the city's heart beats most strongly in the evenings, with an array of pubs, bars, restaurants and places of entertainment. The Elbe, plied by the famous White Fleet of pleasure steamers, forms a link between city and countryside, its banks lined by palaces, vineyards and the astonishing rocky landscapes of Saxon Switzerland (▷ 174).

RATINGS	
Historic interest	●●●●●
Cultural interest	●●●●●
Photo stops	●●●●

BASICS

⊞ 439 J9 🛈 Dresden-Werbung und Tourismus GmbH, Postfach 120952, 01010 Dresden, tel 0351 491920
🚆 Dresden Hauptbahnhof and Dresden Neustadt
www.dresden-tourist.de

HIGHLIGHTS

ZWINGER

⊞ 157 A2 ✉ Theaterplatz 1, Dresden 01067 ☎ 0351 491 4619 🕐 Tue–Sun 10–6
🎟 Gemäldegalerie Alte Meister/Old Masters Picture Gallery: adult €6, child €3.50; Porzellansammlung/Porcelain Collection: adult €5, child €3; Rüstkammer/Armoury: adult €3, child €2; Mathematisch–Physikalischer Salon/Mathematical–Physical Sciences Salon: adult €3, child €2

Arranged around a spacious courtyard with lawns, pools and fountains, the spectacular group of baroque buildings known as the Zwinger was built from 1709 onwards by Saxony's most flamboyant ruler, Augustus the Strong, and his court architect, Matthäus Daniel Pöppelmann. Augustus had recently acquired the additional title of King of Poland, and the Zwinger was intended as a setting for the lavish pageants and festivities appropriate to his greatly enhanced status,

The clock and porcelain bells at the entrance to Dresen's baroque Zwinger (opposite)

DEUTSCHES HYGIENE-MUSEUM

off 157 B3 • Lingnerplatz 1 ☎ 0351 484 6670 ◷ Tue–Sun 10–6 🎫 Adult €2.50, child €1.50

Founded by the inventor of Odol, Germany's best-selling mouth-wash, this unusual establishment tells you everything you could possibly want to know about hygiene and health. The most popular exhibit is the famous Glass Human, with a nervous system made of 13km (8 miles) of wiring.

GOLDENER REITER

157 B1 • Neustädter Markt

The imposing gilded figure greeting you as you enter the Neustadt district on the far bank of the Elbe is Augustus the Strong. He is shown in Roman dress on a rearing horse looking towards the city that he embellished so extravagantly, mostly at the expense of the townsfolk.

SEMPEROPER

off 157 A2 • Theaterplatz 2 ☎ 0351 491 1496 ◷ Entry by guided tour only (times vary) 🎫 Adult €5, child €3

Dresden has one of the greatest opera houses in Europe, named for its architect, Gottfried Semper. Destroyed in 1945, it was rebuilt in exemplary fashion by the GDR authorities. It reopened in 1985.

SCHLOSS PILLNITZ

off 157 C2 ☎ 0351 491 4619 ◷ May–end Oct daily 10–6 🎫 Adult €3, child €2 (decorative arts collection)

On the banks of the Elbe in its park among the vineyards, Pillnitz Palace was built by Augustus the Strong in 1720 in a delicate mock-Chinese style. It makes a wonderful home for a collection of decorative arts from earliest times to the 20th century.

VERKEHRSMUSEUM/ TRANSPORT MUSEUM

157 B2 • Johanneum, Augustusstrasse ☎ 0351 86440 ◷ Tue–Sun 10–5 🎫 Adult €6, child €3

This major museum deals with all kinds of transport, by rail, river, automobile, aircraft, even bicycle. There are fascinating vehicles of all kinds, including Dresden's oldest surviving tram. Try to catch the showing of a 1930s film of a tourist trip around the city before its destruction.

as well as a home for the royal collections of art and porcelain. It remains one of the great sights of Germany, attracting visitors from around the world who fill it with something of the animation it was originally conceived for. Many are on their way to see the artworks in the Old Masters Gallery, but the Zwinger is a great work of art in its own right. Enter through the magnificent Kronentor, topped by the golden crown of Poland, or through the Glockenspielpavillon, with a carillon made from Meissen porcelain. Opposite is Pöppelmann's masterpiece, the Wallpavillon, a building of almost unbelievable exuberance with decoration by the sculptor Balthasar Permoser (1651–1732), who was also responsible for many of the delightful figures in the adjoining Nymphenbad (Nymphs' Bathing Place).

Augustus and his successors amassed huge quantities of art, most of which survived the 1945 bombing and temporary exile in the Soviet Union 'for safe keeping'. The pictures in the Gemäldegalerie Alte Meister (Old Masters Gallery) make up one of the world's great collections. The gallery's most outstanding painting, its equivalent of the *Mona Lisa*, is Raphael's *Sistine Madonna*, the tenderest possible evocation of maternity, and the cheeky cherubs at the foot of the picture have become almost as well known as the serene Madonna herself. There are other first-rate Italian Renaissance canvases as well, such as Giorgine's *Sleeping Venus* (1510), which shows the goddess as an earthly looking young woman slumbering in an open landscape. There are also fine examples of Dutch art like Jan Vermeer's *Girl Reading a Letter at an Open Window* (1657), and much more besides. Meticulously detailed townscapes by Canaletto show Dresden at the summit of its beauty in the 18th century. As if this was not enough, the Zwinger has other fabulous collections: the Rüstkammer (Armoury), the Porzellansammlung (Porcelain Collection) and the Mathematisch–Physikalischer Salon (Mathematical–Physical Sciences Salon), with its array of finely crafted scientific instruments.

HOFKIRCHE

157 B2 • Schlossplatz, 01067 Dresden ☎ 0351 484 4712

Overlooking the Elbe, the elegant Hofkirche (Court Church) of 1755 was the last great baroque edifice to be completed in Dresden. In this otherwise solidly Protestant city, it is a Catholic place of worship, built by the Saxon rulers who changed their religion in order to qualify for the crown of Poland. No local architect could be found for the task, so an Italian master builder, Gaetano Chiaveri, was brought in, along with his work force, which was housed in the Italienisches Dörfchen (Italian Village), now a popular riverside restaurant. Despite its size—it is the largest church in Saxony—the Hofkirche is a joyful and elegant edifice, the parade of sandstone saints along its balustrades giving it a particular air of gaiety. Inside, the organ is the masterpiece of the great Saxon organbuilder Silbermann, while the crypt houses the sarcophagi of Saxon rulers.

RESIDENZSCHLOSS

✚ 157 B2 • Taschenberg 2, 01067 Dresden ☎ 0351 491 4619 ⏰ Fri–Wed 10–6 💶 Adult €6, child €3.50

The palace of the Saxon rulers began as a medieval fortress commanding the crossing of the Elbe and was extended and modified in Renaissance and neo-Renaissance styles right up to the abdication of the last king of Saxony in 1918. Comprehensively destroyed in 1945, it is still being rebuilt and is destined to house a number of museums. It is already home to the Grünes Gewölbe (Green Vault), a fabulous array of jewels and the exquisitely crafted objects to which Augustus the Strong seems to have been particularly addicted. The most extraordinary item is the 'Hofstaat von Delhi am Geburtstag des

Grossmoguls/Court of Delhi on the Birthday of the Great Moghul', an utterly over-the-top tableau of gold, silver, enamel and precious stones that cost Augustus twice the price of a princely palace. You can climb the 100m (328ft) to the top of the palace's tower (Tue–Sun 10–6, summer only), but its most striking feature is the famous frieze on an outside wall; made up of 25,000 Meissen porcelain tiles, it is an impressive parade of the Saxon rulers' 800-year dynasty.

BRÜHLSCHE TERRASSE

✚ 157 B2

The best way to appreciate Dresden's wonderful setting is to

TIPS

● Conscientious the rebuilding of Dresden's Altstadt may have been, but something of the city's old spirit has inevitably been lost. Parts of suburban Dresden have, however, kept their traditional character: Take the No. 11 tram past the opulent villas along the Bautzener Strasse to the Waldschlösschen stop and enjoy the classic vista of the city's skyline rising over the Elbe.

● Few cities list a car factory as one of their attractions, but Dresden's ultra-modern Volkswagen works, known as the Gläserne Manufaktur (Transparent Manufactory) and built on a prominent site on the edge of the Grosser Garten park has to be seen to be believed.

Riverboats moored alongside the Brühlsche Terrasse (left)

THE SIGHTS

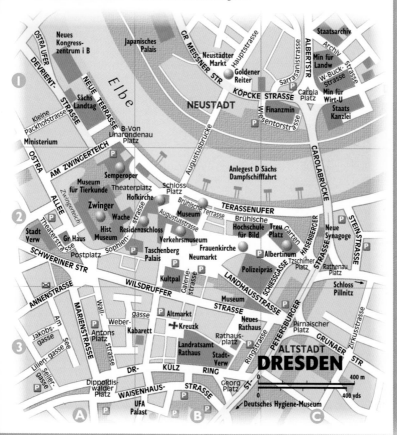

DRESDEN

THE LAST KING

After the unification of Germany in 1871, Saxony remained a kingdom, though its monarch had no real power. The last Saxon king, a member of the Wettin dynasty, which had first come into prominence here 800 years before, was Friedrich August III, a popular figure with a common touch. Along with Kaiser Wilhelm II, he was forced to abdicate at the end of World War I. Dresdeners lined the streets to bid him farewell, but Friedrich August's comment—in broad Saxon dialect—was *'Macht Euren Dreck alleene!*—roughly translated as 'Now you'll have to make your own mess!'

Eating alfresco in the Altmarkt

The Semperoper opera house

take a stroll along this superb elevated terrace overlooking the Elbe. To one side are the historic buildings making up the city's famous skyline, and to the other the great river, graced by the white steamers along the quayside. Beyond the Neustadt on the far bank rise the gentle hills colonized by the city's affluent villa suburbs. Sometimes known as the Balcony of Europe, the terrace owes its official name to the 18th-century Count Brühl, who converted the old fortifications here into a splendid and strictly private garden for his palace; it wasn't opened to the public until the early 19th century.

FRAUENKIRCHE

🔲 157 B2 • Neumarkt, 01067 Dresden ☎ 0351 498 1131 ⏰ Hourly tours by prior arrangement 💲 Donation requested

No other building in Dresden embodies the city's history and beauty so poignantly as the glorious Frauenkirche (Church of Our Lady). A masterpiece of baroque architecture, it was consecrated in 1736 with music directed by Johann Sebastian Bach. The great building's lovely, bell-shaped dome formed the focus of Dresden's skyline. It withstood the bombs of 13 to 14 February 1945, but two days later, as the tortured stonework cooled, it collapsed. Its fall seemed to spell the end of everything the city had ever stood for. For years the church remained a gigantic pile of rubble, a monument to disaster. Then the awesome decision was taken to rebuild, a process begun in 1994 and destined for completion in 2005. The Frauenkirche has become a symbol of reconciliation between former enemies, with some of the costs of reconstruction funded by British contributions; the golden cross that will crown the dome was made in Coventry, itself severely war-damaged, and was handed over by the Duke of Kent on 13 February 2000. Much of the original, blackened stonework has been reused, giving the edifice a patchwork appearance.

ALBERTINUM

🔲 157 C2 • Georg-Treu-Platz2, 01067 Dresden ☎ 0351 491 4619 ⏰ Fri–Wed 10–6 💲 Adult €6, child €3.50

The sombre architecture of this late-19th-century palace gives little idea of the riches within, among them some of Dresden's finest artistic treasures. If you are a lover of modern art, head for the Galerie Neue Meister (Modern Masters), which is especially rich in German painting of the 19th and 20th centuries. Look out for evocative works by Romantic artists like Caspar David Friedrich (1774–1840) and Ludwig Richter, both inspired by Dresden and its surroundings, and marvel at the *1000-Jährige Reich* painted by Hans Grundig in 1938, an extraordinary prophecy of the horrors of war which were shortly to engulf Europe and lead eventually to Dresden's destruction.

The largest of its kind outside Italy, the Skulpturensammlung (Sculpture Collection) covers the whole history of European sculpture and is particularly rich in Classical Greek and Roman works.

BACKGROUND

From a modest riverside settlement of Slav fisherman and farmers, Dresden evolved in the 15th century into the residence of the rulers of Saxony. Its glory days began in the reign of Elector Augustus the Strong (1670–1733), so-called because of his prodigious siring of children. King of Poland as well as Elector of Saxony, Augustus spent lavishly on buildings and works of art, and he and his immediate successors gave the city its predominantly baroque character. In the 19th and early 20th centuries, Dresden expanded, but remained a city of art, escaping the worst effects of industrialization. This, so reasoned its inhabitants as World War II drew to its close, was why it had not been bombed to destruction like other German cities. They were wrong; on the 13th to 14 February 1945, the firestorm unleashed by British and American planes laid waste to a vast area, killing tens of thousands. The devastation was so great that shocked city planners thought seriously about abandoning the site altogether and building a new Dresden elsewhere.

Erfurt's Krämerbrücke is lined with buildings

The Kaisertrutz, Görlitz: home to temporary art exhibitions

A carving of a loving couple on the Rathaus doorway in Gotha

EISENACH AND THE WARTBURG

See page 160.

ERFURT

🚗 434 F9 ℹ️ Tourismus GmbH Erfurt, Benediktplatz 1, 99084 Erfurt, tel 0361 66400; Apr–end Dec Mon–Fri 10–7, Sat 9–6, Sun 10–4; Jan–end Mar Mon–Sat 10–6, Sun 10–4 🚆 Erfurt
www.erfurt.de

The cathedral city and capital of the *Land* of Thuringia, Erfurt escaped the worst that war damage and forty years of Communism could do, and it is a pleasure to stroll through its old streets, with their fascinating mix of buildings of all ages. Sooner or later you will find yourself at the River Gera, crossed by the medieval stone bridge known as the Krämerbrücke, a survivor from an age when bridges had to earn their keep by providing sites for shops and other buildings. This one supports an array of souvenir shops, and you can climb its tower. Eventually you will emerge from the labyrinth of streets and lanes into the vast Domplatz, dominated by two great churches, Erfurt's cathedral and the church of St. Severus rising from the opposite slope. Climb the monumental flight of steps to see the cathedral's treasures, including sculptures of the Wise and Foolish Virgins that grace the portal.

FREIBERG

🚗 439 J9 ℹ️ Tourist-Information, Burgstrasse 1, 09599 Freiberg, tel 03731 2732 6466; Apr–end Dec Mon–Fri 8–6, Sat 9–12; Jan–end Mar Mon–Fri 8–5, Sat 9–12 🚆 Freiberg
www.freiberg.de

Spared wartime destruction, Freiberg owes its fame to its silver mines, the main source of Saxony's wealth for many years. Its mining connections gave it extra credibility in the eyes of the GDR's rulers, who spent scarce resources on restoring the patrician houses in the Altstadt. But the town's great treasure is its Dom, modest outside, but with one of the most glorious interiors in Germany. Come, if you can, on a Thursday evening, when the sublime sound of the great organ fills the space. It was built in the mid-18th century by Gottfried Silbermann, claimed by some to be the master organ-builder of all time. Look, too, for the lavish mausoleums of Saxon rulers, happy to be buried in the town whose silver had financed their extravagant lifestyle in nearby Dresden. You can trace the story of silver mining at the Stadt- und Bergbaumuseum (Town and Mining Museum, Tue–Sun 10–5) or follow in the footsteps of the old miners by descending the shaft of the Reiche Zeche mine (3 tours daily).

GÖRLITZ

🚗 435 L9 ℹ️ Görlitzinformation, Obermarkt 29, 02826 Görlitz, tel 03581 47570; Mar–end Dec Mon–Fri 9–6.30, Sat 10–4, Sun 10–1; Jan, Feb Mon–Fri 9–6.30, Sat 10–4 🚆 Görlitz
www.goerlitz.de

The Altstadt of Germany's easternmost town was miraculously spared by war, its wonderfully harmonious mixture of buildings ranging from medieval to modern. The town's suburbs on the far bank of the little River Neisse were detached from Germany in 1945 and are now the Polish town of Zgorelec. Far from seeing its frontier location as a disadvantage, Görlitz looks forward to a positive, bridging role in the era of eastward European Union expansion (▷ 22). As you stroll from one square to another, Görlitz reveals its treasures, from massive remnants of fortifications with immensely thick walls to an array of medieval churches and splendid Renaissance and baroque mansions. The most exquisite area is around the Untermarkt, with a Neptune fountain and arcaded town houses; it is dominated by the Rathaus, which has a two-faced clock and an elegant outside stairway with a figure of Justice lacking her customary blindfold.

GOTHA

🚗 434 F9 ℹ️ Gotha-Information, Hauptmarkt 2, 99867 Gotha, tel 03621 222138; Apr–end Oct Mon–Fri 9–6, Sat, Sun 10–2; Nov–end Mar Mon–Fri 9–6, Sat 10–2 🚆 Gotha
www.gotha.de

Celebrated in GDR times as a shrine of Socialism, Gotha's greater claim to fame is its aristocratic, even royal, past. For many years it was the seat of the Saxe-Coburg-Gotha dynasty, which included Prince Albert, Queen Victoria's husband, so the British Royal family were called Saxe-Coburg-Gotha until they changed it to Windsor in World War I. The town also gave its name to the Almanac de Gotha, the Who's Who of German nobility, and it remains a fascinating examples of those little courtly cities so characteristic of Germany. The town itself huddles respectfully at the foot of the steep slope leading up to Schloss Friedenstein, the imposing residence built in the mid-17th century by Duke Ernst the Pious. This formidable structure, with its arcaded courtyard and massive corner towers, stands in the middle of a vast park covering an area almost as extensive as the Altstadt itself. The austere exterior of the great building belies its contents: a succession of gorgeous rooms in every style from baroque to Empire, with collections reflecting the wealth and refined taste of successive dukes.

Bach's statue (above).
From its commanding position,
Wartburg (top) watches
over Eisenach

RATINGS

Historic interest	●●●●●
Cultural interest	●●●
Walkability	●●●

BASICS

✚ 438 F9
🛈 Tourist-Information, Markt, 99817
Eisenach, tel 0369 167 0263; Mon 10–6,
Tue–Fri 9–6, Sat, Sun 10–2
🚃 Eisenach
www.eisenach-tourist.de

TIPS

● The Wartburg attracts several
million visitors a year. Parking
is at a premium, and it is still
quite a walk (or donkey ride)
up to the castle. Why not start
your walk from the town itself,
beginning at the information
point near the Predigerkirche?
● You don't have to go very
far from Eisenach to get the
feel of the dramatic landscapes
of the Thuringian Forest. Just
south of the town are a
number of well-laid-out walks
through rocky ravines like the
Drachenschlucht and the
Landgrafenschlucht.

EISENACH AND THE WARTBURG

A historic town, forming the gateway to the attractions of the Thuringian Forest.
Wartburg is the archetypal German castle.

Crowning one of the wooded spurs of the vast Thuringian Forest,
Wartburg Castle (Mar–end Oct daily 8.30–5; Nov–end Feb daily
9–3.30) looks like a vision of the Middle Ages, with stone walls rising
from the bare rock. At its foot spreads Eisenach, a fine little city in its
own right, rich in associations with figures as diverse as Martin Luther
(1483–1546) and Johann Sebastian Bach (1685–1750).

WARTBURG

The origins of the Wartburg go back to the 11th century, when it was
founded by Count Ludwig of Thuringia. His successors built the splendid 12th-century *Palast*, one of the country's few surviving examples
of a Romanesque palace. In 1521, the Protestant Duke Frederick of
Saxony, gave Luther a false identity, and provided him with lodgings
where he could complete his translation of the Bible in peace. Soon,
pilgrims were toiling up the slope to the castle, eager to see the mark
on the wall where Luther is supposed to have hurled his ink-pot at
the Devil. But the Wartburg's fame failed to halt its slide into decay.
After patriotic students added their layer of symbolism to the castle at
the end of the Napoleonic Wars, great efforts were made not just to
repair it but to rebuild it from scratch where necessary. Much of what
you see today dates from this time.

EISENACH

Once you have completed your visit to the Wartburg, descend to
Eisenach, and enter the town through the imposing Nikolaitor, a
formidable remnant of the old fortifications. Don't miss the tall-
towered Georgenkirche (St. George's Church): Luther preached in
the church, and it was here that Bach was baptized in 1685. Both are
celebrated nearby. The rebuilt late-medieval residence of the Cotta
family, where Luther lodged for several years as a schoolboy, is now
the Luther-Haus (Apr–end Oct daily 9–5; Nov–end Mar daily 10–5),
with displays on his life and work. A fine statue of the composer
stands by the 600-year-old Bach-Haus (daily 10–6), which has a collection of contemporary musical instruments used for demonstrations
and concerts. An equally interesting collection is at the Automobilbau-
museum (Tue–Sun 10–5), which has examples of the cars that have
been built here for over a century, among them the GDR's prestige
model, the Wartburg.

Georg Friedrich Händel, Halle's most famous son

The Universitätshochhaus, Jena: a modern icon

Contemporary and Romanesque at Magdeburg's convent

HALLE

434 G8 Tourist Information Halle, Roter Turm, Marktplatz, 06108 Halle, tel 0345 472330 Halle
www.halle.de

This bustling place is the biggest city in Sachsen-Anhalt, but lost out to Magdeburg when the *Land* capital was chosen after reunification. Its historic prosperity was based on the extraction of salt, and one old saltworks—the Technisches Halloren-und Salinenmuseum (Tue–Sun 10–5)—is now a museum. Such works were the forerunners of the vast and polluting chemical industry that caused so much environmental devastation in Communist times. Nowadays, Halle concentrates more on cultural offerings.

The city's greatest son was Georg Friedrich Händel (1685–1759). His life and work is evoked in the baroque house where he was born (Mon, Wed, Fri 9.30–5.30, Thu, Sat, Sun 9.30–7), where there are occasional chamber concerts, though the city's big annual *Handelfest* is in June. Händel's statue is in the central square, the Marktplatz, which is otherwise dominated by the spires of the Marktkirche and the city's main landmark, the Roter Turm (Red Tower, 80m/260ft), which you can climb.

JENA

438 G9 Tourist-Information Jena, Johannisstrasse 23, 07743 Jena, tel 03641 806400; Mon–Fri 9–6, Sat 9–2 Jena
www.tourismus.jena.de

Surrounded by high green hills where vines used to grow, this old university city is in the beautiful valley of the River Saale. Wartime bombing and insensitive urban development in GDR times have left only fragments of Jena's former charm. The most prominent building now is the Universitätshochhaus, a cylindrical skyscraper (120m/395ft) dominating the central Eichplatz. Nevertheless, there are plenty of reminders of an illustrious academic and cultural past, with houses and museums devoted to Johann Wolfgang von Goethe, Friedrich von Schiller and other luminaries, while contemporary Jena is a lively place, proud of the continuing high-tech traditions associated with the name of Carl Zeiss, who set up his optics workshop here in the middle of the 19th century. In celebration of his life, a formidable piece of optical equipment graces the glittering new Goethegalerie shopping mall, and you can also visit the Zeiss Planetarium, the world's oldest and still Germany's biggest, as well as in the Optisches Museum (Optical Museum, Tue–Fri 10–4.30, Sat 1–15), with the original Zeiss workshop.

LEIPZIG

See pages 162–165.

MAGDEBURG

434 G7 Tourist-Information-Magdeburg, Ernst-Reuter-Allee 12, 39104 Magdeburg, tel 0391 19433; Jun–end Sep Mon–Fri 10–7, Sat 10–4; Oct–end May Mon–Fri 10–6, Sat 10–1 Magdeburg
www.magdeburg-tourist.de

Magdeburg's fortunes took a turn for the better on the fall of Communism, when it became the capital of the newly re-created *Land* of Sachsen-Anhalt. It is now a thriving, forward-looking place, though still proud of the fragments of its past that survived an often catastrophic history of fires and wanton destruction. Of these fragments, the finest is the superb Dom (daily 10–6, 4 in winter), one of the greatest of Germany's Gothic cathedrals, with a beautiful riverside setting. Built on foundations established in the 10th century by Emperor Otto the Great, it is not only an architectural jewel in its own right but has a wealth of sculpture, ranging from a truly regal 13th-century representation of a royal couple (possibly Otto and his consort Editha) to a poignant memorial to the victims of World War I by Expressionist sculptor Ernst Barlach. There's more sublime sculpture in the Romanesque Convent of Our Lady (Tue–Sun 10–6).

MORITZBURG

435 J9 • Schloss Moritzburg, 01468 Moritzburg, ☎ 035207 8730 Apr–end Oct daily 10–5.30; Nov, Dec, Feb, Mar Tue–Sun guided tours only 10–4; Jan Sat, Sun guided tours only 10–4 Adult €6, child €4
www.moritzburg.de

Its round corner towers reflected in the waters of a broad lake, approached across a causeway and a gently rising ramp, the palace at Moritzburg is a formidable presence in the game-rich woods and heaths northwest of Dresden. The area was one of the best-loved hunting grounds of the rulers of Saxony, one of whom, Elector Moritz, built a Renaissance hunting lodge here in 1542. In the 18th century, this building proved far too small for the expansive tastes of Elector Augustus the Strong, who extended it and added the huge corner towers with their domed caps. The interior is equally grandiose, though most of the original furnishings disappeared in the chaos of 1945. Augustus' hunting trophies are still here; one set of horns is claimed to be the largest of its kind in the world; another monster specimen was acquired by Augustus from Frederick the Great in exchange for a platoon of soldiers.

Leipzig

**This lively city has strong cultural traditions.
There are many mementoes of the leading role Leipzigers played
in bringing down the GDR regime.**

All the trappings of a modern city: shopping in Leipzig

A tram takes passengers past Leipzig's Bahnhof

Bach was choirmaster at Thomaskirche

RATINGS

Historic interest	● ● ●
Cultural interest	● ● ● ●
Walkability	● ● ●

BASICS

✚ 434 H8 ℹ Leipzig Tourist Service eV, Richard-Wagner-Strasse 1, 04109 Leipzig, tel 0341 7104 260/265; Mon–Fri 10–6, Sat and Sun 9–4
🚆 Hauptbahnhof

TIP

● Leipzig's trade fairs have an 800-year history, though the annual fair that brought the world here even in GDR times has now been replaced by a changing schedule of special-ized events. They are held in the Neue Messe (New Trade Fair) on the northern outskirts, a spectacular complex of futuristic buildings that are the most up to date of their kind in the world. Check with Tourist Information about guided visits outside fair times.

Leipzig's über-modern trade fair venue: the Neue Messe (opposite)

SEEING LEIPZIG

Saxony's second city may be smaller, more down to earth and less glamorous than the state capital, Dresden, but it is a bustling, forward-looking place of strong character, with a long and proud civic history. Its cultural life is second to none, not least because of its glorious musical tradition stretching back to the Middle Ages, which is still very much alive today. When Germans are asked how they feel about their native city, Leipzigers come out top in terms of affection and unwillingness to move elsewhere; after a stay here you will appreciate why. The city attracts plenty of visitors, but nowhere do they outnumber locals, a refreshing contrast to other popular destinations. A wealth of places to eat, drink, shop and be entertained more than makes up for the relatively small number of conventional monuments, though the ones that do exist are fascinating enough. The city is exceptionally compact and easy to explore on foot, its network of arcades providing all-weather cover. These are the successors to the traditional courtyards in which merchants from all over Europe once displayed their wares, the origin of the city's great trade fairs. The fairs now take place in a state-of-the-art complex on the edge of the city, not far from the international airport, which has replaced Leipzig's famous railway station as the gateway for business visitors.

HIGHLIGHTS

HAUPTBAHNHOF/MAIN STATION

The area around Leipzig has one of the densest rail networks in the world, and its monumental main station is claimed to be the largest rail terminus in Europe, with 26 platforms handling local, regional, national and international trains. It was completed in 1913, at a time when the city was served by not one but two state railways, the Prussian and the Saxon; consequently, the building had duplicated facilities—two main entrances, two great halls, two clocks and two waiting rooms. Prussian trains used platforms 1 to 13, the Saxon trains 14 to 26. Local people are proud to have such a grand gateway

MORE TO SEE

GEWANDHAUS

• Augustusplatz 8, 04109 Leipzig
☎ 0341 12702-80

Leipzig's world-class symphony orchestra gave its first performances in 1781 on the upper floor of the 'Clothmakers' Guild House' in 1781. Completed 200 years later, its present home is one of the GDR's prestige buildings, a modern structure, lavishly decorated and with fine acoustics, characteristics it shares with the Opera on the far side of the spacious Augustusplatz.

GRASSI-MUSEUM

• Johannesplatz, Leipzig

The Bauhaus-style buildings of this famous museum with its three departments—Musical Instruments, Ethnography and Decorative Arts—are undergoing a thorough renovation; it is due to reopen in 2005. Meanwhile, a selection of its treasures are on show in a variety of locations around the city.

MENDELSSOHN-HAUS

• Goldschmidtstrasse 12, 04103 Leipzig
☎ 0341 1270294

Appropriately furnished and with much evocative personal memorabilia, the family home of Felix Mendelssohn is a magnet for his many admirers. During his time as conductor of the Gewandhaus orchestra (1835–45), Mendelssohn was responsible for reviving the reputation of many forgotten composers, not least that of the strangely neglected Johann Sebastian Bach.

to their city, and there was much opposition to the post-unification idea of incorporating a huge shopping mall into the complex and converting some platforms for parking. Today, however, the shops of the Bahnhofspromenaden beneath the main concourse are as much an accepted part of the city as the station itself (▷ 268).

ALTES RATHAUS

• Markt 1, 04109 Leipzig ☎ 0341 96513-0 ⏰ Tue–Sun 10–6 💶 Adult €3, child (under 6) free

With its steep roof, six gables, arcades and splendid tower, the immensely long Old City Hall of 1556 is one of Germany's finest Renaissance civic buildings, expressive of local pride and of the need to impress visitors to the great trade fairs. It was completed in the interval between two fairs, in the extraordinarily short time of nine months, to designs by Hieronymus Lotter, the city's burgomaster. The interior has a superb ceremonial hall, and houses many of the treasures of the Stadtgeschichtliches Museum (City History Museum). To the west, the Rathaus dominates the marketplace, while to the east it overlooks one of Leipzig's most appealing historic buildings, the Alte Börse (Old Stock Exchange). This resplendent little baroque structure is now used for lectures and concerts. In front of it stands a statue of the youthful Johann Wolfgang von Goethe, gazing towards Auerbachs Keller, his best-loved watering hole and the inspiration for a famous scene in his *Faust* (▷ 33).

THOMASKIRCHE

• Thomaskirchhof 18, 04109 Leipzig ☎ 0341 9602855 ⏰ Daily

The church of St. Thomas goes back to the early 13th century, though the present structure dates largely from a Gothic rebuilding in the 15th century. But the building is less famous for its architecture than for its music. The angelic voices of the Thomaner, the boys of its choir, were to be heard as long ago as the 13th century. In 1723, they acquired a new choirmaster, none other than Johann Sebastian Bach, who as 'the cantor of cantors' directed the church's music until his death in 1750. He is buried inside the church, and his statue outside is a focal point for all visitors to Leipzig. The Thomaner usually sing at services on Fridays at 6pm and Saturdays at 3pm (▷ 269). Bach was a frequent visitor to one of the houses opposite, the house of his great friend and godfather to his children, Georg Heinrich Bose. Today the Bosehaus contains a Bach archive and a Bach Museum (daily 10–5), though none of the original furnishings have been preserved.

NIKOLAIKIRCHE

• Nikolaikirchhof 3, 04109 Leipzig ☎ 0341 9605270 ⏰ Daily

With the simple sign *Offen für Alle* (Open to all) still hanging at its door, the Church of St. Nicholas is indissolubly linked to the events of late 1989, when it was a focal point of the non-violent revolution which toppled the GDR's regime. Prayers for peace had been said here since 1981, and gradually the church became a place for those whose voices could not otherwise be heard in that oppressive society. On 9 October 1989, the 2,000 people leaving the church were greeted by tens of thousands of candle-holding demonstrators in the streets outside. In the face of this fearlessness, police and troops withdrew; a month later the regime opened the Berlin Wall.

ZEITGESCHICHTLICHES FORUM
• Grimmaische Strasse 6, 04109 Leipzig ☎ 0341 22200 🕐 Tue–Fri 9–6, Sat, Sun 10–6 💷 Free

'Mr Gorbachev, open this gate'. Spoken in the shade of Berlin's Brandenburg Gate when he visited Berlin in 1987, these words of the late US President Ronald Reagan greet visitors as they enter the Forum of Contemporary History. Other voices eerily evoke decades of Cold War and the division of Germany, among them John Kennedy's, with his famous cry of 'Ich bin ein Berliner!'. A branch of the German History Museum in Bonn, the Forum brings to vivid life the realities of existence in eastern Germany under the dictatorship of the Socialist Unity Party, and is designed to appeal to visitors from abroad as well as to the local schoolchildren for whom it forms part of the curriculum. A wealth of posters, photographs, newsreels, uniforms and other exhibits recall key events like the popular uprising of 1953 and the regime's eventual collapse in 1989, but there are plenty of reminders of the culture of everyday life, like a prominently displayed Trabant, painted bright purple.

VÖLKERSCHLACHTDENKMAL
• Prager Strasse, 04299 Leipzig ☎ 0341 878 0471 🕐 Apr–end Oct daily 10–6, Nov–end Mar daily 10–4 💷 Adult €3, child €2 🅿

The colossal granite-clad memorial to the Battle of Nations of 1813 looms like a man-made mountain over Leipzig's southeastern suburbs. Its intimidating presence is accentuated by the vast rectangular pool at its foot, by the broad flights of steps by which it must be approached and by the gigantic figures gracing the summit. A dome soars an astonishing 68m (223ft) above the crypt. The monument was completed in 1913 on the one hundredth anniversary of the defeat of Napoleon by an alliance of mostly German armies. The battle, which raged around Leipzig for several days in mid-October 1813, was the biggest and bloodiest hitherto experienced in Europe, involving half a million soldiers. With its glorification of death in battle, the monument represents the militaristic values that were to plunge Europe into the deadliest conflict of all time a mere year later. Nowadays, it functions mainly as a tourist attraction, offering a splendid panorama over Leipzig from its summit.

BACKGROUND

Leipzig's international profile traditionally depended on the markets and trade fairs whose origins go back to the 12th century, and perhaps even further. But the city has long played a key role in Germany's intellectual and cultural life. The book trade developed early, and many of the country's foremost publishers settled here. Musical life thrived, and many of the great masters of German music worked here, foremost among them Johann Sebastian Bach, Felix Mendelssohn and Robert Schumann. Even in GDR times, the famous Gewandhaus orchestra flourished under the inspired leadership of Kurt Masur. The university, founded in 1409, is only one of a number of academic institutions maintaining Leipzig's reputation as a hub of scientific achievement. While Dresden's life was focused on a royal court, Leipzig's depended on its citizens, whose sense of responsibility put the city in the vanguard of the movement that led to the fall of the Communist regime in 1989.

MUSEUM DER BILDENDEN KÜNSTE
• Katharinenstrasse 10, 04109 Leipzig ☎ 0341 216990 🕐 Tue, Thu and Sun 10–6, Wed 12–8

Leipzig boasts one of the finest art collections in Saxony, particularly strong in Old Masters and in German art of the 19th century, as well as in graphic works and sculpture. The collections are currently in store, waiting to move to a new home.

MUSEUM IN DER RUNDEN ECKE
• Dittrichring 24, 04109 Leipzig ☎ 0341 961 2443 🕐 Daily 10–6 💷 Free

In December 1989, citizens stormed the headquarters of the Leipzig branch of the GDR's secret police (the Stasi), determined to preserve the vast records its occupants were busy shredding. The building now houses a compelling exhibition, Power and Banality, revealing the Communist regime's neurotic obsession with keeping track of everything about the public and private lives of its subjects, down to bottling their personal smells.

RUSSISCHE KIRCHE
• Philipp-Rosenthal-Strasse 51a, 04103 Leipzig ☎ 0341 878 1453 💷 60c

This extraordinary Russian Orthodox church, with its single tower (55mm/180ft high) and richly decorated interior, would dominate the landscape of southeastern Leipzig were it not for the overwhelming presence of the Völkerschlachtdenkmal not far away. The church was built in memory of the 22,000 Russian soldiers who fell in the 1813 Battle of the Nations.

Modern bronze sculpture (far left) in the rebuilt Altstadt. This Smart Car (below) helps police get around Leipzig's narrow streets

Meissen is famous foremost for its porcelain (top), but the town itself (above) is also worth visiting

RATINGS

Historic interest	●●●●
Cultural interest	●●●●
Specialist shopping	●●●●●

TIP

● For the classic view of castle and cathedral looking imperiously down on the town from their crag, cross the bridge over the Elbe to the far bank.

BASICS

✚ 435 J9 ℹ Meissen Tourist Information, Markt 3, 01662 Meissen, tel 03521 41940; Apr–end Oct Mon–Fri 10–6, Sat, Sun 10–4; Nov, Dec, Feb, Mar Mon–Fri 10–5, Sat 10–3; Jan Mon–Fri 10–5
www.touristinfo-meissen.de

MEISSEN

Well-preserved historic city, with a castle and cathedral overlooking the River Elbe. The home of Meissen porcelain.

Founded as a bulwark against the Slavs almost 1,100 years ago, Meissen still presents a defiant image of castle and cathedral on their rocky spur. Its red roofs are huddled defensively at the foot of the citadel, and, as one of eastern Germany's best preserved little cities, its streets, squares and flights of steps are well worth exploring for their wealth of fine old buildings. But it is above all the reputation of its porcelain that makes Meissen an essential destination for visitors to this part of Saxony.

THE FIRST AND FINEST PORCELAIN

In the early 18th century, the court alchemist Johann Friedrich Böttger seemed on the point of cracking the age-old problem of how to convert base metal into gold. His master, Augustus the Strong, locked him up with instructions to get on the job or else. Unsurprisingly, the wretched Böttger failed to produce gold, but his efforts yielded something almost as valuable and aesthetically far more pleasing— fine porcelain, up to then an impenetrable Oriental enigma. Determined to keep the process secret, Augustus decreed that production of porcelain should only take place within the secure walls of Meissen's citadel. It was only in 1863 that the factory moved to its present valley site on the edge of the town centre. Nowadays it's popular with all lovers of fine porcelain; you can view all the stages of production in the course of expertly guided tours.

THE BURGBERG

This is the name given to the crag crowned by the castle and cathedral. Regarded as the cradle of the Saxon state, there was a fortress here from the earliest times, but the present stronghold dates mostly from the late 15th or early 16th century. Following the removal of the porcelain works in 1863, the castle was given a thorough make-over, the aim being to give it what the 19th century considered to be an authentically medieval appearance. The walls were covered with paintings of heroic deeds from the Germanic past in an exaggerated style that soon went out of fashion, but that today is seen as historic in its own right. The lovely Gothic cathedral was begun in 1250 on the site of a Romanesque predecessor, and only completed in 1908, when the twin western towers were added.

A peaceful inner courtyard at Mühlhausen's town hall

Naumberg's town walls surround its historic heart

Quedlinburg's crest on the door of the town hall

MÜHLHAUSEN

⊞ 438 F8 ℹ Tourist-Information, Ratsstrasse 20, 99974 Mühlhausen, tel 03601 452321; May–end Oct Mon–Fri 9–5, Sat 10–2; Nov–end Apr Mon–Fri 9–5
www.muehlhausen.de

Seen from afar, miraculously preserved Mühlhausen still looks much as it did in the Middle Ages, with church spires rising over a ring of medieval walls and the red rooftops of patrician mansions and humbler homes. Although dominated by kings and emperors in its early days, by the 13th century the town had won a degree of independence that was to express itself 200 years later in enthusiastic embrace of the radical ideas of the fiery Protestant preacher Thomas Müntzer, bitter opponent of Martin Luther (▷ 31). Under Müntzer's leadership, the town became the focus of the Peasants' Revolt of 1523–25, but Müntzer himself ended badly; after leading his followers to defeat, he was dragged back to Mühlhausen, tortured and executed. Inevitably, the GDR acclaimed him as a pioneer of Socialism, even renaming the town Thomas-Müntzer-Stadt after him. You can find out more about him and the Peasants' War in the Kornmarktkirche (Tue–Sun 10–4.30). But even if you have little interest you should interrupt your stroll through old streets and alleyways and look into the church where he preached, the lovely Marienkirche (daily 10–5).

NAUMBURG

⊞ 434 G8 ℹ Tourist und Tagungsservice, Markt 6, 06618 Naumburg, tel 03445 201614; Apr– end Oct Mon–Fri 9–6, Sat 9–4, Sun 10–1; Mar, Nov, Dec Mon–Fri 9–6, Sat 9–2 🚆 Naumburg
www.naumburg-tourismus.de

Overlooking the meeting point of the rivers Saale and Unstrut, this thousand-year-old little city is a real surprise: Europe's northern-most wine-growing area. The climate is dry, the soil good and the steep slopes of the river-banks act as a suntrap as well as creating an unusually attractive landscape, though you will have to decide for yourself whether it quite justifies the epithet of 'Tuscany of the North'.

Visitors come this way not just for wine, but for art and architecture. Naumburg's attractive old streets and squares form the setting for one of Germany's great treasures: its cathedral (Apr–end Sep Mon–Sat 9–6, Sun 12–6; Mar, Oct till 5; Jan, Feb, Nov, Dec till 4), whose four-towered silhouette is recognizable from far away. Harmoniously combining Romanesque with Gothic, it contains an outstanding array of sculpture, much of it far in advance of its time. There are poignant scenes of Christ's Passion, but the outstanding figures are those of Margrave Ekkehardt and his consort Uta, seen by generations of Germans as embodying the ideals of medieval chivalry.

POTSDAM

See pages 168–173.

QUEDLINBURG

⊞ 434 G7 ℹ Tourist Information, Markt 2, 06484 Quedlinburg, tel 03946 905624/25; Apr–end Sep Mon–Fri 9–7, Sat 10–4, Sun 10–3; Oct–end Mar Mon–Fri 9.30–6, Sat 10–2
www.quedlinburg.info

Little Quedlinburg is perhaps the place where you come closest to Germany's deepest past, most of all in the Burgberg, the citadel of the country's earliest kings. Here, in the 10th-century crypt of St. Servatius' church, are the tombs of King Heinrich I and his wife, Mathilde, as well as the effigies of the abbesses who ruled the town for centuries. Gold and ivory objects and rare tapestries make the church's treasury one of Germany's richest. The town itself, clustered beneath the citadel, is an unparalleled array of historic stone and timber-framed houses, just one of the reasons Quedlinburg was given Unesco World Heritage Status in 1994. Some of the best buildings are in Breite Strasse and Steinweg, but almost every street and lane in the Altstadt is worth exploring. The Markt has a Renaissance town hall and customary statue of the knight Roland, guardian of civic liberties. **Don't miss** The corner known as the Finkenherd is particularly picturesque.

Musicians statue in Quedlinburg

Potsdam

●

**Come here to see art and architecture embodying the spirit of
Prussia and Imperial Germany.
The German 'Hollywood' is an essential complement to a stay in Berlin.**

*The theatrical entrance to
Schloss Sanssouci*

*A cloudless sky, seen through the roof of the gazebo, means a
great opportunity for exploring Potsdam's parks and gardens*

RATINGS	
Historic interest	● ● ● ● ○
Cultural interest	● ● ● ○
Photo stops	● ● ● ○

TIPS

● An economic alternative to a
guided tour around Sanssouci
is the very useful 695 bus,
which connects Potsdam's railway station with several points
around the edge of the park
(Schloss Sanssouci, Orangerie,
Drachenhaus, Neues Palais).
Hop on and off at will, using
the *Tageskarte*/Day Ticket
(unless you already have an
ABC Berlin regional public
transportation ticket, which
is also valid for travel in
Potsdam).
● Use your *Tageskarte* to visit
Schloss Cecilienhof. Take Tram
90 or 92 to the Stadthaus stop
in Friedrich-Ebert-Strasse,
where you change to Bus 692,
getting off at the Schloss
Cecilienhof stop. From
Cecilienhof walk back to the
town along the lakeside, then
through the Dutch Quarter.

SEEING POTSDAM

The capital of the *Land* of Brandenburg, Potsdam is to Berlin
what Versailles is to Paris: a small town to the west of the
metropolis transformed by successive monarchs into their idea of
an earthly paradise. The town sits in the middle of a lavishly landscaped realm of lakes, parks and gardens—a superlative setting
for an extraordinary array of edifices, ranging from pompous
palaces with sumptuous interiors to fanciful garden follies.
  Potsdam is the most popular day trip from Berlin, easily
reached by main-line rail, S-Bahn, bus and tram, and, most
appealingly, by pleasure steamer. Once in Potsdam, consider
carefully what you want to see and decide on priorities. The town
is not large, but parks, gardens and palaces are quite widely
separated (it is 6km/4 miles from the Neues Palais in the west to
Cecilienhof in the east) and you would need several days to take
in everything of note.
  Babelsberg, a suburb of Potsdam, enjoys worldwide fame
as Germany's Hollywood, and was particularly prominent in
the silent movie era of the 1920s. A variety of theme-park
experiences have made Filmstadt Babelsberg one of Germany's
most popular visitor attractions (▷ 270).

HIGHLIGHTS

SCHLOSS SANSSOUCI

• Park Sanssouci, 14469 Potsdam ☎ 0331 969 4190 ◷ Apr–end Oct Tue–Sun 9–5;
Nov–end Mar Tue–Sun 9–4 🎫 Adult €8, child €5 by guided tour only
Crowning a terraced hillside, Friedrich the Great's summer retreat
seems a modest affair, a single-storey building topped by a shallow
central dome. Nevertheless, it is one of the supreme achievements of
18th-century German architecture, a rococo jewel based on
Friedrich's own designs, which he commanded his court architect,
Knobelsdorff, to follow scrupulously. The King was an impatient client,
and work was completed quickly; beginning in 1744, the terraces
were laid out and planted with fruit trees and vines, while the palace
itself was finished by 1746.

The best approach to the palace is from the park, up the splendid flight of steps in the middle of the terraces. The light-hearted tone desired by the King is set by the lively expressions and attitudes of the caryatids holding up the cornice, no doubt a reference to the wine produced by the terrace grapes. Frederick's guests could saunter in and out of the palace through the doors beneath the dome, but today's visitors must go round the building and enter it from the colonnaded courtyard to the north. The guided tour leads through a succession of sumptuously decorated rooms that formed the setting for the monarch's private pleasures, principally music-making (he was a proficient flautist) and learned conversation with literary companions and other intellectuals. Among these was Voltaire, whom Friedrich hoped to persuade to stay here as his court philosopher. Despite all inducements, the Frenchman declined, and the affronted

BASICS
✚ 435 J6 ℹ Friedrich-Ebert-Strasse 5, 14467 Potsdam, tel 0331 275580; Apr–end Oct Mon–Fri 9–8, Sat 9–6, Sun 9–4; Nov–end Mar Mon–Fri 10–6, Sat, Sun 10–2
🚉 Potsdam
www.potsdam.de

For information about Potsdam's palaces and parks
ℹ Besucherzentrum, An der Orangerie 1, 14469 Potsdam, tel 0331 9694202; Mar–end Oct daily 8.30–5; Nov–end Feb 9–4

King took his revenge by decorating the guest room assigned to him with playful figures of apes and parrots. Other interiors include the circular Library with its collection of mostly French books, the gorgeous Marble Hall beneath the dome and the Concert Room. This riotous confection of rococo gilt and mirrors is in a famous painting by Adolf von Menzel of Friedrich entertaining his guests in his role as flautist.

PARK SANSSOUCI
The grand staircase and vineyard terraces making such a splendid formal approach to Schloss Sanssouci are a mere fragment of a vast park extending westward from the edge of the town centre to Friedrich's other, far larger residence, the Neues Palais. The park is gloriously varied, both in terms of buildings and landscape, a true reflection of how the tastes of Prussia's rulers changed over two centuries. It's a good idea to decide on priorities before setting out, as there is more than enough in the park to keep you busy for days on end. You can explore the parkland on either side of the long avenue and discover some of the fascinating buildings set among the generous greenery.

If you have enough time, follow the circular walk beginning at Schloss Sanssouci, taking in most of the main features of the park. Flanking the Schloss is a pair of structures. To the east the Bildergalerie of 1764 (mid-May to mid-Oct Tue–Sun 10–5),

The observatory at Albert Einstein Science Park (above). Dutch-style houses in the Holländisches Viertel (far left). The Glienicker Brücke (middle left).

BRIDGES
Of the seven bridges connecting the island on which Potsdam is built to the outside world, the Glienicker Brücke, marking the boundary with Berlin, is the best known. It carries what was once Reichsstrasse (Imperial Highway) No.1, which linked Aachen on the Belgian border to far-off Memel (now Klaipeda in Lithuania) in the east. As the Cold War boundary between West Berlin and the German Democratic Republic, it was closed to all but Allied military vehicles, making its then name, 'The Bridge of Unity' particularly ironic. On more than one occasion, the green-painted steel span was the scene of tense exchanges of valuable prisoners, the most sensational being that in 1962 of the American U2 pilot Gary Powers for the Soviet spy Rudolf Abel.

Park Schloss (left)

THE SIGHTS

ALEXANDROWKA
• Russische Kolonie Alexandrowka
Contrasting with Potsdam's prevailing Classical architecture is this charming group of Russian timber houses, authentic copies of those used to house Russian prisoners from the Napoleonic wars. They were formed into a choir by King Friedrich Wilhelm III. The choristers also had a Russian-style place of worship, the onion-domed Alexander Newski Chapel.

Friedrich the Great's grandiose Neues Palais (above)
Sunburst detail on the gazebo (opposite)

BELVEDERE AUF DEM PFINGSTBERG
• Pfingstberg ☎ 0331 292468
🕐 Jun–end Aug daily 10–8; Apr, May, Sep daily 10–6; Oct daily 10–4; Nov, Mar Sat, Sun 10–4 💶 Adult €3.50, child €2.50
Now rescued from the decay to which Communism had consigned it, the monumental Roman-style Belvedere of 1863 provides one of the best views over Potsdam's surroundings.

Germany's first purpose-built picture gallery, housing the royal collection of fine Old Master paintings. To the west the Neue Kammern, originally an orangery, then a royal guest house. Farther west, the last edifice to be built in the park is the Neue Orangerie of 1864, still used to nurse tender plants through the winter months. Farther west still on the high ground is the pagoda-like Drachenhaus, then the lovely rotunda of the Belvedere, built to offer a prospect over the whole area. After a pause to admire the main façade of the immense Neues Palais, you can continue through the parkland south of the main axis, where you will find two of the park's most intriguing structures. Schloss Charlottenhof was designed in 1826 in the form of an Italian Renaissance villa by the celebrated Berlin architect Karl Friedrich Schinkel as a summer palace for Crown Prince Friedrich Wilhelm IV. Nearby are the Roman Baths, originally a gardener's residence, another attempt by Schinkel to implant the spirit of Italy in the heart of Prussia. But perhaps the most appealing of all the buildings in the park is the Chinesisches Haus of 1754 (mid-May to mid-Oct Tue–Sun 10–5), a fantastical tent-like structure that exemplifies the 18th century European passion for all things Chinese and which was used by Friedrich to show off his porcelain collection. Gilded figures sit and stand around the building, whose spreading roof is supported by columns in the form of palm trees. The circular lantern rising from the roof is topped by another gilded figure, a mandarin clutching a parasol. Inside, look up at the theatrically painted ceiling to see Chinese faces grinning down at you from the balcony.

NEUES PALAIS
• Park Sanssouci, 14469 Potsdam ☎ 0331 969 4255 🕐 Apr–end Oct Sat–Thu 9–5; Nov–end Mar Sat–Thu 9–4 💶 Apr–end Oct adult €5, child €4 (€1 extra with guided tour); Nov–end Mar adult €5, child €4 (only by guided tour)
What a contrast between little Schloss Sanssouci and this colossal edifice! By far the largest building in the park, it was completed in 1768 to celebrate Friedrich the Great's triumphs in the Seven Years War and proclaim Prussia's new-found status as one of the great powers of Europe, tasks it fulfils with overwhelming confidence. Behind the immensely long main façade with its cupola and its army of balustrade statues, there are some 200 rooms, many of them apartments originally intended to house Friedrich's guests. In addition, there is a superb baroque theatre and a number of richly ornamented cermonial halls and salons, among them the Marble Gallery and the Marble Hall with its magnificent inlaid floor. The most extravagant interior however is the Grotto Hall; connecting palace to park, it is decorated with a mix of minerals, fossils, shells, glass and stonework. On the far side of the palace, the west front consists of two wings partly enclosing a spacious courtyard and facing the so-called Communs, two sizeable blocks linked by a colonnade which were built to house the palace's numerous staff.

NEUER GARTEN AND MARBLE PALACE
Potsdam's extensive 'New Garden' was laid out in the last years of the 18th century as a setting for the Marble Palace, the summer residence of Crown Prince Friedrich Wilhelm. Eager to catch up on the latest fashions in landscaping, the Prince employed the garden designer Johann August Eyserbeck, fresh from working on the innovative English-style park at Wörlitz. The Neuer Garten is a lovely landscape, benefiting enormously from its lakeside setting, with cleverly contrived views across the water to other eye-catching features, such as the mock castle on Peacock Island far to the northeast. As at Sanssouci, the park is enhanced by a number of fanciful follies and other structures; they include a Gothic Library marking the boundary between town and park, a wonderful neo-Egyptian Orangerie, a splendid stone Pyramid, which served as an icehouse, and a group of gabled brick buildings in Dutch style for retainers.

BRANDENBURGER TOR
• Am Luisenplatz

Potsdam has a varied collection of city gates, but this is the most impressive. A triumphal arch, built on the orders of Friedrich the Great in 1770, it is actually older, though less famous, than Berlin's Brandenburg Gate, and forms a satisfying terminal feature to one of the city's main shopping streets, Brandenburger Strasse.

The Marble Palace itself is a modest neoclassical red-brick rectangle projecting out into the waters of the Heiliger See. It soon proved far too small for the Crown Prince and his family, and side wings were quickly added. It suffered bomb damage in 1945 and was ill-treated in GDR times, when it was used as the Museum of the People's Army. Its interior of lovely wall-paintings and gorgeous floors has now been restored.

SCHLOSS CECILIENHOF
• Neuer Garten, Potsdam ☎ 0331 969 4244 ◉ Apr–end Oct Tue–Sun 9–5; Nov–end Mar Tue–Sun 9–4 ◉ Apr–end Oct adult €4, child €3 (€1 extra with guided tour); Nov–end Mar adult €4, child €3 (by guided tour only)

The New Garden's main attraction is Schloss Cecilienhof, built for Crown Prince Wilhelm, Kaiser Wilhelm II's son. It is an extraordinary

Bacchanalian figures on the façade of Schloss Sanssouci, watching over the vines at the front of the palace

Nikolaikirche and the Altes Rathaus in Potsdam

THE SIGHTS

DAMPFMASCHINENHAUS
• Breite Strasse 28, 14467 Potsdam ☎ 0331 969 4248 ◉ Mid-May to mid-Oct Sat, Sun 10–7 ◉ Adult €2, child €1.50 (by guided tour only)

The answer to the problem of providing water to feed the fountains of Sanssouci, this lakeside pumping station, disguised as a mosque, is one of the city's most fanciful structures. Its tall tower was not built to call the faithful to prayer but to conceal the chimney serving the steam engine in the boiler hall.

EINSTEINTURM
• Wissenschaftspark Albert Einstein, Albert-Einstein-Strasse, 14473 Potsdam ☎ 0331 2880 ◉ Admission by guided tour only (tel 0331 291741)

An icon of modern architecture, and more a piece of expressionist sculpture than a functional building, the Einstein Tower was built in 1924 by Erich Mendelssohn to house equipment investigating the Theory of Relativity, and is still in use today.

building, an early 20th-century reproduction of a half-timbered English Tudor manor house, all gables, steep roofs and a skyline of brick chimneys (most of which are purely decorative). It was completed in 1917, in the middle of World War I, a time when German admiration for things English was hardly at its height. At the end of the next war, in the summer of 1945, Cecilienhof was the setting for the Potsdam Conference, when the Big Three, US President Harry S. Truman, Soviet Political Leader Joseph Stalin and British Prime Minister Winston Churchill (later succeeded by Clement Attlee) met to shape the fate of the postwar world. The panelled interior has many mementos of their deliberations. The GDR regime turned Cecilienhof into a luxury hotel, a role it continues to fulfil, playing host to eminent guests such as former American president George H. W. Bush.

EINSTEINTURM

ALTER MARKT
Despite the disappearance of some of the buildings that once surrounded it, the Old Market is still the place where Potsdam presents itself to its public. The most prominent building is the Nikolaikirche (Tue–Sat 10–5, Sun 11.30–5, Mon 2–5) with its portico, corner

towers and its great dome. Begun in 1826, the church was a pet project of Friedrich Wilhelm IV while still Crown Prince; his stingy father, King William III, refused to release money for the construction of the dome, and the building had to make do with an undistinguished flat roof until the old King passed away. Flanking St. Nicholas's to the east is the baroque Altes Rathaus, Potsdam's old city hall, built in 1755 on the orders of Friedrich the Great, its tower topped by a gilded figure of Atlas. To the west is a huge and undistinguished megastructure of the 1970s, housing a variety of offices and institutions, including the city's tourist information centre, while to the south…is a gap, only partly filled by the recently reconstructed Fortuna Portal. This is a fragment of the mostly 18th-century Stadtschloss (City Castle), which once dominated the square, and indeed Potsdam itself. The principal Potsdam residence of Prussian kings, it was laid out around a great

MORE TO SEE

FILM-MUSEUM

✉ Marstall am Lustgarten, 14467 Potsdam ☎ 0331 271810

🕐 Daily 10–6 💶 €1–5 (depending on exhibitions)

While the Filmstadt in the suburb of Babelsberg provides cinematic experiences designed to appeal to all ages (▷ 270), the Film Museum in the stables pays serious tribute to German cinema, with displays, costumes, posters and clips from classic films.

THE SIGHTS

courtyard, but fell victim first to World War II bombing, then to the whims of GDR city planners, who considered it an unwanted symbol of Prussian militarism and demolished what was left of it in 1959.

This golden griffin marks the entrance to Schloss Klein Glienicke, near Babelsberg

BACKGROUND

Potsdam celebrated its thousandth anniversary in 1993, but its rise to royal fame really began after 1640, during the reign of the Great Elector, at a time when Prussia had been devastated by the Thirty Years War. He revived the fortunes of his realm by bringing in industrious immigrants from France and the Netherlands. His successors extended the city, making it their preferred residence after Berlin, not least because of its appealing location among lakes and woods rich in fish and game. As Prussia rose to European eminence as a military power in the 18th century, Potsdam took on the character of a garrison town, its citizens obliged to provide lodgings for the soldiers. More Dutch migrants arrived in the reign of the Soldier King, Friedrich Wilhelm I, who accommodated them in the charming brick-built houses of the Holländisches Viertel (Dutch Quarter). But the beautification of the town and its surroundings really began in the mid-18th century under his son, Friedrich the Great, who built the palaces and laid out the parkland of Sanssouci. In the first decades of the 19th century, Friedrich's successors added to his vision, enlisting the expertise of designers such as architect Karl Friedrich Schinkel and the great landscape architect, Peter Joseph Lenné.

Under both Nazism and Communism, the city was fated to continue its symbolic role in the nation's life. On his accession to power in 1933, Hitler cosied up to Germany's military aristocracy with elaborate ceremonies focused around the Garrison Church. The GDR took a negative view of Potsdam's superlative heritage, allowing much of it to moulder away or deliberating demolishing buildings like the Stadtschloss.

A scenic river view (above)

*The Königstein fortress (top)
dominates the landscape*

RATINGS	
Good for kids	● ● ●
Photo stops	● ● ● ● ●
Walkability	● ● ●

BASICS

✚ 435 K9
ℹ Nationalparkhaus Sächsische
Schweiz, Dresdener Strasse 2B, 01814
Bad Schandau, tel 035022 50230
🕐 Apr–end Oct daily 9–6; Nov–end
Mar daily 9–5
www.lanu.org

TIP

● The Elbe Sandstone
Mountains continue across the
border into the Czech
Republic, where they are
known as Bohemian
Switzerland. You can easily
make day trips, either by
steamer or by train, usually as
far as the town of Děčín
(Tetschen in German).

SÄCHSISCHE SCHWEIZ (SAXON SWITZERLAND)

This is the most spectacular scenery in Saxony: A gloriously wooded
sandstone upland through which the River Elbe has carved a winding
course between Dresden and the border with the Czech Republic.
The sandstone has been eroded into cliffs and ravines, and sculpted
into fantastical shapes, including pinnacles, stacks, towers and natural
bridges. In the past, few ventured deep into the Elbe Sandstone
Mountains except for woodmen and villagers seeking refuge in time
of war. But in the late 18th century, the area's picturesque qualities
were discovered by a pair of landscape painters from Switzerland
(hence its popular name), as well as by Romantic artists like Caspar
David Friedrich (1774–1840).

PIRNA AND KÖNIGSTEIN
Beneath its fortress, the old town of Pirna is the natural gateway to
the area. The Markt remains almost as it was portrayed in a painting
of 1755 by Canaletto. St. Marien's, the town's parish church, is a hall-
church, which has particularly fine vaulting.
   One of the most distinctive features of Saxon Switzerland is its table
mountains—isolated massifs rising sheer from the surrounding countryside. One of the most spectacular, the Königstein, had its already
formidable natural defences strengthened in the late 16th century by
the addition of walls, ramparts and gateways, making it the strongest
fortress in Germany (daily from 9).

BAD SCHANDAU AND THE BASTEI
Ever since visitors started coming to the area, the little riverside spa
town of Bad Schandau has been a popular destination. Schandau has
a wonderful open-air elevator that whisks 10 people at a time up to a
high viewpoint, and also a rustic tramway running along the picturesque Kirnitzsch valley to the Lichtenhain waterfall.
   Far and away the best known feature of Saxon Switzerland is the
Bastei (Bastion), where a sheer cliff rises 190m (623ft) from the
river. The spectacular rock formations here have attracted crowds of
visitors ever since refreshment huts were built on the summit in
1826. Since then a network of paths, catwalks and bridges has been
laid out, making it a simple matter for everyone to experience this
weird world without suffering unduly from vertigo. And the refreshment huts have long since been replaced by a smart hotel, cafés
and a panoramic restaurant.

Take to the water to enjoy the Spreewald

Trabants as far as the eye can see, at Automobilmuseum 'August Horch' in Zwickau

THE SPREEWALD

435 K8 Spreewald-Touristinformation Lübbenau e.V., Ehm-Welk-Strasse 15, 03222 Lübbenau, tel 03542 3668
www.spreewald-online.de

Downstream from Cottbus, the River Spree divides into countless tree-shaded channels, a tranquil inland delta designated a Unesco Biosphere Reserve because of its extraordinarily diverse wildlife. The Spreewald is also home to some of the Sorb minority, whose ancestors cleared the once dense woodland to make a delightful mosaic of meadows, orchards and market gardens. The most famous crop is the gherkin, marinated in herbs to give it a special tang. Transport here is traditionally by punt, and there are some settlements still inaccessible by road; even the mail is delivered by boat. The appeal of the area to outsiders goes back a long way. It was discovered by Berlin artists and intellectuals early in the 19th century, and today it attracts millions, the majority of whom come to the little Spreewald capital of Lübbenau to enjoy a punt trip. Many of the villages have punt stations too, or you can avoid the crowds by walking or hiring a bicycle or canoe.

WEIMAR

See page 176.

WITTENBERG

434 H7 Wittenberg-Information, Schlossplatz 2, 06886 Lutherstadt Wittenberg, tel 03491 414848; Mar–end Oct Mon–Fri 9–6, Sat 10–3, Sun 11–4; Nov–end Feb Mon–Fri 10–4, Sat 10–2, Sun 11–3 L Wittenberg
www.wittenberg.de

This attractive small town on the River Elbe is also known as Lutherstadt Wittenberg: Of all the places that claim a connection with Martin Luther, this is the one most intimately associated with this leading figure of the Protestant Reformation. It was here Luther taught and preached, here in 1517 he nailed up his famous 95 theses denouncing church corruption, here he burned the papal bull condemning him, here he married and was buried. The central place of pilgrimage for Wittenberg's many visitors is the authentically furnished Lutherhaus (Apr–end Oct daily 9–6, Nov–end Mar Tue–Sun 10–5), with its interesting museum of the Reformation, but there are many other sights connected with the great man.

Wittenberg is also home to an attraction of a very different kind, a unique set of meticulously recreated interiors in the Haus der Geschichte (Tue–Fri 10–5, Sat, Sun 11–6) showing what everyday life was really like under Communism.

ZITTAU

435 K9 Tourist-Information Zittau, Rathaus, Markt 1, 02763 Zittau, tel 03583 752137/38; May–end Oct Mon–Fri 8–6, Sat 9–1, Sun 1–4; Nov–end Apr Mon–Fri 8–6, Sat 9–1
www.zittau.de

Separated from Poland only by the River Neisse, this attractive town once belonged to what is now the Czech Republic, the border with which is formed by the crest of the Zittauer Gebirge, the line of invitingly wooded hills a short distance to the south.

Zittau itself is not just a gateway to the hills but an atmospheric place of old streets, squares and fountains with more than a touch of Italy about it. For a fine overall view, climb the tower of the Johanneskirche (Apr–end Oct Mon–Fri 12–6, Sat, Sun 1–6; Nov–end Mar Mon–Fri 10–4.30, Sat 10–4) and meet the watchman who marks the passing time with a blast from his trumpet. In the Kirche zum Heiligen Geist hangs the town's greatest treasure, the Zittauer Fastentuch (Lenten Veil, Tue–Sun 10–5). Dating from 1472, the veil (8.2m high by 6.8m across) shows 90 biblical pictures painted directly onto the cloth, an achievement of medieval story-telling comparable to France's Bayeux Tapestry.

ZWICKAU

439 H9 Tourist Information Zwickau, Hauptstrasse 6, 08056 Zwickau, tel 0375 27259-10; Mon–Fri 9–6.30, Sat 10–4 Zwickau
www.kultur-z.de

A town inextricably identified with that icon of the GDR, the noisy, wobbly, smelly Trabant, would seem a place to be avoided. But don't be put off: Zwickau's recent fortunes may have been built on heavy industry, but its traditions go back centuries to the silver mines found in the wooded Erzgebirge/Ore Mountains to the south. The town itself was first mentioned as long ago as 1118. So as well as many handsome structures from the 19th and early 20th centuries, there are plenty of far older fine buildings, mainly around the central Markt and the cathedral close. A must for music-lovers is the rebuilt birthplace of the composer Robert Schumann (Tue–Sun 10–5), born here in 1810, while Zwickau's most fascinating museum is the well-stocked and newly reopened Automobilmuseum 'August Horch' (Tue–Thu 9–5, Sat, Sun 10–5) in the north of the town. It celebrates the name of the automobile pioneer who, in 1904, founded the works that turned out elegant limousines and classic racing cars as well as Audis, DKWs and, latterly, the Trabant.

The Buchenwald memorial
(above).
The garden at the Goethehaus
(top)

WEIMAR

**This miniature ducal capital city is suffused with the
atmosphere of the Golden Age of German culture.**

Otherwise just one of Germany's countless little courtly cities, Weimar
occupies a special place in German life because of the unique flower-
ing of literary and cultural life that took place here in the late 18th to
early 19th century. It was started by Duchess Anna Amalia, who
wanted to get the best education possible for her son. A search for
tutors led to an invitation to the 26-year-old Johann Wolfgang von
Goethe (1749–1832). The two young men got on well, forming an
enduring partnership; Goethe served under Carl August for the rest of
his life as a government official. His fame drew other luminaries here,
including the playwright Friedrich von Schiller (1759–1805). Weimar
acquired a Europe-wide reputation for intellectual excellence that
lasted throughout the 19th century. Franz Liszt (1811–86) became
musical director and Richard Wagner (1813–83) also visited. Henry
van der Velde (1863–1957) founded the school of art and design
that, under Walter Gropius (1883–1969), was to evolve into the
Bauhaus. In 1919, the government fled here from revolutionary chaos
in Berlin, and the town gave its name to the short-lived democratic
republic, destroyed by Hitler in 1933. By then, Weimar was a stronghold of Nazism, whose aversion to the left-leaning ideas of the
Bauhaus had forced the movement to relocate to Dessau.

RATINGS

Historic interest	●●●○
Cultural interest	●●●●○
Walkability	●●●○

BASICS

🔲 434 G9 ℹ️ Tourist-Information
Weimar, Markt 10, 99423 Weimar, tel
03643 24000; Apr–end Oct Mon–Fri
9.30–6, Sat, Sun 9.30–3; Nov–end Mar
Mon–Fri 10–6, Sat, Sun 10–2
🚆 Weimar
www.weimar.de

TIP

● A walking tour with an
English-speaking guide will
enormously enhance your
appreciation of the heritage of
this delightful little city.

THE GOLDEN AGE

Almost anywhere you wander through Weimar's streets and squares
will reveal something evoking the spirit of the town's Golden Age. The
famous statue of Goethe and Schiller in front of the Deutsches
Nationaltheater is a compulsory stop for every German visitor. Other
Goethe shrines include his main residence, the Goethehaus
(Apr–end Oct Tue–Sun 9–6; Nov–end Mar Tue–Sun 9–4), with a
fine modern museum that deals with the phenomenon of Weimar
Classicism. There's also Goethes Gartenhaus (Apr–end Oct daily
10–6; Nov–end Mar daily 10–4), an attractive building among the
greenery of the Park an der Ilm, which Goethe helped to landscape.

BUCHENWALD

Many visitors make the trip to the remains of Buchenwald concentration camp, 8km (5 miles) to the north of the town, where there are
museums and memorials evoking the camp's use under the Nazis, as
well as during the postwar Soviet occupation (Gedenkstätte Buchenwald, May–end Sep Tue–Sun 9.45–6; Oct–end Apr Tue–Sun 8.45–5).

MUNICH

Historic Munich is known as the beer capital of Germany. Visitors flock to the city's lively beer halls and annual *Oktoberfest*, but also to the world-class art galleries, magnificent palaces, Olympic stadium, impressive churches and the Englischer Garten, the largest city park in Europe.

THE SIGHTS

MAJOR SIGHTS

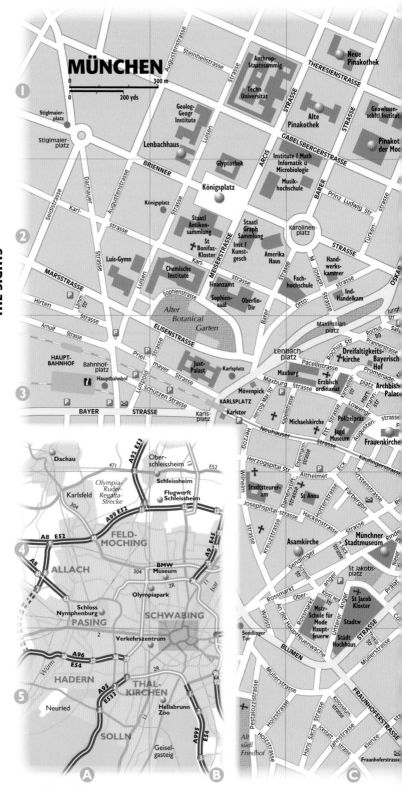

MÜNCHEN

0   300 m
0   200 yds

THE SIGHTS

178   **MUNICH**

Veterinär-strasse
Tierärztl Kliniken
British University
Schelling
strasse
Strasse
LUDWIG STRASSE
Ludwigs Kloster Ev Waisenhaus
Dolmetscher Institute
Kaulbachstrasse
Königinstrasse
Schwabinger Bach
Englischer Garten
Theresienstrasse
VHS
Staats-bibliotheken
Bayer Ob-Rechng-hof
Amalien
Fürstenstrasse
Rheinberger-strasse
Haupt-Staats-archiv
Schönfeld Strasse
Himmel-reich-strasse
Glückstr
Finanz-Min
K Döpfnerstr
VON-DER-TANN STRASSE
Landw-Min
Prinz-Carl-Palais
Haus der Kunst
F J STRAUSS RING
PRINZREGENTEN
Eisbach
Seeau Strasse
strasse
Galeriestrasse
elsbacher-platz
Innen-Min
Odeonsplatz
Theater Museum
Hofgarten
Pilotystr
Sigmundstr
STRASSE
Bruder Strasse
Unsöldstrasse
Wagmüllerstrasse
Wirt Min
Bayerisches Nationalmuseum
Lerchenfeld
Himbselstrasse
amira-platz
Odeonsplatz
Hofgarten
strasse
Christophstr
Liebigstrasse
St Anna Kloster
St Anna
Bez Fin Dir
LVA
OETTINGEN STRASSE
Theatiner
Kaiserhof Residenz
Residenz
Max Planck Institute
Theater im Marstall
Cuvilliés-theater
Marstallplatz
Marstallstrasse
SCHARNAGL RING
St Anna Platz
Lehel
Anna
St Anna
Triftstrasse
Tattenbachstr
Koch
Liebig-strasse
STRASSE
rasse
Joseph platz
National-theater
Perusastrasse
Maximilian
Wurzerstrasse
H Rudolph-strasse
Bürkleinstrasse
Reg v Oberbayern
Gewürzmühl
Pfar strasse
Bayers Yers Ka
STERN
WIDENMAYERSTRASSE
Schramm Strasse
Marienhof
Bayer Ld Amt ehem
Falkentstr
Pfisterstr
MAXIMILIANSTRASSE
MAXIMILIANBRÜCKE
Neues Rathaus
Alter Hof
Hofbräu-haus
Münz-strasse
Brauh-strasse
Neuturm str
Hildegardstrasse
WIMMER RING
Museum für Völkerkde
Knöbel strasse
Adelgrundenstrasse
Mariannstr
Alp Museum
Altes Rathaus
enplatz
Diener
Burgstrasse
Sparkassenstrasse
Ledererstr
Madlerbr
Hochbrückenstr
THOMAS
Stollberg
Marstall
Stollbergstr
Maximilan-anlagen
ualienmarkt
TAL
Küchlbäck-strasse
Dürnbräu-gasse
Marien Strasse
Herrnstrasse
Mannhardt Strasse
Thierschstrasse
Isar
Dreifalt-platz
Heiligestr
Radlsteg
Westenrieder Strasse
Isartor-platz
Pilug-strasse
ISARTOR
FRAUEN STRASSE
Zwinger Str
Rumfordstrasse
ZWEIBRÜCKEN-STRASSE
Liebherrstrasse
STEINSDORFSTRASSE
Länd
St Nik Volks
INNERE WIENER STRASSE
Preysingstrasse
Reichen-bach-platz
Kienze
Buttermelcherstrasse
Baaderstrasse
Baader-platz
Morassi Strasse
LUDWIGSBRÜCKE
Am Lilien
Semmer Str
Gasteig Zentrum Bibliotheken
eater
Europ-Patent-amt
Kohl strasse
Deut-Patent-u Markenamt Bundespatent-gericht
Forum d Technik (Planetarium)
ERHARDTSTRASSE
Boch brücke
Zenneck brücke
Zeppelinstrasse
Lilien strasse
Herbertstrasse
Rosenheimer Strasse
reichenbach
Corneliusstrasse
Deutsches Museum

D   E   F

MUNICH 179

Munich

✚ 182 A3 🛈 Hauptbahnhof, Bahnhofsplatz 2, 80331, tel 089 2339 6500; Mon–Fri 9–5 🚇 Hauptbahnhof
✚ 183 D4 🛈 Marienplatz, 80331, tel 089 2339 6500; Mon–Fri 10–8, Sat 10–4 🚇 Marienplatz

GETTING AROUND

● Munich has an underground/subway (U-Bahn), an overground railway (S-Bahn), trams and buses. For more details, look up www.mvv-muenchen.de.
● The München Welcome Card is valid for 1 or 3 days and allows you unlimited use of all public transportation, as well as discounts on tours and entry to attractions. Buy it anywhere that displays the München Welcome Card poster. The 1-day card costs €6.50; the 3-day card costs €16.
● The Partner Card is valid for up to 5 adults (2 children aged 6–14 count as one adult) and costs €11 for a 1-day card and €23.50 for a 3-day card.

Inside the Pinakothek der Moderne (above right). A statue at Schloss Nymphenburg (right). Munich's Rathaus (below)

SEEING MUNICH

Munich (München in German) is a thousand-year-old city that is extremely proud to be Bavarian. And while the traditional beer-and-*Lederhosen* image still exists, it doesn't reflect the city's world-class art galleries, Italian-designer-clad citizens and fashionable bars and restaurants. Two days is enough to get a taste of the city, but it would take you two weeks to get round all the galleries, museums, castles and other sights.

The best way to see Munich is on foot—many of the main attractions are within an area bounded by Odeonsplatz to the north, the old city gates of Isartor to the east, Sendlingertor to the south and Karlstor to the west. A good way to get your bearings is to stroll round the Old Town (Altstadt), following the walk on pages 310–311. If you have less time, take a bus tour (▷ 277).

The heart of the city is Marienplatz (▷ 193). Be there at 11am to see the famous *Glockenspiel* come to life. For great views, go up the tower of the Rathaus in Marienplatz, or climb the 300 steps to the top of Alter Peter, the tower of Peterskirche. This is Munich's oldest church and is between Marienplatz and the Viktualienmarkt. For the best views of the city and the surrounding area, head out to Olympiapark and take the elevator up the Olympiaturm (▷ 197) where, on a clear day, you can see as far as the Alps.

THE SIGHTS

BACKGROUND

In the 10th century, monks established a settlement on the banks of the River Isar, which became known as Munichen. The city's monastic origins are still evident in Munich's coat of arms, which depicts a monk.

In 1158, Heinrich der Löwe (Henry the Lion), the Duke of Saxony, took control of Bavaria. He ensured his own power over the growing city of München by destroying his rival's toll bridge and building his own nearby. A century later, Munich became the main residence of the Wittelsbach dynasty, and in 1505 the city became the capital of Bavaria.

From 1618 until 1648, during the Thirty Years War, Gustav Adolph of Sweden occupied the city. The statue of the Mariensäule was erected in Marienplatz to give thanks to God because the Swedes did not destroy the city during their occupation. In fact, Munich had to pay Sweden not to destroy the city.

In the first half of the 19th century, Ludwig I commissioned the construction of many classical buildings, such as those in Königsplatz, leading to Munich's alternative name of Athens-on-the-Isar. Many of these buildings have now been turned into museums, such as the Glyptothek (▷ 194).

The November Revolution of 1919 led to the last Wittelsbach ruler, Ludwig III, and his family fleeing the city in the middle of the night. Ludwig abdicated a few days later. Political unrest continued through the early 20th century, and in 1923, a young Adolf Hitler attempted to instigate a socialist revolution by storming a beer hall with armed troops. The *putsch* failed and Hitler spent the next year in prison, where he began writing *Mein Kampf* (*My Struggle*). After suffering heavy bomb damage during World War II, Munich was rebuilt and during the second half of the 20th century, it became the economic heart of Germany, with companies such as BMW and Siemens choosing the city for their headquarters. In the 21st century, construction of a new stadium is underway for the 2006 Football World Cup.

TIPS

● Be aware that many pavements (sidewalks) have a dividing line painted down the middle, with one half designated for pedestrians and the other half for cyclists. To rent a bicycle ▷ 277.
● Jaywalking (crossing the street without regard for traffic) is a crime in Germany and the citizens of Munich obey pedestrian crossing signals faithfully, even when there are no cars in sight. Do the same or you face prosecution.
● The easiest way to buy transportation tickets is from the ticket machines at stations. Remember to validate your ticket in the machine before you start your journey.

THE SIGHTS

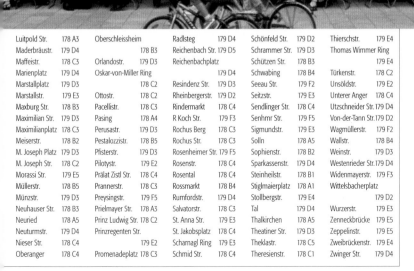

Who needs the sea? Surfing in the Englischer Garten

Alte Pinakothek

●

With more than 850 Old Masters, this huge gallery can compete with the Louvre, Prado, Uffizi and the Metropolitan as one of the oldest and most important galleries in the world.

The Lamentation of Christ (c1490) by Sandro Botticelli

Self-Portrait at the Age of 28 (1500) by Albrecht Durer

Something new: A bronze sculpture on the front lawns

The Melon Eaters *(1645)* by Bartolome Esteban Murillo (top)

SEEING ALTE PINAKOTHEK

The Alte Pinakothek is a magnificent gallery, with paintings by European artists from the 14th to the 18th centuries. The gallery is arranged by schools—for example Room IX on the Upper Floor contains works by 17th-century Dutch artists such as Rubens and van Dyck. The collection is of the same high quality as the Louvre in Paris or the Uffizi in Florence, but unlike those galleries, it is a manageable size and it is possible to see everything in one visit. That said, the gallery is large and there is a wealth of paintings, so make sure you leave enough time to see everything.

The entrance is set back from Theresienstrasse, opposite the entrance to the Neue Pinakothek. When you arrive, you can hand your coat into the cloakroom (free) and you should put any bags or umbrellas in one of the lockers to the left of the entrance (€2 deposit). Pick up the free floor plan, which is available in English, and the free audioguide, available in English, German, French or Italian. On Sundays, when entry to the gallery is free, the audioguide costs €4. There are no explanatory notes next to paintings, so if you want to know more about what you're looking at, buy a gallery guide from the shop beforehand or make use of the audioguide.

HIGHLIGHTS

RUBENS

The gallery houses the finest collection of paintings by the Flemish painter Peter Paul Rubens (1577–1640) in the world, so if you are a fan, you will not be disappointed. There's even a self-portrait of him and his second wife in the collection. One highlight (and one to steer the children past) is the graphic, horrific depiction of *The Fall of the Damned into Hell* (1620), showing the bodies of the damned being sucked down into the everlasting fire. *Drunken Silenus* (1616–17), with the clear warning against the perils of too much wine, shows a ruddy-faced Silenus staggering along amid mythical animals and not-so-allegorical bunches of grapes. Rubens' range and versatility as an artist are evident in *Lion Hunt* (1621), an allegory for life and death.

ITALIAN PAINTING FROM THE 15TH TO THE 16TH CENTURIES

Renaissance masters such as Raphael (1483–1520), Titian (1488–1576), Leonardo da Vinci (1452–1519) and Sandro Botticelli (1445–1510) are all well represented. Raphael's *Canigiani Holy Family* (1505–06) shows the Holy Family arranged in the form of a pyramid, with angels looking down from clouds at the top of the painting. These angels were painted over and were only uncovered in 1983. If you look closely at Venetian artist Jacopo Tintoretto's *Vulcan Surprising Venus and Mars* (1555), you'll see Mars, the mighty god of war, hiding under a table, trying to stop Venus' dog barking and revealing his presence.

17TH-CENTURY DUTCH PAINTING

This period is often referred to as the Golden Century of Dutch painting, as the success of the Dutch against the Spanish brought about an independent middle-class with a penchant for paintings, leading to a large body of work produced by Dutch painters in this period. One of the most well-known painters of this time is Rembrandt (1606–69) and the gallery has a self-portrait painted when the artist was only 23, as well as two of his paintings with biblical themes—*The Raising of the Cross* and *The Deposition*. Caravaggio fans will find something familiar in Gerrit von Honthorst's *Conviviality* (1622), as the artist uses the *chiaroscuro* effect made famous by the Italian artist in his picture of a morally dubious group enjoying too much wine. Portraits were also popular at this time and you can see the arrogant stance of Haarlem yarn-trader *Willem van Heythuysen*, painted by Frans Hals in about 1625.

MORE TO SEE

Italian art from the 18th century is represented in elegant scenes of Venice's Canal Grande, piazza San Marco and Rialto bridge by Venetian artists Canaletto (1697–1768) and Francesco Guardi (1712–93). There is only a fairly small collection of paintings by 16th- and 17th-century Spanish artists, although all of the major artists are represented—Juan Pantoja de la Cruz (1553–1608), Diego Rodriguez de Silva (1599–1660), El Greco (1541–1614) and Bartholomé Esteban Murillo (1618–82). Murillo's representations of children in *Urchins Playing Dice* (c.1675) and *Beggar Boys Eating Grapes and Melons* (c.1645) show suspiciously healthy-looking beggars.

In the section devoted to French art, rococo artist François Boucher's *Portrait of Madame de Pompadour* (1756) depicts Louis XV's mistress reclining in her boudoir in a sumptuous green dress decorated with countless pink roses. She is surrounded by objects that represent her interests (sheets of music, books and writing materials), and has her King Charles Spaniel by her tiny feet. By the same artist is the erotic *Reclining Girl* (1752), which shows one of Boucher's models, Louise O'Murphy, who also later became the mistress of Louis XV.

Work by one of Rubens' contemporaries, Sir Antony van Dyck (1599–1641), is in the Flemish section. There's van Dyck's self-portrait and a depiction of the Bible story from Daniel 13 of Susanna being surprised in her bath by two Elders. For an earlier, and entirely different, depiction of the same story, go to the Early German section for Albrecht Altdorfer's interpretation (1480–1538).

BACKGROUND

Many of the works in the Alte Pinakothek used to be in a much smaller gallery in the Residenz, but when the collection outgrew it, Ludwig I commissioned architect Leo von Klenze to design a new building to hold the collection. The gallery, which took 10 years to construct, was designed in the style of a Venetian Renaissance palace and was finished in 1836. The building itself was so well received that other galleries in Europe have used it as a model. Like many other buildings in Munich, it suffered extensive bomb damage in World War II, but restoration work in the 1950s and 1990s revived the gallery.

TIPS

● You can't take bags or umbrellas into the gallery so make sure you have €2 for the deposit for the locker.
● You are allowed to take photographs as long as you do not use a flash.
● There is free entry to the gallery on Sunday, so it can get crowded.

Two Satyrs *(detail)* by *Peter Paul Rubens*

THE SIGHTS

GALLERY GUIDE

GROUND FLOOR

Early German paintings, Brueghel paintings, temporary exhibitions, café and bookshop.

UPPER FLOOR

Dutch, German, Italian, Flemish, French and Spanish paintings from the 14th to 18th centuries.

Adoration of the Magi *by Hans Holbein the Elder*

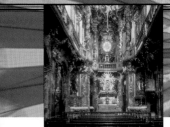

The lavishly decorated Asamkirche

Decorated panelling, in the Bayerisches Nationalmuseum

Cars of all ages are displayed at the BMW Museum

THE SIGHTS

ASAMKIRCHE

178 C4 • Sendlingerstrasse 62, 80331 Munich ◷ Daily 8–5.30
U-Bahn Sendlinger Tor ⬆ Free

The narrow (9m/29.5ft) façade of this church gives little hint of the magnificence inside. Before you go in, notice the unhewn rock on either side of the columns and, above the door, the statue of St. John Nepomuk, who gave the church its official name. The church is commonly known as Asamkirche after the Asam brothers who designed, built and decorated it between 1733 and 1746. The brothers' efforts have resulted in a lavish rococo interior with sculptures of angels and gold leaf that makes the walls gleam on a sunny day.

The church is only 30m (98ft) long, but is crammed with ornamentation. Look out for the ceiling fresco by Cosmas Damian Asam, the portraits of the brothers and the gallery altar, which portrays the Trinity.

Remember that the church is still a place of worship; when services are in progress, a sign is hung on the door asking you not to disturb those at prayer.

BAYERISCHES NATIONALMUSEUM

179 F2 • Prinzregentenstrasse 3, 80538 Munich ☎ 089 211 2401
◷ Tue, Wed, Fri–Sun 10–5, Thu 10–8
U-Bahn Lehel ▣ Tram 17, bus 53
⬆ Adult €3, under 18 free, free to all on Sundays ▦ ▢
www.bayerisches-nationalmuseum.de

The Bavarian National Museum is an art and cultural history museum with collections of arts and crafts from Bavaria and farther afield. When you arrive, you'll be asked to leave your bag and coat in the cloakroom (free), then you should pick up a plan of the museum, available in English. This is invaluable, as the museum has large collections spread over three floors. These include musical instruments, porcelain (including faience from Schloss Nymphenburg), suits of armour (look out for the child-size suit), traditional clothes, furniture, baroque and rococo tapestries, Gothic sculpture and paintings from the 13th century through to art nouveau.

The museum is well known for its collection of 18th- and 19th-century German and Italian cribs (*Krippe*). There are temporary exhibitions on the upper floor, with themes such as The World in Miniature (Bavarian toys). **Don't miss** The shop in the basement has beautiful hand-crafted Christmas decorations and ornaments with scenes of market stalls and people in traditional Bavarian costume.

BMW MUSEUM

178 B4 (inset) • Am Spiridon-Louis-Ring, Parkdeck, 80809 Munich ☎ 089 3822 3307 ◷ Apr–end Oct daily 10–10; Nov–end Mar daily 10–8
U3 to Olympiazentrum or Petuelring ▣ Tram 27 to Petuelring, bus 36 or 80 to Petuelring ⬆ Adult €2, child €1.50
www.bmw-mobiletradition.com

Within walking distance of the Olympiapark, this unusual building, shaped like four cylinders and designed by Karl Schwanzer in 1970, is the headquarters of BMW. The windowless silver building shaped like a bowl next to it is the BMW Museum, the most popular company museum in the country. The 'Time Horizons' exhibition traces the company's history and technological developments in the last 80 years through films and slide shows. There are plenty of shining models to admire, including rare and new sports cars and motorcycles. At the time of writing, the museum was closed for a major redesign and is not due to reopen until 2007. In the meantime, an

Heilige Barbara, a wonderful woodcarving from the Bayerisches Nationalmuseum

This large memorial dwarfs the old watchtower in the former concentration camp at Dachau

Oompah music and German beer at the Hofbräuhaus

interim exhibition is in place, its entrance behind the Olympiaturm (▷ 197).

DACHAU

✚ 178 A3 (inset) • Alte Römerstrasse 75, 85221 Dachau ☎ 08131 669970 🕐 Tue–Sun 9–5 🚇 🚌 S2 to Dachau, bus 724 or 726 to KZ-Gedenkstätte 💷 Free

Until 1933, Munchners used to come to the pretty town of Dachau to stroll along its picturesque cobbled streets and visit the Renaissance castle, but in that year, the Third Reich designated the town as the site of a concentration camp (KZ-Gedenkstätte). Between 1933 and 1945, around 200,000 people were interned here, and about 32,000 of them died. Several of the camp's buildings have been turned into a museum and memorial, which is at the eastern edge of the town.

The Renaissance castle, Schloss Dachau (Apr–end Sep Tue–Sun 9–6; Oct–end Mar Tue–Sun 10–4), on a hill above the town and the River Amper, was a summer residence of the Bavarian royal family, the Wittelsbachs. The castle is known for the exquisitely carved wood ceiling from the 16th century in the banqueting hall and for the views of Munich and the Alps from the terrace.

DEUTSCHES MUSEUM

See pages 186–191.

ENGLISCHER GARTEN

See page 192.

FRAUENKIRCHE

✚ 178 C3 • Frauenplatz 12, 80331 Munich ☎ 089 290 0820

The enduring image of Munich is the Italian Renaissance onion domes of the twin towers (100m/330ft high) of the city's

cathedral, the Frauenkirche. The church was built between 1468 and 1488, although what you see today was rebuilt after the church was reduced to rubble in World War II. The distinctive green onion domes were originally only added to the towers in 1524 as a temporary measure, but proved so popular that they became a permanent feature. You can climb the south tower of the cathedral (Apr–end Oct Mon–Sat 10–5) for wonderful views of the city.

The cathedral is huge—109m (350ft) long and 41m (135ft) wide—and has a beautifully light interior with simple white walls and vivid stained-glass windows. Behind the choir, a staircase leads down to the crypt, where there are the tombs of Bavaria's rulers, the Wittelsbachs. At the front entrance you can see a footprint in the stone—legend has it that it was left by the Devil himself when he stamped his foot. For music recitals in the cathedral, pick up a leaflet inside, ask at the tourist office or see the website www.muenchner-dommusik.de.

HELLABRUNN ZOO

✚ 178 B5 (inset) • Tierparkstrasse 30, 81543 Munich (Thalkirchen) ☎ 089 625080 🕐 Apr–end Sep daily 8–6; Oct–end Mar daily 9–5 🚇 U3 Thalkirchen (arrives at Isar entrance) 🚌 Bus 52 (arrives at Flamingo entrance) 💷 Adult €9, child (4–14) €4.50, under 4 free 🏢 🍴 🍽 Pizzeria, self-service café with beer garden and snack stands throughout the zoo www.zoo-munich.de

Hellabrunn is different from many other city zoos in that it is a 'geo-zoo', which means that the animals live in surroundings as close as possible to their natural habitat. The way the enclosures are designed means that you very often get a view of the

animals without looking through a cage or a fence.

The zoo has a coral reef, a primate house with monkeys and gorillas, a South American area with anteaters and vicunas and an Australian area with wallabies and kangaroos. There are plenty of activities for children, such as camel rides, elephant shows and the seal show. At the Isar entrance there is an enclosure where children can touch non-threatening animals, such as dwarf goats.

HOFBRÄUHAUS

✚ 179 D3 • Platzl 9, 80331 Munich (Altstadt) ☎ 089 290 1360 🕐 Daily 9am–midnight 🚇 U-Bahn and S-Bahn Marienplatz 🚌 Bus 52, tram 19 www.hofbraeuhaus.de

If you're looking for traditional dirndl-clad waitresses serving frothy steins of beer and thigh-slapping oompah-band music, then this beer hall is where to go. The Hofbräuhaus is one of the world's most famous pubs, and certainly no visit to the city would be complete without a visit to this Munich institution. Just don't expect it to be full of locals.

The brewery was founded in 1589 when Wilhelm V wanted a dark beer to drink at court. The beer remained unavailable to the public until the brewery became an inn in 1828. The Hofbräuhaus also has a political history—the first mass meeting of the Nationalist Socialist Workers' Party (which later became the Nazi Party) took place here in 1920. Hitler spoke here many times including at the infamous Battle of the Hofbräuhaus, where he finished his speech despite the throwing of steins and chairs going on around him.

Deutsches Museum

●

With 18km (11 miles) of galleries, this is one of the world's biggest museums of science and technology, with everything from submarines to sundials and model railways to mines.

Cut-away models help you understand the technology

This 1886 model put Carl Benz on the road to car manufacturing

It takes a large building (above) to house this fishing wherry (right)

RATINGS	
Cultural interest	● ● ●
Good for kids	● ● ●
Value for money	● ● ●

BASICS
✚ 179 E5 • Museuminsel 1, 80538 Munich
☎ 089 21791
🕐 Daily 9–5; closed 1 Jan, Fasching Tuesday (usually last Tue in Feb), Good Friday, 1 May, 1 Nov, 24, 25 and 31 Dec; closes at 1pm on 2nd Wed in Dec
🚇 S-Bahn Isartor
🚋 Tram 18 Deutsches Museum
🎟 Adult €7.50, child €3, under 6 free, family €15; Tower lift €2. Planetarium €2. Combined ticket for Deutsches Museum, Flugwerft Schleissheim, Verkehrszentrum and shuttle bus to Verkehrszentrum €10
📖 Guidebook €4
🚶 Guided tours in German only
📚 Large book and giftshop outside
🍴 On most floors
💻 Internet café on 3rd floor, self-service restaurant

www.deutsches-museum.de
Very detailed site in German, English and Italian, with information on all of the permanent exhibition halls, temporary exhibitions, photographs, diagrams and maps.

SEEING THE DEUTSCHES MUSEUM

This is Germany's most visited attraction and one of the largest science and technology museums in the world, but you don't need to be a science buff or have any specialist knowledge to appreciate the cars, planes, helicopters, model railway or re-creation of a mine, to name just a few of the 18,000 exhibits. The museum is in the heart of the city, on an island on the Isar, and is accessible from either side of the river. Before you buy your ticket, decide whether you also want to visit the other museums, as it may be worth getting a combined ticket, which gives you entry to the main Deutsches Museum, the Transport Museum (Verkehrszentrum), which is in town, and the Museum of Flight (Flugwerft Schleissheim), which is farther out at Schleissheim. There is a free shuttle bus from here to the Verkehrszentrum, but not to the Flugwerft. If you want to visit the Planetarium (sixth floor) or the Tower, which cost extra, you'll need to buy your tickets at the Deutsches Museum.

If you want to know more about what you're looking at in the Deutsches Museum, consider buying the guidebook (€4), although it's not essential because of the explanatory notes in German and English next to many of the exhibits. The floor plan, available in English, German, Italian, French, Spanish and Japanese, is essential, because the museum really is huge. After you've bought your ticket and it has been checked by the museum attendant, turn left and go up the ramp towards the cloakroom, where you can leave your coat (€1) and bag (50c). It's not possible to see everything—you'll need to be selective.

HIGHLIGHTS

MINE, BASEMENT

You reach this re-creation of a mine via a staircase past the cloakroom, and the museum recommends that you allow an hour to follow the underground route. The mine is realistic enough that very small children and those who are claustrophobic may find the dim tunnels a little unnerving. Piles of coal and rock, pistons and pulleys and

- The Deutsches Museum, unlike most other museums and galleries in Munich, is open on Mondays.
- You can bring your own food into the museum and there is a dining area on the ground floor where you can eat your picnic—particularly useful if you have young children with you.
- You are allowed to use video cameras and take photographs, even with a flash.

life-size models of miners, pick-axes in hand, add to the experience. Diagrams and models explain (mostly in German) the mining process as well as what life is like for miners.

AERONAUTICS, ROOM 17 (GROUND FLOOR) AND ROOM 26 (FIRST FLOOR)

Even if you're not particularly fond of planes, you should be impressed by the huge collection of aircraft in this hangar-like exhibition room. There are hang-gliders, helicopters, jet fighters and even a rocket, with information on the German space programme. You can get into a Junkers JU-52 transport plane and into the front section of a Lufthansa Boeing 707 with its 1970s-style interior decoration. One fascinating exhibit is the cross-section of a passenger aircraft suspended from the ceiling, which makes you realise exactly how little there is separating you from the outside when you are flying. If it all gets to be a bit much, you can sit down on (what else?) aircraft seats. Make sure you go upstairs to room 26, where you can get a better view of the aircraft and see the old-style flying machines with canvas wings and even bicycle wheels.

SHIPS AND BOATS (MARINE NAVIGATION), ROOM 10 (GROUND FLOOR)

If you can think of a way to travel across water, then you are likely to find it in this well-stocked collection. When you enter the room, you are immediately struck by the size of the 19th-century fishing wherry the *Maria* (60m/197ft long), which, despite its size, had a crew of only three. Other craft include a Venetian gondola, canoes from the Amazon, kayaks and many model ships.

If you go down the staircase by the *Maria*, you'll find a huge area devoted to the sea. Here, there's the re-creation of a cruise liner, complete with sundeck, the noise of seagulls and officers' cabins. There are also many model sailing ships and war ships, huge anchors, old-fashioned diving suits, jet skis and a complete World War II German U-Boat. The side has been cut away so you can see exactly what's inside, including the engine room and the area where the seamen and officers slept when they were off duty.

Jet fighters (below) and early cars (bottom) are just some of the larger exhibits at this museum

TRAINS AND AUTOMOBILES, ROOM 13 (GROUND FLOOR) AND ROOM 22 (BASEMENT)

See huge, shiny steam trains in the Railways exhibition room, although unfortunately you can't go inside any of them. In summer,

you can go outside to an old-fashioned railway car that has been converted into a café. Other modern trains include the prototype for a train that runs above the track on an electromagnetic cushion. Nearby is a very steep mountain railway used in the Alps and a large model railway, which is always popular with children.

If trains aren't for you, head down the escalator to the automobiles, which include Carl Benz's 1886 motorized tricycle, 1920s American automobiles that wouldn't look out of place in a gangster film, VW

Beetles and, of course, BMWs. If you want to get into a car, go to the end of the corridor, with its displays of coaches and bicycles, where you can climb inside a BMW or test your skills in a driving simulator (€2). If you still haven't had enough cars, take the shuttle bus to the Deutsches Museum's new Museum of Transport or go to the BMW Museum (▷ 184).

FOR CHILDREN

There are plenty of exhibits that will entertain children. The Planetarium on the sixth floor (not suitable for children under 6) has a commentary in German but is still an exciting visual experience.

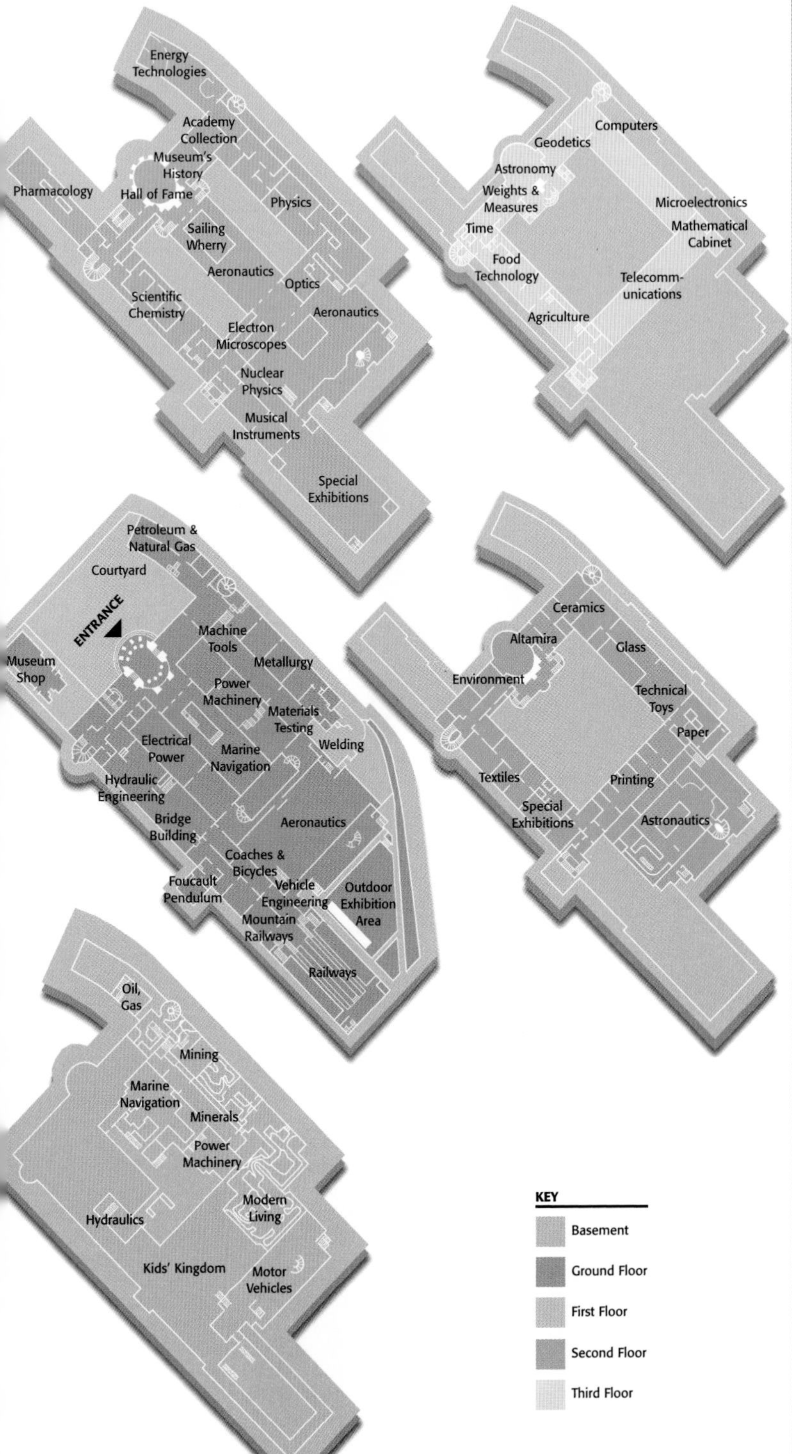

Energy
Technologies

Academy
Collection

Museum's
History

Computers

Geodetics

Pharmacology

Hall of Fame

Physics

Astronomy

Weights &
Measures

Time

Microelectronics

Mathematical
Cabinet

Sailing
Wherry

Aeronautics

Optics

Food
Technology

Telecommunications

Scientific
Chemistry

Aeronautics

Agriculture

Electron
Microscopes

Nuclear
Physics

Musical
Instruments

Special
Exhibitions

Petroleum &
Natural Gas

Courtyard

ENTRANCE

Machine
Tools

Ceramics

Altamira

Glass

Metallurgy

Environment

Technical
Toys

Museum
Shop

Power
Machinery

Materials
Testing

Welding

Paper

Electrical
Power

Marine
Navigation

Hydraulic
Engineering

Textiles

Printing

Bridge
Building

Aeronautics

Special
Exhibitions

Astronautics

Foucault
Pendulum

Coaches &
Bicycles

Vehicle
Engineering

Outdoor
Exhibition
Area

Mountain
Railways

Railways

Oil,
Gas

Mining

Marine
Navigation

Minerals

Power
Machinery

Hydraulics

Modern
Living

Kids' Kingdom

Motor
Vehicles

THE SIGHTS

KEY

	Basement
	Ground Floor
	First Floor
	Second Floor
	Third Floor

Basement Mining, automobiles, Kids' Kingdom.

Ground floor Cloakroom, petroleum and natural gas, metal, welding and soldering, materials testing, machine tools, power machinery, machine components, electrical power, marine navigation (including canoes, boats and ships), buses and bicycles, vehicle engineering, trains and the model railway, tunnels, planes and helicopters, bridge building, hydraulic engineering, Foucault pendulum, snack bar and picnic area.

Mezzanine floor Self-service restaurant near the entrance.

Outside Exhibition area with lifeboat, windmill, train-carriage café (summer only), museum shop (in front of the museum).

First floor Energy technologies, physics, aeronautics, musical instruments, chemistry, pharmacology, special exhibitions, small coffee bar.

Second floor Altamira cave, ceramics, glass, paper and printing, astronautics, technical toys, textiles, the environment.

Third floor Astronomy, geodesy, computers, microelectronics, mathematical cabinet, telecommunications, agriculture, food technology, chronometry, weights and measures, internet café.

Fourth to sixth floors Amateur radio, astronomy, Zeiss Planetarium (buy tickets on the ground floor), sundial garden.

Learning about the history of the bicycle (above right).
An early Mercedes Benz (below)

The model railway will be particularly appealing to children and it runs at 11, 2 and 4. For smaller children, the Kids' Kingdom in the basement is a great place to play and run around. Older children may appreciate the driving simulator (€2) or getting into a BMW or fork-lift truck. In summer, the Outdoor Exhibition is the best place to be; you can go on board an ocean-going lifeboat and into a windmill. There are baby changing facilities on the ground floor near the entrance.

VERKEHRSZENTRUM
(TRANSPORT AND MOBILITY MUSEUM)
🔟 178 B5 (inset) • Theresienhöhe 14a, 80339 Munich ☎ 089 5008 06140 or 089 217 9529 🕐 Fri–Wed 9–5, Thu 9–8 🚇 U4 and U5 to Theresienwiese 🚌 Bus 62 or 66 to Theresienhöhe; shuttle bus from Museumsinsel (the main Deutsches Museum) 💶 Adult €2.50, child €1.50, under 6 free 🚻 📷 www.verkehrszentrum.deutsches-museum.de

The Deutsches Museum also has two other museums—the Verkehrszentrum and Flugwerft Schleissheim. The Verkehrszentrum is a transport museum designed from a 21st-century point of view, and it contains every kind of car and bicycle imaginable, as well as buses and steam locomotives. The museum explores the concept of motion, with exhibits on engineering, city travel and journeys.

FLUGWERFT SCHLEISSHEIM
(AIRCRAFT MUSEUM)
🔟 178 B4 (inset) • Effnerstrasse 18, 85764, Oberschleissheim ☎ 089 315 7140 🕐 Daily 9–5 🚇 S1 to Oberschleissheim 🚗 Take the A99 to the Neuherberg exit 💶 Adult €3.50, child €2.50, under 6 free 🚻 📷

If you like anything to do with flight, this extension of the Deutsches Museum's collection of civil, military and sport flying machines is for you. The site, on an old airfield at Schleissheim, 13km (8 miles) from downtown Munich, was originally built for the Bavarian Royal Flying Corps. There are helicopters (including one used by the police), gliders, planes, including a MiG fighter jet, and even a rocket. If you want to feel as if you are flying, try out the flight simulator. Keep your children entertained by letting them loose on the model planes. For good views, go up the control tower.

BACKGROUND

The museum was founded in 1903 by the engineer Oskar von Miller. The collection moved to its present home in 1925. Since then, the number of exhibits has topped 18,000 and will continue to grow when the Centre for New Technologies opens in 2005. It will focus on genetic engineering and nanotechnology as well as hosting temporary special exhibitions.

In September 1992, the Deutsches Museum opened a separate branch, dedicated to aircraft and flying, at a former airfield at Schleissheim, 13km (8 miles outside town). The expansion continued with the opening of a museum devoted to transport and mobility, the Vehrkehrszentrum, in 2003. This museum is still being added to, with new exhibition halls due to open at the end of 2005.

● Take the elevator (65m/213ft) to the top of the tower (€2, under 6 free) at 10, 11, 12, 2, 3 and 4 for views of the city and, on a clear day, the Alps.

● The Environment exhibition on the second floor shows how much rubbish (garbage) the average German family produces in a year and how Germany's production of waste compares with other countries.

● On the third floor, the Agriculture section is in a room created to look like a barn, and is filled with tractors, ploughs and other farm machinery.

● To see what a traditional wooden mountain chalet looks like, go to the Food Technology exhibits on the third floor, although unfortunately you can't actually go inside the chalet.

● Although only a reconstruction, the Altamira cave is very dark. The exhibition shows the cave-paintings of wild animals and hunting scenes that archaeologists found in this Spanish cave, and explains what they discovered about these hunters from their cave art.

● Look out for special temporary exhibitions.

THE SIGHTS

From the air, the museum's island location is more obvious, as is its vast size. Much of the complex was rebuilt after bomb damage during World War II

The history of speed at a glance (above left)

This 'people's park' is a great place for walking and bicycling (top), or even surfing (above)

RATINGS	
Good for kids	● ● ● ●
Photo stops	● ● ●
Value for money	FREE

BASICS

➕ 179 F1 • Stretching from Prinzregentenstrasse in the south to the outskirts of the city in the north

☎ 089 3866 6390

🕐 Daily dawn to dusk

🚇 U6 Universität or Münchener Freiheit

🚃 Tram 17

🍴 Seehaus restaurant and beer garden, Chinese Tower restaurant and beer garden, Japanese tea house, Aumeister beer garden at the northern edge of park.

🚻

www.schloesser.bayern.de

TIP

● You can rent bicycles at Kleinhesseloher See to explore more of the gardens.

ENGLISCHER GARTEN

The largest city park in Europe, ideal for sunbathing, surfing, rowing, having a beer or simply enjoying being outside.

At 5km (3 miles) long and a kilometre (0.6 miles) wide, the Englischer Garten is more to the people of Munich than just a large park. Often referred to as 'the lungs of Munich', the English Garden is a place to relax, an aspect of life that is very important to Münchners, who flock here on weekends and sunny days. Prince Elector Karl Theodor commissioned the park, which had been the hunting grounds of the Wittelsbach dynasty, in the 18th century. The design was unusual for its time; it broke away from the fashion for more formal, manicured gardens and was instead an open, natural-looking *Volksgarten* (people's park), evident in the fields, woodland, lake, rivers and many kilometres of footpaths.

ACTIVITIES

With such large open spaces, the park is ideal for a range of activities, such as bicycling, jogging, playing soccer, having a picnic, feeding the ducks and boating or paddling in the lake. Some paths are suitable for pushchairs and there are playgrounds, making this a great place for children. You should be aware that in summer it is not unusual (nor illegal) for Münchners to sunbathe nude by the river. You'll also see canoes on the Eisbach, and even surfers who challenge each other to stay upright as they surf *against* the flow of the crest of a permanent wave, which is at the stretch of water by Prinzregentenstrasse.

THINGS TO SEE

Most of the attractions are in the section south of the main road—the Isar Ring. Here is the Kleinhesseloher See, where you can rent a boat, or enjoy a beer or a meal at the Seehaus restaurant, where brass bands play and there's a festival atmosphere. If you follow the Eisbach creek south, you'll come to the Chinesischer Turm (Chinese Pagoda), where there's a 7,000-seater beer garden, as well as mulled wine stalls in winter and a children's playground. When you pay for your drinks at the supermarket-style cash desk in the beer garden, you must also pay a small deposit (*pfand*) for each glass. (You are given a token that you hand back with your empty glass when you've finished your drink.) You can eat simple food in the beer garden or have something more sophisticated at the Restaurant am Chinesischen Turm (Mon–Sun 10am–midnight). At the very south of the garden is the Japanese Tea House, a gift to the city of Munich from Japan for the 1972 Olympic Games.

MARIENPLATZ

This square, the heart of the city, is surrounded by historical buildings and home of the world-famous Glockenspiel.

If the Englischer Garten represents the lungs of Munich, then Marienplatz is surely its heart. The square has many purposes, not least as a central point where Münchners meet up with their friends, but is also the place where citizens converge to hold political demonstrations. Many years ago, public executions took place here, and the Viktualienmarkt was here until it grew too big and was moved to its present site nearby (▷ 202). Today the place has a lively buzz about it, with visitors taking photos of the City Hall and the famous Glockenspiel, locals sitting outside enjoying a beer in summer and, in December, the traditional Christmas market.

STATUES AND FOUNTAINS
Marienplatz takes its name from the Mariensäule, the golden figure of the Virgin Mary on a column, 11m (36ft) high, in the middle of the square. It was created by Hubert Gerhart and was erected in Marienplatz at the request of Elector Maximilian in 1638. It marks the saving of the city during the period of Swedish occupation in the Thirty Years War. On the statue's pedestal are four winged children who represent the fight against the plagues of humankind—Heresy, War, Plague and Famine. The *Fischbrunnen* (Fish Fountain) nearby is named for the fish market that stood here. It was built in 1865, and it is said that if you wash your wallet here on Ash Wednesday, it will never be empty. Munich takes this tradition seriously and the Lord Mayor still douses the city purse in the fountain every year.

NEUES AND ALTES RATHAUS
The 19th-century Neues Rathaus (New City Hall) dominates the square. Under the eaves at the front of the building is the Tourist Information Centre and at basement level is the Ratskeller, a huge restaurant and beer house. On the front of the main tower is the Glockenspiel. Get here at 11, noon or 5 to see the brightly painted figures move and chime. You can climb the tower (May–end Oct Mon–Fri 9–7; Sat, Sun 10–7; Nov–end Apr Mon–Thu 9–4, Fri 9–1) for great views of the city.

At the east side of the square is the Altes Rathaus (Old City Hall). It dates from the 15th century but had to be reconstructed after bomb damage during World War II. It contains the Spielzeug-Museum (the toy museum), which has collections of teddy bears, dolls, doll's houses and model railways. It's open daily from 10 to 5.30.

From the Neues Rathaus, there are great views of the square (top), which is home to the Mariensäule (above)

RATINGS	
Photo stops	●●●●
Specialist shopping	●●●
Historic interest	●●●

BASICS
⊞ 179 D3 • Marienplatz
Ⓤ U-Bahn and S-Bahn Marienplatz
🚌 52
🍴 Plenty of restaurants and cafés, including the Glockenspiel Café (▷ 365) and Ratskeller (▷ 367)
ℹ Marienplatz; Mon–Fri 10–8, Sat 10–4, closed Sun

TIPS
● You'll probably pass through Marienplatz several times during your stay. Be there at 11, noon or 5 to see the Glockenspiel chime.
● For good views of the city, climb up the City Hall tower or the Alter Peter in Peterskirche nearby.

Italian gardens in the heart of Munich at Lenbachhaus

Maximilianstrasse, dominated by the Maximilianeum, is famous for its designer shopping

KÖNIGSPLATZ

🕂 178 B2 • Königsplatz, 80333 Munich
☎ Glyptothek 089 286100;
Antikensammlung 089 598359
🚇 U2 and U8 Königsplatz
🍴 In the Glyptothek and
Antikensammlung

Königsplatz is a majestic royal square enclosed on three sides by neoclassical buildings, commissioned by Ludwig I in 1817. The Greek style of these buildings gave the square its alternative name, Athens-on-the-Isar. The Propyläen, on the west side of the square, is an imposing temple built for purely aesthetic reasons. It was based on the entrance to the Acropolis in Athens and was finished in 1862 by Leo von Klenze. The Ionic-style building on the north side is the Glyptothek (Tue, Wed, Fri–Sun 10–5, Thu 10–8), a sculpture gallery with more than 160 Greek and Roman statues. Among the finest are the *Barberini Faun*, the bust of Augustus and Tenea's *Apollo*. On the square's south side is the Staatliche Antikensammlung (Tue, Thu–Sun 10–5, Wed 10–8), the State Collection of Antiquities, with ancient bronzes, jewellery, Greek vases, ceramics and sculpture.

LENBACHHAUS

🕂 178 B1 • Luisenstrasse 33, 80333 Munich ☎ 089 2332 3002 🕐 Tue–Sun and hols 10–6 🚇 U-Bahn Königsplatz 🚋 Tram 27 to Karolinenplatz 🎫 Adult €5, child €3, under 6 free, family €7.50
🏛🍴🛍📷
www.lenbachhaus.de

The Städtische Galerie im Lenbachhaus is in a beautiful dark yellow Florentine High Renaissance-style building with a

A Greek helmet from Münchner Stadtmuseum, dating from 500BC

small formal garden, with statues and a fountain. It was built in 1887 for the Bavarian painter Prince Franz von Lenbach, who was very much in vogue at the time. After his death, the building became the property of the State and was converted into an art gallery, which now charts the development of painting in Munich.

If you turn left when you reach the top of the stairs on the upper floor, you'll see the gallery's collection of Bavarian landscapes, with many paintings showing how Munich used to look. However, most people come for the paintings by the Munich-based expressionist group Der Blaue Reiter, founded by Wassily Kandinsky (1866–1944) and Franz Marc (1880–1916). There are many vibrant, abstract paintings by Kandinsky, his partner Gabriele Münter (1877–1962) and August Macke (1887–1914), as well as some by Paul Klee (1879–1940).

MARIENPLATZ

See page 193.

MAXIMILIANSTRASSE

🕂 179 E3 • Maximilianstrasse
🚇 West end: U-Bahn Odeonsplatz or Marienplatz, S-Bahn Marienplatz; east end U-Bahn Max-Weber-Platz
🚌 West end: bus 52 to Marienplatz, bus 53 to Odeonsplatz or tram 19 to Nationaltheater; east end tram 19 to Maximilianeum

Maximilianstrasse, named for its creator King Maximilian II, begins with Munich's opera house, the Nationaltheater (▷ 275), and ends on the other side of the Isar

with the Renaissance-style Maximilianeum building. Built between 1857 and 1874, it used to be a school before it became the Bavarian State Parliament in 1949. These grand buildings set the tone for the avenue, where Munich's designer-clad citizens (and there are many) come to shop. Window shop (or indulge) at Gucci, Dior, Bulgari, Gianfranco Ferre, Versace and Hermès, or watch VIPs unload their Louis Vuitton luggage outside Munich's top hotel, the Kempinski Vier Jahreszeiten.

Maximilianstrasse's reputation as a fashionable street is evident in its bars and restaurants—Café Roma, open until 3am, is owned by a German actress and is visited by German actors and actresses when they are in town.

MÜNCHNER STADTMUSEUM

🕂 178 C4 • St-Jakobs-Platz 1, 80331 Munich ☎ 089 2332 2370 🕐 Tue–Sun 10–6 🚇 S-Bahn Marienplatz or U-Bahn to Marienplatz or Sendlinger Tor 🚌 Bus 52 and 56 Blumenstrasse 🎫 Adult €2.50, child (6–15) €1.50, under 6 free, family €4; free for all on Sun 🍴 Stadtcafé
www.stadtmuseum-online.de

The Stadtmuseum, in what was Munich's armoury, traces the city's history with a permanent exhibition and changing special exhibitions. It covers Munich's royal history through to the devastation of the city in World War II. You'll find paintings, furniture, toys, costumes, ancient weaponry and Bavarian handcrafts, as well as hundreds of musical instruments and a photography and film museum. Well-known aspects of the collections include Erasmus Grasser's Gothic Moriske dancers, which he made in the 16th century. They were originally carved for the Altes Rathaus in Marienplatz.

A shadow puppet from the Münchner Stadtmuseum

The puppet theatre museum (Münchner Marionettentheater) is one of the biggest in the world, with mechanical toys and glove puppets. Its collection covers Bavaria's important role in the production of puppets and toys. Alongside this is the fairground museum. When you're finished, head for the museum café, the Stadtcafé, with its delicious cakes and international newspapers.

NEUE PINAKOTHEK

See page 196.

ODEONSPLATZ

➕ 179 D2 🚇 U-Bahn Odeonsplatz

This grand square, with wide Ludwigstrasse leading off to the north, is surrounded by impressive buildings. The most striking and beautiful is the mustard yellow baroque Theatinerkirche which was designed by several Italian architects, including Agostino Barelli (1627–87), and was commissioned by Bavarian Elector Ferdinand Maria (1636–79) to celebrate the birth of his son and heir Max Emanuel. The church was based on, and takes its name from, the home of the Theatine order in Rome, Sant'Andrea della Valle, and has an incredibly light interior decorated with white stuccowork.

On the south side of the square is the Feldherrnhalle, or General's Hall, presided over by two lions, and on the east side behind the wall is the Hofgarten (Court Garden). This was designed in a baroque Italian style, with a pavilion in the middle and arcades with frescoes depicting Bavarian history. If you head south along Residenz-strasse, you'll come to the entrance to the opulent Residenz (▷ 198–199), which takes up the entire block and was the home of the Wittelsbach dynasty and government for centuries.

A time capsule of 20th-century design

PINAKOTHEK DER MODERNE

One of the largest areas in the world for 20th- and 21st-century art and design, which opened in 2002.

The Pinakothek der Moderne brings Munich's art collection right into the 21st century. The gallery's collection of 20th- and 21st-century art and sculpture, architecture, design and works on paper is displayed in a modern building designed by Stephan Braunfels. When you enter the building on the ground floor (Level 2), pick up an orientation guide, which is available in German and English.

ART

On Level 3 you'll find a superb collection of modern and contemporary art with several rooms devoted to expressionism. The most influential movements of the 20th century are here—cubism by Pablo Picasso (1881–1973), surrealism by Salvador Dalí (1904–89) and pop art by Andy Warhol (1928–87). There are also paintings by Paul Klee (1879–1940) and Wassily Kandinsky (1866–1944) of the Blaue Reiter movement, which started in Munich.

DESIGN

The exhibition in the basement (confusingly named Level 1), traces the history of design, taking in the avant gardes of the 1920s and pop art design. There are areas dedicated to automobile design, computer culture (think huge computers from the 1980s), and design of everyday objects such as furniture. There is a strong focus on the humble chair—guaranteed to make you think more about the design of what you're sitting on. Other exhibits to look out for include the perpetual motion machines full of designer trainers and video installations.

Don't miss The huge, bright, jellyfish-like sculpture on the staircase to Level 3 is an arresting sight.

RATINGS	
Cultural interest	●●●●
Good for kids	●●
Shopping (art books)	●●●

BASICS
➕ 178 C1 • Barerstrasse 40, 80333 Munich
☎ 089 2380 5360
🕐 Tue, Wed, Sat, Sun 10–5, Thu, Fri 10–8; closed Shrove Tue, 1 May, 24, 25, 31 Dec
💶 Adult €9, child €5; free to all on Sun; day ticket for all three Pinakothek galleries adult €12, child €7
🚇 U2 and U8 to Königsplatz or Theresienstrasse
🚋 Tram 27 to Pinakothek, bus 53 to Schellingstrasse
🔲 🏛 🏠
📖 €7.50 (German or English), large guidebook €16.80 (German, English, French or Italian)
www.pinakothek-der-moderne.de

BASICS

✚ 178 C1 • Barerstrasse 29, 80799 Munich (Schwabing)
☎ 089 2380 5195
🕐 Thu–Mon 10–5, Wed 10–8; closed Tue, Dec 24, 25, 31, Shrove Tue, 1 May
💶 Adult €5, child €3.50; free to all on Sun; day ticket for all three Pinakothek galleries adult €12, child €7
🚇 U-Bahn Königsplatz or Theresienstrasse
🚋 Tram 27
🍴 Caffè Greco
🗣 In German only
📖 Bookshop by entrance
♿
📕 €9.95, €14.50 and €17.90
www.neue-pinakothek.de
Detailed site in German and English with practical information, biographies of artists and pictures of the building and paintings.

TIPS

● All Munich's Pinakotheks are free on Sunday, and as a result the gallery and restaurant can get very busy, particularly in the afternoon.
● If you are considering buying the day ticket, bear in mind that visiting all three galleries in one day may test the staying power of even the most artistically minded.

The Neue Pinakothek (top), at the heart of the student quarter

NEUE PINAKOTHEK

The largest post-war art gallery in Germany is packed with outstanding works of European art and sculpture from the late 18th to the early 20th centuries.

The Neue Pinakothek is in a glass, granite and concrete building designed by Munich architect Alexander von Branca, and is sometimes referred to as Palazzo Branca. It contains hundreds of European paintings and sculptures from the late 18th to the early 20th centuries, focusing on the development of German art. There are particularly fine collections of 19th-century German art, landscapes by French, English and Spanish painters and a sizeable French Impressionism section. Throughout the gallery are sculptures, including works by Auguste Rodin, Edgar Degas and Pablo Picasso.

LANDSCAPES AND PORTRAITS BY EUROPEAN PAINTERS

Several rooms are devoted to landscapes by European artists, with English painters particularly well represented. *Landscape with Shepherd, Sheep and Cattle* (1783) was inspired by a visit Gainsborough made to the Lake District in the north of England. In his day, Gainsborough was a well-known painter of high society figures, and here you can see examples of his portraits such as *Mrs Thomas Hibbert* from 1786. Other paintings to look out for include the unpretentious depiction of the *Marquise de Sorcy de Thélusson* by French portraitist Jacques Louis David (1748–1825) and still lifes and portraits by the Spanish painter Goya (1746–1828).

19TH-CENTURY GERMAN ART

The art in this gallery focuses on German Romanticism, Realism and Impressionism, with works by Caspar David Friedrich, Wilhelm von Kaulbach and Carl von Piloty, among others. Highlights include The *Schmadri Falls* (1822) by Joseph Anton Koch, which depicts dramatic snow-covered mountains and waterfalls, and German Impressionist Max Liebermann's *Munich Beer Garden* (1884), a scene that, apart from the style of dress, could be found in Munich today.

IMPRESSIONISM ONWARDS

Rooms 19 to 22 contain paintings by the French Impressionists. Highlights include Manet's painting *The Boat* (1874), which shows his friend Monet painting a picture while on a boat with his wife. In rooms 21 and 22 you'll find examples of more modern art, notably Vincent van Gogh's extremely well-known *Sunflowers* (1888) and the beautiful blues and greens of his *View of Arles* (1889).

OLYMPIAPARK

The hub of Munich's sporting life and home of the Olympic stadium has views as far as The Alps from the Olympic Tower.

When it was announced that the 1972 Olympic Games were to be held in Munich, the city set about building a comprehensive set of sports facilities on the site of the old airport. The site, which you can tour on the park train in the summer, is known for its unusual and expensive roof, which looks like a spider's web. It covers the Olympic Hall, where rock and pop concerts are held, the Olympic swimming pool and the stadium, which is home to Munich's two soccer teams, FC Bayern München and TSV 1860. Other facilities include the ice rink, gym and spa complex, which are all open to the public.

If you prefer spending time outside, you can walk around the artificial lake, the Olympiasee, or climb 53m (174 ft) up the man-made hill, made of rubble from World War II and now covered with alpine vegetation.

TOURS

There are several different tours you can take at the Olympiapark. The soccer tour, which lasts an hour, is at 11am and takes in the Olympic stadium, the changing rooms and the VIP area of Munich's two soccer teams. The tour costs €5 for adults and €3.50 for children (6–15). The Adventure Tour, at 2pm and lasting an hour and a half, takes in the sights that you see on the football tour, as well as the Olympic Hall and the swimming pool, and includes a ride on the park train. It costs €7 for adults and €5 for children (6–15). If you're not afraid of heights, there's the Roof Climb Tour at 2.30, which involves climbing up to the roof of the Olympic stadium (wear rubber soled shoes), where a guide explains the stadium's architecture and you get a different view of the Frauenkirche. This tour costs €25 during the week and €30 on weekends for adults, and €20 for children (5–15).

OLYMPIATURM

Built between 1965 and 1968, and standing 290m (951ft) high, the Olympic tower is now as much part of the Munich skyline as the twin onion domes of the Frauenkirche. You whizz up to the top in a matter of seconds in the high speed lift (elevator), and it is certainly worth the trip as, on a clear day, you can see as far as the Alps. When you get to the top, make sure you go outside for unimpeded views over the whole city and fantastic photo opportunities. There's also a (very slowly) revolving restaurant which is open in the summer only.

RATINGS

Good for kids	● ● ●
Photo stops	● ● ● ●
Activities	● ● ● ●

BASICS

✚ 178 B4 (inset) • Spiridon-Louis-Ring, Munich

☎ 089 3067 2414;
information hotline 0180 530 6730

🕐 Stadium: summer daily 8.30–6, winter daily 9–4.30. Olympiaturm: daily 9am–11.30pm. Tours: Apr–end Oct daily

💰 Entrance to the site free. Tower: adult €3, child €2, under 6 free, family €8. For pool and ice skating ▷ 278

🚇 U3 Olympiapark, then 10 min walk

🍴 Revolving restaurant

☕ Self-service café, beer garden and ice-cream stalls in summer

🎫 Daily 9.30–7 ♿

www.olympiapark-muenchen.de
Comprehensive site in English and German with maps of the park, details of prices for sports and tours and information on concerts in the Olympiahalle.

TIPS

● When you arrive at the U-Bahn station, follow signs for Eissportzentrum, Olympia-stadion, Besucherdienst or Olympiahalle, rather than Olympiadorf, which is on the wrong side of the motorway.
● It's worth bringing your swimming costume and a towel, so you can have a swim or use the sauna and steam room after the tour.

The Olympiapark (top), with the Olympiaturm in the foreground

Residenz

A sumptuous palace demonstrating the wealth and power of the
Wittelsbach dynasty, rulers of Bavaria for nearly 800 years.
The Residenz is decorated in a fusion of styles, from Renaissance to rococo.

Look out for the variety of decorated ceilings

The intricate white-and-gold decoration of the State Bedroom

The Antiquarium, built to house Duke Albrecht V's antiques

TIPS

● The Residenz is large, so why not make a day of it? After visiting the rooms that open in the morning, have a leisurely lunch before going back to see the afternoon rooms (▷ 263–268 for suggestions).
● There is a free cloakroom for bags and coats, although you may want to keep your coat on in winter; some of the larger rooms are quite cold.
● You can take photographs as long as you don't use a flash.

GALLERY GUIDE

GROUND FLOOR

The Treasury, Ancestral Gallery, Grotto Courtyard, Antiquarium, Nibelungen Halls, Court Chapel, Sacred Vestment Rooms, bookshop and cloakroom.

UPPER FLOOR

Black Hall, Porcelain Chambers, Rich Rooms, Reliquaries Chamber, Rich Chapel, Stone Rooms, Four White Horses Hall, Imperial Hall, Royal Apartments.

SEEING THE RESIDENZ

The Munich Residenz, the largest building in Munich's Altstadt, was the residence of the dukes and kings of Bavaria for more than 400 years, from the beginning of the 16th century to the early 20th century. The complex includes the Antiquarium (a large Renaissance Hall), a rococo theatre, Royal Apartments in the Königsbau (Royal Palace), museums and the Treasury, filled with priceless jewels, crowns, chains and ornaments.

There are two entrances to the Residenz, one on Max-Joseph Platz and one around the corner on Residenzstrasse. Decide before you arrive what you would like to see and what you realistically have time for. You have the option of buying a ticket for the Treasury only, the Residenz only, or a combined ticket, which lets you see both. In the Residenz itself, about half the rooms are open to the public in the morning, then closed in the afternoon, when the rest of the rooms are open. This means that to see all the rooms you will have to visit before and after lunch or go straight through at the changeover time (12.30 in winter and 1.30 in the summer). You should allow at least an hour for each set of rooms. In addition, you will need at least half an hour to see the Treasury. Pick up a free floor plan (available in English), which has a plan of the complex and numbers for each room.

TREASURY

The Wittelsbachs' Treasury (Schatzkammer) is in ten rooms of the Königsbau, opposite the cloakroom, and contains hundreds of precious and priceless crowns and insignia, jewels, shrines, religious art and tableware. An audioguide (available in German, English, Italian and French) is included in the price of your ticket and gives a detailed commentary on most of the pieces in the Treasury. You'll need to be selective, as the commentaries cover so many of the items that the running time of the tape is several hours! Highlights include the magnificent statuette of St. George, the patron saint of the Wittelsbach family. The incredibly detailed statuette, which shows St. George on horseback slaying the dragon, is exquisitely decorated in gold, silver, precious stones and large pearls. Other pieces to look out for include the rock crystal shrine with scenes from the Old Testament in room 6 and the beautiful table in room 7, commissioned by Elector Maximilian I and his first wife. The table is inlaid with gold, agate, lapis lazuli and jasper, and has a landscape picture in the middle, made from flat slices of precious stones.

ANTIQUARIUM (HALL OF ANTIQUITIES)

This magnificent hall, the largest Renaissance hall north of the Alps, was built by Duke Albrecht V between 1568 and 1571 to house his collection of antiques and later became a banquet hall. It's 66m (216ft) long, with a beautiful, low, barrel-vaulted ceiling, painted with scenes of old Bavarian towns and allegorical paintings of Fame and the Virtues. As you walk through the hall you have an eerie sensation of being watched by the collection of more than 100 busts, which are mostly from Rome and Venice.

ALTES RESIDENZTHEATER (CUVILLIÉS THEATRE)

Said by some to be the finest rococo theatre in the world, the Italian-style Old Residence Theatre was built between 1751 and 1755 by François Cuvilliés, and for this reason is also known as the Cuvilliés Theatre. One claim to fame is that in 1781 it hosted the world premiere of Mozart's *Idomeneo*. The building was destroyed by bombing in World War II, but the tiers of boxes had been removed for safekeeping beforehand, and you can still see them today. The theatre continues as a performance venue and so it is sometimes closed for rehearsals.

OTHER HIGHLIGHTS

The Residenz has a dizzying array of styles of interior decoration. Other interesting pieces to look out for include the Grottenhof, which you pass before going into the Antiquarium, with its unusual fountain encrusted with shells, and the Ancestral Gallery filled with portraits. On the upper floor is the Schwarzer Saal (Black Room), named after the black marble that surrounds the doorways. It has a beautiful *trompe l'oeil* ceiling painted by Hans Werl, which gives the illusion of an upper gallery supported by pillars. In the Green Gallery of the Rich Rooms, strategically placed mirrors make the rooms look as if they go on forever. The Kaisersaal, which you'll come to at the end of your visit, is large and impressive with its marble floor, chandeliers, tapestries and ornate ceiling. The light pastel ceilings of the Royal Apartments, such as King Max II's living room (Wohnzimmer) are a pleasant antidote to the heavy opulence of rooms such as Ludwig I's sumptuous gold and deep red Throne Room. Also on the upper floor is the Rich Chapel, Maximilian I's private oratory, which lives up to its name by being richly decorated. The highlights are the oval-shaped tambour with stained-glass windows and the walls, which appear to be made of red marble, but are in fact lined with stucco, designed to simulate marble.

BACKGROUND

The Residenz was built as a small castle and was begun in 1385. The Wittelsbach dynasty, which ruled Bavaria for nearly 800 years, added to the original building over the years until it became the palace, with more than 130 rooms, that exists today. The complex is built around seven courtyards, decorated in a number of different styles (Renaissance, baroque, rococo and neoclassical) and filled with valuable paintings and sculptures, furniture, clocks, tapestries, porcelain and even sacred vestments. The Wittelsbach family used the Residenz as their luxurious private home, but also as the seat of government for 400 years. Today, the complex is run by the Bavarian Department for State-Owned Palaces, Gardens and Lakes (which also looks after the Nymphenburg and Schleissheim palaces). This department oversaw the rebuilding of the complex after the devastation of World War II.

The entrance to the Residenz is flanked by verdigris lions

Schloss Nymphenburg

One of Germany's largest baroque palaces, set in beautiful parkland, yet within easy reach of the city.
Home of the famous Nymphenburg porcelain factory.

Detail of the ornate decoration on a carriage

After visiting the palace, take time to relax in the park

A ceremonial carriage from the Marstallmuseum's collection

SEEING SCHLOSS NYMPHENBURG

This baroque castle, 15 minutes from downtown Munich by tram, was used by the kings of Bavaria as a summer residence in the days when the journey from Munich took two hours. There is plenty here to fill a day, including the palace rooms (filled with frescoes, paintings, chandeliers and fine furniture), three museums and landscaped parkland with four pavilions, each of which merit a visit. If you arrive by tram (which is more convenient than taking the U-Bahn), you'll need to walk to the Palace, past the ornamental ponds, which takes about 10 minutes. Head towards the shop in the main Palace building (the tall square building in the middle), where you buy your entrance ticket. Once you have your ticket, head outside and up the steps to the Palace entrance. Here you can rent an audioguide (for the Palace only), which costs €2.50 and is available in English, German and French.

HIGHLIGHTS

THE MAIN PALACE

The first thing you notice when you enter the Palace is the large ceiling fresco in the Great Hall or Steinerner Saal (Stone Room), which was painted by Johann Baptist Zimmermann between 1755 and 1757 and was commissioned by Max Joseph, who wanted a fresco with themes of peace and reconciliation. In the middle is Apollo's sun chariot, with Olympian gods riding over a rainbow, and to the right is Diana, goddess of hunting, whose presence reflects the palace's role as a hunting lodge.

Other rooms you can see in the palace, most of which have a board with explanatory notes in German, English and Italian, include the Queen's Bedroom, where Ludwig II was born in 1845, and, in the south wing, Ludwig I's Gallery of Beauties, with paintings that were originally on show in the Residenz (▷ 198–199). Ludwig I (ruled 1825–1848) was a great admirer of beauty and commissioned the artist Joseph Stieler to paint the portraits of many beautiful young women. Between 1827 and 1850 Stieler painted 36 portraits of women from various countries, including England, Italy and Bavaria, and his subjects included the daughter of a shoemaker as well as Ludwig I's sister and daughter.

PARK AND PAVILIONS

The park, 300ha (740 acres) in size, is a wonderful place to walk at any time of the year. Originally in Italian style, the park was relaid in French baroque style. In the 19th century, it was transformed into an English park with waterways, a large and a small lake, the Monopteros (a Greek-style temple), statues and the long central canal, which ends in a waterfall. Amalienburg is the little rococo hunting lodge designed by the architect François Cuvilliés the Elder in 1734 and built by Karl Albrecht for his wife Electress Maria Amalia. It has a grand Hall of Mirrors with gold stuccowork, and its Hunting Room is full of landscape paintings.

MUSEUMS

At Schloss Nymphenburg there are three museums, each with a different themed collection. The Marstallmuseum (Coach Museum) is in the former stables: The large building is needed to show the sumptuous coaches (including some designed for children), sleighs and portraits of the royal thoroughbred horses. The ornate gold New Dress Coach of King Ludwig II has to be seen to be believed.

The Porcelain Museum, above the stables, displays the exquisite porcelain manufactured at the Nymphenburg porcelain factory, founded in 1761. There are plates, ornaments and urns, paintings and, surprisingly, an extensive collection of porcelain bridles. Both museums have the same opening hours as the palace.

In the north wing is the Museum Mensch und Natur (Museum of Man and Nature, Tue–Sun 9–5), which, unusually for a palace museum, does not showcase objects from the royal household. It explains how the Earth was created and traces the origin of species. It's designed as a 'hands-on' museum, and should appeal to children.

BACKGROUND

Between 1664 and 1757, five rulers from the Wittelsbach family—Ferdinand Maria, Max Emanuel, Karl Albrecht, Max III Joseph and Max IV Joseph—contributed to the construction of the baroque palace and gardens at Nymphenburg, which served as the rulers' summer residence. The Palace was begun by Elector Ferdinand Maria (ruled 1651–1679) in 1664 to celebrate the birth of his son and heir Max Emanuel, who himself later added a gallery and side wings to the original building. The palace was based on designs by the Italian architect Agostino Barelli (who also worked on the Theatinerkirche in Odeonsplatz), who was succeeded in 1673 by Enrico Zuccalli. From 1714 the German architect Joseph Effner took over, adding the pavilions Pagodenburg, Badenburg and Magdalenenklause (Hermitage of Mary Magdalene).

GALLERY GUIDE

MAIN PALACE
Ground floor: lockers, giftshop, ticket desk, toilets.
Upper floor: Palace rooms, including The Stone Room (Steinerner Saal) and The Gallery of Beauties.

PARK
Pavilions (Amalienburg, Badenburg, Pagodenburg and Magdalenenklause), Monopteros, greenhouses, fountain, canal, waterfall and café.

SOUTH OF THE PALACE (FORMER STABLES)
Marstallmuseum and Porcelain Museum.

NORTH OF THE PALACE
Museum Mensch und Natur.

THE SIGHTS

TIPS

● The Badenburg, Pagodenburg and Magdalenenklause pavilions are closed in winter.
● The park is a wonderful place to explore, so bring your walking shoes and a camera. You can even go jogging here.
● The atmospheric café/restaurant Schlosscafé im Palmenhaus (▷ 367) is a great place for a coffee or lunch between museums.
● Classical music concerts are held at the Palace. Ask at the tourist office or call 089 179 08444 for details.

The main palace, at the middle of the Schloss Nymphenburg complex, includes the ticket office

The Altes Schloss at Schleissheim was the earliest palace built on this site, which is 15km (9 miles) from Munich

Viktualienmarkt—Munich's largest food market

PRINZREGENTEN-STRASSE

🕂 179 F2 📷 U-Bahn Lehel (west end) or Prinzregentenplatz (east end) 🚋 Tram 17 to Haus der Kunst and Nationalmuseum

This long avenue, laid out in the 19th century, begins at the foot of the Englischer Garten and ends in Prinzregentenplatz in the fashionable Bogenhausen district, where many Munich celebrities have their homes (Boris Becker lives here). By the Englischer Garten is the Haus der Kunst art gallery (daily 10–8, Thu 10–10), which used to display German art of the Third Reich, but now houses changing exhibitions of contemporary art. Just beyond the gallery you cross the stretch of river in the Englischer Garten where surfers surf *against* the flow of water.

Farther on is the Bayerisches Nationalmuseum (▷ 184), which contains items relating to Bavarian history, including tapestries, paintings and sculpture. Heading east along the avenue, cross the River Isar and, if you are on foot, go down the underpass to cross the road. You come out at the golden Friedensengel (Angel of Peace), which faces toward Paris and was erected to commemorate the 25th anniversary of the Treaty of Versailles. Farther along, art lovers have another treat in the elegant, white Villa Stuck (Wed–Sun 11–6), which specializes in art nouveau.

An example of Meissen porcelain at Schloss Lustheim, Schleissheim

SCHLEISSHEIM

🕂 178 B4 (inset) • Max-Emanuel-Platz 1, 85764, Oberschleissheim ☎ 089 315 8720 🕐 Palace: Jun–end Sep Tue–Sun 9–6; Oct–end May Tue–Sun 10–4. Fountains: Apr to mid-Sep daily 10–4 📷 S1 to Oberschleissheim 🚌 Bus 292 (Mon–Sat only) to Freisingerstrasse or Schloss Lustheim 🎫 Schleissheim only: adult €4, child €3. Lustheim only: adult €3, child €2. Combined ticket: adult €5, child €4 🎫 🍴 🛍 closed Mon www.schloesser.bayern.de

To the north of Munich are the three palaces and gardens that make up Schleissheim. The original palace was built in the late 16th century for Duke Wilhelm V and was expanded considerably by Maximilian I. The more flamboyant palace is the Neues Schloss (the New Palace), begun in 1701 by Prince Elector Max Emanuel as 'the Bavarian Versailles'. The cost of building the palace drained Bavaria's resources, but resulted in an impressive building in Bavarian baroque and rococo styles, with stuccowork and frescoes by François Cuvilliés (1696–1768) and the Asam brothers, whose work you can also see in Asamkirche in the city centre (▷ 184). Max Emanuel was also a great collector of paintings, and in the Grand Gallery there are works by Anthony van Dyck (1599–1641) and Peter Paul Rubens (1577–1640), among others. The Lustheim Palace was also built by Max Emanuel as a grand hunting lodge to celebrate his marriage to Maria Antonia, the daughter of the Austrian

emperor. It is worth visiting for the Ernst Schneider Meissen porcelain collection alone. Once you've seen the palaces, you can enjoy the formal baroque gardens, which follow the strict rules set down by Versailles garden designer André Le Nôtre.

VIKTUALIENMARKT

🕂 179 D4 • By Peterskirche near Marienplatz 🕐 Mon–Fri 7–6, Sat 7–4, closed Sun 📷 U-Bahn and S-Bahn Marienplatz 🍴 Plenty of stalls selling take-away food

The Viktualienmarkt (with a Latin derivation meaning 'food market') is the food market in Munich. It used to be in Marienplatz but grew so big that it was moved to its present site by Peterskirche 200 years ago. Anything and everything you could want to eat is here: Fruit, vegetables, fish, meat, sausages, cheese, honey, bread, cakes and wine are just some of the things on sale. There is also plenty of non-German produce on sale, including Italian cheeses and French wines, and in recent years more exotic stalls and shops have opened, such as the South American shop and the kosher shop where you can buy kosher red wine and soups as well as filled bagels for about €3.50. The freshly squeezed juice stands are a must—choose from any combination of raspberry, orange, apple, carrot, pineapple and celery, to name a few, with a small juice costing upwards of €1.30.

The market is a good place to come for a quick bite to eat, with stalls selling pork sandwiches, pretzels, soup and *weissbier* (a pale, refreshing beer). Don't leave without admiring the tall, brightly painted Maypole in the middle of the market.

SOUTHERN GERMANY

The landscape of Southern Germany rises through densely-forested uplands to the Alpine backdrop of Bodensee, Germany's largest lake. Now and then the forests clear to reveal sights such as Regensburg, a city with Germany's greatest concentration of medieval buildings; Baden-Baden, Germany's oldest spa town; romantic Heidelberg and the fairytale turrets of Schloss Neuschwanstein. Motorsport fans will probably prefer the Porsche and Mercedes-Benz museums in Stuttgart.

MAJOR SIGHTS

The formal façade of Ansbach's Residenz, guarded by statues and a sentry box, hides a rococo interior

On the lake, at Aschaffenburg's Schloss Schonbusch

ALTMÜHLTAL (AND EICHSTÄTT)

✚ 442 F12 🛈 Naturpark Altmühltal, Kardinal-Preysing-Platz 14, Eichstätt, tel 08421 98760 🛈 Tourist Office, Domplatz 8, Eichstätt, tel 08421 98800 🚉 Eichstätt
www.altmuehltal.de
www.eichstaett.de

Altmühltal is Germany's largest nature park. Castles and fortresses nestle on wooded hills, and rugged crags overlook the rolling river valleys with their unspoiled towns and villages. The pretty town of Solnhofen is noted for its quarries of Jurassic limestone, holding numerous fossils. Pappenheim is an old-world little town with the 15th-century Gothic Stadtkirche and Galluskirche, which dates from Carolingian times.

The elegant town of Eichstatt is an architectural showpiece. The spires of its 14th-century cathedral and numerous other churches dominate the skyline, and remains of medieval fortifications sit alongside brightly painted rococo mansions. A mix of Romanesque, Gothic and baroque, the cathedral of St. Wilibald (first bishop of Eichstatt) houses the tomb of the saint and many pictures and relics, including the Pappenheim Altar, a late medieval depiction of the Crucifixion.

ANSBACH

✚ 438 F12 🛈 Johann-Sebastian-Bach-Platz 1, 91522 Ansbach, tel 09 8151243 🚉 Ansbach
www.ansbach.de

The city of Ansbach is more than 1,250 years old. Now the administrative and cultural hub of central Franconia, its historic Old Town has attractive houses moulded over the years by its history as a former residence of the margraves of Brandenburg-

Ansbach. The Margrave Residenz, one of the most important 18th-century palaces in Franconia, is a superb Renaissance structure with a magnificent rococo interior and beautiful gardens. It now houses the Bavarian State collection of Ansbach faience and porcelain and the Staatsgalerie.

You can see art nouveau buildings on Judttstrasse and baroque façades at Karlsplatz. The tranquil Hofgarten has a magnificent 250-year-old lime tree alley. Its Orangerie is one of the most remarkable Park palaces of Franconia, and the Kasper-Hauser-Memorial reminds you of the mysterious death of the 'Child of Europe'.

Don't miss In Johann-Sebastian-Bach-Platz, see the three-towered Gumbertus Church, with a Romanesque crypt, the Schwanenritterkapelle (Chapel of the Swan Knight) and the burial vault of the margraves.

ASCHAFFENBURG

✚ 437 D10 🛈 Schlossplatz 1, 63739 Aschaffenburg, tel 06021 395800 🚉 Aschaffenburg
www.aschaffenburg.de

Tucked away in the northwest corner of Bavaria, Aschaffenburg is on the banks of the River Main and bordered by the rolling hills of the Spessart. The town is dominated by the mighty Schloss Johannisburg, a magnificent Renaissance palace built at the beginning of the 17th century by the bishop of Mainz. Inside are the State Art Gallery, Palace Museum and state departments. There are fine views of the Main from the Palace Gardens and from the Pompejanum, a reproduction of the Villa of Castor and Pollux in Pompeii.

In the middle of town is the Stiftskirche, with its late Romanesque cloister. The church has a number of important works

of art, including *Lamentation* by Matthias Grunewald, with its tender portrayal of grief. In the former chapter house is the Stiftsmuseum, with church art and a collection of faience. More modern treasures can be seen in the Automuseum (Rosso Bianco); there are over 200,000 cars on display, making this the world's largest permanent exhibition of racing and sports cars.

BADEN-BADEN

See page 206.

BAMBERG

See page 207.

BAYERISCHER WALD

✚ 443 H12 🛈 Hans-Eisenmann-Haus, Böhmstrasse 35, Neuschonau, tel 08558 96150 🚉 Bayerischer Wald
www.nationalpark-bayerischer-wald.de

The Bayerischer Wald (Bavarian Forest) is the largest stretch of woodland in Central Europe. The first national park in Germany, it stretches over 6,000 sq km (2,300sq miles) between the Danube valley and merges into the Bohemian Forest in the Czech Republic and Austria. This wonderful park is popular with German visitors; it shelters pretty towns and villages with pastel-tinted houses, cobbled squares and winding lanes, quiet corners and pavement cafés, museums and galleries.

Near the information centre at Neuschonau is the Tier-Freigelande Nature Park where wild animals roam freely, while Furth im Wald is noted for its annual Slaying of the Dragon and Dragon Museum. The route of the Glass Road begins in Neustadt an der Weinstrasse and runs south through the forest to Passau (▷ 314–315).

To the west of the park, Amberg is a charming little town concealed within city walls.

AUGSBURG

Bavaria's oldest city.
A cultural city, with 15 museums and art galleries to visit.

Augsburg's cityscape has been formed by its 2000-year history; within it you'll find styles of all the major architectural periods. The Renaissance in particular flourished here, and rococo became known as the Augsburg style. The city has many great buildings, monumental fountains and grand boulevards. Maximilianstrasse is the grandest of all: The impressive Renaissance and baroque façades of stately patrician mansions line this broad avenue leading to the pedestrianized Rathausplatz. The imposing twin-domed spires of the Renaissance Rathaus dominate the square, and inside the restored Goldener Saal (golden hall) is famous for its magnificent portals, coffered ceiling and mural paintings. On Frauentorstrasse is Mozart House, the birthplace of Leopold Mozart, father of Wolfgang Amadeus, and now a Mozart museum. The Romanesque and Gothic St. Mary's Cathedral (Domkirche St. Maria) has impressive bronze doors with 35 relief panels presenting Old Testament scenes, a Romanesque crypt, medieval frescoes and the so-called Prophets' Windows from the 12th century.

HISTORY

Augsburg came to the fore in the 15th century when it became established as an important trading hub linking northern Europe to Italy. Augsburg enjoyed its heyday during this period, when the city was highly prosperous as a result of the international trade in gold, silver and copper. Also, the financial businesses of the wealthy Fugger and Welser merchant families evolved here, making Augsburg second only to London as a banking hub. Augsburg's three magnificent fountains were erected in 1594 on the occasion of the city's 1,600th anniversary in memory of its Roman founders.

FUGGER FAMILY

Augsburg owes much to the Fugger family. In 1516, Jakob Fugger founded the Fuggerei, the world's oldest welfare settlement for the poor, and still it houses around 200 residents in a picturesque gated complex with modernized apartments. Residents are expected to pray daily for the Fugger family and in return they pay a minimal rent. The gates of the complex are closed from 10pm until 6am (5am in summer), and residents returning late are fined. The former family town house, the 16th-century Fuggerhaus, sits alongside many grand houses on Maximilianstrasse.

The pine-cone on top of the Altes Rathaus is a town symbol

RATINGS

Historic interest	●●●●●
Good for kids	●●●
Photo stops	●●●●

TIPS

● Augsburg is an ideal base from which to visit Munich, especially during the *Oktoberfest* (▷ 279). It's just a half-hour ICE train ride from Munich and there are also hourly nonstop regional trains, which are cheaper.
● Hire a bicycle or tandem to tour the city and see the sights. There are many good bicycle rental companies with a range of adult and children's bicycles to suit all requirements.
● Next to the Town Hall, the Perlachturm (Perlach Tower) offers a spectacular panoramic view of Augsburg. It is open from May to October.

BASICS

✚ 442 F13 ℹ Bahnhofstrasse 7, 86150 Augsburg, tel 0821 502 0721; Mon–Fri 9–6
🚆 Augsburg
🚌 Augsburg

www.augsburg.de
Lots of useful information (in English) about the city and its attractions. Also check out www.regio-augsburg.de for comprehensive details (in English) of sights (including opening times), hotels and restaurants.

The modern Caracalla Spa

RATINGS

Historic interest	● ● ●
Cultural interest	● ● ● ●
Specialist shopping	● ● ●

TIPS

● Dining out in Baden-Baden can be expensive; take a short trip across the Rhine into France, where you will find some excellent restaurants in small villages that serve fine French cuisine at very reasonable prices.

● Take the funicular railway to the top of Baden-Baden's own mountain, the Merkur. There are wonderful views of the town and the surrounding area, plus a nature trail and waymarked footpaths.

BASICS

✚ 440 C12 🛈 Trinlchalle, Kaiserallee, Baden-Baden, tel 07221 275200; Mon–Sat 10–5

🚆 Baden-Baden–The Hauptbahnhof Baden-Baden is a stop for ICE/EC/IC/IR trains, as well as all other regional trains
🚌 Baden-Baden

www.Baden-Baden.de
Good website with lots of useful information (in English).

BADEN-BADEN

**The gateway to the Black Forest is renowned for its spa, casino and horse racing.
It has a townscape of elegant villas, stately 19th-century hotels, tree-lined avenues and expensively groomed parks.**

Once known as the Summer Capital of Europe, Baden-Baden has for many years been a popular destination with the rich and famous. Renowned for its spa, casino and horse racing, the town attracts visitors from all over the world who come here to sample the waters or lose their fortunes. Despite its upper class image, the elegant town has much to offer the casual visitor. Its temperate climate and wonderful location in the lush valley of the River Oos at the gateway to the Black Forest add much to its attraction.

WHAT TO SEE

Today, Baden-Baden is a popular all-year resort with elegant villas, stately 19th-century hotels. With its tree-lined avenues and expensively groomed parks, you can see evidence of its noble and elegant past everywhere; the white neoclassical Kurhaus (spa building) and impeccably maintained Kurgarten are the hub of fashionable life. The casino's interior is as opulent as its visitors, and have attracted the glitterati through its doors for many years. Close by, you can test the saline waters at the Trinkhalle and then follow the lovely Lichtentaler Allee, passing the magnificent Baden-Baden Theatre, Kunsthalle (state art gallery) and Alleehaus (City Museum) to the medieval Cistercian Lichenthal Abbey. The ruined castle (Old Palace), originally built in 1102, was the seat of the margraves of Baden-Baden. The Paradise is a complex of waterfalls, fountains and cascades.

SPAS

Baden-Baden is best known for its thermal springs, Europe's hottest with a temperature of 69ºC. You can see the restored ruins of a 2,000-year-old Roman bath used by Roman emperor Caracalla in AD213 from below Römerplatz. Built on either side of the Römerplatz are the 19th-century Friedrichsbad and modern Caracalla Baths. Friedrichsbad has stunning interiors, especially the circular pool ringed by columns and arcades. Caracalla has a variety of hot and cold water grottoes, indoor and outdoor pools, and whirlpools.

Don't miss In the suburb of Iffezheim is the racecourse that hosts the International Horse Races of Baden-Baden each September.

BAMBERG

The Altstadt is a UNESCO World Heritage Monument.
There are over 90 breweries in and around Bamberg.

Bamberg has everything for those prepared to linger and inhale the magic of the past that still hangs in the air. A thousand years of turbulent history are on display in this city, with historic buildings that read like an encyclopedia of architecture. The list is endless, but pride of place has to go to the amazingly situated Altes Rathaus (Old Town Hall), an unusual, picturesque mixture of rustic half-timbering and rococo elegance in the middle of the Regnitz.

In 1993, the Old Town was declared a World Heritage Monument by UNESCO.

HISTORY

After Heinrich II, the Holy Roman Emperor, was elected King of Germany in 1002, he decided to found a diocese in Bamberg to consolidate his power. By the 11th century, a trading settlement began to emerge on the Regnitz below the cathedral, and the citizens later built a town hall on an island in the river. In parts of the city today you can still see the imperial endowment Heinrich gave to the diocese and the cathedral, and the city's division into two distinct districts is evident; the Burgerstadt (merchants' town) is close to the river, and the Bischofsstadt (ecclesiastical quarter) is on the slopes above.

KAISERDOM

The Kaiserdom (Emperor Cathedral) sits majestically on one of Bamberg's seven hills, its four great towers piercing the skyline above the town. Built between the late Romanesque and early Gothic periods, its interior has some of the most remarkable sculpture to be found in Germany. In front of St. George's Choir is the impressive tomb of Emperor Heinrich II and his wife, Queen Kunigunde, by the great Tilman Riemenschneider, while on the left-side pier of the choir is the mysterious Bamberger Reiter (Bamberg Knight), whose identity is still the subject of much speculation. The most intriguing feature outside is the Furstentor (Prince's Portal), with a sculpture showing Christ and the Last Judgement. Looking over the Domplatz (Cathedral Square) is the Alte Hofhaltung, a fine example of German Renaissance construction, built as the Bishop's Palace in 1576: It now houses the Historisches Museum. On the other side is the Neue Residenz with its superb baroque interior and cobbled courtyard.

This rococo gatehouse hangs over the River Regnitz

RATINGS

Historic interest	●●●●●
Cultural interest	●●●●●
Walkability	●●●●

TIPS

● The best way of seeing Bamberg's treasures and experiencing the town's history is to stroll through the romantic lanes of the Old Town on foot. Most sights of interest are within a comfortable walking distance.

● There are over 90 breweries in and around Bamberg, the highest density of breweries in the world. The local brew is the Rauchbier, a dark red ale with a smooth, smoky taste that you will find served in Schlenkerla, a traditional inn in the Old Town. There's an interesting Beer Brewing Museum in rebuilt historic caves of the former Benedictine monastery's brewing cellars.

BASICS

✚ 438 F11 ⓘ Geyerswörthstrasse 3, 96047 Bamberg, tel 0951 871161; Apr–end Dec Mon–Fri 9.30–6, Sat, Sun 9.30–2.30; Jan–end Mar Mon–Fri 9.30–6, Sat 9.30–2.30
🚆 Bamberg

www.bamberg.info (also in English)

Berchtesgadener Land

Berchtesgaden National Park is one of the oldest protected areas in the Alps. It is a health resort with a wealth of unusual natural features.

Looking across the still waters of the Königssee

The view from the area's mountain tracks is stunning

The baroque church of Maria Gern, deep in the forested valley

RATINGS

Good for kids	●●●○
Historic interest	●●●○
Outdoor pursuits	●●●●●
Photo stops	●●●○

BASICS

✚ 443 H15

ℹ Königsseer Strasse 2, 83471 Berchtesgaden, tel 08652 9670; late May to mid-Oct Mon–Fri 8.30–6, Sat 8.30–5, Sun 8.30–3; mid-Oct to late May Mon–Fri 8.30–5, Sat 8.30–12

🚌 Bus to Eagle's Nest: from bus station Berchtesgaden to Obersalzberg adult €3.70, child €1.70. From Obersaltzberg to the Eagle's Nest (inc. elevator) adult €12.50 with visitors pass, €13.50 without, child €7 with visitors pass, €7.50 without. Schellenberg Ice Caves adult €4.50 with visitors pass, €5 without, child €2 with visitors pass, €2 without

🚉 Berchtesgaden

www.berchtesgadener-land.com
(also in English)

SEEING BERCHTESGADENER LAND

Berchtesgadener Land protrudes into Austria from southeastern Bavaria, just 20km (12.5 miles) from Mozart's Salzburg. In the south of the area, the Berchtesgaden National Park, with its massive landmark the Watzmann peak (2,713m/8,900ft), has a wealth of unusual natural features, and is one of the oldest protected areas in the Alps. The park is dotted with interesting small towns, places to visit and things to do. Topping the list are the Kehlsteinhaus (Eagle's Nest), Mount Jenner, Königsee (the Kings Lake), the 480-year-old salt mines and the Schellenberg Ice Caves. The historical town of Berchtesgaden has a number of interesting sights. The Royal Palace, formerly an Augustinian Priory, is now a museum with superb pieces of furniture, artwork and weapons. The Museum of Folklore (Heimatmuseum) has displays of local woodcrafts. The heart of the town is mostly a pedestrianized zone; the Kurgarten is a pleasant place to sit and watch the world go by.

HIGHLIGHTS

THE ROYAL PALACE

✉ Königliches Schloss, Berchtesgaden ☎ 08652 947980 ⏰ Late May–15 Oct Sun–Fri tours on the hour 10–12, 2–4; 16 Oct–late May Mon–Fri tours at 11, 2 💶 Adult €6 with visitors card, €7 without; child €3 with visitors card, €3.50 without
The Royal Palace has an interesting tour encompassing many different periods. From the Romanesque cloisters, you proceed through the periods of Gothic, baroque, rococo and Biedermeier: Though the Royal Palace was extended throughout the centuries, the older sections were left practically intact. Crown Prince Rupprecht decorated many of the rooms with valuable objects from the royal Wittelsbach family's art collection, including hunting weapons and trophies, furniture, fine porcelain and paintings by famous Bavarian artists.

THE KEHLSTEINHAUS (EAGLE'S NEST)

✉ Kehlsteinstrasse, Berchtesgaden ☎ 08652 2969 (Eagle's Nest Restaurant) ⏰ Mid-May to end Oct

Don't miss the trip to the Kehlsteinhaus (Eagle's Nest) mountain top restaurant. The restaurant was opened in 1952, and from May to October special mountain buses take you from Obersalzberg to a parking area 150m (165yd) below the mountain summit. From there a tunnel guides you to an elevator that takes you inside the mountain directly to the restaurant; the views are spectacular. The road leading 6.5km (4 miles) from Obersalzberg to the Eagle's Nest parking area (Kehlsteinstrasse) is itself an amazing feat of engineering: Built by Hitler to give access to his holiday house, it has five tunnels and gradients of up to 28% or 1 in 4.

DOKUMENTATION OBERSALZBERG

✉ Dokumentation Obersalzberg, Salzbergstrasse 41 83471 Berchtesgaden
☎ 08652 947960 ⏰ Apr–end Oct daily 9–5 (last admission 4); Nov–end Mar Tue–Sun 10–3 (last admission 2). Closed 1 Jan, 1 Nov, 24 & 31 Dec 💶 Adult €2.50, child €1.50.

Perched at 1,834m (6,017ft), this building near the parking area at Obersalzberg was a project of Martin Bormann's and was given to Adolf Hitler for his 50th birthday as a holiday house and teahouse for diplomats. It was expanded after 1933, becoming the southern headquarters for Hitler's Nazi government. The exhibition documents the history of the Obersalzberg and links the local historical aspects with a portrayal of the central phenomena of the National Socialist dictatorship. There are over 900 photos, documents, posters, films and sound recordings on display, some of which have been made accessible to the public for the first time. There's also access to part of the underground bunker system.

THE SALT MINES

✉ Bergwerkstrasse 83, 83471 Berchtesgaden
☎ 08652 600220 ⏰ May–15 Oct daily 9–5; 16 Oct–end Apr daily 11.30–3 💶 Adult €12.50, first child (4–16) €6.80, further children €4.20

In former times, only privileged dignitaries were allowed to visit Berchtesgaden's salt mines, but today this fascinating underground world can be visited by all. Tours are given by knowledgeable guides. Don't miss the opportunity to get dressed in miner's clothing and travel deep into the mountain on a mining train. Via slides and dark passages you will visit a glowing salt grotto, learn about mining history and techniques thanks to a film and numerous exhibits, traverse the subterranean lake on a raft and ride on the funicular. The tour takes about an hour and heavy-duty trousers are provided for the trip down slides. You need to wear warm clothing and good walking shoes for the tour.

BACKGROUND

Prior to AD700, the area that is today known as Berchtesgaden was largely uninhabited. In 1106, Augustinian monks from Salzburg began building their monastery where the royal palace stands today. For the next seven centuries, Berchtesgaden was an independent state ruled by prince-provosts, who were heads of both the Church and the State. The area flourished thanks to the discovery of salt, locally known as white gold. In 1803, Napoleon controlled this area, making Berchtesgaden part of Austria until 1810, when it was secularized and incorporated into Bavaria. Later, the royal family of Bavaria, the Wittelsbachs, used the area for fishing and hunting, and the monastery was redesigned as a royal palace. Although a large part of the building in open to the public as a museum, the monastery-palace of Berchtesgaden is still owned by the Wittelsbach family.

The 17th-century pilgrimage church of St. Bartholomew (below) nestles into the mountainous landscape

Alpine gentians (bottom)

Bodensee (Lake Constance)

Often called the Swabian Sea because of its enormous size, this is the largest lake in Germany and third largest in Central Europe. From the German shore, the backdrop of the Swiss Alps is breathtaking.

Taking shelter in Lindau harbour, at the southern end of the lake

A great day's fishing at Meersburg

The area around Bodensee is a rich agricultural landscape

RATINGS	
Historic interest	● ● ● ○
Cultural interest	● ● ● ○
Outdoor pursuits	● ● ● ○
Walkability	● ● ● ○

BASICS

✚ 441 D14

🎫 Lake of Constance Card (Bodensee Erlebniskarte): 3 days adult €54, child (6–15) €29. 7 days adult €67, child €39. 14 days adult €93, child €49, under 6 free

www.lake-constance.com (in English) The English version has just one page with a sketch map and little information. Try www.bodensee-tourismus.com: It's in German only but much more informative.

SEEING BODENSEE

Bodensee (Lake Constance) has 273km (170 miles) of shoreline shared between three countries. At 173km (107 miles), Germany has the largest shoreline, and it gets very busy here during the high season, but the rewards far outweigh the inconvenience of heavy traffic and crowded towns. Part of the area's attraction is the temperate climate; the mild, dry weather is ideal for visitors and the surrounding orchards and vineyards. The historic city of Konstanz, with its bustling Altstadt (Old Town), has many interesting places to visit. Around the lake, Mainau is a paradise island of tropical plants with a fairytale castle; Reichenau Island has three Romanesque churches; in Singen you can explore the largest castle ruins in Germany; a prehistoric lake dwellers' village has been wonderfully reconstructed in Unteruhldingen; Meersburg has two formidable castles; in Friedrichshafen there's the interesting Zeppelin Museum; and the island town of Lindau has many nooks and crannies to explore.

HIGHLIGHTS

KONSTANZ

🚉 Bahnhofplatz 13, Konstanz, tel 07531 133030; Apr–end Oct Mon–Fri 9.15–6.30, Sat 9–4, Sun 10–1; Nov–end Mar Mon–Fri 9.30–12.30, 2–6 🚊 Konstanz

This historic city sits on a spit of land separating the Obersee, the main area of the lake, from the Untersee where the mighty Rhine flows from the lake into Switzerland before beginning its long journey north through Germany. Konstanz avoided bombing attacks during WWII because of its close proximity to neutral Switzerland, so the city's historical buildings were spared the structural damage suffered elsewhere. At the harbour, you can see the city's most famous historic building, the Konzil, and its most controversial monument, the gigantic *Imperia* statue. The late-20th-century *Imperia*, a massive female figure by sculptor Peter Lenk, rotates on the base of a former light tower enabling onlookers to view the provocatively clad woman from all angles. Initially the cause of much controversy but now widely accepted, the figure symbolizes the power of the many courtesans who followed the male participants to Konstanz at the time of the Council of Constance. Nearby, the impressive historic council building, a former warehouse known as the Konzil, is where the 1417 papal election was held. The historic part of the city holds many delights: Don't miss the Marktstätte and Kaiserbrunnen (Emperor's Fountain, 1897), the 16th-century Rathaus, St. Stephen's Church, the five-floor Hohe Haus and the oldest building in Konstanz, the Cathedral.

LINDAU

🔹 Ludwigstrasse 68, Lindau, tel 08382 260030; Apr to mid-Jun, mid-Sep to mid-Oct Mon–Fri 9–1, 2–6, Sat 10–2; mid-Jun to mid-Sep Mon–Fri 9–6, Sat, Sun 10–2; mid-Oct to end Mar Mon–Fri 9–12, 2–5 🔹 Lindau

The tiny island town of Lindau is linked to the mainland by a bridge on the northeastern corner of the lake. Owing to its location on a major trading route, Lindau was a bustling trading post in the Middle Ages, and consequently wealthy merchants built grand, gabled, Italian-style houses on the town squares. Half-timbered buildings from all eras lean over the narrow streets, and Maximilianstrasse, with its patrician houses, fountains and shaded walks, is particularly beautiful. Stroll around the Altstadt and see the Old Town Hall with its stepped gables and garish murals, the Diebsturm (Thieves' Tower) and St. Peter's Church, with fine frescoes showing scenes from the Passion story. Parking is a big problem here, so try leaving your car on the mainland and taking the free shuttle bus to the island.

MEERSBURG

🔹 Kirchstrasse 4, Meersburg, tel 07532 431110; May–end Sep Mon–Fri 9.30–12, 2–6, Sat 10–2; Oct–end Apr Mon–Fri 9–12, 2–5

Beautifully baroque, Meersburg is often described as a jewel of European architecture. The Unterstadt (Lower Town) consists of only two streets, which are sandwiched between the shore and the tower-ing Altes and Neues Schloss (old and new castles) above. At the western end is the Seetor (Lake Gate) and at the eastern side the promenade is dominated by the massive tithe barn. The narrow streets in the historic Oberstadt (Upper Town) are lined with half-timbered houses and stately baroque buildings. Try to visit the Altes Schloss, Neues Schloss (which houses the Municipal Gallery) and Weinbaumuseum (Museum of Wine Making).

FRIEDRICHSHAFEN

🔹 Am Bahnhofsplatz 2, Friedrichshafen, tel 07541 30010; May–end Sep Mon–Fri 9–6, Sat 9–1; Oct–end Apr Mon–Fri 9–12, 2–5, Sat 9–12 🔹 Friedrichshafen

Although an industrial town, its association with the Zeppelin airships make this a worthwhile place to visit. The Friedrichshafen Zeppelin Museum opened in the former port railway station in 1996, and has the world's largest exhibition on the history and technology airships. While you are here, visit the twin onion-domed Schlosskirche, built in 1695 in the early baroque style by Christian Thumb.

BACKGROUND

Lake Constance is Germany's largest stretch of inland water and is also Europe's largest water reservoir, supplying water to most of southern Germany. The vineyards and orchards on the northern side thrive in the mild climate, while from the southern banks you get spectacular scenes of the snow-capped Alps. The Rhine enters the lake at its southeastern corner and flows out through the Untersee into Switzerland before crashing over the largest waterfall in Europe, the mighty Rhine Falls (23m/75ft high and 150m/490ft wide) in Schaffhausen. This spectacular expanse of water has served trade, culture and leisure for centuries, and today it continues to offer a wide range of opportunities to all its visitors.

THE SIGHTS

A friendly face in Konstanz's Altstadt

Fountains in front of Ludwig II's
Schloss Herrenchiemsee

Coburg's Stadthaus is the
backdrop for a busy market

Ramparts and a watchtower still
guard Dinkelsbühl

THE SIGHTS

BAYREUTH

✚ 438 G11 ℹ️ Kongress-und
Tourismuszentrale Bayreuth,
Luitpoldplatz 9, 95444 Bayreuth,
tel 0921 69001 🚆 Bayreuth
www.bayreuth-tourismus.de

Bayreuth's history can be traced
to the late 12th century, but it
was from 1735 to 1763, during
the rule of Margrave Friedrich
and his enterprising wife,
Wilhemine (older sister of
Frederick the Great), that the
town came to prominence.
Wilhemine was the force behind
the construction of the magnificent palaces and gardens you
can see in Bayreuth today.

Although you can still see
traces of Bayreuth's medieval
past—the original residence of
the margraves, the Altes Schloss
(Old Palace), dates back to the
14th century—the baroque age
contributed most to the town's
architectural character. The
Neues Schloss (New Palace),
built in 1753, houses several
museums and has an interesting
grotto and garden rooms.
Composer Richard Wagner
(1813–83) is responsible for
Bayreuth's eminence today; his
former home, Villa Wahnfried, is
now a national museum dedicated to his life and works, and is
also the site of the annual
Bayreuth Wagner Festival. In the
gardens are the graves of Wagner
and his wife.

Fresh fish on Fraueninsel, Chiemsee

CHIEMSEE

✚ 443 H14 ℹ️ Chiemsee Infocenter,
Felden 10, D-83233, Bernau am
Chiemsee, tel 08051 965550
🚆 Prien/Bernau
www.mychiemsee.de

Bavaria's largest lake is a popular
resort surrounded by pretty
towns and villages and has two
principal islands. There's much to
see and do here, and Chiemsee
has something for everyone, with
good hiking, cycling, boating and
bathing facilities, as well as many
museums and galleries.

Herreninsel (Men's Island) and
Fraueninsel (Women's Island)
are both interesting places to
visit. On the mostly wooded
Hereninsel is the magnificent
Schloss Herrenchiemsee, an
unfinished palace of Ludwig II.
Between 1878 and 1885, the
King decided to build a replica of
Versailles, but ran out of funds
before the palace was completed. What does exist is
impressive, especially the long
Hall of Mirrors, palatial rooms
and museum. Fraueninsel, the
smaller island, has a Benedictine
nunnery, founded in the 8th century, and a picturesque little
fishing village.

COBURG

✚ 438 F10 ℹ️ Herrengasse 4, 96450
Coburg, tel 09561 74180 🚆 Coburg
www.coburg-tourist.com

The stark exterior of the massive
Veste (fortress) towers above
this lively town with its
wealth of tradition. For
many years this was the seat
of the dukes of Saxe-Coburg
and a popular meeting place
of the European aristocracy.
Coburg Castle, known as the
Crown of Franconia because
of its hilltop position and towers, was founded in the 11th

century and much rebuilt during
the Renaissance. This impressive
stronghold, with its double ring of
defensive walls, was never taken
by force. Today, there is a display
of weapons and copperplate
engravings, plus a world-
renowned art collection.

The Hofgarten (Court Garden),
which houses the Museum of
Natural History, is one of the
most beautiful parts of the town
and owes a lot to Coburg's ducal
heritage. The garden stretches
from the castle to the Ehrenburg
Palace, which has an impressive
Riesensaal (Giants' Hall)—a
baroque chamber decorated with
stucco ornamental plasterwork.

DINKELSBÜHL

✚ 442 E12 ℹ️ Marktplatz, Dinkelsbühl,
tel 09851 90240 🚆 Dinkelsbühl
www.dinkelsbuehl.de

Dinkelsbühl is a cultural monument: a distinctive townscape,
perfectly preserved town walls
and magnificent patrician houses.
The Hezelhof, with its tiered balconies, and the Renaissance
half-timbered Deutsches Haus
are a reminder of the town's
glorious era in the 15th and 16th
centuries, when its industrious
craftsmen and flourishing trading
activities enhanced its wealth.

There are four gates in the
town walls, the most impressive
being the Rothenburger Tor on
the north side. Martin Luther
Strasse leads to the Marktplatz
and the late gothic St. George's
Minster, one of the most beautiful hall churches in Germany. The
tower of the Minster offers the
best panoramic views of the
town. Behind the church is the
Old Town Hall, with prison cells
and courtyard. A walk around the
ramparts at night is an ideal way
to experience the town's vibrant
ambience, especially in the
company of the nightwatchman
as he does his rounds.

FREIBURG IM BREISGAU

The capital of the Black Forest is surrounded by lush green hills and vineyards.
The Cathedral is a masterpiece of Gothic architecture.

The sloping roofs and narrow streets of Freiburg

Known as the capital of the Black Forest, Freiburg sits neatly in the midst of lush green hills and vineyards close to the borders of France and Switzerland. The historic Altstadt with numerous historical monuments, museums, theatres and lively squares with intimate restaurants and quaint bars all make this vibrant city popular with students and visitors alike. Look out for the Freiburg Bächle, the small streams of water that flow through the streets in open gullies. Nearby are the vineyard and wine villages of the Margrave, Kaiserstuhl and Tuniberg regions.

FREIBURG MUNSTER

The magnificent Gothic Cathedral takes pride of place as Freiburg's main landmark. It took over 300 years to build and it ranks among the masterworks of Gothic architecture. The unique 116m (381ft) tower dominates the city, and if you are fit enough, you can climb to the viewing platform for magnificent views. The highlights of the lavish interior are its high altar with a famous altar-piece by Hans Baldung Grien, the choir chapels with their 16th-century windows, fine altars and monuments and the wonderful 14th-century stained glass in the aisles.

OTHER SIGHTS

The Augustiner Museum is a former monastery of the Augustinian hermits, with artistic and historical collections of the city and Upper Rhine region from the 9th to 20th centuries. The Museum for Town History is in the Wentzinger House, built in 1761 by the artist Johann Christian Wentzinger. The Adelshauser Kloster, an old convent now occupied by the Natural History Museum, has interesting geological, zoological and mineralogical collections. In the unusual Carnival Museum, the Breisgau Jesters' Guild shows the history of carnival from the Middle Ages to the present day. The Cathedral Square is surrounded by impressive buildings, the tallest of which is the historical Kaufhaus (Merchants Hall), with statues of Habsburg rulers on its façade. Other sights worth seeing are the baroque Erzbischöfliches Palais (Archbishops' Palace), Haus zum Walfisch (House of Whale) with its superb late Gothic portal, Basler Hof (Basle Court), the restored 15th century Kornhaus (the original was destroyed in World War II) and the two medieval city gates, Martinstor and Schwabentor.

RATINGS				
Historic interest	●	●	●	
Walkability	●	●	●	●
Good for food	●	●	●	●	●

BASICS

🗺 440 B13

ℹ Rotteckring 14, 79098 Freiburg, tel 0761 388 1880; May–end Oct Mon–Fri 9.30–8, Sat 9.30–5, Sun 10–2; Nov–end Apr Mon–Fri 9.30–6, Sat 9.30–2, Sun 10–12

🚃 Freiburg

🚆 Freiburg

www.freiburg.de (in German)
www.fwt-online.de (in German)

TIPS

● The best way of seeing Freiburg is to take one of the many guided city tours with the Freiburg Kulture tour-guide team. They begin at the tourist office and cover a wide variety of sights and themes.
● Freiburg is an excellent base to tour the Black Forest and visit Germany's largest family theme park, the amazing Europa Park in Rust.
● The 1284m Schauinsland mountain provides the perfect platform for viewing both the city and the Rhine Valley. The 15-minute cable car ride from the valley station is majestic, the lush Black Forest spreads out below as you head for the top of the world.

Heidelberg

Romantic Heidelberg is celebrated in song and poetry. The large ruined castle is one of the finest examples of German Renaissance architecture.

Heidelberg's Altstadt is a dominating presence

This ancient university town has a vibrant student life

Although now in ruins, Schloss Heidleberg is worth a visit

RATINGS	
Cultural interest	●●●○
Specialist shopping	●●●○
Walkability	●●○
Good for food	●●●○

BASICS

✚ 437 D11

🛈 Willy-Brandt Platz 1, Heidelberg (outside the main train station), tel 06221 194 33; Apr–end Oct Mon–Sat 9–7, Sun and hols 10–6; Nov–end Mar Mon–Sat 9–6

🚌 🚇 Heidelberg
www.cvb-heidelberg.de (in English)

TIPS

● For the best views of Heidelberg, take a stroll along the Philosophers' Path, one of Europe's most beautiful walks, high above the town and the Neckar River.

● Look out for the popular 'Made in Heidelberg' designs such as Lamy writing tools and Gil Brett and Betty Barclay ladies' fashion.

SEEING HEIDELBERG

The enchanting location of Heidelberg on the meandering Neckar River amid wooded hillsides and sloping vineyards does much to explain its romantic appeal to artists, poets and visitors. The towers and bridges, Old Town and majestic towering castle cast their magical spell on all who enter, the only problem being that there are many people that do. This is a busy university town with lots of cultural activities going on throughout the year. The Hauptstrasse is a pedestrianized shopping thoroughfare 1.5km (1 mile) wide, with many narrow side streets full of interesting shops, rowdy student pubs, bistros and intimate restaurants—it's a great place to explore but be prepared for the crowds. Perched high above this, the magnificent red sandstone Heidelberg castle crowns the city: Enjoy the walk through steep cobbled lanes from the Kornmarkt to the ruins. Allow at least half a day to poke around and shop in the Altstadt and the same to explore the castle ruins. Other places of interest include the Botanical Garden of the University of Heidelberg, one of the oldest in Germany, and the University Museum, which displays Heidelberg's academic history. Near by is the Students' Prison, where from 1778 until 1914 students were imprisoned for so called *Kavaliersdelikte* (minor transgressions). There are more than fifteen museums in Heidelberg, including the Palatinate Museum with interesting regional items and works of art. In this vibrant city, there are several theatres, private galleries, concerts and festivals throughout the year.

HIGHLIGHTS

SCHLOSS HEIDELBERG

✉ Heidelberg ☎ 06221 538431 ◷ Daily 8–5.30 🎫 Interior: adult €3, senior €1.50. Castle Yard, Great Vat and German Pharmacy Museum: adult €2, senior €1

This impressive ruin on a granite rock 90m (300ft) above the city is one of Germany's finest examples of a Gothic-Renaissance fortress. Construction began in the 13th century and continued over a period of 400 years, with ramparts, buildings and palaces added in a variety of styles. The prince electors of the 16th and 17th century turned the fortress into a castle, and the two dominant buildings at the eastern and northern side of the courtyard are considered to be two of the most important buildings in German architectural history. The castle was destroyed during the Thirty Years War and again in the late 17th century by invading French troops. Local people began using castle sandstone to build houses in Heidelberg, but fortunately this was stopped in 1800 by Count Charles de Graimberg. The King's Hall was added in 1934 and is used today for dinner banquets, balls and theatrical performances. During the Heidelberg Castle Festival, the amazing Renaissance courtyard is used for open-air musicals, operas, theatre performances and classical concerts, such as the famous Castle Serenades performed by the Heidelberg City Orchestra. From the terrace there are fantastic views across the town and Neckar valley: Look out for the huge footprint said to have been made by a knight who had to make a hasty escape from a third-floor window when caught by a prince in his wife's bedroom.

CASTLE GARDENS

⚑ Free
In former times, the geometrically designed terraces of the Renaissance garden stood out against the wooded background of Heidelberg Castle; before its destruction during the Thirty Years War, contemporaries even considered the Hortus Palatinus to be the Eighth Wonder of the World. The remains of the Great Grotto, where the water flows in time with music, is amazing, and in the nearby pond is a great sandstone sculpture of Father Rhine.

OLD UNIVERSITY AND THE BOTANICAL GARDEN

🕑 Museum: Tue–Sat 10–4. Library: Mon–Sat 10–6. Botanical Garden: Mon–Thu 9–4, Fri 9–2.30, Sun 9–12, 1–4 ⚑ Free.
Germany's oldest university was founded here in 1386. Dominating the University Square are the Old and New University buildings, along with the Löwenbrunnen, a fountain crowned by a lion symbolizing the power of the Palatinate. The ceiling in the Old Assembly Hall holds paintings depicting the four university faculties: philosophy, medicine, law and theology. The university museum explains Heidelberg's academic history and the library holds huge electronic archives. The Botanical Garden, one of the oldest in Germany, was originally established in 1593 as a *hortus medicus* for the cultivation of medical herbs. Nowadays, this institution is noted for plant biology and the greenhouses contain rare plant collections.

THE PHILOSOPHERS' WALK

Enjoy a stroll along the famous Philosophenweg and follow in the footsteps of Heidelberg's philosophers and university teachers. The views are outstanding, as are the exotic trees, shrubs, parks, gardens and memorial stones along the path.

BACKGROUND

This historic university town and former capital of the Palatinate is beautifully located at the point where the Neckar emerges from the wooded Odenwald hills into the Rhine plain. The town was destroyed during the Thirty Years War and sacked again by invading French troops in the late 17th century. Careful rebuilding has created a friendly, romantic city that has become one of Germany's most popular destinations. The magic of the Castle, the Old Bridge and the Old Town has attracted such notable characters as Mark Twain and English artist J. M. W. Turner: Today they attract countless visitors from throughout the world.

HEIDELBERG CARDS

Heidelberg Cards come with a city guide and map, and give free or reduced-priced access to some attractions and museums, plus discounts in many shops, restaurants and bars.
● Heidelberg Card 2 days is valid all year, costs €12 and includes: public transportation in Heidelberg; admission to Heidelberg Castle; a guided tour of the castle interiors the Old Assembly Hall; German

From its hillside location, the Schloss looks down on the town

Pharmaceutical Museum; University Museum; Student Prison; Museum of the Palatinate; Ethnographical Museum; reductions at other places of interest, restaurants and discounted shopping.
● Heidelberg Card 4 days is also valid all year, and costs €20. As well as all the benefits of the HeidelbergCard 2 days, you get free admission to the Prinzhorn Collection, Museum Art Brut Haus Cajeth and the German Packaging Museum.
● Heidelberg Card Family 2 days is valid from 1 March 1 to 31 October and covers either 2 adults and 2 children or 1 adult and 3 children. It costs €24 and it includes all the benefits of the HeidelbergCard 2 days, plus Heidelberg Zoo and the Fairy Tale Theme Park on Köenigstuhl Mountain.

Germany's highest peak, the Zugspitze, Garmish-Partenkirchen

The formidable walls of Burg Trausnitz, near Landshut

The sumptuous dining room at Schloss Linderhof

FURTWANGEN

✠ 440 C13 🛈 Marktplatz 4, 78120 Furtwangen, tel 07723 939111
🚉 Furtwangen
www.furtwangen.de

The Black Forest is the heart of the German clockmaking region, and Furtwangen is one of the industry's major towns. The Deutsches Uhrenmuseum (German Clock Museum) is the place to go to see fine examples of timepieces from around the world. With over 5,000 exhibits, the museum has the largest collection of clocks in Germany, and the world's largest collection of Black Forest clocks, including Renaissance ones and examples of clockmasters' art. Many of the factories and workshops in the area are open to visitors.

If you are particularly interested in clocks, visit the nearby town of Villingen-Schwenningen and the Uhrenindustriemuseum, which housed the former factory of the oldest clock company in Wurttemberg.

GARMISCH-PARTENKIRCHEN

✠ 442 F15 🛈 Richard Strauss Platz 2, Garmisch-Partenkirchen, tel 08821 180700 🚉 Garmisch-Partenkirchen
www.garmisch-partenkirchen.de

Garmisch-Partenkirchen is undoubtedly Germany's winter sports capital. The town comprises two villages that were merged together for the Winter Olympics of 1936, the older Partenkirchen and the more modern Garmisch. Garmisch is the ritzier of the two, with plenty of fashionable shops and cafés. Its Kurpark regularly hosts open-air concerts, and the Kurhaus contains a collection of Meissen porcelain and historic toys. Pfarrkirche St. Martin, built by Joseph Schmuzer in 1733, has a rich baroque interior.

Partenkirchen is characterized by the traditional painted houses, and one of these, a former merchant's residence at Ludwigstrasse 47, is the only house in the street not to be devastated by a terrible fire in 1865. The house contains the Werdenfelser Heimatmuseum, which vividly brings the region's distinctive culture to life. You are still likely to see country folk in traditional costumes and cattle being driven from their mountain-grazing grounds through the streets here.

The towns straddle the River Partnach, surrounded by mighty mountain massifs. Most impressive is the Zugspitze, the highest mountain in Germany at 2,962m (9,724ft), easily conquered nowadays by rack railway from Garmisch. There's also the option of taking the cable car from Erwald past the imposing West Wall, or the Eibsee cable railway from Grainau at Lake Eibsee.

HEIDELBERG

See pages 214–215.

LANDSHUT

✠ 443 G13 🛈 Altstadt 315, 84028 Landshut, tel 0871 922050
🚉 Landshut
www.landshut.de

This historical ducal town has retained much of the appearance and character of the provincial capital that it once was. The cobbled squares and town boulevards are ideal for exploring the cultural highlights of this medieval town. Landshut is on the banks of the River Isar, and the pattern of the town is set by two wide market streets, Altstadt and Neustadt, lined with late medieval town houses. In the Altstadt, the town's main street lined with late Gothic gabled houses, is the church of St. Martin, its slender tower rising to

133m, the highest brick steeple in the world.

Dominating the skyline above the town is the imposing Trausnitz Castle, founded by Duke Ludwig I in 1204. In the 16th century, the castle was rebuilt by Prince William of Bavaria in an Italian style. He retained the 13th-century chapel with its Romanesque statuary, and had the famous Narrentreppe, or Fools' Staircase, decorated with wall paintings. The castle terrace gives a spectacular panorama over the town.

LINDERHOF

✠ 442 F15 🛈 Linderhof 12, 82488 Ettal, tel 08822 920349 🚉 Linderhof
www.linderhof.de

Set among magnificent mountain scenery and surrounded by forest, Schloss Linderhof is perhaps the most appealing of King Ludwig's castles. The Royal Villa of Ludwig II began as a hunting lodge belonging to his father, Maximilian II, and was based on the Petit Trianon at Versailles. Completed in 1878, the lavish interiors are not as spectacularly bizarre as Ludwig's Schloss Neuschwanstein (▷ 224–227), but are nevertheless pretentious, with a large private bedroom, Hall of Mirrors and an enormous crystal chandelier weighing 500kg (1,000lb), all decorated in a mixture of Renaissance and baroque styles. Ludwig used the palace as a retreat and rarely received visitors here.

The formal French gardens, with fanciful fountains, pools and follies, are a wonderful place to explore. The grand cascade is a water jet that shoots higher than the palace itself, the grotto is an artificial stalactite cave inspired by the Venusberg of Wagner's opera *Tannhauser*, and the oriental-style Moorish Kiosk has a grandiose peacock throne.

KARLSRUHE

**An unusual town, laid out in the shape of a fan.
Superb collections from the Baden State Museum are on
display in the Schloss.**

In 1715, Margrave Karl Wilheim decided to build a residential retreat close to the Rhine in the northern foothills of the Black Forest. Tired of living in a decaying medieval castle, the Margrave is said to have dreamed of building a city laid out in the shape of an oriental fan with a palace at the axis. When his son, Karl Friedrich, took up regency, he commissioned Albert Friedrich von Kesslau to build a new palace. Von Kesslau designed it in close consultation with his mentor La Guépière from Paris. The building work was completed in 1770. From the beginning, Karlsruhe was designed as a city without walls, and the unusual pattern of streets running in straight lines from the palace still exists today. Master builder and architect Weinbrenner created the numerous classical buildings around the city. In 1951, Karlsruhe lost its status as regional capital of Baden, but its importance is still recognized; today it is home to Germany's two highest courts, the Federal Constitutional Court and the Federal Supreme Court.

SIGHTS
The Marktplatz, designed by Weinbrenner in 1797, is a neoclassical square. The red sandstone pyramid (1825) that has become the emblem of Karlsruhe marks the burial vault of the town's founder. On either side of the square are the Stadtkirche, the municipal church for the state of Baden-Württemberg, and the Rathaus. The market fountain is a monument commemorating the merits of Grand Duke Ludwig in establishing the first spring water mains in Karlsruhe. The Natural History Museum (Naturkundemuseum), State Art Gallery (Staatliche Kunsthalle), Municipal Gallery (Städtische Galerie) and Museum of Modern Art (Museum für neue Kunst) all have wide ranges of interesting exhibits. The Kaiserstrasse, the first main street running parallel to the Schloss, is a popular spot on a sunny day.

SCHLOSS
The Schloss displays superb collections of the Baden State Museum: Greek, Roman and near-Eastern art, the Margrave of Baden's treasure chamber, a famous collection of Turkish trophies and art and cultural history from the Middle Ages to the modern era. Behind the palace, in the extensive Schlossgarten, is the Orangery, with exhibits, paintings and sculptures from the end of the 19th century through to the more contemporary, and the Botanic Garden.

*Duke Karl Friedrich overlooks
that town that carries his name*

RATINGS
Historic interest	● ● ●
Cultural interest	● ● ● ●
Walkability	● ● ● ●

BASICS
✚ 441 C12
🛈 Bahnhofsplatz 6, Karlsruhe, tel 0721 3720 5383; Mon–Fri 9–6, Sat 9–1
🚈 Karlsruhe
🚌 Karlsruhe

www.karlsruhe.de (in English)

TIPS
● The best vantage point from which to see the layout of this fan-shaped city is the palace tower. Here you are standing right at the axis and can look over the whole town from a height of 42m (138ft).
● Many German cities have a Christmas market, but the Karlsruhe Christkindl Markt (Christmas craft market) is exceptional. Beginning in November, a small village of stalls takes over the market square and the smell of *Glühwein* (mulled wine) and *Lebkuchen* (gingerbread) fills the air.

Nürnberg (Nuremberg)

**The second largest city in the state after Munich.
Once a city of medieval elegance, Nürnberg has the dubious distinction
of being the ideological heart of the Third Reich.**

The stark, modern exterior of the Germanisches National Museum

Children will love Nürnberg's toy museum

Many of Nürnberg's old building have been reconstructed

RATINGS	
Historic interest	●●●○
Cultural interest	●●●○
Walkability	●●●○
Good for food	●●○

BASICS

🔁 438 F11

ℹ️ Hauptmarkt 18, Nürnberg, tel 0911 233 6135; Mon–Sat 9–6; also Sun 10–4 May–end Oct. Open during Christkindlesmarkt Mon–Sat 9–7, Sun 10–7

ℹ️ Künsterhaus, Bahnhofsplatz, tel 0911 233 6135; Mon–Sat 9–6; also Sun 10–4 May–end Oct. Open during Christkindlesmarkt Mon–Sat 9–7, Sun 10–7

🚶 Walking tours of the Old Town (in English) May–end Oct, late Nov–early Jan. Adult €7.50 (includes admission to Kaiserburg), child (under 14) free

🚇 Nürnberg
🚉 Nürnberg

www.nuernberg.de (also in English)

SEEING NÜRNBERG

Nürnberg is an interesting mix of the quaint and the cosmopolitan. The Altstadt is a medieval walled city with large pedestrian walkways. The River Pegnitz divides the old town into its Sebald and Lorenz districts, named after the two main churches. The narrow streets and alleys lined with timber-framed houses are ideal places to explore and shop. In November, the Marktplatz is invaded for the famous Christkindlesmarkt, the open-air Christmas Market. Apart from the variety of Christmas decorations, don't miss the *glühwein* (warm spiced wine) and lebkuchen (similar to gingerbread). The city's three main churches, Frauenkirche, St. Lorenz Kirche and St. Sebaldus Kirche, are prominent landmarks adorned with magnificent works of art. The painter Albrecht Dürer lived in Nürnberg from 1509 to 1528, his house is now a museum with interesting guided tours by an actress dressed as Dürer's wife. The climb to the Kaiserburg (Imperial Castle), which dates back to the city's founding in the 11th century, is well worth the effort. Try to visit the cellars and bunkers, especially the Kunstbunker (World War II Art Bunker) and labyrinth of underground cellars below the castle.

HIGHLIGHTS

KAISERBURG (EMPEROR'S CASTLE)

✉️ Auf der Burg 13, 90403 Nürnberg ☎ 0911 2446 59115 🕐 Apr–end Sep daily 9–6; Oct–end Mar daily 10–4 🎫 Adult €5, child free. The rooms can only be visited with a guided tour, which takes about 1.5 hours. Combination ticket for Palace with Double Chapel, Deep Well, Sinwell Tower and Imperial Castle Museum: adult €6, child free

Nürnberg's Kaiserburg is an important imperial palace dating from the Middle Ages: From 1050 to 1571 a variety of kings and emperors of the Holy Roman Empire stayed in it during their reign. You can visit the Romanesque double chapel, a two-level chapel, the upper floor of which was reserved for the emperor and court, while the lower floor was for the lower ranks. The *Brunnenhaus* (covered well) has a well, 48m (157ft) deep, where you can watch lighted candles being

THE SIGHTS

lowered to demonstrate the depth of this rocky chasm. The mighty Sinwell Tower dominates the courtyard, and there are great views of the city's pointed rooftops and towering churches from here. Also here is the Kaiserburg Museum, which shows the construction history of the castle and its significance, as well as the evolution of weapons and defense techniques.

GERMANISCHES NATIONALMUSEUM

✉ Kartausergasse 1, 90402 Nürnberg ☎ 0911 13310 ⏰ Tue, Thu–Sun 10–6, Wed 10–9 💶 Adult €5, child €4, under 6 free, family €9. Free on Wed 6–9
Allow plenty of time to visit this, the largest and most important museum of Germanic art and culture, spanning from prehistoric times to the present. Founded in 1852, the museum's collections illustrate the high points of German art and history. Highlights include great works by Albrecht Dürer and Veit Stoss, the world's earliest globe, by Martin Behaim and a self-portrait by Rembrant.

HISTORISCHER KÜNSTERBUNKER

✉ Obere Schmiedgasse 52, 90403 Nürnberg ☎ 0911 227066 ⏰ Guided tours daily 3pm (not bank hols). Tours only run if there are three or more adults. In German only 💶 Adult €4, child €3, under 6 free, family €10.
It is hard to imagine Nürnberg nowadays without the famous works of art that decorate its churches and fill its streets and museums. The devastating bombing attacks during World War II leveled 90 per cent of the architecture of the old town, but thanks to the foresight of town officials, much of Nürnberg's artistic heritage survived. At the start of the war, they transformed the former beer cellars, 24m (79ft) beneath the castle hill, into a secure art shelter with a simple but effective system of air-conditioning and moisture-proof storage cells. The original installations can still be seen on the tour, but dress warmly because even in summer it's cool in the rock-cut cellars.

TIERGARTEN (ZOO)

✉ Am Tiergarten 30, 90480 Nürnberg ☎ 0911 54546 ⏰ Easter–end Oct daily 8–7.30; Oct–Easter daily 9–5 💶 Adult €6.50, child €3.50, family €15
This magnificent landscaped zoological garden with large open-air enclosures is a great place for a stroll. There are animal houses, aviaries and a children's zoo, plus the Adler miniature train, a model of Germany's first railway, which operates from Easter to October.

BACKGROUND

Nürnberg is a place risen from the rubble of wartime destruction and restored to its Middle Ages heyday. This was Germany's greatest surviving medieval city and, thanks to careful reconstruction, it has recaptured much of its former appeal. It's unfortunate, however, that Nürnberg's most recent history is associated with its links to the National Socialists, the infamous Nuremberg Laws and the post-World War II Nuremberg Trials. Today, the city attracts many visitors, especially during the summer and for the Christmas market, and is one of the leading industrial and commercial towns in Southern Germany.

TIPS
● The Nürnberg Card (adult €18, child under 12 free) gives you two full days of unrestricted use of public transport and free admission to 34 museums and sights. It also entitles you to 10–20 per cent off theatre tickets.
● You will get good views of Nürnberg from the Sinwell Tower, but as an alternative, go into the Castle Garden, turn left and follow the garden down to a door that leads onto a walkway: The views from here are equally spectacular.
● You cannot visit Nürnberg without sampling the famous Bratwurst. Try the Bratwurst-häusle, Rathausplatz (next to the Sebaldus Church). Sausages are made fresh every day in the factory below the restaurant.

THE SIGHTS

The Documentation Centre (above left), built inside the former Nazi Party Rally Grounds
This work of modern art (below) is made up from street name signs from the former East Berlin

A detail of the carvings on Schoner Brunnen (below left)

The gardens of the Schloss, at Ludwigsburg

Don't criticize the food at this Maulbronn restaurant

Oberammergau is known for its tradtional woodcarvings

THE SIGHTS

LUDWIGSBURG

➕ 441 D12 ℹ Marktplatz 6, Ludwigsburg, tel 07141 917555
🚉 Ludwigsburg
www.ludwigsburg.de

Picturesque Ludwigsburg is on a plateau above the River Neckar. In 1704, it was chosen as the location for a royal summer residence, but under the rule of Duke Eberhard Ludwig this plan quickly expanded. It became a city of palaces, and the magnificent Residential Palace is the largest surviving baroque palace in Germany. Often called the Swabian Versailles, it has 452 rooms in 28 buildings. In the new wing is a section of the Württemberg Provincial Museum, and on the ground floor are examples of finely crafted porcelain still being produced by the factory first established in the palace in 1758.

In the beautiful park there's an aviary and a Fairytale Garden (Märchengarten), where mechanical figures act out fairytales. North of the palace is the Favoritepark (a game park and nature reserve), with the baroque Palace of Favorit, the former summer residence built by Ludwig for his mistress. The Monrepos Lakeside Palace is the former hunting lodge of Duke Eberhard Ludwig; it is a rococo masterpiece, with the interior decorated in the style of the Napoleonic era.

MANNHEIM

➕ 437 C11 ℹ Willi-Brandt-Platz 3, Mannheim, tel 0621 101012
🚉 Mannheim
www.tourist-mannheim.de

Mannheim was founded in 1606 by the Prince Elector Friedrich IV to establish a strong commercial base for the collecting of taxes. He built a formidable fortress, with residential blocks that stretch out from its base like the squares on a chessboard. Streets define the 144 squares, each of which is designated by a letter and a number, a logical system unique in Germany.

Mannheim is the second largest river port in Europe and a commercial and industrial hub. Little of the city survived World War II, and most of the rebuilding was for practical rather than aesthetic purposes. In the Friedrichsplatz stands the symbol of the city, the Wasserturm (water tower), built in 1886 and rising over 60m (200ft) high. It is watched over by a statue of Amphitrite, wife of the sea god, Poseidon. Also worth visiting are the Kunsthalle, housing one of Germany's leading displays of 19th- and 20th-century art; the Palace, with more than 400 rooms (now the main campus of Mannheim University); and the huge Jesuit Church, a fine baroque building, now restored.

MAULBRONN

➕ 441 D12 ℹ Klosterhof 31, Maulbronn, tel 07043 1030
🚉 Maulbronn
www.maulbronn.de

The little town of Maulbronn is in the vine-covered foothills of the Stromberg. It grew up around one of the earliest and most beautiful of Cistercian monasteries to survive in Germany. According to folklore, a group of monks stopped here in 1147 to water their mules (the name originally meant 'mule well') and stayed on to found the abbey. This story is depicted in sketches for a fresco on the wall of the Brunnenkapelle (Well Chapel).

Half-timbered buildings surround the abbey courtyard, inside which are the kitchens, inner chambers and cloisters. You can also see the Paradise, the porch of the church of St. Mary, which has a stone crucifix from 1473 and 15th-century choir stalls.
Don't miss A nice place for a stroll is the Philosophers' Walk.

NÜRNBERG

See pages 218–219.

OBERAMMERGAU

➕ 442 F14 ℹ Eugen-Papst-Strasse 9a, 82487 Oberammergau, tel 08822 92310 🚉 Oberammergau
www.oberammergau.de

World renowned for its fairy-tale houses and woodcarvings, but particularly for its Passion Play, Oberammergau is a popular resort throughout the year. The woodcarving tradition goes back to the 17th century and fine examples can be seen in the town's many craft shops.

The Passion Play was first performed in 1634 in fulfillment of a vow made in 1633, when the village was stricken by plague. After months of suffering, the Oberammergauers swore an oath that they would perform the *Play of the Suffering, Death and Resurrection of Our Lord Jesus Christ* every ten years. The next production is in 2010. Now, more than 2,000 actors, singers, instrumentalists and technicians are involved in staging the play. Local policemen are even allowed to grow beards.

Many houses in the town are decorated with frescoes by Franz Zwirk (1748–92). Fine examples of painted façades include the Forsthaus and the magnificent Pilatushaus, with its ornate architectural fantasies. The Hänsel and Gretel House in Ettaler Strasse is a modern 20th-century creation.

PASSAU

See page 230.

REGENSBURG

See pages 222–223.

ROTHENBURG OB DER TAUBER

**One of Germany's best-preserved medieval towns.
At the intersection of the Castle Road and the Romantic Road,
it's ideally placed for touring the area.
Visit the German Christmas Museum and Christmas Village,
where its Christmas every day.**

*Even the fortifications have
charm in this medieval town*

RATINGS				
Historic interest	●	●	●	● ●
Cultural interest	●	●	●	● ●
Walkability	●	●	●	●

BASICS

✚ 438 E11

ℹ Markplatz 2, 91541 Rothenburg ob
der Tauber, tel 09861 404800; May–
end Oct Mon–Fri 9–12, 1–6, Sat–Sun
10–3; Nov–end Apr Mon–Fri 9–12, 1–5,
Sat 10–1

🚉 Rothenburg ob der Tauber

www.rothenburg.de
Good website with lots of useful
information (in English).

TIPS

● Visit the Deutsches
Weihnachtsmuseum (German
Christmas Museum), with
fascinating exhibits that show
Christmas in different eras,
with explanations about
ornaments and traditions.
● There are some lovely walks
here, including a stroll along
the Tauber Valley to Detwang
and St. Peter und Pauls Kirche.
There's a lovely riverside beer
garden and restaurant about
halfway along. On a rainy day,
you can still wander along the
Wehrgang (Sentry walk), as it
is roofed for over 2.5km (1.5
miles) between the Klingen
Bastion and Kobolzell Gate.

Rothenburg ob der Tauber is a fascinating town at the intersection of
the two most important tourist routes in Germany: the Castle Road
and the Romantic Road. Completely ringed by ramparts, this is one of
Germany's best-preserved medieval towns, and its silhouette high
above the lush Tauber valley has earned Rothenburg the nickname of
the 'Franconian Jerusalem.' A leisurely stroll through this delightful
town will take you back in time, whether you wander through the
cobbled streets and winding alleys lined with picturesque, half-timbered houses with red- tiled roofs, or walk along the fortifications,
with mighty battlements and towers.

ROTHENBURG'S TOWNSCAPE

The intricate wrought iron signs on shops and restaurants are evidence of the craftsmanship that gave Schmiedgasse (Smithy's Lane)
its name. Today, these signs still have to be made from wrought iron
and approved by the town council. The Plonlein (Little Square), with
its changing street level and half-timbered house framed by Siebers
Tower and the Kobolzell Gate, is one of the most famous (and most
photographed) places in the town. The Thirty Years War is brought to
life in the Historical Vaults of the Town Hall. The dark dungeons are
where Rothenburg's most powerful Lord Mayor, Heinrich Toppler, met
his death in 1408. St. Jacob's Church is the most important church in
town, not only because of the towers, but also because of its interior
with two altars by the famous woodcarver Tilman Riemenschneider.

THE MARKET SQUARE

The Marktplatz is the main focal point of the town and the beautiful
Rathaus with its superb Imperial Hall is one of the finest in South
Germany. The City Councillors' Tavern (Ratstrinkstube) is probably
one of the most famous buildings in Rothenburg. The main clock was
installed in 1683, and since 1910, the two windows to the right and
left open every hour between 11 and 3 and 8 and 10 to show the
Meistertrunk (Master Draught). This commemorates an event in
1631 when Rothenburg was taken by Imperial troops, and only saved
when the mayor was challenged to drink the welcome draught, over
three litres (almost one gallon) of wine.

Regensburg

The best preserved medieval city in Germany, with more
than 1,300 medieval buildings packed into an Old City barely
a kilometre (half-mile) square.

*The Stone Bridge, crossing the
River Danube*

*Detail of the Laughing Angel in
Dom St. Peter*

*You're never too young to tour
Regensburg by bicycle*

RATINGS	
Historic interest	●●●●○
Cultural interest	●●●○○
Walkability	●●●●○
Good for food	●●●○○

*Myth looms large in
Regensburg's Altstadt*

SEEING REGENSBURG

Regensburg is a city steeped in history and rich with relics from
many periods. This cathedral city sits neatly beside the romantic
Danube, its church spires sharing the skyline with the palaces of
great noble families and the 13th- and 14th-century patrician
houses. Remarkably, the city escaped the wartime devastation
suffered by nearby cities, so its many historical buildings are
unscathed, and its narrow cobbled streets and lively squares are
a joy to explore. The city's leading families built towers in competition with each other, the most impressive being the
Kastenmayerhaus with its four-floor tower, and the Goldener
Turn with its imposing golden tower and Renaissance courtyard
in the Wahlenstrasse, the city's oldest street. The buildings you
see near the central marketplace are all part of the Old Town
Hall, which was begun in the 13th century and evolved through
many additions and alterations into what you see today. The
middle part is formed by the old Patrician Castle, consisting of
the Tower and the Great Hall, to the left are the historic rooms of
the Perpetual Imperial Diet, and the baroque town hall is on the
right. The Stone Bridge, as impressive today as it was when it
was built in the 12th century, is the perfect platform to view the
city's spires, towers and steep sloping roofs.

HIGHLIGHTS

PRINCE OF THURN AND TAXIS MUSEUMS

✉ Emmeramsplatz 5, 93047 Regensburg ☎ 0941 504 8133 🕐 Guided tours (in
German) of Palace and Cloisters (approx 1.5 hours): Apr–end Oct daily 11, 2, 3 & 4.
Sat, Sun, holidays additional tour at 10; Nov–end Mar Sat, Sun, holidays 10, 11, 2 &
3. Museum: Apr–end Oct, Mon–Fri 11–5, Sat, Sun, holidays 10–5; Nov–end Mar,
Sat, Sun, holidays 10–5. 💰 Palace and Cloisters: Adult €8, concession €7. Cloisters
only: Adult €4, concession €3.50. Marstallmuseum (Coach House) & Thurn and
Taxis Museum: Adult €4.50, concession €3.50. Combined ticket: Adult €10, conces-
sion €8.50

In the 18th century, the princes of Thurn and Taxis, founders of the
first large-scale postal service in Europe, created a magnificent palace

here built around a former 8th-century monastery. The apartments are adorned with magnificent 19th-century furnishings, as well as some brought from the family's older residences. There's a branch of the National Museum of Bavaria in the Palace, with art collections of the Thurn and Taxis dynasty. The Cloisters, built in a combination of Romanesque and Gothic styles, are considered to be among the most impressive in Germany.

DOM ST. PETER (ST. PETER'S CATHEDRAL)

✉ Unter den Schwibbogen 17, 93047 Regensburg ☎ 0941 597 1002 ◷ Guided tours (in German) May–end Oct Mon–Sat at 10, 11 & 2, Sun, holidays 12.30 & 2. Nov–end Apr Sat 11, Sun, hols 12.30 💷 Cathedral: Free. Tours: adult €2.50, concessions €1.50

Considered to be Bavaria's finest example of Gothic architecture, the cathedral originates from the 13th century, although the distinctive spires are a 19th-century addition by King Ludwig I. The cloisters have magnificent examples of Gothic rib-vaulting from the 15th century, while the 13th- and 14th-century stained-glass windows are sublime.

Regensburg enjoys an attractive riverside setting

CATHEDRAL TREASURY (DOMSCHATZMUSEUM)

✉ Emmeramsplatz 1, 93047 Regensburg ☎ 0941 57645 ◷ Apr–end Nov Tue–Sat 10–5, Sun, hols 12–5; Dec–end Mar Fri, Sat 10–4, Sun 12–4 💷 Adult €1.50, child (under 14) 80c

In the Cathedral Treasury, the former bishop's residence, there's an assortment of 11th- to 18th-century church treasures on display. These include gold plate, vestments and tapestries.

DOCUMENT NEUPFARRPLATZ

✉ Neupfarrplatz, Regensburg ◷ Thu, Fri, Sat by guided tour only 💷 Adult €3, concession €2. Tickets and information from Tabak Gotz, Neupfarrplatz 3.

Between 1995 and 1998, archaeologists carried out excavations in the Altstadt, where they unearthed the remains of cellars belonging to the houses and buildings of the Jewish quarter, as well as sections of the Roman legionary fortress Castra Regina. You can visit this underground site to see the relics from the Roman age and the medieval Jewish quarter.

BACKGROUND

Regensburg's written history dates back to AD179, when the Roman camp Castra Regina was established here. Following the Roman withdrawal, Regensburg became a popular site for Imperial diets and with this rise in its political fortune, the city enjoyed an economic boom. The ministry officials of the Frankish kings became wealthy merchants, who built elaborate patrician homes in the style of Italian fortresses. Each showed off his wealth and prestige by trying to build higher towers, of which 19 remain today to give the city its famous skyline.

One of Regensburg's famous towered houses (below left)

BASICS

✚ 443 G12

🛈 Altes Rathaus, Rathausplatz 4, Regensburg, tel 0941 507 4410; Apr–end Oct Mon–Fri 9.15–6, Sat. 9.15–4, Sun 9.30–4; Nov–end Mar Mon–Fri 9.15–6, Sat. 9.15–4, Sun 9.30–2.30

🚆 Regensburg

www.regensburg.de (also in English)

TIPS

● The compact Altstadt and an extensive pedestrianized zone make Regensburg perfect for walking. Early mornings are the best time to explore and shop before the hordes arrive.

● Take the boat trip from the Stone Bridge to Walhalla, the imposing Greek-style marble temple built for King Ludwig I on a hillside overlooking the Danube. (Boats run Apr–end Oct daily 10.30 and 2. Adult €9.50, child (under 14) €4.50.) The trip takes around three hours, including a stay at Walhalla.

● You cannot visit Regensburg without sampling the famous *Bratwurst* at the Historische Wurstkuche (Historic Sausage Kitchen). They serve more than 100,000 Regensburger Bratwurst every day.

● Take a tour in English, starting at the City Hall. They include patrician homes, restored areas, Old Stone Bridge, Porta Praetoria, St. Peter's Cathedral and Old Town Hall. (May–end Sep Wed, Sat. Adult €6, child €3.) Buy your tickets at the Tourist Information Office.

Schloss Neuschwanstein

A fairy-tale come true, and inspiration for Walt Disney's *Sleeping Beauty* Castle. King Ludwig's most famous castle, built 200m above the valley floor. One of the most popular of all the palaces and castles in Europe.

Salve—welcome to Schloss Neuschwanstein

Flora and fauna decorate the walls of Ludwig's castle

Christ surrounded by angels, in a wall painting from the castle

RATINGS		
Historic interest	●●●●●	
Cultural interest	●●●●○	
Walkability	●●●●●	

St. George and the Dragon (below), from Wagner's Die Meistersinger von Nürnberg *Schloss Neuschwanstein, in its fairy-tale setting (right)*

SEEING SCHLOSS NEUSCHWANSTEIN

The magnificent Neuschwanstein is one of the most popular of all the castles in Europe and is always busy: 1.3 million people visit it every year, and in the summer around 6,000 visitors a day stream through its rooms. You can only get tickets from the ticket office in the village of Hohenschwangau below the castle, and you need to allow plenty of time to get up to the castle and find the right queue at the entrance for the start of your tour. The entrance system is automated and you can only go through the gates at the allotted time and take a guided tour, so if you miss your slot, you miss your tour. The 35-minute walk up the winding hill to the castle is very enjoyable, but if the weather is bad or you don't wish to tackle the climb there are other options. The horse-drawn carriage ride is a pleasant alternative, or there's a bus that will take you to the spectacular Marienbrücke observation point, leaving you with just a 10-minute walk to the castle entrance.

You can only visit 15 of the castle's rooms; the rest lies bare and eerie. On the second floor in particular you wander through empty room after empty room: Even the throne room doesn't have a throne in it. However, the rooms on view are amazing and once inside the castle you will appreciate the enormity of the building and understand why it is known as the Fairy-tale Castle of a Fairy-tale King. The architecture and decoration are an interesting mixture of historical styles: Byzantine for the Throne Hall, Romanesque for the private apartments and Gothic for the impressive Singers' Hall. In every room you will see tributes to the Wagner operas: Look out for taps shaped like swans, illustrations from the *Lohengrin* saga and amazing stalagmites in the Grotto based on the *Venusberg* in *Tannhäuser*.

HIGHLIGHTS

THE SÄNGERSAAL (SINGERS' HALL)

The heart of the castle is the lavish Singers' Hall, the first room to be planned, which was created so Ludwig could feed his obsession with

BASICS

✚ 442 F15 🛈 Kaiser-Maximilian-Platz 1, Füssen, tel 08362 93850; May–end Oct Mon–Fri 8.30–6, Sat 10–1, Sun 10–12; Nov–end Apr Mon–Fri 9–6

✉ Ticketcenter Neuschwanstein, Hohenschwangau, Alpseestrasse 12, 87645 Hohenschwangau

☎ 08362 930830

🕐 Apr–end Sep 8–6; Oct–end Mar 9–4. First tour at 9 Apr–end Sep, 10 Oct–end Mar

💶 Adult €9, senior €8, Konigsticket (combination day ticket covering Neuschwanstein and Hohenschwangau castles): adult €17, senior €15, child (under 18) free if accompanied by an adult, otherwise €8. There's a non-refundable booking fee of €1.50 per ticket. Horse carriage from Muller Hotel: uphill €5, downhill €2.50. Bus from Schlosshotel Lisl to Jugend/ Marien-brücke observation point (Not suitable for disabled or elderly visitors): uphill €1.80, downhill €1.00, round trip €2.60 (buses do not run in snow or ice)

🚌 Füssen

www.neuschwanstein.de (in English)

WALKS

There are some beautiful walks around the grounds, none more so than across Marienbrücke (Mary's Bridge) from where you can enjoy Ludwig's best-loved view of the castle and waterfall. The bridge spans a deep gorge, and from the path between it and the castle is a lovely view of Hohenschwangau and the Alpsee. In fine weather, take the cable car up the Tegelberg (1,720m/5,645ft) from where you get outstanding views of the Alps.

Schloss Neuschwansteinsits, surrounded by woods (above left).
A tapestry in the Sangersaal (above middle).
A wallpainting typical of the 'stage set' decoration of the castle (above right)

Wagner. It is based on the Singers' Hall in the Wartburg, which was supposedly the setting for the singing contest in Wagner's opera *Tannhäuser*. Wall frescoes in the hall depict scenes from the opera, and on the end wall you will see a magnificent mural portraying Klingsor's magic garden from the opera *Parsifal*. Wagner concerts are held here every September, and even if you are not fortunate enough to get tickets, you will be able to imagine how wonderful they are when held in such a magnificent setting.

THRONE ROOM

The Byzantine Throne Room resembles the Court Chapel in Munich's Residenz, and is the most sumptuous room in the castle. Of particular interest are the wall paintings showing royalty performing holy acts, and a large image of Christ surrounded by nine canonized kings from

the Middle Ages in the apse. Ludwig's throne was to be placed under this huge painting, but sadly it was never built. Even without a throne, this room was probably the most expensive to create, and savings were made by using mosaics instead of paintings and tinted stucco instead of marble for the pillars.

From the balcony, there are magnificent views of the gardens.

SERVANTS' ROOMS

Moving upstairs, the tour takes you through five of the servants' rooms, all simply fitted out with oak furniture and designed for two people. Between 10 and 15 servants were employed to look after the castle on a day-to-day basis, but if the King was in residence, double this number was needed.

DINING ROOM

The small dining room is indicative of King Ludwig's solitary existence. A unique feature of this room is the Tischlein-deck-dich mechanism, based on a fairy-tale about a table that would serve a meal by itself. The dining table, in the middle of the floor, is mounted on an elevator, which goes directly into the kitchen below. The King's meal was laid on the table and sent back up into the dining room so that he could dine alone and wouldn't have to see any of the servants. The interesting wall pictures show the world of the Minnesingers, German lyric poets and singers in the troubadour tradition who flourished between the 12th and 14th centuries. A magnificent gilt bronze sculpture portraying Siegfried's fight with the dragon Fafnir dominates the room.

BEDROOM

The first thing you see when you enter the bedroom is the King's huge bed, carved with spires and intricate tracery windows that resemble a late Gothic church. The elaborate oak carvings in the chamber took 14 woodcarvers over four years to complete. Ludwig was in this room when he was arrested on the night of 11th June 1886, before he was taken to Berg Palace on the banks of Lake Starnberg (see Background).

DRESSING ROOM

When you enter the dressing room, look up at the *trompe l'oeil* ceiling, which gives the appearance of looking up through a garden bower, with a background of blue sky and birds and a trellis of vines.

SALON

After touring a series of small rooms, entering the enormous salon, the largest room in the King's apartments, has quite an impact. In the far corner there are four columns that separate the main room from a secluded area where the king could retreat to read, known as Swan Corner. Wagner's influence is in evidence here too, with numerous images from the *Lohengrin* saga, painted onto coarse linen so they look like tapestries, and the swan motifs on the textiles and doors. There is also a beautiful life-size swan made of china.

GROTTO

Next to the Salon, the artificial grotto is yet another allusion to *Tannhäuser*, and it even has a concealed opening in the ceiling that let the King to listen to music from the Singers' Hall, directly above.

The exit door into the conservatory actually slides down into rock, but for safety reasons this exit is always open.

KITCHEN

Prepare to be amazed at the equipment in the basement kitchens, which demonstrates the technically high standard of the castle's facilities. The crockery was added later, but everything else you see is original and would still be serviceable in a large modern kitchen. It's equipped with hot and cold running water, automatic spits and cupboards that could be heated with hot air from the large kitchen stove. Its pristine condition is partly owing to the fact that the kitchen was only in use for two years, from 1884 to 1886.

HOHENSCHWANGAU

Less famous, but no less worth seeing, Hohenschwangau was the castle where Ludwig spent his happy childhood. It stands above the village, romantically enthroned between centuries-old yews and weeping beeches. At its foot are the emerald waters of the moody Alpsee. If you are planning to visit Hohenschwangau, come here first, as it pales next to Ludwig's fantasy castle.

BACKGROUND

The 18-year-old Prinz Otto Ludwig Friedrich Wilhelm ascended the Bavarian throne in 1864. Although initially an enthusiastic leader, following the creation of the German Reich in 1871 he became merely a puppet king. He was introduced to the world of German sagas and legends through Wagner's operas, and this, combined with his love of French culture, led to the creation of three fantastical palaces: Linderhof (▷ 216) was built in the French style, Herrenchiemesse (▷ 212) was inspired by Versailles, but Neuschwanstein was King Ludwig's own personal fantasy. Its turrets and mock-medievalism were based on Wartburg (▷ 160), and the interior styles, ranging from Byzantine to Gothic and Romanesque, are a real fairy-tale fantasy come true. This imposing structure was built between 1868 and 1886 but only about a third of it was actually completed. The fairy-tale appearance of the castle is due to the original designs being painted by Christian Jank, a scenery designer at the Court Theatre, which were later translated into architectural plans by Eduard Riedel. Loved by his people but despised by his ministers, Ludwig was declared insane and deposed in 1886. He was taken from Neuschwanstein to Berg Palace on the banks of Lake Starnberg where he died in suspicious circumstances. Just seven weeks after his death, Neuschwanstein was opened to the public to pay off the enormous debts he had incurred building the castle.

● An ideal base for your visit is Füssen, a renowned holiday and health resort. This attractive mountain town in the eastern Allgäu has a lovely historical Altstadt, and stands at the southernmost end of the Romantic Road.

Candelabra (above) add atmosphere to the Sangersaal Figures from Wagner's operas (below) decorate the castle's walls

THE SIGHTS

Stuttgart

Sprawling parks and woods account for almost a quarter of the entire city area. The state capital of Baden-Wurttemberg, and best known as the home of Mercedes-Benz.

Beautiful modern curves of the Staatsgalerie

Local bread on sale at the Emporemarkt Halle

Cars built for speed at the Porsche Museum

RATINGS	
Historic interest	● ● ●
Cultural interest	● ● ●
Specialist shopping	● ● ● ●
Good for food	● ● ● ● ●

These pink and blue tubes run all around the Staatsgalerie

SEEING STUTTGART

The city is beautifully located deep in a valley, with its streets climbing steeply to meet the surrounding hills covered with orchards, vineyards, forests and meadowland. Its associations with the motor industry through such famous names as Daimler, Bosch and Benz give the city an image of industrialization, but in reality its inner city parklands and surrounding landscape make Stuttgart a very enjoyable place to be. The Mercedes star proudly adorns the Hauptbahnhof tower and the Mercedes platform is open to visitors (admission free). You can take a free tour of the Mercedes-Benz Museum and factory, while the Porsche Museum has a grand display of 'Toys for Boys' (free tours). For such a large city of regional importance, it has a wonderful relaxed atmosphere; maybe this is connected with the surrounding vineyards!

The motor industry aside, the city has some fine museums and galleries: The Staatsgalerie is one of Europe's great modern art galleries; the Stiftsfruchtkasten, a former wine depot, has a wonderful collection of musical instruments; the reconstructed Stiftskirche has two very different late-Gothic towers, each 61m (200ft) high, and the Market Hall, built in 1914 by Martin Elsaesser in the art nouveau style, is one of the most beautiful in Germany: a trip to the theatre is a must and where better than the Stuttgart State Theatre, incorporating the world-famous Stuttgart Ballet and the Stuttgart State Opera.

HIGHLIGHTS

ALTES SCHLOSS–WÜRTTEMBERG STATE MUSEUM
✉ Schillerplatz 6, Stuttgart ☎ 0711 279 3400 🕐 Wed–Sun 10–5, Tue 10–1
💶 Adult €3, concession €2, child free (includes instrument museum)
The Old Palace has one of the most beautiful inner courtyards in the Renaissance style. It is the venue for summer concerts, theatre performances and the opening ceremony of the Christmas Market. The Wurttemberg State Museum (Landesmuseum) has a wide variety of interesting exhibits of the House of Wurttemberg; look out for the elk on the clock tower that ram their horns on the hour.

SCHLOSSPLATZ
In the middle of Schlossplatz is the Jubilee Column, erected in 1841 to commemorate the silver jubilee of the reign of King Wilhelm I. Be sure to visit the two fountains dating from 1863, a cast iron music pavilion and a number of pieces of modern sculpture. Also here is the House of Art (currently in the process of rebuilding works, telephone 0711 216 2188 for details) and the baroque Neues Schloss, behind which is the magnificent Schlossgarten. These gardens are exceptional and always busy with locals and visitors wandering along the many footpaths, admiring the fountains and vibrant gardens.

MERCEDES-BENZ MUSEUM
✉ Mercedesstrasse 137/1, Stuttgart ☎ 0711 172 2578 🕐 Tue–Sun 9–5 💶 Free
Recorded commentaries tell the history of the Daimler-Benz merger as you wander around an amazing array of magnificent cars. Free tours of the factory (at Sindelfingen, tel 07031 907 0403) are given twice a day, Monday to Friday, in English and German. They last 1.5 hours and must be booked at least 3 weeks in advance. Minimum age is 6 years.

WILHELMA ZOO
✉ Neckartalstrasse, Stuttgart–Bad Cannstatt ☎ 0711 54020 🕐 May–end Aug daily 8.15–6; Apr, Sep daily 8.15–6.30; Mar, Oct daily 8.15–5; Nov–end Feb 8.15–4
💶 Adult €10.20 (Mar–end Oct) or €7 (Nov–end Feb), child €5.10 (Mar–end Oct) or €3.50 (Nov–end Feb)
Germany's largest Zoological and Botanical Gardens, on the northern edge of Rosensteinpark, are some of the most beautiful in Europe. Laid out for King Wilhelm I of Württemberg between 1842 and 1853 as a Moorish garden, the zoo has more than 10,000 animals of around 1,000 species. The mix of animal and plant life is exceptional and with approximately two million visitors every year, the Wilhelma is one of the most popular places to visit in Baden-Württemberg.

BACKGROUND

The name Stuttgart originates from a stud farm (Stutengarten) established in the 10th century by the Duke of Swabia. By the 12th century it had become a thriving trading hub, and by 1427 was the capital and residence of the counts of Württemberg. Prosperity and fortune continued through the centuries and by the turn of the 20th century it had a population of 175,000. Stuttgart suffered badly during World War II and none of its landmarks or historic buildings survived intact. After the war, buildings were quickly restored and Stuttgart became the capital of the newly formed state of Baden-Württemberg (although many still call it Swabia). Today the population is about 600,000, and unlike many large industrial cities, Stuttgart is not a concrete jungle. Its association with the manufacture of high-class, up-market cars gives the city a refined air, which you'll find in its streets, squares, parks and gardens.

BASICS
🏠 441 D12
ℹ Königstrasse 1a, Stuttgart, tel 0711 222 8240; Mon–Fri 9–8, Sat 9–6; Sun 11–6 Apr–end Oct & 1–6 Nov–end Mar
🚇 🚆 Stuttgart

www.stuttgart-tourist.de (in English)

TIPS
● The Bohnenviertel (bean quarter) is so called because it was formerly the area where workers or poorer people lived, and they reputedly ate mainly beans. It is now filled with many excellent bars and restaurants that are not on the tourist trail.
● The Stuttcard Plus three-day ticket is good value at €17. It entitles one adult and two children (6–14) to free entry to all public museums, discounts on admission charges to other attractions and city tours and free travel on all inner-city public transportation for three days. If you don't want to use public transportation, the standard Stuttcard costs €8.50.
● For the best panoramic view of Stuttgart, visit the Television Tower (Fernsehturm). It is 217m high and has a four-floor complex with a gourmet restaurant and viewing platform at 150m. On a clear day there are wonderful views of the Black Forest and Swabian Alps.

THE SIGHTS

An exhibition of Hegel's work, at the house where he was born

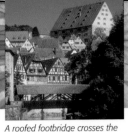

Passau's domed towers can be seen across the Danube

A roofed footbridge crosses the River Kocher at Schwabisch Hall

A Triberg local, no doubt enjoying the pure air

THE SIGHTS

PASSAU

✚ 443 J13 🛈 Rathausplatz 3, Passau, tel 0851 95598 🚉 Passau
www.passau.de

The old Episcopal city of Passau is at the confluence of the blue Danube, green Inn and black Ilz rivers. Over the centuries, this spectacular setting has been responsible for many floods in the town, but it has also made it one of Germany's main river gateways to Austria and beyond.

The baroque design of Passau is dominated by large squares, riverside promenades and narrow winding lanes, framed by the Veste Oberhaus castle and the pilgramage monastery Mariahilf. The old town lies on a narrow tongue of land between the Danube and the Inn, its houses huddled around a hill topped by the magnificent St. Stephen's Cathedral, from which narrow lanes spiral down to the two rivers. The cathedral houses the world's largest church organ, which is actually five organs played from one main keyboard.

SCHWÄBISCH HALL

✚ 441 E12 🛈 Am Markt 6, Schwäbisch Hall, tel 0791 751246 🚉 Schwäbisch Hall
www.schwaebischhall.de

This is a popular little town on the north-eastern fringes of the Swabian Forest, overlooking the River Kocher. The buildings of the old town grow upwards from the river valley, and the sloping Marktplatz with its 16th-century fountain is one of the most impressive market squares in Germany. Around the square, the baroque town hall, rebuilt after fire damage in 1945, has a magnificent clock and bell tower, and an imposing flight of 54 stone steps, on which festival performances are given in summer, lead up to the Pfarrkirche

(St. Michael's Church). The church has an interesting interior and the tower is the perfect place for panoramic views.

Hall, meaning place of salt, was a wealthy town in the 15th century because of its trade in salt, wine and corn. The Haller pfennige was minted here as early as the 11th century and gave its name to coins elsewhere in Germany and Austria. The town was called Hall until 1934, when Schwäbisch was added to the name.

TRIBERG

✚ 440 C13 🛈 Luisenstrasse 10, Triberg, tel 07722 953230 🚉 Triberg
www.triberg.de

Triberg is in the heart of the cuckoo clock region, and this is the main draw for the visitors who flock to this busy area all year round. The business launched by Josef Weisser in 1824 gave the town the title of the *Haus der 1,000 Uhren* (House of 1,000 Clocks). Triberg can also lay claim to having two of the largest cuckoo clocks in the world and the highest waterfall in Germany (163m/ 535ft). The Gutach Falls are a spectacular sight after heavy rain or snow melt, as the water plunges in seven cascades down the mountain. The walk to the top of the falls is well worth the effort. The Schwarzwald Museum has a large collection of Black Forest clocks on display, as well as local costumes, wood carvings and clock-making memorabilia.

Triberg—cuckoo clock land

Deep in the Black Forest, Triberg is also renowned for the purity of its air and has become a popular health and spa resort.

TÜBINGEN

✚ 441 D13 🛈 An der Neckarbrücke 1, Tübingen, tel 07071 9136 14 🚉 Tübingen
www.tuebingen-info.de

Winding cobbled alleys, stone walls, half-timbered houses and pointed gables shape the silhouette of the university town of Tübingen. The Platanenallee (Avenue of Plane Trees) is a wonderful place to stroll along the picturesque Neckarfront. The Renaissance Hohentübingen Castle (now part of the university) gives the best views across the valleys of Neckar and Ammer, the red-tiled rooftops of the Altstadt and its surroundings. Burgsteige (Castle Way) is one of the earliest streets with the oldest houses.

The Holzmarkt (Timber Market) and St. George's Fountain give an excellent view of the late-Gothic Stiftskirche, with its handsome monuments commemorating members of the princely house of Württemburg. Beyond the church are the oldest parts of the Karl Eberhard University and the Karzer (students' prison). On the banks of the Neckar stands the Hölderlin Tower, and in the nearby Marktplatz are the Neptune fountain and Rathaus, a half-timbered building dating from 1435.

ULM

Ulm's Münster spire is the highest church spiire in the world. This is the birthplace of Albert Einstein.

The old and the new: the minster and the Stadthaus

Ulm's strategic location on the Danube brought it to prominence as early as the 12th century, but today, river traffic brings mainly tourists to this city divided by the blue water. Much of the old city was destroyed during a bombing raid in 1944, but many of the historic buildings have been carefully restored, making this an interesting place to visit.

SIGHTS TO SEE

Pride of place has to go to the Ulm Münster, the second largest example of Gothic ecclesiastical architecture in Germany, and its spire, the tallest in the world. But it's not just the building that's worth seeing: There are many works of distinction inside the Cathedral, too, particularly the 15th-century choir stalls by Jörg Syrlin the Younger, and Hans Multscher's *Man of Sorrows* on the main portal. The Rathaus was built as offices in 1370 but has been the town hall since 1419. Inside is a replica of Albrecht Berblinger's flying machine. In 1810, Berblinger built a flying machine and on 31 May 1811, he attempted, in presence of the King, to glide over the Danube, but failed. However, in 1986, a replica was built and made the crossing successfully. The extensive Ulmer Museum has an emphasis on Gothic art in Upper Swabia, plus works by 20th-century artists.

THE ULM SPARROW

The legend of the Ulm Sparrow tells the story of citizens transporting wooden beams into the city for the construction of the Cathedral. The beams were loaded crosswise on the carriages, so they were too wide to go through the narrow city gate. Then they suddenly noticed a sparrow carrying a long straw in its beak and observed it inserting this straw lengthwise into a niche of the tower. The citizens realised that if they repositioned the beams lengthwise on the carriages they would go through the gate, so in gratitude they placed a memorial to the sparrow on the Munster's roof.

E=mc², said local boy Albert Einstein

RATINGS

Historic interest	●●●○
Cultural interest	●●●○
Good for food	●●●○

BASICS

🔢 441 E13

ℹ️ Stadthaus, Münsterplatz 50, Ulm, tel 0731 161 2830; May–end Oct Mon–Fri 9–6, Sat 9–4, Sun 11–2; Nov–end Apr Mon–Fri 9–6, Sat 9–1

🚆 🚋 Ulm

www.tourismus.ulm.de (also in English)

TIPS

● Apart from having magnificent views of the city, the Danube and, on a clear day, across the Black Forest to the Swiss Alps, its well worth climbing the 768 steps to the top of the Münster spire so you can say that you have conquered the world's highest church spire (161m/528ft).

● At €6 for a one-day ticket, (or €10 for a family), the Ulm Card is good value for exploring the city. You get free travel on all Ding buses, trams and trains; a 50 per cent reduction on guided city tours; reduced fees for visits to the Münster, spire, museums and theatres; and a number of other benefits. Two-day tickets are also available.

The Residenz has painted ceilings by Tiepolo

RATINGS	
Historic interest	●●●●
Cultural interest	●●●
Walkability	●●●
Good for food	●●●●

BASICS

✚ 437 E11

🏠 Falkenhaus, Am Markt, 97070 Würzburg, tel 0931 372398; Apr–end Dec Mon–Fri 10–6, Sat 10–2; Jan–end Mar Mon–Fri 10–4, Sat 10–1

🚉 🚋 Würzburg

www.wurzburg.de
Good website with lots of useful information (in English).

TIPS

• The best way of seeing Würzburg is on foot. Various routes are clearly waymarked, giving you a choice of tours through the Altstadt, trails through the vineyards and Landesgartenschau Park to the Fortress Marienberg, or a stroll (4km/2.5 miles) along a panoramic route above the city, passing through one of the most famous wine areas of Germany.

Madonna and Child by Riemenschneider, in the Mainfränkisches Museum

WÜRZBURG

**A city of architecture, culture and wine.
The gateway to the Romantic Road.**

The lively university city of Würzburg is surrounded by productive vineyards and dominated by the massive Marienberg fortress. The origins of this fortress date back to around 1000BC when Celtic tribesmen first fortified the site, but it was in AD689 that the town really came to prominence with the martyrdom of three Irish missionaries, Kilian, Kolonat and Totnan, who tried to convert the local people to Christianity. Würzburg was severely damaged during World War II, but after careful rebuilding, the city today has re-established itself as a popular destination renowned for its architecture, culture and wines.

THE BISHOPRIC AND CHURCHES
Since the foundation of the Würzburg bishopric in AD742, the city has been the religious heart of the region. Würzburg is notable for its many churches, and one of the oldest is the Marienkirche, built on the site of the fortress in AD704 and surrounded by the first fortification in the 13th century. The Juliusspital, an impressive, castle-like baroque building dating back to 1576, was founded by Prince Bishop Julius Echter and contains a hospital, home for the elderly and a winery that supports both. The Marienkapelle on the Marktplatz is an interesting late-Gothic Bavarian church and the magnificent Dom St. Kilian is the fourth largest Romanesque church in Germany.

Veitshochheim, the prince bishops' summer resort (7km/4 miles north-west), is a jewel of baroque architecture and has an exquisite rococo garden.

THE RESIDENZ
The Würzburg Residenz (1719–44), designed by Balthasar Neumann, is the greatest baroque building of its kind in Germany. The enormous and lavish interiors of this 'Palace of Palaces' are amazing, especially the vast fresco painted by the Venetian artist Tieplo on the ceiling above the grand staircase, the largest painting in the world. The palace has more than 300 baroque and rococo rooms, although many are still being renovated and may be closed. Behind the Residenz, the terraced Hofgarten's English- and French-styled gardens are carefully manicured and filled with whimsical rococo sculptures.

This chapter gives information on things to do in Germany other than sightseeing. Germany's best shops, arts venues, nightlife, activities and events are listed region by region.

What to Do

SHOPPING

Shopping is practically a national pastime in Germany, and visitors keen to spend a few euros won't be disappointed by the quality and variety of goods on offer. Most towns are home to at least one major shopping mall and a handful of indoor *Passagen* (literally 'passageways') lined with shops. Commercial hubs like Frankfurt and Düsseldorf are home to some of the most exclusive and lucrative shopping districts in Europe, while cities such as Cologne and Berlin have a more eclectic feel. Bargains (and a great deal of junk) can be found at flea markets and Christmas markets all over the country, while souvenirs range from the distressingly tacky to the reassuringly expensive.

DEPARTMENT STORES

The biggest department store chain in Germany—and indeed the whole of Europe—is Karstadt, although you'll also

Designer clothing at Escada on Berlin's Friedrichstrasse

find Galeria Kaufhof and other chain department stores in most major cities. All of these stores sell an overwhelming range of high-quality goods, from clothes and kitchenware to sports equipment and electrical supplies. Many stores also have a restaurant or café in which shoppers can rest tired limbs, and where the food is usually excellent. The biggest department store on the European mainland, incidentally, is Berlin's famous KaDeWe (Kaufhaus des Westens), which has eight different levels, a legendary delicatessen and a tropical café on the top floor.

LOCAL MARKETS

All major towns in Germany have at least one weekly market (usually held on a Saturday, but sometimes on a Sunday), and many smaller towns do too. Berlin holds numerous flea markets at weekends, the most popular of which takes place in Charlottenburg every Saturday. Stuttgart hosts a number of markets at weekends and during the week; the biggest is probably its food market, which takes place two or three times a week (contact the local tourist office for up-to-date information). Even more popular than the weekly markets, however, are the Christmas markets, which are held just about everywhere. The best are in Munich and Dresden, both of which are famous for their handmade wooden toys and Christmas decorations.

SUPERMARKETS

Until reunification in 1990, supermarkets in East Germany sold completely different brands from those in the West, but these days shops all over the country are stocked to the rafters with everything you could possibly need. Many of the bigger supermarkets, or hypermarkets, also sell things like clothes, basic sports equipment and electrical goods, and they're often part of a bigger retail complex. In

smaller places, supermarkets are usually in or near the middle of town, while elsewhere they're more likely to be on the outskirts.

OPENING HOURS

Germany's shops used to be regulated by draconian laws covering opening times, but these days things are much more relaxed. Most shops in the major cities stay open until 7 or 8pm on weekdays and 5 or 6pm on Saturdays. In smaller towns, shops tend to close at 6pm on weekdays. Markets usually call it a day at around 4pm, apart from during

Friedrichstadt Passage in Friedrichstrasse, Berlin

the run-up to Christmas. Souvenir shops in resort towns may stay open later than usual in the high season, but will close earlier in the winter.

PAYMENT

Credit cards are not as widely accepted as they are in, say, the UK or US, although bigger shops and department stores will usually accept most major cards. If in doubt, ask before you buy to avoid disappointment. Personal cheques and traveller's cheques are not generally accepted, and smaller shops may refuse to change large denomination notes (bills).

TAX REFUNDS

MwSt (sales tax or VAT) stands at 16 per cent, and is added to most goods and services. Non-EU citizens can request a tax-free shopping cheque for big purchases, which can then be cashed at customs on leaving the country. Not all shops offer this service, so check before you buy (participating shops should display a sticker saying 'tax-free for tourists' in the window; see page 412).

WHAT TO BUY

Beer Steins and Glasses

No trip to Germany would be complete without sampling the beer, and assuming you

enjoy the experience, the stein the beer is served in makes an excellent souvenir. Steins are basically beer mugs, and they come in all shapes and sizes. Most are made from pewter or porcelain and have elaborate emblems on the side, and you can get them from department stores, beer halls and souvenir shops. Beer glasses in Germany are all very similar, but those that Cologne's *Kölsch* is served in are unique, and are well worth searching out (*Kölsch* glasses are small and slender with completely straight sides).

Ceramics and Porcelain

Germany is well known for the quality of its porcelain. Its two

most famous manufacturers are Villeroy & Boch, based in Mettlach, and Meissen (▷ 269), based near Leipzig. Both have outlets all over Germany (and throughout Europe), but the best place to pick up a bargain and see how everything is made is at the factory outlets in their home towns (worldwide delivery can be arranged at both). To see Villeroy & Boch's goods in use before you buy, look no farther than the vast mosaic that forms the choir floor of Cologne Cathedral, or the interior of the Pfunds Molkerei dairy shop in Dresden, which is made up of over 3,000 hand-painted tiles (▷ 267). High-quality porcelain is also produced in Thuringia.

Food and Wine

Every region in Germany has its local recipe when it comes to sausages, but unless they're cured or sealed, they're quite difficult to take home. The same is true for chocolates, particularly if you haven't got access to a fridge while you're travelling—but that doesn't mean you shouldn't try them. Some of the best chocolate truffles in the world can be found at Fassbender and Rausch, in Berlin (▷ 260) and elsewhere, and Leonidas Pralinen, which has outlets all over Europe, including Aachen (▷ 252).

The best places to try local wines are the Rhine and the Mosel valleys, which produce some excellent Rieslings. Also worth tasting if you're in the area is the velvety-smooth Spätburgunder from the Eifel's Ahr valley, and Sekt (Germany's answer to champagne) from Saale, Germany's northern-most wine-producing region.

Leather Goods

If you looked around any German main street on any given day in the winter, you

could be forgiven for thinking that everyone has shares in the country's cows. Leather jackets are available everywhere, and come in all shapes and sizes, although you may have to shop around to find a bargain. More traditional jackets (such as those worn by Bavarians in oompah bands) can be bought in Munich or its environs.

Shoes

You only have to look at a cut-away diagram of a pair of Birkenstock shoes to realize that the Germans take their footwear seriously. Layer after layer of felt and leather help to create shoes that shape themselves to your feet as you wear them. Birkenstocks will set you back as much as £80 in the UK, and at least the same in dollars in the US, so if you're coveting a pair, look for one of the many outlets in major towns and cities.

Toys and Christmas Decorations

Christmas markets are a national institution in Germany, as are stalls selling seasonal decorations. These range in quality from tacky trinkets to handmade (and usually quite expensive) treasures crafted out of wood. Other items on offer include candles, chinaware and traditional wooden serving boards (used for cold meats and cheeses).

Toys are also a serious business in a country that's packed with toy museums and factories. Seiffen, in the Erzgebirge Mountains near the Czech border, has 100 master craftsmen, and is the place to go for traditional wooden toys, as are Nuremberg, Dresden and Leipzig, particularly at Christmas time. The Harz Mountains, right in the middle of Germany, are renowned for their wooden puppets, while the Black Forest is the place to head for cuckoo clocks.

ENTERTAINMENT

The range of entertainment on offer in Germany is vast. From classical music and opera to rock and pop, from art house cinema to traditional caberets, you're sure to find something that appeals. Berlin is, of course, the best place for nightclubs and cutting-edge entertainment, but all Germany's cities have their highlights. Most cities have their own orchestra, theatre or opera companies, and many capitalize on famous citizens, such as Beethoven in Bonn or Wagner in Leipzig and Dresden. Cinema is popular with Germans, and you will often be able to find an *originalversion* of the latest blockbuster.

CINEMA

Going to the cinema is a popular pastime (there are over 80 cinemas in Munich alone) and most towns and cities have large multiplexes. The bad news is that films are usually

The Film Museum at the Sony Centre in Potsdamer Platz, Berlin

dubbed into German, and even in bigger towns you may be hard pushed to find a film showing in its *originalversion*, or OV (*Original mit Untertiteln*, original with subtitles, or OmU, means 'original language with subtitles'). If a film is showing in its original version, it should say OV or OmU on the poster outside the cinema, although if you can't see it, it's always worth asking. Major cities such as Berlin, Munich, Hamburg and Frankfurt all have cinemas that show original-language films, and Hollywood blockbusters are usually released at the same time as they are elsewhere in Europe. Many

cinemas also offer discounted admissions one evening a week—ask at the local tourist office for details.

CLASSICAL MUSIC AND OPERA

The Germans can't seem to get enough of classical music, which is hardly surprising given their track record. Germany has produced more famous composers than any other country in the world, among them Johann Sebastian Bach, Ludwig van Beethoven, Johannes Brahms, Georg Händel, Richard Strauss and Richard Wagner, to name just a few. It goes without saying that the cities most associated with these names host internationally important music festivals every summer, but even smaller towns and villages put on regular classical concerts throughout the year.

The best time to catch a concert is in the summer, when most music festivals are in full swing, although the weeks leading up to Christmas are also well served with seasonal offerings. Details can usually be found at the local tourist information office.

The best-known concert venues in Germany are the Beethovenhalle in Bonn, the Sächsische Staatsoper (known as the Semperoper) in Dresden, the Gewandhaus in Leipzig and the Philharmonies in Berlin and Cologne. The best-known opera venues are the Nationaltheater in Munich

and the Staatsopers in Berlin and Hamburg (see individual entries in the What to Do listings on pages 246–286).

(see individual entries in the What to Do listings on pages 246–286).

BERLIN FILM FESTIVAL

The Berlin Film Festival (*Internationale Filmfestspiele Berlin,* or *Berlinale*) is one of the biggest celebrations of cinema in the world, and although it doesn't match the glitz and glamour of Cannes, it certainly enjoys a much bigger audience, with locals and visitors attending screenings in their droves. During the decades before reunification, the *Berlinale* was one of the few forums where East and West came together, and because of this it was overtly political and often highly controversial. These days, of course, things are a bit calmer, but visitors can always be sure of seeing the very best in world cinema. The festival takes place in February each year. For more details check the website www.berlinale.de (in English and German).

Churches and cathedrals also provide ideal venues for choral concerts—have a look at their noticeboards or ask at the nearest tourist office for details of forthcoming events.

CONTEMPORARY LIVE MUSIC

Hard rock and heavy metal are extremely popular in Germany, as are mainstream pop and rock. Major international acts tend to perform in the bigger cities of Berlin, Cologne and Hamburg, but you'll find national and local rock bands performing just about anywhere, from the smallest pub to the biggest concert hall. Many cities also host an

A drumming band in Dresden

annual pop festival, such as the RheinKultur concert in Bonn. For information on what's on, check local listings magazines or at the nearest tourist information office.

JAZZ AND BLUES

Most jazz and blues music is performed in bars or clubs, but there are also a number of jazz festivals held in towns and cities throughout the country. Chief among these are the Stuttgart Jazz Festival in April, the Dresden Jazz Festival in May and JazzFest Berlin in early November, all of which attract the best in local and international talent.

FOLK AND REGIONAL MUSIC

Traditional regional music doesn't enjoy the same popularity in Germany as it does in, say, Spain, but there's no explaining the almost universal appeal of the ubiquitous oom-pah band. Although these brass and drum ensembles aren't popular with Germany's younger generation, the old guard invariably know all the words, and they generally don't need much encouragement to sing them. This can be a little overwhelming at first, but many songs have an easy-to-remember refrain that's repeated ad infinitum until the band members run out of breath. A few glasses of the local beer usually helps, but if you're still struggling, just stamp your feet and bang the table at the same time as everyone else. Oompah bands perform in pubs and beer halls year-round, but the best time to experience them is during the various Lenten carnivals that are held in January or February. Traditional folk festivals are also held across Germany in July and August.

THEATRE AND DANCE

Germany enjoys a rich and varied theatre scene, particularly in the larger cities. Unless you speak German, of course, you're unlikely to want to see a play, but that doesn't mean you can't take in a cabaret, a ballet or a dance performance. Check out Deutsche Oper in Berlin, the Deutsche Theater in Munich, the Niedersächsisches Staatstheater in Hannover or the Staatsoper in Hamburg for the best in ballet and the Tigerpalast in Frankfurt or the Friedrichstaadtpalast in Berlin for the cream of cabaret. Many smaller cities and towns, especially those with a thriving university scene, are full of more intimate venues that stage mainstream and alternative acts all year round (see pages 246–286 for full listings).

If you do want to see something in English, Frankfurt's aptly named English Theatre is reputed to be the largest of its kind in mainland Europe, and puts on a full schedule of plays and musicals, many of them from Broadway and London's West End (▷ 253). There is also a smaller English-speaking theatre in Hamburg (▷ 248). For an authentic traditional German spectacle, look no farther than the famous puppet theatre in Cologne (▷ 255) or Lübeck (▷ 250).

TICKETS

Munich
Tickets for concerts and shows in Munich can be obtained from the box office of the venue concerned, or from München Ticket at www.muenchenticket.de (the desk in the main tourist information office at Marienplatz also has up-to-date information on last-minute tickets and deals ▷ 180).

Berlin
There are ticket outlets all over Berlin, although since most are likely to charge 15 per cent commission on top of the price of the ticket, it is a good idea to go to the relevant box office in person if you want to keep the cost down. You can also purchase tickets for most shows, concerts and sporting events on-line at the comprehensive and informative www.berlin.de (but note that although this website does have an English listings section, the booking facility is available only in German).

NIGHTLIFE

Despite their reputation for being a serious-minded lot, the Germans know how to have a good time, whether they're singing along with an oompah band at a traditional beer hall or immersing themselves in trance and techno at some hip new club.

Given that Germany is the home of techno, it's perhaps not surprising that clubs and discos are hugely popular in all of the major towns and cities, although even in smaller towns and villages the locals don't need much of an excuse to let their hair down and have

The Adagio in Berlin

a good sing-song. Berlin and Hamburg are arguably the hottest of Germany's hotspots when it comes to cutting-edge clubs, but university cities such as Dresden, Leipzig, Münster and Cologne can certainly hold their own. You'll find music and venues to suit all trends and tastes. In addition to techno and trance clubs, there's no shortage of excellent jazz and blues bars in Germany, and most mainstream clubs put on at least one rock and pop night a week. Salsa, reggae and hard rock bands are also popular. Traditional music, which tends to be of the folk or brass band variety, is usually restricted to beer halls and pubs, and is particularly prevalent in smaller towns, where it's often the only form of after-hours

entertainment. Most cities in Germany also boast a casino—one of the most luxurious is in Weisbaden, where gamblers can place their chips beneath the crystal chandeliers and coffered ceilings of the city's magnificent neoclassical Kurhaus (▷ 258).

Germany goes to bed much earlier than many other European countries, with bars and clubs often closing as early as 1 or 2am, so if you're hell-bent on pulling an all-nighter, your best bet is probably to head for Hamburg or Berlin.

BARS

There are American-style bars in most major cities, but more traditional pubs in Germany often double as something else, such as a restaurant, bistro or music venue. In smaller towns and villages, pubs and beer halls are the norm, with or without live music. They invariably serve traditional German food in addition to local dishes.

BERLIN'S GAY SCENE

The gay club scene in Berlin dates back to the early 1920s and originated in the dance halls and salons of Schöneberg. Along with London and Amsterdam, Berlin is one of the major gay capitals in Europe, home to about 300,000 gays and lesbians. The scene is no longer restricted to Berlin's subculture and is a fully integrated part of mainstream culture and nightlife, so most clubs and bars are gay-friendly and many of the larger clubs have a gay night. The borough of Schöneberg should be the first place that visitors head for. There is a high density of clubs and bars welcoming gay visitors around the Fuggerstrasse, Motzstrasse

and Eisenacherstrasse area. Lesbenberatung (Lesbian Advice Centre) on Kulmer Strasse has the latest details of lesbian-friendly parties and events (Kulmer Strasse 20a, Berlin (Schöneberg), tel 030 215 2000), while the gay shop Mann-O-Meter in Motzstrasse provides information and tips on the gay scene (Bülowstrasse 106, Berlin (Schöneberg), tel 030 216 8008; www.mann-o-meter.de).

Prenzlauer Berg is a popular student borough that attracts a very diverse crowd. Most of the cafés, bars and nightclubs are concentrated between Greifenhagener Strasse and Gleimstrasse. In Kreuzberg, the gay scene

is focused around Oranienburgerstrasse and parts of Mehringdamm, where you will also find the Schwule Museum (Gay Museum; Mehringdamm 61, 10961 Berlin (Kreuzberg), tel 030 6959 9050; www.schwulesmuseum.de; Wed–Sun 2–6, Sat 2–7). In Friedrichshain there is also a lively party scene near East Side Gallery—the paintings are on the remains of the Berlin Wall. The Gay-Lesbian City-Festival (▷ 265) takes place every year at the end of June around Nollendorf Platz and culminates with the CSD: Christopher Street Day gay and lesbian parade through the city.

HEALTH AND BEAUTY

Given the number of towns that have the world Bad (literally 'bath') in their names, it's perhaps not surprising that spas are something of a national obsession in Germany.

Unlike in the UK and the US, however, the term spa doesn't necessarily refer to an exclusive (and expensive) pamper palace—in fact, most spas in Germany are open to the public and won't cost you much more than a trip to your local swimming pool. Facilities usually include numerous indoor and outdoor pools at various temperatures, plus water jets, Jacuzzis and extensive sauna areas. Changing facilities are invariably immaculate, and most spas also have at least one café or restaurant overlooking the main pool area (this is often open to bathers only). But the highlight of any spa experience has to be the water itself, which is usually salty and is supposed to work wonders on aching limbs. It's

worth pointing out, however, that a few spas encourage what they call 'textile-free' (i.e. nude) bathing, so if you're at all concerned about this you

might want to check before you go in. Massage, acupuncture and other therapies may also be offered at an additional cost.

Spas are popular in Germany and treatments are sometimes available as part of a health plan

WHAT TO DO

HOW TO FIND OUT MORE

Most major towns and cities in Germany publish listings for what's on and local papers may also have up-to-date details in their entertainment sections. Tourist information offices are another good source of information, particularly in smaller towns.

Munich
• *München im…* (*München im Februar*, *München im März* and so on) is a free monthly paper with complete listings for museums, galleries, concerts, theatres and cinemas. The free fortnightly *In München* provides similar information. Both are in German only, but it's relatively easy to figure out what's what, and both are available in bars,

restaurants and similar venues.
• Listings information in English can be found in *New in the City Today*, which is a free paper, and the more useful monthly magazine *Munich Found*, which costs €3. The latter contains restaurant reviews and other articles in addition to detailed listings.

Berlin
• The best listings magazines in Berlin are *Zitty* (€2.50) and *Tip* (€3), both of which are packed with up-to-the-minute information on everything that's happening in Germany's capital city. They're published bi-weekly in German only. The monthly magazine *Berlin Programm* (€2) provides a more general overview of

what's on where, while *Prinz*, another monthly magazine (€1), picks out the month's best parties, gigs and concerts, and gives details of the latest film and music releases. It also reviews new restaurants, bars and club nights. In addition, *Prinz* publishes a yearly magazine that rates the top shops, restaurants, nightclubs, bars, health spas, gyms and hotels in the city (€4.50).
• *030* is a free two-weekly listings magazine, which you can pick up at tourist information offices, shops, bars, restaurants and hotels. It has all the latest information about the up-and-coming parties and club nights, plus reviews of recent gigs. It also has a good film review and cinema listings section.

SPORTS AND ACTIVITIES

In general, Germans take good care of their health, and many take part in some kind of sports activity. Walking and cycling are popular, and most cities have large parks where you can exercise without coming into contact with car fumes. Skiing and other winter sports are available in the mountainous south, while sailing is popular on the limited northern coastline, as well as on the many lakes and rivers.

Soccer is often seen as the national sport, although ice hockey and American football also have a great following, as do motor racing heroes Michael and Ralph Schumacher.

SPECTATOR SPORTS

American Football
American football is becoming increasingly popular, with four teams competing against outfits from Scotland and Holland over the country competing in the national Basketball Bundesliga (BBL). The season runs from the end of October until the end of June, with most games taking place on Friday, Saturday and Sunday

Ice Hockey is a popular sport, with teams throughout the country

for the coveted World Bowl Championships between April and June each year. The German teams in the NFL European League are Berlin Thunder, Frankfurt Galaxy, the Cologne Centurions and Rhein Fire (from Düsseldorf). Berlin Thunder won World Bowl XII in 2004. And to give you an idea of what the standard is like, 34 European League players were signed to American NFL teams in 2004. For tickets, go to www.nfleurope.com.

Basketball
Basketball is much more popular in Germany than it is elsewhere in Europe, with 11 professional teams from all

nights. The Berlin Albatrosses were league champions for seven years in a row before being beaten by GHP Bamberg in the 2004 semi-finals; Bamberg then went on to lose 3–2 to Frankfurt's Opel Skyliners. For schedules go to www.basketball-bundesliga.de.

Formula One Motor Racing
As befits the home of the legendary Schumacher brothers, Germany is the only country in the world to host two Grand Prix races per season, namely the European Grand Prix, held at the infamous Nürburgring in the spectacular Eifel region of western Germany (▷ 253),

and the German Grand Prix, held at Hockenheim, near Heidelberg in the south of the country. These races are hugely popular, so it's a good idea to book tickets well in advance to avoid disappointment. Of course, more minor motor racing events take place at both tracks throughout the year and are much easier to get tickets for. For more information on events at both venues, go to www.nuerburgring.de or www.hockenheimring.de.

Horse Racing
Although not quite the national institution it is in England, horse racing in Germany continues to have an enthusiastic following, thanks to big weekend meetings at major race courses, such as the Mariendorf Derby in Berlin (▷ 263), Rennbahn Grafenberg in Düsseldorf (▷ 253), Rennbahn Verden near Bremen (▷ 250) and the Internationaler Club at Baden-Baden (▷ 281). Dressing up is the order of the day at weekends, but Fridays tend to be a bit more relaxed, and are sometimes free of charge.

Ice Hockey
Ice hockey in Germany is probably second only to soccer when it comes to the dedication and enthusiasm of its fans. It's also big business, with 14 professional teams competing in the national Deutschen Eishockey Liga (DEL), and dozens more taking part in the lesser leagues. The season runs from September through to April, and games are usually played on Friday, Saturday and Sunday nights. In 2004, the Frankfurt Lions beat the Berlin Ice Bears three games to one to win the national league championships. For a current schedule of games, take a look at www.del.org.

WHAT TO DO

Soccer

Thanks to the success of its national team, soccer is arguably Germany's national sport, although a recent hiccup saw them knocked out of Euro 2004 at the group stage. In addition to a (usually) strong national side, Germany also boasts one of the best leagues in Europe, with teams like Bayern Munich and Bayern Leverkusen regularly battling it out on the national and international stage. The season lasts from August until June, and games are usually played on Wednesday evenings or at weekends. For a full match schedule, log onto www.bundesliga.de and click on the link that says 'Spieltermine'.

Many stadiums in Germany are currently being renovated or rebuilt to stage the 2006 World Cup. For more details and ticketing information, go to www.fifaworldcup.com.

Tennis

The biggest event of the country's tennis calendar is the German Masters in Hamburg, one of the key competitions on the international circuit. This is a popular event and tickets sell out quickly. Order yours through www.masterseries.com.

ACTIVITIES

Cycling

Cycling is extremely popular in Germany. Berlin has more than 750km (465 miles) of cycle paths. In most major towns in Germany, bicycles can be rented in Berlin at the local *Fahrradstation*, which may also offer themed bicycle tours with English-speaking guides (▷ 336). Cycle lanes are often separate from the road and tend to be much more user-friendly than those in the UK or the US.

Outside of the cities, the most popular cycle paths in Germany are those that line

the Rhine and Mosel. These paths are continuous and run for most of the length of both rivers. The north of the country is generally quite flat and is well suited to family cycling (again, bicycles can be rented in many towns), while the south is more hilly.

The German Tourist Board (www.germany-tourism.co.uk) publishes the useful guide *Discovering Germany by Bike*. For those who wish to tour, the ADFC (German Cyclists' Federation) offers trail and route information; log onto www.adfc.de (German only).

Fishing

Germany has some of the most picturesque lakes, rivers

Golfers at Chiemsee, one of Germany's quality courses

and streams in Europe, and there is plenty to offer both the expert angler and the first-time fisherman. Trout fishing is popular, but other catches include pike, carp, salmon, perch and bream. The best areas for fishing are the Black Forest, the Harz Mountains, Bavaria and, of course, the Rhineland and North Rhine Westphalia. Hamburg and Kiel are well placed for sea fishing, as are many of the towns and villages along Germany's coastline.

An angling permit (*Angelschein* in German) is required, and can be obtained from the local rural district council (*Landratsamt*) on payment of a small fee (usually €5–10).

A similar fee may also be required for a local permit, payable to the owners of the fishing ground. For information on where to fish, and for advice on where to get the relevant permits, ask at your nearest tourist office.

Golf

German enthusiasm for golf is reflected in the number and quality of golf courses that are scattered throughout the country. The course at Gut Kaden, 47km (30 miles) north of Hamburg, and the Club Zur Vahr course in Bremen, former home of the German Open, are among the most famous, but equally impressive are the Klostermannshof course at

Niederkassel in the Rhineland, and the Hohen Wieschendorf on the Baltic Sea between Lübeck and Wismar.

Many private clubs welcome non-members, although proof of your handicap (usually a minimum of 32) is often required. Clubs and carts can be rented at most courses. Green fees near major towns and cities such as Düsseldorf or Frankfurt are typically in the region of €60–80 per round (although weekends are often cheaper), but clubs in the countryside charge a lot less. For a listing of selected courses in Germany, log onto www.golfeurope.com or www.linksgolf.co.uk.

In-line Skating

In-line skating is extremely popular in Germany, and an increase in demand in the last five years has resulted in the establishment of designated skating paths in a number of cities. In fact, skating is so popular that in many cities the downtown area is closed to traffic for one night a week to make way for those dashing about on eight wheels. Your nearest tourist information office can tell you the best places to skate, and advice on where to rent equipment.

Trekking and Climbing

You could spend a lifetime trekking in Germany and you still wouldn't get close to

Make sure you're well equipped for walking in areas like the Brocken

covering all the country's way-marked paths. Popular areas include the Black Forest, with its well-signed trails and pretty, half-timbered villages; Upper Bavaria, with its fairy-tale castles and ancient monasteries; and the area known as Saxon Switzerland, which has around 700km (435 miles) of trails and no fewer than 700 different rock faces for climbers of all abilities.

The Bavarian Alps form the heart of Germany's mountaineering scene, and the Zugspitze, the highest mountain in the country at 2,963m (9,721ft), is regularly tackled by experienced climbers in both summer and winter.

Well-established long-distance trails in Germany include the Rennsteig, a ridge walk through the Thuringian Forest, and the Oberlausitzer Bergweg, on the border with the Czech Republic. Culture buffs and wine aficionados may prefer the more romantic Rheinhöhenweg, which follows the right bank of the Rhine between Bonn and Oppenheim, or the Moselhöhenweg, which travels along both banks of the Mosel between Koblenz and Trier. And there's also the much shorter Rotweinwanderweg, between Altenahr and Bad Badendorf in the Ahr valley (▷ 96 for information on accessing this trail). An excellent resource for walks throughout Europe is www.walkingworld.com.

Watersports

Germany's coastline is awash with windsurfing and sailing opportunities: Sylt, Amrum and St. Peter-Ording are the best-known windsurfing spots on the North Sea coast, while the more sheltered Baltic coast towns are ideal for those with less experience. Kiel Bay, Lübeck Bay and Flensburg Firth are perfect for combining sailing with some city sightseeing. Elsewhere, Germany's numerous lakes provide plenty of potential for watersports in the summer: Bodensee (Lake

Constance), in the far south of the country, is popular, as are Müggelsee in Berlin and Alster in Hamburg. Rafting, kayaking and canyoning are all available in the mountainous regions, with Berchtesgaden, Thuringia and the Harz Mountains offering the best in the way of white water. Germany is also home to Europe's biggest scuba-diving venue, the Dive-Gasometer in Duisburg. It welcomes divers of all abilities, and its on-site facilities include an underwater wreck and an artificial reef. Lake Constance is another well-loved diving destination. For those with suitable experience and qualifications, however, the Baltic Sea offers some of the best wreck and cave diving in Europe.

Winter Sports

Opportunities to enjoy winter sports abound in Germany, particularly in the south. The biggest and best-known skiing area in the country is at Garmisch-Partenkirchen (▷ 282) in the Bavarian Alps, an hour's drive from Munich. This world-class resort has hosted the Winter Olympics, the Alpine World Ski Championships and numerous world cup winter sports events. Almost as impressive is Berchtesgaden National Park in the southeast corner of the country, near Salzburg. Winterberg, in the Arnsberger Wald to the east of Düsseldorf, is Germany's northernmost ski resort, and is home to an Olympic bobsleigh run that is open the public (▷ 258). There's also a bobsleigh run at Oberhof, the biggest resort in the Thuringian Forest. Other popular skiing areas include the Black Forest and the Harz Mountains. Ski rental is available in all areas, and the ski season usually runs from late November until late March (although it's generally shorter the farther north you go).

WHAT TO DO

NATIONAL PARKS

There are 15 national parks, 14 biosphere reserves and no fewer than 90 nature parks in Germany. Below is a list of the parks, with a brief description of each. For more detailed information, visit the tourist board's website at www.germany-tourism.de, choose the English-language version, and look for 'National Parks' in the pull-down menu under the blue 'Destination' heading at the top of the page.

Nationalpark Bayerischer Wald (Bavarian Forest National Park)
Near the Czech border, and characterized by densely forested mountains, central Europe's largest protected closed woodland area has some good hiking trails.

Nationalpark Berchtesgaden (Berchtesgaden National Park)
Rising more than 2,700m (8,860ft), Berchtesgaden is an important area for winter sports (see below) and is arguably Germany's most scenic national park (also ▷ 208–209).

Nationalpark Eifel (Eifel National Park)
Not far from Bonn and Cologne, Eifel forms the westernmost of Germany's upland massifs, and comprises scenic river valleys and rolling, forested hills (also ▷ 96).

Nationalpark Hainich (Hainich National Park)
In the Thuringian mountains to the south of Weimar. It contains Europe's largest mixed deciduous forest and is rich in wildlife.

Nationalpark Hamburgisches Wattenmeer (Hamburg National Park)
Straddles the banks of the Elbe River in the far north of Germany, and is rich in sea life and birdlife.

Nationalpark Harz (Harz National Park) and Nationalpark Hochharz (Upper Harz National Park)
Both of these parks are to the southeast of Hannover. They contain several spectacular caves and crags, plus the Brocken, northern Germany's highest peak at 1,142m (3,747ft).

Nationalpark Jasmund (Jasmund National Park)

Enjoy the landscape of Germany's National Parks

Comprises just 30sq km (11sq miles) of chalk cliffs and forested creeks on Rügen island, off Germany's northeast coast, but contains a variety of flora and fauna.

Nationalpark Kellerwald-Edersee (Kellerwald National Park)
Germany's newest national park is a haven of rolling hills and deciduous woodland just a short drive to the west of Kassel.

Nationalpark Müritz (Müritz National Park)
An amazing and inviting landscape made up of dozens of small lakes in the northeast of Germany, and an important breeding ground for migratory birds. There are numerous hiking and cycling paths.

Nationalpark Niedersächsisches Wattenmeer (Wadden Sea National Park)
Protects a series of islands to the northeast of Bremen that are famed for their beaches and birdlife.

Nationalpark Sächsische Schweiz (Saxon Switzerland National Park)
Just to the south of Dresden, near the Czech border. The park's craggy sandstone rock formations are popular with hikers and climbers alike. There are also boat tours.

Nationalpark Schleswig-Holsteinisches Wattenmeer (Schleswig-Holstein National Park)
Between Kiel and Lübeck. This park is known for its dunes, salt-marshes and *Halligen* (small islands that become flooded whenever there is a high spring tide or heavy storm).

Nationalpark Unteres Odertal (Lower Oder Valley National Park)
Spilling over into Poland, this park is a unique wetland area offering some great birding opportunities, and is home to 37 different types of fauna.

Nationalpark Vorpommersche Boddenlandschaft (Vorpommern Lagoon National Park)
On the coast between Rostock and Stralsund, this park is dominated by dunes, coves and *Bodden* (shallow bays cut off from the Baltic.

FOR CHILDREN

A family day out is a frequent event for many Germans, so there's no shortage of things for kids to do. In addition to some world-class theme parks (see box below), Germany has plenty of excellent zoos, aquariums, planetariums and science sites, not to mention a handful of film museums, two or three car museums and even a chocolate museum with a working chocolate factory (▷ 256). More traditional are the various toy and puppet museums that are dotted around the country, which give an insight into the life and times of children in Germany.

THEME PARKS

There are dozens of different theme parks scattered throughout Germany. The biggest are described below, but more are listed under the regional sections, accompanied by the symbol shown above, and on the German tourist board's website, www.germany-tourism.co.uk.

TAKING YOUR KIDS

● Children are welcome almost everywhere in Germany, as long as they're well behaved. German social life is very family-orientated, so pubs and beer halls are often frequented by families, particularly at lunchtime and in the early evening. Classier restaurants may be less amenable to welcoming children late at night, but on the whole it shouldn't be a problem. Most restaurants have a limited number of high chairs.

● Children's discounts are commonplace everywhere from museums to zoos, although the age limit varies both for very young children (who often get in free) and for school-age children. The upper age limit is normally 18, although 16 or even 14 is not uncommon. Children under 18 are also eligible for discounts on all public transportation.

● Infant products (baby food, milk formulas and so on) are widely available in supermarkets throughout Germany, but you might want to bring your own brand with you anyway.

● Most hotels are happy to put up additional beds in rooms for kids, and some of the bigger hotels have a babysitting service for parents who want an evening on their own.

Enjoy a family boat trip on Bodensee (Lake Constance)

Children at play often overcome the language barrier

GERMANY'S BIGGEST AND BEST THEME PARKS

Europa-Park, Freiburg
The aptly named Europa-Park allows you to travel around Europe in a single day, in addition to offering the usual white-knuckle rides, rollercoasters and other forms of family entertainment. It's also Germany's most popular leisure park and is probably best avoided during June, July and August. It's situated near Freiburg, in the south, and is open daily 9–6. More details can be found on page 281 and at www.europapark.de.

Legoland, Günzburg
The fourth theme park of Danish toy manufacturer Lego is in Günzburg, near Ulm in southern Germany. More than 50 million Lego blocks have been used to create a miniature version of the world's greatest cities and landmarks. In addition to the park's 40 different attractions, there are also entertainment shows for kids and adults alike. Closed Nov–Mar. For more details, see page 282 and www.legoland.de.

Phantasialand, Brühl
Phantasialand near Cologne is one of Germany's most popular theme parks, with a range of white-knuckle rides and family entertainment. Among its annual highlights are the Festival of Lights in October and Winter Dream, a special performance put on during the weekends leading up to Christmas. Open daily Apr–Oct 9–6. For more details, and for Christmas openings, click on www. phantasialand.de.

A visit to any of the festivals listed here will show that not only do the Germans know how to have a good time, they know how to do it in style. Even the most raucous celebrations have a well-deserved reputation for being friendly and good natured, though, and visitors are made to feel especially welcome. As well as the major festivals there are literally thousands more held in every town, village and hamlet in the country—see individual sight entries for up-to-date details. The list below is restricted to general festivals; information on the major music and arts festivals can be found in the listings on pages 246–286.

GERMANY'S BIGGEST AND BEST FESTIVALS

Carnival, Cologne
February
Pre-Lenten celebratations take place all over Germany, but none is more spectacular than the week-long knees-up held each year in Cologne. It includes endless parades, processions and brass bands, all enjoyed by millions of party-goers in fancy dress; the result is one of the world's biggest street parties.

Dom Festival, Hamburg
Takes place three times a year, usually in March, July and August
Dating back to the 14th century, when traders and minstrels were offered refuge in St. Mary's Cathedral in bad weather, Hamburg's Cathedral Festival is one of the largest funfairs in Germany. Thrill rides, beer tents, live music and family entertainment are all part of the fun. It attracts a staggering 9 million visitors.

Rhine in Flames, Bonn, Bingen, Koblenz, Oberwesel and St. Goar
Summer; dates vary—see www.germany-tourism.co.uk
At five different venues throughout the valley on five different nights throughout the summer, the romantic Rhine provides the backdrop to one of the most spectacular fireworks displays in the world.

Love Parade, Berlin
July
One of the world's biggest raves, attracting around a million people. A procession is followed by two or three days

Munich's Oktoberfest: 7 million visitors in just over two weeks

of partying in clubs and on the streets. The event began in 1989, but controversy concerning the damage caused by the parade led to the cancellation of the 2004 event. It is hoped that the parade will be reinstated in 2005.

Oktoberfest, Munich
October
The most famous festival in Germany needs little introduction. An opening parade—in which everyone wears traditional regional costume and there is entertainment for all the family—is followed by 16 straight days of eating and drinking. Despite the fact that around 6 million litres (1.5

million US gallons) of Wies'n beer is consumed by the same number of visitors in a little more than two weeks, it's all very good natured.

Weinfeste (Wine Festivals)
Autumn; for information on individual festivals, see www.deutscheweine.de
Although Germany is better known for its beer festivals, the country also hosts hundreds of wine festivals to celebrate the annual grape harvest. The biggest are held in northern Bavaria, and in the Rhine and Mosel regions, and comprise the usual eating and drinking, accompanied by dancing and live music, but there are also smaller-scale parties in the wine-growing villages.

Weihnachtsmärkte (Christmas Markets)
Last week of November–Christmas Eve
Mulled wine, roasted chestnuts and grilled sausages; market stalls festooned with carvings, candles and lambskin shoes; children clutching toys, gingerbread men and marzipan—these are the things that make Germany's traditional Christmas markets unique. They're held every year in cities, towns and villages throughout the country.

NORTHERN GERMANY

The Hanseviertel shopping arcade in Hamburg

All possible variations on the shopping theme are to be found in northern Germany. Hamburg is one of the country's style capitals, with a range of clothing stores to suit. Although Bremen is not so noted, it does not lag far behind, while Hannover at first glance seems to be just one big shopping mall. Some towns, like Jever and Einbeck, are famed for their brews, and Rostock has an excellent schnapps. Look out also for maritime knick-knacks and beachwear at the coastal resorts.

Hamburg leads the field in northern Germany in terms of performance venues—the Hamburgische Staatsoper and its associated opera and ballet companies, and the Musikhalle concert hall with its pair of home-based orchestras, are shining stars in the nation's cultural firmament. Bremen and Hanover also have excellent venues and performers, and Rostock and Shwerin, both culturally important in the former East Germany, retain that character today. Lübeck, meanwhile, has a superb heritage of church and choral music that dates back at least as far as the life of composer and organist Dietrich Buxtehude (1637–1707).

Undoubtedly the most notorious nightlife area in the country is Hamburg's red-light district, focused on the Reeperbahn, but this by no means represents all the city has to offer. Its clubs have a reputation for cutting-edge music that dates back to the time when the Beatles were learning their trade here. Nowhere else in northern Germany can match the range and vigour of this port city's nightlife, although the other big cities have good scenes.

While many other activities are focused on the big cities, children's entertainment options are legion. The cities and towns do, of course, have a greater concentration of adventure and amusement parks—Bremen is particularly well endowed in the former category—but plenty of small towns and country areas have their own noteworthy attractions for children.

In 2004, Werder Bremen became champions of Germany's soccer Bundesliga, eclipsing more fancied outfits such as Bayern München and Borussia-München-Gladbach. The clubs in Hamburg and Hannover are also national achievers. Cycling and hiking are popular in the region, and the generally unchallenging terrain helps to make them feasible for most age groups. Since the north boasts all of Germany's coastline, sailing, windsurfing and other water sports are a big attraction. But as there are no mountains, and not even many high hills, open-air winter sports are limited to ice-skating when waterways and lakes freeze, and some *langlauf* (cross-country) skiing.

KEY TO SYMBOLS	
🌐	**Shopping**
🎵	**Entertainment**
👁	**Nightlife**
🏅	**Sports**
✪	**Activities**
♡	**Health and Beauty**
⊗	**For Children**

BREMEN

🎭 BREMER THEATER
Am Goetheplatz 1–3, 28203 Bremen
Tel 0421 36530
www.bremertheater.com
This large venue, just outside and to the southeast of the Altstadt, is actually a multi-theatre complex, the different elements of which stage opera, dance, musicals and theatre (occasionally in English) among other events.
🕐 Mon–Fri 11–5, Sat 11–2 💶 €7–51 🚊 Tram 2, 3 ♿

🎭 DIE GLOCKE
Domsheide 4–5, 28195 Bremen
Tel 0421 336699
www.glocke.de
The old Die Glocke concert hall just south of the Dom, is the home of two fine orchestras—the Deutsche Kammer-philharmonie Bremen, for chamber music, and the Bremer Philharmoniker symphony orchestra. The venue was described by the late conductor Herbert von Karajan (1908–89) as being one of the three finest in Europe.
🕐 Box office: open 1 hour before performances 💶 €6.50–106.50 🚊 Tram 2, 3, 4, 6, 8 ♿

🎭 THEATER AM LEIBNIZPLATZ
Leibnizplatz 28, 28199 Bremen
Tel 0421 500333
www.shakespeare-company.com
The Bremer Shakespeare Company is unique in Germany and attracts visitors from all over the country to its interpretations of works by the great English playwright, William Shakespeare (1564–1616). All performances are in German.
🕐 Tue–Sat 3–6 💶 €14–30 🚊 Tram 4, 5, 6

🎲 CASINO BREMEN
Böttcherstrasse 3–5, 28195 Bremen
Tel 0421 329000
www.casino-bremen.de
Try your luck here at French and American roulette and blackjack. The casino is housed in a fine building dating from 1927, just off Martinistrasse in the Altstadt's pedestrian zone. You'll need to take your passport, and men are required to wear a jacket and tie.
🕐 Daily 5pm–3am 💶 Admission €2.50 🚊 Tram 2, 3, 4, 6, 8 ♿ ⚠

🍺 SCHÜTTINGER
Hinter dem Schütting 12–13, 28195 Bremen
Tel 0421 337 6633
www.schuettinger.de
Although it has only been around since 1990, the Erste Bremer Gasthausbrauerei home brewery, in the Altstadt, has a reputation for its fine Schüttinger pilsener and a range of special occasional

Ice cream and other sweet treats on sale in a Bremen street

beers. The bar has a rustic atmosphere and you sit at long wooden tables. There's also simple pub food, and the kitchen can rustle up something for groups of six or more.
🕐 Mon–Fri noon–midnight, Sat, Sun 11am–2am 🚊 Tram 2, 3, 4, 5, 6

⚽ SV WERDER BREMEN
Am Weserstadion 7, 28205 Bremen
Tel 01805 937337
www.werder-online.de
www.weserstadion.de
The home ground of the Bundesliga soccer champions and winners of the 2004 German Cup is the fine Weserstadion, just north of the River Weser.

🕐 Information: Mon–Fri 9–6. Tickets: Mon–Fri 10–6, Sat 11am–30 minutes before the game, Sun 3pm–30 minutes before the game 💶 €6.50–105 🚊 2, 3, 10 ♿

🚀 SPACE CENTER
Space Park Plaza 1, 28237 Bremen
Tel 0421 840000
www.space-center-bremen-de
Bremen is one of the head-quarters of Europe's space industry, reflected in this space adventure park. Kids of all ages can take part in a simulated rocket launch and virtual tours of the moon, planets and the galaxy, as well as watch films on the super-wide IMAX screen.
🕐 Tue–Thu 10–5, Fri–Sun 9–6 💶 Adult €22, child (6–18) €18 🚊 Tram 3 ♿

🔬 UNIVERSUM SCIENCE CENTER BREMEN
Wiener Strasse 2, 28359 Bremen
Tel 0421 33460
www.universum-bremen.de
Visit this high-tech, interactive facility for an introduction to the mysteries of the universe and the way humans act to uncover the truth. Some 250 different hands-on exhibits explore problems and solutions in three main scientific areas: planet Earth, the human race and the cosmos.
🕐 Mon–Fri 9–6, Sat, Sun 10–7 💶 Adult €10, child (6–18) €6 🚊 Tram 6 ♿

BREMERHAVEN

🐾 ZOO AM MEER BREMERHAVEN
H.-H.-Meier-Strasse 5, 27568 Bremerhaven
Tel 0471 42071
www.zoo-am-meer-bremerhaven.de
The primary focus of this marine-orientated zoo beside the Weser is its aquarium, home to seals and sea lions, but there are also animals from the Arctic and the northern seas, such as polar bears, Arctic foxes and Arctic hares.
🕐 Apr–end Sep daily 9–7; Mar, Oct daily 9–6; Nov–end Feb daily 9–4.30 💶 Adult €6, child (4–14) €3.50 ♿

HAMBURG

⊞ ALSTERHAUS

Jungfernstieg 16–20, 20354 Hamburg
Tel 040 359010
www.alsterhaus.de
Under the ownership of the
Karstadt chain, Hamburg's
long-established flagship
department store took a leap
into the future and a further
step towards chicdom during
2004. Rebuilding gave it a
more modern look, and the
product range was refined to
focus on quality fashion and
accessories, perfumes, lifestyle
items and gastronomy.
🕐 Mon–Sat 10–7 🚇 Jungfernstieg 🚇

⊞ FISCHMARKT

Fischmarkt (and nearby streets), 22767
Hamburg
www.hamburger-fischmarkt.de
The venerable St.-Pauli fish
market is renowned throughout Germany, so much so that
it has gone on the road, taking
its inimitable brand of street-
trader charm (and cheek) to
other cities. But back home on
the Elbe waterfront is where it
makes its principal mark, selling not only fish but also many
other different kinds of food
products and flea-market
goods.
🕐 Apr–end Oct Sun 5am–10am;
Nov–end Apr Sun 7am–10am
🚇 Landungsbrücken

**🎭 ENGLISH THEATRE OF
HAMBURG**

Lerchenfeld 14, 22081 Hamburg
Tel 040 227 7089
www.englishtheatre.de
Founded by two Americans in
1976, this is the only dedicated
English-language theatre
company in northern Germany.
It puts on both modern and
classic works. The theatre
building, in the Uhlenhorst
district east of the Aussenalster,
has just 160 seats. Most performances are in the evening,
but there are matinees on
Tuesdays and Fridays.
🕐 Box office: Mon–Fri 10–2, 3.30–7.30,
Sat 3.30–7.30 💰 €7 (previews)–26
🚇 Mundsburg

**🎭 HAMBURGISCHE
STAATSOPER**

Grosse Theaterstrasse 34, 20354
Hamburg
Tel 040 356868
www.hamburgische-staatsoper.de
The home of the
Hamburgische Staatsoper and
Ballettcompagnie John
Neumeier (Hamburg's ballet
company) was built in the
1950s and is in the northern
part of the Neustadt. The opera
company itself was founded in
1678 and stages everything
from classics to contemporary
works; the ballet company
specializes in modern dance.
🕐 Box office: Mon–Sat 10–6.30 and 1
hour before performances 💰 €4–77
🚇 Gänsemarkt 🚇

*Watching the water-borne traffic in
Hamburg*

🎭 MUSIKHALLE HAMBURG

Johannes-Brahms-Platz, 20355
Hamburg
Tel 040 357 6660
www.musikhalle-hamburg.de
On the northwest edge of
the Neustadt, beside the
Wallanlagen gardens, is this
ornate concert hall dating from
1908. It is the home of the
Hamburger Symphoniker, the
Philharmonisches
Staatsorchester Hamburg and
the NDR Sinfonieorchester,
and attracts some of the
world's great ensembles.
🕐 Box office: Mon–Fri 10–6 and 1
hour before performances 💰 €5–38
🚇 Stefansplatz, Gänsemarkt 🚇

🎷 COTTON CLUB

Alter Steinweg 10, 20459 Hamburg
Tel 040 343878
www.cotton-club-hamburg.de
Hamburg's oldest jazz club
was founded in 1959 and has
been called the Cotton Club
since 1963. It has changed
venue several times, before
ending up at its present location across the Herrengraben
canal from the middle of town.
Live jazz is performed by highly
regarded local combos and
international names.
🕐 Daily from 8.30pm (music from
9pm) 💰 €5–15 🚇 Stadthausbrücke

🎷 GROSSE FREIHEIT 36

Grosse Feiheit 36, 22767 Hamburg
Tel 040 3177 7811
www.grossefreiheit36.de
Big, brash and beautiful, this
club just off of the Reeperbahn
in the city's red-light district is
world famous, not least for its
connection with the early
days of the Beatles. It is a top
venue for visiting performers
of international renown.
There is live music by less
well-known performers in the
downstairs Kaiserkeller, and a
dance club.
🕐 Concerts: from 7 or 8pm (in the
Kaiserkeller, from 10pm) 💰 €5–20
🚇 Reeperbahn

🎾 AM ROTHENBAUM

Hallerstrasse 89, 20148 Hamburg
Tel 040 4117 8210
www.dtb-tennis.de
The German Tennis Masters
tournament, one of the key
competitions on the international tennis circuit (though it's
not a Grand Slam event), takes
place here every May. The
venue is in the north of the
city, off Rothenbaumchaussee
and close to the Aussenalster,
and can seat 13,000 spectators.
🕐 Tickets: Mon–Fri (also some Sat and
Sun) 10–6 💰 From €40
🚇 Hallerstrasse 🚇

🎾 HAMBURGER GOLF-CLUB

In de Bargen 59, 22587 Hamburg
Tel 040 812177
www.hamburgergolf-club.de

WHAT TO DO

This is a top-notch, 18-hole course, in the suburb of Blankenese west of the city on the north bank of the Elbe.
🕐 Daily 9–5 💰 Green fees: €45–55
🚇 Sülldorf 🚾

😊 HAMBURG DUNGEON
Kehrwieder 2, 20457 Hamburg
Tel 040 3600 5500
www.hamburgdungeon.com
An underground boat trip at this attraction in the Speicherstadt takes you on a tour through some of the grislier aspects of Hamburg's 1,200 years of history. Ghosts, torture, death, the Black Death, the Inquisition, fire and flood are depicted by actors and through displays, making for a pretty scary show. Not recommended for children under 10 or those of a squeamish disposition.
🕐 Daily 10–6 💰 Adult €12.95, under-14s €9.95 (must be accompanied by an adult) 🚇 Baumwall

😊 TIERPARK HAGENBECK
Lokstedter Grenzstrasse, 22509 Hamburg-Stellingen
Tel 040 540 0010
www.hagenbeck.de
Dating back to 1907, this large and impressive zoo in northwest Hamburg was a pioneer in the more modern presentation of exotic animals in habitats modelled on those in the wild, rather than simply behind bars. On its 27ha (67-acre) site, it continues to develop novel approaches to keeping animals, and there are numerous activities for children.
🕐 Mar–end Oct daily 9–5 (as late as 7 when the weather is fine); Nov–end Feb daily 9–4.30 💰 Adult €14.50, child (4–16) €8.50 🚇 Hagenbecks Tierpark

HANNOVER

🍴 AALRÄUCHEREI HODANN
Alter Winkel 1, 31515 Steinhude
Tel 05033 8246
www.hodann.de
Smoked eel from the Steinhuder Meer is a byword for taste throughout Germany,

and no one does it better than this traditional smoke-house. Find it in the fishing village and resort of Steinhude, some 30km (18 miles) west of Hannover (▷ 82–83). You can visit the smoking facility and buy some of the finished goods at the on-site shop.
🕐 Mon–Sun 8–6

🛍️ LEIBNIZUFER FLOHMARKT
Leibnizufer, 30169 Hannover
A long stretch along the west bank of the Leine, just outside Hannover's Altstadt (old town), is taken up every Saturday with the stalls of this popular general market and flea market.
🕐 Sat 7–2 🚾 Markthalle

Enjoying the sunshine at the Herrenhäuser Gardens, Hannover

🎭 NIEDERSÄCHSISCHES STAATSTHEATER
Opernplatz 1, 30159 Hannover
Tel 0511 9999 1111
www.staatstheater-hannover.de
This palatial and centrally located neoclassical theatre from 1857 is Hannover's premier venue for opera, classical music, ballet and theatre. Concerts are often given by its affiliated symphony orchestra, the Niedersächsisches Staatsorchester.
🕐 Mon–Fri 10–7.30, Sat 10–4
💰 €8–40 🚇 Kröpcke 🚾

😊 REGENWALDHAUS
Herrenhäuser Strasse 4a, 30419 Hannover

Tel 0511 1260 4210
www.regenwaldhaus.de
Part of the Herrenhäuser Gärten complex (▷ 82), this thoroughly modern attraction re-creates a piece of the world's fast-disappearing rainforest. Its hands-on approach makes it particularly interesting for children. The high-tech setting is somewhat incongruous, but 6,000 different species of tropical plants, along with birds, butterflies and other animals, help to lend realism to the experience.
🕐 Nov–end Mar Mon–Thu 10–4, Fri–Sun 10–6; Apr, May, Sep, Oct Mon–Thu 10–5, Fri–Sun 10–8; Jun–Aug Mon–Thu 10–6, Fri 10–10, Sat, Sun 10–8
💰 Adult €8.50, child (6–14) €4.50
🚇 Herrenhäuser Gärten 🚾

LÜBECK

🛍️ NIEDEREGGER
Breite Strasse 89, 23552 Lübeck
Tel 0451 530 1126
www.niederegger.de
Lübeck has been famed for its marzipan since Hanseatic times, and nowhere in the city makes it better than this jewel of a place across from the Rathaus, in business since 1806. Downstairs, marzipan is available in an astonishing range of pastries and confections; upstairs, you can eat it in an elegant café; and in the top-floor museum you can chew over its provenance.
🕐 Mon–Fri 9–7, Sat 9–6, Sun 10–6
🚌 5, 7, 11, 14, 16 🚾

🎭 LÜBECKER MARIONETTENTHEATER FRITZ FEY
Kolk 20–22, 23552 Lübeck
Tel 0451 70060
www.fritzfey.de
Just off Holstenstrasse, and a few doors along from the Theaterfiguren Museum (▷ 250), is this superb puppet theatre, which is aimed as much at adults as it is at children. The magical performances of pieces like *The Little Prince* and *The Barber of Seville* will appeal to all

ages, although they are spoken and sung in German.
🕐 Tue 9–noon, Wed–Fri 9–noon, 1.30–3, Sat–Sun 1.30–3 (except 1st Sun of month ⬛ €4–9.50 🚊 1, 3, 11

🔅 SEA LIFE TIMMENDORFER STRAND
Kurpromenade 5, 23669 Timmendorfer Strand
Tel 04503 358888
www.sealife-timmendorf.de
This is one of five Sea Life venues in Germany, at a Baltic coast resort just north of Lübeck. Rays, small sharks and sea horses are among the denizens of the deep in the various display tanks. A unique part of the exhibition is a section on the endangered sea that was organized in cooperation with Greenpeace.
🕐 Jul, Aug daily 10–7; Apr–end Jun, Sep, Oct daily 10–6; Nov–end Mar Mon–Fri 10–5, Sat, Sun and school hols 10–6 ⬛ Adult €10, child (3–14) €6.50

🔅 THEATERFIGUREN MUSEUM
Kolk 14–16, 23552 Lübeck
Tel 0451 78626
This appears to be associated with the nearby Lübecker Marionettentheater Fritz Fey (▷ 249), but in fact it is a fascinating collection of more than 2,000 puppets from around the world, both antique and modern. The proprietors are accomplished puppetmasters and their love

for their subject shows in the range and quality of the exhibits.
🕐 Daily 10–6 ⬛ Adult €3, child (5–15) €1.50 🚊 1, 3, 11 🛒

ROSTOCK

🔅 ZOO ROSTOCK
Rennbahnallee 21, 18059 Rostock
Tel 0381 20820
www.zoo-rostock.de
This zoo is the largest in northern Germany, with some 1,500 animals in woodland and gardens. Every year a different theme from the natural world is explored through exhibitions and educational activities.
🕐 Daily, 10–6 ⬛ Adult €11.50, child (3–16) €5 🚊 Tram 11 🍴 🛒

Dining alfresco German style at this open-air sandwich stall

VERDEN

🔅 RENNBAHN VERDEN
Lüneburger Weg, 27266 Verden
Tel 04236 1368
www.rennverein-verden.de
The town of Verden, southeast of Bremen, is so closely connected with horses that it is known as Reiterstadt (Horse-Riders' Town) Verden. The connection dates back centuries and encompasses the German army's cavalry, along with stud farms and various horse-racing and other events. Racing meetings are held here at the town's racetrack.
🕐 On race days 1–6 ⬛ From €5 🛒

WILHELMSHAVEN

🔅 OCEANIS
Bontekai 63, 26382 Wilhelmshaven
Tel 04421 755055
www.oceanis.de
The port town that was Germany's most important naval base through two world wars is an appropriate place to host an introduction to the sea. Here, you enter a virtual underwater research station—it's actually onshore, in a purpose-built harbour facility. Innovative technology and a hands-on approach help illuminate the wonders of the sea and its creatures.
🕐 Daily 10–6 ⬛ Adult €11.50, child (6–14) €5 🛒

FESTIVALS AND EVENTS

JULY

TRAVEMÜNDER-WOCHE
Tel: 01805 882233
www.luebeck-tourism.de
Lübeck's Sailing Week has been attracting sailors to this maritime town for over one hundred years. More than 800 boats from 16 countries attend this annual sailing regatta and yachting event.
🕐 Late Jul

JULY/AUGUST

SCHLESWIG-HOLSTEIN MUSIC FESTIVAL
Jerusalemsberg 7, Lübeck
Tel 0451 389570
www.shmf.de
Germany's northernmost *Land* celebrates classical music with one hundred concerts held in a variety of locations, from barns and stables to churches and country estates.
🕐 Jul and Aug ⬛ Varies

OCTOBER

BREMEN FREIMARKT
Bürgerweide and Marktplatz
Tel 01805 101030
www.bremen-tourism.de
Although primarily based around the Bürgerweide and Marktplatz, the oldest folk festival in Germany takes over the whole city, with music, dancing and general gaiety. The highlight of the festival is the parade on the second Saturday.
🕐 Two weeks from mid-October

WHAT TO DO

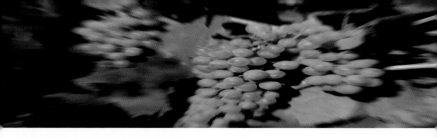

WESTERN GERMANY

You'll find images of Beethoven are everywhere in Bonn

Given the affluence enjoyed by many of western Germany's cities, it's perhaps not surprising that the area abounds in things to see and do beyond its best-known buildings, monuments and museums. In terms of retail therapy, both Düsseldorf and Frankfurt are known for their exclusive designer districts, while Essen and Cologne offer browsers a wide choice of mainstream stores and small, independent boutiques. The latter is also the place to sample eau de Cologne, the world's most famous perfume.

Culturally speaking, Bonn—the birthplace of composer Ludwig van Beethoven (1770–1827)—is hard to beat when it comes to classical music, although Cologne's two world-class symphony orchestras certainly give it a run for its money. Cologne is also home to one of the most famous—not to mention most popular—puppet theatres in the world, while those who are feeling a little homesick can visit Frankfurt's English-language theatre, the largest such venue on the Continent.

When it comes to nightlife, jazz and blues get top billing, although Frankfurt's wonderfully named King Kamehameha club is a must for anyone who likes to eat, drink and dance his or her way into the wee small hours. Children, meanwhile, are spoiled for choice: While their parents are nursing sore heads after all that enjoying themselves, they can explore a

chocolate factory, ride in a bobsleigh and wander around a genuine U-boat (in addition to dozens of other planes, trains and automobiles).

Finally, no trip to western Germany would be complete without a round of golf, a day at the races or an evening out at a luxury thermal spa. If all that sounds a little too relaxing, there's always the legendary Nürburgring, one of the few places in the world where members of the public can drive their own car around a former Formula 1 racing circuit (and all for less than €15 a lap, which isn't bad when you consider that each lap is a staggering 21km, or 13 miles, long).

And for those who'd rather watch than take part, the region is home to two premier league soccer teams (at least, they were at the time of writing!) and Germany's only professional American football team.

AACHEN

⊕ FORUM M

Buchkremerstrasse 1–7, 52062 Aachen
Tel 0241 477 7145
www.mayersche.de

This great bookshop is just a stone's throw to the north of the tourist information office. Although most of its books are in German, it does have a big newspaper and magazine section that stocks foreign editions of a variety of mainstream publications, and many of its books on subjects such as art, photography and travel are in English, too. It also sells gifts, such as postcards, and there is an inviting café.
🕐 Mon–Sat 9.30–8 🔲

KEY TO SYMBOLS	
⊕	Shopping
🎭	Entertainment
🍸	Nightlife
⚽	Sports
✪	Activities
♥	Health and Beauty
☺	For Children

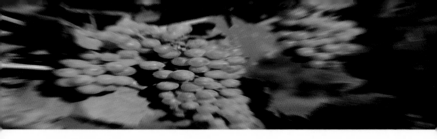

🏛 LEONIDAS PRALINEN
Markt 45, 52062 Aachen
Tel 0241 20296
www.leonidas.com
Leonidas pralines are probably the most delicious—and the most calorific—chocolates in the world. They taste so smooth and creamy because they're made with cream instead of milk, which also means that they have to be kept refrigerated. They're available in dozens of different sizes and guises, but, at around €5 for 200g (7oz), they're not cheap.
🕐 Mon–Fri 9.30–6.30, Sat 9.30–4

🏛 MAASMECHELEN VILLAGE
Zetellaan 100, 3630 Maasmechelen, Belgium
Tel 00 32 (0)8977 4020
www.maasmechelenvillage.com
Stores at this compact outlet shopping village, 40km (25 miles) to the west of Aachen across the border in Belgium, include Versace, Diesel, Benetton and Pepe Jeans, plus dozens of top-end Dutch, Belgian and German retailers. Snacks, cakes and coffees are served by a handful of classy bistros and cafés. Take your passport or ID card to cross the border.
🕐 Mon–Thu 10–6, Fri–Sat 10–7
🍴🖥

💜 CAROLUS THERMEN
Passstrasse 79, 52070 Aachen
Tel 0241 182740
www.carolus-thermen.de
Built in 2001 to look like an original Roman bath, Carolus Thermen is the perfect place to pamper aching limbs and tired muscles. This cutting-edge spa complex features 10 outdoor and indoor pools (all filled with thermal mineral water at a balmy 38°C/100°F), outdoor sun terraces, a Baltic sauna landscape, an oriental bathing world, a solarium and an inviting café serving light snacks, salads and fruit juices. There's also a Mediterranean restaurant and beer garden.

🕐 Daily 9am–11pm (last entry 9.30pm) 💷 €9 without sauna, €17 with sauna, €26 day pass 🚌 Bus to Carolus Thermen 🍴 🖥

BONN

🎵 BEETHOVENHALLE
Wachsbleiche 16, 53111 Bonn
Tel 0228 72220
www.beethovenhalle.de
This modern domed building on the banks of the Rhine has been Bonn's main concert arena and congress hall since it opened in 1959, and today is home to the world-renowned Beethoven Orchestra. The biggest of the building's four halls can seat 2,000.

Relaxing in the sunshine at the Rhine Meadows in Bonn

🕐 Performances most days 💷 €10–40 🚋 Tram to Willhelmsplatz

🎵 KAMMERMUSIKSAAL
Bonngasse 18–26, 53111 Bonn
Tel 0228 981750
www.beethoven-haus-bonn.de
Two doors down from the Beethoven House (▷ 95) is the Beethoven Chamber Music Hall. The focal point of the building is the Hermann J. Abs Music Hall, named after a former president. An unusual schedule includes performances especially for children. It's also home to the Beethoven Archive, the Beethoven House collection and the Beethoven Library.

🕐 Performances every 7–14 days 💷 €5–20 🚋 Tram to Bertha-v-Suttner Platz

🍸 EN'TE BAR
Kaiserpassage, 53113 Bonn
Tel 0228 639322
www.en-te.de
The En'te Bar is tucked away in Kaiserpassage, a tiny mall just to the north of Bonn's main bus station. It's more of a bistro than a bar, with its menu of snacks and main meals, but it also serves a comprehensive range of cocktails, shots and beers. The intimate candlelit atmosphere makes it ideal for a romantic drink. There is live jazz every Wednesday night from 9pm to 1am.
🕐 Mon–Sat 10am–1am, Sun and hols 10am–8pm 🍴 Snacks €3–7, main courses €7–12 🚋 Tram to Busbahnhof

✴ RHEINAUE FREIZEITPARK
Windeckstrasse 1, 53103 Bonn
Tel 0228 374030
www.rheinaue.de
This lovingly landscaped park on the banks of the Rhine boasts 45km (28 miles) of footpaths (the riverside promenade alone is over 5km/3 miles long), a boating lake (ideal for rowing on in the summer), a Japanese garden and a garden for the blind. For kids there's a crazy golf course and a playground. The park is open 24 hours year-round.
🕐 Daily 24 hrs 🚋 Tram to Rheinaue 🍴

DÜSSELDORF

🏛 KÖNIGSALLEE
Düsseldorf's tree-lined Königsallee, known locally as the Kö, prides itself on being a shoppers' paradise. The street itself is lined with achingly fashionable boutiques, while nearby malls take shopping to a whole new level. Almost every designer label you can think of is represented here, and the Kö's cafés and restaurants are every bit as chic as its shops.
🚇 Königsallee 🍴 🖥

GOLFPLATZ LAUSWARD

Auf der Lausward 51, 40221 Düsseldorf
Tel 0211 410529

Within sight of downtown Düsseldorf and the Rheinturm (▷ 97) is Lausward Golf Course, established in 1978 as the first public golf course in Germany. It has a nine-hole, par 35 course and a 250m (275 yard) driving range. Clubs and hand carts can be rented.

Mar–Nov daily 18 holes: Mon–Fri €18, Sat, Sun €24 Tram 708 to D-Hamm, then bus 725 to Auf der Lausward

RENNBAHN GRAFENBERG

Rennbahnstrasse, 40629 Düsseldorf
Tel 0211 363466
www.duesseldorf-galopp.de

Established in 1844, Düsseldorf Galopp is one of the oldest and most important races in Germany. Race meetings are held from March to October, but check the website before you go. The track is on the B7, about 6km (4 miles) to the west of the A3 autobahn.

Race meetings: Mar–end Oct Sat, Sun Adult €5, under-18s free Tram to Staufenplatz, then shuttle bus 894 to the Rennbahn (racecourse)

AQUAZOO

Kaiserswerther Strasse 380, 40200 Düsseldorf
Tel 0211 899 6150
www.duesseldorf.de/aquazoo

This superb sealife attraction combines the presentation techniques of a zoo with the sort of information you'd usually expect to find at a natural history museum. Exhibition rooms from A to Z are alphabetically ordered and themed according to region or species, making them easy to explore.

Daily 10–6 Adult €5.50, student €3.50 Aquazoo

EIFEL

NÜRBURGRING

Nürburgring GmbH, 53520 Nürburg
Tel 02691 3020
www.nuerburgring.de

The world-famous Nürburgring is in the heart of Germany's Eifel region. Built between 1925 and 1927 it is 21km (13 miles) long and contains no fewer than 73 bends. It was the venue for the German Grand Prix from 1950 to 1976, when it was finally deemed too dangerous following Niki Lauda's spectacular crash into the cliff face at Bergwerk. Today, Nürburgring is still used as a test track and occasional race track, and at certain times it can be driven by the public. For those who'd prefer not to be in the driving seat, it is possible to be chauffeured round the circuit in a Ringtaxi, a snarling BMW M5 that will do up to 330kph (205mph).

Luxury shopping in one of Frankfurt's beautifully lit arcades

There's also a motoring museum here, plus a 450m (1,475ft) indoor go-cart track.

Track: most weekends year-round, plus some additional days Self-drive: €14 per circuit. Ringtaxi: €160 for up to three people

ESSEN

CITY CENTER ESSEN

Porscheplatz 67, 45127 Essen
Tel 0201 747670
www.citycenter-essen.de

With its vast downtown shopping precinct, Essen is rightly regarded as a magnet for shopaholics. In the heart of it all is City Center Essen, a state-of-the-art mall with a multiplex cinema, fast-food outlets and more than 80 shops, selling everything from sports equipment to lingerie. There's little in the way of designer gear on offer, however.

Mon–Sat 10–8 Porscheplatz

FRANKFURT AM MAIN

MARKETS

Frankfurt's popular Saturday flea market has kitsch art and assorted knick-knacks. Those who like their food fresh will relish a tour of Kleinmarkthalle, a vast, indoor grocery market selling meat, fish, vegetables, fruit and exotic herbs and spices from all over the world.

SHOPPING DISTRICTS

Frankfurt is home to some of Germany's most profitable shopping districts. Chief among these is the famous Zeil Promenade, lined with department stores, retail outlets and specialist shops. Nearby is Goethestrasse, which has exclusive designer boutiques and expensive jewellery stores. Also worth exploring is Schweizer Strasse, in Frankfurt's Sachsenhausen district. And for those who prefer to do all their shopping under one roof, the gleaming Zeilgalerie, at the west end of the Zeil, features more than 50 shops on eight levels.

ENGLISH THEATRE

Kaiserstrasse 34, 60313 Frankfurt am Main
Tel 069 2423 1620
www.english-theatre.org

Billed as the largest English-language theatre in mainland Europe, Frankfurt's English Theatre presents a varied schedule of plays and musicals throughout the year. Many of the shows performed here have come from Broadway or London's West End, and they regularly feature famous faces from television and film.

Shows Tue–Sat 7pm, Sun 6pm Plays: €19–29. Musicals: €25–39 Willy Brandt Platz

WHAT TO DO

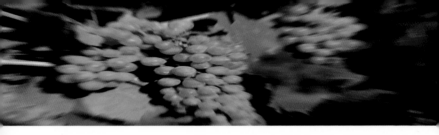

🎭 TIGERPALAST

Heligkreuzgasse, 60313 Frankfurt am Main

Tel 069 920 0220

www.tigerpalast.com

Frankfurt's famous Tigerpalast is a variety theatre for the new millennium. Accompanied by a resident orchestra, five to seven different artists from all over the world feature in a performance that lasts around two hours. It's great fun if you're in the mood for something a bit different. Tigerpalast is also home to a Michelin-starred restaurant (Tue–Sat 6pm–1am), an American cellar bar (Tue–Sun 5pm–3am) and an underground bistro (Tue–Sun 5pm–2am).

🎭 Two performances per night Tue–Sun, plus midnight reviews Mon–Fri 🎟 Adult €47.50, under-12s half-price, student 25 per cent discount (subject to availability) 🚇 Konstablerwache

🎵 JAZZKELLER

Kleine Bockenheimer Strasse 18a, 60318 Frankfurt am Main

Tel 069 288537

www.jazzkeller.com

Established in 1952, this jazz club in the heart of the city's shopping district, is the oldest in Germany. Over the years it has played host to such luminaries as Louis Armstrong, Dizzy Gillespie and Frank Sinatra. A small, intimate venue with a relaxed, earthy feel, it continues to present the very best in local and world jazz on an almost nightly basis.

🎵 Wed–Sun from 9pm 🎟 €4–14 🚇 Opernplatz

🎵 KING KAMEHAMEHA

Hanauer Landstrasse 192, 60314 Frankfurt am Main

Tel 069 480 0 70

www.king-kamehameha.de

The King Kamehameha club, specializing in Latin jazz and house music, is one of the most popular clubs in Frankfurt. This vast contemporary venue attracts a trendy crowd and some of the

country's best bands and DJs. There's also a restaurant (food until 11pm) and cocktail bar (drinks until 4am). King Kamehameha is to the east of Ostbahnhof on Hanauer Landstrasse.

🎵 Mon–Fri 3.15–midnight, Sat, Sun 10–midnight 🎟 Around €10, depending on show 🚇 Ostbahnhof

⚽ EINTRACHT FRANKFURT

Gustav-Behringer-Strasse 10, 60386 Frankfurt am Main

Tel 069 955030

www.eintracht-frankfurt.de

Although the Eintracht Frankfurt soccer team has had a yo-yo career in recent years, its die-hard fans continue to

Eating, drinking and shopping, all under one roof in Frankfurt

turn out in their droves to show their support. Eintracht is due to move to its new home at the impressive World Cup stadium (being built for the 2006 event), just to the south of the city off Junction 51 of the A3 autobahn.

⚽ Home games: Aug–late May Sat or Sun every few weeks 🎟 €11–35.20 🚇 Tram to Sportfeld

⚽ FRANKFURTER GOLF CLUB

Golfstrasse 41, 60528 Frankfurt am Main

Tel 069 666 2318

www.fgc.de

There are more than half a dozen golf courses in and around Frankfurt that welcome non-members, but the one

closest to the downtown area is the Frankfurt Golf Club. It's also one of the oldest, having been established in 1913. During the 1970s and 1980s, the German Open was held here on a number of occasions. Guests must have a handicap of 32 or better. Carts and caddies are available.

⚽ Daily 🎟 €60 Mon–Fri, €70 Sat–Sun 🚇 Tram to Niederrad

🔬 EXPLORA MUSEUM

Glauburgplatz 1, 60318 Frankfurt am Main

Tel 069 788888

www.exploramuseum.de

Hidden in a former air-raid bunker is the brilliant Explora Museum, with an outstanding collection of interactive exhibits, including optical illusions, puzzle pictures and holograms, 3D photography, 3D stereo art and 3D magic-eye dots (you'll have to go to find out what these are) and even a famous Ames room, where things are never quite what they appear. The museum is about 1km (0.5 mile) to the north of the Römerberg, and is a must for both curious kids and adults.

🔬 Tue–Sun 11–6 🎟 Adult €8, student €6 🚇 Glauburgstrasse

🔬 NATURMUSEUM SENCKENBERG

Senckenberganlage 25, 60325 Frankfurt am Main

Tel 069 75420

www.senckenberg.de

The Senckenberg Natural History Museum, about 1km (0.5 mile) west of the city, is one of the largest museums of its kind in Europe. As well as an impressive display of free-standing dinosaur skeletons, it has exhibitions on animals, vegetables and minerals, on specific mammal species and on the origins of the Earth and the evolution of humans.

🔬 Mon–Tue, Thu–Fri 9–5, Wed 9–8, Sat–Sun and holidays 9–6

🎟 Adult €5, child (5–15) €2.50, under 5 free 🚇 Bockenheimer Warte

WHAT TO DO

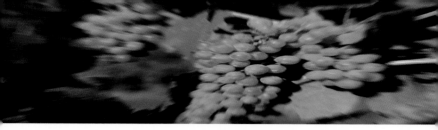

ZOO FRANKFURT

Alfred-Brehm-Platz 16, 60316 Frankfurt am Main

Tel 069 2123 3735

www.zoo-frankfurt.de

Frankfurt Zoo is in a spacious park just beyond the east end of the Zeil (▷ 253). It has a big cat jungle, elephant and hippo enclosures, and an impressive free-flying aviary, plus a sea-cliff environment (visible from both above and below water) and a specially designed house for nocturnal animals. Water-filled ditches or panes of glass are used around the zoo, so visitors don't feel cut off from the animals.

🕐 Apr–end Oct daily 9–7; Nov–end Mar daily 9–5 💶 Adult €8, child €4, under 6 free 🚋 Alfred-Brehm Platz ⬛

KÖLN (COLOGNE)

🏛 4711

Glockengasse 4711, 50667 Köln

Tel 0221 925 0451

www.4711.com

Eau de Cologne was first man-ufactured in the city at the start of the 18th century by Italian immigrant Paolo Feminis (▷ 104). Soon dozens of other companies began distilling the so-called *eau admirable* using similar methods. One of the biggest of these companies was run by the Mülhens family, whose laboratory on Glockengasse was given the number 4711 by Napoleon's troops during the French occu-pation of Cologne in 1794. This number went on to become a world-famous trademark, although the building itself was destroyed during World War II. It was rebuilt in 1964 in neo-Gothic style and is now the flagship store for 4711.

🕐 Mon–Fri 9.30–8, Sat 9.30–4 🚋 Tram to Appellhofplatz

🏛 BIRKENSTOCK

Breite Strasse 80–90, 50667 Köln

Tel 0221 252529

www.birkenstock.de

As anyone who's ever owned a pair of these well-designed and enduringly popular shoes

will tell you, the numerous felt and leather layers used to make up the soles soon mould themselves to your feet, result-ing in a perfect fit. There are dozens of different designs, and they're much cheaper in Germany than elsewhere.

🕐 Mon–Fri 10–8, Sat 10–4 🚋 Tram to Domplatz

🏛 SHOPPING DISTRICTS

Bearing in mind Cologne's size (it's the fourth-largest city in Germany), it has a reassuringly compact downtown area. Its three main shopping precincts are the area around Domplatz, at the northern end of the Altstadt; Hohe Strasse and its

All Germany's major cities have their own orchestra

offshoots, stretching to the south of Domplatz for almost 1km (0.5 mile); and the area around Neumarkt, about 1km (0.5 mile) to the west of Hohe Strasse. Domplatz itself is dominated by glitzy designer shops, but as you head south, you'll see the more main-stream stores of Hohe Strasse, including Benetton, Gap and Zara. Neumarkt, meanwhile, is home to the Neumarkt Passage, a small, street-like mall specializing in gifts, clothes and shoes. Beyond Neumarkt, dozens of little side-street shops sell everything from fine art to furniture.

🎵 PHILHARMONIE

KölnMusik, Bischofsgartenstrasse 1, Köln 50667

Tel 0221 204080

www.koelnmusik.de

This vast, cavernous concert hall, next door to the cathedral beneath Heinrich-Böll-Platz (▷ 101), is home to two world-renowned orchestras: the Gürzenich Orchestra Cologne and the WDR Symphony Orchestra Cologne. It puts on more than 350 concerts a year.

🎭 Performances almost daily year-round 💶 €5–35 depending on concert/seat 🚋 Tram to Domplatz or Hauptbahnhof

🎭 PUPPENSPIELE

Kölsch Hänneschen Theatre, Eisenmarkt 2–4, 50667 Köln

Tel 0221 258 1201

www.haenneschen.de

This historic puppet theatre dates from 1802 and is a Cologne institution. Tickets for the annual *Puppensitzung*, or puppet festival at the begin-ning of February go on sale at the end of September, and are so popular that people have been known to camp outside the theatre for days to ensure they don't miss out. Tickets for other shows are easier to get, but it's still worth booking well in advance. There are two matinees a day for kids and an evening show for adults. The shows aren't performed in English, but you can easily follow what's going on.

🎭 Children's performances: twice daily Wed–Sun. Adult shows: once daily Wed–Sun 💶 €10–25 🚋 Tram to Heumarkt

🍷 BRASSERIE BREUGEL

Hohenzollernring 17, 50672 Köln

Tel 0221 252579

www.bruegel.de

The effortlessly cool Brasserie Breugel, just to the north of Rudolfplatz, doubles as a jazz bar from 11pm until late every night. One end of its elegantly furnished main dining area is overlooked by a lofty gallery

WHAT TO DO

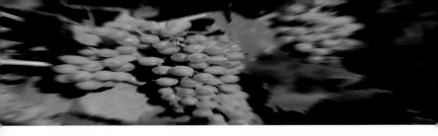

lined with candlelit tables for two. The seasonal menu focuses on fish dishes, and theme nights help to spice things up a little. Aside from the food, of course, Breugel also serves up some of the country's biggest names in jazz and soul. For the best seats in the house, book ahead and ask for a table in the gallery.

🕐 Mon–Fri noon–3am, Sat, Sun 6pm–3am 🍴 Starters €6–12, main courses €15–22.50 🚊 Tram to Rudolfplatz

🍸 HOTELUX SOVIETBAR

Rathenauplatz 22, 50674 Köln
Tel 0221 241136
www.hotelux.de

This plush, bright red bar, steeped in Soviet nostalgia, serves 28 different sorts of vodka and over 40 different cocktails. A *Potemkin* sailor greets guests as they arrive, and the bar area is clad in replicas of military paintings and posters. At Von-Sandt-Platz, on the other side of town, is the Hotelux Soviet Restaurant (Mon–Thu 6pm–1am, Sat–Sun 6pm–3am), part of which looks like the inside of the Moscow Metro in the 1920s and 1930s. It serves lovingly prepared Russian staples such as *pelmeni* (a kind of stuffed pancake) and borscht.

🕐 Sun–Thu 6pm–1am, Fri–Sat 6pm–3am 🚊 Tram to Zülpicher Platz

⚽ STADION KÖLN

RheinEnergieStadion, Aachener Strasse 999, 50933 Köln
Tel 0221 7161 6150
www.stadion-koeln.de

The RheinEnergieStadion, situated in Müngersdorf to the west of the city, is home to Cologne's professional soccer team, Cologne FC, and to its professional American football team, the Cologne Centurions. The site will also be one of the match venues for the 2006 soccer World Cup. For tickets and additional information, log onto the website.

🕐 Cologne FC games: Aug–late May generally Sat or Sun every few weeks. Cologne Centurions: Apr–early Jun 5–6 home games per season 🎫 Soccer tickets: €7–20. American football tickets: €10–35 🚊 Tram to Stadion

♨ CLAUDIUS THERME

Sachsenbergstrasse 1, 50679 Köln
Tel 0221 981440
www.claudius-therme.de

Tucked away in a corner of Cologne's restful Rheinpark, these thermal baths are an oasis of calm. Characterized by bright tiles, marble paving and stone columns, the facilities here include a spa area with massage jets, neck showers and a whirlpool, plus a sauna

Enjoy being pampered at one of Germany's many spas

area offering all kinds of steam rooms. The thermal water is state-accredited, and comes from two springs 364m (1,194ft) and 1,027m (3,370ft) underground. There's a café overlooking the main pool.

🕐 Daily 9am–midnight 💶 €13 for 2 hours, €18 for 4 hours, €23 for day pass 🚊 Bus to Claudius Therme

🏆 DEUTSCHES SPORT UND OLYMPIA MUSEUM

Rheinauhafen 1, 50678 Köln
Tel 0221 336090
www.sportmuseum-koeln.de

This cleverly conceived museum is on the banks of the Rhine just a short walk south of Cologne's Altstadt (▷ 104).

Sports-mad kids can enjoy the museum's numerous interactive exhibits, from the cycling wind tunnel and the triple-jump runway to the boxing ring and soccer cinema. Curiously, though, the most popular exhibit is a simple reaction-time test, made from two plates that have to be pressed one after the other in quick succession.

🕐 Tue–Fri 10–6, Sat–Sun 11–7 💶 Adult €5, student €2.50 🚊 Tram to Heumarkt 🚇

🍫 IMHOFF-STOLLWERCK MUSEUM

Rheinauhafen, 50678 Köln
Tel 0221 931 8880
www.schokoladenmuseum.de

Cologne's chocolate museum is right next door to the sports museum (see above), and is equally popular with kids of all ages. The beauty of this museum lies in watching the inner workings of a fully functioning, miniature chocolate factory, which takes visitors through the various stages of chocolate production, from mixing the raw ingredients to wrapping the final truffle.

🕐 Tue–Fri 10–6, Sat, Sun 11–7 💶 Adult €6, child €3.50, under 6 free 🚊 Tram to Heumarkt 🚇

🍫 WOLTERS SCHOKO EXPRESS

Malteserstrasse 28, 50859 Köln
Tel 02234 77226

Kids young enough to appreciate the finer things in life should try the Bimmelbahn, or 'small train', which winds its way through Cologne's Altstadt to either the chocolate museum (see above) or zoo (▷ 257). The round trip takes around two hours and departs from Roncalli Platz, just to the south of the cathedral (▷ 101). Expert commentary on points of interest is provided in both English and German.

🕐 Mar–end Nov daily 10–6; Dec–end Feb Sat, Sun 10–6 💶 Round trip: adult €4, schoolchild €2 🚊 Tram to Domplatz or Hauptbahnhof

WHAT TO DO

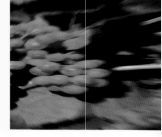

🐾 ZOOLOGISCHER GARTEN KÖLN

Riehler Strasse 173, 50735 Köln
Tel 0221 77850
www.zoo-koeln.de

Set in magnificent parkland to the north of the cathedral, Cologne's zoo houses a huge variety of animals from all over the world. It is best known for its primate collection, aquarium and big-cat enclosure. Next door is the city's botanical garden, which contains around 12,000 different plant species.

🕐 Apr–end Oct daily 9–6; Nov–end Mar daily 9–5. Aquarium: daily 9–6. Botanical Gardens: daily 8–dusk
💶 Adult €11, child (4–17) €5.50
🚃 Tram to Zoo or Flora 🍴 🅿

MÜNSTER

🎷 HOT JAZZ CLUB

Hafenweg 26b, 48155 Münster
Tel 0251 6743727
www.hotjazzclub.de

In a basement next door to Grosse Freiheit 26, the Hot Jazz Club, one of Münster's premier music venues, has international jazz and blues on an almost nightly basis. Staff members are friendly and knowledgeable, and resident DJs keep things moving. There's also a menu with original Italian cooking.

🕐 Tue–Sat 7pm–late, Sun 3pm–late
💶 Around €8–10; some gigs are free

🚲 RADSTATION MÜNSTER

Berliner Platz 27a, 48153 Münster
Tel 0251 484 0170

You can rent bicycles at a number of places, but the outlet with the biggest stock is the Radstation, a vast, underground bicycle park enclosed by a striking glass triangle opposite the city's main train station. Numerous numbered routes crisscross the city and the surrounding area—maps are available at the Radstation and the tourist information office (▷ 110).

🕐 Mon–Fri 5.30am–11pm, Sat, Sun and holidays 7am–11pm 💶 Bicycles: €6 per person per day. Tandems: €10 per day

🐾 ALLWETTERZOO, DOLPHINERIUM UND PFERDEMUSEUM

Sentruper Strasse 315, 48161 Münster
Tel 0251 89040
www.allwetterzoo.de

A few kilometres southwest of the city is Münster's All-Weather Zoo, also home to the Dolphinarium and Horse Museum. Zoo highlights include the orang-utan enclosure, with its unique tropical forest and 6m-high (19ft) viewing platform, and two walk-through enclosures housing smaller primates. There is also a roofed, all-weather route that goes past all the main enclosures.

Take a break from sightseeing at the Markt Café in Münster

🕐 Apr–end Sep daily 9–6; Oct–end Mar daily 9–4 💶 Adult €11.50, child (3–17) €5.75 🚃 To Allwetterzoo 🍴

🐾 LWL LANDESMUSUEM UND PLANETARIUM

Sentruper Strasse 285, 48161 Münster
Tel 0251 59105
www.naturkundemuseum-muenster.de

Right next door to the zoo (see above) is the State Museum and Planetarium. Inside, the natural history of the Rhine is brought to life by a beautifully presented display on dinosaurs and other regional prehistoric life. There's also an ongoing schedule of temporary exhibitions. The planetarium features a varied selection of shows for both kids and adults, although they're only in German; ask at the information desk to find out which show is the easiest to follow for those who don't speak the language.

🕐 Tue–Sun 9–6 💶 Planetarium, adult €4, child €2; Landesmuseum, adult €3.50, child €2 🚃 To Allwetterzoo 🅿

SPEYER

🐾 SEA LIFE SPEYER

Im Hafenbecken 5, 67346 Speyer
Tel 06232 69780
www.sealife.de

This brand new facility on the banks of the Rhine reflects the 'learning can be fun' philosophy that's common to other European Sea Life venues. Imaginative displays take visitors on an underwater journey from the upper reaches of the Rhine to the depths of the Atlantic. Among Sea Life Speyer's highlights are its shark population, and a hands-on tank for curious children.

🕐 Mon–Fri 10–5, Sat, Sun 10–6
💶 Adult €10, schoolchild €7 🍴

🐾 TECHNIK MUSEUM SPEYER

Am Technik Museum 1, 67346 Speyer
Tel 06232 67080
www.technik-museum.de

Visitors to Speyer can't miss the sprawling Technology Museum, just to the south of the town, with its enormous collection of trains, planes and automobiles. Among the displays that kids can explore are a full-size, walk-in jumbo jet (raised up as if coming in to land), a U-boat and a gigantic Antonov 22 transporter, the largest propeller-powered plane in the world. Additional attractions include 70 more aircraft and helicopters, 50 vintage cars, 40 fire engines and 20 trains. A good-value café serves snacks and hot meals, and the museum also features two IMAX cinemas (though unfortunately, all films are dubbed into German).

🕐 Mon–Fri 9–6, Sat, Sun 9–7
💶 Museum only: adult €11, child (under 14) €9 🅿

WHAT TO DO

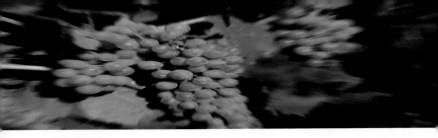

SAUERLAND

🎿 BOBBAHN WINTERBERG HOCHSAUERLAND

Unterm Dumel 30, 59955 Winterberg
Tel 01805 007263
www.bobbahn.de
The Olympic bobsleigh run at Winterberg is 1,600m (1,750 yards) long and has an average gradient of 10 per cent. It has been the venue for a number of German and European championships, and for just €75, you too can discover exactly what it feels like to be fired down a narrow barrel of rock-hard ice at speeds of up to 130kph (81mph). All participants are accompanied by an experienced driver, and all training and equipment are provided. You must be at least 16 years old and 1.5m (5ft) tall, and have no heart or spinal problems.
🕐 Nov–end Feb daily 💶 €78 per person 🚌 Winterberg

TRIER

🍸 COYOTE BAR

Nikolaus Koch Platz, 54290 Trier
Tel 0651 994 7606
www.coyote.de
This centrally located bar, on a quiet street near Marktplatz, is popular with well-heeled students and young professionals alike. For those who've had enough of sausages, schnitzel and sauerkraut, it serves a reassuringly Tex-Mex menu of burgers, burritos and steaks, plus an all-day breakfast menu and a changing lunch menu. The theme is continued in the terracotta-toned vents that snake around the ceiling and in the large mural of Arizona's Monument Valley opposite the entrance. But the focal point for late-night visitors is the long and well-stocked bar, which serves dozens of different cocktails, spirits and beers. There's also a daily happy hour and regular cocktail specials.
🕐 Sun–Thu 10am–1am, Fri, Sat 10am–3am 💶 Breakfasts, burgers and main courses €5–12.50

🧸 SPIELZEUGMUSEUM

Hauptmarkt 14, 54290 Trier
Tel 0651 75850
www.spielzeugmuseum-trier.de
Do you remember Meccano? And the USS *Enterprise*? And the scale model of the space shuttle with the working bay doors? All of these toys and thousands more like them at this splendid toy museum take curious kids and nostalgic adults on a journey back in time. Other highlights include an astonishingly detailed model railway, a clockwork animal kingdom and some life-size 19th-century dolls. Note that the museum can now be found above the Restaurant

Restaurant Zur Steipe, home to the Spielzeugmuseum

Zur Steipe, and not on Nagelstrasse.
🕐 Daily 10–6 💶 Adult €4, child (11–18) €2, under 11 €1.50

WIESBADEN

🎰 SPIELBANK WIESBADEN

Kurhausplatz 1, 65189 Wiesbaden
Tel 0611 53 100
www.spielbank-wiesbaden.de
With its opulent red carpet, enormous crystal chandeliers and lofty coffered ceiling, the Spielbank Wiesbaden is the oldest casino in Germany, not to mention one of the most lavish, and a night out here will make you feel like a king (or a pauper, depending on whether your luck is in). It's housed in the magnificent, neoclassical Kurhaus, which was built in 1907 and lovingly restored in 1987 in accordance with the plans of original architect Friedrich von Thiersch. Men are required to wear a jacket and tie, and guests must be at least 21. For those who've never played before, free taster sessions take place every Friday and Saturday night.
🕐 Daily 2pm–3am 🚌 Bus to Kurhaus

FESTIVALS AND EVENTS

APRIL/MAY

MUSIKTRIENNALE
Bischofsgartenstrasse1, 50667 Köln
Tel 0221 925 7160
www.musiktriennalekoeln.de
This musical extravaganza is held every three years: the next event is in 2007. Orchestras from all over the world come here to take part in some of the 130 concerts at 14 venues around the city.
🕐 Mid-Apr to early May

AUGUST

CHIO INTERNATIONAL EQUESTRIAN CHAMPIONSHIPS
Aachen-Laurensberger Rennverein
P O Box 500101, 52085 Aachen
Tel 0241 917 1111
www.chioaachen.de
Held over five days in August, Aachen's premier equestrian event covers both show jumping and dressage. Each year, the show is themed around a foreign country.
🕐 Late August
💶 €6–35

SEPTEMBER/OCTOBER

BEETHOVEN FESTIVAL
www.bonnticket.de
Inaugurated in Bonn by composer Franz Liszt in 1845, the festival features some 50 concerts performed in a variety of venues all over the city and the surrounding region.
🕐 Three to four weeks, September/October

BERLIN

Berlin's Sony Centre has all kinds of entertainment under one roof

Berlin is a paradise for shopaholics, with everything from expensive and unique designer luxuries to weird and wonderful bargains. The bustling boulevard of Kurfürstendamm in the western part of the city, known as the Ku'damm for short, has a diverse array of shops and is lined with designer boutiques, cafés, theatres, museums, cinemas, art galleries, bars and clubs. On the eastern side of the city, halfway down Unter den Linden, is the shopping street of Friedrichstrasse (www.friedrichstrasse.de), also with designer boutiques, department stores, restaurants, theatres and bars.

Wilmersdorferstrasse, known as 'Wildo' by Berliners, is one of the oldest and longest-established shopping streets in the city, with department stores, and individual boutiques and designer shops. In general, shops open between 9am and 8pm on weekdays, and 9am and 6pm on Saturdays, closing on Sundays.

Berlin's shopping arcades and department stores cater for every taste and consumer trend. The latest styles and alternative fashions can be found in some of the quirky shops at Savignyplatz in Charlottenburg, on Akazienstrasse in Schöneberg, on Bergmanstrasse in Kreuzberg, on Kastanienallee in Prenzlauer Berg and on Alte Schönhauser Allee in Mitte. Berlin's flea markets also yield some unusual purchases, while street markets are a great place to buy fresh produce for a hearty picnic or

sample some Turkish, Greek or Italian delicacies.

Berlin's cultural scene is buzzing. From traditional cabaret to experimental theatre, and from opera to new metal bands, the city's entertainment and live events line-up caters for all tastes.

Hackescher Markt, Oranienburger Strasse, Linienstrasse and Torstrasse in Mitte are good places for exploring Berlin at night, as there are plenty of bars and clubs. Pariser Strasse in Wilmersdorfer is great for pubs, bars and high-tech clubs.

Charlottenburg's night scene revolves around Savignyplatz, Kantstrasse and Schlosstrasse, where there are plenty of bars and Latin, jazz and funk clubs. The area between Ostbahnhof and Ostkreuz in Friedrichshain is becoming very popular with students, while a young international crowd is attracted to the clubs in Kreuzberg.

KEY TO SYMBOLS

⊞	**Shopping**
ⓐ	**Entertainment**
ⓥ	**Nightlife**
ⓚ	**Sports**
✪	**Activities**
♡	**Health and Beauty**
✱	**For Children**

⊞ SHOPPING

DEPARTMENT STORES AND SHOPPING ARCADES

KADEWE—KAUFHAUS DES WESTENS

Tauenzienstrasse 21–24, 10789 Berlin (Schöneberg)
Tel 030 21210
www.kadewe.de

KaDeWe is the largest department store in mainland Europe. This consumer paradise is spread over eight floors. Its legendary delicatessen is popular with visitors and locals alike, who are attracted by the feast of luxury chocolates, vintage wines and spirits and gourmet ingredients.

Exhibitions, fashion shows and book signings are regular occurrences. There is a great view across the rooftops of the Kurfürstendamm from the top-floor café.
🎟 Mon–Fri 10–8, Sat 9.30–8
Ⓢ Wittenbergplatz 🚌 185, 219

GALERIES LAFAYETTE
Friedrichstrasse 76–78, 10117 Berlin (Mitte)
Tel 030 209480
www.lafayette-berlin.de
www.galerieslafayette.de
This glass-roofed shopping arcade dominates the stylish shopping district of Friedrichstrasse. Every exclusive item you desire is here, from designer shoes to fine porcelain. In the delicatessen you can sip champagne, sample exquisite pastries and track down some of the smelliest French cheese in the city.
🎟 Mon–Fri 9.30–8, Sat–Sun 9–4
Ⓢ Friedrichstrasse, Französische Strasse 🚌 147

FASHION AND LINGERIE

SERGEANT PEPPERS
Kastanienallee 91–92, 10435 Berlin (Prenzlauer Berg)
Tel 030 448 1121
www.sgt-peppers-berlin.de
Sergeant Peppers, in the funky Kastanienallee shopping street, is the place to shop for authentic 1960s clothing. It has an excellent selection of original antique clothing for men and women.
🎟 Mon–Fri 11–8, Sat 11–6
Ⓢ Eberswalder Strasse, Senefelder Strasse

FOOD AND DRINK
FASSBENDER AND RAUSCH
Charlottenstrasse 60, Ecke Mohrenstrasse, 10117 Berlin (Mitte)
Tel 030 2045 8440
www.fassbender-rausche.de
Founded in the 19th century, this luxury chocolate shop and confectioners near the Gendarmenmarkt (▷ 129) is always busy. Treat yourself to their delicate truffles and chocolate cake.

🎟 Mon–Fri 10–8, Sat 10–4
Ⓢ Stadtmitte, Französische Strasse

GIFTS AND SOUVENIRS
FACHHANDELSGESCHÄFT RASCHKE
Neuer Hackescher Markt, Dircksenstrasse 50, 10178 Berlin (Mitte)
Tel 030 2838 8010
www.erzgebirge-berlin.de
If you miss out on Berlin's Christmas markets (▷ 265), you can still find traditional wooden, handmade Christmas decorations in this magical shop, which is stuffed from floor to ceiling with painted wooden toys, figurines, advent carousels and armies of wooden soldiers.

Ties for sale on Kurfurstendamm, Berlin's busy shopping street

🎟 Mon–Fri 11–7, Sat 11–4
Ⓢ Hackescher Markt

POSTKARTEN
Oranienburger Strasse 51, 10117 Berlin (Mitte)
Tel 030 2809 6230
www.post-art.de
This shop has a huge range of unusual postcards and cards. There is also an entertaining and kitsch collection of gifts, trinkets and accessories, such as souvenirs bearing the green and red 'Ampelmann' logo, the cult hat-wearing celebrity from Berlin's pedestrian crossings.
🎟 Mon–Fri 12–8, Sat 12–10, Sun 2–7
Ⓢ Oranienburger Tor, Oranienburger Strasse

MARKETS
MARKT AM WINTERFELDPLATZ
Winterfeldplatz, Berlin (Schöneberg)
This bustling market attracts a diverse crowd in search of organic fruit and vegetables, freshly baked wholemeal bread and freshly squeezed juices. There are clothes and craft stalls, but the highlights are the delicatessen stalls.
🎟 Wed and Sat 8–2
Ⓢ Nollendorfplatz

TÜRKISCHER BASAR
Maybachufer, Berlin (Neukölln)
The Turkish Bazaar, popular since the 1970s, is the liveliest and cheapest market in Berlin. It is a great place to sample Turkish cuisine, soak up exotic sights and smells, and get a genuine feel for Berlin's multicultural way of life.
🎟 Tue and Fri noon–6.30
Ⓢ Schönleinstrasse

🎭 ENTERTAINMENT
CABARET
FRIEDRICHSTADTPALAST
Friedrichstrasse 107, 10117 Berlin (Mitte)
Tel 030 2326 2264 (box office)
www.friedrichstadtpalast.de
This is Berlin's largest cabaret theatre and the largest costume revue venue in Europe. The show is a fantastic glitzy spectacle of dance, circus, music and chorus. They have their own high-kicking troupe of 66 dancers, plus an orchestra.
🎟 Ticket hotline: Mon 9–6, Tue–Sat 9–8 and 1 hour before performance.
Main revue: Tue–Fri 8, Sat 4 and 8, Sun 4 💶 €17–61 Ⓢ Oranienburger Tor, Friedrichstrasse 🚌 Bus 147; tram 1, 50

POMP, DUCK AND CIRCUMSTANCE
Möckernstrasse 26, 10963 Berlin (Kreuzberg)
Tel 030 2694 9200
www.pompduck.de
Pomp, Duck and Circumstance pays tribute to the glory days of cabaret. In the big top, with its white tablecloths and sparkling glasses, you will be served some of the best gourmet food in Berlin. During the four-course

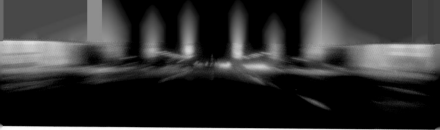

meal and a 3.5-hour show you are treated to a bizarre ensemble of acts that makes for a surreal dining experience. Not for the fainthearted.

🕐 Wed–Sat 6.30pm, Tue and Sun 7pm 💶 Tue–Thu, Sun €110, Fri–Sat €120 🚇 Möckernbrücke, Anhalter Bahnhof

CINEMAS

ARSENAL
Potsdamer Strasse 2, 10785 Berlin (Tiergarten)
Tel 030 2695 5100
www.fdk-berlin.de
This art-house cinema screens films by up-and-coming German directors during the Berlin International Film Festival (▷ 265). For the rest of the year, its shows classic films, historical documentaries and cinematic lectures.

🕐 Daily, 4, 5, 7, 7.30, 9, 9.30 💶 Adult €6, child €3 🚇 Potsdamer Platz

CINEMAXX
Potsdamer Strasse 5, Berlin (Tiergarten)
Tel 01805 2463 6299
www.cinemaxx.de
A modern mutiplex showing a selection of the latest film releases in their original version. As it is easy to end up in the wrong screening, make sure you get the 'OV—Originalversion' (original version) ticket for your film, and check it and the screen number carefully. There is a café and a bar. No credit cards.

🕐 Daily, performance times vary 💶 Tue adult €4.50, child €3; Mon, Wed, Thu and Sun after 5pm €5.90; Fri, Sat adult €7.30, child €4.50 🚇 Potsdamer Platz 🅿

CLASSICAL MUSIC, DANCE AND OPERA

DEUTSCHE OPER BERLIN
Bismarkstrasse 35, 10585 Berlin (Charlottenburg)
Tel 030 348 8401
www.deutscheoperberlin.de
The Deutsche Oper company has been staging classical and modern opera and ballet, plus symphony and chamber concerts, since 1912. Performances since World War II have been held in Fritz Bornemann's contemporary glass-fronted building. Even in the cheap seats you get a great view of the stage and can appreciate the fantastic acoustics.

🕐 Mon–Sat 11–1 hour before performance, Sun 10–2 and 1 hour before performance 💶 €10–112 🚇 Deutsche Oper, Bismarkstrasse, Charlottenburg 🚌 101, 109

PHILHARMONIE
Herbert-von-Karajan-Strasse 1, 10785 Berlin (Tiergarten)
Tel 030 254880, 030 2548 8999 (tickets)
www.berliner-philharmoniker.de
Hans Scharoun's eye-catching yellow building was built

Funky women's fashion—just the ticket for Berlin's club scene

between 1960 and 1963. The Philharmonie is now home to the Berlin Philharmonic Orchestra, and plays host to classical and modern orchestral concerts, chamber music and solo performances.

🕐 Mon–Fri 3–6, Sat–Sun and holidays 11–2 💶 €7–330 🚇 Potsdamer Platz 🚌 129, 148, 200, 248, 348

CONTEMPORARY LIVE MUSIC

B-FLAT
Rosenthaler Strasse, 10119 Berlin (Mitte)
Tel 030 283 3123
www.b-flat-berlin.de
This club in the heart of the city has acoustic music and jazz. Drinks are cheaper before 10pm, and happy hour is between 1am and 2am. There are open-mike sessions on Wednesday nights; the club screens art-house films and shorts on Thursday; and Sunday night from 10pm is 'Tango Time'. Live music schedules change weekly.

🕐 Sun–Thu from 8pm, Fri–Sat from 9pm 💶 €4–8, free Wed–Thu 🚇 Hackescher Markt, Weinmeisterstrasse 🚊 Tram 13, 53

SO 36
Oranienstrasse 190, 10999 Berlin (Kreuzberg)
Tel 030 6140 1306
www.so36.de
Besides the regular weekly line-up of club nights—techno, Asian vibes, 1980s revival, hip-hop and house—this club also plays host to ska, rock, new metal and punk bands. Up-and-coming German bands make their mark here, as well as a few headline acts.

🕐 Electric Ballroom: Mon from 11pm. Gay/Lesbian Party: Wed from 11pm. Café Fatal, variety show and dances: Sun from 5pm (7pm in summer) 💶 €3–7. Concerts: €10–25 🚇 Görlitzer Bahnhof, Kottbusser Tor 🚌 129, 140, N8, N129

THEATRE

BERLINER ENSEMBLE
Bertolt-Brecht-Platz 1, 10117 Berlin (Mitte)
Tel 030 2480 8155
www.berliner-ensemble.de
In 1952, this theatre became the home of the Berliner Ensemble, founded by Bertolt Brecht and Helene Weigel in the late 1940s. It focuses on the works of Brecht, William Shakespeare and Austrian playwrights. There are also film screenings and exhibitions.

🕐 Mon–Fri 8–6, Sat–Sun and holidays 11–6 💶 €5–30 🚇 Friedrichstrasse 🚊 Tram 1, 50

MAXIM GORKI THEATER
Am Festungsgraben 2, 10117 Berlin (Mitte)
Tel 030 2022 1129, 030 2022 1115 (box office)
www.gorki.de

WHAT TO DO

Built between 1825 and 1827 by Karl Theodor Ottmer, this former singing academy, with its beautiful classical façade, has been a theatre since 1952. The main theatre stages plays by contemporary dramatists and classical German playwrights, while experimental theatre and performance art is held at the Gorki Studio.

🕐 Mon–Sat 12–6.30 and 1 hour before performance, Sun and holidays 4–6.30 💶 €12–30 🚇 Friedrichstrasse 🚌 Bus 100, 157, 348; tram 1, 50, 1E

🟥 NIGHTLIFE

CLUBS

90 GRAD
Dennewitzstrasse 37, 10785 Berlin (Schöneberg)
Tel 030 2759 6231
www.90grad.com
It's a tradition for visiting stars, such as George Clooney and Dustin Hoffman, to have a party at this retro 1980s institution at some point during their stay. At weekends, it becomes a trendy joint for rich kids and chic champagne-sipping revellers. Dress to impress.

🕐 Wed from 10pm, Fri–Sat from 11pm 💶 €10 🚇 Kurfürstenstrasse 🚌 N5, N52

HAVANNA
Hauptstrasse 30, 10827 Berlin (Schöneberg)
Tel 030 784 8565
www.havanna-berlin.de
This welcoming Latin club in Schöneberg has three floors, and you can dance the night away to salsa, merengue, bachata, funk and soul. They also hold dance classes.

🕐 Fri–Sat from 10pm, Wed from 9pm 💶 Fri €6.50, Sat €7, Wed €2.50 🚇 Kleistpark 🚌 148, 348

PUBS AND BARS

BAR AM LÜTZOWPLATZ
Lützowplatz 7, 10785 Berlin (Tiergarten)
Tel 030 262 6807
www.baramluetzowplatz.com
Designed by architect Jürgen Sawade, this sophisticated cocktail bar is one of the largest in Berlin and boasts 126 different varieties of champagne. The happy hour attracts many of Berlin's business types seeking a tipple in stylish surroundings after work. The bartenders have made serving drinks an art form.

🕐 Daily 2pm–4am. Happy hour: 2pm–9pm 🚌 100, 129, 187

PONY BAR
Alte Schönhauser Strasse 44, 10119 Berlin (Mitte)
Tel 030 9798 4778
Pony Bar is the brainchild of a couple of unemployed architecture students. They have completely transformed this bar in Mitte, creating a post-

Berlin's Sony Centre, Potsdamer Platz, lights the night sky

modern 1970 to '80s-inspired interior with floral tablecloths and funky lamps.

🕐 Mon–Sat from noon, Sun from 6pm 🚇 Richard-Luxemburg Platz, Weinmeisterstrasse

ZAPATA
Oranienburger Strasse 54–56a (in Tacheles art gallery), 10117 Berlin (Mitte)
Tel 030 281 6109
www.cafe-zapata.de
This chilled-out café by day and offbeat bar and music venue by night attracts hundreds of people to listen to experimental DJs or up-and-coming live music acts. It is decorated with barbed wire,

tins and artworks made from recycled materials. Wide selection of beers, and a beer garden open in the summer.

🕐 Daily noon–late 🚇 Hackescher Markt

SPORTS AND ACTIVITIES

AMERICAN FOOTBALL

BERLIN THUNDER
Stadium: Olympiastadion, Olympischer Platz 3, 14053 Berlin (Charlottenburg). Club: Footballteam Betriebs-GmbH, Manns-Braun-Strasse (Friesenhof 1), 14053 Berlin (Charlottenburg)
Tel 030 3006 4400, 0800 300 6444 (ticket line)
www.berlin-thunder.de
The black, red and white-clad players of Berlin Thunder compete in the NFL European League and were World Bowl Champions in 2001 and 2002. Established in 1998, the team moved to its current home in the Olympiastadion in 2003.

🕐 Season: Apr–end Jun 💶 €7.50–30 🚇 Olympiastadion

BASKETBALL

ALBA BERLIN
Cantianstrasse 24, 10437 Berlin (Prenzlauer Berg)
Tel 030 300 9050 (Alba hotline, Mon–Sat 10–8)
www.albaberlin.de
The Albatrosses won the German basketball championships for the seventh time running in 2003. If you fancy checking out their skills, head for the Max Schlemming Hall, one of the best sports venues in the world.

🕐 One midweek and one weekend match per week year-round 💶 €6.50–27 🚇 Schönhauser Allee, Eberswalder Strasse

CYCLING

CALL-A-BIKE
Tel 0700 0522 5522
www.callabike.de
If you have a mobile phone and fancy renting a bicycle to explore the city, you can hop on one of the red-and-white hi-tech bicycles distributed around the city. Deutsche Bahn's fleet of 2,000 bicycles

are found near S-Bahn and long-distance train stations, and at major crossroads. You need to register by ringing Call-a-Bike's hotline, giving them your credit card details or bank account number. Then call the number in the red circle on the cover of the lock of the bicycle you want to rent, and you will be given a code to unlock it. Once you have finished pedalling, return the bicycle to any major crossing and lock it to a fixed object such as a traffic sign or one of the stands provided. Open the protective cover of the lock and a message will appear in the electronic display reading '*Rückgabe Ja/Nein*' ('Return Yes/No'). Press '*Ja*' to return the bike and you will be given a receipt code. Dial the number circled in red on the cover of the lock again, and give Call-a-Bike the receipt code and the location of the bicycle (the names of both roads at the crossing). Your credit card or bank account will then be charged for the amount of time you used the bicycle.
🚲 6c a minute, €15 per day

BOAT TRIPS

STERN- UND KREISSCHIFFAHRT GMBH
Puschkinallee 15, 12435 Berlin
Tel 030 536 36 00
www.sternundkreis.de
Berlin is intersected by the River Spree and crisscrossed with a network of canals, so there are plenty of opportunities to view the city from the water. Take in the contrasting historical and modern sights on a boat trip from Treptow to Charlottenburg, or explore the heart of Berlin on a one-hour boat tour with commentaries in German and English departing from/to Nikolaiviertel. Alternatively, join one of the short tours of the River Spree and Landwehr canal that leave every half hour from Jannowitzbrücke.

⏰ Treptow–Charlottenburg: daily 9.45, 2.10. Nikolaiviertel: daily 10.30–5. Jannowitzbrücke: daily 10, 10.15, 11.10, 11.30, 12.20, 2, 2.30, 3.10, 3.30, 4.20, 7
🚢 Treptow–Charlottenburg: €10 one way, €15.50 return. Nikolaiviertel: €5 one way, €8.50 return.
Jannowitzbrücke: €10 one way, €15.50 return 🚉 Jannowitzbrücke for tours of the River Spree and Landwehr canal; Alexanderplatz for departures from the Nikolaiviertel; Treptower Park for departures from Hafen Treptow

HORSE RACING

TRABRENNBAHN MARIENDORF
Mariendorfer Damm 222–298, 12107 Berlin (Mariendorf)
Tel 030 7610 0111
www.berlintrab.de

The IMAX cinema at the Sony Centre, Potsdamer Platz

The betting is fast-paced and the tension high during trotting meetings at the Mariendorf Derby Course. Ladies and gents come out in their hats on summer weekends, while on Fridays entry is free and things are more relaxed.
⏰ Sun 1.30, Fri 6 🎫 Sun €2.50, Fri free 🚌 176, 179

ICE HOCKEY

BERLIN CAPITALS
Eissporthalle, Jaffestrasse, 14055 Berlin (Charlottenburg)
Tel 030 3038 4223
www.berlin-capitals.de
Ice hockey is very popular in Germany and is a big-money game. The Berlin Capitals, or

'The Prussians', as they are more affectionately known, play through the winter at the Eissporthalle in Charlottenburg. If you fancy watching an action-packed match in among a noisy and energetic crowd, email tickets@berlin-capitals.de for more details.
⏰ Jan–end Mar Fri, Sat or Sun nights 🎫 €18–70 🚉 Eichkamp 🚌 X21

RUNNING

RBB LAUFBEWEGUNG
RBB-Laufbewegung, 14046 Berlin
www.rbb-laufbewegung.de
Run with the crowd and participate in this weekly communal event. This is the largest running and walking club in Berlin, and meets every Saturday at 2pm at the Siegessäule. Yellow-clad crew members are on hand to guide runners on a circuit of the Tiergarten. Whether you are old or young, training for a marathon or a complete beginner, there is a time and pace to suit you.
⏰ Every Sat at 2 🎫 Free 🚉 Bellevue, Tiergarten, Hansaplatz 🚌 100, 187, 341

SOCCER

HERTHA BSC
Hanns-Braun-Strasse (Friesenhaus 2) 14053 Berlin
Tel 01805 189200
www.herthabsc.de
Berlin's largest soccer club has moved away from its past, which was dogged by allegations of bribery and match fixing. The club battled back from bankruptcy in 1994 with the aid of media giant UFA, and the team are now fighting to stay at the top end of the Bundesliga table. Hertha has had a good run in the European Champions League and is due to move to the renovated stadium of the Olympiastadion complex, to be completed in time for the 2006 soccer World Cup.
⏰ Alternate Sats during the season (Aug to mid-May) 🎫 €8–50
🚉 Olympiastadion

WHAT TO DO

SWIMMING

FREIBAD MÜGGELSEE
Fürstenwalder Damm 838, Köpenick
Tel 030 648 7777
You can wallow and splash to your heart's content in this open-air bathing area on the Müggelsee, Berlin's largest natural lake (20ha/50 acres). There are plenty of sandy beaches to lie on, footpaths to explore and sports facilities to make use of, and if it isn't hot enough for you, you can even have a sauna.
🕐 Jun–Aug daily 10–7. Phone for opening times in Apr, May and Sep
💶 Free 🚇 Friedrichshagen then tram 61

❤ HEALTH AND BEAUTY

THERMAL POOLS AND SPAS

THERMEN AM EUROPA-CENTER
Nürnberger Strasse 7, 10787 Berlin (Charlottenburg)
Tel 030 257 5760
www.thermen-berlin.de
Indulge yourself in some cosmetic treatments or a massage, and enjoy the warm salt springs and chlorine-free rooftop pool of the Europa Center in the western area of town. With aqua aerobics, Jacuzzis, saunas, steam rooms, solariums and mud baths, there is all you need here to help you relax.
🕐 Mon–Sat 10am–midnight, Sun 10–9
💶 Standard day ticket: €17.90
🚇 Zoologischer Garten, Kurfürstendamm, Augsburger Strasse, Wittenburgplatz

❸ FOR CHILDREN

MUSEUMS

MUSEUM FÜR NATURKUNDE
Invalidenstrasse 43, 10115 Berlin (Mitte)
Tel 030 2093 8591
www.museum.hu-berlin.de
Pick up a free audioguide and explore the 6,000sq m (64,500sq ft) of this natural history museum, filled with geology, palaeontology and zoology exhibits. Get close to the largest assembled skeleton of a brachiosaurus in the world and Germany's biggest collection of meteorites.

🕐 Tue–Fri 9.30–5, Sat–Sun and holidays 10–6 💶 Adult €3.50, child €2, family €7 🚇 Zinnowitzer Strasse, Nordbahnhof 🚌 Bus 157, 245, 340; tram 6, 8, 13, 50 🍴

PLANETARIUMS

ZEISS GROSSPLANETARIUM
Prenzlauer Allee 80, 10405 Berlin (Prenzlauer Berg)
Tel 030 4218 4512
www.astw.de
The shows in the planetarium's auditorium transport you into space on a star-gazing journey. Learn more in the 'Star Sagas of the Greeks', 'Cosmic Shadow Games' or 'The Earth on the Way Through Space and Time' shows.

Classical entertainment at the Opernpalais on Unter den Linden

🕐 Shows: Mon–Fri 9.30am, 11am (also afternoon shows Wed, Sat, Sun) 💶 Adult €5, child €4, family €15 🚇 Prenzlauer Allee 🚌 Bus 156; tram 1

THEME PARKS

FILMPARK BABELSBERG
August-Bebel-Strasse 26–53 (entrance on Grossbeerenstrasse), 14482 Berlin
Tel 0331 721 2750/55
www.filmpark.de
This theme park on the outskirts of the city is in the former UFA Studios, where Marlene Dietrich began her career. A guided tour takes you behind the scenes of the movie industry, revealing the secrets of special effects, stunts, pyrotechnics, action

scene choreography, make-up and costume.
🕐 May–end Sep 10–6; Mar, Apr, Oct, Nov daily 10–4 💶 Adult €15, child (4–16) €9 🚇 Babelsberg 🚌 690, 698 🍴 🅿

WATER PARKS

BLUB-BADEPARADIES
Buschkrugallee 64, 12359 Berlin (Neukölln)
Tel 030 609060
www.blub-berlin.de
Burn off some energy on the Crazy River, wave pools and water rapids, and then relax over a picnic in the beautiful gardens of this water park on the outskirts of the city. There is plenty to keep kids occupied while parents relax in the Palmgarten (palm garden) or retreat to the wellness suite for a session in the Egyptian sauna or Turkish bath.
🕐 Daily 10am–11pm 💶 Sat, Sun and school holidays adult €10.70, under 12 €8.20; Mon–Fri adult €9.20, under 12 €7.10 🚇 Grenzallee 🚌 141

ZOOS AND AQUARIUMS

ZOOLOGISCHER GARTEN
Hardenbergplatz 8, 10787 Berlin (Tiergarten)
Tel 030 254010
www.zoo-berlin.de
Berlin's central zoo has lots of interest for children. There is a playground with monkey bars, slides and swings near the brown bears, plus the Tierkinder Zoo (Children's Zoo) beside the Vogelhaus (Bird House), where kids can wander around a mini farm, stroking the goats, sheep, Shetland ponies and donkeys. The Zoo-Aquarium, accessed at Budapester Strasse 32, is home to insects, fish, reptiles and amphibians.
🕐 Daily 9–6 💶 Either zoo or aquarium: adult €8, child €6.50. Combined zoo and aquarium ticket: adult €13, child €10.50 🚇 Zoologischer Garten 🚌 100, 109, 119, 129, 145, 146, 149, 245, X9, X34 🍴

FESTIVALS AND EVENTS

JANUARY

LANGE NACHT DER MUSEEN
Tel 030 90 26 99 444
www.mdberlin.de
More than 100 museums stay open until midnight. Accompanying events include concerts, readings, lectures, theatre and parties.
🕒 Late January and late August

FEBRUARY

INTERNATIONALE FILMFESTSPIELE BERLIN
Tel 030 259200
www.berlinale.de
Two weeks of classic films, lectures, previews and directorial debuts are held around the Filmhaus (▷ 144) in Potsdamer Platz and in various other city cinemas.
🕒 Early–mid-February

MAY

KARNEVAL DER KULTUREN
Tel 030 6097 7022
www.karneval-berlin.de
This three-day festival in Kreuzberg celebrates the city's multicultural character. Enjoy the parades, singing and dancing.
🕒 Late May (Whitsun)

JUNE

GAY-LESBIAN CITY-FESTIVAL
Tel 030 2362 8632
www.berlin-tourist-information.de
The Gay-Lesbian City-Festival takes place every year at the end of June around Nollendorf Platz. The carnival spreads down Motzstrasse, Fuggerstrasse, Kalkreutstrasse and Eisenacherstrasse, and the party culminates with the CSD: Christopher Street Day gay and lesbian parade.
🕒 Late June

JULY

LOVE PARADE
Strasse des 17 Juni, 10785 Berlin (Charlottenburg)
Tel 030 284620
www.loveparade.de

This parade, celebrating tolerance among nations through music, has evolved from 150 participants and one truck in 1989 into a huge festival with over a million ravers, 50 floats and 250 techno DJs. It begins at 2pm at Ernst-Reuter-Platz and the Brandenburg Gate, at either end of Strasse des 17 Juni, and meets in the middle of the Tiergarten at the Siegessäule (Victory Column), where there is a massive rave. However, its future is unclear.
🕒 Mid-July

The Filmhaus, home to the famous Internationale Filmfestspiele Berlin

SEPTEMBER

BERLIN MARATHON
Tel 030 3012 8810
www.berlin-marathon.com
Over 38,000 runners, wheelchair competitors and power walkers from 99 countries take part in the Berlin Marathon every year, which starts and finishes near the Brandenburg Gate, the Federal Chancellery and the Reichstag, and passes many of Berlin's major sights. An inline skating marathon is held around the course on the Saturday before the main Sunday marathon.

🕒 Late September
📍 Unter den Linden

NOVEMBER

JAZZFEST BERLIN
Tel 030 254890
www.berlinerfestspiele.de
This annual jazz festival attracts famous artists from all over the world and takes place at various venues across the city.
🕒 Early November

NOVEMBER/ DECEMBER

WEIHNACHTSMÄRKTE (CHRISTMAS MARKETS)
www.weihnachtsmarkt-berlin.de
During the month before Christmas, Berlin's squares are filled with fairground rides and market stalls selling traditional Christmas decorations and *Glühwein* (warm spiced wine). The largest Christmas market in Europe is in Altstadt Spandau, while the market around the Gedächtniskirche is great for an evening stroll. Alexanderplatz has a fairy-tale market selling sweets, warm punch and *Brockwurst*, and there is an outdoor skating rink to get you in the mood. For more nostalgia, head for the market at the Opernpalais on Unter den Linden.
🕒 24 November–28 December

DECEMBER

SILVESTERPARTY AM BRANDENBURGER TOR
Tel 030 2460 3252
www.weihnachtsmarkt-deutschland.de/silvester-berlin.html
Every year on the evening of 31 December there is a huge party around the Brandenburg Gate to welcome in the New Year. Expect huge crowds and plenty of fireworks, light shows and live music.
🕒 31 December

WHAT TO DO

EASTERN GERMANY

Messing around in boats at Schloss Wörlitz

WHAT TO DO

Eastern Germany has been rapidly westernized in terms of what there is to buy; long gone are the days when, armed with a jangling pocketful of aluminium GDR coins, you could expect to find beautifully produced books at bargain prices or superlative recordings of some of the world's best orchestras at a fraction of their cost in the West (not that there was much else to buy). Nowadays, shops look and charge exactly as they do in the rest of Germany, though because purchasing power is still less here, choice of goods is likely to be more restricted—at least outside the major cities.

Rather than hang around the shops, check what is on in the way of concerts and other performances. Eastern Germany's theatres, opera houses and concert halls are some of the best in the country, and an evening spent at the Semperoper in Dresden or the Gewandhaus concert hall will be memorable.

Culture of another kind is on offer in the student clubs of the region's university cities. Lively complexes like the Moritzbastei in Leipzig, the Rosenkeller in Jena and the Kasseturm in Weimar owe their existence to the self-help tradition during GDR times and are worth visiting. Eastern cities are far livelier at night than they once were, as you will see from an evening stroll along Dresden's Münzgasse or Leipzig's 'Drallewatsch'.

The region has wonderfully varied countryside with tempting recreational opportunities:

rock-climbing in Saxon Switzerland; hiking in the Harz or Thuringian Forest; or messing around in boats more or less everywhere, but particularly in watery Brandenburg, with its lakes and slow-flowing rivers. Rail buffs are well catered for, with several lines still served by steam. There is also the occasional survivor from the children's 'Pioneer Railways' of the Communist era (Cottbus and Dresden).

Strong local musical traditions mean that there are several first-rate classical music festivals, while Dresden's annual Dixieland jamboree is one of the biggest of its kind in the world. Folk traditions survived and often flourished under Communism. Miners parade through the streets of Freiberg arrayed in their traditional finery, while old customs and costumes survive among the Sorbs, the Slav population of the Spreewald and Lusatia.

KEY TO SYMBOLS
- ⊕ **Shopping**
- ⊘ **Entertainment**
- ⊘ **Nightlife**
- ⊗ **Sports**
- ✪ **Activities**
- ♡ **Health and Beauty**
- ✷ **For Children**

BAD SAROW

♡ **DIE THERME**
Am Kurpark 1, 15526 Bad Sarow
Tel 03363 18680
At this little spa town you get the chance to bob around in an enclosed salt-water pool at a temperature of 35°C (95°F), then swim outside in an open-air pool. There are also saunas, mud-baths and massages.
🕓 Mon–Thu 9am–9pm, Fri–Sat 9am–11pm 🛁 Treatments from €10

BAD SULZA

TOSKANA THERME
Wunderwaldstrasse 2a, 99518 Bad Sulza
Tel 036461 91080
www.liquid-sound.com

A luxurious and unusual spa experience that the ancient Romans would have envied. Your immersion is accompanied by light and 'liquid sound' and, if you wish, by an 'Aqua-Wellness Bodyworker'.

⏰ Thu 10am–10pm, Fri–Sat 10am–midnight
💶 Treatments from €16

BAUTZEN

✪ SAURIERPARK KLEINWELKA
Bautzen OT Kleinwelka, 02625 Bautzen
Tel 0359 353036
www.saurierpark.de
Lurking in this leafy park just 4km (2.5 miles) north of Bautzen are terrifying creatures from Jurassic times. Convincingly life-like, despite being modelled in steel and concrete, they are said to make up the biggest collection of its kind in the country. There is also a playground.

⏰ Late Mar–early Nov daily 9–6
💶 Adult €8, child €5 🅿

COTTBUS

✪ PARKEISENBAHN COTTBUS
Am Eliaspark 1, 03042 Cottbus
Tel 0355 756170
www.cmt-cottbus.de
One of the more attractive features of Soviet-style Communism was the setting up of narrow-gauge railways 'run by children', where nearly all the work of getting the trains run to time was carried out by well-drilled Young Pioneers. The Pioneers may have disappeared, but their young successors still attend to the little trains that chuff (steam) or chug (diesel) for more than 3km (2 miles) through the town's parkland.

⏰ May–end Aug daily 10–5; Apr, Sat, Sun and hols 10–5; Sep, Sat, Sun 10–5; service every 15–45 mins 💶 Adult €3, child €. 🅿

DESSAU-WÖRLITZ

✪ ANTONOV 2 FLIGHTS
Flugplatz, Tower, Alte Landebahn 27, 06846 Dessau
Tel 0340 619751

Dessau was famous in aviation history as the home of Junkers aircraft; today, you can take a trip aboard an Antonov 2, the archaic-looking but extremely robust nine-seater Soviet biplane featured in many a film. The trip is expensive, so try to make up a group.

⏰ On demand 💶 €287.60 for 15 min

DRESDEN

🏛 PFUNDS MOLKEREI
Bautzner Strasse 79, 01099 Dresden
Tel 0351 808080
www.pfunds.de
This wonderful dairy shop is considered by local people (as well as by the *Guinness Book*

Dresden's busy Altmarkt shopping arcade

of Records) to be the 'most beautiful dairy in the world'. Founded in 1880, it is embellished with more than 3,500 hand-painted tiles made by the firm of Villeroy & Boch. You can choose from a range of more than 100 different kinds of cheese, and there's a very pleasant café upstairs.

⏰ Mon–Sat 10–6, Sun 10–3 🚋 Tram 11 to Pulsnitzer Strasse 🅿

🏛 STRIEZELMARKT
Altmarkt, Dresden
www.dresden-tourist.de
This is the name given to Dresden's Christmas market, one of Germany's largest and liveliest, held every year on the

Altmarkt. Originally, in the 15th century, only *Stollen* (fruit bread) was allowed to be sold, but gradually other goods crept in, such as the famous wooden toys and implements from the Ore Mountains (▷ 270).

⏰ Late Nov to 24 Dec Sun–Thu 10–8, Fri, Sat 10–9 🚋 Tram 1, 2, 4, 6 to Altmarkt

🎭 KULTURPALAST
Kulturpalast am Altmarkt, 01067 Dresden
Tel 0351 486 6306
www.dresdnerphilharmonie.de
Closing off the north side of Dresden's Altmarkt is the city's Palace of Culture. As well as being the home base of the renowned Dresden Philharmonic Orchestra, the Kulturpalast is the venue for a whole range of entertainments, and comes into its own during the city's classical music festival and the International Dresden Dixieland Jazz Festival (▷ 272).

⏰ Mon–Fri 10–7, Sat 10–4 (concert weekends) 💶 Varies 🚋 1, 2, 4, 6 to Altmarkt

☾ M.5 NIGHTLIFE
Münzgasse 5, 01067 Dresden
Tel 0351 496 5491
www.m5-nightlife.de
More sophisticated than your normal disco, M.5 has top DJs, go-go girls and boys, a fabulous range of drinks and good food, intimate niches where you can escape and free entrance for ladies.

⏰ Wed–Sat 9–late 💶 €6–7, ladies free 🚋 Tram 1, 2, 4, 49 to Neumarkt; tram 3, 7, 9, 12 to Pirnaischer Platz

✪ GROSSER GARTEN
Hauptallee 5, 01219 Dresden
Tel 0351 445 6795
www.schloesser-dresden.de
The Great Garden has a 34km (21-mile) network of footpaths (including skating paths), a palace, a boating lake, an open-air theatre, a puppet theatre and the city zoo, home to some 3,000 animals. One

way of exploring it is to take the Parkeisenbahn (Park Railway, Apr–Oct), which runs for 5.6km (3.5 miles) through the greenery past many of its features, including Volkswagen's staggering new 'transparent' factory. The railway is run almost entirely by children.

🕐 Daily 🔲

🎭 PUPPENTHEATERSAMMLUNG

Barkengasse 6, 01445 Radebeul
Tel 0351 491 4619
www.skd-dresden.de
In the suburb of Radebeul is this wondrous collection of marionettes, stage sets and all kinds of puppet theatre memorabilia. The puppets spring to life in shows on the last Sunday of every month.

🕐 Tue–Fri 9–4, last Sun in month 10–5
🎟 Adult €2, child €1

GÖRLITZ

🏬 KARSTADT

An der Frauenkirche 5–7, 02826 Görlitz
Tel 03581 4600
German retailers were among the pioneers of department stores, and some of those built in the early 20th century were architectural monuments in their own right. Most were destroyed in wartime, but the Karstadt *Jugendstil* (art nouveau) store escaped intact. Opened in 1913, it's a fabulous creation, with retail space opening off the central atrium beneath a stained-glass roof.

🕐 Mon–Fri 9.30–6.30, Sat 9–4 (sometimes 9–6)

🎭 SPIELZEUGMUSEUM

Rothenburgerstrasse 7, 02826 Görlitz
Tel 03581 405870
www.spielzeugmuseum-goerlitz.de
This little museum has a fascinating array of the typical wooden toys traditionally made in the region, some up to 150 years old, some new. Children can watch a toymaker at work and even have a go at creating playthings themselves.

🕐 Adult Mon–Fri 10–noon, 2–4,
Sat–Sun 2–5 🎟 €2, child €1

HALLE

🎭 TURM

Friedemann-Bach-Platz 5, 06108 Halle
Tel 0345 202 3737
www.turm-net.de
With its large student population, Halle is a young city, and the 'Tower' of the Moritzburg has had a hot reputation for decades. There is live music, plus disco, party nights and cabaret-type entertainment.

🕐 Events: Wed–Sun 🎟 €2.50–12
🚋 Tram 7 to Moritzburgring

JENA

🎭 ROSENKELLER

Johannisstrasse 13, 07743 Jena
Tel 03641 931190
www.rosenkeller.org

Jugendstil style makes shopping at Görlitz's Karstadt a chic activity

Jena's ancient wine cellars were cleared out by voluntary student workers and turned into a lively and friendly place to meet, flirt and enjoy all sorts of cultural (lectures and discussions) and other (live bands, disco and jazz) offerings. There is a great choice of drinks, and a beer garden.

🕐 Tue–Sat from 9pm 🎟 Events: €2–8

LEIPZIG

🏬 BAHNHOFSPROMENADEN

Willy-Brandt-Platz 7, 04109 Leipzig
Tel 0341 141270
The huge multi-level retail mall, which was cleverly inserted into Leipzig's main railway station in the 1990s,

continues the city's tradition of all-weather shopping arcades. There are 140 shops, covering everything from A (an Aldi supermarket) to Z (Zoo Richter, selling pet requisites), as well as restaurants offering every kind of cuisine.

🕐 Mon–Sat 6am–10pm, Sun 6–4
🅿 €3 all day (no parking on Sat)
🍴 🔲

🎄 WEIHNACHTSMARKT

Markt, Leipzig
The Christmas market on the square in front of Leipzig's Altes Rathaus is one of the oldest (from 1767) and largest in Germany. It has a huge range of stalls and a panoply of related attractions, including Father Christmas, seasonal music concerts, and fanfares from the Rathaus tower.

🕐 Stalls: late Nov–Christmas Eve daily 10–8 🚋 Tram 9 to Thomaskirche

🎵 GEWANDHAUS ZU LEIPZIG

Augustusplatz 8, 04109 Leipzig
Tel 0341 12700
www.gewandhaus.de
Leipzig's great powerhouse is the Gewandhaus and its world-famous orchestra, directed since 1998 by Herbert Blomstedt. The 600-plus annual events held here include orchestral concerts in the 1900-seat Main Hall, and there are organ recitals, choral and chamber music and other events in the Mendelssohn Hall.

🕐 Mon–Fri 10–6 or to start of concert, Sat 10–2 and 1 hour before concert
🎟 €4–11

🎵 OPER

Oper Leipzig, Augustusplatz 12, 04109 Leipzig
Tel 0341 126 1261
www.oper-leipzig.de
Leipzig has had an opera house since 1693, and its musical directors have included the likes of Austrian composer and conductor Gustav Mahler (1860–1911). The present building, a strange mixture of the classical and the modern, was completed in

1960, and was one of the GDR's most prestigious cultural and architectural projects. It is also home to the Leipziger Ballett.
🕐 Mon–Fri 10–8, Sat 10–4 💶 €9–48

🎭 THOMASKIRCHE
Thomaskirchhof, 04109 Leipzig
Tel 0341 960 2855
www.thomaskirche.org
www.thomanerchor.de
It's an unforgettable experience to listen to the choir of St. Thomas's Church; composer Johann Sebastian Bach (1685–1750) was once choirmaster here. The Thomaner, as the boys are known, perform on Friday evening and Saturday afternoon, except during school holidays and when they are on tour.
🕐 Motets: Fri 6, Sat 3 💶 Free, but programme purchase obligatory (€1)

🎵 MB-MORITZBASTEI
Universitätsstrasse 9, 04109 Leipzig
Tel 0341 702590
www.moritzbastei.de
In the 1970s, students voluntarily spent hours digging out the rubble clogging the Moritz Bastion, a remnant of Leipzig's fortifications. Now it is possibly the largest student club in Europe, a top place for young people to mix in a laid-back atmosphere. There are three levels of cellars and other spaces, home to cafés and bars and all kinds of concerts.
🕐 Daily 💶 Free; charge for events
🚋 Tram 4, 7, 8, 10, 11, 12, 15, 16 to Augustusplatz; tram 2, 8, 9, 10, 11 to Wilhelm-Leuschnerplatz

🎭 WERK II KULTURFABRIK
Kochstrasse 132, 04277 Leipzig
Tel 0341 308 0140
www.werk-2.de
This old gas-meter factory in Leipzig's southern suburb has been converted into a splendid 'social-cultural' venue, with a head-spinning line-up of parties, live music, experimental theatre, discos, dances, children's events and exhibitions.
🕐 7pm 💶 From €4 🚋 Tram 9, 10, 11 to Connewitzer Kreuz

🎢 BELANTIS
Zur Weissen Mark 1, 04249 Leipzig
Tel 01805 694694
www.belantis.de
The Belantis theme park is the largest attraction of its kind in eastern Germany. It comprises re-creations of historical eras, such as the Ancient Greek 'Beach of the Gods' and the 'Valley of the Pharaohs', all with specialized rides, entertainments and refreshments.
🕐 Early Apr–early Nov Wed–Sun (school holidays Mon–Sun) 10–6
💶 Adult and child more than 1.45m (4ft 9in) tall €17, child 1m–1.45m (3ft 4in–4ft 9in) tall €15, child under 1m (3ft 4in) tall free 🚋 Tram 3 to Knauthain terminus, then bus 118 🚌

Shop before you travel, at the Promenaden in Leipzig's station

🎢 ZOO LEIPZIG
Pfaffendorfer Strasse 29, 04105 Leipzig
Tel 0341 593 3500
www.zoo-leipzig.de
One of the world's oldest zoos (1877), Leipzig Zoo also considers itself a 'zoo of the future' and plans to extend its range of habitats for the 1,000-plus species of animals that live here. There is already the Tiger Taiga, the Valley of the Sloths and Pongoland, a landscape of rocks, savannah and primeval forest populated by gorillas, chimpanzees and orang-utans.
🕐 May–end Sep daily 9–7; Apr, Oct 9–6; Nov–end Apr daily 9–5 💶 Adult €7.50, child €4 🚋 Tram 12 to Zoo Leipzig 🚌

LUTHERSTADT WITTENBERG

🚗 RENT-A-TRABI
Event und Touring AG, Dessauer Strasse 38, 06886 Lutherstadt Wittenberg
Tel 03491 660195
www.trabi-abi.de
After spending an hour driving a Trabant, you may wonder why several million of them were made and why many eastern Germans still feel nostalgic about them. Or, you could let yourself be seduced by the car's charms and spend a whole day testing its capabilities on a 'Trabi Safari'.
🕐 9am–5.30pm 💶 €22 per hour

MEISSEN

🏛 MEISSENER PORZELLAN
Meissener Porzellan in der Schauhalle, Talstrasse 9, 01662 Meissen
Tel 03521 468332
www.meissen.de
Perhaps the most appropriate place to select an exquisite Meissen porcelain souvenir is in the exhibition hall of the factory itself. A fine range of products is on show, and arrangements can be made for postal delivery worldwide. There's also an outlet in downtown Meissen at Burgstrasse 6.
🕐 Daily, May–Oct 9–6, Nov–Apr 9–5

NAUMBERG

🏛 NAUMBURGER WEIN UND SEKT MANUFAKTUR
Blütengrund 16, 06618 Naumburg/Henne
Tel 03445 202042
www.naumburgerweinundsekt.de
webmaster@naumburgerweinundsekt.de
In the heart of Europe's northernmost vineyards, the oldest *Sekt* (sparkling white wine) production site in Germany has been restored and reopened. Visitors are taken around the cellars (which are hewn out of the local sandstone) to view the production process in all its traditional complexity, before being invited to purchase wines and *Sekt* from the shop.
🕐 Mon–Fri 8–6, Sat, Sun 1–6

✪ MODELLBAHN-ZENTRUM-WIEHE

Am Anger 19, 06571 Wiehe
Tel 01805 909011
www.mowi-world.de
The tiny town of Wiehe, 34km (21 miles) from Naumberg, is home to what is claimed to be the biggest model railway attraction in the world. There are various layouts, including a miniature version of the famous steam train that puffs its way to the top of the Brocken mountain.
◎ Daily 9–6 (24 Dec–31 Dec daily 9–2) 🎫 Adult €8.50, child (4–14) €4.50 🍴 Gastronomy Zone

POTSDAM

✪ FILMPARK BABELSBERG

Grossbeerenstrasse, 14482 Potsdam
Tel 0331 721 2750
www.filmpark.de
The hub of Germany's film industry for 90 years, the vast studios in the suburb of Babelsberg were responsible for such classics as *Metropolis* (1927) and *The Blue Angel* (1930). You can enjoy a studio tour and marvel at special effects, while experiencing the cinema of the future at one of Germany's most visited attractions.
◎ Apr–Oct daily 10–6 🎫 Adult €17, child €10 🚌 Bus 601 from Potsdam train station to 'Filmpark' 🍴 Choice of eating places

SÄCHSISCHE SCHWEIZ

✪ FELSENBÜHNE RATHEN

Amselgrund 17, 01824 Kurort Rathen
Tel 035024 7770
www.dresden-theater.de
This open-air theatre is reckoned to be one of the most beautiful and atmospheric of its kind. It stages plays, musicals, operas and spectacles from May to September. Adaptations of Karl May's stories of cowboys and Indians are popular. Check access details when booking; it is on the opposite bank of the Elbe from the station and car park.
◎ May–Sep 🎫 €4–20 🚉 Kurort Rathen

✪ ARNOLDS BERGSPORTLADEN

Obere Strasse 35, 01848 Hohnstein
Tel 035975 81246
www.bergsport-arnold.de
With around 400km (250 miles) of waymarked footpaths, Saxon Switzerland is great for hikers, while there are no fewer than 700 rock faces open to rock climbers, for all grades of proficiency. A good introduction to these remarkable sandstone mountains and their climbing opportunities (including courses and guided tours) is offered by the well-known climber Bernd Arnold from his shop in Hohnstein.

Germany's nightlife ranges from classical to modern

◎ Mon–Fri 9–6, Sat 9–2 🎫 3-day introductory course €150

SEIFFEN

✪ ERZGEBIRGISCHES SPIELZEUGMUSEUM

Hauptstrasse 73, 09548 Seiffen
Tel 037362 8239
www.seiffen.de
In years gone by, the harsh winter climate of the Erzgebirge (Ore Mountains) drove the inhabitants indoors for several months, and they became expert woodcarvers, making toys whose fame spread worldwide. With around 100 craftsmen still at work, Seiffen is central to this activity. You can visit the Erzgebirgische Spielzeugmuseum (Ore Mountains Toy Museum) or watch the woodcarvers at work around the village—nutcrackers and 'Christmas pyramids' are particular to Seiffen.
◎ Daily 9–5 🎫 Adult €6, child €3

THÜRINGER WALD

✪ OBERHOF

Kurverwaltung/Oberhof-Information, Crawincklerstrasse 2, 98559 Oberhof
Tel 036842 2690
www.oberhof.de
At 800m (2,625ft), Oberhof is the most important winter resort in the Thuringian Forest. It has sports and recreational facilities and downhill and cross-country skiing. In summer, you can whizz downhill at nearly 80kph (50mph) on the 1,130m (1,235-yard) bobsleigh run (tel 01733 90 15 64; www.rennsteigthermen.de; E11). There are also 4,000 species of plants to investigate in the famous Rennsteiggarten.

✪ RENNSTEIG

Haus des Gastes, Bad Vilbeler Platz 4, 98599 Brotterode
Tel 036840 3333
The Rennsteig ridge walk atop the heights of the Thuringian Forest is the most famous of all Germany's many long-distance trails. You can do the whole trail or sections of it without the bother of carrying a backpack by booking a tour, which organizes your hotel and collects you at the end of each day's walking.
◎ Apr–end Oct Mon–Fri 9–5.30, Sat 10–2; Nov–end Mar Mon–Fri 10–4 (Thu 10–5.30) 🎫 €100 for 7-day tour

✪ THÜRINGENWALDBAHN

Thüringerwaldbahn und Strassenbahn Gotha GmbH, Waltershäuserstrasse 98, 99867 Gotha
Tel 03621 4310
www.waldbahn-gotha.de
A ride aboard this rural tramway will give you a taste of the woods and mountains of the Thuringian Forest. After grinding through the streets of Gotha, it rattles along before

reaching the upland resort of Tabarz at the foot of the Grosser Inselberg, one of the area's highest summits.

🎫 Adult €1, child or senior 70c

WEIMAR

🎭 DEUTSCHES NATIONALTHEATER WEIMAR
Theaterplatz 2, 99401 Weimar
Tel 03643 7550
www.nationaltheater.de

Weimar's German National Theatre is the place to experience competent productions from the classical German repertory, such as Goethe's *Faust*. For non-German-speakers, there are operas, the occasional musical and concerts by the Weimar Staatskapelle.

🕐 Mon 2–6, Tue–Fri 10–6, Sat 10–6 (Nov–end Mar 10–1, 4–6), Sun 10–1 🎫 €8–55

🎵 KASSETURM
Goetheplatz 10, 99423 Weimar
Tel 03643 851670
www.kasseturm.de

Once part of the town's medieval defences, this formidable round tower is now the liveliest meeting place for students and young people in Weimar. Like other such clubs in the old GDR, it owes its existence to the students, who rescued it from decay and

misuse in the 1960s. There's a varied schedule of jazz, disco and live music, plus an atmospheric beer cellar.

🕐 Closed Sun 🎫 Free; charge varies for events

ZITTAU

🥾 OBERLAUSITZER BERGWEG
Fremdenverkehrsgemeinschaft Zittauer Gebirge, Markt 1, 02763 Zittau
Tel 03583 752200
www.zittauer-gebirge-tour.de

The mountains forming the border between Germany and the Czech Republic are a popular hiking destination for locals. Choose a tour with the company listed above and walk this long-distance

Meissen don't just make figurines, as this ferocious-looking cat testifies

footpath along granite ridges and picturesque valleys, and past strangely shaped rock formations and volcanic outcrops. You stay in villages characterized by the timber-framed houses that are unique to the area.

🕐 Mon–Fri 8–6, Sat 9–1 🎫 €299 (includes 7 nights' B&B accommodation in hotels or guesthouses, plus picnic lunches, luggage transfer and full route information)

ZWICKAU

🌍 MINIWELT
Chemnitzer Strasse 43, 09350 Lichtenstein
Tel 037204 72255
www.miniwelt.de

Halfway between the cities of Zwickau and Chemnitz is Mini-World, an open-air collection of scaled-down famous buildings and other structures, from the Eiffel Tower to the Great Wall of China. Watch the skilled model-builders at work—you can even have a go yourself.

🕐 Apr–end Aug daily 9–7; Sep, Oct daily 9–6 🎫 Adult €5, child €4, under-6s free 🚗 From Zwickau, head east on the B173, turning left just beyond Lichtenstein 🍴

FESTIVALS AND EVENTS

FEBRUARY/MARCH

KURT WEILL FEST
Kartenservice Kurt Weill Dessau, Rossdeutscher und Bartel GbR, Jahnallee 38, 04109 Leipzig
Tel 0180 556 4564
Theaterkasse im Anhaltischen Theater Dessau, Friedensplatz 1a, 06844, Dessau
Tel 0340 251 13 33
www.kurt-weill-fest.de

Among its most famous sons Dessau numbers the composer Kurt Weill (1900–50), whose music for Berthold Brecht's *Threepenny Opera* so tellingly evokes the deca-

dent spirit of the Weimar era. This 10-day annual festival celebrates Weill's work in the context of its time with first-rate concerts, films, dances and other entertainments, including a lavish '1920s Berlin Ball'. Hotel/concert packages available.

🕐 Late February/early March

MARCH

TELEMANN FESTIVAL
Magdeburger Telemann-Festtage, Telemann-Zentrum, Regierungsstrasse 4–6, 39104 Magdeburg
Tel 0391 540 6755

In March every even year, Magdeburg celebrates its most famous son, composer Georg Philipp Telemann (1681–1767). A performance of one of Telemann's choral works in the setting of the city's oldest building, the 11th-century Convent of Our Lady, is a sublime experience.

MARCH/APRIL

OSTERREITEN
Srbska kulturna informacija, Postplatz 2, 02625 Bautzen
Tel 03591 42105
www.bautzen.de

The members of the Sorb ethnic group celebrate Easter in a distinctive way. Villages stage an *Osterreiten* (Easter Ride), in which festively clad riders process around the parish proclaiming the tidings of the Resurrection. Bautzen has a display of the traditional craft of Easter egg painting.

⊙ Easter

APRIL

WALPURGISNACHT

Thale-Tourist-Information,
Bahnhofstrasse 3, 06502 Thale
Tel 03947 2597
Walpurgisverein, Harz
Tel 03947 23 24

Virtually all the communities in and around the Harz Mountains make the most of the area's connection with *Walpurgisnacht*, the Witches' Sabbath, which attracts thousands of revellers and is held as April gives way to May. Some of the most outrageous happenings occur at the Hexentanzplatz above the resort of Thale, when the devil greets the witches who have arrived on brooms, pitchforks, goats and pigs, and weds the prettiest of them.

⊙ Last weekend in April

MAY

INTERNATIONALES DIXIELANDFESTIVAL

Kulturpalast, Schlossstrasse 2, 01067 Dresden
Tel 0351 486 6666
www.dixieland.de

Dresden's International Dixieland Jazz Festival is one of the most lavish events of its kind in the world. Far more bands wish to participate than there is room for, despite the variety of venues, many in the open air and aboard the city's White Fleet paddlesteamers.

⊙ Mid-May

ROLANDFEST

Brandenburg Information:
Hauptstrasse 51, 14776 Brandenburg
Tel 03381 19433
www.stadt-brandenburg.de

During *Rolandfest* the streets and squares of Brandenburg are given over to medieval festivities celebrating the knight Roland, guardian of civic liberties, who stemmed the advance of the Arabs into France. There are jugglers and other medieval characters, tournaments, ancient crafts on display, and a lively procession.

⊙ Third weekend in May

River trips on the River Spree at Spreewald

MAY/JUNE

MUSIKFESTSPIELE

Ticketzentrale Kulturpalast Dresden,
Schlossstrasse, 01067 Dresden
Tel 0351 478560
www.musikfestspiele.com

Dresden's classical music festival stars first-rate performers and ensembles from around the world. Concerts are given in some of the city's finest interiors, and also in outdoor locations like the Grosser Garten, the grounds of Pillnitz Palace on the banks of the Elbe and more distant venues, such as Meissen's cathedral.

⊙ Late May/early June

JUNE

HÄNDEL-FESTSPIELE

Direktion der Händel-Festspiele,
Händel-Haus-Halle, Grosse
Nikolaistrasse 5, 06108 Halle
Tel 0345 5009 0222
www.haendelfestspiele.halle.de

Halle's Händel Festival is a major event in the musical calendar, drawing not only fans but serious students of his music to the city where the great composer was born. Ten days of opera, oratorio, orchestral and chamber music by George Händel (1685–1759) and his contemporaries are complemented by seminars and conferences.

⊙ Ten days in June

SANSSOUCI MUSIC FESTIVAL

Wilhelm-Staab-Strasse 10/11, 14467 Potsdam
Tel 0331 288 8817

Midsummer concerts of classical music are held in some of the loveliest interiors of the historic Prussian city of Potsdam, including Schloss Sanssouci itself, the Chinese Teahouse and the baroque theatre of the Neues Schloss. There is an extensive line-up of other events, plus guided walks and exhibitions.

⊙ June

BERGSTADTFEST

Fremdenverkehrsamt der Stadt Freiberg, Burgstrasse 1, 09599 Freiberg
Tel 03731 273266
www.freiberg.de

The silver miners of Saxony are proud folk, with traditions going back to medieval times. Freiberg's main festival is the Miners' Festival, held on the last weekend in June. The miners wear their distinctive uniforms and carry banners, making a splendid spectacle as they parade through the city streets on the Sunday on their way to worship in Freiberg's lovely cathedral.

⊙ Last weekend in June

WHAT TO DO

MUNICH

Münchners use the Englischer Garten for relaxing or sunbathing

Munich has no shortage of shopping opportunities, particularly as downtown stores stay open until 7.30 or 8pm during the week and no longer close early on a Saturday. For designer labels, head straight to Maximilianstrasse, Theatinerstrasse and the Fünf Höfe (five covered courtyards between Maffeistrasse and Theatinerstrasse). For chain stores selling clothes, cosmetics, books and music, and for Munich's many department stores, go to the main pedestrianized shopping area on Neuhauserstrasse, Kaufingerstrasse and around the Marienplatz. Nearby Sendlingerstrasse has interesting boutiques selling clothes and items for the home.

Nightlife is not as lively as in Berlin, but there's still plenty to do—for starters, there are more than 50 theatres and 80 cinemas in the city. Check out the free monthly listings brochure *München im…* (*München im Februar, München im März* and so on), which is in German, or *In München*, also in German, which comes out every two weeks. For listings magazines in English, try the free newspaper *New in the City Today*, or the monthly magazine *Munich Found* (€3), which also has restaurant reviews and articles. You can buy theatre and concert tickets from box offices or from München Ticket (tel 089 5481 8181; www.muenchenticket. de), which has a desk in the tourist information office in Marienplatz.

If you're feeling active, head for the Olympiapark, built for the 1972 Olympic games. Here

you can swim, ice-skate or use the gym, as well as walk, jog, climb up the Olympic Tower for fantastic views, or tour the football stadium. Munich's open spaces are particularly good for restless children (and their parents!), and the city has many beautiful (and free) places to walk, jog or power walk; the Englischer Garten is the most popular place locals go to stretch their legs. Southwest of the Hauptbahnhof is the open green area of the Theresienwiese, where the *Oktoberfest* is held in late September. A little farther from the downtown area are the Olympiapark and Schloss Nymphenburg—surprisingly, you are allowed to jog through the beautiful landscaped gardens of the latter.

Of course, this being Munich, you're never far from a beer garden, where it's very easy to while away an afternoon.

KEY TO SYMBOLS	
🌐	**Shopping**
🎭	**Entertainment**
🎵	**Nightlife**
⚽	**Sports**
✪	**Activities**
♡	**Health and Beauty**
✪	**For Children**

🌐 SHOPPING

BOOKS

HUGENDUBEL
Marienplatz 22, 80331 München
(Altstadt)
Tel 01801 484484
www.hugendubel.de
There are several other branches of this large bookstore chain in the city—in Theatinerstrasse, Salvatorplatz and Karlsplatz. It sells DVDs, books (including fiction, cookery, travel guides and dictionaries), and magazines in English and French as well as German.
🕐 Mon–Sat 9–8 🚇 Marienplatz

WORDS'WORTH
Schellingstrasse 21a, 80799 München (Schwabing)
Tel 089 280 9141
www.wordsworth.de
There's a large selection of English-language literature, audio-books, videos, DVDs and postcards at this Schwabing store. As well as Pooh Corner for children, there's also a National Trust shop.
🕐 Mon–Sat 10–7 🚇 Universität

FASHION AND LINGERIE
7 HIMMEL
Hans-Sach-Strasse 17, 80469 München (Isarvorstadt)
Tel 089 267053
www.siebterhimmel.com
Siebter Himmel (Seventh Heaven) is a women's clothing store with bright, funky, individual clothes at reasonable prices. Across the street is Schuhhimmel (Shoe Heaven).
🕐 Mon–Fri 11–7, Sat 10–6
🚇 Sendlinger Tor

FOOD AND DRINK
DALLMAYR
Dienerstrasse 14–15, 80331 München (Altstadt)
Tel 089 213 5130
www.dallmayr.de
This traditional high-quality Munich delicatessen is rather like Harrods' food halls in London. Separate counters sell such delicacies as beautifully decorated cakes, cold meats and sausages, chocolate, tea leaves, coffee beans and fruit. There is also a cigar shop and a small champagne bar.
🕐 Mon–Fri 9–6, Sat 9–4
🚇 Marienplatz 🚋 Marienplatz

GIFTS AND SOUVENIRS
ALLES AUS HOLZ
Viktualienmarkt 15, 80331 München (Altstadt)
Tel 089 268248
Everything in this store is made out of wood. Items that might fit in your suitcase include chess sets, toys, pens, large bowls and salad servers.
🕐 Mon–Sat 10–7 🚇 Marienplatz
🚋 Marienplatz

MAX KRUG
Neuhauserstrasse 2, 80331 München (Altstadt)
Tel 089 224501
www.max-krug.com
Lined from floor to ceiling with beer steins, musical boxes, toys, Christmas decorations and wooden cuckoo clocks, handmade in Bavaria's Black Forest, this is the shop for you if you're looking for a cute Bavarian gift. Buying larger items is made easier as they accept credit cards, there's tax-free shopping for non-EU visitors and they can send purchases overseas for you.
🕐 Mon–Sat 9.30–8 🚇 Karlsplatz Stachus, Marienplatz 🚋 Karlsplatz Stachus, Marienplatz

The Dallmayr Delicatessen, purveyors of fine food since 1880

HOME FURNISHINGS
KARE CITYHAUS
Sendlingerstrasse 37, 80331 München (Altstadt)
Tel 089 230 8735
Spread over three floors, this store sells funky accessories and items for every room, including cushions, blankets, Italian Alessi kitchen implements, psychedelic ashtrays and even business-card holders. When you're in need of sustenance, go downstairs to the Yambai Thai Garden, which serves delicious dishes such as coconut curry and chicken or vegetable chop suey.
🕐 Mon–Sat 10–8 🚇 Sendlinger Tor

MARKETS
VIKTUALIENMARKT
See page 202

SHOPPING MALLS AND DEPARTMENT STORES
GALERIA KAUFHOF
Marienplatz, 80331 München (Altstadt)
Tel 089 231851
www.galeria-kaufhof.de
Kaufhof is a well-known Munich department store (with branches in Marienplatz, Karlsplatz and Rotkreutzplatz), and is not as expensive as the more classy Ludwig Beck and Loden Frey. It has several floors with menswear, womenswear, a perfumery, books, stationery and food. As with Kaufhof's rival department store Karstadt, head to the basement for the best bargains.
🕐 Mon–Sat 9–8 🚇 Marienplatz
🚋 Marienplatz

KARSTADT
Neuhauserstrasse 18, 80331 München (Altstadt)
Tel 089 290230
www.karstadt.de
This huge department store, housed in more than one building on Neuhauserstrasse, sells a range of different items: Karstadt Sportshaus Oberpollinger stocks sports clothing and equipment; Oberpollinger am Dom sells electrical appliances, things for the home, books and DVDs; and Karstadt am Karlstor has clothes, perfume and beauty products.
🕐 Mon–Sat 9–8 🚇 Karlsplatz
🚋 Karlsplatz

LODEN FREY
Maffeistrasse 7, 80331 München (Altstadt)
Tel 089 210390
www.loden-frey.de
The first things you will notice about this extremely elegant department store is the door handles, one in the shape of a woman wearing the traditional dirndl skirt and the other a Bavarian man in lederhosen. It is more classy than Kaufhof

but not as cutting edge as its department store rival Ludwig Beck. Expect to find designer-clad women shopping for Armani, Dolce&Gabbana, Escada, Burberry, Valentino and Ralph Lauren.
🕐 Mon–Wed 10–7, Thu–Fri 10–8, Sat 10–7 🚇 Marienplatz

LUDWIG BECK
Marienplatz 11, 80331 München (Altstadt)
Tel 089 236910
www.ludwig-beck.de
A Munich store of choice, with several floors of clothes, lingerie, expensive cosmetic brands, handbags and accessories. Don't miss the music department on the top floor, which is loved by Munich's classical music fans; in the relaxed atmosphere here you can listen before you buy on one of the many sets of headphones. There are also several cafés in Ludwig Beck, so you could easily find yourself spending several hours here.
🕐 Mon–Sat 10–8 🚇 Marienplatz
🚉 Marienplatz

SPORTS
SPORT-SCHECK
Sendlingerstrasse 6, 80331 München (Altstadt)
Tel 089 21660
www.sportscheck.com
Here you will find six floors of clothing and equipment, as well as anything else you could ever possibly need for just about any sport. You can buy gear for surfing, tennis, golf, running or the gym, and fit yourself out for a skiing or snowboarding weekend in the Alps. The store also organizes day trips to the snow for winter sports.
🕐 Mon–Sat 10–8 🚇 Marienplatz
🚉 Marienplatz

SUPERMARKETS
BASIC
Westenriederstrasse 35, 80331 München (Altstadt)
Tel 089 242 0890
www.basic-ag.de

If you prefer eating organic food then you'll love this supermarket-style shop, which is packed with organic fruit and vegetables, pasta, beer, wine, fruit juices, bread and even doughnuts (*krapfen*). Upstairs, you can buy unbleached cotton clothes for children, handbags, natural cosmetics, and face and body products. There's also a vegetarian restaurant, a health and beauty treatment clinic (▷ 278) and a snack and juice bar.
🕐 Mon–Fri 9–8, Sat 8.30–6 🚉 Isartor

Dressing up to shop on Munich's Maximilianstrasse

🎭 ENTERTAINMENT
CINEMA
CINEMA
Nymphenburgerstrasse 31, 80335 München (Neuhausen)
Tel 089 555255
www.cinema-muenchen.com
The appropriately named Cinema, which shows only original-language films, is the meeting place for Munich's English-speaking residents and is where Münchners come to improve their English. There is only one screen, but there are plenty of films in English. Be sure to arrive early (or book by phone) for Sunday evening screenings and also on 'Cinema Days' (Monday and

Tuesday), when movies starting before 5.30pm are €4 and after 5.30pm €5. Another bonus is that you can take your drinks into the cinema with you.
🕐 Box office noon–11pm 💷 €4–9
🚇 Stigmaierplatz

MATHÄSER
Bayerstrasse 5, 80335 München (Hauptbahnhof)
Tel 089 515651
www.mathaeser.de
Munich's latest cinema complex is near the main train station (Hauptbahnhof). It has 14 screens, one or two of which usually show the latest Hollywood blockbusters in English.
🕐 Box office 10.30am–10.50pm
💷 €7–9 🚇 Karlsplatz Stachus
🚉 Karlsplatz Stachus

CLASSICAL MUSIC, DANCE AND OPERA
GASTEIG
Rosenheimerstrasse 5, 81667 München (Haidhausen)
Tel 089 5481 8181
www.gasteig.de
www.muenchnerphilharmoniker.de
The huge Gasteig complex is the home of the Munich Philharmonic Orchestra and it also plays host to visiting orchestras such as the English Chamber Orchestra and the London Philharmonic Orchestra. Many other different kinds of performances are also held here, from the Chinese State Circus to Frank Sinatra tributes, *The Phantom of the Opera* and jazz.
🕐 Box office: Mon–Fri 9–9, Sat 9–4, Sun 10–4 💷 Varies 🚊 Tram 18 to Am Gasteig; tram 15, 25 to Rosenheimerplatz
🚉 Rosenheimerplatz

NATIONALTHEATER
Max-Joseph-Platz 1, 80539 München (Altstadt)
Tel 089 2185 1920
www.staatstheater.bayern.de
www.staatsoper.de
The Nationaltheater, in a building reminiscent of a Greek

temple in Max-Joseph-Platz, is home to the Bavarian State Opera and stages performances of Verdi, Wagner and Strauss during the opera season. You can watch a performance or join a tour, which takes in the foyer, the plush auditorium with its large chandelier and the machinery, essential for today's high-tech productions.

🕐 Box office: Mon–Fri 10–6, Sat 10–1. Tours: 2pm 💶 €6–240
🚇 Marienplatz, Odeonsplatz
🚌 Bus 52 to Marienplatz; bus 53 to Odeonsplatz; tram 19 to Nationaltheater
🚊 Marienplatz

CONTEMPORARY LIVE MUSIC

OLYMPIAHALLE

Olympiapark, Spiridon-Louis-Ring 21, 80809 München (Olympiapark)
Tel 089 30670
www.olympiapark-muenchen.de
This huge venue at the Olympiapark, north of the downtown area, stages concerts by big names such as Ozzy Osbourne, Pink and Phil Collins, as well as performances like *Lord of the Dance*. For tickets, contact Olympiapark's ticket service kiosk (opposite the ice rink).

🕐 7pm–11pm 💶 Varies (tickets from München Ticket, Tel 089 954 81 81 81)
🚇 Olympiapark

THEATRE

DEUTSCHES THEATER

Schwanthalerstrasse 13, 80336 München (Hauptbahnhof)
Tel 089 5523 4444
www.deutsches-theater.de
The Deutsches Theater hosts ballet performances, musicals and revues, and during *Fasching* (Carnival; ▷ 279) there are many fancy-dress balls and events held here.

🕐 Box office Mon–Fri noon–6, Sat 10.30am–1.30pm 💶 €19–54
🚇 Karlsplatz 🚊 Karlsplatz

MÜNCHNER KAMMERSPIELE

Schauspielhaus: Maximilianstrasse 26–28, 80539 München. Neues Haus: Falckenbergstrasse 1, 80539 München. Werkraum: Hildegardstrasse 1, 80539

München
Tel 089 2339 6600
www.muenchner-kammerspiele.de
This theatre company is housed in three locations in Munich. It stages high-quality productions, including contemporary plays and updated interpretations of Shakespeare.

🕐 Box office Mon–Fri 10–6, Sat 10–1
💶 €7.60–39.40 🚊 Tram 19 to Maximilianstrasse 🚇 🚊

🎵 NIGHTLIFE

BARS

BAR CENTRALE

Ledererstrasse 10, 80331 (Altstadt)
Tel 089 223762
www.bar-centrale.com
Centrale is a small, intimate

The classical façade of the Nationaltheater

Italian bar, great for a late-night coffee or grappa. The room at the back is full of conversation and gets very smoky.

🕐 Mon–Sat 8am–1am, Sun 11am–1am 🚊 Isartor

COCCODRILLO

Hohenzollernstrasse 11, 80801 München (Schwabing)
Tel 089 336639
This bar is in the atmospheric cellar of Caffè Florian in the university area of Schwabing, and has live music on Tuesdays and Thursdays. Happy hour is 8pm–9pm every evening.

🕐 Sun–Thu 8pm–1am, Fri–Sat 8pm–3am. Live music: Tue and Thu

from 8pm (from 9pm Sep–May)
🚇 Giselastrasse, Münchner Freiheit
🚊 Tram 12, 27 to Kurfürstenplatz; bus 33

DEUTSCHE EICHE

Reichenbachstrasse 13, 80469 München (Glockenbach)
Tel 089 231 1660
www.deutsche-eiche.de
This hotel is home to Munich's oldest gay bar, where Freddie Mercury used to have a beer when he was in Munich.

🕐 Daily 7.30am–1am 🚊 Tram 17, 18 to Reichenbachstrasse

NEKTAR

Stubenvollstrasse 1, München (Haidhausen)
Tel 089 4591 1311
www.nektar.de
An evening in Nektar is a unique experience, starting with the slippers you are given to wear to your dinner, which you eat horizontally, lying down on cushions. Expect films, cabaret and live music.

🕐 Sun–Thu 7pm–2am, Fri–Sat 7pm–3am 🚊 Tram 15, 25 to Rosenheimerplatz
🚊 Rosenheimerplatz

SCHUMANN'S

Ludwigstrasse 2, 80331 München (Altstadt)
Tel 089 229060
www.schumanns.de
This is a good-looking bar frequented by good-looking people drinking cocktails served by staff in old-fashioned white coats. Dress up.

🕐 Mon–Fri 5pm–3am, Sun 6pm–3am. Closed Sat 🚇 Odeonsplatz

VER O PESO

Rosenheimerstrasse 14, München (Haidhausen)
Tel 089 4449 9799
The Brazilian owner of Ver o Paso has created a small bar with classy cocktails, a lively atmosphere and tasty food.

🕐 Daily 5.30pm–2am 🚊 Tram 18 to Am Gasteig; tram 15, 25 to Rosenheimerplatz
🚊 Rosenheimerplatz

BEER GARDENS

CHINESISCHER TURM
Englischer Garten, 80538 München (Schwabing)
www.chinaturm.de
You can't beat the setting of this beer garden at the Chinese Tower in the Englischer Garten, where there are plenty of people and there's always a good atmosphere, even in winter. It can seat up to 7,000 people at its trestle tables, and there are food stalls and children's playparks.
Daily 10am–midnight Bus 54, 154

HIRSCHGARTEN
Hirschgartenallee 1, 80639 München (Nymphenburg)
Tel 089 172591
The 200-year-old Hirschgarten is Munich's largest beer garden, seating up to 8,500. It's near Schloss Nymphenburg outside the downtown area, and is in a huge park with a deer enclosure, so the children should be happy too.
Daily 9am–11.30pm Tram 17; bus 41, 68, 83

CLUBS

ATOMIC CAFÉ
Neuturmstrasse 5, 80331 München (Altstadt)
Tel 089 228 3052
www.atomic.de
A strict door policy ensures that only the beautiful people get into this club, so it's a good idea to dress up. It is known for playing plenty of Britpop, as well as reggae, punk, soul and hip-hop.
Tue–Thu, Sun 10pm–3am, Fri–Sat 10pm–4am €2 before 11.30pm
Tram 19 to Kammerspiele

MUFFATHALLE
Zellstrasse 4, 81667 München (Haidhausen)
Tel 089 4587 5010
www.muffathalle.de
This cultural venue on the other side of the Isar hosts a constantly changing line-up of gigs. There are also club nights on Thursdays, Fridays and Saturdays, with DJs playing reggae, rare groove, funk, Latin, drum and bass, and hip-hop. See the website for what's on. Muffathalle also has a café and a beer garden selling organic beer.
Beer garden: Mon–Fri 4pm–1am, Sat–Sun 11am–1am. Club nights: Thu 10pm–4am, Fri–Sat 11pm–5am
€7–25 Tram 18 to Gasteig

P1
Prinzregentenstrasse 1, 80538 München (Lehel)
Tel 089 211 1140
www.p1-club.de
If you get past the doormen to this club in the Haus der Kunst,

Chinesischer Turm, the beer garden in the Englischer Garten

you'll find yourself in the company of soccer players and their entourages.
Daily 9.30pm–5am Tram 17, bus 53 to Nationalmuseum/Haus der Kunst

🏃 ⭐ SPORTS AND ACTIVITIES

CITY TOURS

MIKE'S BIKE TOURS
Hochrukenstrasse, 80331 Munich
Tel 089 2554 3987
www.mikesbiketours.com
You can tour the city by bicycle with a native English-speaking guide. The ride, which lasts four hours, is almost entirely on bicycle-only paths and includes a stop at the beer garden in the Englischer Garten. There are bicycles available for children, as well as trailers and child seats. Meet at the Altes Rathaus in Marienplatz.
Mar–mid-Apr, Sep–mid-Nov 12.30; mid-Apr–end May, Aug 11.30 and 4; Jun–end Jul 10.30, 11.30, 3, 4, plus 6-hour tour departing at 12.30 with two breaks at Olympiapark and Schloss Nymphenburg Adult €22, child (6–14) €11, under 6 free

MÜNCHENER STADT RUNDFAHRTEN
Arnulfstrasse 8, 80331 Munich (Hauptbahnhof)
Tel 089 5502 8995
www.muenchenerstadtrundfahrten.de
On this open-top double-decker bus tour, you'll see the main sights of Munich in just under an hour. The route takes in Königsplatz, Maximilianstrasse, the Viktualienmarkt, Deutsches Museum, Hofbräuhaus and Residenz, among other sights, and a guide gives live commentary in German and English. You board the bus at the Panorama bus stop outside Hertie department store, opposite the Hauptbahnhof. Buses are air-conditioned and the top deck is covered in winter. Buy your ticket at the tourist information office in Marienplatz or the Hauptbahnhof.
Daily 10, 11, noon, 1, 2, 2.30, 3, 4; extra tours Apr–end Oct 11.30, 5
Adult €11, child (4–14) €6, under 4 free Marienplatz

MUNICH WALKING TOURS
Hochrukenstrasse, 80331 Munich
Tel 089 2554 3987
www.mikesbiketours.com
Take a three-hour walking tour of the city with a native English-speaking guide, learning about Munich's history from the Middle Ages to the 20th century. For tours in the morning, meet outside the tourist information office at the Hauptbahnhof, and for afternoon tours meet outside the Altes Rathaus in Marienplatz.

Mid-Apr to mid-May, mid-Aug to end Oct daily 10.45am; mid-May to mid-Aug daily 10.15, 4.45 👣 Adult €9, child free 🚇 Hauptbahnhof, Marienplatz

RIKSCHA-MOBIL

Postfach 10126, München (Marienplatz)
Tel 077 8090 1020
www.rikscha-mobil.de
If walking or cycling seem a bit strenuous, hop into the back of a rickshaw, and create your own itinerary. Tours start at the Fish Fountain in Marienplatz.
Apr–Nov 👣 30-minute tour from €19; 45-minute tour from €29; 60-minute tour from €37 🚇 Marienplatz

ICE SKATING
EISSPORTZENTRUM

Olympiapark, Spiridon-Louis-Ring 21, 80809 München (Olympiapark)
Tel 089 3067 2150
www.olympiapark-muenchen.de
Skate in the tracks of Olympic skaters at the Olympiapark. Check before you set off that there isn't a training session or class in progress when you intend to go.
Daily 9.30–noon, 1–4, 7–10 👣 Adult €3, child (6–15) €2.50, under 6 free, family €8 🚇 Olympiazentrum

SOCCER
OLYMPIASTADION

Olympiapark, Spiridon-Louis-Ring 21, 80809 München (Olympiapark)
Tel 089 699310 (FC Bayern München), 0180 560 1860 (TSV)
www.fcbayern.t-online.de
www.tsv1860.de
Watch one of Munich's two soccer teams (Bayern München and TSV 1860) play at the Olympiastadion, north of downtown Munich.
Aug–May 👣 €10–40 🚇 Olympiazentrum

SWIMMING

Olympia-Schwimmhalle
Olympiapark, Spiridon-Louis-Ring 21, 80809 München (Olympiapark)
Tel 089 3067 2290
www.olympiapark-muenchen.de
If you're visiting the Olympiapark, you should bring your swimming costume and

towel, as you may be tempted by the Olympic-size pool and the Sauna-Paradies. The sauna area has four saunas, a steam bath and a plunge pool.
Pool: daily 7am–11pm. Sauna: Mon 10am–11pm, Tue–Sun 8am–11pm (women only on Tue). Ticket office: closes at 10pm 👣 Pool: adult €3, child (6–16) €2.50, under 6 free, family €8. Sauna plus swim: adult €11, child (6–16) €8 🚇 Olympiazentrum

♥ HEALTH AND BEAUTY
BEAUTY SPAS
BEAUTY AND NATURE

Westenriederstrasse 35, 80331 München (Altstadt)
Tel 089 2423 1234
www.beautyandnature.de

Seeing the Englischer Garten on two wheels

This spa is on the first floor of the organic supermarket Basic (▷ 275), and uses only natural products. Choose from aromatherapy massage, Tibetan massage or foot massage, as well as the usual beauty treatments.
Mon–Fri 9–8, Sat 8.30–4 👣 60-minute aromatherapy massage €55; manicure €23; pedicure €25 🚉 Isartor

SANTA MARGARITA SCHÖNHEITSSALON

Reichenbachstrasse 24, 80469 München (Glockenbach)
Tel 089 201 0961
www.santa-margarita.de
This salon uses Aveda and Vagheggi products for facials

and different types of massage, including the Aveda mood massage with essential oils.
Mon by appointment only, Tue–Fri 9–7, Sat 10–2 👣 1-hour body massage €55; 1-hour Aveda mood massage €60; pedicure €55 🚇 Fraunhoferstrasse

😊 FOR CHILDREN
FILM STUDIOS
BAVARIA FILMSTADT

Bavariafilmplatz 7, 82031 München (Geiselgasteig)
Tel 089 6499 2304
www.filmstadt.de
The Bavaria Filmstadt is designed for children, with a stunt show and motion cinema, where your seat moves with the action in the film.
Mar–end Oct daily 9–4; Nov–end Feb daily 10–3. Guided tours in English: Mar–end Nov daily 1pm. 3D cinema: Mar–end Oct daily 9–5; Nov–end Feb daily 9–4 👣 90-minute tour: adult €10, child (4–14) €7, family €29.50. Stunt show: €7. 3D cinema: €4. Combined ticket (including tour, stunt show and 3D cinema): adult €17, child €14, family €57 🚉 Tram 25 to Bavariafilmplatz 🚇

MUSEUMS
DEUTSCHES MUSEUM
▷ 186–191

PARKS
ENGLISCHER GARTEN
▷ 192.

PUPPET THEATRES
MARIONETTENTHEATER

Blumenstrasse 32, 80331 München (Sendlinger Tor)
Tel 089 265712
www.muenchner-marionettentheater.de
There are puppet shows and storytelling held here all year round.
Wed, Sat, Sun; show times 3pm, 8pm 👣 Afternoon shows: adult €8, child €6. Evening shows: adult €15, child €10 🚇 Sendlinger Tor

ZOOS
TIERPARK HELLABRUNN
See page 185.

WHAT TO DO

FESTIVALS AND EVENTS

JANUARY/FEBRUARY

FASCHING
www.muenchen-tourist.de
Many balls are held across the city during *Fasching* (Carnival). You'll see people dressed in their finery for the classic evening balls, and entire families dressed in fancy dress for less formal events. On the third Sunday in February (*Fasching Sonntag*), there is music and dancing in the heart of the city.
Second week in January–end of February

APRIL/MAY

AUER DULT
Mariahilfplatz, München (Au)
www.muenchen-tourist.de
The *Dult* is a street market and funfair held three times a year. It has been running since the Middle Ages and takes place in the Mariahilfplatz, with its distinctive red-brick church, in the district of Au (meaning 'meadow') on the other side of the Isar. There's an antiques market, a large funfair with a Ferris wheel and bumper cars and traditional Bavarian food and beer stalls. Also late July to early August and the third week in October.
Late April–beginning of May
Tram 27; bus 52, 56

JUNE/JULY

MÜNCHNER FILMFEST
www.filmfest-muenchen.de
Munich is a major focus of film-making and home to numerous film production companies. During the Munich Film Festival, international movies—particularly German and European productions—are premièred in some of the city's 84 cinemas.
Late June–early July

AUGUST

SOMMERFEST IM OLYMPIA-PARK
Olympiapark, Spiridon-Louis-Ring 21, 80809 München (Olympiapark)
Tel 089 3067 2414, 0180 530 6730
www.olympiapark-muenchen.de
This family-friendly summer festival is held at Munich's sports ground, Olympiapark. During the day there are activities and attractions such as fishing competitions on the lake and beer stalls for the parents, then when the sun goes down there are fireworks displays and live bands.

Supporters of internationally known soccer team Bayern Munich

Two weeks in August
Olympiazentrum

SEPTEMBER/OCTOBER

OKTOBERFEST
Theresienwiese, 80336 München (Theresienwisese)
www.muenchen-tourist.de
Munich's legendary and the world's biggest beer festival, *Oktoberfest*, is held every year at the Theresienwiese, known to Münchners as the Wiesn. A festival for all ages, here you'll find the world's biggest funfair, with rides and an impressive Ferris wheel, and, of course, 14 vast beer tents serving up litres of beer

and hearty Bavarian food to the sound of brass oompah bands. You will need to make sure you book your accommodation months in advance.
Mid-September to beginning October
Theresienwiese

OCTOBER

DIE LANGE NACHT
Tel 089 3061 0041
www.die-lange-nacht.de
For one night only, more than 70 churches, museums and galleries stay open very late and organize concerts, guided tours and performances. To obtain information see the website, and to buy tickets contact München Ticket (tel 089 54 81 81 81; www.muenchenticket.de).
One night in mid-October

NOVEMBER/DECEMBER

CHRISTKINDLMARKT
Marienplatz, München (Altstadt)
www.muenchen-tourist.de
Dating back to the 14th century, Munich's Christmas market, held in the heart of the city, is legendary—visitors come from abroad especially to spend the weekend shopping in the city. There are more than 140 stalls, where you can buy Christmas tree decorations, crafts, toys made of wood, a Christmas post office and even figures from the Crib Market to make your own Nativity scene. There's also live music, Advent music at 5.30pm on the balcony of the town hall, and food stalls selling baked apples, *Glühwein* (hot spiced wine) and roasted almonds.
Last Friday of November–24 December
Marienplatz Marienplatz

SOUTHERN GERMANY

Snowboarders prepare to take on the Zugspitze

WHAT TO DO

Southern Germany has a variety of activities on offer that will make your visit to the region all the more enjoyable. You will find a wide choice of shops and markets in every city and town, an abundance of entertainment and nightlife and lots of opportunities to watch or participate in sports and activities. The area is famous for its festivals and events, with everything from rowdy beer festivals to serene ballet and operatic performances. Children are well catered for, and parents can enjoy relaxing in one of the numerous spas and specialist wellness clinics.

In the south, there's a varied choice of handicrafts. Department stores are in the larger cities, while regional crafts are available throughout the area. Of special interest are the cuckoo clocks of the Schwarzwald (Black Forest), quality Nürnberg (Nuremberg) toys, crystal glassware from the Bayerischer Wald (Bavarian Forest) and regional wines. Major stores open at 8.30 or 9am and can legally stay open until 8pm on weekdays, but not all do so. Some stores stay open until 8pm on Saturdays, but shops in general close on Sundays.

You can also watch or do almost any sport: there are many waymarked bicycle and walking routes, excellent winter sports facilities throughout the mountain and forest regions and water sports on lakes such as Bodensee (Lake Constance) and Chiemsee, as well as international events.

There are many spa towns and health resorts, such as the thermal baths in Baden-Baden and the mineral baths in Stuttgart, and many of the larger hotels have specialist beauty treatment facilities.

Children are well provided with sporting activities (especially winter sports), theatrical performances (including puppet theatre), concerts, zoos and theme parks. Europa-Park, Germany's largest family theme park, is between Baden-Baden and Freiburg.

There are festivals and events throughout the year. Highlights include the *Mozart Festival* in Würzburg (May), the *Richard-Wagner-Festspiele* in Bayreuth (July), wine festivals throughout the Rhineland area (August) and the *Cannstatter Volksfest* (Stuttgart Beer Festival, in September), as well as traditional Christmas markets (*Weihnachtsmärkte*) in the region's towns and villages.

KEY TO SYMBOLS	
🛍	Shopping
🎭	Entertainment
🍸	Nightlife
⚽	Sports
✪	Activities
♥	Health and Beauty
✷	For Children

BADEN-BADEN

🎭 FESTSPIELHAUS

Beim Alten Bahnhof 2, 76530 Baden-Baden
Tel 07221 301 3101
www.festspielhaus.de

In 1998, Baden-Baden's neo-classical train station was transformed into the second-largest opera house in Europe. The modern concert hall has 2,500 seats and acoustics that are considered among the best in the world.

🕐 Booking office: Mon–Fri 10–6, Sat–Sun and public holidays 10–2, and 2 hours before events 💶 Varies
🚌 Special bus transfers (check website) 🍴

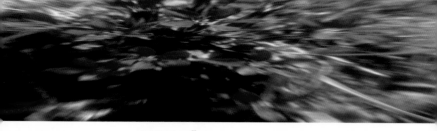

🏃 INTERNATIONALER CLUB
Lichtentaler Allee 8, 76530 Baden-Baden
Tel 07221 21120
www.baden-galopp.de
The village of Iffezheim is home to the track that hosts Baden-Baden's International Horse Races. The Spring Meeting (late May/early June), the Grand Festival Week (late August/early September) and the Sales and Racing Festival (late October) attract the rich and famous, and even if you don't gamble, these meetings are spectacular events.
🕐 Meetings start 12.30 or 1.30
💶 €6–200

💧 CARACALLA THERME
Romerplatz 1, 76530 Baden-Baden
Tel 07221 275940
Baden-Baden is renowned for its thermal springs, Europe's hottest at 69°C (156°F). The modern Caracalla Therme has a choice of relaxing and health-promoting treatment stations, including whirlpools and indoor and outdoor pools, all further enhanced with underwater jets and waterfalls. There is also a spacious, well-lit environment that has seven different types of sauna and an aromatic steam bath.
🕐 Daily 8am–10pm, last admission 8.30pm 💶 €12 (2 hours), €14 (3 hours), €16 (4 hours) 🔲 🏢

BERCHTESGADEN

💧 WATZMANN THERME
Bergwerkstrasse 54, 83471 Berchtesgaden
Tel 08652 94640
www.watzmann-therme.de
This modern swimming complex is an oasis of water fun, as well as a spa whose locally produced brine has curative and health-giving properties. Here, you will find numerous pools, including indoor and outdoor pools enriched with brine from the nearby salt mines, plus a sports pool and giant water slide.
🕐 Daily 10–10 💶 €8 (2 hours), €10.50 (4 hours), €15 (day)

DINKELSBÜHL

⊕ DINKELSBÜHLER KERAMIK
Segringer Strasse 53–55, 91550 Dinkelsbühl
Tel 09851 7596
www.dinkelsbuehler-keramik.de
Dinkelsbühl is noted for its arts and crafts (ceramics), souvenirs and trendy clothes, nearly all of which can be found in the little shops in the heart of the town. Join the arts and crafts tour, which will take you to some of Dinkelsbühl's retail outlets.
🕐 10–1, 2–6 🔲 🏢

🎵 SUNDAY CONCERTS
Town Park, 91550 Dinkelsbühl
A free concert is held in the

Horse racing at Iffezheim, near Baden-Baden

town park music pavilion every Sunday from May to September at 11.15am. This is a wonderful place to sit and relax, enjoying a varied play list of music that includes traditional, jazz and folk.
🕐 May–end Sep Sun 11.15am 💶 Free

FRAUENAU

⊕ GLASSHÜTTE EISCH
Am Steg 7, 94258 Frauenau
Tel 09926 1890
www.eisch.de
Frauenau is just one of numerous towns and villages along the famous Glasstrasse where you can stop and buy glass from the many outlets or watch the craftsmen at work.

At the Glasshütte Eisch you can purchase products direct from the factory outlet. The items sold are current products, discontinued lines and remainders, most with minor flaws, which means they come at reduced prices.
🕐 Shop: Mon–Fri 9–6, Sat 9–4, Sun and hols 10–4 🔲 Guided tours: Mon–Thu 9–11.30, 1–2.45, Fri–Sat 9–11.45

FREIBURG

🎭 THEATER FREIBURG
Bertoldstrasse 46, 79098 Freiburg
Tel 0761 201 2853 (information and ticket office)
www.theaterfreiburg.de
Freiburg's largest theatre has four performance areas, where you can see opera, ballet, musicals and plays. Freiburg Philharmonic Orchestra concerts take place in the Konzerthaus. An impressive range of productions is held throughout the year, and the theatre stages around 25 premières each season.
🕐 Information and ticket office: Tue–Fri 10–6, Sat 10–1 💶 Varies 🔲

🎵 JAZZHAUS
Schnewlinstrasse 1, 79098 Freiburg
Tel 0761 34973
www.jazzhaus.de
This historic cellar attracts both locals and visitors. The traditional jazz nights are very popular, but there's also a varied line-up of other themed fun nights, such as a salsa night, reggae summer party, funky dance night and 1960s and '70s nights.
🕐 Fri–Sat 9pm–2am (doors open at 7pm on concert nights) 💶 €12–15

⚡ EUROPA-PARK
Europa-Park-Strasse 2, 77977 Rust
Tel 01805 776688; ticket line 01805 788997
www.europapark.de
With more than 100 attractions and shows set in 65ha (160 acres) of parkland, this is Germany's largest family theme park. You can visit 11 beautifully decorated

WHAT TO DO

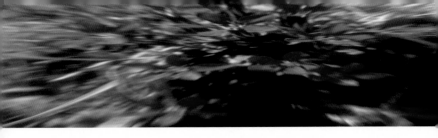

European themed areas in one day, seeing the landmarks of each nation, meeting people dressed in traditional costume and discovering interesting architecture and you can also ride on the Silver Star, Europe's biggest roller-coaster. The park gets very busy at weekends and during holiday periods.

 Apr–end Oct, Dec daily 9–6 (extended hours during peak season) 💶 Adult €26, child (4–11) €23, under 4 free

GARMISCH-PARTENKIRCHEN

❄ WINTER SPORTS

Garmisch-Partenkirchen-Tourism, Richard-Strauss-Platz 1a, 82467 Garmisch-Partenkirchen
Tel 08821 180700
www.garmisch-partenkirchen.de
This is a paradise for winter sports enthusiasts, as there's something here to suit all levels of experience and preference. The skiing season begins in November with the Viva Winter Fun-Festival, a weekend of fun and action. There are 110km (68 miles) of ski trails for cross-country skiers, including the floodlit Loipe at Kainzebad, while the glacier skiing region atop the Zugspitze is ideal for alpine skiers, snowboarders and freestylers. A special delight for the family is sledging down the 3.9km (2.4-mile) run on Hausberg mountain; you can also sledge by night on the illuminated track on Wednesday and Friday 5–8pm.
💶 Ski-pass from €104; sledge-trip details tel 08821 94 29 20

GÜNZBURG

🎢 LEGOLAND

Legoland Allee, 89312 Günzburg
Tel 08221 700700
www.legoland.de
Hugely popular with both children and adults, Germany's Legoland is at Günzburg, 50km (31 miles) west of Augsburg. There are plenty of models to marvel at—including one of Neuschwanstein, made from 300,000 bricks—plus the largest Lego shop in the world and many other attractions.
🕐 Apr–end Nov 10–6 💶 Adult €24, child (3–11) €19, under 3 free
🚌 Günzburg (shuttle service) 🍴 🛒

HEIDELBERG

🎵 SCHWIMMBAD MUSIK CLUB

Tiergartenstrasse 13, 69121 Heidelberg
Tel 06221 470201
www.schwimmbad-musik-club.de
This excellent venue caters for all musical styles and is one of the most popular clubs in town. It has an interesting range of themed nights, including Gothic rock nights, concert nights and fun music nights in the main disco.

There's something for everyone at Karlsruhe's open-air market

🕐 Wed–Thu 10pm–3am, Fri, Sat 10pm–4am 💶 €1.50–12 🛒

🎭 HEIDELBERGER MÄRCHENPARADIES

Königstuhl 5a, 69117 Heidelberg
Tel 06221 23416
www.maerchenparadies.de
Translating it as 'Heidelberg Fairy-tale Paradise', this recreational park provides lots of entertainment for both adults and children. Set amid woodlands, it has fairy-tale themes that are both well presented and fun to explore. There's also a large play area for children, a horseback-riding school, a park railway and a café.

🕐 Mar–end Jun, Sep–end Nov Mon–Fri 10–6, Sat, Sun 10–7; Jul, Aug daily 10–7. Closed Dec–end Feb 💶 Adult €3, child (2–12) €2 🚠 Bergbahn ('mountain train') from Heidelberg 🛒

KARLSRUHE

🛍 POSTGALERIE

Europaplatz, 76133 Karlsruhe
Tel 0721 180 5860
www.postgalerie-karlsruhe.com
Karlsruhe's Postgalerie is a modern shopping mall in the pedestrian zone around Kaiserstrasse, an area with a varied choice of shops. On Mondays, Wednesdays and Fridays, a market is held on Stephanplatz behind the mall.
🕐 Mon–Fri 10–8, Sat 10–6

🎬 FILMPALAST-AM-ZKM

Brauerstrasse 40, 76137 Karlsruhe
Tel 0721 205 9200
www.filmpalast-am-zkm.de
This is the largest and most modern cinema multiplex in the city. There's lots of choice here because this complex has ten air-conditioned and highly modern theatres and numerous restaurants.
🕐 Box office: daily 11am–midnight 💶 Adult €4–8.70, child under 12 €3.50–4.80. Tram 6 🍴

🐾 ZOOLOGISCHER GARTEN KARLSRUHE UND STADTGARTEN

Ettlinger Strasse 6, 76137 Karlsruhe
Tel 0721 133 6801
www.karlsruhe.de/zoo
Karlsruhe Zoo is home to more than 1,000 animals of 150 species from all over the world, from elephants to prairie dogs and from chimpanzees to penguins. The beautiful Municipal Gardens have 800 large trees from a wide diversity of countries, as well as roses, tulips and summer flowers, shrubs and climbing plants. You can spend a pleasant day enjoying the zoo, gardens, park, children's zoo, railway and playground, as well as the cable-guided pleasure boat ride that connects the large Schwanensee (Swan Lake) with the

WHAT TO DO

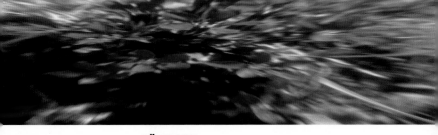

Stadtgartensee (Municipal Garden Lake). There are many events held every year on the lakeside stage in the park.

🕐 May–end Sep daily 8–6; Feb–end Apr, Oct daily 9–5; Nov–end Jan daily 9–4 💶 Adult €4, child (6–15) €2, under 6 free 🍴 🚻 ♿

KONSTANZ

🏛 WEINMARKT AN DER LAUBE

Untere Laube 17, 78462 Konstanz
Tel 07531 22131
www.weinmarkt-konstanz.de

This wine market is a joy to visit. It has a large selection of local and international wines to taste and buy, plus champagnes and spirits, and an assortment of glassware, baskets and accessories.

🕐 Tue–Fri 9–6.30, Sat 9–1.30

💜 BODENSEE-THERME

Wilheim-von-Scholz-Weg 2, 78464 Konstanz
Tel 07531 61163

This leisure and recreation area has a thermal bath with a temperature of 33°C (91°F), swimming pools with slides, a shallow pool for children, a solarium, a restaurant and a children's playground.

🕐 Daily 9–9 💶 Adult €4.60, child €3 ♿5 🚻

🐟 SEA LIFE KONSTANZ

Hafenstrasse 9, 78462 Konstanz
Tel 07531 12827-0
www.sealife.de (English summary)

At Konstanz's Sea Life centre, enormous glazed aquariums trace the aquatic life of the Rhine from its source in the Gotthard massif to the North Sea. It's an amazing world, with around 3,000 freshwater and sea-water fish ranging from perch to sharks. In the same building is the interesting Bodensee Naturmuseum (Lake Constance Natural History Museum).

🕐 Jul–mid Sep daily 10–7; May, Jun, mid Sep to end Oct daily 10–6; Nov–end Apr Mon–Fri 10–5, Sat, Sun and hols 10–6 💶 Adult €10.50, child €7 🍴 ♿

NÜRNBERG

🛍 WMF-FACHGESCHÄFT

Karolinenstrasse 27, 90402 Nürnberg
Tel 0911 206860

This shop specializes in wonderful Meissen porcelain. It stocks a comprehensive range of tableware, figurines, gifts and souvenirs.

🕐 Mon–Sat 10–7

🎬 CINECITTA

Gewerbemuseumsplatz 3, 90403 Nürnberg
Tel 0911 206666 (box office)
www.cinecitta.de

Germany's largest multiplex cinema has 21 theatres that seat more than 5,000 people, three restaurants, cafés, bars

A beer stein makes a great souvenir of southern Germany

and a film shop. Next door is an IMAX cinema that can project onto a screen the height of a seven-floor building.

🕐 Daily 10am–midnight 💶 €5.90–8.40 🍴 🚻 ♿

🎷 JAZZ-STUDIO

Paniersplatz 27–29, 90403 Nürnberg
Tel 0911 935 0880 (tickets)
www. jazzstudio.de

The Jazz-Studio first opened in 1954 and over the years has hosted many young, talented artists as well as regional and international stars. All forms of jazz are played here, including blues, swing and soul.

🕐 Fri–Sat from 8.30pm (concerts begin at 9pm) 💶 €6.50–15 🚌 46, 47

🧸 SPIELZEUGMUSEUM

Karlstrasse 13–15, 90403 Nürnberg
Tel 0911 231 3164
www.spielzeugmuseum-nuernberg.de

Nuremberg has a long tradition of toy-making, from the *Dockenmacher* (doll-makers) of medieval times to the outstanding tin-figure manufacturers and tin-toy producers of the industrial age. Both adults and children will enjoy the comprehensive collection of historic toys (train sets and steam engines, dolls and dolls' houses and tin figures) displayed on four floors of the Toy Museum, hidden behind the Renaissance façade of a Nuremberg town house.

🕐 Tue–Fri 10–5, Sat, Sun 10–6 💶 Adult €5, child €2.50 🚌 Guided tours €3.50 🚇 U1, U11 🚌 36 🚻

OBERAMMERGAU

🎭 PASSIONSTHEATER

Oberammergau
Tel 08822 945 8833 (for guided tour); 08822 9231-0 (for info on 2010 Passion Play and other events)
www.oberammergau.de

Every year, opera performances are staged in the wonderful setting of Oberammergau's Passion Play Theatre. From May to October you can also take a guided tour of this amazing venue to see the costumes, dressing rooms and backstage areas. The Passion Play itself is held every 10 years; the next one will be performed in 2010. Tickets for this historical performance are very much in demand and will not go on sale until 2008.

🕐 Passion Play: next performance is in 2010 💶 Varies. See above for contact details

🎿 WINTER SPORTS

Oberammergau Tourismus, Eugen-Papst-Strasse 9a, 82487 Oberammergau
Tel 08822 92310
www.oberammergau.de

Oberammergau has good skiing facilities (nine ski-lifts) to suit all levels of experience.

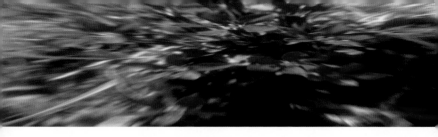

The spacious Ammer valley is ideal for cross-country skiing, while the Kolben is a great downhill area for the entire family. The descent from the saddle of the Kolben (1,280m/4200ft) is only suitable for more advanced skiers; beginners can stay on the lower slopes near the parking area.
🎿 Ski-lifts in winter 9–4.30 (every 30 mins) 🎫 Ski-pass €12 (until noon), €14 (afternoon)

RAVENSBURG

✪ RAVENSBURGER VERLAGSMUSEUM
Marktstrasse 26, 88212 Ravensburg
Tel 0751 82324
www.ravensburg.de/content/artikel_tourist/3322.htm
The Ravensburg company is renowned throughout the world for its games, puzzles and children's books, and here in the Ravensburg Games Museum you will discover everything about its history. The entrance is free, and you can see old books, puzzles and games that have been produced since the company started up in 1883, all interestingly laid out in the old Ravensburg building in the heart of the town.
🕐 Apr–end Sep Thu 2–6 (summer holidays Tue–Fri 2–6, Sat, Sun 11–2 🎫 Free

ROTHENBURG OB DER TAUBER

🏛 TEDDYS LOVE ROTHENBURG
Obere Schmiedgasse 1, 91541
Rothenburg ob der Tauber
Tel 09861 933444
www.teddys-rothenburg.de
This is no ordinary teddy bear shop, for the teddies here are exceptional, coming in all shapes and sizes and clothed in many forms of amazing dress. Both children and adults will admire the huge collection on display, particularly the snoring bear that actually moves as it breathes.
🕐 Mon–Fri 9am–10pm, Sat 9–9, Sun 9–7 (after Christmas to end Apr closed Sun, except Easter)

🏛 WEIHNACHTSDORF
Herrngasse 1, 91541 Rothenburg ob der Tauber
Tel 09861 4090
www.wohlfahrt.com (also in English)
Rothenburg is fortunate to have a selection of the wonderful Wolfahrt shops. The Weihnachtsdorf, Käthe Wohlfahrt's Christmas Village, is where the year-round sale of Christmas decorations started in 1977. Here, you will find an enormous selection of traditional German Christmas decorations and knick-knacks, including nutcrackers, incense burners, *Schwibbogen* (candle arches), music boxes, Christmas pyramids, nativity

The Staatsgalerie in Stuttgart has an interesting souvenir shop

sets, Christmas lights, festive decorations for windows and doors, and tree ornaments of glass, wood, pewter and straw.
🕐 Mon–Sat 9–6, Sun 10–6 (Jan–end Apr closed Sun)

✪ FIGURENTHEATER
Herrngasse 38 am Burgtor, 91541
Rothenburg ob der Tauber
Tel 09861 3333
www.figurentheater-rothenburg.de
This is a wonderful little theatre with an entertaining puppet show that is ideal for all ages. There are two performances each day in summer, so you have the choice of an afternoon show, or an evening performance.

🕐 May–end Aug, Dec 3pm, 8pm; Apr, end Sep–Nov 8pm 🎫 Adult €6, child €4 (3pm); adult €8, child €6 (8pm)

STUTTGART

🏛 BREUNINGER
Marktstrasse 1–3, 70173 Stuttgart
Tel 0711 2110
www.breuninger.de
Breuninger is a huge department store, set out over six floors. It is an impressive shopping experience, renowned for its excellent service and regarded as a fashion and lifestyle authority for shoppers with an interest in high-quality items. Here, you will find a large range of international and sometimes exclusive fashion brands. The restaurant has a varied menu and is an ideal place to relax.
🕐 Mon–Fri 10–8, Sat 9.30–8 🍴

✪ SI-ERLEBNIS-CENTRUM
Plieninger Strasse 100, 70567
Stuttgart
Tel 0711 222 8243
www.si-centrum.de
This unique entertainment complex has everything for all age groups and tastes. There are two luxurious theatres showing successful musical productions, six state-of-the art cinemas, a 6,000sq m (64,500sq ft) spa, a casino and two hotels. Also here are 19 attractively appointed themed restaurants; particularly popular is the Backstage restaurant, where visitors can dine among the backdrops of famous musicals. You can hear live music daily in The Dubliner and traditional music every Friday in the Hausbräuerei.
🕐 Contact/check website for details
🎫 Varies 🚇 U3, U5, U6 🚌 74, 75, 77, 809, 826, 827 🍴 💻 ☎

🎶 ZAPATA
Pragstrasse 120, 70376 Stuttgart
Tel 0711 956 1544
www.zapata.de
With four dance floors and a capacity for 1,600 people, this stylish disco is one of the largest in Stuttgart. The music

includes reggae, funk and soul, and there are also live gigs. Zapata also has a theatre and concert and exhibition rooms.
🕐 Fri, Sat 10pm–5am 💶 €5

🔱 MINERALBAD BERG
Am Schwanenplatz 9, 70190 Stuttgart
Tel 0711 923 6516
Very popular with locals, this bath complex has been owned by the same family for more than 140 years. It has a nostalgic atmosphere reminiscent of the 1950s, and you take baths in copper tubs that are decades old. There are indoor and outdoor mineral

swimming and therapeutic pools, a solarium and restaurant.
🕐 Mon–Fri 6–8, Sat 6–7, Sun 6–1
💶 Adult €6, child (6–17) €5.10 🚇 U1, U2, U14 🚌 56, 402 🚋 S1, S2, S3 🍴

✳ WILHELMA
Neckartalstrasse, 70376 Stuttgart-Bad Cannstatt
Tel 0711 54020
www.wilhelma.de
Europe's largest zoological and botanical gardens are home to more than 10,000 animals and plants from all over the world. Here, you will see around 1,000 species of animals in

one of Baden-Württemberg's most popular visitor attractions. Note that it gets very busy during main holiday periods and weekends.
🕐 Zoo: May–end Aug daily 8.15–6; Apr, Sep daily 8.15–5.30; Mar, Oct daily 8.15–5; Nov–end Feb daily 8.15–4. Gardens: daily 8.15–dusk 📅 Mar–end Oct adult €10.20, child (6–17) €5.10; Nov–end Feb adult €7, child €3.50
🚇 U13, U14 🚌 52, 55, 56 🍴

FESTIVALS AND EVENTS

MAY

DER MEISTERTRUNK
Rothenburg ob der Tauber
Tel 09861 4611
www.meistertrunk.de
According to legend, in 1631 Mayor Nusch of Rothenburg saved the town from being destroyed by the imperial troops of Count Tilly when he won the challenge to drain a tankard containing more than 3 litres (6 pints) of wine. This episode was first re-enacted as the festival play *Der Meistertrunk* (*The Master Draught*) in 1881, and is still celebrated every Whitsuntide by hundreds of townspeople.
🕐 Whitsuntide (last Sun in May)
💶 Adult €9–18, child (6–14) €5–18

JUNE

RICHARD-STRAUSS-TAGE
Garmisch-Partenkirchen-Tourism, Richard-Strauss-Platz 1a, 82467 Garmisch-Partenkirchen
Tel 08821 752545
www.richard-strauss-tage.de
Richard Strauss lived in Garmisch-Partenkirchen from 1908 until his death in 1949. Each June, Garmisch honours the distinguished composer with the Richard Strauss Festival. Famous artists from all over the world perform at this musical extravaganza,

Schloss Heildelberg, the setting for the Schlossfestspiele

and the festival hosts many other events such as master classes, lectures, an introduction to the maestro's works (including orchestral and vocal highlights) and discussions with the artists.
🕐 June
💶 €11–66 depending on event

JUNE/AUGUST

SCHLOSSFESTSPIELE
Schloss Heidelberg, Schlossberg, 69117 Heidelberg
Tel 06221 582000
www.schlossfestspiele-heidelberg.de
The ruins of Heidelberg Castle provide the picturesque setting for this

world-famous festival. The courtyard is the site of open-air musicals, operas and theatre performances, as well as classical concerts (such as the famous 'Castle Serenades') performed by the Heidelberg City Orchestra.
🕐 End Jun to mid-Aug
💶 Adult €15–45, reduction for child or senior depends on event

JULY

INTERNATIONAL ZELT-MUSIK FESTIVAL
Freiburg Mundenhof
Tel 0761 504030
www.zmf.de
This music festival has gained international recognition for its spectacular variety of presentations. More than 100 events over 19 days, with artists and stars from all over the world contribute to provide a menu of classical, rock, jazz, circus and variety performances in venues just outside the town.
🕐 First three weeks in July
💶 Varies

DIE KINDERZECHE
Dinkelsbühl
Tel 09851 90240
www.kinderzeche.de
The historic festival play *Die Kinderzeche* (performed

since 1897) is one of Germany's oldest and most interesting. According to legend, when Swedish hordes laid siege to the town in 1632, the gatekeeper's daughter, Lore, together with the children of the town, pleaded for mercy and saved Dinkelsbühl from pillage and destruction. Hundreds of children are involved in the 10 days of festivities, and the event is accompanied by a diverse peripheral schedule, making it ideal for families.
🕐 10 days in July
💶 €2–9

RUTENFEST
Ravensburg
Tel 0751 82324
www.ravensburger-rutenfest.de
Ravensburg's local history festival begins every July with the firing of a small cannon from the Mehlsack tower, marking the start of a traditional event that attracts visitors from all over the world. The highlight is Monday's historical parade, when schoolchildren in historical costumes, music bands, horses and wagons pass through Ravensburg in a display of the town's history.
🕐 July

AUGUST

KONSTANZER SEENACHTFEST
Tourist Information Konstanz, Fischmarkt 2, 78462 Konstanz
Tel 01805 133030
www.seenachtfest.com
The Konstanzer Seenachtfest is the largest summer event held around Lake Constance, and takes place along the lakeshore of the city of Konstanz and the neighbouring Swiss city of Kreuzlingen. The Seenachtfest is mostly known for its fireworks on the lake, the biggest display in Germany. Events held during the festival include street theatre, water-ski shows and live music on seven stages.

🕐 Second weekend in Aug
💶 Adult €10, child (14–17) €8, under 14 free

SEPTEMBER

REICHSSTADT-FESTTAGE
Rothenburg ob der Tauber
Tel 09861 404800
www.rothenburg.de
The Imperial City Festival is one of the highlights of Rothenburg's calendar. The entire history of the town is brought alive by more than 1,000 participants—you will see knights, riflemen and peasants, witness a medieval trial, or suddenly find yourself in the midst of an ancient cattle market. The opening is

The Emporemarkt Halle in Stuttgart

marked by a torchlit procession of all the participants, along with music and fireworks along the façade of the impressive town hall. On the Saturday, don't miss the spectacular fireworks display in the Tauber valley.
🕐 Early Sep

SEPTEMBER/OCTOBER

CANNSTATTER VOLKSFEST
Cannstatter Wasen, Stuttgart
Tel 0711 222 8240 (Stuttgart Tourist Office)
www.cannstatter-volksfest.de
This is one of the largest and best beer festivals in the world, originally established

in 1818 as a harvest festival—hence the 24m-high (80ft) fruit column, which is the focal point and symbol of the festival. Three huge brewery tents cater for more than 4,500 visitors, and traditional brass bands keep everyone's spirits high. Don't miss the delicious Swabian food, such as cheese *Spätzle* (a kind of pasta), roast beef, *Schupfnudeln* with sauerkraut, roast chicken and crispy roast leg of pork. There's also a firework display, plus a grand opening parade of lavishly decorated brewery floats and groups of people in traditional dress from all over Baden-Württemberg.
🕐 End Sep/beg Oct Mon–Fri noon–11, Sat, Sun 11–11 💶 Free

NOVEMBER/ DECEMBER

CHRISTKINDLESMARKT
Hauptmarkt, Nürnberg
Tel 0911 233 6135
www.nuernberg.de
Nuremberg's Christmas Market is the oldest and one of the best in Germany. The highlight is the opening ceremony, when the *Christkind* (Christ Child) speaks from the gallery of the Frauenkirche.
🕐 Last week in Nov–24 Dec

WEIHNACHTSMARKT
Marktplatz and Shillerplatz, Stuttgart
Tel 0711 222 8240 (Stuttgart Tourist Office)
www.stuttgart-tourist.de
At Stuttgart's market, more than 200 brightly decorated stalls sell a wide range of seasonal goods and culinary treats, including gingerbread, cinnamon waffles and mulled wine. For the children there's an enchanting fairy-tale land on Schlossplatz, while everyone can take a turn on the ice-skating rink.
🕐 Last week in Nov–23 Dec Mon–Sat 10–8.30, Sun 11–8.30

WHAT TO DO

This chapter describes 14 driving tours and 10 walks that explore Germany's scenic areas and major cities. Their locations are marked on the map on page 288. In each area, the walk starts from a point on the driving tour, (except those within cities), and are marked by a red star on the tour. Walks follow clearly defined, waymarked paths or the most interesting parts of the city.

Out and About

KEY TO THIS MAP

- ❷ Drive
- ❹ Walk
- ▪ City
- ● Town

OUT AND ABOUT

1. Walk
Brodtener Steilufer (▷ 289)

2. Drive
The Baltic Coast (▷ 290–291)

3. Drive
Weserbergland (▷ 292–294)

4. Walk
Hameln (▷ 295)

5. Drive
Sauerland and Winterberg (▷ 296–297)

6. Walk
Berlin Mitte (▷ 298–299)

7. Drive
Around the Brocken: Into the Harz Mountains (▷ 300–302)

8. Walk
The Ravine of the River Bode (▷ 303)

9. Drive
Highlights of Saxony (▷ 304–305)

10. Walk
To the top of the Pfaffenstein in Saxon Switzerland (▷ 306–307)

11. Drive
The Thuringian Forest: A circular tour from Eisenach (▷ 308–309)

12. Walk
Munich's Old Town (▷ 310–311)

13. Drive
Bavaria's Altmühl Valley (▷ 312–313)

14. Walk
Northern Bavaria: The Glasstrasse through the Bayerischer Wald (▷ 314–315)

15. Drive
Southern Bavaria: Garmisch-Partenkirchen and Oberammergau (▷ 316–318)

16. Walk
Garmisch-Partenkirchen: The Partnachklamm (▷ 319)

17. Drive
The Alps in Southern Bavaria (▷ 320–322)

18. Walk
The Breitachklamm near Oberstdorf (▷ 323)

19. Drive
Around Lake Constance (▷ 324–326)

20. Walk
Along the shore of Lake Constance (▷ 327)

21. Drive
The Black Forest: A circular drive from Freiburg im Breisgau (▷ 328–330)

22. Walk
The Black Forest: Triberg and the Gutach Falls (▷ 331)

23. Drive
The Neckar Valley and the Bergstrasse: A circular drive from Heidelberg (▷ 332–334)

24. Walk
Through the Margarethenschlucht in the Neckar Valley (▷ 335)

KEY TO ROUTE MAPS IN THIS CHAPTER

- ★ Start point
- ━ Route
- ▪▪ Alternative route
- ► Route direction
- ❷ Walk start point on drive
- ❻ Featured sight along route
- ● Place of interest in Sights section
- ● Other place of interest
- ☀ Viewpoint
- 621▲ Peak (height in metres)

BRODTENER STEILUFER

The curving, Brodtener promontory jutting into the Lübecker Bucht between Travemünde and Niendorf is rimmed with low sea-cliffs. The easily managed walk along here gives you superb views of the Baltic coast.

THE WALK

Distance:	4km (2.5 miles)
Allow:	1–2 hours
Start at:	Travemünde
End at:	Niendorf

Note: You can follow the clifftop path or walk on the beach, directly alongside the sea. Both routes end at the same place. However, the beach route is rocky and the going hard in places, while the views are less spectacular. The descriptive detail that follows is based on a walk along the clifftop path. In either case, as long as you keep the sea to your right, you can hardly get lost.

Start at the Mövenstein parking area alongside the sailing school at the north end of Travemünde beach (there is a public toilet here). Go up on Helldahl, a path that ascends easily into the trees. You're soon on the clifftop path, the start of which is marked near a sign that says *Landschafts-schutzgebiet*, indicating that this is a protected landscape. The cliffs and the sea are just off to your right.

On the clifftop, try to resist the temptation to peer over the cliff edge. Signposts warn of an *abbrechendes Steilufer*—meaning that the edge is subject to collapse and that you approach it at your own peril. The cliffs are no more than 20m (66ft) high, but a fall from that height could easily prove fatal.

As you come level with the practice range of a golf course off to your left, an information board (in German) provides background about the geography and wildlife of the Brodtener coastline.

About 100m (110 yards) beyond the intersection of the cliffside path with a path that goes off to the left through a forested area—the Heidenhof—you'll see a stone inscribed with the text of Psalm 93, verse 4, which extols the greater power of the Lord in comparison even with that of the sea. Some 50m (55 yards) beyond here is a section of the cliff that is lower and less steep, where it's possible to scramble down to the beach and back up again—as long as you go carefully.

Back on top, little side paths branch off from the main path through the trees to the cliff edge.

Hermannshöhe, a café-restaurant that sits on a wide lawn overlooking the sea, is at about the midpoint and is a good spot for a break.

Continuing, the path curves away from the sea a little and you pass what looks like a broken-down vacation home on your right, before regaining the shore.

Sunset over the Baltic coast

Large broken concrete blocks down on the beach, and others a little way inland, are the remnants of an old coastal defence work, the Buschkoppel. In this more open country, you'll see a pond in a field off to your left, and beyond that the village of Brodten. As the promontory curves westward, a view over another arm of the Lübecker Bucht opens up, across to Timmendorfer Strand and beyond.

Some 50m (55 yards) after passing, on your left, a holiday home for young people, the red-brick Jugendheim 'Seeblick', a flight of wooden steps leads down to the beach. Staying on the path, you emerge from a cluster of bushes, with Niendorf just ahead. The path becomes enclosed and seaside homes appear on the left as you enter the resort.

OUT AND ABOUT

WHEN TO GO

The best season for this walk is undoubtedly summer, but you could also tackle it on a fine spring or autumn day. In winter, be prepared for wind and cold temperatures; in bad weather, conditions could be positively unpleasant.

WHERE TO EAT

Café-Restaurant Hermannshöhe (tel 04502 73021) is the ideal point for a mid-walk break, either inside or on the outside terrace.

The 15th-century Holstentor gateway at Lübeck—officially a district of nearby Travemünde

THE BALTIC COAST

Beginning near Lübeck and ending near Rostock, this tour covers a scenic section of eastern Germany's fast-developing Baltic coast and its agricultural hinterland. At about the midpoint, it passes through the particularly attractive small town of Wismar.

THE DRIVE

Distance:	160km (100 miles)
Allow:	6–8 hours
Start at:	Travemünde
End at:	Heiligendamm

In Travemünde ★, you cross from the west to the east bank of the River Trave on a vehicle ferry, the Priwallfähre. On the east bank, go straight ahead; after about 2km (1.2 miles), you cross the old border with East Germany, which is marked by a memorial stone with the inscription *Nie Wieder Geteilt* (Never Again Divided).

Go right, following the signs for Pötenitz and Dassow, with intermittent views of the waters of the Dassower See off to your right, into Dassow. At the first major intersection, go left onto the B105 in the direction of Wismar, but only for 200m (220 yards) or so before going left again, following signs for Neuenhagen and Kalkhorst. Pass through Neuenhagen and continue to Kalkhorst.

❶ The handsome village of Kalkhorst is worth stopping at to look at its impressive red-brick Gothic Sankt-Laurentius church, dating from 1230.

Just beyond the church turn left, then quickly right again, onto the road to Brook. This brings you to the coastal forest of Naturschutzgebiet Brooker Wald (Brook Forest Nature Reserve). The minor road continues through Warnkenhagen and Elmenhorst before regaining the coast road to Wismar just short of Klütz (watch for the Dutch-style windmill on your left just before you enter the village).

❷ In Klütz, the 13th-century Sankt-Marienkirche is of interest, as is Schloss Bothmer, and, for railway enthusiasts, there are the steam trains of the Klützer–Ostsee–Eisenbahn. A pleasant diversion from the village is north to the Baltic resort of Boltenhagen.

From Klütz the coastal road runs southeast towards Wismar, making a gentle curve around the coast of the Wohlenberger Wiek. Part of this section of the drive is on scenic roads lined by avenues of trees—Alleenstrassen. Just beyond the village of Proseken, turn left onto the E22/B105 for the run into Wismar.

❸ The old heart of Wismar (▷ 92), a former Hanseatic town, is one of the most handsome on the Baltic coast.

Klütz's Dutch-style windmill

Take the coast road north out of town, following the signs for Insel Poel. Some 10km (6 miles) farther, the road splits at Gross Stromkendorf and you follow the signs left for Poel, across a causeway to the island.

❹ Once on Poel, follow the signs for Wangern and Timmendorf along a road between wide, flat fields dotted with large farmhouses. At Kirchdorf, park next to the fishing harbour, where you may find fishermen selling freshly caught fish. Stroll around the harbour and into the remnants of a star-shaped fortification next to it, which dates from 1620. Driving on, you eventually come to the end of the road at Timmendorfer-Strand, a small resort with a fine, sandy beach.

Retrace your route back over the causeway to Gross Stromkendorf, where you head north once more along the coast road, following the signs for Neubukow. At Wodorf, you pass several fine Heidekaten—traditional thatched farmhouses—and at Stove there, is a Dutch-style windmill from 1889. At Boiensdorf, take the road to your left for a diversion of 2km (1.2 miles) to the Boiensdorfer Werder peninsula, where there's parking right beside the beach. Back on the coast road, the run up to Neubukow is on a scenic Alleenstrasse.

❺ Neubukow, where there is another old windmill, was the birthplace of Heinrich Schliemann (1822–90), the archaeologist who discovered and excavated the sites of ancient Troy and Mycenae.

Take the road north to Kühlungsborn, passing the lighthouse at Bastorf on the way.

❻ The seacoast resort of Kühlungsborn is a curious mix

OUT AND ABOUT

of decrepit old buildings, evidently allowed to rot by the East German government, and well-restored art nouveau and belle époque villas.

Drive 9km (5.5 miles) east to Heiligendamm.

❼ Heiligendamm was founded in 1793 as a bathing resort, and is even more exclusive than nearby Kühlungsborn.

From here it's just 6km (3.5 miles) to Bad Doberan along the E22/B105, for a fast return via Wismar, or on to the autobahn interchanges around Rostock.

PLACES TO VISIT

Klützer–Ostsee–Eisenbahn
Bahnhofstrasse 4, 23948 Klütz
☎ 038825 3201

Poel Island
🛈 Wismarsche Strasse 2, 23999 Kirchdorf/Poel ☎ 038425 2-03-47
www.insel-poel.de

Kühlungsborn
🛈 Ostseeallee 19, 18225 Ostseebad Kühlungsborn ☎ 038293/84-90
www.kuehlungsborn.de

Bad Doberan (for Heiligendamm)
🛈 Alexandrinenplatz 2, 18209 Bad Doberan ☎ 038203/6-21-54
www.bad-doberan.de

WHEN TO GO

Any time between spring and autumn is ideal, but note that the roads and resorts are at their busiest in summer. In winter, many attractions in the coastal regions are closed, but if the weather conditions are good, the coast does have more of an untamed beauty then.

WHERE TO EAT

Lübeck and Rostock, respectively close to the start and the end of the drive, and Wismar in the middle all have good eating possibilities (▷ 345). There are places to eat in the resorts of Travemünde, Kühlungsborn and Heiligendamm too, though they tend to be more tourist oriented. A great choice is the Alter Schwede (▷ 345) in Wismar.

Reeds line the shore at Wohlenberg Bay (far left)

Gabled houses on Wismar's cobbled market square (below)

OUT AND ABOUT

THE WESERBERGLAND

Beginning and ending close to the E45/A7 north-south autobahn, this route winds through the gentle hill country of the Weser river valley. This is an inland holiday area, rich in nature parks and other protected landscapes, and dotted with towns full of interest for their literary associations, romantic half-timbered buildings and architectural treasures in the style known as Weser Renaissance.

THE DRIVE

Distance: 166km (103 miles)

Allow: 5–8 hours

Start at: Hildesheim

End at: Hannoversch Münden—from here to Hildesheim along the E45/A7 is 110km (68 miles)

Hildesheim ★ (▷ 75), an important ecclesiastical town during the Middle Ages, retains a quartet of fine churches from that period, two of which are UNESCO World Heritage Sites. The partially reconstructed central Marktplatz is a reminder of what was one of Germany's largest and finest collections of centuries-old *Fachwerkhäuser* (half-timbered houses) before it was destroyed in World War II.

From central Hildesheim, follow the signs west for Hameln, leaving town along the B1. About 6 km (3.5 miles) along the road, as you pass the twin villages of Gross Escherde and Klein Escherde, you can see off to your left the low forested hills of the Hildesheimer Wald. After a further 6km (3.5 miles), you cross over the River Leine at Burgstemmen, before pressing on through the village towards Elze and the southern edge of the Osterwald. From here the B1 curves northwest through Coppenbrügge in the valley between the Osterwald and the Oberberg (494m/1,620ft). It then angles westward for the final 14km (8.5 miles) into Hameln. You get to the old heart of the town by following signs to *Historische Altstadt* and *Zentrum*.

❶ Hameln (▷ 74), on the banks of the River Weser and at the southern edge of the Naturpark Weserbergland-Schaumburg-Hameln, is known worldwide for its legend of the Pied Piper (Rattenfänger). The attractive, bustling heart of town is invariably filled with visitors.

Distinctive Weser Renaissance architecture adorns Hameln's Abbot's House (above) and Hann. Münden's Rathaus (below)

There are various popular sites associated with the tale of the ratcatcher who enticed away the town's children, but there are enough other places of interest to justify an hour or two's to a stroll around the old part of Hameln (▷ 295).

You leave Hameln to the south, along the B83, following the signs for Höxter. This road hugs the west (left) bank of the Weser all the way to Höxter, so it's hard to go wrong, even though the river is not always in view. The road twists through the alternately flat and hilly country of the Weserbergland. Sometimes you are looking down on the river, while at other times it is hard to see it as you drive along the river floodplain. Small ferries take cars and passengers across the stream at several points, and tour boats call at some of the riverside towns and villages. At the hamlet of Risch, 8km (5 miles) south of Hameln, signs point off to the right for the village of Hämelschenburg, with its fine Weser Renaissance Schloss dating from 1613. A visit here makes a worthwhile diversion of just 4km (2.5 miles) in total. Some 19km (11.5 miles) southeast of Hameln, you arrive at Bodenwerder.

❷ Bodenwerder is a moderately attractive village that would be scarcely distinguishable from many other Weser villages were it not for its connection with Baron Karl Friedrich Hieronymus von Münchhausen (1720–97). This native of Bodenwerder and spinner of incredibly tall tales has been immortalized in literature and film, and you can visit his family seat, now the Rathaus, which has a museum devoted to him and his greatly exaggerated memories.

Continued on page 294

OUT AND ABOUT

WHEN TO GO

Spring and autumn are good times to go, as the roads are then generally quieter than in summer. The advantages of a summer trip are that more places to visit are open, as are restaurant and café outdoor terraces.

The picturesque, lush, green countryside and hills of the Weser valley

WHERE TO EAT

The riverside towns and villages of the Weserbergland have many hotels, restaurants and cafés. Good choices are the Knochenhauer Amtshaus in Hildesheim (▷ 344), the Rattenfängerhaus in Hameln (▷ 344) and the restaurant of Hotel Schlosschänke (Vor der Burg 3–5, 34346 Hannoversch Münden tel 05541 70940), across from the River Werra and the Welfenschloss on the northern edge of the Altstadt. It serves traditional German cuisine in an English colonial setting, and has outdoor tables in fine weather.

PLACES TO VISIT

Museum Hameln
Osterstrasse 8–9, Hameln
☎ 05151 202215
🕐 Tue–Sun 10–4.30
💶 Adult €3, child €1.50

Münchhausen Museum
Münchhausenplatz 1, Bodenwerder
☎ 05533 40541
🕐 Apr–end Oct 10–12, 2–5
💶 Adult €1.50, child €1

Hameln's 'Wedding House' carillon plays and enacts the Pied Piper legend daily

Decorative façades line Hildesheim's market square

After the village of Stahle, 29km (18 miles) farther south, you can either go left into Holzminden for a look at its *Fachwerkhäuser* or keep to the right on the B83 and continue for 8km (5 miles) into Höxter to do the same. At Godelheim, 5km (3 miles) south of Höxter, watch for a left turn (difficult to see) near the end of the village, signposted for Hann. Münden. You need to take this to remain on the B83 riverside road. Continue through Beverungen and Herstelle (where there's a small tour-boat jetty). At Bad Karlshafen, you go left across a bridge over the Diemel, a tributary of the Weser, and on into the town. At this point you leave the B83 for the B80 (signposted for Hann. Münden).

❸ Elegant Bad Karlshafen is a spa town that was founded in 1699 as a community for French Protestant Huguenot refugees, and some of its original baroque buildings survive. Among these is the centrally situated Rathaus, which was formerly the hunting lodge of Landgrave Karl von Hessen. Close to here, in a former cigar factory, is the Deutsches Hugenottenmuseum, which records the town's history and the role of the German Huguenots. A stroll around downtown Bad Karlshafen and along the waterfront is a pleasure. The town's intrinsic attractiveness is enhanced by its position in an area of natural beauty, between the Naturpark Solling-Vogler and the extensive Reinhardswald forest.

The B80 continues through Bad Karlshafen and emerges once more alongside the Weser. The road curves generally east and south, between the river and the Reinhardswald, sometimes passing over hills and sometimes through flat country. After a drive of about 40km (25 miles), you approach Hannoversch Münden, which you enter by staying on the B80 when it turns sharply left, crossing the Weser. Follow the signs that point to *Innenstadt* and *Zentrum*.

❹ Hannoversch Münden (or Hann. Münden) lies at the foot of wooded hills in the gorge where the Fulda and Werra rivers merge to form the Weser. The Reinhardswald is to the

Among Hann. Münden's many half-timbered buildings is the handsome gabled Rathaus

northwest, the Bramwald to the northeast and the Naturpark Münden to the east and south. The town's wealth of centuries-old half-timbered houses (it possesses more than 700) gives it a distinctive character, even though there are few outstanding examples. The 14th-century Rathaus has a later, Weser Renaissance façade facing the market square.

From Hannoversch Münden, it is 10km (6 miles) along the B496 to intersection 76 on the E45/A7 autobahn if you are heading south, and 20km (12 miles) to intersection 75, for those going north.

Hann. Münden's Gothic church of St. Blasius has a late-14th-century bronze font

HAMELN

Associations with the Pied Piper, the legendary medieval ratcatcher immortalized in English in Robert Browning's much-loved poem, are a big part of Hameln's attractions. But they are not the whole story, as this tour goes to show.

THE WALK

Distance: 3km (2 miles)

Allow: 1 hour

Start/end at: Tourist Information Hameln, Deisterallee, at the eastern end of the Altstadt (Old Town)

From outside the tourist office, cross busy Kastanienwall via the pedestrian tunnel at the top end of Deiserallee. This brings you onto Osterstrasse, the Altstadt's main thoroughfare. Walk to the corner with Bungelosenstrasse.

The Rattenfängerhaus, on the corner was built in 1602 to 1603 in Weser Renaissance style. The Pied Piper's House, which takes its name from an inscription recounting the legend, is now a restaurant. On the other side of Osterstrasse is the Garrisonkirche (1713), the baroque former garrison church, now a bank. A few doors along at Osterstrasse 18, is a building dating from 1577 (now a health food store) with a bas-relief carving of a dragon and a lion on the façade.

Continuing along Osterstrasse, pass the post office and a bronze sculpture of the Pied Piper.

The richly ornamented Weser Renaissance Leisthaus, at Osterstrasse 9, was built between 1585 and 1589. It houses the Museum Hameln, which has a collection of items from the town's history including exhibits relating to the Pied Piper. The museum continues in the next house, known as the Stiftsherrenhaus (Canon's House, 1556–58), which has a café on the ground floor.

At Osterstrasse's western end, on the other side of the street, is the massive bulk of the Hochzeitshaus.

The 'Wedding House', built in Weser Renaissance style from 1610 to 1617 as a ceremonial hall, now fulfils a rather dull purpose as civic offices. But crowds gather outside every day at 1.05, 3.35 and 5.35 to hear its carillon play and to watch mechanical figures re-enact the legend of the Pied Piper. Facing this building across Osterstrasse, in Pferdemarkt, is the Gothic Marktkirche St.-Nicolai. Originally dating from 1200, the church was rebuilt in the 1950s. It's well worth a visit, as is Pferdemarkt itself, especially on a Saturday, when there is a lively market. Adjoining Pferdemarkt is Am Markt.

The Dempterhaus on the corner of Am Markt is a graceful sandstone and half-timbered house built in Weser Renaissance style in 1607 to 1608 for Tobias van Dempter, who in 1629 was mayor of Hameln.

Take Zehntopfstrasse at the side of the Dempterhaus and at its end cross over to the Weser-promenade, where there's an uninspiring view of the river from the bridge. Go south along the riverfront for 100m (110 yards) or so, past the Pfortmühle, a 19th-century mill that houses the library, and cross over Sudeten-strasse to Kupferschmiedestrasse.

The Weser Renaissance Bürgerhaus at Kupfer-schmiedestrasse 13 dates back to 1560. Once a brewery, this rambling building now houses

Hameln rat statue, among many associations of the legend

Hameln's rats now play an important part in tourism

a restaurant, the Kartoffelhaus. Around the corner at Wendenstrasse 8 is the half-timbered Lückingsches Haus (1638–39), with painted motifs and an inscription from Psalm 127 on its façade.

Turn right into Bäckerstrasse for a look at the Löwenapotheke, dating from 1300, directly ahead, and at the Rattenkrug (1250, rebuilt 1568–69), Hameln's oldest café-restaurant. A few steps on, go left on Alte Marktstrasse, a street of half-timbered residential houses. This leads back by way of Bungelosenstrasse to the Rattenfängerhaus and Osterstrasse, from where you retrace your steps to return to the tourist office.

WHEN TO GO

You can do this walk at any time of the year. The streets are quieter in winter but you miss out on the outdoor café terraces and other street animation.

WHERE TO EAT

The Rattenfängerhaus (▷ 344) and the Kartoffelhaus (▷ 343) are both excellent choices.

PLACES TO VISIT

Museum Hameln (▷ 293)

OUT AND ABOUT

SAUERLAND AND WINTERBERG

This drive takes you across the gently rolling hills of the Naturpark Arnsberger to the lively ski resort of Winterberg and to Kahler Asten, the highest peak in western Germany. From here, the drive crosses back over the Arnsberger Wald to reach Möhnesee-Damm, which was destroyed by the RAF's 'Dambuster' Squadron during World War II.

THE DRIVE
Distance: 180km (112 miles)
Allow: 8 hours
Start/end at: Soest

To find your way out of the labyrinth that is central Soest ★, follow signs for Route 1 towards Bad Sassendorf and then Route 475 towards the A44. Continue straight under the A44, following signs to Meschede. Over the next few kilometres you'll pass a series of wind turbines.

❶ The wind turbines you see are evidence of the German government's ongoing commitment to green energy. Germany leads the world in wind-power production, generating enough electricity to satisfy the needs of around three million households.

When you have gone 10km (6 miles) beyond the A44, you'll come to an angled crossroads; turn left here, following the 516 towards Brilon. After a further 20km (12 miles) the route starts to wind up into the Arnsberger hills. At the traffic lights just before Brilon, turn right towards Winterberg, along Route 7. In Altenbüren, turn left at the lights. A steep climb brings you to the brow of a hill with impressive views over Olsberg.
Continue through Olsberg as far as the traffic lights, then turn left along the 480. The next stretch follows the bottom of a pretty wooded valley, and is lined with car parking areas and footpath signs. At Winterberg, follow signs for *Zentrum* and park where you can.

❷ Winterberg is a friendly resort town with some of the best winter sports facilities north of the Alps. There's also great hiking and bicycling in the summer months.

From Winterberg, take the 236 towards Kahler Asten. To reach the top of Kahler Asten

Möhnesee-Damm, destroyed by RAF bouncing bombs in 1943

(841m/2,758ft), take the first right after the Bob-Bahn and then first left up a steep hairpin road.
To continue the drive, return to the 236 and turn right towards Olpe. Stay on the 236 for the next 20km (12 miles). After about 10km (6 miles), some exciting hairpin driving provides fine views. Drive through the tiny, half-timbered villages of Oberkirchen and Winkhausen and continue as far as the traffic lights in Gleidorf. Turn right here, towards Bad Fredeburg. After 3km (2 miles), take the first right to get to the heart of Bad Fredeburg.

❸ Bad Fredeburg's spa is Sauerland-Bad, which you reach by continuing along the 511 until you see it signed to the right. Spas are still very much part of the health and leisure scene in Germany.

Beyond Bad Fredeburg, a fast, sweeping road winds along the Wenne Valley as far as Bremke. At Bremke, turn left on route 55 and, after 2km (1.2 miles), take the left turn that doubles back under the 55 towards Freienohl. Just after you cross the Ruhr into

Freienohl, turn left at the traffic lights and continue to Arnsberg.
If you want to visit the town, continue as far as the traffic lights at the end of the road and head right, following signs for *Zentrum*. At the end of a tunnel turn left up a gentle hill, and park as close to the top as you can. The town square is at the end of this road.

❹ Arnsberg is a pleasant place to stop for a stroll. History enthusiasts might like to visit the Sauerland-Museum in a whitewashed neoclassical building just off Altermarkt. The poorly signed tourist office (which publishes some leaflets in English) is on the north side of the town square.

To continue to Soest along the 229 without stopping in Arnsberg, turn hard right up a hill at the first traffic lights as you come into the town. This is a steep, winding road, taking you over a pass and into the heart of the Naturpark Arnsberger. Just beyond the first Möhnesee bridge, at the top of a hill, is an information board with a map of the reservoir. At the end of the second bridge, turn left at the roundabout to reach the Möhne Dam.

Boating on Möhnesee Dam waters

OUT AND ABOUT

❺ The Möhnesee-Damm was one of a number of dams in the region targeted by the RAF's 617 Squadron during World War II. They famously used bouncing bombs to destroy it, a feat later documented in the 1954 film *The Dambusters*. There's ample parking, and an information board at one end explains (in English and German) exactly what happened to the dam—and to the villages below it—on the morning of 17 May 1943.

To return to Soest, retrace your route from the dam, and go left along the 229 for 10km (6 miles).

WHEN TO GO

Although January and February are probably the best months for skiing, driving can be a bit hazardous in the hills after particularly heavy snow. The summer is the best time for driving, bicycling, walking and water sports. If you want to avoid the crowds, May is recommended (also for trekking before the weather gets too warm) along with September, which is good for sailing and windsurfing too (when the water has had the whole summer to warm up).

PLACES TO VISIT

Sauerland-Bad
Sportzentrum 1, 57392 Bad Fredeburg
☎ 02974 96800 🕐 Mon–Fri 10–10, Sat, Sun and holds 9am–10pm
🎫 Adult €9 child (4–14) €7 for 2 hours 30min, including pool and sauna

Sauerland-Museum
Altermarkt 24–26, 59821 Arnsberg
☎ 02931 4098 🕐 Tue–Fri 10–5, Sat 2–5, Sun 10–6 🎫 Adult €1, child 50c, under 6 free
www.sauerland-museum.de

Möhnesee
ℹ Kürbiker Strasse 1, Körbecke
☎ 02924 4971414
www.moehnesee.de

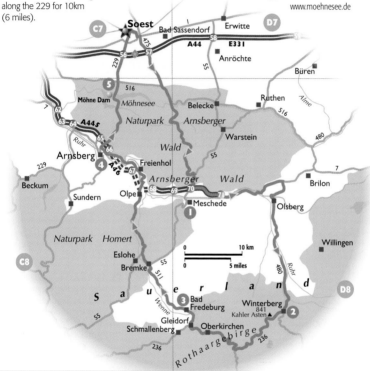

Sauerland's rolling countryside is just a stone's throw from the industrialized Ruhr valley

OUT AND ABOUT

WHERE TO EAT

In Winterberg, the bistro Täglich Café (Hellenstrasse 2, tel 02981 820990) is a welcoming eatery, serving anything from snacks and coffees to cocktails.
The Goldener Stern in Arnsberg (Altermarkt 6, tel 02931 530020), a luxurious café/restaurant, has an impressive range of starters and mains, plus cakes and waffles.

BERLIN MITTE

This route takes in all the major sights in Berlin Mitte, from the Brandenburg Gate and the historic Unter den Linden avenue in the west to Alexanderplatz and the towering Fernsehturm around the former heart of the city in the east.

THE WALK

Distance:	5.5km (3.5 miles)
Allow:	1 hour 30min (not including stops)
Start at/end at:	Brandenburg Tor
How to get there:	Unter den Linden S-Bahn station

Walk down the left-hand side of Unter den Linden with your back to Pariser Platz and the Brandenburg Gate ★ (▷ 128). After 150m (165 yards), pass Hotel Adlon and the Russian embassy on the right. Cross Neustädtische Kirchstrasse. A little farther on, you'll see, on the left, the courtyard of the Staatsbibliothek zu Berlin (the Berlin State Library). Just ahead on the left is Humboldt University, and in the middle of the street is Christian Daniel Rauch's equestrian statue of Frederick the Great (1851). On the opposite side of Unter den Linden is Bebelplatz.

Bustling Unter den Linden runs through the heart of Berlin

❶ Bebelplatz was where, on 10 May 1933, the group naming itself 'Action Against the Non-German Spirit' burned huge piles of books and journals by authors who appeared on Hitler's 'black list'.

Another 50m (55 yards) down Unter den Linden, is the Neue Wache (New Guardhouse).

❷ The Neue Wache was built by Karl Friedrich Schinkel between 1816 and 1818. A large sculpture by Käthe Kollwitz (1867–1945) stands in the middle as a memorial to the victims of war and tyranny.

Cross Hinter dem Griefhaus, passing the Zeughaus (Arsenal) on the left, now the Deutsches Historisches Museum.

❸ The Arsenal was designed in 1706 by Johann Arnold Nering. The exhibits in the square, baroque-style building provide insights into the country's turbulent past.

Unter den Linden now becomes Schinkelallee, which takes you over the River Spree. Continue ahead, keeping Museum Island and the Berliner Dom (▷ 127) on the left. Pass over the Liebknecht bridge and cross to the right-hand side of the road to the Marx-Engels-Forum.

❹ The statue by Ludwig Engelhart of the two influential Communist thinkers, Karl Marx and Friedrich Engels, was placed in the square in 1986.

Face the Fernsehturm (TV Tower, ▷ 125). Cross Spandauer Strasse, walk past the Neptunbrunnen (Neptune Fountain) and round to the main entrance of the Fernsehturm. This is a good place to stop for a break.
Go back south, re-crossing Spandauer Strasse at the crossing nearest the Rotes Rathaus. Turn left, with the arcades on the right. At Am Nussbaum turn right into the pedestrian-only Nikolaiviertel (▷ 150). Walk towards the twin spires of the Nikolaikirche **❺**.
From the Nikolaikirche, turn right onto Propstrasse and walk west. Continue towards the River Spree until you reach the

equestrian statue of St. George slaying the dragon. At the river turn right and walk down Spree Ufer towards the Berliner Dom. Head northwest along the river, turn left onto Rathausstrasse and cross the bridge.

❻ The Palast der Republik, the large building on the right, is the former headquarters of the German Democratic Republic parliament. It is now empty and its fate undecided.

Walk west towards the red-brick twin towers of the Friedrichswerdersche Kirche, crossing Breite Strasse. On the right is the Bauakademie monument, a reconstructed corner section of a building designed by Schinkel. Next to this is the Friedrichswerdersche Kirche.

❼ The Friedrichswerdersche Kirche, designed by Schinkel and built between 1824 and 1830, was the first neo-Gothic church in Berlin.

Proceed along Werderscher Markt. The Hedwigskirche is on the right.

❽ Berlin's Catholic Cathedral was consecrated in 1773. It was rebuilt in 1952 and 1963 after damage during World War II and has a modern interior.

Head back onto Werderstrasse on the right; this becomes Französische Strasse. Continue for a little more than 150m (165 yards) and then turn left into Markgrafenstrasse and cross over into the square known as Gendarmenmarkt **❾** (▷ 129). From the Schinkel monument in the middle, walk northwest, leaving the square between the Schauspielhaus (Playhouse) and the Französische Dom. Turn right on to Charlottenstrasse. Cross over to the other side of the road and walk until the road rejoins Französische Strasse. Turn left and keep going as far as the traffic lights. You can end the walk here, at the Französische Strasse U-Bahn station. Alternatively, turn right into Friedrichstrasse, which leads back to Unter den Linden and the Brandenburg Gate.

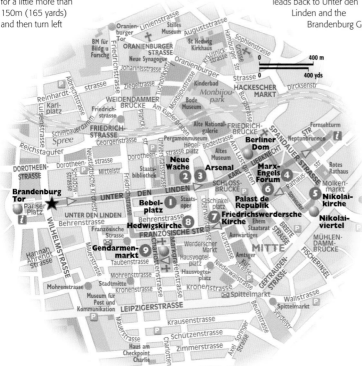

WHEN TO GO

This walk can be done any time of day, all year round. The major sights, such as the Brandenburg Gate and the Gendarmenmarkt, are illuminated at night.

PLACES TO VISIT

Deutsches Historisches Museum
Unter den Linden 2, 10117 Berlin (Mitte)
☎ 030 20 30 40 ⏰ Daily 10–6 💶 €2
🚇 Unter den Linden, Friedrichstrasse

Friedrichswerdersche Kirche
Schinkelmuseum, Werderscher Markt, 10117 Berlin (Mitte) ☎ 030 208 13 23
⏰ Tue–Sun 10–6 💶 Free
🚇 Hausvogteiplatz

Sankt-Hedwigs-Kathedrale
Bebelplatz, 10117 Berlin (Mitte) ☎ 030 203 48 10 ⏰ Mon–Sat 10–5, Sun 1–5
💶 Free 🚇 Französische Strasse, Hausvogteiplatz, Stadtmitte 🚌 147, 257

Ancient and modern; the city's 1960's TV Tower sits next to the Gothic Marienkirche

WHERE TO EAT

At the top of the Fernsehturm is the Telecafé, where you can enjoy a snack or a light meal and take in the 360° view in the revolving restaurant (TV Turm Alexanderplatz, Panoramastrasse 1A, 10178 Berlin (Mitte), tel 030 242 33 33). The ice-cream sundaes, and coffee and cake selections are particularly good. If you don't like heights there is also the Tourist Info Café at the base of the tower (Unter dem Fernsehturm am Alexanderplatz). Café Einstein on Unter den Linden is something of a German institution and a great place to stop for a snack. Sit back and enjoy a special coffee or tea and—to revitalize you on a cold, wet day—warm apple strudel with vanilla sauce.

AROUND THE BROCKEN: INTO THE HARZ MOUNTAINS

This drive skirts the Harz Mountains, then climbs to give you a view of central Germany's highest point, the Brocken. For a closer look at its summit, you can leave your car and the 21st century behind, and make an ascent by steam railway.

Wernigerode is famous for its timber-framed buildings

OUT AND ABOUT

THE DRIVE

Distance: 100km (62 miles)	
Allow: 2 hours	
Start at: Quedlinburg	
End at: Wernigerode	

Drive west out of Quedlinburg ★ and follow signs that take you along minor roads to Thale, where you should look for directions to *Seilbahn* (cable car).

❶ Thale's early fortunes were based on the iron ore extracted from the Harz Mountains, which form a dramatic rocky backdrop to the town. The iron- and steelworks are now in an advanced state of decay, but Thale still provides its visitors with mineral water from its spa. A big attraction is the gorge of the River Bode (▷ 303), a cable car and chairlift and a summer toboggan run around the entrance to it. There are also play facilities.

Continue west, following signs to the town of Blankenburg, then taking the B6 towards Wernigerode.

❷ Wernigerode has one of Germany's most extravagant town halls—the extraordinary spiky towers of the Rathaus overlook the marketplace—and a wealth of timber-framed buildings. The Old Town is a popular starting point for exploration of the Harz and is the northern terminus of the narrow-gauge railway which threads its way through the mountains (▷ 302).

Carry on west along the B6, making a brief diversion south to go through the Altstadt of Ilsenburg, a pleasant, low-key resort popular with hikers. The B6 leads to Bad Harzburg.

❸ Bad Harzburg is one of the area's main resort towns, with plenty of spa facilities for its guests. The exhibits in the Haus der Natur provide a lively introduction to the natural riches of the mountains.

From Bad Harzburg, follow signs towards Braunlage, driving south along the B4 limited-access highway, which climbs into the heart of the Harz. After 11km (7 miles), turn east into the large car parking area at Torfhaus.

❹ Torfhaus, at 798m (2,618ft), is the most popular spot for viewing the Brocken. From here there's a superb panorama over the forested foothills towards the mountain's rounded summit (1,142m/3,747ft), some 5km (3 miles) away. During the Cold War, Torfhaus, which was in the Federal Republic, was one of the places where West Germans could easily gaze into the forbidden territory of the German Democratic Republic. If you are unlucky with the weather, visit the Nationalparkhaus Altenau-Torfhaus on the far side of the road (take care in crossing). The multimedia exhibits give a virtual tour of the Brocken, and you can even hear the call of the

Cable cars traverse high above the River Bode between Thale and Hexentanzplatz

lynx, one of the area's more elusive inhabitants.

Descend south along the B4 for 9km (5.5 miles), and take the exit signposted 'Braunlage Nord'.

5 Braunlage is a busy upland resort, popular in both summer and winter, with a dense network of waymarked trails and a good range of visitor facilities. A cableway whisks visitors up to the top of the Wurmberg (972m/3,189ft), with fine views northwards.

Continued on page 302

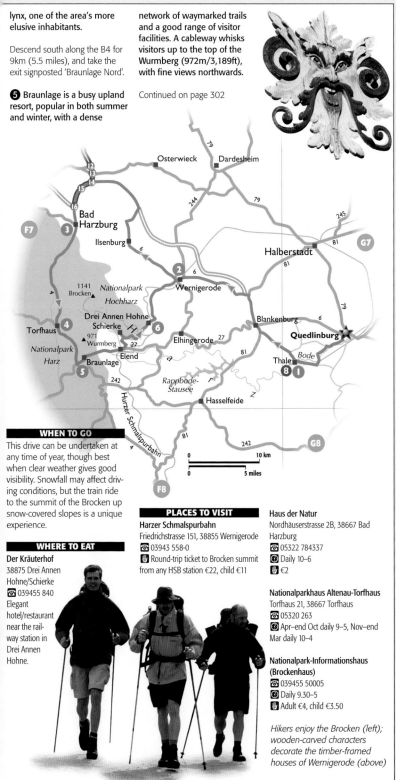

WHEN TO GO

This drive can be undertaken at any time of year, though best when clear weather gives good visibility. Snowfall may affect driving conditions, but the train ride to the summit of the Brocken up snow-covered slopes is a unique experience.

WHERE TO EAT

Der Kräuterhof
38875 Drei Annen Hohne/Schierke
☎ 039455 840
Elegant hotel/restaurant near the railway station in Drei Annen Hohne.

PLACES TO VISIT

Harzer Schmalspurbahn
Friedrichstrasse 151, 38855 Wernigerode
☎ 03943 558-0
🖐 Round-trip ticket to Brocken summit from any HSB station €22, child €11

Haus der Natur
Nordhäuserstrasse 2B, 38667 Bad Harzburg
☎ 05322 784337
🕐 Daily 10–6
🎟 €2

Nationalparkhaus Altenau-Torfhaus
Torfhaus 21, 38667 Torfhaus
☎ 05320 263
🕐 Apr–end Oct daily 9–5, Nov–end Mar daily 10–4

Nationalpark-Informationshaus (Brockenhaus)
☎ 039455 50005
🕐 Daily 9.30–5
🖐 Adult €4, child €3.50

Hikers enjoy the Brocken (left); wooden-carved characters decorate the timber-framed houses of Wernigerode (above)

OUT AND ABOUT

STEAMING UP THE BROCKEN

The station at Drei Annen Hohne is the most convenient starting point for a trip to the top of the Brocken by an HSB steam train—the Brockenbahn. Schierke, the next stop up the line, is nearer the summit, but lacks parking, while leaving from Wernigerode adds 40 minutes.

The ride is an exhilarating experience. A massive 2-10-2 locomotive, especially built for the line in the 1950s to tackle the steep 1:25 gradient, pulls the train, which consists of old-fashioned coaches (cars) with open platforms at each end. The 16km (10 mile) trip, including a 5-minute stop at Schierke, takes 45 minutes. At the top, there are cafés and the Brockenhaus, a modern museum devoted to explaining the mountain's history and ecology. Exhibits illustrate the GDR's treatment of its highest mountain as forbidden territory; from the early 1960s, the railway was closed to the public and only used to supply the listening posts.

If you have time, take the 2km (1.2 mile) walk laid out around the summit; it gives superb, ever-changing views over much of the Harz and the lowlands at its foot and takes you past the granite outcrops nicknamed the Witches' Altar and Devil's Pulpit, reminders of the Brocken's place in legend.

Let the train take the strain to the top of the Brocken

From Braunlage, drive northeast along the B27, following signs to Schierke. After 5km (3 miles), turn north in the village of Elend up a minor road, still following signs to Schierke, and after 2km (1.2 miles), turn east towards Drei Annen Hohne. In 4km (2.5 miles), the road crosses the Brocken railway. Drive past the station and turn south into the large parking area.

6 Drei Annen Hohne station is a busy place in summer (though trains run all year round), as it is an intersection on the Harzer Schmalspurbahn (HSB), Germany's most extensive narrow-gauge rail system. Trains run north to Wernigerode and south to Nordhausen, as well as to the summit of the Brocken (see box).

From Drei Annen Hohne, drive north for 11km (7 miles) towards Wernigerode. The road drops down through the forest and enters the town through extensive suburbs.

Devil's Pulpit and Witches' Altar sign (above) and Goethe plaque (right), both on the summit of the Brocken (below)

THE RAVINE OF THE RIVER BODE

This mostly level walk penetrates deep into the core of the Harz massif along what has been justly described as the 'most rugged valley north of the Alps'. The walk follows part of a longer trail leading through the Bode ravine to the resort town of Treseburg and is waymarked with blue triangles on a white background. The numbers in the text correspond to numbered posts along the course of the walk.

THE WALK

Distance: 8km (5 miles)

Allow: 2 hours

Start/end at: *Seilbahn* (cable railway) parking area in Thale

How to get there: See page 300

From the *Seilbahn* parking area, walk south along the riverbank and turn west across two bridges towards the cable railway.

The cable railway whisks you high over the river to Hexentanplatz, named for the witches thought to have danced there.

Continuing through the valley, turn south along the side of the cable railway terminus and walk through the wood alongside the river. The rocky scenery becomes more dramatic as you approach the footbridge known as the Katersteg (Tomcat Bridge).

On the other side of the Katersteg are a large youth hostel and the Kleiner Waldkater restaurant and guest house.

Without crossing the bridge, continue upstream. Sheer rock walls rise 300m (1,000ft) and in places the path is aligned directly above the rushing river. It rounds a projecting rock face known as Goethe-Felsen (Goethe Rock).

The Goethe-Felsen was renamed in 1949 in honour of the great writer, who came here in 1784.

Carry on upstream to the Königsruhe restaurant, with the figure of a witch on its roof.

The Königsruhe stands on a spot where refreshments have been served since 1820.

The area around the River Bode is popular with families

Continue upstream through the Königsruhe group of buildings.

Herr von Bülow, commemorated in the plaque here, was the forestry superintendent.

A sign just beyond the plaque reminds you that you are on a Wanderweg—a hiking path with difficult stretches. However, with proper footwear you need not worry. A carefully constructed path leads up to the Rosstrappe viewpoint in 45 minutes, but our walk continues to the Teufelsbrücke (Devil's Bridge).

The Teufelsbrücke crosses the Bode at the narrowest point in the ravine. It was once planned to build a dam here to generate hydroelectricity.

Cross the bridge and continue for 70m (76 yards) on the far bank of the river to Bodekessel (Bode Cauldron).

The Bodekessel got its name from the turbulent water in the depths that the river has carved out of the granite.

Germany's waymarked paths are clearly signposted

Many walkers turn back at this point, but it is worth taking a deep breath and tackling the zigzag path that climbs up towards the rim of the plateau, just below the area known as the Prinzensicht. From the path's summit there is a commanding view over the ravine. Return to your starting point in Thale.

WHEN TO GO

This walk can get very crowded during school holidays and in the summer months, especially at weekends.

WHERE TO EAT

Gastätte Königsruhe

Hirschgrund 1, 06502 Thale

☎ 3947 2726

Attractive, rustic restaurant and café overlooking the River Bode. Enjoy game, fish and homemade pastries.

PLACES TO VISIT

Hexentanzplatz

☎ 03947 2500

Reached by road or cable railway (weekends only in winter). Spectacular viewpoint, zoo, open-air theatre, summer toboggan run.

Rosstrappe

☎ 03947 2500

Reached by road or chairlift (weekends only in winter). Spectacular viewpoint.

OUT AND ABOUT

HIGHLIGHTS OF SAXONY

This drive starts off in lowland landscape, but the scenic highlight of the tour is the wooded valley of the Elbe known as Saxon Switzerland. The route also takes in several of the historic cities of Saxony, each with its own character. On either side of Dresden, the route forms part of the Saxon Wine Road.

THE DRIVE

Distance: 360km (224 miles)	
Allow: 8 hours	
Start/end at: Leipzig	

Leave Leipzig ★ eastwards on the B6 towards Wurzen. In Wurzen turn north into the Altstadt and park the car.

❶ Wurzen proclaims itself from far off with two huge grain elevators, but it's an old place with a stately market square. Although the cathedral dates from the 12th century, it is most remarkable for its 1932 refurbishment, which includes a Crucifixion scene in bronze.

Retrace your route along the B6 for 2km (1.2 miles), turning south onto the B107 to Grimma.

❷ The 800-year-old small town of Grimma calls itself the 'Pearl of the Mulde Valley', but the river wrought havoc in terrible floods in 2002. The lovely baroque bridge designed by Mathaes Daniel Pöppelmann now lacks its central span, but has a splendid Saxon coat of arms adorning the parapet.

Continue south for 15km (9 miles) along the B107 through attractive countryside to Colditz. Here follow signs to *Zentrum*.

❸ The international fame of Colditz rests on the role of its crag-top castle in World War II, when its massive walls imprisoned the most recalcitrant of Allied prisoners of war.

Colditz Castle (above); River Elbe cuts through Dresden (above right)

Drive east from Colditz along the B176 towards Döbeln. On the approach to this town follow signs to Dresden and the autobahn. Leave the autobahn at exit 78 and follow signs to *Zentrum*.

❹ Dresden's historic heart was completely destroyed in the Allied bombing raids of 13 February 1945, but heroic rebuilding has restored at least some of the charm of Saxony's venerable capital.

Take the B172 southeast from Dresden and follow signs to Pirna. In Pirna turn north and follow signs to *Historische Altstadt*.

❺ Pirna has a charming market square that remains almost exactly as it was depicted in a famous painting of 1750 by Canaletto. The old town promotes itself as the gateway to Saxon Switzerland.

Return to the B172 and drive east for 12km (7.5 miles), turning south off the main road towards the parking area for Königstein.

❻ The great fortress of Königstein occupies the whole of the summit of one of the strange tabletop hills characteristic of Saxon Switzerland, a sandstone plateau that wind

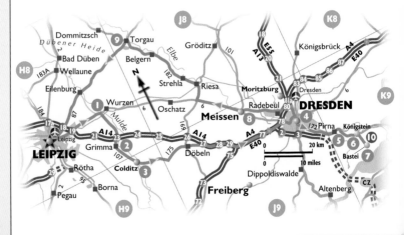

OUT AND ABOUT

Narrow streets and steps climb up the castle hill in Meissen

and water have eroded into fantastic shapes. There are superb panoramas from its ramparts.

Return to the B172 and continue east, dropping down to the River Elbe. In 5km (3 miles), the road crosses the Elbe into Bad Schandau, but before entering the town turn south off the bridge approach and follow signs to Hohenstein, driving north up a minor road through a wooded ravine. Continue west through tiny Hohenstein, following signs to *Bastei*. Turn south in 2.5km (1.5 miles) towards the Bastei. Leave your car at the park-and-ride station, or continue south to the main parking area. Walk past the hotel to the main viewpoint.

WHEN TO GO

This drive can be undertaken at any time of year, but take care when walking around the Bastei in icy conditions.

PLACES TO VISIT

Pirna

🛈 Am Markt 7, 01796 Pirna

☎ 03501 46570

🕒 Apr–end Oct Mon–Fri 9–6, Sat 9.30–1, Sun 11–2; Nov–end Mar Mon–Fri 9–6, Sat–9.30–1

7 The Bastei (bastion) is a spectacular place, where rock columns and pillars plunge nearly 200m (650ft) to the water's edge. The vertiginous views over the valley of the Elbe from the top of these sandstone formations equal those from the Königstein fortress.

Return to the road and turn west towards Pirna, but after 9km (5.5 miles) follow signs towards Pillnitz, then Dresden. You are now on the Saxon Wine Route, and the road runs for a while at the foot of vineyards of a fascinating wine region now emerging from the obscurity it suffered under the GDR regime.

Back in Dresden, follow signs to Radebeul, then Coswig and Meissen. As you finally emerge from Dresden's extensive built-up area you will see, on the north side of the road, Schloss Wackerbarth, the revived Saxon state winery, its terraced vineyards rising steeply behind the castle. Continue northwest for 10km (6 miles) to Meissen, following signs to *Zentrum* and enjoying the view of castle and cathedral before crossing the Elbe into the heart of the city.

8 Meissen has a well-preserved Altstadt worth a stroll, but highlights of a visit here are a walk up to the castle and a tour of the world-famous porcelain factory.

From Meissen, drive northwest along the B6 towards Oschatz, turning northeast after 20km (12 miles) towards Riesa. Avoiding the middle of Riesa, follow signs north to Torgau, which is reached in 39km (24 miles).

9 Torgau is proud of Schloss Hartenfels, its vast and splendid Renaissance castle. The town is also famous as the point where the American and Soviet armies met on the banks of the River Elbe in the closing days of World War II, splitting Hitler's Third Reich in half.

Return southwest to Leipzig (52km/32 miles) along the B87.

WHERE TO EAT

Berghotel und Panoramarestaurant Bastei (tel 0350 247790) is a hotel complex with several restaurants, including one perched on the edge of the Bastei rocks with fabulous views.

Near Dresden, you can enjoy refined but not expensive eating in Schloss Wackerbarth (Wackerbarther Strasse, 101445 Radebeul, tel 0351 8955 200), the spacious restaurant attached to the Saxon state winery.

Paths, catwalks and railings line the Bastei rocks above the Elbe

OUT AND ABOUT

TO THE TOP OF THE PFAFFENSTEIN IN SAXON SWITZERLAND

This hike in Saxon Switzerland gives you the chance to enjoy the bizarre beauty of this world of weirdly eroded sandstone. Protected by sheer 60m (200ft) cliffs, the Pfaffenstein, which rises to 434m (1,424ft), appears impregnable, but its formidable natural ramparts are split by fissures through which steps have been carved and metal stairways hung, making the great crag accessible to walkers.

THE WALK

Distance: 4.5km (3 miles); total ascent: 110m (360ft)

Allow: 1 hour, 30 min

Start/end at: Pfaffendorf car parking area

How to get there: The village of Pfaffendorf is 3km (2 miles) south of Königstein town. From the roundabout on the B172 in Königstein, drive south, turning left (east) at the sign for Pfaffendorf up a steeply climbing minor road. Turn right (south) into the parking area, which is just past the built up part of the village.

Note: Bear in mind that the sheer drops from the top of the Pfaffenstein are mostly unprotected by railings and that small children should not be allowed to run around unsupervised on the summit.

Walk south from the parking area, turning half-right (south-west) up a path made of concrete slabs towards the wooded cliffs of the Pfaffenstein. At the edge of the wood, turn half-left (southeast) into the trees and climb across the boulder-strewn slope. This is the beginning of the Nadelöhr.

The Nadelöhr (Eye of the Needle) is aptly named: At first sight it looks impossible to thread your way up through the narrow clefts in the cliffs. However, the fissures have been artificially enlarged in places, and steps, metal stairways and handrails make the ascent of this flank of the Pfaffenstein

Natur-schutzgebiet

Nature reserve sign on the Pfaffenstein

Pfaffenstein straightforward (if somewhat breathless). This approach was first opened in 1894.

At the top of the climb you reach the more-or-less flat summit of the Pfaffenstein.

Much of the summit is covered with open woodland of silver birch and other trees, some apparently growing directly out of the bare rock. In places there is a substantial layer of loamy soil, up to 1.5m (5ft) thick, which retains water, and it was this that made it possible for prehistoric people to set up permanent camp here.

Follow the timber railing round, turning left (southeast) at a sign indicating *Aussichtspunkt/Goldschmidthöhle* (Viewpoint/Goldsmith's Cave). The magnificent view extends beyond other table mountains, such as the Papststein straight ahead, to old volcanic peaks far away in the Czech Republic.

Go back the way you came and turn left (south) at the sign indicating 'Barbarine', then right (west) towards 'Opferkessel-Dom-Luftballon'.

The views from the summit of the Pfaffenstein are stunning, but take care of the edge

OUT AND ABOUT

'Sacrificial Cauldron', 'Cathedral' and 'Air Balloon' are the fanciful names given to the variously shaped rocks forming the western ramparts of the Pfaffenstein. There are popular climbing faces nearby and a fine view of the Königstein fortress.

Go back the way you came, turning right (south) to the Gaststätte (Restaurant) and the viewing tower.

The Pfaffenstein lodge/restaurant has been enlarged several times since it was established on this spot in 1880. The stone-built tower, 27m (89ft) high, built in 1904, replaced a timber structure erected in 1894. Its structural condition may mean that it is sometimes closed to the public.

As you continue south, you descend into a natural amphitheatre, climb through rocks and narrow clefts and ascend stone steps to reach a viewpoint facing southeast. The Pfaffenstein cliffs are at their most dramatic here—precipitous walls with great masses of fallen rock at their feet. Metal stairways lead down through the rocks to a flat area with extensive views to the southwest. A cleft to the east gives access to a narrow platform directly facing the Barbarine needle rock.

The Barbarine, an immensely tall and thin rock, seems an impossible climb to the layman, but it was very popular until its dangerous state led to its closure to climbers in 1975. The precarious summit has now been stabilized by the injection of resins and silicon. The rock owes its name to a tall tale about a disobedient little girl who was turned to stone by her angry mother.

Go back towards the tower and lodge, turning left (west) where a sign indicates *Klammweg/ Bequemer Abstieg* (cleft path/ easy descent). The path goes down via steps and through a spectacularly deep cleft, emerging into a flat open area.

A medallion high on the rockface commemorates Karl Gottlob Jäckel, a local

Man-made steps aid your passage through the Eye of the Needle

landowner who was responsible for opening up the Pfaffenstein to the public in the 19th century.

Continue down, turning right (north) when you emerge from the trees. Follow the flank of the Pfaffenstein north, then east, turning left (north) in 650m (710 yards) to descend the concrete path to the parking area.

WHERE TO EAT

Snacks may be available at the lodge on top of the Pfaffenstein. Otherwise there is a selection of places to eat in Königstein town or Bad Schandau (5.5km/3 miles east). In Pfaffendorf village, next to the car park, is the simple Gasthaus und Pension Zum Pfaffenstein (tel 035021 67951).

WHEN TO GO

This walk is best enjoyed when clear autumn weather gives good visibility.

PFAFFENSTEIN

The Pfaffenstein was inhabited in the Bronze Age, then served as a refuge in unsettled times for people from the valley. In the mid-19th century, one of its caves was used as a hideout by a counterfeiter who had escaped from the prison on the Königstein. Not long after his recapture, the rock's delights were discovered by walkers and climbers; in 1880 the refreshment hut was built followed by the viewing tower in 1904. The Pfaffenstein's most famous feature, the extraordinary needle rock called the Barbarine, was climbed for the first time by the well-known alpinists Rudolph Fehrmann and Englishman Perry Smith.

THE THURINGIAN FOREST:
A CIRCULAR TOUR FROM EISENACH

A glorious hilly area running some 100km (60 miles) southeast from Eisenach, the Thuringian Forest mixes deep beech and spruce woodland with open areas of field and meadow. This drive through the Forest takes in a whole string of historic towns, beginning with Eisenach, the imperial city where this route begins and ends, while Goethe and J. S. Bach provide literary and musical associations.

Wild flowers and dense woodland characterize the Thuringian Forest

OUT AND ABOUT

THE DRIVE

Distance:	170km (106 miles)
Allow:	4 hours
Start/end at:	Eisenach

From Karlsplatz in the middle of Eisenach ★, take the B19 southwards and follow signs towards Wartburg, turning east at the first set of traffic lights onto Johann-Sebastian-Bach-Strasse. Drive up steeply, following small green signs towards Burschenschafts-denkmal and Berghotel. Park where the road ends and walk up to the memorial.

❶ The huge stone Burschenschaftsdenkmal (Fraternities Memorial) was built in 1902 to commemorate the great rally on the Wartburg in 1817, during which patriotic students called for freedom and national unity. The vast wooded panorama gives a foretaste of the landscapes of the Thuringian Forest.

Return to the heart of town, first following signs for *Alle Richtungen* (all directions), then signs towards Gotha and the B7. In 4.5km (3 miles), turn south

onto the B88, and stay on this road following signs towards Ohrdruf and Ilmenau. After 19km (12 miles), at 2km (1.2 miles) beyond the spa town of Tabarz, turn south into the car parking area of the Marienglashöhle.

❷ The Marienglashöhle is one of the largest crystalline caves in Europe, featuring magical patterns formed by gypsum crystals as well as stalactites and stalagmites.

Continue 2km (1.2 miles) along the B88 to Friedrichroda.

❸ Like Tabarz, Friedrichroda is a summer resort and spa town, much developed in GDR days with oversized buildings for subsidized vacationers, but now recovering much of its attractive turn-of-the-century character.

Continue along the B88 to Ohrdruf. When you exit the town, leave the B88 and take the B247 towards Oberhof. To the east of the road, in 1.5km (1 mile), you'll see the car parking area for the Tobiashammer.

❹ The Tobiashammer is a fascinating technical museum, with exhibits that include a monster 1920's steam engine.

Continue south along the B247 towards the winter resort of Oberhof. The resort, with its huge hotels and ski slopes, is to the west, while there are views to the southeast of the Schneekopf (978m/3,209ft). Beyond Oberhof, turn southeast onto a minor road signposted Schmücke. The road winds through the forest, close to the famous Rennsteig long-distance trail. After 16km (10 miles), turn north along the B4 towards Ilmenau. As the road descends to Stützerbach, there are fine views of houses hung with slate tiles. After 10km (6 miles) you'll reach the old town of Ilmenau.

❺ Ilmenau is known for its glass and porcelain, and above all for its associations with one of Germany's greatest writers, Johann Wolfgang von Goethe, who came here no fewer than 28 times, finding inspiration in the hills, woods, valleys and ravines all around.

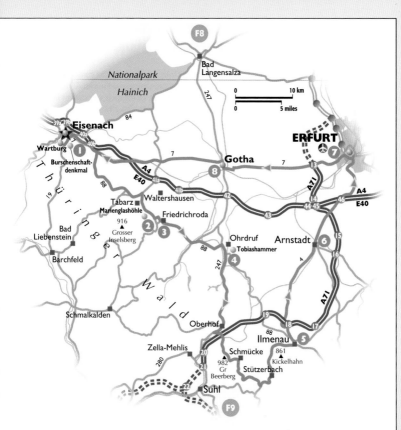

Continue north on the B4 to Arnstadt, where the hills of the Thuringian Forest descend to the plain.

6 Well-preserved Arnstadt is one of Germany's most venerable small cities. J. S. Bach was organist here between 1703 and 1707; the town museum pays tribute to him. But Arnstadt's great attraction is Mon Plaisir, a collection of 400 costumed dolls, assembled in the 18th century by the widowed Princess Augusta Dorothea and occupying a floor in the Neues Palais.

Continue north along the B4 for 19km (11.5 miles) to Erfurt. In the city, follow signs to 'Dom' and park on the Domplatz.

7 In Erfurt, the capital of Thuringia, take time to appreciate its dramatically sited Gothic cathedral, well-preserved old buildings and a famous horticultural exhibition at the Cyriaksburg castle, just outside town.

From the middle of Erfurt, follow the B7 for 21km (13 miles) to Gotha. On the approach to the town, look for signs to Schloss Friedenstein. Park in front of the castle, with its massive twin towers, and walk through the spacious courtyard for a wonderful view over the old city below.

8 The princely city of Gotha has an old core focused on the high-gabled town hall, and rich art collections displayed in the 17th-century baroque Schloss Friedenstein.

Return to Eisenach along the B7.

Arnstadt gave Johann Sebastian Bach his first job as an organist

OUT AND ABOUT

WHEN TO GO

This drive can be undertaken at any time of year, but check on driving conditions in winter when the mountian roads may be affected by snowfall as well as crowded with winter sports traffic.

WHERE TO EAT

Thuringian sausages are famed far beyond their place of origin, and in the most visited parts of the Forest you will find plenty of stalls selling them.

Halfway along the route is Gasthof Jägerstube Meyersgrund (Ilmenauerstrasse 7, 98714 Stützerbach, tel 036784 50235/50750), a roadside restaurant specializing in trout.

PLACES TO VISIT

Marienglashöhle
99894 Friedrichroda
☎ 03695 614101
🕐 Daily Apr–end Oct 9–5; Nov–end Mar 9–4

Tobiashammer
Suhler Strasse 34, Ohrdruf
☎ 03624 402792
🕐 Daily 9–5

MUNICH'S OLD TOWN

The walk starts on Munich's grand square, Odeonsplatz, and ends in the heart of the city on Marienplatz. It takes in several churches, including the twin-towered Frauenkirche, which has become emblematic of the city. En route you also pass one of Munich's grandest hotels and walk through one of the former gates to the city.

THE WALK

Distance:	2km (1.25 miles)
Allow:	2 hours
Start at:	Odeonsplatz
How to get there:	Odeonsplatz U-bahn
End at:	Marienplatz

Begin at Odeonsplatz and walk west along Briennerstrasse, where there are exclusive shops selling antiques, jewellery and designer clothes. Remember that most shops here don't open until 10am, so if you come before then, it'll be window-shopping only. Very soon you'll come to Wittelsbacherplatz.

❶ Wittelsbacherplatz, named after the dynasty that ruled Bavaria from 1180 until 1918, has an impressive equestrian statue of Elector Maximilian I.

Opposite Wittelsbacherplatz, on the other side of the road, is Amiraplatz, which looks more like a street than a square. Go down here past the Literaturhaus.

❷ The Literaturhaus is the home of Munich's literary scene, with book readings and a wonderful café (▷ 365). Opposite it is the city's ubiquitous bookstore, Hugendubel: You'll see other branches all over the city. A little further down the street is the Greek Orthodox church, the Salvatorkirche.

Continue straight on to Kardinal Faulhaberstrasse, where you have a good view of the distinctive green onion domes of the Frauenkirche at the end of the street.

❸ The Archbishop's Palace on Kardinal Faulhaberstrasse has been the residence of the archbishops of Munich and Freising since 1818. Also in this street, near the end, is an unusual grille on the pavement

The red roof and onion-domed towers of the Frauenkirche

(sidewalk), in the shape of a dead man's body. It marks the spot where Bavaria's first prime minister, Kurt Eisner, was assassinated in February 1919.

At the end of Kardinal Faulhaberstrasse, turn right into Promenadeplatz. Walk past one of Munich's most glamorous hotels, the five-star Bayerischer Hof (▷ 397), with its livery-clad doorman outside.

❹ On the other side of Promenadeplatz on Karmeliterstrasse is the Carmelite church, the earliest baroque church in the city. Almost opposite on

Pacellistrasse is the Dreifaltigkeitskirche (Church of the Holy Trinity), with its ornate gold and green door.

Continue to the end of Pacellistrasse. Opposite you, in the middle of the main road in Lenbachplatz, is the Wittelsbach Fountain dating from 1885. Don't cross over the road—stay on the same side and turn left. On the left you'll pass the gleaming BMW showroom, which has 4x4 models from Munich's most popular car manufacturer. Cross over Maxburgstrasse to reach Mövenpick.

❺ Mövenpick is well known in Munich for its enormous

breakfast buffet and Sunday brunch, which are served in the café. It also has a cocktail bar, a restaurant and even a cigar smoking room, and it's a good place to stop for coffee and cake.

When you come out of Mövenpick, turn left and continue along the main road until you come to Karlstor, formerly the west gate to the city, on the left. Go through the gate into the pedestrianized shopping area on Neuhauserstrasse. Pass Michaelskirche and, at the statue of a wild boar, turn left up Augustinerstrasse to the Frauenkirche.

6 The mighty Frauenkirche (Church of Our Lady) acts as Munich's cathedral. Its twin towers, topped by distinctive green onion domes, which can be seen from all over the city, are the symbol of Munich.

Go down Thiereckstrasse and continue into Marienplatz, where there are plenty of options for lunch.

Interior of the Baroque Dreifaltigkeitskirche (above); detail from the coat of arms on the portal of the Archbishop's Palace (left)

The Altes Rathaus (Old Town Hall) now houses a toy museum

WHEN TO GO

You can do this walk at all times of the year.

PLACES TO VISIT

Salvatorkirche
Salvatorplatz
⏰ Daily 10–5
💶 Free

WHERE TO EAT

For a quick bite standing up, go to one of the food stands at the Viktualienmarkt (▷ 202), or for good traditional Bavarian fare, try Spatenhaus an der Oper (▷ 367). To get there, walk up Dienerstrasse to Max-Joseph-Platz. For something more exclusive (and expensive), indulge yourself at Dallmayr (▷ 365) on Dienerstrasse.

OUT AND ABOUT

BAVARIA'S ALTMÜHL VALLEY

From cosmopolitan Nürnberg, Bavaria's second largest city, this route takes you deep into the Naturpark Altmühltal, one of Germany's largest nature parks, and on into the Franconian Lake District. You will pass castles and fortresses on wooded hills and rugged crags overlooking rolling river valleys dotted with unspoiled towns and villages.

The River Altmühl runs through the historic town of Eichstätt

THE DRIVE

Distance:	187km (116 miles)
Allow:	6 hours
Start/end at:	Nürnberg

Leave Nürnberg ★ by the B4 going southeast. After 9km (5.5 miles) turn off south to Feucht, then after 2km (1.2 miles) turn southeast onto the B8 and follow it for 27km (17.5 miles) to Neumarkt.

❶ Neumarkt's museum gives an interesting insight into the town's history, from its golden age as a town of residence for the Counts Palatine to its destruction in World War II.

Leave Neumarkt on the B299 and continue south for 29km (18 miles) to Beilngries.

❷ Beilngries is the gateway to the Altmühltal Naturpark, and is also a town noted for its baroque town hall, its rococo church—and its beer. There are some lovely walks here alongside the rivers Sulz and Altmühl, south of the town, and the Main–Danube Canal to the north. Within the Altmühltal Nature Park, which covers an area of 3,000sq km (1,150sq miles), are palaces, castles, churches and monasteries that are testimony to the long history and rich cultural heritage of this scenic region. Along the way, be sure to stop and admire the scenery.

From central Beilngries, take a right turn onto a minor road and follow the signs for Kinding and Eichstätt. Continue on this quiet road for 32km (20 miles) through the heart of the Altmühltal Naturpark to Eichstätt.

❸ Eichstätt is worth exploring. The spires from its 14th-century cathedral and numerous churches dominate the skyline, and remains of medieval fortifications sit alongside rococo mansions. The cathedral of St. Wilibald (first bishop of Eichstätt) houses the Pappenheim Altar, a late medieval depiction of the Crucifixion.

From Eichstätt, join the B13 and head northwest for 24km (15 miles) to Weissenburg, where there are plenty of places to park near the town walls.

❹ Old Weissenburg still bears the character of an Imperial city. The town walls, with their 38 towers and one remaining town gate (Ellinger Tor), are almost intact and rank among the finest in Bavaria. The medieval core of the town has many timber-framed houses, baroque façades and fine public buildings, including the late Gothic town hall and the Andreaskirche. The remnant of Roman baths and the Roman Museum add another aspect.

Leave Weissenburg on the B2 north towards Roth. Now you are heading out of the Naturpark and into the Franconian Lake District, the area of reservoirs made up of the Altmühlsee, the Brombach lake system, which consists of the idyllic Igelsbachsee and the Little and Great Brombachsee, and the Rothsee. All the lakes have beaches for swimming and sunbathing, excellent facilities for water sports and waterfront restaurants serving Franconian and Bavarian cuisine. The area is ideal for walking and cycling too. After 28km (17 miles), you come to Roth.

5 Roth has always been a busy little city. Today it's the seat of the county administration and a garrison town of the German armed forces, while its location in the Franconian Lake District brings many visitors. Sights in the town include one of the finest timber-framed buildings in Franconia—the Riffelmacherhaus in the market square—and Schloss Ratibor, which contains a museum. If you have time, take a look at the valley of the River Roth, particularly beautiful between Hilpoltstein and Roth. Near Eckersmühlen, 4km (2.5 miles) from town, there's a museum that demonstrates the use of water as a power source for the local industry.

Continue north along the B2 for 36km (22 miles) to Nürnberg. Watch on the right for large ships drifting leisurely across the horizon as they navigate the Main–Danube Canal, a massive project completed in 1992, enabling vessels to operate between the Rhine and the Black Sea.

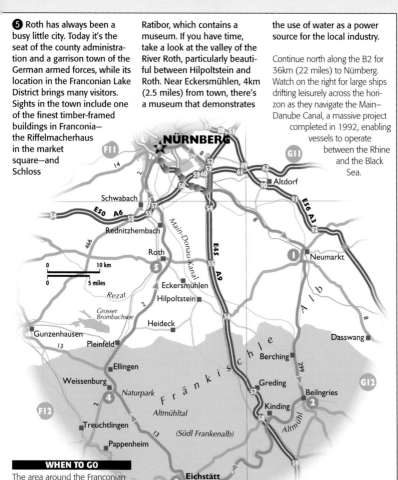

WHEN TO GO

The area around the Franconian Lake District gets extremely busy in summer. However, if you are planning to do the drive without stopping there, the route is enjoyable at any time of year.

WHERE TO EAT

There are many excellent places to eat around the medieval heart of Eichstätt, including the Ratskeller (Am Graben 8, tel 08421 901258), which serves a good choice of local dishes and beers in pleasant surroundings. In Weissenburg there are two lovely cellar restaurants: Waldgaststätte Araunerskeller (An den Sommerkellern, tel 09141 92933) and Sigwartskeller (Eichstätter Landstrasse, tel 09141 874885). In Roth, the Ratsstuben (Schloss Ratibor, Haupstrasse 1, tel 09171 853585) is a large café/restaurant in a historic location.

PLACES TO VISIT

Stadtmuseum (Town Museum)
Adolf-Kolping-Strasse 4, Neumarkt
☎ 09181 2401
🕐 Mar–end Jan Wed–Fri, Sun 2–5
💶 Adult €2, child €1

Römermuseum
Martin-Luther-Platz 3, Weissenburg
☎ 09141 907124
🕐 Apr–end Dec daily 10–12.30, 2–5
💶 Adult €2, child €1.50

Museum Schloss Ratibor
Haupstrasse 1, Roth
☎ 09171 848 513
🕐 Apr–end Sep Sat, Sun 1–4
🎟 Free

Historischer Eisenhammer
Eckersmühlen
☎ 09171 81329
🕐 Apr–end Oct Wed–Sun 1–5

Weissenburg's medieval town square

NORTHERN BAVARIA: THE GLASSTRASSE THROUGH THE BAYERISCHER WALD

Glass is the theme of this drive. From Passau, 'the city of three rivers', this route follows the 'Glass Road' through the Bavarian Forest National Park. Roads wind their way through dense upland forests, passing attractive towns and villages, many of them associated with glassmaking.

THE DRIVE

Distance:	267km (166 miles)
Allow:	10 hours
Start/end at:	Passau

Leave Passau ★ on the B85 and head north for 22km (13.5 miles) to Tittling.

1 Tittling is the gateway to the Bavarian Forest. Visit the Museumsdorf Bayerischer Wald (Museum Village), where reconstructed farms show traditional life.

Continue north along the B85 for a further 16km (10 miles), then turn right onto the B533 and head northeast for 5km (3 miles) to Grafenau.

2 Grafenau, an attractive town in mountainous countryside, has an unusual snuff museum, with over 400 snuff bottles (*Schmalzliergläsl*).

Leave Grafenau on the minor road north signposted to Spiegelau. To detour to the National Park's excellent visitor headquarters, look for a signpost to turn right after 3km/2 miles. It's in the Hans-Eisenmann-Haus

Glass blowing in Frauenau, the heart of glassmaking in Germany

in Neuschönau, and has much information (including some in English) about the park.

Spiegelau is 8km (5 miles) from Grafenau. It has a variety of glass shops selling glasses of all shapes and sizes. From here, the Glass Road continues north through lush forests, passing old glassworking towns, for a further 16km (10 miles) to Frauenau.

3 Frauenau is the historical focus of glass production in the Bavarian Forest, with glass produced here since the 15th century. The Glasmuseum is the perfect place to discover more about the history and culture of glassmaking, both locally and worldwide.

From Frauenau continue northwest for 8km (5 miles) to reach the 'glass town' of Zwiesel.

4 Zwiesel is dominated by the red-brick steeple of St. Nicholas's Church, where the brilliant *Jugendstil* (art nouveau) glass bears witness to the quality of the former plate glassworks in the area.

When leaving Zwiesel, turn right at the intersection and head north to join the B27 for 16km (10 miles) to Bayerisch

Eisenstein. As you approach the Czech border, take the left turn and follow the winding mountainous road for 26km (16 miles) to Lohberg and Lam. This is a spectacular drive along a ridge-top road with the towering Grosser Arber (1,456m/4,776ft) to your left and the green forests of the Bayerischer Wald falling away into the Czech Republic on your right. There are many lovely spots to stop and walk or admire the scenery. One of the best places for this is the Hindenberg viewpoint shortly before you descend into Lam. After leaving Lam, continue heading north for 23km (14 miles) towards Furth im Wald. You will soon pass through the small town of Engelshütt.

5 Engelshütt's long history of glassmaking is enshrined in its name—En Glashutt (a glassworks). There are still parts of the town with names like 'Schmelz' (melt) and 'Glaserbauer' (glass builder).

The next town you come to after 10km (6 miles) is Neukirchen bei Heiligen Blut.

6 Neukirchen bei Heiligen Blut is a place of pilgrimage that came to fame thanks to a legend about a miracle from about 1450. A Hussite (follower of the Bohemian religious reformer Jan Hus) struck a venerated figure of the Virgin Mary with his sword, and blood is said to have flowed from the wooden statue.

After a further 11km (7 miles) you reach the frontier town of Furth im Wald.

7 Furth im Wald is the home of the mirror glass industry, and the City Museum has displays illustrating the history of glass. August sees the spectacular *Drachenstich* (Dragon Slaying)

OUT AND ABOUT

pageant, when visitors flock to see part of a 500-year-old play in which a huge (18m/60ft) animated dragon is 'slain'.

From Furth im Wald head south-west along the B20 for 19km (11.5 miles) to Cham.

❽ Cham might appear to have slipped into the wrong country every day at five minutes past noon, when the

French national anthem (the 'Marseillaise') rings out from the town hall's tower. The Glockenspiel plays in tribute to the town's best-known son, Nikolaus Graf von Luckner, who became a marshal in the French Army, and to whom the anthem was dedicated.

Return to the B20 and head east for 2km (1.2 miles) before turning right onto the B85 and

driving south through the heart of the Bayerischer Wald for 47km (29 miles) to Regen.

❾ Regen is noted for the production of optical glasses and lenses. Above the town in the direction of Passau are the castle ruins of Weissenstein, the former home of writer Siegfried von Vegesack (1888–1974). Today it houses the Museum Burgkasten collection of more than 1,300 snuff bottles demonstrating the range of traditional hand-crafted glass.

Continue south along the B85 for 59km (37 miles) to Passau.

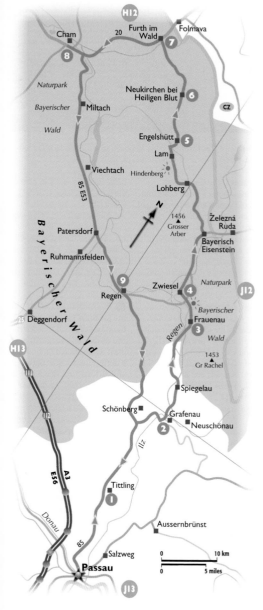

WHEN TO GO
Except on public holidays and some weekends in the high season, this route is untroubled by hoards of visitors. The most popular glass factories are busy throughout the year, but there are plenty to choose from along the Glass Road.

WHERE TO EAT
In Passau, Zur Triftsperre Waldrestaurant (Triftsperre 15, tel 0851 51162) is in a lovely situation in the nature reserve near the River Ilz.
Close to the lake in Tittling is the Hotel Dreiburgensee (Am Dreiburgensee, tel 08504 760), with a good choice of restaurants serving Bavarian and international meals.
Many of the glass factory outlets and museums have excellent coffee shops, but the Café Glashüttenbistro in Glaszentrum Spiegelau is particularly good (tel 08553 24191).

PLACES TO VISIT
Glasmuseum (Frauenau)
Am Museumspark 1, Frauenau
☎ 09926 9400-35
🕐 Due to reopen May 2005

Glasmuseum (Passau)
Haus Wilder Mann, Am Rathausplatz, Passau
☎ 0851 35071
🕐 All year, daily 1–5
💶 Adult €5, child (12–18) €3

Veste Oberhaus–Oberhausmuseum
Veste Oberhaus 125, 94034, Passau
☎ 0851 493351
🕐 Apr–end Dec Mon–Fri 9–5, Sat, Sun 10–6
💶 Adult €5, child (6–18) €4

OUT AND ABOUT

SOUTHERN BAVARIA: GARMISCH-PARTENKIRCHEN AND OBERAMMERGAU

This circular drive takes you from Garmisch-Partenkirchen, Germany's winter sports capital, to Oberammergau, a village renowned for its fairy-tale painted houses, woodcarvings and, above all, its Passion Play. The route also takes in Schloss Linderhof, one of the castles built by 'Mad' King Ludwig of Bavaria in the 19th century, and the Wieskirche, among the greatest rococo buildings in Europe.

The magnificent scenery close to Linderhof is framed by a backdrop of brooding Alpine peaks (left and above)

OUT AND ABOUT

THE DRIVE

Distance: 210km (130 miles)	
Allow: 8 hours	
Start/end at: Garmisch-Partenkirchen	

Leave Garmisch-Partenkirchen ★ east past the Olympic Stadium and follow the B2 for 12km (7.5 miles) to Klais. From the village, follow the signs to Schloss Elmau, which is a right turn onto a narrow toll road (€3) This is a winding gravel road passing through spruce forests; after 5km (3 miles) it opens out to farmland and the castle.

❶ Schloss Elmau is now a private hotel and open to staying guests only, but the exterior and grounds are worth seeing.

Return to Klais and head southeast from the village on a minor road for 5km (3 miles) to Mittenwald.

❷ Mittenwald is a photogenic small town surrounded by snow-capped Alpine peaks. Famous for violin-making, this busy visitor resort has retained much of its old-world charm. Look for the statue of violin-maker Matthias Klotz near the baroque church with its fine

frescoes. The Geigenbau Museum has a good collection of old violins and other stringed instruments on display.

Leave Mittenwald north on the B2. After 7km (4.4 miles) the road bends sharp left; continue straight ahead north onto the B11 and follow this road for 36km (22 miles). Look for the viewpoint over the Walchensee on your right to get wonderful views of the lake. Shortly before Bichl, turn left onto the B472 and continue for 18km (11 miles) to the intersection with the B2. Turn right then left, and after 3km (2 miles) rejoin the B472 west for 27km (17 miles) to the attractive small town of Schongau.

❸ Schongau, perched on a hill above the River Lech, is still partly surrounded by its town walls. On the Marienplatz are the Ballenhaus, a former warehouse of 1515, and the parish church of St. Mary of the Ascension, a Romanesque-Gothic building with a tower and choir dating from the 17th century.

Leave Schongau going west, and just outside town turn left at the B472 intersection, then head southeast for 7km (4 miles)

before taking a right turn onto the B23. After 10km (6 miles), take a right turn signposted to the Wieskirche and continue on this minor road for 9km (5.5 miles) before turning left again. Follow this narrow road through open countryside for 3km (2 miles). Suddenly, you will see the great dome of the Wieskirche.

❹ The Wieskirche ('Church in the Meadow') stands alone in the midst of green meadows, just as its name suggests, a plain white church embodying a perfect harmony of nature and architecture. This is one of the great rococo buildings of Europe, a pilgrimage church built to house a figure representing the Scourging of Christ, which had allegedly shed tears. This became known as 'the miracle in the meadows' and a surge of pilgrimages began. A chapel was built in 1740, but as the flood of pilgrims increased, the Abbot of Steingaden decided it was necessary to build a larger church, and in 1745 the

Continued on page 318

The village of Oberammergau (right) is famous for its Passion Play and woodcarvings

This whole area is popular with visitors, so there's a wide choice of restaurants and cafés in the towns and villages around the route. In the Kurpark in Garmisch-Partenkirchen, the Adlwärth (Richard-Strauss-Platz 1, tel 08821 3177; open May–end Oct) is an excellent café and restaurant in pleasant surroundings. One of the best places in Mittenwald is the Restaurant Arnspitze (Innsbrucker Strasse, tel 08823 2425), serving good local fare. If you fancy a British pub meal, try the Rose and Crown in Schongau (Weinstrasse 4, tel 08861 7242).

Garmisch-Partenkirchen, Oberammergau and the Wieskirche attract large numbers of visitors and are exceptionally busy all year; avoid visiting on weekends and during public holidays.

Geigenbau Museum (Violin-making Museum)
Ballenhausgasse 3, Mittenwald
☎ 08823 2511
🕐 Tue–Fri 10–1, 3–6, Sat, Sun 10–1
💶 Adult €2.50, child (7–14) €0.50

Passions Theater, Oberammergau
Passionswiese 1, Oberammergau.
☎ 08822 92310
🕐 Daily 9–6
💶 €2.50

Schloss Linderhof, Ettal
☎ 08822 92030
🕐 Apr–end Oct 9–6, Nov–end Mar 10–4
💶 Apr–end Oct adult €7, child €6, Nov–end Mar adult €6, child €5

Käthe Wohlfahrt
(Traditional German Christmas decorations and ornaments)
Marienplatz 4, Garmisch-Partenkirchen
☎ 08821 79448
🕐 Mon–Fri 9–6, Sat 9–4

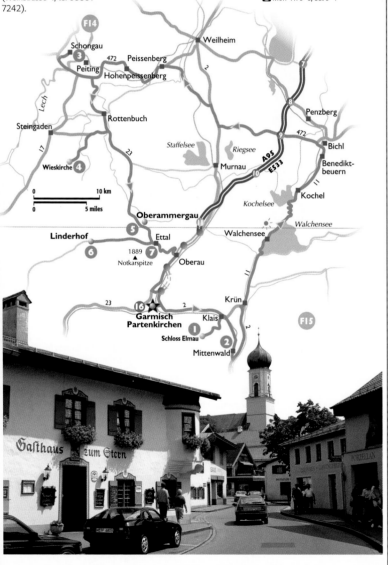

OUT AND ABOUT

The aptly named Wieskirche ('Church in the Meadows'—top)

The dome of Ettal's Benedictine monastery is by Joseph Schmuzer

OUT AND ABOUT

Schloss Linderhof's Renaissance-inspired gardens (above)

architect Dominikus Zimmermann built his masterpiece. The interior, flooded with light, is a glorious assemblage of stuccowork and fresco, notably the frescoed dome, which depicts the Gate to Paradise. The Wieskirche attracts almost a million visitors a year, so if possible avoid peak times for your visit.

Leave the Wieskirche and return to the B23. Turn right and head south for 16km (10 miles) to Oberammergau. Turn left off the main road to enter the town.

❺ Oberammergau is well described as a fairy-tale town: As soon as you enter, you are confronted by house façades painted with a varied mixture of religious, fairy-tale and

secular themes. Although renowned for its Passion Play, Oberammergau is a popular resort at all times of the year.

Leave the town on the continuation of the minor road by which you entered, heading southwest for 8km (5 miles) to Schloss Linderhof.

❻ Schloss Linderhof, amid magnificent mountain scenery and surrounded by forest, is arguably the most pleasing of Ludwig II's castles, and even if you don't visit the palace, the grounds—full of surprises, including a 'Moorish' kiosk—are a great place to wander.

Leave Linderhof on the minor road heading east across the wide valley floor at the foot of the Notkarspitze (1,889m/ 6198ft) for 11km (7 miles) to

Ettal. This beautiful countryside is popular in winter with cross-country skiers, and the sight of trains of skiers in bright ski-suits scurrying across the valley floor is entertaining.

❼ Ettal is known for its Benedictine abbey and Ettaler Klosterlikör, a fragrant herb liqueur made by monks using an ancient recipe. The abbey, founded in 1330 by Emperor Ludwig the Bavarian and converted into a domed baroque church in the 18th century, has an unusual 12-sided nave and fine frescoes in the dome. The complex in front of the church is the abbey's boarding school.

From Ettal, head southeast along the B23 for 6km (3.5 miles) to Oberau, then turn right and follow the B2 south for 10km (6 miles) to Garmisch-Partenkirchen.

GARMISCH-PARTENKIRCHEN: THE PARTNACHKLAMM

This is a spectacular walk along a man-made path that snakes along the bottom of a ravine. The sheer walls of the Partnach gorge rise to 80m (260ft) and the foaming river roars through the narrow gorge. Tunnels have been cut into the rock to give safe access and views of the turquoise water below; in winter, spectacular ice formations cling to the rock faces. Before following the path through the gorge, you can view it from above by taking a cable car ride and walking back from the top of the gorge to one of the entrances.

THE WALK

Distance: 5km (3 miles)

Allow: 2 hours

Start/end at: Olympic Ski Stadium, Partenkirchen

How to get there: The Olympic Ski Stadium is just off the B2 in Partenkirchen and is well signposted. There is ample free parking at the stadium. Admission to gorge: Adult €2, child (6–16) €1

Note: You will need good walking shoes and a jacket for this walk. Even in the height of summer the temperature drops dramatically in the gorge and water constantly drips from the high rocks above the walkway.

You are not allowed to drive beyond the Olympic Ski Stadium. From here, you can either walk along the road (1.5km/1 mile) to the gorge entrance, or take a horse-drawn carriage ride (€2.50 per person). The road follows the course of the river, which flows quite sedately at this point in comparison to its furious passage through the gorge.

WHEN TO GO

The path through the gorge is well maintained and open all year. During spring when the snow begins to melt, the water reaches its peak level and roars through the gorge, but summer is also a spectacular time to visit. Although the path is cleared of snow and gritted in winter, extreme care needs to be taken in icy conditions.

The cable car ride to the summit of the Zugspitze from Garmisch-Patrenkirchen is as obligatory as the Partnachklamm walk

Opposite the Forsthaus Graseck hotel is the Graseckbahn automatic cable car, which will take you 130m (430ft) up to the small hamlet of Vordergraseck. The short cable car ride takes you directly above the gorge, giving spectacular views below of the sheer rock faces and turbulent waters of the Partnach river.

From Vordergraseck you can follow the signs to the Hohe Brücke (High Bridge), approximately 1km (0.5 mile) away, then follow the signs to take you downhill back to the lower gorge entrance, approximately 2km (1.2 miles). Alternatively, from the Hohe Brücke, follow the track up the valley for 1km (0.5 mile) to the top entrance.

From the lower gorge entrance, continue to the ticket gate (300m/330 yards) and enter the ravine. Almost immediately, you pass through a series of tunnels cut into the rock face. The noise of the water roaring through the narrow gorge below is deafening. The path is safe and the barriers are good, but you need to be cautious if you have young children with you, as the noise may frighten them. It's not feasible to take a pushchair (stroller) along.

Early walkways through the gorge once helped forestry workers to float timber down to the sawmills, while the path visitors walk today involved the difficult task of blasting tunnels through the rock face.

After 700m (770 yards), you emerge from the gorge through another ticket gate into a wide forested valley where the river ambles serenely across the valley floor before being squeezed through the narrow gorge and converted into a raging torrent. This is a pleasant place to rest and relax before retracing your footsteps to the start of the walk.

WHERE TO EAT

Hotel Leiner (Wildenauerstrasse 20, tel 08821 95280), just 200m (220 yards) from the Olympic Stadium, is an ideal place to eat and stay. It has a restaurant, beer garden, terrace café, sauna and swimming pool. About halfway along the road between the stadium and the gorge entrance there's a café on the riverside, serving ice cream, teas, coffee and snacks. At the entrance to the gorge is the Forsthaus Graseck hotel, where you can get good food and drink. There's also a beer garden between this entrance and the ticket gate.

The weather station and viewing platforms atop the Zugspitze

OUT AND ABOUT

THE ALPS IN SOUTHERN BAVARIA

This drive follows the Alps along the Austrian border in southern Bavaria, from the southernmost end of the Romantic Road at Füssen to Isny, a border town between Bavaria and Baden-Württemberg.

THE DRIVE

Distance: 190 km (118 miles)

Allow: 7 hours

Start/end at: Füssen

The attractive mountain town of Füssen ★, with its handsome old quarter, stands at the end of the Romantische Strasse (Romantic Road), which links it with Würzburg 350km (215 miles) to the north. Nearby are Ludwig II's extraordinary medieval fantasies, the castles of Neuschwanstein and Hohenschwangau.

Leave Füssen and head northwest along the B310 for 12km (7.5 miles) to join the B309 for 14km (8.5 miles) to Mittelberg, a tranquil village at the far end of the Kleinwalsertal valley. Continue northwest along the B309 for a further 16km (10 miles) to Kempten.

Neuschwanstein, Ludwig II's fairy-tale castle, dominates the skyline

❶ Kempten, despite being a busy commercial town, has much that is worth seeing. The Archäologischer Park (Archaeological Park) occupies the former site of the Roman town of Cambodunum, while museums and galleries include the Allgäu-Museum für Kunst und Kulturgeschichte (for local history), Römisches Museum (the Romans), Alpinmuseum (people and mountains of the Alps) and the Alpenländische Galerie (Alpine arts). The Burghalde, one of the oldest parts of the town, was originally a late Roman fort. Other sights are the Gothic church of St. Mang (1426) and an art nouveau fountain (1905), both in St. Mang-Platz; the Fürstäbtliche Residenz, a baroque palace with a magnificent rococo interior; and the St. Lorenz basilica, the first major church built in southern Germany after the Thirty Years War (1652).

From downtown Kempten, head west along the old B12 signposted to Wengen and Isny. Follow this scenic route for 25km (15.5 miles) as it climbs and twists to Wengen and the great Schwarzer Grat, before dropping down to Isny.

❷ Isny, a border town between Bavaria and Baden-Württemberg, is relatively quiet, ideal for a stop and a stroll. The clean air and climate around the town, an officially designated health resort, is known to be beneficial and, although many people visit to take advantage of the resort's facilities, it doesn't get overrun. Main points of interest are the Rathaus, which has a massive tiled stove that reaches as high as the ceiling, and St. Nicholas's Church, with a library housed in its spire. Parking is reasonably easy to find and there are some pleasingly old-fashioned little cafés and restaurants in the squares and narrow streets.

From Isny, take the minor road marked with brown signs, which show it is a designated scenic route, south for 19km (11.5 miles) to join the Deutsche Alpenstrasse (German Alpine Highway) at Oberstaufen.

❸ Oberstaufen, a popular resort in the western Allgäu, is also noted for its *Schrotkur*, a cure for the effects of overeating and drinking that involves fasting. A pleasant detour here is to visit nearby Steibis (2km/1.2 miles south) where you can take the cable car and walk to the summit of Hochgrat (1832m/5,023 ft), from where there are stunning views.

Now head east along the B308 for 16km (10 miles) to Immenstadt.

Continued on page 322

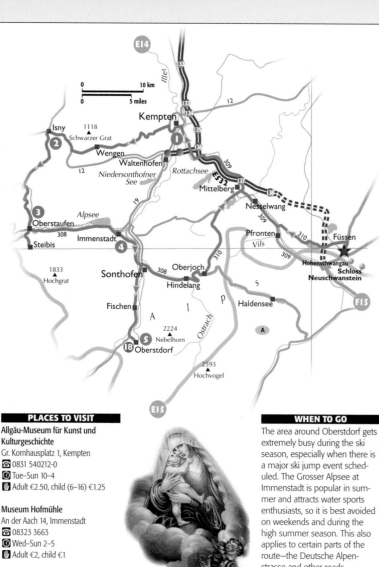

PLACES TO VISIT

Allgäu-Museum für Kunst und Kulturgeschichte
Gr. Kornhausplatz 1, Kempten
☎ 0831 540212-0
◷ Tue–Sun 10–4
▥ Adult €2.50, child (6–16) €1.25

Museum Hofmühle
An der Aach 14, Immenstadt
☎ 08323 3663
◷ Wed–Sun 2–5
▥ Adult €2, child €1

Heimat-Museum
Oststrasse 13, Oberstdorf
☎ 08322 5470
◷ Tue–Sat 10–12, 2–5.30
▥ Adult €2.50, child €1.50

The architectural detail of Schloss Hohe (below) is a fine example of trompe-l'oeil

WHEN TO GO

The area around Oberstdorf gets extremely busy during the ski season, especially when there is a major ski jump event scheduled. The Grosser Alpsee at Immenstadt is popular in summer and attracts water sports enthusiasts, so it is best avoided on weekends and during the high summer season. This also applies to certain parts of the route—the Deutsche Alpenstrasse and other roads designated for their stunning scenery.

WHERE TO EAT

The main towns along the route, such as Kempten and Oberstdorf, have a good choice of cafés and restaurants, but these are often busy. Look in the smaller towns and villages to find places to eat with local character. Try the Hotel Bistro Restaurant Baren (Obertorstrasse 9, Isny, tel 07562 2420), Hotel Restaurant Krone (Rottachbergstrasse 1, Immenstadt, tel 08323 96610) or, for its wonderful views, the Inn's Panorama Hotel and Restaurant (Reute, Oberstdorf, tel 08322 3074).

Neo-Gothic Schloss Hohenschwangau, Ludwig II's other spectacular castle near Füssen, is set high among the mountain crags

4 Immenstadt, idyllically positioned at the foot of the Immenstadter Horn, is another much-visited resort. The nearby Grosser Alpsee, an Alpine lake 3km (2 miles) long stretching below the towering mass of the Gschwendner Horn, is ideal for water sports and swimming. Sights in and around the town include the 17th-century ruins of Schloss Königsegg and the nearby Laubenbergstein castle.

Leave Immenstadt on the B19 and head southeast for 7km (4 miles) to Sonthofen, an attractive little town in the wide valley of the Iller noted for its winter sports facilities. Continue southeast along the B19 for a further 13km (8 miles) to Oberstdorf.

5 Oberstdorf has a famous ski jump and draws the crowds for its winter sports. In summer there's rock climbing, hiking, bicycling, hang-gliding and parasailing (a spectacular sight). The many cable cars (including the largest cable car in Germany, holding up to 100 passengers) take less energetic visitors to mountain summits for spectacular views and walks. The Sollereckbahn is Germany's longest continuous monocable elevator, with comfortable six-seater cabins allowing for tremendous views. No fewer than seven valleys join the Iller valley at Oberstdorf, each one with its own character and charm. The Heimat-Museum (Museum of Local History) in

the town has some fascinating displays, including the largest shoe in the world, made by Oberstdorf shoemaker Josef Schatt, who used 18 cowhides to make it.

Return to Sonthofen along the B19, then turn right onto the B308 and head east for 15km (9 miles), via Hindelang, to Oberjoch. This road twists and winds with many hairpin bends; it is also a designated tourist route because of the stunning scenery, particularly along the stretch between Hindelang and Oberjoch. From Oberjoch take the B310 north for 16km (10 miles) to Mittelberg and continue along the B310 southeast for 24km (15 miles) back to Füssen.

THE BREITACHKLAMM NEAR OBERSTDORF

This walk through and above the Breitach gorge near Oberstdorf takes you close to the Austrian border. The path is cut deep inside the gorge and gently climbs above spraying water and extraordinary rock formations. At the end of the gorge, the path climbs steeply through mixed woodland before emerging into open countryside with superb views of the Alps and Oberstdorf.

THE WALK

Distance: 5km (3 miles)
Time: 2 hours, 30 min
Start/end at: Lower entrance to the Breitachklamm
How to get there: From the B19, take the turn to the Breitachklamm 2km (1.2 miles) north of Oberstdorf. Follow this minor road for 3km (2 miles) to the parking area (plenty of space, parking fee €1) and lower entrance to the gorge.

The walk begins from the lower entrance gate (Kasse 1) and follows a tarmac path to the Breitachklamm. The path through the gorge is undulating but not steep and has good safety barriers; the surface is generally safe but will be slippery in icy or snowy conditions. The turquoise waters of the River Breitach squeeze through the narrow gorge with a deafening roar, crashing against boulders and sending sprays of water high into the air. The unusual hue of the water is the result of melting snow that feeds into the river from the surrounding mountains. In summer, water cascades from the overhanging rocks, creating fine spray and droplets that glisten in the sunlight; in winter, spectacular curtains of ice form as the cascading water freezes.

The Breitachklamm was formed during the last ice age, when glaciers forced away the soft rock, leaving the deep gorge we see today. The pathway through the gorge was officially opened to the public on 4 July 1905.

After 800m (880 yards), at the end of the gorge you come to a flight of steps up to the top entrance gate. Go through the ticket booth and make a U-turn, then continue uphill for a further 1km (0.5 mile) to the Walserschanz restaurant. The Walserschanz is on a clear path uphill and you follow the clearly marked loop to return to the top entrance gate to the gorge

(make sure you have kept the entrance ticket you bought at the lower gate because you will need it to be readmitted through this entrance). Continue through the ticket booth and straight ahead up steps to the bridge. After the bridge, the path becomes very steep as it zigzags uphill through dense woodland, but there are plenty of seats for a rest. At the top, you will come out of the woodland onto a tarmac road, where you turn right downhill.

The open countryside is beautiful as you walk downhill between traditional farmhouses surrounded by fields. In summer the sound of cowbells echo and the meadows are lush with green grass and wild flowers. On your left you will see the Dornach-Alpe, which serves refreshments.

Shortly after the Dornach-Alpe, you will come to a sign giving you a choice of ways to return to the starting point. For a shorter walk bear right—this will take 15 minutes. Otherwise continue straight ahead on the tarmac road for half an hour. The shorter route is quite steep and can be slippery in wet conditions, while the longer route is a much easier walk back to the parking area.

WHEN TO GO

A summer weekday is the best time for the walk. The path may be closed at times during the thaw in spring because of the high water level, so it's advisable to check with the tourist office in Oberstdorf if you are planning to visit around this time. Avoid winter: Oberstdorf is a popular spot at this time of year and regularly hosts major winter sports events.

WHERE TO EAT

There's plenty of choice for food and refreshments on this walk. There's a good café/restaurant (tel 08322 4643) at the start of the walk, but this can get busy, especially when tour buses arrive. The Walserschanz restaurant (tel 05517 5359) is an ideal halfway point and has spectacular views. But if you want to visit a traditional Alpe (alpine farmhouse) and sample some home baking, the Dornach Alpe (tel 08322 988110) is perfect.

PLACES TO VISIT

Breitachklamm
☎ 08322 48 87
🕐 May–end Sep 8–5, Oct–end Apr 9–4
🎟 Adult €2.50, child (under 15) €1.20

The lush, green countryside and the busy valley resort of Oberstdorf in the Allgäuer Alps

OUT AND ABOUT

AROUND LAKE CONSTANCE

Beginning in historic Konstanz, scene in the 15th century of one of the most important councils of medieval Christianity, this route takes you around the shores of Germany's largest lake, the Bodensee (Lake Constance).

THE DRIVE

Distance:	157km (98 miles)
Allow:	7 hours
Start/end at:	Konstanz

among the finest examples of early Romanesque buildings in Germany. After crossing the causeway, the first village you reach is Oberzell, which has one of the oldest Romanesque churches in Germany (St. George's), with several interior wall frescoes painted in the 10th and 11th centuries. In Mittelzell is the eighth-century Minster of St. Mary and St. Mark, which has examples of 1,000-year-old stained glass, while the church of St. Peter and St. Paul in Niederzell has a series of Romanesque frescoes.

Return to the B33 and continue northwest for 15km (9 miles)

Konstanz's Old Town has retained much of its medieval charm

towards Radolfzell. Shortly after rejoining the B33 you will come to Hegne, where the restored Renaissance palace once served as the summer residence of the bishops of Constance. In nearby Allensbach, look for the wild animal and recreational park, home to many animals that were once indigenous to the area. Follow the signs off the B33 to the historic city of Radolfzell.

❸ The Old Town of Radolfzell is focused on the Münster Unserer Lieben Frau (St. Mary's

Meersburg's landmark Altes Schloss overlooks Lake Constance

Minster), erected in the Gothic style starting in 1436 with subsequent baroque modifications. The splendid Österreichische Schlösschen (Austrian Palace), begun in 1620 as the residence of Archduke Leopold Wilhelm, now houses the city library.

Leave Radolfzell and follow the B34 north to Ludwigshafen, then turn right onto the B31 and head southeast for 10km (6 miles) towards Überlingen. The scenery here is superb as the road winds its way through vineyards overlooking the Überlingen See. Shortly before Überlingen, take a short detour off the highway to visit the village of Goldbach.

❹ Goldbach's early Romanesque Chapel of St. Sylvester has remnants of medieval mural paintings.

From Konstanz head northwest along the B33 for 5km (3 miles), then turn left onto the causeway to Reichenau Island. Before the causeway, nature lovers may want to look at the Wollmatinger Ried (Wollmating Marsh).

❶ Wollmatinger Ried wildlife preservation area may only be entered on Naturschutzbund Deutschland (Nature Conservation Union of Germany) organized tours. Their information office is in Reichenau's former train station.

Drive for 2km (1.2 miles) along the poplar-lined causeway to Reichenau.

❷ Reichenau, the largest island on Lake Constance, was made a UNESCO World Heritage Site in 2000 for the three churches on the island belonging to the great monastery of Reichenau, founded in 724. They are

While you're in the village, take a look at the amazing Gletschermühle (Glacier Mill), a hole carved by a glacier out of the Molasse sandstone rock during the last ice age.

Return to the highway and drive on to Überlingen.

❺ The imperial town of Überlingen became such a popular holiday and health resort in the mid-19th century that it was known as 'Little Nice on Lake Constance'. Nobility, the gentry and artists and poets visited the town. Look for the fountain crowned by the legendary 'Rider of Lake Constance', immortalized by the poet Gustav Schwab in a 19th-century ballad.

Continued on page 326

Because the area is so popular with visitors, all the towns and villages around the lake have a good selection of cafés and restaurants. Many restaurants serve fresh local fish when in season, together with fresh vegetables grown on Reichenau and local wines. Good choices are: Roter Knopf (Paradiesstrasse 7, Konstanz, tel 07531 25696); Restaurant Strandcafé Mettnau (Strandbadstrasse 1, Radolfzell, tel 07732 1650); Spitalkeller im Steinhaus–Weinkeller Restaurant (Steinhausgasse 1, Uberlingen, tel 07551 66020); and Hotel Löwen (Marktplatz 2, Meersburg, tel 07532 43040).

The main roads around Lake Constance are always busy, not only with visitors but also with people heading for Austria and Switzerland. July and August are exceptionally busy; pleasanter times to visit are April–May when the fruit trees are in blossom, or during the autumn wine harvest.

Affenberg (Ape Mountain)
☎ 07553 381
◉ Apr–end Nov daily 9–6
🎟 Adult €7, child €4

Schloss Salem
☎ 07553 814 37
◉ Apr–end Oct Mon–Sat 9.30–6, Sun 10.30–6
🎟 €12 (park and guided tour of castle)

Plying Lake Constance, the Meersburg to Konstanz ferry

Zeppelin Museum
Seestrasse 22, Friedrichshafen
☎ 07541 38010
◉ Apr–end Oct Tue–Sun 10–6; Nov–end Mar Tue–Sun 10–5
🎟 Adult €7, child €4

Meersburg–Konstanz Ferry
◉ Crossings every 15 minutes
🎟 Approximately €10 for a car with two passengers (varies according to length of car)

OUT AND ABOUT

Continue following the lakeshore southeast for 8km (5 miles) along the B31 to Unteruhldingen. As the route climbs through magnificent woods, orchards and vineyards it passes two places of particular interest, Nussdorf and Birnau. The former fishing village of Nussdorf has streets named after Lake Constance fish species, beginning with Asche (grayling) through to Zander (lake perch). The Nussdorf Chapel contains a carved altar from the 15th century and frescoes from the 16th century. The famous pilgrimage church of Birnau stands on a hill in the middle of vineyards; the views from here are spectacular.

From Unteruhldingen take the minor road northeast for 7km (4 miles) to Salem. Don't be surprised when, after 3km (2 miles), you pass Affenberg (Ape Mountain), where more than 200 Barbary apes swing freely from tree to tree in the woodland.

❼ Salem Abbey, founded in 1137, was the largest and wealthiest abbey in southern Germany. In 1700, part of the huge abbey complex was rebuilt and renamed as the Schloss, and an elite boarding school was founded in part of

The Benedictine Kloster in Weingarten

Princes of Fürstenberg), built in 1575 on the site of a medieval castle. The Rittersaal (Hall of Knights), which occupies two floors of the south wing, has a wonderful Renaissance ceiling with carvings reckoned to be the finest of their kind in Germany. There are splendid views out to Lake Constance.

Carry on north from here for a further 5km (3 miles), then take a right turn followed shortly by a left turn to Illmensee, and drive via Pfrungen for 10km (6 miles) to Wilhelmsdorf. Turn right here and follow the road south for 21km (13.5 miles) to Ravensburg.

❾ Ravensburg is a town of towers and gates, 17 in all, mostly built in the 14th and 15th centuries. The town developed around its 11th-century castle, but it was its evolution into one of the leading merchant towns of upper Germany at the end of the Middle Ages that brought the wealth and opulence that resulted in the construction of many of the rich buildings that line the Marienplatz and Marktplatz. Of particular interest are the Kornhaus (Corn Exchange), Waaghaus (Weighing Office), Lederhaus (Leatherworkers' Guildhouse) and Mehlsack (Flour-Sack Tower) a tower standing 50m (165ft) high, from where you will get magnificent views to Lake Constance and the Alps.

❻ In Unteruhldingen a prehistoric lake-dwellers' village has been wonderfully reconstructed on the shore of Lake Constance. The Pfahlbaumuseum provides a unique insight into the lives of these early settlers. Beware: This is a popular destination and pedestrians have right of way everywhere. Leave your car in the large parking area outside town and catch the *Kurbähnle* (mini-train) to the harbour.

the west wing. The Kaisersaal (Emperor's Hall) is a magnificent sight.

Continue north up the winding Salem Valley for 10km (6 miles) to the health resort of Heiligenberg, sitting on a plateau at more than 700m (2,300ft). The views here are superb.

❽ Heiligenberg's main attraction is the Schloss der Fürsten von Fürstenberg (Palace of the

Just 4km (2.5 miles) north of Ravensburg along the B30 is Weingarten, which has one of Germany's largest baroque basilicas. Return to Ravensburg and head southwest along the B30 for 20km (12 miles) to Friedrichshafen. During World War I the famous Zeppelin airships were deployed here, and there's a museum that tells the Zeppelin story. From Friedrichshafen follow the scenic B31 shore road northwest for 18km (11 miles) to Meersburg, an attractive town with a formidable feudal castle and a baroque palace. On the busy lakeside promenade in the Unterstadt (lower town) is the terminal for the ferry crossing to return to Konstanz.

ALONG THE SHORE OF LAKE CONSTANCE

The Bodensee (Lake Constance) is actually part of the course of the River Rhine. Konstanz, the largest town on the lake, sits on a spit of land separating the Obersee, the main area of the Bodensee, from the Untersee, where the Rhine leaves the lake to enter Switzerland. This walk follows the waterside promenade into the heart of the town. You will walk between grand houses that overlook the harbour and marinas filled with expensive yachts before you visit some of the town's historic sights and buildings. You can even put a foot into Switzerland!

THE WALK

Distance: 8km (5 miles)

Time: 3 hours

Start/end at: Bodensee Stadion, Konstanz

How to get there: Take the route signposted to Meersburg and Mainau from Konstanz. About 500m (550 yards) after the Rhine bridge, turn right into Eichhornstrasse and follow this road to the Bodensee Stadion, where there is plenty of free parking.

This is a comfortable level walk. Leave the parking area from the east or south footpath and head for the promenade ahead. Turn right along the promenade and continue along this tree-lined walkway to the Rhine bridge.

From the promenade there are pleasing views across the lake; in the distance you will see Konstanz and the cathedral spire. The high, ugly building dominating the skyline is a block of flats on the Swiss side of town. On your right are grand houses and hotels; on the left, you will pass the yacht marina.

At the Rhine bridge, turn right up the steps and left to cross the bridge. Keep to the left of the railway line and follow the promenade through the public gardens to the Konzil and the *Imperia* statue. There is a superb café/restaurant at the Konzil, ideal for coffee or lunch.

The Konzil was built in 1388 as a grain store and warehouse for trade with southern

Europe. It was here in 1417, during the Council of Constance, that the rift in Christendom known as the Great Schism (when rival popes had vied for power) was brought to an end. The *Imperia*, a massive female figure by sculptor Peter Lenk, rotates on the base of a former lighthouse, the figure symbolizing the power of the many courtesans who followed the male participants to Konstanz at the time of the Council of Constance.

Continue along the promenade for a further 500m (550 yards) and you will come to the Swiss border. Return to the Konzil, turn left over the railway line and take the underpass into the Marktstätte. Continue straight ahead through the market square and Kanzlestrasse, then turn right into Obermarkt, which becomes Wessenbergstrasse. Ahead of you is the Münster.

Konstanz's rotating Imperia *statue on the end of the pier*

Konstanz escaped war damage and high-rise construction

The Münster Unserer Lieben Frau (Minster of Our Dear Lady) stands on the site of a Roman fortress. If you have time, explore inside the impressive cathedral. Also worth seeing are St. Maurice's church, built around 940AD, and the Silvesterkapelle (Silvester chapel) and Konradikapelle (Konrad chapel).

When you leave the cathedral, head back to the harbour and turn left along the promenade to retrace your route to the Bodensee Stadion.

WHERE TO EAT

The ground-floor Konzil restaurant (Hafenstrasse 2, tel 07531 21221) is in a great position overlooking the harbour, and is a good place to stop for refreshments or a meal. Once you cross the road into the market square you will find plenty of excellent little coffee shops and restaurants with seating out on the square.

WHEN TO GO

Although Lake Constance is a busy area in summer, especially on weekends, the promenade in Konstanz is reasonably quiet even in the height of summer. However, being flat and free of traffic, it is popular with local joggers and skaters. The town itself may be busy, but seeing the sights should not be a problem.

OUT AND ABOUT

THE BLACK FOREST: A CIRCULAR DRIVE FROM FREIBURG IM BREISGAU

This drive follows the southern fringes of the Black Forest before heading into the heart of the German clockmaking region. Leaving behind the lush green hills and vineyards surrounding Freiburg, the route heads north deep into the forest before passing the Gutach Falls, the highest waterfall in Germany, and the placid waters of the Titisee and Schluchsee lakes.

THE DRIVE

Distance: 184km (114 miles)
Allow: 6 hours
Start/end at: Freiburg im Breisgau

Take the busy B31 from Freiburg ★ and head southeast for 25km (15.5 miles) to Hinterzarten. Turn north onto the quieter B500 and drive for 26km (16 miles) to Furtwangen, one of the major clockmaking towns in the Black Forest.

❶ In Furtwangen you can visit the Deutsches Uhrenmuseum (German Clock Museum), which has the largest collection of clocks in Germany. In addition, many factories and workshops in the area open their doors to visitors, providing a great opportunity to see how clocks are made.

Continue north from Furtwangen along the B500 for 17km (11 miles) to Triberg.

❷ Triberg is another place dominated by clocks—there are cuckoo clocks everywhere, including two of the largest in the world. The Schwarzwaldmuseum here (also see page 331) has a large collection of Black Forest clocks on display, as well as local costumes, woodcarvings, ceramics and clockmaking memorabilia.

The roar of the nearby Gutach Falls, the highest waterfall in Germany (163m/535ft), is a welcome relief from the sound of cuckoos. This is a popular area for visitors at all times of year and finding somewhere to park can be difficult at times.

From Triberg take the B33 southeast for 25km (15.5 miles) to Villingen.

❸ The double town of Villingen-Schwenningen was formed in 1972. It's a curious hybrid of spa, medieval town and local industry— clockmaking, of course. You will find an interesting mix of attractions. Villingen is still surrounded by its original defensive walls and towers, and the Old Town is focused on the 12th-century Münster Unserer Lieben Frau (Minster of our Dear Lady). In Münsterplatz is the Altes Rathaus, which contains a museum with a collection of art and antiquities, and west of the Old Town is the Franziskaner Museum, in a former Franciscan monastery. In Schwenningen, you can visit the Uhrenindustriemuseum in what was the factory of the oldest clock company in Württemberg.

Continue south from Schwenningen along the B33/27 for 13km (8 miles) as the road gently climbs along the eastern fringe of the Black Forest to Donaueschingen.

Statue detail at Villingen (above); Cuckoo clock at Titisee (top left)

④ Donaueschingen is where the rivers Breg and Brigach unite to form the source of the Danube. A monumental fountain in the Schlosspark marks the site of the Donauquelle (source of the Danube). From 1723 the baroque Schloss was the seat of the princes of Fürstenburg, whose territories passed to Baden and Württemberg in 1806. The castle was altered considerably during the 19th century, and the interior has fine furnishings This is a pleasant small town and parking facilities are good. There are also some agreeable walks through the Schlosspark and alongside the rivers.

Take the minor road south out of Donaueschingen for 5km (3 miles) to Hüfingen, then join the B31 west for 27km (17 miles) to Titisee. This road links the E41 and E35 autobahn routes and is used by commercial vehicles.

⑤ Titisee is the resort village for the lake of the same name. Because of the easy direct access from a major road, it has become both busy and commercialized. The lake itself is attractive and the path around its shore makes a pleasant walk on a quiet day—if you can find one!

There are plenty of recreational and water sports facilities around and on the lake itself, and equipment is available to rent.

Continued on page 330

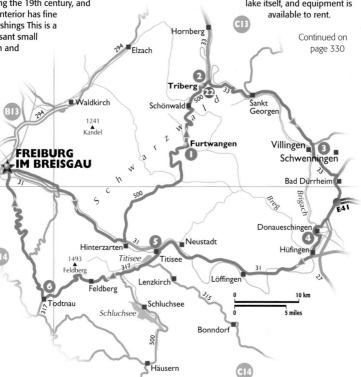

OUT AND ABOUT

WHERE TO EAT

Being a university town, Freiburg has a whole range of excellent places to eat. Try the oldest inn (established 1120), the historic Zum Roten Bären (Oberlinden 12, tel 0761 387 870), or the Schlossbergrestaurant Dattler (Am Schlossberg 1, tel 761 31729), which is just out of town, next to the upper cable station and with lovely views. In Triberg, the Bergcafe (Hermann-Schwer-Strasse, tel 07722 866 490) has good value and good views, and in Villingen, the Ratskeller (Obere Strasse 37, tel 07721 40 47 94) has a satisfying menu.

WHEN TO GO

This is a busy area throughout the year. In summer especially, the forests, mountains, lakes and clock museums attract hoards of visitors, so try to avoid the main holiday periods.

PLACES TO VISIT

Deutsches Uhrenmuseum (German Clock Museum)
Gerwigstrasse 11, Furtwangen
☎ 07723 920 117
🕐 Apr–end Oct daily 9–6, Nov–end Mar daily 10–5
💶 Adult €3, child €2.50

Uhrenindustriemuseum
Burkstrasse 39, Schwenningen
☎ 07721 380 44
🕐 Tue–Sun 10–12, 2–6
💶 Adult €3, child €2

Schwarzwaldmuseum, Triberg
See panel on page 331 for details

Gutach Falls footpath, Triberg

A gateway to the Black Forest, Freiburg im Breisgau has a sunny climate, venerable university and magnificent münster

Schluchsee, about 10km (6 miles) south, off the B500, is a much quieter spot.

From Titisee, return to the B31, then take the B317 southwest for 21km (13 miles) to Todtnau.

6 The small town of Todtnau is tucked away in the southwest corner of the Black Forest, close to the borders of France and Switzerland. It is officially classified as a health resort, partly thanks to its spectacular situation surrounded by mountains, all of which exceed 1,000m (3,300ft) in height. Don't miss the opportunity to take the chairlift to the summit of the Hasenhorn (1065m/ 3,495ft) to get fantastic views over the Alps and Black Forest. Just north of Todtnau, on the road to the village of Todtnauberg, is a dramatic waterfall that thunders down the mountainside from a height of 90m (300ft).

Leave Todtnau on the B317 and almost immediately turn right to follow a minor road for 25km (15.5 miles) to return to Freiburg. The scenery you pass through is a glorious mixture of towering mountains rising amid wooded ridges, alternating with peaceful valleys and meadows.

The Münster Fountain in the Altstadt (old town) at Villingen

THE BLACK FOREST: TRIBERG AND THE GUTACH FALLS

Deep in the southern reaches of the Black Forest is Germany's highest waterfall, one of the natural highlights in a region better known for its cuckoo clocks. Triberg is surrounded by forest and famous for its waterfall, the Gutach Falls. This walk takes you up these spectacular falls, where the water plunges in seven cascades down the mountainside, and to the pilgrimage church of Maria in der Tanne.

THE WALK

Distance: 3.2km (2 miles)

Allow: 2 hours

Start/end at: Parking area 4 in Triberg

How to get there: Triberg is on the B33 between the E35 and E41 autobahns. The Gutach Falls are well signposted on all approaches to the town. Follow the signs to P4 (parking area 4), which is street parking close to the main entrance to the falls (ticket parking €1 for 2 hours).

Set off from the main entrance to the Gutach Falls in Triberg, and follow the path that winds steeply uphill alongside the waterfall. The paths are clearly marked, each with its individual markers; you will be following the culture trail, which has red markers with a symbol of a church. There are plenty of places to sit and rest on the steep ascent, and there are excellent viewing points where you can admire the water cascading down a series of falls. Many of these points have attractive hand-painted enamel signs presenting useful information (in English and German). The path bears right and crosses a bridge between two waterfalls, from where you can look down and back towards Triberg.

The River Gutach winds its way through high spruce trees and granite rocks before it plunges 163m (535ft) down a series of seven waterfalls into the valley below. This natural phenomenon is known worldwide and has attracted visitors to Triberg for more than 100 years. Energy has been generated from the falls since 1884, and Triberg was the first German town to have electric street lamps.

From the bridge follow the path gently downhill through conifer-ous woodland. From this high path you will see to your right the rooftops of Triberg spread out below. The path levels out as you approach a small boating lake (Bergsee), where there's a café with tables and chairs pleasantly spread out along the waterside. Here you turn right and walk alongside the café downhill for approximately 50m (55 yards) to join a road, then turn right again and continue for about 60m (66 yards) to the pilgrimage church of Maria in der Tanne.

The baroque pilgrimage church of Maria in der Tanne (Our Lady in the Fir Tree) was built on the site where a large fir tree with low-hanging branches once stood. The story goes that in 1644 a seven-year-old girl was passing the fir tree and picked up a painting of the Virgin's Immaculate Conception that had fallen from the tree. The girl took the painting home and prayed to it, but three days later she was struck by an eye disease that almost blinded her. In her sleep the girl heard a voice telling her that if she returned the painting to its original place on the tree she would be cured. Next day her parents took her and the picture back to the fir tree and bathed her eyes with water from the nearby spring. From that moment the girl's eyesight improved and two days later the disease had completely disappeared.

Continue downhill along the narrow road from the church to join a main road. Follow the road ahead for approximately 200m (220 yards) to the Schwarzwald-museum (Black Forest Museum, ▷ 328), which you will see on your left, housed in the former trade hall of Triberg. Cross the Gutach River bridge and return to the parking area.

WHEN TO GO

The walk can be completed at most times of the year, but snow and ice may make it impassable in winter.

WHERE TO EAT

The café at Lake Bergsee is an ideal place to stop for refreshments and snacks. For more substantial fare, there are many excellent restaurants in Triberg that serve a variety of local and international dishes.

PLACES TO VISIT

Schwarzwaldmuseum

Wallfahrtstrasse 4, 78098 Triberg

☎ 07722 4434

🕐 Daily 10–5

💶 Adult €2.50, child (5–13) €2, family €9.50, combined family ticket (museum and waterfall) €11

Gutach Falls

Triberger Wasserfälle, Gutach

🕐 Daily 8.30–5.30

💶 Adult €1.50, child (8–18) 50c, under 8 free

📖 You are given a free leaflet (in English) with your admission fee. It includes a good map of the walk and information about the falls

The footpath winds its way alongside the Gutach Falls

OUT AND ABOUT

THE NECKAR VALLEY AND THE BERGSTRASSE: A CIRCULAR DRIVE FROM HEIDELBERG

From the romantic city of Heidelberg, you follow the winding Neckar valley with its attractive towns and castles before heading into the wooded hills of the Neckartal–Odenwald Nature Park, which stretches northwards from the Neckar. The route also takes in the historic Bergstrasse and the wine region of the Upper Rhine.

THE DRIVE	
Distance: 242km (150 miles)	
Allow: 9 hours	
Start/end at: Heidelberg	

Looking down on the popular town of Heidelberg

Head east from Heidelberg ★ along the B37 for 13km (8 miles) to Neckargemünd, an attractive town with 16th-century half-timbered houses. Just 5km (3 miles) farther on, take a right turn signposted *Feste Dilsberg*.

❶ The mighty fortress (*Feste*) of Dilsburg was never conquered. Its keep towers over the rooftops of the Old Town, providing excellent views of the Neckar Valley.

From Dilsberg, return to the B37 and continue east along the river valley for 10km (6 miles) to Neckarsteinach.

❷ Neckarsteinach, known as the 'Town of Four Castles', is where the rivers Neckar and Steinach meet. It is the only

town in Germany with four castles and you can enjoy a pleasant walk from one to another. Two of the castles are in ruins; the others are inhabited and private.

Still on the B37, after a further 12km (7.5 miles) you'll come to Hirschhorn, a nice place to stop and watch boats pass through locks alongside the terraced Neckar dam. From here, the road follows a long bend in the river to Eberbach, for 10km (6 miles).

❸ Eberbach has several interesting places to explore, and an enjoyable way to see the sights is by horse-drawn carriage. Of particular interest are the castle ruins, Thalheim House (former palace of the royal house of Leiningen), the medieval bathhouse (the only one of its kind in Baden-Württemberg) and the Pulverturm (powder tower).

You continue along the B37 for 29km (18 miles) southeast from Eberbach, passing by Zwingenberg and Neckargerach, before taking a left turn onto the B27 for Mosbach.

❹ Mosbach is a splendid little town sandwiched between the Neckar and the Odenwald range. This former free city of the Holy Roman Empire is more than 1,200 years old. Take time to see the Renaissance town hall and the Palm House (1610), which has been used as a church since 1705 and is considered one of the most beautiful half-timbered houses in Germany.

The small town of Miltenberg has many half-timbered buildings

After leaving Mosbach follow the B27 for a further 21km (13 miles), then take a left turn onto a minor road signposted to Mudau and Amorbach. The

Continued on page 334

OUT AND ABOUT

The towns along the Bergstrasse get extremely busy from the end of April through to the end of September because of the blossom and the various festivals. The Neckar Valley and Neckartal–Odenwald Nature Park may get busy during peak times and weekends in summer, but are rarely too crowded to enjoy.

All the towns along the Neckar have a good choice of cafés and restaurants. Zum Schiff Restaurant in Neckarsteinach (Neckargemünder Strasse 2, tel 06229 324) has a beautiful situation on the banks of the Neckar. Eberbach's Café Viktoria (Friedrichstrasse 5–9, tel 06271 2018) is noted for its delicious Viktoria-Gateau (▷ 370). The villages and towns between Amorbach and Bensheim are less commercialized and the food is more traditional.

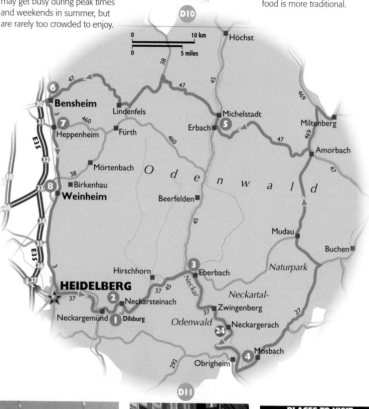

OUT AND ABOUT

Museum für Stadtgeschichte und Volkskunde
Kurzmainzer Amtshof, Amtsgasse 5, Heppenheim
☎ 06252 69112
🕐 Wed–Thu, Sat 2–5, Sun and hols 2–6
🎫 Free

Odenwald Museum and Toy Museum
Im der Kellerei, 64720, Michelstadt
☎ 06061 706139
🕐 Mar–end Oct Tue–Fri 10–12, 2–5, Sat, Sun 11–6; Nov–end Feb Fri–Sun 11–6
🎫 Adult €3, child €1.50

Bookstall in picturesque, half-timbered Miltenberg

Heidelberg's graceful Alte Brücke (old bridge) gateway has long been a city landmark (far left)

scenery here is spectacular as you head north and climb out of the Neckar Valley into the heart of the Neckartal–Odenwald Nature Park. There are some lovely places to stop and walk, with wonderful views across the wooded upland clothed with beech and spruce. Follow the minor road north for 20km (12 miles) to Amorbach. At the crossroads with the B47 go straight ahead along the B469 for 10km (6 miles) to Miltenberg, a pleasant small town. From Miltenberg, return along the B469 to the crossroads and turn right onto the B47 and continue west for 22km (13.5 miles) to Michelstadt and Erbach.

5 Outstanding in Michelstadt is the picturesque Rathaus with its oak columns and pointed corner turrets; this is one of the oldest oak-beamed buildings in Germany. In the Kellerie (a relic of the old castle) are the Odenwald Museum and the Toy Museum. Erbach is just south of the B47 and has a unique museum of ivory carving. The Schloss, with a round tower dating from 1200, has fine collections of art and weapons.

Leaving Erbach, continue west along the B47: You are now following a tourist route known as the Nibelungenstrasse, which runs between Worms and Würzburg. After 28km (17 miles) you will pass the village of Lindenfels, with its castle, and another 18km (11 miles) brings you to the intersection with the B3, known as the Bergstrasse. This historic route, the former Strata Montana of the Romans, runs for 58km (36 miles) along the rift valley of the Upper Rhine. The region is famed for its mild climate, its fruit and its almond trees that flower earlier here than anywhere else in Germany. The Bergstrasse is something special in spring—a sea of blossom all the way from Darmstadt to Heidelberg. Bensheim, the largest town in the Bergstrasse region, lies at the intersection of the B47 and the Bergstrasse.

6 Bensheim is a vibrant town, busy throughout the year. The drama productions in the international summer festival

at Schloss Auerbach and Fürstenlager Park are recognized worldwide. In a region renowned for its wine, the Bergstrasse Spring Wine festival (end of April) and the Bergstrasse Winegrowers festival (September) draw crowds.

It's a pleasant drive south along the B3 from Bensheim. For most of the year the surrounding slopes seem to glisten and glow with the various fruits, vines, figs, almonds and even exotic trees. Just 3km (2 miles) from Bensheim is Heppenheim.

7 Heppenheim is known for its drama festival and wine market. Overlooked by the ruins of Schloss Starkenburg, the town has an attractive heart with timber-framed buildings and a large neo-Gothic church. Take a break

to visit the history and folklore museum at the Kurmainzer Amtshof and the state observatory in the castle ruins.

Still heading south along the B3, 13km (8 miles) from Heppenheim is Weinheim.

8 Weinheim, a lovely little town, is the green heart of the Bergstrasse. It has castle gardens, parks and woodland with an abundance of exotic plants and trees. The castle, old town hall, narrow Obertor arch and ruins of the town walls are all well preserved. There is also a local history museum in the House of the Teutonic Order.

The final part of your journey continues south along the B3 for 18km (11 miles) to Heidelberg.

Much photographed, delightful Michelstadt's Town Hall (Rathaus)

THROUGH THE MARGARETHENSCHLUCHT IN THE NECKAR VALLEY

This walk from the village of Neckargerach takes you high into the tree-lined slopes above the River Neckar, from where you will see the valley cutting its way through distant hills dominated by romantic castles. There is a choice of routes: For the more energetic, a spectacular scramble up the steep Margarethenschlucht gorge, with the alternative of a gentle stroll along the river for less adventurous walkers.

THE WALK

Distance: 4.5km (2.8 miles) for route 3; 7km (4.4 miles) for route 6 (see Note below)

Allow: 2 hours for route 3; 2 hours 30 min for route 6

Start/end at: Hotel Grüner Baum, Neckargerach

How to get there: Neckargerach is on the B37, 41km (25.5 miles) east of Heidelberg, 14km (9 miles) northwest of Mosbach. There's plenty of parking at the Hotel Grüner Baum on Neckarstrasse.

Note: Ortsplan Neckargerach mit Wanderkarte (in German only) is an excellent small leaflet available from the tourist office. It includes a street plan and details of all the walking routes around Neckargerach, which are numbered. You will be following route 3 with an option to include part of route 6.

From the Hotel Grüner Baum's parking area, walk along Neckarstrasse to the first intersection. Turn right, then take the second turn left into Bahnhofstrasse. As you continue uphill, the road bends right past the old railway station to a new bridge across the railway line. Cross the bridge and turn right along a tarmac path marked with green signs to the Margarethenschlucht, and follow it between houses and the railway line. Continue straight ahead along this path, which eventually becomes a gravel track, then a dirt path running between woodlands and the river below. There are spectacular views on your right of the river and its valley with, peeping out of the trees, the ruins of the Minneburg.

The ruins of the 11th-century Minneburg are accessible via a steep path through woodlands from near the village of Guttenbach, which became part of Neckargerach in 1973

The path continues to climb gently away from Neckargerach. When you have walked 2km (1.2 miles) from the beginning of the route, you will come to an information board and the entrance to the Margarethenschlucht waterfall. The path, which climbs for 600m (660 yards) to the top of the waterfall, is very steep (ascent 100m/330ft) and slippery in places; good walking shoes are essential. Continue uphill on the narrow path and cross the lower waterfall. Approximately 50m (55 yards) from this point, the path forks.

For a gentler route back to Neckargerach, continue straight ahead at this point and follow route 6 through the woods and along the river. Route 6 takes you right downhill, crosses the B37 and a small footbridge over the Neckar at the locks, then turns right and follows the river to Guttenbach before crossing the road bridge and river to return to Neckargerach.

To continue on route 3, head left at the fork, up the steps, and follow the narrow dirt path uphill. There is a double safety rope on one side of this path, but as you ascend into the gorge the drop down becomes very steep.

The path through the Margarethenschlucht zigzags across small waterfalls as it climbs high through the woodland to the top of the gorge.

At the top of the gorge you come out of the woodland into open countryside and join a narrow tarmac road. Turn left here and head downhill for approximately 300m (330 yards) to an intersection, then turn left again and follow this road to return to Neckargerach.

WHEN TO GO

Parts of this walk are possible at any time of year and it is not often busy. You should not attempt to walk through the gorge when there is ice or snow. Also be aware that after particularly heavy rainfall the volume of water over the falls may make the paths that cross them impassable. At such times, the walk along the river and through Guttenbach to Neckargerach is a pleasant alternative.

WHERE TO EAT

The hotel/restaurant Grüner Baum (Neckarstrasse 13, tel 06263 706) in Neckargerach is an excellent place to eat. The Greek owners provide a wide choice of refreshments, including Greek and German dishes.

The ruins of Minneburg, surrounded by lush landscape

OUT AND ABOUT

Whether you're into art and architecture, food and wine, or walking and cycling, Germany has something for everyone, and there's certainly no shortage of tour operators to cater for every taste. Below is a short selection of established operators who organize a variety of specialist tours in Germany, or you can check out the official websites of the German tourist board, www.germany-tourism.co.uk and www.cometogermany.com.

Ace Study Tours
Tel 01223 835055 (UK)
www.study-tours.org
This UK-based charity offers guided art, architecture and music trips, with profits going to restoration projects throughout the world. Itineraries include the Handel Festival at Göttingen and exploring the art and architecture of Berlin. Acknowledged experts are employed as guides.

Arblaster & Clarke
Tel 01730 893344 (UK)
www.arblasterandclarke.com
The UK-based Arblaster & Clarke specialize in wine tours. One of their scheduled itineraries takes in the valleys and vineyards of the Mosel, providing ample opportunity to sample some of Germany's finest wines.

British Trust for Conservation Volunteers (BTCV)
Tel 01302 572 244 (UK)
www.btcv.org.uk
The BTCV runs hundreds of affordable conservation breaks. One involves conservation work (such as scrub clearance, pond building and haymaking) on the shores of Lake Ammersee in Bavaria. Training is provided.

Eurobike
Tel 800/321-6060 (US)
www.eurobike.com
Eurobike is a US-based tour operator offering a number of guided walking and bicycling tours in Germany. Choose between bicycling along the Rhine or the Mosel, or walking in Bavaria. There's also a longer, two-week bicycle tour that crosses into Austria and Hungary.

Explore Worldwide
Tel 01252 760000 (UK)
www.exploreworldwide.com
Explore Worldwide is a UK-based company that organizes activity holidays all over the world, including a 15-day tour of the former East Germany.

Freedom Tour
Tel 212/202-5130 (US)
www.freedom-tour.com
A US-based company offering general tours within Germany.

German Travel Centre
Tel 020 8429 2900 (UK)
www.german-travel-uk.com
The London-based German Travel Centre offers a comprehensive range of holidays to destinations throughout Germany, from short city breaks to extended tours. Possible options include beer festivals, Christmas markets and carnivals.

Headwater
Tel 01606 720099 (UK)
www.headwater.com
Headwater is a UK-based company that arranges guided walking and bicycling tours all over Europe. At the time of writing, the highlight in Germany was a week's walking in the Oberammergau region.

Martin Randall
Tel 020 8742 3355 (UK)
www.martinrandall.com
The UK's leading art and architecture specialists offer a wide variety of themed tours throughout Germany, including 'Art Along the Rhine', 'Opera in Munich' and 'Christmas in Berlin'. Tours are led by specialist lecturers and last from three days to three weeks.

Prospect Tours
Tel 020 7486 5704 (UK)
www.prospecttours.com
Prospect Tours is another UK-based specialist operator that organizes a variety of tours to Germany's cultural hotspots. Themes include art and architecture, wine festivals and Christmas markets.

Rick Steves
Tel 425/771-8303 (US)
www.ricksteves.com
Rick Steves is a US-based company offering general bus tours within Germany.

Shearings
Tel 01942 824824 (UK)
www.shearingsholidays.com
Shearings is a UK-based company offering general tours within Germany.

Voyage Jules Verne
Tel 020 7616 1000 (UK)
www.vjv.co.uk
This London-based operator organizes a number of luxury themed tours in Germany, from extended river cruises on the Elbe and the Mosel to short city breaks in Berlin and Munich.

Woods
Tel 01243 868080 (UK)
www.woodstravel.co.uk
A UK-based company offering general tours within Germany.

World Walks
Tel 01242 254353 (UK)
www.worldwalks.com
This UK-based outfit offers a limited number of guided walking holidays in Germany; destinations include the Bavarian Alps, the Black Forest and the romantic Rhine.

OUT AND ABOUT

This chapter lists places to eat and places to stay, broken down by region, then alphabetically by town, or in the cities by establishment.

Eating and Staying

GERMAN CUISINE

Eating and drinking well is more or less compulsory in Germany.
Traditional dishes tend to be wholesome and hearty, with pork products—
particularly sausages—the mainstay. Potatoes also feature highly, as
does *sauerkraut*, which seems to be served with almost everything.
But you will also find a wide variety of exquisite local dishes served
alongside a growing range of international cuisine.

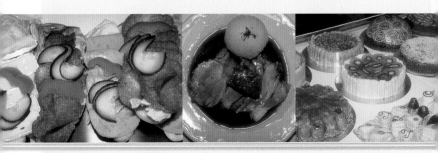

A salami salad, ideal for a quick lunch (left); roast pork and dumplings, a traditional German main course (middle); a selection of tempting gateaux (right)

MEALTIMES

● Breakfast (*Frühstück*) typically includes a selection of rolls and sliced bread (light and dark), served alongside various cheeses, sliced meats and conserves, all washed down with a glass of juice and a cup of coffee or tea. Many hotels include a buffet breakfast in the room price—the quality of the spread can vary considerably, but it's usually pretty good.

● Alternatively, if breakfast isn't included in your room rate, try one of the dozens of mouth-watering pastries that are on display in every bakery in Germany.

● Lunch (*Mittagessen*) is traditionally the main meal in Germany, and most restaurants are open all day and not just in the evening (▷ 418 for opening times). In major towns and cities, many restaurants offer set-price menus at lunchtime, which are usually excellent value for money. A big, hearty meal and a beer or two is the norm rather than the exception here, although Germans don't seem to be too big on desserts, particularly at lunchtime. If this all sounds a bit heavy, light snacks can always be found at cafés and bistros, and all manner of sandwiches and sausage-based bites can be bought at bakeries (*Bäckerei*) and snack bars (*Imbissstube*).

● Dinner (*Abendessen*) in many German homes consists of platters of breads, cheese and cold meats, accompanied by a chilled beer or a glass of wine. Restaurants, however, serve a full menu from 6pm onwards (▷ 418).

WHERE TO EAT

● Bakeries (*Bäckerei*) are usually the first eateries to open in the morning, so are useful if you are making an early start. They serve an overwhelming array of pastries, cakes and coffees, and sometimes rolls and sand-wiches. All are freshly prepared and are at very reasonable prices. Nuts and/or fruit are high on the agenda when it comes to treats, while ham, cheese and salami are the staples of the sandwich scene. Many bakeries also have a small seating or standing area, so you can eat your purchases there.

● Snack bars (*Imbissstube*) usually serve a few varieties of sausage in a bread roll, and may also offer things like fries, burgers and kebabs. Most have a standing area. They're inexpensive and friendly, and great if you're in a hurry or on a tight budget.

● Cafés in Germany often open as early as 7 or 8am, and tend to serve a wide range of light snacks and hot and cold fast food, in addition to the ubiquitous *Kaffee und Kuchen* (coffee and cakes), which are usually enjoyed mid-morning or late in the afternoon.

● Bistros and restaurants are generally the last to open, but most will be up and running by midday at the latest. In bistros, snacks are served alongside main meals, and cocktails alongside coffee. Restaurants, meanwhile, follow the more traditional starter, main course and dessert format, and offer a similar range of beers, wines and spirits.

● Beer halls (*Brauhäuser*) are the place to try traditional German food and sample some of the local beer. In most places, local dishes are served alongside countrywide staples, but you can be sure that the beer is always brewed on the premises or (occasionally) in a nearby brewery.

EATING

FAST FOOD

● The likes of McDonald's, Burger King and Pizza Hut can be found in Germany's larger towns and cities. There are also nationwide chains, such as Kamps bakery, which serve value-for-money food.

INTERNATIONAL CUISINE

● Many parts of Germany are flush with foreign restaurants, of which Italian (serving pizza and pasta), Latin American (with tortillas and fajitas) and Greek (dishing up shish kebabs and tzatziki) are the most popular. In the pubs and restaurants, although most places tend to be a bit more adult-oriented after 7 or 8pm.

WHAT TO DRINK

● Beer (*Bier*) is a national institution in Germany and there are literally hundreds, if not thousands, of breweries, beer halls and pubs producing their own. German beer traditionally tastes stronger than other European, American and Australian beers, and it can be light (*Helles*) or dark (*Dunkles*). Many regions take great pride in their particular special brew, such as *Altbier*

Fresh vegetables are plentiful at the market (left); you can't visit Germany without trying one of the famous sausages (middle); fruit liqueurs (right)

larger towns and cities, however, you'll find restaurants representing all four corners of the globe, from Armenia to Vietnam. Thai and Chinese are particularly popular in the major financial hubs, such as Frankfurt and Düsseldorf.

SPECIAL REQUIREMENTS

● Vegetarians should look for the words '*vegetarische Gerichte*' (vegetarian dishes) on the menu, although vegetarianism isn't that widespread in Germany, so don't expect to be offered much in the way of choice. In beer halls in particular, you may be lucky to find anything that doesn't include meat. Similarly, many seemingly innocuous options, such as soups, rice and vegetable dishes, may have been prepared or spiced up with meat stock— if in doubt, ask. Things are changing, however, and in the major cities there are increasing numbers of restaurants catering specifically to vegetarians.

CHILDREN'S FOOD

● German children eat out with their parents from an early age, particularly in beer halls (*Brauhäuser*), which during the day and in the early evening are often patronized by the whole family.

● Smaller portions are offered as *Kinderteller*. As a result, children tend to be well looked after. The food is often of the omelette or burger-and-fries variety, so you shouldn't get any complaints from your offspring, but if they (or you) are a bit more adventurous, starters or smaller portions of main meals are ideal. Even small children won't look out of place in many

(from the Rhine region) or *Kölsch* (from Cologne). Glasses are often smaller than they are in the UK or US, and in some cases they may contain only a few mouthfuls (although the price generally reflects this). Unlike English bitter, German beer is almost always served cold.

● Wine (*Wein*) is not as popular a drink as beer at mealtimes, but that's not to say it isn't widely appreciated, particularly around the major wine-producing regions. Some 80 per cent of the wine produced in Germany is white, and the basic categories are *trocken* (dry), *halb-trocken* (medium) and *lieblich* (sweet). Wines are also further categorized into *Tafelwein* (table wine), *Qualitätswein* (quality wine) and *Qualitätswein mit Prädikat* (literally 'with distinctive features'). Among the most popular grape varieties are Riesling (a fresh, fruity white from the Mosel area), Silvaner (a full-bodied white from Pfalz) and Spätburgunder (a velvety-smooth red from the Ahr). Rightly or wrongly, the most famous German wine is probably Liebfraumilch, originally named after the 14th-century Liebfrauenkirche convent in Worms and now produced throughout the Rhine region. Wine-tasting, which is usually very good value for money, is widely available in all of the country's wine-producing areas.

● Ice wine (*Eiswein*) is made from specially selected grapes that are actually allowed to freeze on the vine in the autumn, and is considered to be something of a luxury, with half-bottle prices starting from around €30. *Sekt*, meanwhile, is Germany's version of champagne, and although it's not in the same league, some brands are of a very high

EATING

quality. Finally, *Apfelwein* is a sweet, heady cider with a strong, sweet aftertaste. It is brewed particularly in Frankfurt and the southern Hesse palatinate.

● Schnapps (*Schnaps*) translates as 'spirits', but it's more usually used to describe sweet, fruit-based drinks that are taken as aperitifs or digestifs. Apple, pear and plum are the most common ingredients, and the drinks are traditionally downed in shots.

● Soft drinks can be found everywhere in Germany, as can bottles of mineral water—with the latter, be sure to ask for carbonated

(*mit Kohlensäure*) or still (*still*), depending on what you prefer.

● Coffee (*Kaffee*) is served everywhere, and is relatively inexpensive (unless you're in a chain coffee shop, it which case you can easily pay a euro or more over the odds). It usually comes in a cup (*Tasse*), and is served with sugar and milk (or cream) on the side.

● Tea (*Tee*) tends to be served in a glass, with the tea-bag left in the water, and sugar and/or lemon served on the side. If you want tea with milk (*Milch*), ask for it on the side, so that you can add it after the tea-bag has stewed a little.

A Bavarian dish of roast pork and dumplings (left); asparagus (middle); rounds of rye bread (right)

MENU READER

USEFUL WORDS
Gerichte plate/dish
hausgemacht home-made
heiss hot
kalt cold
Speisekarte menu
Tageskarte specials menu
vegetarisch vegetarian

ESSEN—MEALS
Abendessen dinner
Frühstück breakfast
Mittagessen lunch

GANG—COURSES
Suppen soups
Vorspeise starter
Hauptgericht main
Nachtisch dessert

COOKING METHODS
nicht durchgebraten rare
Brat fried
gebacken baked/roasted
gebraten (pan) fried
gedämpft steamed
gefüllt stuffed
gegrillt grilled
gekocht boiled
geräuchert smoked
geschmort braised
paniert breaded

FLEISCH—MEAT
Ente duck
Fasan pheasant

Gans goose
Gyros kebab
Hackfleisch mince (ground) beef
Hähnchen chicken
Hirsch venison
Kalbfleisch veal
Kaninchen rabbit
Kotelett (pork) chop
Lammfleisch lamb
Rindfleisch beef
Schaschlik kebab
Schinken ham
Schnitzel escalope
Schwein pork
Speck bacon
Truthahn turkey
Zunge tongue

WURST—SAUSAGES
Bierwurst beer sausage
Blutwurst black pudding (blood sausage)
Bockwurst boiled sausage
Bratwurst fried sausage
Brühwurst thick sausage
Knackwurst spicy sausage
Leberwurst liver sausage
Wiener frankfurters

FISCH—FISH
Barsch perch
Dorsch cod
Forelle trout
Hering herring
Karpfen carp

Lachs salmon
Makrele mackerel
Sardinen sardines
Schellfisch haddock
Scholle plaice
Seezunge sole
Tunfisch tuna

MEERESFRÜCHTE—SEAFOOD
Austern oysters
Hummer lobster
Krabben prawns
Muscheln mussels

GEMÜSE—VEGETABLES
Artischocken artichoke
Bohnen beans
Erbsen peas
Gewürzgurken gherkins (pickles)
Grüne Bohnen green beans
Gurke cucumber
Karotten carrots
Kartoffeln potatoes
Kohl cabbage
Paprika peppers
Pilze mushrooms
Spargel asparagus
Tomaten tomatoes
Zwiebeln onions

OBST—FRUIT
Apfel apple
Aprikose apricot
Banane banana

EATING

Brombeeren blackberries
Erdbeeren strawberries
Himbeeren raspberries
Kirschen red cherries
Mandarine mandarin
Melone melon
Orange orange
Pfirsich peach
Pflaumen plums
Trauben grapes
Zitrone lemon

SPECIAL DISHES
Bulette a type of meat pie that's typical of Berlin
Gulasch beef stew with paprika, often served up as a soup
Hackepeter German-style steak tartare, common in Berlin
Handkäse mit Musik strong, medium-soft cheese from Frankfurt, served with pickled onions and bread
Jägerschnitzel cutlet served in a mushroom and wine sauce
Kaiserschmarren pancakes served with raisins, cinnamon and sugar
Kartoffelpüree mashed potato (often served with *sauerkraut*)
Kasseler Rippe mit Sauerkraut smoked saddle of pork with *sauerkraut*; a variation on knuckle of pork (see Schweinhaxe, right)
Labskaus sailor's stew, with cured beef, mashed potato, pickled beetroot and fish; from the north, where meat and fish are often combined
Matjeshering salted herring, another special dish in the

north of Germany; often served pickled and rolled in sour cream as rollmops
Rippenbraten mit Backpflaumen spare ribs with prunes; this splendidly named dish is typical of the German tendency for combining sweet and savoury flavours
Rösti diced potatoes pan-fried with onion and bacon; a staple
Sauerkraut shredded white cabbage that's been pickled; another German staple
Schlesisches Himmelreich literally 'Silesian heaven', a stew made of pork and dried fruits
Schwarzwälder Kirschtorte Black Forest gateau (literally 'Black Forest cherry cake')
Schwarzwälder Schinken Black Forest ham, reputedly among the best in Germany
Schweinshaxe knuckle of pork. A special dish of the northern Rhine region, although invariably available elsewhere; usually served with mashed potato and *sauerkraut*
Thüringer Rostbratwurst a coarse, fatty sausage that's typical of eastern Germany
Wiener Schnitzel practically synonymous with German cuisine; basically a pork chop that's been pounded flat and then pan-fried in breadcrumbs. The quality varies, but arguably the best place to try it is in Frankfurt, where it'll come with a healthy helping of the city's justly famous 'green sauce'
Westphälischer Schinken fine ham from the Düsseldorf/Westphalia region

CONDIMENTS
Knoblauch garlic
Mayonnaise mayonnaise
Pfeffer pepper
Salz table salt
Senf mustard
Zucker sugar

SIDE DISHES
Brot bread
Brötchen roll
Ei egg (uncooked)
gemischter Salat mixed salad
Kroketten (potato) croquettes
Nudeln noodles (also pasta)
Pommes frites chips/fries
Pumpernickel rye bread
Rührei scrambled egg
Spiegelei fried egg

NACHTISCHE–DESSERTS
Apfelstrudel apple and pastry
Berliner jam doughnut/jelly doughnut
Eierkuchen/Pfannkuchen pancakes
Eis ice cream (also ice)
Käsekuchen cheesecake
Kekse biscuits (sweet)
Krapfen ring doughnut
Linzer Torte lattice tart
Obstsalat fresh fruit salad

Delicious plum pie

GETRÄNKE–DRINKS
Apfelsaft apple juice
Bier beer (any sort)
Dunkles dark beer
Fruchtsaft fruit juice
Helles light beer
Kaffee coffee (black)
Kaffee mit Milch coffee with milk
Kaffee mit Sahne coffee with cream
Kölsch light, fizzy beer from Cologne
Limonade lemonade
Mineralwasser mineral water
Mineralwasser mit Kohlensäure carbonated mineral water
Pils strong-tasting lager
Schnaps strong spirit
(Zitronen) Tee (lemon) tea
Weinkarte wine list

WEIN–WINE
Apfelwein apple wine/cider
Glühwein mulled wine
Hauswein house wine
Roséwein rosé wine
Rotwein red wine
Sekt sparkling wine
Weisswein white wine

ZAHLEN–THE BILL/CHECK
Wir möchten zahlen, bitte Can I have the bill, please?
Bedienung (nicht) inklusive service charge (not) included

EATING

NORTHERN GERMANY

Northern Germany is the only region of the country that borders the sea and here you can eat fish fresh—accompanied by the salty tang of sea air—rather than frozen. *Matjes* (young salted herring) are a particular delicacy. These can be eaten on a bread roll with by onions, served pickled and rolled in sour cream as rollmops or in *Matjestopf*, where they are served with onions, cream and potatoes. A local Hamburg dish is *Labskaus*, a stew in which salted herring is combined with beef, pork, potatoes and other vegetables. Many other kinds of fish are also available, with *Scholle* (sole) and *Zander* (pike-perch) among the most popular. Grey North Sea *Krabben* (shrimp) taste far better when they are freshly landed. *Aalsuppe* (eel soup), meanwhile, is served sweet and sour, with vegetables, bacon and fruit. Typical meat-based and other traditional foods and dishes from around Germany are also served in the north. Ethnic options are available, particularly in the larger cities of Hamburg, Bremen and Hannover, but are less common in the area that used to be part of East Germany.

PRICES

The prices given are for a two-course lunch (L) and a three-course dinner (D) for two people, without drinks. The wine price is for the least expensive bottle.

BRAUNSCHWEIG

BRODOCZ

Stephanstrasse 1–2, 38110 Braunschweig
Tel 0531 42236

If you relish vegetarian and vegan food, you'll enjoy this small restaurant a few blocks west of the Rathaus. The atmosphere inside its stone walls and half-timbered frame, softly illuminated by spotlights and candles, is informal. A non-smoking policy adds a hallowed air. There is a play table for children. Some of the interior seating is fixed, and the swivel chairs could be a little more comfortable, but in fine weather, you can't beat sitting out on the tree-shaded terrace. The menu changes daily, and is Meditteranean with some Asian flourishes.
🕐 Mon–Fri 11–10.30, Sat 11–5
🍴 L €30, D €50, Wine €12

BREMEN

RATSKELLER

Rathaus, Am Markt, 28195 Bremen
Tel 0421 321676

Often considered the best of Germany's many traditional

SPECIAL IN BREMEN

MEIEREI IM BÜRGERPARK

Bürgerpark, 28209 Bremen
Tel 0421 340 8619

In an area northeast of the Hauptbahnhof, where 19th-century villas abound, you can combine a stroll in the English-style Bürgerpark (1866) with lunch or dinner at this smart but casual restaurant. The gabled Swiss-style wood-built villa dates from 1881 and was once an aristocrat's summer hideaway. Tranquillity and relaxation are guaranteed while you choose from the fine seafood, meat (the sautéed squab is particularly good) and vegetarian dishes on the varied Continental menu. Eat in one of the four traditional interior rooms, or on the verandah with a garnish of fresh air and a view of the park. Coffee and cake are served between mealtimes. Visa is the only card accepted.
🕐 Tue–Sun noon–10pm
🍴 L €50, D €70, Wine €21

Ratskeller (town-hall cellar) restaurants, Bremen's vaulted establishment, with secluded niches, has been in business since 1408. A curious drawback is that it's not allowed to serve beer, but the astonishing feat of stocking more than 600 different German wines, some served from barrels, makes up for that deficiency. Seafood—including smoked fish—has a prominent place on the menu, but so too does that Hamburg favourite, *Labskaus*. A bistro section has a simpler menu.
🕐 Restaurant: daily 11–3, 6–midnight. Bistro: daily 11am–midnight
🍴 L €40, D €50, Wine €18.90

CELLE

HISTORISCHER RATSKELLER

Markt 14, 29221 Celle
Tel 05141 29099

Rustic, wood-hewn, and decorated with old paintings and antiques, the atmospheric restaurant in this vaulted cellar of the stone-built town hall is plush in a faded kind of way. It serves German cuisine such as local roast game and *Heidschnucken* lamb, but also includes some international dishes—if items such as steak with various sauces and scallops au gratin can be so described—and a mixed seafood platter that's a bit of both. Dustin Hoffman passed this way once and apparently departed satisfied, and there's every reason to suppose you will too. It's also popular with locals. Be sure to sample one of the fine German wines.
🕐 Mon–Sat 10am–midnight, Sun 10–3
🍴 L €20, D €40, Wine €19

GOSLAR

DIE WORTH

Kaiserworth Hotel, Markt 3, 38640 Goslar
Tel 05321 7090

The in-house restaurant of this 500-year-old lodging is a touch of class on the venerable market square. Gothic arches define the interior, but far from being gloomy it is bright and elegant, with fine table settings and attentive service. Given the

EATING

proximity of the Harz mountains, with their forests, rivers and lakes, it is no surprise that roast venison and other game is on the menu in season, and grilled trout year-round. If the weather is fine try for a seat on the outside terrace, under the building's arches on the square.

🕐 Daily 6–11
🍴 L €30, D €50, Wine €14

HAMBURG

CASA MADEIRA

Ditmar-Koel-Strasse 14, 20459 Hamburg
Tel 040 7404 1880

Amid an enclave of ethnic restaurants on a bustling street just inland from the Landungsbrücken, this small but personable place stands out for its authentic Portuguese cuisine. The plain interior recalls many such simple but satisfying local eateries in Portugal. Resident and visiting Portuguese dine here, and not just because the prices are attractive. The atmosphere achieved by having a television set tuned to a Portuguese satellite station won't appeal to every diner, but menu items such as garlic scampi certainly should.

🕐 Mon–Fri 9.30am–2am, Sat–Sun 8am–2am
🍴 L €25, D €40, Wine €8
🚇 Landungsbrücken

LANDHAUS DILL

Elbchaussee 94, 22763 Hamburg
Tel 040 390 4387
www.landhausdill.com

A country-style villa across a wide street from the Elbe is the setting for this elegant restaurant, focusing mainly on German and Austrian cuisine. Despite the proximity to the river, there's no real view of the water, which is masked by buildings. The garden terrace separated from the traffic by a hedgerow is a fine place to dine on a warm summer's day, while at other times, the bright, flower-bedecked interior is a better choice. Seafood dishes, including sushi, complement standards such as roast lamb with herbs. The wine list has 250 choices.

🕐 Tue–Sun noon–10.30
🍴 L €60, D €90, Wine €20
🚇 Altona
🚌 Bus 36 Susettestrasse

SPECIAL IN HAMBURG
FISCHEREIHAFEN

Grosse Elbstrasse 143, 22767 Hamburg
Tel 040 381816
www.fischereihafen-restaurant-hamburg.de

Just off the England-Kai in Altona, this modern, family-owned seafood restaurant has been a fixture of the Hamburg cuisine scene since 1981. The extensive menu covers traditional and some international dishes, including the popular grilled fillet of zander (pike-perch) on spinach with a caper and tuna sauce and potatoes. The mixed seafood platter (for two) is a good way to sample different items from the menu at once. You can have a pre-meal drink in the *gemütlich* (friendly) Oysterbar, and dine indoors or (from May to September) on the balcony, which has a fine view of the river.

🕐 Sun–Thu 11.30–10, Fri–Sat 11.30–10.30
🍴 L €40, D €90, Wine €25
🚇 Königstrasse

OLD COMMERCIAL ROOM

Englische Planke 10, 20459 Hamburg
Tel 040 366319

It would be difficult to find a place that's more replete with traditional Hamburg atmosphere than this venerable seamen's tavern not far from the harbour, facing the landmark Michaeliskirche. With its intimate wood-panelled interior, with tables in convivial proximity to one another and old photographs adorning the walls, this is *the* place to sample that traditional Hamburg dish of *Labskaus* (▷ 341). Seafood dishes, including fine sole and wild salmon, are prominent on the menu, and meat-eaters won't go wrong by choosing a simple steak with all the trimmings.

🕐 Daily noon–midnight
🍴 L €40, D €80, Wine €25
🚇 St. Pauli

VAPIANO

Hohe Bleichen 10, 20345 Hamburg
Tel 040 3501 9975

Ideal for a break while shopping, or for a quick but far from bland dinner, this breezy self-service Italian restaurant is a cut above a mere fast-food joint and has a trendy cachet all its own. Freshly made pasta and pizza, and some interesting wines, make Vapiano stand out from the crowd. You don't pay directly but put your purchases on a house card.

🕐 Mon–Sat 11.30am–midnight, Sun 4–10.30pm
🍴 L €6.50, D €8.50, Wine €13.50
🚇 Gänsemarkt

HAMELN

KARTOFFELHAUS IM BÜRGERHAUS

Kupferschmiedestrasse 13, 31785 Hameln
Tel 05151 22383
www.kartoffelhaus-hameln.de

You might find it difficult to persuade yourself to enter this restaurant, so handsome is the exterior of the old half-timbered townhouse on the west side of the Altstadt, close to the River Weser. The scene is equally good among the wooden beams on the two floors inside, where you dine

on unambitious but tasty traditional fare such as the *Kartoffelhaus pfanne*, which is based around tender grilled pork fillet and the restaurant's signature potatoes. There's a good view of the nearby *Fachwerkhäuser* (half-timbered houses) from the window tables upstairs, but the downstairs nooks are perhaps cosier.

🕐 Tue–Sat 11.30–2.30, 6–10.30, Sun 11.30–2.30, 6–9
🍴 L €20, D €40, Wine €17

EATING

RATTENFÄNGERHAUS

Osterstrasse 28, 31785
Hameln
Tel 05151 3888
www.rattenfaengerhaus.de

Indelibly associated with the Pied Piper, if for no other reason than the inscription on its 1603 façade, this bustling and touristy but memorable restaurant on the town's main street takes full advantage of Hamelin's legend. Things are perhaps taken too far, as some dishes and set-price menus contain the rather unappetizing word 'rat' in their names—though happily not the real thing in the food

itself. Traditional German dishes such as *schnitzel* and roast game, in season, abound on the menu, but you can also choose light snacks.

🕐 Daily 11–2.30, 6–11
🍴 L €20, D €45, Wine €14

HANNOVER

BASIL

Dragonerstrasse 30a, 30163
Hannover
Tel 0511 622636

This chic restaurant is in the unlikely but graceful setting of a former Prussian army riding establishment in the northeast of Hannover.

Up to 100 diners can be seated here among iron pillars, under a vaulted brick ceiling in a room suffused with natural light. The menu is hard to define—'international fusion'

would be one way—since it changes every few weeks and the chef roams Europe and Asia in spirit for inspiration. Cuisines, styles and ingredients are mixed and matched to intriguing effect, complemented by wines from around the world. In good weather, there's a fine outdoor terrace.

🕐 Mon–Sat 6.30–11
🍴 L €40, D €80, Wine €15
🚋 Tram 8

CLICHY

Weissekreuzstrasse 31, 30161
Hannover
Tel 0511 312447

This downtown restaurant is one of the most admired and consistent in Hannover, pulling in local foodies, business people and visitors alike for a dining experience that's

memorable without being overly formal. The owner-chef speaks of trying to create an elegant bistro ambience, and there seems little doubt that he succeeds, aided by waiters who are attentive, but not to a fault. Goose livers, truffle sauces and similar gourmet fare have their place on the menu, but so too does pan-fried chicken in a curry sauce with vegetables. American Express and Visa are accepted.

🕐 Mon–Fri noon–2.30, 6–11, Sat 6–11
🍴 L €60, D €90, Wine €20
🚋 Tram 3, 7

HILDESHEIM

KNOCHENHAUERAMTSHAUS

Markt 7, 31134
Hildesheim
Tel 05121 288 9909

Dining at this café-restaurant in the central square of Hildesheim is something of an event thanks to the building it is in. The medieval masterpiece *Fachwerkhaus* (half-timbered house), the old Butchers' Guildhouse, was one of the loveliest buildings in Germany. Destroyed during World War II, it was rebuilt faithfully in the 1980s, and has plenty of nooks and crannies where you can keep apart from fellow diners, and open spaces where you can join them. You can settle for just a beer and a snack inside or, in good weather, outside on the cobbled square. Alternatively, you can also have a plain but satisfying meal from the limited menu. Visa is the only card accepted here.

🕐 Daily 9am–10pm
🍴 L €20, D €30, Wine €10

LÜBECK

MIERA

Hüxstrasse 57, 23552
Lübeck
Tel 0451 77212

Hidden away up a flight of stairs in an old merchant's townhouse just east of the Markt, Miera shines both as a setting and for its food. Graceful dining rooms edged with stucco display touches of artful shabbiness and are adorned with works of modern art that veer towards the risqué. The menu changes every few days, drawing on a mix of Continental influences and paying significant homage to Mediterranean cuisine and wines, although it deliberately eludes easy categorization— venison might share the day's list with bouillabaisse and rocket (arugula) salad. The restaurant is only open for dinner, but there is also a bistro, which is open all day (Mon–Sat 9.30–11).

🕐 Wed–Sat 6–midnight
🍴 L €40, D €80, Wine €15
🚋 1, 4, 11, 21, 24, 31, 32, 34, 39

EATING

SCHIFFERGESELLSCHAFT

Breite Strasse 2, 23552
Lübeck
Tel 0451 76776
www.schiffergesellschaft.de
An armada of old sailing
ships is suspended from
the ceiling and other antique
maritime memorabilia
graces the wood-panelled
walls in this restaurant
of the step-gabled Hanseatic
League-era Haus der
Schiffergesellschaft
(Seafarers' Guild House),
dating from 1535. You can
dine convivially at long oak
tables, or at your own
four-person table. Expect
hearty servings of heavy
but tasty traditional fare,
such as grilled pork fillets
and roasted lamb with
thick sauces and all the
trimmings, alongside lighter
fish dishes and salads.
🕐 10am–1am
🍴 L €40, D €70, Wine €20.50
🚌 1, 2

RATSKELLER ZU LÜBECK

Markt 15, 23552
Lübeck
Tel 0451 72044
This cellar restaurant, with an
entrance at the side of the
medieval Rathaus, has a
choice of dining spaces: in
an open room, in a more
discreet space close to the
kitchen, and in total privacy in
a series of booths whose
doors are marked with the
insignia of once prominent
local families. Whichever you
choose, you'll be basking in
traditional style and dining
on old-fashioned northern
German cuisine. Meat dishes
predominate, but there are a
few vegetarian choices; among
the fish options, the grilled
zander (pike-perch) is a special
house dish, and the smoked-
fish soup is also well worth
trying. The restaurant accepts
Visa and MasterCard.
🕐 Daily 11am–midnight
🍴 L €40, D €60, Wine €15
🚌 1, 2

LÜNEBURG

NEPTUN'S FISCHHAUS/ MARISQUEIRA

Bei der Abtspferdetränke 1, 21335
Lüneburg
Tel 04131 408528
That 'Marisqueira' tag reveals
the Portuguese roots of this
fine little seafood restaurant,
close to the old Wasserviertel
river port, though much of
the fish comes from the North
Sea and the Baltic. You choose
your fish from a glass-fronted
cabinet in which the day's
offerings are displayed on
ice, and you can watch the
lady of the house as she cooks
your selection. The interior is
plain, but the plants on the
tables and decorations have
been made from mussel and
oyster shells. In fine weather,
you can dine outside. Fish
soup, grilled scampi, *matjes*
(fresh raw herring) and grilled
tuna are just a few of the
dishes on offer. The restaurant
doesn't accept credit cards.
🕐 Mon–Thu 11–9.30, Fri, Sat 11–10,
Sun 5–9.30
🍴 L €30, D €40, Wine €10

ROSTOCK

ZUR KOGGE

Wokrenterstrasse 27, 18055
Rostock
Tel 0381 493 4493
www.zur-kogge.m-vp.de
If a location at the harbour
and a name that recalls the
Hansekoggen (Hanseatic
League cog ships) of yore
isn't enough of a give-away,
you'll be convinced that
you've entered a maritime
world the moment you step
through the door. This 150-
year-old sailors' bar-turned-
restaurant is Rostock's oldest
such establishment. Model
sailing ships hang from the
ceiling, and life jackets join all
kinds of seagoing mementos
among the polished wood
and burnished brass. The
menu takes its inheritance
seriously, as is shown by the
pan-fried Baltic herring and
the Labskaus, and by the
many different pork dishes,
but it manages to fit in
some vegetarian choices too.
American Express is not
accepted here.
🕐 Daily 11.30am–11pm
🍴 L €30, D €50, Wine €14.30
🚌 Tram 11, 12

SCHWERIN

WEINHAUS UHLE

Schusterstrasse 13–15, 19055
Schwerin
Tel 0385 562956
www.weinhaus-uhle.de
This restaurant in the old town,
close to the cathedral, is in an
elegant rococo building dating
from 1740 that later became a
wine shop and tasting house.
The main dining room is decorated in a bright, *Jugendstil*
(art nouveau) style. Upstairs is
the medieval-style Rittersaal
(Hall of the Knights), used
on special occasions and for
groups. Regional dishes
include pan-fried Schweriner
eel and zander (pike-perch)
from the Baltic and nearby
Mecklenburg lakes, as well
as roast Mecklenburg duck.
The young couple who run
the restaurant are notable
for their classy German
Gastfreundschaft (hospitality).
🕐 Daily noon–3, 6–midnight
🍴 L €40, D €70, Wine €17.50

WISMAR

ALTER SCHWEDE

Am Markt 20, 23966 Wismar
Tel 03841 283552
The oldest building in town
(1380) and a visitor attraction
in its own right contains one
of the most characterful
restaurants on the Baltic
coast—if not in all Germany.

The 'Old Swede' has a
traditional, wood-panelled
interior and a warm and
sophisticated atmosphere. The
portions of Baltic seafood,
marinaded roast pork and
other traditional dishes are
hearty, which is especially
welcoming on cold days. In
warm, sunny weather, you can
dine outdoors on the square,
with a view of the Wasserkunst
pavilion just across the street.
🕐 Daily 11.30am–late
🍴 L €30, D €30, Wine €23

EATING

WESTERN GERMANY

Western Germany, with Nordrhein-Westfalen at its heart, is rightly proud of its culinary heritage—its trademark dish, knuckle of pork with mashed potato and *sauerkraut* (pickled while cabbage), seems to be on the menu of every tavern. Other traditional dishes include *Sauerbraten* (marinated beef in a sour cream sauce) with bread dumplings, and *bratwurst* with savoy cabbage and fried potatoes. Look for Frankfurt's delicious *Grüne Sosse* (green sauce), made with dill and sour cream, and served with egg and potatoes alongside meat dishes; and *Handkäse mit Musik* (literally 'hand cheese with music'), a soft, succulent cheese marinaded in pickled onions and served with dark bread. The latter is traditionally washed down with a glass of Frankfurt's heady *Apfelwein* (cider). Across the region, home-brewed beers are excellent; highlights include the dark *Alt* beer, typical of Düsseldorf, and the light frothy *Kölsch* of Köln.

Spanish and Italian cuisines are well represented, while the bigger cities are home to a smorgasbord of restaurants. In the Rhine and Mosel valleys, welcoming *Weinstubes* (wine rooms) have tastings of local wines, from the Spätburgunder of the Ahr valley to the Rhine's fresh and fruity Riesling.

PRICES

The prices given are for a two-course lunch (L) and a three-course dinner (D) for two people, without drinks. The wine price is for the least expensive bottle.

AACHEN

BESITOS

Kapuzinergraben 19, 52062 Aachen
Tel 0241 445 3682
www.besitos.sportkneipe.de

Although it is part of a chain, this bustling bistro feels like a family-run restaurant, with its warm lighting, Spanish music and imaginatively decorated interior. It is on the broad sweep of the Kapuzinergraben, near the imposing neoclassical theatre. Diners can choose to sit either at tall wooden tables with stools (ideal for a quick snack) or at more formal tables with cushioned chairs. The menu includes tapas and main courses, from succulent Iberian ham to mouthwatering paella.

🕐 Sun–Fri 10am–1am, Sat 10am–2am
🍽 L €25, D €35

NOBIS PRINTEN

Münsterplatz 3, 52062 Aachen
Tel 0241 968000
www.nobis-printen.de

Nobis Printen, at the southeast corner of the cathedral, takes its name from a local culinary delicacy—a soft, spicy gingerbread called *Printen*. As well as baking the gingerbread by the bagful, this popular bakery also serves a huge range of freshly prepared sandwiches and baguettes, plus the traditional *Kaffee und Kuchen* (coffee and cakes). Upstairs is a snug café with bouncy leather seats and great views of the cathedral square. Credit cards are not accepted.

🕐 Mon–Fri 7–7, Sat 7–6, Sun 9–6
🍽 Cakes, rolls €2–€3

BONN

CAFÉ BISTRO PENDEL

Vivatsgasse 2a, 53111 Bonn
Tel 0228 976 6064
www.cafe-bistro-pendel.de

This intimate little café in the heart of Bonn's Altstadt is just around the corner from the tourist information office. It has a great range of dishes,

from freshly prepared snacks, salads and baguettes to steaming bowls of chilli, gnocchi and pasta. The low lighting and dark wooden interior, complemented by an impressive collection of antique clocks, give the place a snug, old-fashioned feel in winter, while in the summer visitors can sit outside and watch the world go by. Café

Bistro Pendel attracts a young crowd, and it can get a bit smoky, but (as long as it doesn't bother you) this just adds to the ambience.

🕐 Mon–Thu 9am–1am, Fri–Sat 9am–2am, Sun and holidays 10am–1am
🍽 L €20, D €35, Wine €8

ROSES RESTAURANT

Martinsplatz 2a, 53113 Bonn
Tel 0228 433 0653

More classy than the Café Pendel is Roses Restaurant, which serves reasonably priced food in elegant surroundings. Soft lighting and clean lines characterize the interior, while the menu includes a tantalizing array of pasta, fish and meat dishes, from dark tagliatelle with shrimp in a mascarpone sauce to pork medallions draped in orange slices. An extensive breakfast menu (priced from €3 to €7) is served daily until 3pm. A mezzanine looks out over Martinsplatz and the basilica, as does a pretty cobbled patio.

🕐 Sun–Thu 9am–1am, Fri–Sat 9am–2am
🍽 L €25, D €45, Wine €19

DARMSTADT

BORMUTH CAFÉHAUS

Marktplatz 5, 64283 Darmstadt
Tel 06151 170913
www.bormuth.de

This ultra-elegant bakery has a bustling *Stehcafe* (stand-up café) downstairs for quick bites and coffee. There is a seating area upstairs for those who prefer to take their time. The interior is simple yet sumptuous, with dark leather booths, marble-topped tables and subtle yellow lighting. The extensive menu includes

EATING

breakfasts, cakes, baguettes and hot specials, plus more than a dozen sorts of tea, each with a name like 'Sport Cup' (which apparently contains 10 different vitamins). Credit cards are not accepted.

🕐 Mon–Fri 7.30–7, Sat 7.30–6, Sun 10.30–6

🍴 Snacks €3–€5, breakfasts and main courses €5–€8

DARMSTÄDTER RATSKELLER

Marktplatz 8, 64283
Darmstadt
Tel 06151 26444

Although established only in 1989, this centrally located pub overlooking Darmstadt's spacious Marktplatz has an old-fashioned feel, with solid wooden tables and walls, apron-wearing waiters and, of course, home-brewed beer. Ratsbräu Spezial Dunkel is a sweet, slightly malty brew that is wonderful in the cold weather, while Ratsbräu Premium Hell has a more refreshing aftertaste, and is a great warm-weather thirst-quencher. Simple but tasty German food is served all day, every day, and in the summer the pub spills out onto the bustling square.

🕐 Daily 10am–midnight

🍴 L €20, D €35, Wine by the glass only

DÜSSELDORF

RESTAURANT BRAUEREI ZUM SCHIFFCHEN

Hafenstrasse 5, 40213
Düsseldorf
Tel 0211 132422
www.stockheim.de

Founded in 1628, Zum Schiffchen is the oldest restaurant in Düsseldorf, and it's also one of the best. Traditional Alt beer is brewed on the premises and served direct to your table until you say you've had enough; even then, the waiter will probably ask again, just to make sure.

Special local dishes include pork leg with mashed potato and *sauerkraut*: Portions are on the generous side, so make sure you come with a hearty appetite. The restaurant is just off Bergerstrasse, one block to the south of Uerige.

🕐 Mon–Sat 11.30am–midnight

🍴 L €30, D €60, Wine €23

🚇 Heinrich-Heine-Allee

UERIGE OBERGÄRIGE HAUSBRAUEREI

Bergerstrasse 1, 40213
Düsseldorf
Tel 0211 866990
www.uerige.de

Extremely popular with locals in both summer and winter, the Uerige oozes Rhenish charm, from the intricately carved wooden wall panels to the copper detailing that is used almost everywhere else. Deliciously dark beer is

brewed on the premises and is poured from wooden barrels on top of the bar. A wide range of snacks is also available, including platters of *liverwurst* and gouda sandwiches for larger groups. Reserve in advance for *Schweinshaxe* (knuckle of pork). Uerige can be found one block to the south of Marklplatz. Credit cards are not accepted.

🕐 Daily 10am–midnight

🍴 Snacks only: €2.50

🚇 Heinrich-Heine-Allee

EIFEL

WINZERGENOSSENSCHAFT MAYSCHOSS-ALTENAHR

Ahrrotweinstrasse 42, 54508
Mayschoss
Tel 02643 93600
www.winzergenossenschaft-mayschoss.de

Established in 1868, the wine cooperative in Altenahr is a great place to sample the region's renowned Spätburgunder wine, a velvety-smooth red that is considered

to be among Germany's best. The region's white wine, meanwhile, typically comes from Riesling, Müller-Thurgau and Silvaner grapes, while *Eiswein* (ice wine) is made from specially selected grapes that have been allowed to freeze on the vine. The latter is considered an aromatic delicacy, and a half-bottle will set you back at least €30. The cooperative itself is housed in a fine brick building overlooking the Ahr.

🕐 May–end Oct daily 9–6; Nov–end Apr Mon–Fri 8–6, Sat–Sun 10–6

🍴 Tasting costs depend on numbers involved; cellar tour and tasting of four wines costs €6 per person for a group of 20

🚇 Altenahr

ESSEN

CAFÉ SOLO

Kettwiger Strasse 36, 45127 Essen
Tel 0201 747 6666
www.solocation.de

Despite its young, vibrant feel, Café Solo is popular with people of all ages, thanks to its relaxed atmosphere, wholesome food and friendly service. It's always busy but never overwhelmingly so, and the whole place is bathed in a warm, welcoming glow. Snacks such as bagels, panini and salads

are the mainstay of the menu, but burgers and pasta dishes are also available, and the delicious spicy Chinese specials are superb value. Solo's location, at the heart of Essen's main shopping precinct, makes it a great place for alfresco dining in the summer, while in the winter outdoor heaters keep the cold at bay. Credit cards are not accepted.

🕐 Mon–Thu 8am–1am, Fri–Sat 8am–3am, Sun 10am–1am

🍴 L €15, D €15, Wine €11.90

🚇 Hauptbahnhof

CASINO ZOLLVEREIN

Gelsenkirchener Strasse 181, 45309 Essen

Tel 0201 830240

www.casino-zollverein.de

This *über*-chic restaurant and café has an effortlessly elegant dining area and bar among the pipes and pillars of a former industrial boiler room. *Kaffee und Kuchen* (coffee and cakes) are available during the day, but to appreciate the atmosphere here fully it's best to come at night, when crisp white tablecloths and flickering candles provide inviting islands of light in an otherwise dark and cavernous space. The imaginative menu has a mixture of international and German cuisine, which is exquisitely prepared and presented. Zollverein itself is a few kilometres to the northeast of Essen, and can be reached via tram from anywhere in the downtown area. Credit cards are not accepted.

🕐 Tue–Sun 11.30am–midnight (food served noon–2.30 and 6–10.30)

🍴 L €40, D €70, Wine €20.50

🚌 Bus or tram 7 to Zollverein

FRANKFURT AM MAIN

HAUS WERTHEIM

Fahrtor 1, 60311

Frankfurt am Main

Tel 069 281432

This intimate little pub just to the south of the Römerberg is the oldest inn in the city, and was one of the few buildings to survive the Allied bombing raids of World War II. Inside, it looks as if it hasn't changed in centuries: Beer jugs and brass fittings dangle from every available beam, while kitsch, back-lit paintings made of stained glass bathe everything in a warm, ethereal light. The house dish is *Wiener schnitzel* in green sauce (▷ 341), which comes with boiled potatoes and eggs, and is indescribably delicious, not to mention generous to a fault. Because there are only half a dozen tables, it's often a good idea to book ahead.

🕐 Daily 11–11

🍴 L €35, D €50, Wine €22

🚇 Römerberg

SPECIAL IN FRANKFURT

MAIN TOWER RESTAURANT AND BAR

53rd floor, Helaba Building, Neue Mainzer Strasse 52–54, 60311 Frankfurt am Main

Tel 069 3650 4777

www.maintower-restaurant.de

Perched 200m (650ft) above Frankfurt's teeming streets, the Main Tower Restaurant offers a breathtaking dining experience. Tables for two are arranged near floor-to-ceiling windows on the 53rd floor, with superb views of the city and its surroundings. The modern, imaginative menu isn't cheap, with one course starting at €30 and three courses at around €55, but for a treat it's hard to beat. Main courses might include scallops and caviar with beetroot ravioli and horseradish sauce, or breast of duck with creamed potatoes and wild garlic in a honey mushroom sauce. For dessert, choose from the likes of chocolate and rhubarb risotto, or coconut, banana and lime compote. After you've eaten, you can take a stroll on the open-air observation deck. Main Tower itself is just a short walk south of Opernplatz.

🕐 Tue–Sat 5.30pm–1am (bar open until 2am)

🍴 D €100

🚇 Willy-Brandt-Platz

RAMA V

Vilbeler Strasse 32, 60313 Frankfurt am Main

Tel 069 2199 6488

International restaurants abound near the train station and around Fressgasse, the pedestrianized precinct between Opernplatz and An der Hauptwoche, but for a real treat make your way farther east to Rama V, on Vilbeler Strasse. This popular Thai restaurant is characterized by candlelit tables, dark, wood-panelled walls and cool white tablecloths, although its relaxed atmosphere ensures it never feels too formal. The menu is available in English and German, and lists an overwhelming variety of dishes at very reasonable prices. The

service is impeccable, and the portions are more than generous. For a taste sensation, try the deep-fried banana with coconut ice cream.

🕐 Mon–Sat 12–3, 6–11.30, Sun 6–11.30

🍴 L €40, D €60, Wine €16

🚇 Konstablerwache

ZUM GEMALTEN HAUS

Schweizer Strasse 67, 60594 Frankfurt am Main

Tel 069 614559

There are literally dozens of pubs, restaurants and bars in Frankfurt's Sachsenhausen district, to the south of the river, but the best place to sample *Apfelwein* and *Handkäse mit Musik* (▷ 346) is arguably Zum Gemalten Haus. Set back a little from the street, it has wall-to-wall wood-panelled paintings with a distinctly Dutch feel. The cider is served in large, tilting jars that are left on your table. Credit cards are not accepted.

🕐 Tue–Sun 10am–midnight

🍴 Snacks €2–€5, main courses €8–€12, cider €1.50 for 300ml (12fl oz)

🚇 Schweizer Platz

KOBLENZ

KAFFEEWIRTSCHAFT

Münzplatz 14, 56068 Koblenz

Tel 0261 914 4702

www.kaffeewirtschaft.de

The friendly Kaffeewirtschaft is in a prominent position overlooking Münzplatz, in the heart of Koblenz's old town. The café is fronted by a stunning colonnade and has a striking, candlelit interior with dark wooden chairs, marble table

tops and blood-red walls (relieved by occasional swathes of blue). It serves everything from breakfasts and baguettes to pasta dishes and steak specials, so it provides the perfect place to rest tired limbs at any hour of the day or

EATING

night. In the summer, drinks here on the square are a must. Credit cards are not accepted.

🕙 Mon–Thu 9am–midnight, Fri–Sat 9am–2am, Sun and holidays 10am–midnight

🍴 L €15, D €30, Wine €12.50

KÖLN

CAFÉ HOLTMANN'S

Am Museum Ludwig, Bischofsgartenstrasse 1, 50667 Köln

Tel 0221 2509 9977

www.holtmanns.com

Housed in Köln's famous Museum Ludwig, Café Holtmann's is one of the most popular and relaxing eateries in the middle of the city, and as such is worth a visit in its own right. It serves a wide range of freshly made cakes, baguettes, quiches and salads, all at surprisingly reasonable prices considering its location. The sofas lining one of the walls provide the perfect place for burying your head in a book or newspaper, and live jazz is played every Friday, Saturday and Sunday afternoon.

🕙 Tue–Sun 10–6

🍴 Snacks/lunches €3–€7

🚌 Bus/tram to Domplatz

EIS CAFÉ RAFAELLI

Am Hof 28, 50667 Köln

Tel 0221 420 7960

Within sight of the cathedral on the south side of Domplatz is the Eis Café Rafaelli, with soft leather sofas, glitzy chandeliers and floor-to-ceiling windows. This is a great place to grab an ice cream or cold drink in summer, although because of its location it can get quite busy. The themed ice cream sundaes are popular with kids, such as 'Spaghetti Carbonara', with hazelnuts, walnuts and chocolate sauce on stringy ice cream that looks like spaghetti. The menu also includes snacks, waffles, crêpes and other desserts. Credit cards are not accepted.

🕙 Mon–Fri 10am–11pm, Sat–Sun 10am–midnight

🍴 Snacks €2–€5, ice-cream sundaes €5–€8

🚌 Bus/tram to Domplatz

PETERS BRAUHAUS

Mühlengasse 1, 50667 Köln

Tel 0221 257 3950

www.peters-brauhaus.de

Peters Brauhaus, just to the northeast of the Altermarkt, is one of the traditional taverns in Köln's Altstadt, and it's also one of the best, thanks to its friendly service, welcoming atmosphere and excellent

food. Not surprisingly, traditional staples such as *bratwurst* with *sauerkraut* and *Wiener schnitzel* with potatoes are the mainstay of the menu here, and everything is invariably washed down with a few glasses of *Kölsch*, the city's local brew—the number of beers you drink is simply marked on your beer mat with a pencil and added up at the end of the meal.

🕙 Daily 11am–12.30am (food served 11.30am–midnight)

🍴 L €25, D €50, Wine served by the glass only

🚌 Hauptbahnhof

GRANDE MILANO

Hohenstaufenring 29–37, 50674 Köln

Tel 0221 242121

www.ristorante-grande-milano.de

For a culinary treat, head to this chic Italian restaurant on the Hohenstaufenring, a few blocks to the south of Rudolfplatz. The interior is elegant yet understated, characterized by soft spot lighting, crisp white tablecloths and immaculately framed black-and-white prints, giving the whole place a relaxed, informal feel. The restaurant's chef, Dottore Minotti, specializes in truffles. Reservations are recommended. If the main

restaurant seems a bit pricey, there's also a bistro right next door.

🕙 Mon–Fri 12–3, 6.30–midnight, Sat 6.30–midnight

🍴 L €40, D €80, Wine €16

🚌 Bus/tram to Zülpicher Platz

MAINZ

PIZZA PEPE

Augustinerstrasse 21, 55116 Mainz

Tel 06131 229986

www.pizzapepe.de

This tiny pizza place just a short walk to the east of the cathedral may not look like much from the outside, but it's actually one of the most popular places in town. This is largely because of its great-tasting pizzas, which are made to order from fresh ingredients, although the booming voice of the proprietor also helps to keep

the atmosphere fun and frantic. There's a vast array of toppings to choose from, and the mini pizzas (18cm/7in) are ideal for those with smaller appetites. All the staff wear white uniforms and tall paper hats, and can usually be seen flinging dough around the kitchen as though their lives depended on it. Pasta dishes are also available, and food can be ordered until midnight. Credit cards are not accepted.

🕙 Sun–Thu 11am–1am, Fri–Sat 11am–2am

🍴 Small pizzas from €3, large pizzas from €5

MÜNSTER

GROSSE FREIHEIT 26

Hafenweg 26, 48143
Münster

Tel 0251 747 4919

In recent years, Münster's once-derelict docklands have been transformed into a trendy but understated meeting place for students, jazz-lovers and other assorted night owls. At the heart of Hafenweg, the area's main drag, is Grosse Freiheit 26, a romantic, candlelit eatery that rubs shoulders with the Hot Jazz Club, the city's best basement jazz venue, on one side (▷ 257) and a Harley Davidson shop on the other. Overlooking the canal, this vibrant, popular restaurant has intimate but informal seating in a converted industrial space, complete with brick walls and internal piping. The young staff are friendly and attentive, the food is excellent, and the atmosphere is relaxing. Credit cards are not accepted.

🕐 Daily 6pm–1am
🍴 D €50, Wine €21

IPANEMA

Mauritzstrasse 24, 48143
Münster

Tel 0251 40409

Specializing in Latin-American food, this lively restaurant just a short walk to the north of the train station is very popular. Wicker chairs, an artificial waterfall and beach-hut bamboo give a relaxed, infor-

mal feel, and the extensive menu—with everything from generously stuffed tortillas to mouthwatering steaks—is unbelievably good value for money. Fast and friendly service and lively Latino music complete the scene in this inexpensive gem.

🕐 Daily noon–midnight
🍴 L €15, D €20, Wine €11

MARKT CAFÉ

Dom Platz 6–7, 48143
Münster

Tel 0251 57585

The café is opposite the cathedral in the heart of Münster's pedestrian precinct, and is far more inviting than its uninspired façade suggests. Frequented by students, work colleagues and families in equal measure, it serves everything from cake and hot drinks

to baguettes and pizzas, not to mention all manner of beers, cocktails and spirits. In summer, the whole café spills out onto the square, making it a great place to quaff a quick beer or soft drink just a stone's throw from the cathedral. Credit cards are not accepted.

🕐 Mon–Fri 9am–1am, Sat 8am–1am, Sun and hols 10am–1am
🍴 L €15, D €25, Wine €18

RHEINTAL

RESTAURANT ZUM GOLDENEN LÖWEN

Heerstrasse 82, 56329
St. Goar

Tel 06741 1674

With its pink candles and curtains, and its old-fashioned furnishings, this friendly establishment on the banks of the Rhine is like a flashback to the 1950s, although it's no less charming for all that. The menu is a little on the pricey

side, but Goldenen Löwen is one of the few places near Loreley rock and has a terrace

overlooking the river. It is also a hotel, with 12 immaculate double rooms dating from 1728. Credit cards are not accepted.

🕐 Apr–end Nov daily 8am–10pm; Dec–end Mar Fri–Wed 8am–10pm
🍴 L €30, D €45, Wine €12.50
🚉 St. Goar

RISTORANTE DA FRANCO

Rheinpromenade 43, 53424
Remagen

Tel 02642 22422

www.ristorante-dafranco.de

If you find yourself feeling a little peckish in Remagen, look no further than Ristorante da Franco, one of a handful of eateries with a view of the Rhine. It's housed in a fine baroque building painted an eye-catching (if rather incongruous) yellow, while the interior is littered with little knick-knacks, from oversized bottles of wine to giant jars of pasta. Home-made pizza is the order of the day here, but if you just want a snack, the soup—accompanied by freshly baked dough balls—is also excellent.

🕐 Daily 11–3, 5–midnight
🍴 L €20, D €35, Wine €17
🚉 Remagen

SPEYER

DOMHOF HAUSBRAUEREI

Grosse Himmelsgasse 6, 67346
Speyer

Tel 06232 74055

www.domhof.de

With its tendril-clad façade, flower-draped ceilings and solid wooden beams, this historic establishment opposite Speyer's magnificent cathedral is popular with locals and visitors. The Domhof is staffed by friendly female waitresses who are young (or young at heart). A wide range of traditional German food is available, with sausages and *sauerkraut* much in evidence, along with delicious home-brewed beer by the barrelful.

🕐 Mon–Fri 11am–midnight, Sat–Sun 10am–midnight
🍴 Snacks €3–€5, main courses €8–€15, desserts €3–€5

EATING

MAXIMILIAN CAFÉBAR UND RESTAURANT

Korngasse 15, 67346 Speyer
Tel 06232 622648
www.cafe-maximilian.de

With its dark wooden tables, shallow-domed ceilings and art nouveau theme, this intimate bar has all the charm of a busy Parisian café. In addition to snacks and main courses, from buffalo wings to burritos, it also does a fine line in doughnuts and cakes. Its hot drinks include a whole range of teas, plus flavoured hot chocolates with apt names like 'One Night in Heaven' (laced with caramel and toffee). Credit cards are not accepted.

🕐 Mon–Fri 8am–1am, Sat–Sun 9am–1am

🍴 L €20, D €35, Wine €18

SOEST

SPECIAL IN SOEST

LAMÄNG BRASSERIE

Kungelmarkt 4–6, 59494 Soest
Tel 02921 767283

This intimate, welcoming café is decorated in art nouveau style, with deep, comfortable sofas, stained glass and assorted Gustav Klimt prints hung tastefully on the walls. It does a nice

menu of hot baguettes, as well as breakfasts, waffles and *apfelstrudel*. In terms of drinks, it seems your imagination really is the limit here: Beers, wine and cocktails are served alongside coffees, milkshakes and no fewer than 17 different types of tea. Candlelight in the evening adds to the relaxed atmosphere. Credit cards are not accepted.

🕐 Sun–Mon 9am–1am, Fri–Sat 9am–3am

🍴 L €15, D €25, Wine €13.30

TRIER

CAFÉ RESTAURANT ZUR STEIPE

Hauptmarkt 14, 54290 Trier
Tel 0651 145 5456

Zur Steipe is a relaxed restaurant that also has a café and cake shop. It is housed in one of the most historic buildings in Trier: The Steipe itself was built in the 15th century, and has an imposing crenellated façade with a striking colonnade of arches on the

ground floor. Between these arches are statues of the city's patron saints, and above them, at the corners of the building, are two knights, one of whom faces the cathedral with his visor down, an act of defiance that symbolized the animosity between Church and State during the Middle Ages. The restaurant is arranged around a stunning courtyard. Cakes and sandwiches are served in the café, with more substantial fare offered in the main restaurant.

🕐 Mon–Sat 8am–10pm, Sun 10am–7pm

🍴 L €20, D €40, Wine €22, breakfast and snacks €3–€9

ZUM DOMSTEIN

Hauptmarkt 5, 54290 Trier
Tel 0651 74490
www.domstein.de

As well as serving traditional German fare and offering wine-tasting by the glass, Zum Domstein, overlooking Trier's historic Market Place, also has a separate dining area devoted entirely to Roman cuisine. Menus are printed in Latin, English and German, all the dishes are taken from an original Roman recipe book, and the intimate cellar where the food is served is decked out with replicas of Roman objects that were unearthed in the cellar when it was excavated just a few years ago. A typical

set-price menu might include pine-kernel sausages with artichoke hearts, green beans in a fish sauce, lamb cutlets in a wine and date marinade, and soufflé of pears topped with crème caramel and pepper (which, believe it or not, tastes rather good). Meals are accompanied by a wine roll (with a bay leaf baked into the base) and a Roman 'aperitif', a sweet liqueur with a faintly aniseed taste. Credit cards are not accepted.

🕐 Daily 8.30am–midnight

🍴 L €30, D €55, Wine €7

WIESBADEN

LUMEN RESTAURANT

Marktplatz, 65183 Wiesbaden
Tel 0611 300200
www.lumen-gastronomie.de

In the middle of Marktplatz at the base of the imposing Marktkirche is Lumen, a glass and chrome haven in the heart of Wiesbaden. It's popular with smartly dressed business people and ladies who lunch, but it retains a relaxed atmosphere thanks to its light and spacious feel.

It's not particularly cheap, but the constantly changing menu is imaginative, and the food delicious. If you just fancy a snack, the soup, served with warm bread, is highly recommended.

🕐 Tue–Sat 6pm–12.30am

🍴 L €45, D €75, Wine €18.50

EATING

BERLIN

Berlin's cuisine and restaurants reflect the multicultural character of the city. You will find everything here from Australian restaurants to sushi bars, as well as a few creative combinations in the trendy gourmet and fusion restaurants. A growing number of quality Turkish and Persian restaurants are appearing in Prenzlauer Berg and Kreuzberg. Some of the best (and least expensive) food in the city is Italian: Berliners love pizza and pasta.

It can be quite difficult to find traditional German food here, but the most typical Berlin dish is *Bulette*, a type of meat pie, closely followed by *Currywurst* (curried sausage) and *Hackepeter* (German-style steak tartare). The famous *Berliner Weisse* beer is popular too.

Café culture thrives in the capital. Sunday brunch is a tradition among Berliners, and afternoon *Kaffee und Kuchen* is still standard practice. Traditional and independent cafés are doing well, although American-style coffee chains are beginning to make their presence felt. Credit cards are not universally accepted, so it is probably wise to carry cash with you.

PRICES

The prices given are for a two-course lunch (L) and a three-course dinner (D) for two people, without drinks. The wine price is for the least expensive bottle.

AMRIT

Oranienstrasse 202–203, 10117
Berlin (Kreuzberg)
Tel 030 612 5550
www.amrit.de

Warm surroundings, friendly and attentive staff, excellent food and fruity cocktails make this Indian restaurant a popular choice with both locals and visitors. The spicy dishes, whisked to your table on sizzling hot plates are sure to awaken the senses. If you prefer something milder, they also prepare some creamy coconut curries. Pre-dinner drinks, after-dinner citrus liqueurs to cleanse the palette and hot towels are all part of the service. There is another branch in Mitte at Oranienburger Strasse 45.

🕒 Sun–Thu noon–1am, Fri–Sat noon–2am
🍴 L €15, D €35, Wine €17.40
🚇 Görlitzer Bahnhof

AROMA

Kantstrasse 35, 10625
Berlin (Charlottenburg)
Tel 030 3759 1628

If it's dim sum you're after, this large Chinese restaurant on the corner of Kantstrasse is the place to go. The red tablecloths and furnishings may be a little dated, but the Cantonese dishes are first class. The sweet-and-sour soup and chicken soup with fine glass noodles are great lunchtime fillers.

🕒 Daily noon–3am
🍴 L €12, D €27, Wine €18
🚇 Wilmersdorfer Strasse

BOCCA DI BACCO

Friedrichstrasse 167–168, 10117
Berlin (Mitte)
Tel 030 2067 2828
www.boccadibacco.de

This is the most exclusive restaurant in the city for Italian food. The winning combination of gourmet Tuscan cuisine and contemporary elegance continues to attract VIPs and politicians from the nearby diplomatic quarter. The food and the surroundings are stylish, the staff are friendly and welcoming, and the clientele are relaxed. Black chairs, gleaming white tablecloths and fruit-inspired art add to the clean, modern feel. The finest Italian ingredients are lovingly prepared and beautifully presented. Reservations are essential for dinner.

🕒 Mon–Sat noon–midnight, Sun 6–midnight
🍴 L €35, D €65, Wine €25
🚇 Friedrichstrasse

BORCHARDT

Französische Strasse 47, 10117
Berlin (Mitte)
Tel 030 8188 6262

A. F. W. Borchardt founded this top-quality French restaurant on the eastern side of Mitte in 1853. High ceilings, plush maroon benches, art nouveau mosaics and marble columns re-create the 1920s café culture. This well-known celebrity hang-out is popular with politicians, actors and sports personalities, so you may spot a few stars. There is plenty of fresh fish, veal and tender beef on the menu, plus a €48 set-price menu with an excellent choice of dishes for every course. Reservations are essential.

🕒 Daily noon–midnight
🍴 L €20, D €50, Wine €20
🚇 Französische Strasse

CAFÉ BRAVO

Auguststrasse 69, im Kunst-Werke
Berlin e.v., 10117 Berlin (Mitte)
Tel 030 2759 4067
www.cafebravo.de

The American artist Dan Graham created this sculpture garden-cum-café in the new courtyard of the Kunst-Werke Institute for Contemporary Art between 1995 and 1998. The two cube-shaped areas, with their mirrored walls and transparent ceilings, form a contemporary meeting and eating space at the heart of the institute. Enjoy coffee, cake or a light meal in the bright, calm surroundings of this unique gallery café. Credit cards are not accepted.

🕒 Daily 11am–midnight
🍴 L €12, D €26, Wine €12
🚇 Oranienburger Tor

CAFÉ EINSTEIN

Unter den Linden 42, 10117
Berlin (Mitte)
Tel 030 204 3632
www.cafeeinstein.com

Café Einstein is an institution, popular with business lunchers during the week and brunchers on Sunday. It has a touch of art nouveau elegance with a modern twist, and there are some interesting photos

of celebrities and film stars hanging on the walls. Snuggle into one of the booths, or get a table by the window and

EATING

watch the world go by. They have a great selection of exotic teas and coffees, and their homemade apple strudel, served warm with vanilla sauce, is a great comfort on a cold, rainy afternoon. There is another branch in Tiergarten at Kurfürstenstrasse 58 (tel 030 261 50 96).

🕐 Daily 10am–2am
🍴 L €24, D €24, Wine €22
🚇 Unter den Linden

CAFÉ DE FRANCE

Unter den Linden 62–68, 10117 Berlin (Mitte)
Tel 030 2064 1391
www.peugeot-avenue.de
The dishes are traditional French but the surroundings are modern at this popular bistro on Unter den Linden. The excellent food and service come at a reasonable price too. The red chairs, walls and ceilings contrast with the bright white tablecloths and sparkling glasses. Enjoy a pre-dinner drink in their sleek bar area before you order. A meal here is an affordable, stylish and romantic treat.

🕐 Mon–Sat 10–10, Sun 10–6
🍴 L €16, D €30, Wine €17
🚇 Unter den Linden

CAFÉ E GELATO

Potsdamer Platz Arkaden Einkauf-Center, 10785 Berlin (Tiergarten)
Tel 030 2529 7832
www.potsdamer-platz.net
Eat in or take away at this café and ice-cream parlour on the top floor of the Potsdamer Platz Arkaden. Choose from an extensive selection of ice creams and sorbets—try 'Maracuja', 'Pocket Coffee' or chocolate. Alternatively, share a towering sundae or sample their cakes and generous Italian coffees, a great treat after a session of retail therapy. Credit cards are not accepted.

🕐 Sun–Thu 10am–11pm, Fri–Sat 10am–midnight
🍴 €1 per scoop
🚇 Potsdamer Platz

CAFÉ IM LITERATURHAUS 'WINTERGARTEN'

Fasanenstrasse 23, 10719 Berlin (Charlottenburg)
Tel 030 882 5414
On the ground floor of a beautiful 19th-century villa, this traditional coffee house is one of Berlin's most popular

Sunday brunch hot spots. It is a great place to escape the bustling shops on the Kufürstendamm. Waiters in dinner jackets and bow ties introduce you to the extensive cake buffet, and you can sit in the lovely garden in summer. Inside, the ceilings are lined with gilt stucco and there is a wonderful early-20th-century conservatory, so you can enjoy the view out to the garden. Credit cards are not accepted.

🕐 Daily 9.30am–1am
🍴 L €25, D €30, Wine €16
🚇 Kurfürstendamm

CAFÉ AM UFER

Paul-Lincke-Ufer 42, 10999 Berlin (Kreuzberg)
Tel 030 6162 9200
This garden café on the Paul-Lincke-Ufer (*Ufer* means 'riverbank') is a great place to be if the weather is warm, when you can bask in the sunshine over a coffee or iced tea. In spring and summer, the café's terraces are packed, but it is worth waiting for a place so you can enjoy the breakfast, light lunch or an evening meal outside. Credit cards are not accepted.

🕐 10am–late
🍴 Soups from €3.50, main dishes €7–€12
🚇 Paul-Lincke-Ufer, Kottbusser Tor, Schönleinstrasse

CASOLARE

Grimmstrasse 30, 10967 Berlin (Kreuzberg)
Tel 030 6950 6610
www.ilcasolaredikreuzberginrete.it
The staff at this bustling *trattoria* (small Italian restaurant) on a scenic corner in Kreuzberg are very vocal and entertaining, particularly during an Italian soccer final. The service is excellent and everything comes with a smile. The house wine is very good, and the pizzas are the best you will find in Berlin at the most reasonable prices. If you don't fancy pizza, try the venison ragout with mushrooms, which is rich and substantial. Reserve a table in the evenings to avoid disappointment. Credit cards are not accepted.

🕐 Daily noon–midnight
🍴 L €20, D €30, Wine €11
🚇 Schönleinstrasse, Kottbusser Tor

FACIL

Hotel Madison, Potsdamer Strasse 3, 10785 Berlin (Tiergarten)
Tel 030 5900 51234
www.madison-berlin.de
Mediterranean cuisine with a French twist is served at the Hotel Madison's Michelin-starred restaurant. You'll be treated to first-class service in this tranquil glasshouse in a bamboo-filled quadrangle at the heart of the hotel. There is a bubbling fountain, and in the summer they remove the roof to give an alfresco dining feel. Reserve ahead for this popular Zen oasis. A special six-course menu costs €100 per person.

🕐 Mon–Fri 12–3, 7–11
🍴 L €50, D €70, Wine €22
🚇 Potsdamer Platz

GOURMET RESTAURANT LORENZ ADLON

Hotel Adlon, Unter den Linden 77, 10117 Berlin (Mitte)
Tel 030 22610
www.hotel-adlon.de
Sample some of the best

gourmet fusion food in the city at this exclusive experimental restaurant in the historic surroundings of the Hotel Adlon (▷ 384) on Unter den Linden. Seafood from Brittany, Bresse poultry, fine wines, lobster, caviar and regional dishes are all on the menu. Whether you opt for an exquisite breakfast or brunch, a fine afternoon pastry with coffee or a gala dinner you are guaranteed a memorable meal and first-class service. They also have their own cookbook, so you can re-create some of the fine cuisine at home.

🕐 Tue–Sat 7pm–11pm
🍴 D €190–300, Wine prices vary
🚇 Unter den Linden

EATING

HACKESCHER HOF

Rosenthaler Strasse 40–41, 10117
Berlin (Mitte)
Tel 030 283 5293
www.hackescher-hof.de

This wine bar and café has been tastefully modernized, yet still preserves reminders of the 1930s boomtime of Berlin's coffee houses and music halls. There is an excellent selection of wines and the late opening hours are attractive to those seeking a meal when everything else is shut. If you're after a snack, try a delicious cake or pastry baked in their own pâtisserie.

🕐 Mon–Fri 7am–3am, Sat–Sun 9am–3am

🍴 L €20, D €50, Wine €18

🚇 Hackescher Hof

HAKUIN

Martin-Luther-Strasse 1/1a, 10777
Berlin (Schöneberg)
Tel 030 218 2027
www.restaurant-hakuin.de

Hakuin is an Asian restaurant with an excellent reputation and is regarded by many as the best vegetarian eatery in the city. The chefs use organic ingredients to create a huge variety of vegetarian dishes from around the world. A pond filled with Japanese carp and surrounded by plants, combined with a non-smoking policy, help create a calm retreat in the middle of the city.

🕐 Tue–Sat 5–11, Sun noon–11

🍴 L €40, D €52, Wine €24

🚇 Wittenbergplatz

HUGOS

Hotel Inter-Continental, Budapester Strasse 2, 10787 Berlin (Tiergarten)
Tel 030 2602 1263
www.hugos-restaurant.de

Hugos is a gourmet restaurant right at the top of the Hotel Inter-Continental, and has won an impressive list of accolades. It has earned one Michelin star and 17 Gault-Millau points, and was named Der Feinschmecker Restaurant of the Year in 2003. Enjoy a cocktail or a glass of champagne in the sophisticated low-lit bar before you are shown to your table in the panoramic restaurant, which has a 360-degree view over the rooftops of Berlin. Head chef Thomas Kammeler has created a diverse and enticing menu with an emphasis on light Mediterranean food, complemented by a superior wine list. You can start with cold-smoked salmon with leeks and Périgord truffles, and then move on to fillet of sole with salsify and truffle fondue, or saddle of suckling pig on saffron-fennel vegetables and olive gnocchi. For dessert, try the blood-orange terrine with marinated orange fillets and Grand Marnier ice cream.

🕐 Mon–Sat 6–10.30

🍴 D €150 (4 courses), Wine €28

🚇 Zoologischer Garten

KAISERSAAL

Sony Center, Bellevuestrasse 1, Potsdamer Platz, 10785 Berlin (Tiergarten)
Tel 030 2575 1454
www.kaisersaal-berlin.de

Few structures in Potsdamer Platz survived the bombing of World War II. However, this reconstructed building was one of them. With its new glass exterior, it has become one of the top places to eat in Berlin. There are only 40 seats at this exclusive establishments, so reservations are essential, but it is worth making the effort for the superior cuisine, based on the classical German-French style. Begin with tomato cappuccino with king prawns or fried scallop with kohlrabi, then for your main course try the red snapper with bean cassoulet or the poached turbot on fennel with crayfish ravioli. There is a huge variety of delicate desserts, although the marinated figs with praline ice cream stands out.

🕐 Reserve ahead

🍴 D €130, Wine €26

🚇 Potsdamer Platz

KARTOFFEL KISTE

Europa Center, 1 Étage, 10789
Berlin (Mitte)
Tel 030 261 4254
www.katoffelkiste-berlin.de

Kartoffel Kiste serves hearty and wholesome German cooking in traditional surroundings. Every dish contains potato in some shape or form—even the pizza bases are made from potato. The menu proves that a great deal can be done with the humble tuber, although vegetarians will struggle to find something that doesn't contain meat too. Credit cards are not accepted.

🕐 Daily 11.30am–midnight

🍴 L €15, D €25, Wine €19

🚇 Zoologischer Garten

LAFIL

Gormannstrasse 22, 10119
Berlin (Mitte)
Tel 030 2859 9026
www.lafil.de

This Spanish restaurant is great value for money. Its extensive cocktail and wine menu rivals any found in a gourmet restaurant, and the fish and lobster dishes are fantastic. The finest fresh Mediterranean ingredients are used, and the relaxed and friendly staff and clientele make this a great place to start your evening.

🕐 Mon–Fri 1pm–2am, Sat–Sun 6pm–2am

🍴 L €14, D €36, Wine €15

🚇 Weinmeisterstrasse

MAO THAI STAMMHAUS

Wörther Strasse 30, 10405
Berlin (Prenzlauer Berg)
Tel 030 441 9261
www.thaipage.com

This is universally regarded as the finest Thai restaurant in Berlin, with top-class service and elegant surroundings. It is a little bit pricey, but the beautifully presented food is delicious and deserves its excellent reputation. If you can't get a table here, there are other braches in the city: The small Kamala on Oranienburger Strasse, Mao Thai am Fasanenplatz on Meirorrostrasse or Tuans Hütte Thai grill and sushi on Dirksenstrasse. Credit cards not accepted.

🕐 Daily noon–midnight

🍴 L €24, D €50, Wine €20

🚇 Senefelderplatz

MAR Y SOL

Savignyplatz 5, 10623
Berlin (Charlottenburg)
Tel 030 313 2593
www.marysol-berlin.de

Come here for Spanish cooking and the tastiest and fastest tapas in the city. The food is authentic and the crowd is loud. There is an extensive list of Andalucían delicacies to choose from, and at just €2–€4 per dish you can afford to try a few. In summer, the large garden is opened,

EATING

which is filled with palm trees and Spanish furniture. It is always busy, so reservations are essential, particularly on the weekend.

🕐 Daily 11.30am–1am
🍴 Tapas €2.50–€4.50, salad €7.50–€11.50, D €48, Wine €16
🚇 Savignyplatz

MARE BÊ

Rosenthaler Strasse 46–48, 10178 Berlin (Mitte)
Tel 030 283 6545
www.marebe.de

This is a first-class, fashionable eatery for those who appreciate creative Mediterranean-inspired cuisine. Tucked away from the chaos and noise on Hackescher Markt, the restaurant basks in surroundings that are both tasteful and calming. The chefs are on show at the back of the restaurant, carefully preparing fresh and imaginative cuisine from France and southern Europe. There are plenty of choices for fish fans and vegetarians, and the French, Italian and Spanish wine collection is outstanding. There is also an extensive cocktail list. On a warm summer's evening you can relax in the courtyard and listen to the bubbling fountain.

🕐 Mon–Sat noon–late, Sun 1pm–10pm
🍴 L €15, D €25, Wine €19
🚇 Hackescher Markt

MARGAUX

Unter den Linden 78, 10117 Berlin (Mitte)
Tel 030 2265 2611
www.margaux-berlin.de

Head chef Michael Hoffman and his expert team create fabulous avant-garde and classic French dishes at this Michelin-starred restaurant on Unter den Linden. The service is quick, discrete and professional, and the contemporary furnishings, modern art and soft lighting add to the air of sophistication. You can choose from four to eight courses, and the sommelier is happy to help you select from the list of 750 vintage wines. Reserve a table in advance if you want to dine alongside the diplomats and top business people who visit this exclusive establishment.

🕐 Tue–Sat 12–2, 7–10.30
🍴 L €70, D €100, Wine €25
🚇 Unter den Linden

MIRCHI

Oranienburgerstrasse 50, 10117 Berlin (Mitte)
Tel 030 2844 4482
www.mirchi.de

Good food is guaranteed at this Indian and Singaporean fusion restaurant and cocktail bar in Mitte. The dishes have been toned down to suit the Western palate, so it isn't exactly authentic, but the food is still very good. The daily

lunch menu has a good selection of vegetarian, chicken and lamb dishes. There is a greater choice in the evenings, but meals at this time are more expensive.

🕐 Sun–Thu noon–1am, Fri–Sat noon–2am
🍴 L €14, D €40, Wine €18
🚇 Oranienburger Tor, Oranienburger Strasse

OSSENA I

Oranienstrasse 39, Berlin (Kreuzberg)
Tel 030 615 2622
www.ossena.de

Ossena is bustling at any time of day, filled with visitors as well as locals who return again and again for the warm welcome and surroundings, prompt service and excellent Italian food at affordable prices. The wines are very drinkable and the pizzas good, while the spinach and ricotta cannelloni is also recommended if you fancy pasta. For dessert, try the deliciously light tiramisù. Credit cards are not accepted. There is another branch of Ossena, in Mitte, at Rosenthaler Strasse 42 (tel 030 28 09 98 77).

🕐 Daily 5pm–midnight
🍴 D €26, Wine €18
🚇 Kottbusser Tor

OXYMORON

Rosenthaler Strasse 40–41, Hackesche Höfe, Hof 1, 10178 Berlin (Mitte)
Tel 030 2839 1886, 030 2839 1888
www.oxymoron-berlin.de

Classic Italian food is on the menu at this 1920s-style restaurant-bar. The buffalo mozzarella on a bed of salad leaves with chilli and leek cream is delicious, and the rosemary and honey parfait with marinated figs is divine. Enjoy a wonderful meal, relax in the sophisticated lounge and then party into the night on the dance floor of the stylish bar.

🕐 Daily
🚇 Hackescher Markt

SARAH WIENER'S

Hamburger Bahnhof, Invalidenstrasse 50–51, 10557 Berlin (Tiergarten)
Tel 030 7071 3650
www.sarahwieners.de

Sarah Wiener is in a wing of the Hamburger Bahnhof, and is a great place for a meal after a morning's modern art appreciation. Enjoy some classic Austrian cuisine in stylish contemporary surroundings; if you like garlic, try the mushroom soup. There are plenty of newspapers, magazines and art books to browse while you relax with a cup of coffee or a large glass of red wine. Credit cards are not accepted.

🕐 Tue, Wed, Fri 10–6, Thu, Sat 10–at least 8pm, Sun 11–6pm
🍴 L €30, D €40, Wine €12
🚇 Lehrter Bahnhof

SHABU-JO

Kronenstrasse 55–58, 10117 Berlin (Mitte)
Tel 030 2248 7701

The interior design is minimalist, but you get a great deal for your money and wonderful service at this central Japanese restaurant. There is a sushi bar area, but the main attraction here is the Japanese fondue, which is great to share and excellent value for money. Try the *shabu shabu*, a clear meat-broth fondue, or the sukiyaki, a sweet soy sauce fondue, both served with a choice of pork, beef, vegetable or tofu pieces.

🕐 Mon–Fri noon–1am, Sat–Sun 1pm–1am
🍴 L €15.60, D €39, Wine €8.90
🚇 Stadtmitte

EATING

SIXTIES

Oranienburger Strasse 11,
10119 Berlin (Mitte)
Tel 030 2859 9041

This is the best place in the city to grab a burger and fries or a

hearty steak. There is everything here that you would expect to find in a 1960s American diner—red leather seats, booths and jukeboxes. The portions are huge, and in addition to burgers there is a great selection of chicken and Tex-Mex dishes. The milkshakes are thick and creamy. Credit cards are not accepted.

🕐 Sun–Thu 10am–2am, Fri–Sat 10am–4am

🍴 L €12, D €24, Wine €3.50 a glass

🚇 Hackescher Markt

SKALES

Rosenthaler Strasse 13, 10119
Berlin (Mitte)
Tel 030 283 3006

Come to Skales for some of the best Greek food in the city. The huge, high-ceilinged room, once a storage space for uniforms and equipment for the Freie Deutsche Jugend (the GDR's youth organization), has been completely transformed into a modern Greek taverna.

🕐 Daily 6pm–1am

🍴 D €26, Wine €16

🚇 Rosenthaler Platz

SODA

Schönhauser Allee 36–39, 10435
Berlin (Prenzlauer Berg)
Tel 030 4405 6071
www.soda-berlin.de

This 1920s-style restaurant and lounge in Prenzlauer Berg has a very creative kitchen, and in the summer you can cool off in the beer garden. If you fancy dancing off some calories, there is also a club, accessed via a glass elevator, where you can dance to a different type of music every night of the week

until the early hours. Credit cards are not accepted.

🕐 Mon–Sat 10am–midnight, Sun 10–4

🍴 L €20, D €32, Wine €18

🚇 Eberswalder Strasse

SUFISSIMO

Fichstrasse 1, 10967
Berlin (Kreuzberg)
Tel 030 6162 0833
www.sufissimo.de

There is a wealth of Turkish and North African eateries in Kreuzberg, but this café and Persian restaurant is one of the best. Spicy couscous, traditional lamb dishes and freshly prepared, healthy options are on the menu, and vegetarians will also find plenty of interesting choices. Round off your meal with an aromatic and energizing herbal tea.

🕐 Daily 4pm–late

🍴 D €20, Wine €18

🚇 Südstern

SUMO

Bergmannstrasse 89, 10961
Berlin (Kreuzberg)
Tel 030 6900 4963

This modern, stylish sushi bar has an excellent choice of expertly prepared raw fish, along with a great selection of Japanese beers and green teas. All sushi is charged by the plate: Choose from tuna, salmon, red snapper, octopus, shrimp, mackerel or avocado sushi. The Maximino sushi is beautifully made—small pieces of raw fish are surrounded by sticky rice, wrapped in seaweed and cut into little circular parcels. There are also soups and salads—try the *Eiersuppe*, with glass noodles, tofu, seaweed and shrimps. Beware—the wasabi is very hot and the *kimchi* (Korean cabbage salad with chilli sauce) has a kick.

🕐 Daily noon–midnight

🍴 €3 per plate, Wine €3.50 a glass

🚇 Gneisenaustrasse

WEINSTEIN

Lychener Strasse 33,
10437 Berlin (Prenzlauer Berg/Pankow)
Tel 030 441 1842

Weinstein is one of the best wine bars in the city, with the bonus that it is also a bistro and restaurant. The classic German and French food is very good, but customers are happy to come here simply for the quality wine list and the

atmosphere. The elegance and service, reminiscent of the restaurants and brasseries of Paris in the late 19th and early 20th centuries, will make this a meal to remember.

🕐 Mon–Sat 5pm–2am, Sun 6pm–2am

🍴 D €50, Wine €14

🚇 Eberswalder Strasse

WOOLLOOMOOLOO

Röntgenstrasse 7, 10587 Berlin
Tel 030 3470 2777
www.woolloomooloo.de

This exotic Australian bar and kitchen serves delicious grilled meat and fish dishes, including crocodile, kangaroo and ostrich; the sesame tuna and kangaroo with bilberry sauce are particularly good. The marinades are tasty, and the vegetables and side dishes are served with an oriental or Pacific twist. As expected, there is an excellent selection of antipodean wines. Aboriginal-style paintings of animals cover the orange and yellow walls and ceilings. Sunday night is popular with families, when a didgeridoo player entertains the crowd between 7 and 9.

🕐 Daily 5pm–1am (food served 6–11.30)

🍴 D €55, Wine €18

🚇 Richard-Wagner-Platz

DIE ZWÖLF APOSTEL

Georgenstrasse 2, 10117
Berlin (Mitte)
Tel 030 201 0222
www.12-apostel.de

Under the arches of an S-Bahn bridge on Georgenstrasse, this restaurant is an ideal refreshment spot for those visiting Museumsinsel. Red velvet curtains, candlelight, painted ceilings and an open kitchen piled high with fresh ingredients all add to the theatrical experience. You get great value at lunchtime, as all pizzas are reduced in price between noon and 4. The service is speedy—look out for the waiters on roller skates. Credit cards are not accepted. There is another branch, in Charlottenburg at Bleibtreustrasse 49 (tel 030 312 14 33).

🕐 Daily 24 hours

🍴 L €20, D €40, Wine €19

🚇 Friedrichstrasse

EASTERN GERMANY

Gastronomic standards have improved immeasurably in eastern Germany in the last decade. There are restaurants specializing in various international cuisines, but you should try out some of the local dishes. Traditionally, these are on the rather heavy side: Thuringian dumplings are famous, and particularly good when home-made, and there are plenty of hearty stews based on game. *Thüringer Rostbratwurst* is an extremely tasty sausage made from coarsely chopped meat (containing plenty of fat). Leipzigers are proud of *Leipziger Allerlei*, young spring vegetables in a sauce, served as an accompaniment to the main dish. Another Leipzig creation is the *Leipziger Lerche* (Leipzig lark), a marzipan confection representing the little birds that were once caught and consumed by the million. But the Saxon city is best known for its coffee houses. The town of Görlitz sits in a corner of the lost province of Silesia, now part of Saxony; this is the place to try the great Silesian dish *Schlesisches Himmelreich* (Silesian heaven), an intriguing name for a stew made of pork and dried fruits.

Eastern Germany has several flourishing local breweries; the most famous is Radeberger, from near Dresden. The region also makes wine. Considerably upgraded since GDR times, the vineyards along the banks of the Saale and Unstrut, and edging the Elbe around Dresden, produce very palatable wines.

PRICES

The prices given are for a two-course lunch (L) and a three-course dinner (D) for two people, without drinks. The wine price is for the least expensive bottle.

BAUTZEN

SCHLOSS-SCHÄNKE
Burgplatz 5, 02625 Bautzen
Tel 03591 304990
www.schloss-schaenke.net
You have a choice of several attractive places in which to dine in this 600-year-old establishment, including a parlour with an open fireplace, the vaulted Knights' Room and a wine cellar. Dishes are individually prepared, so don't expect instant service. The sautéed calf's liver in Calvados brandy sauce is particularly tempting. The wine list is exceptionally long, with more than 160 items, and includes bottles from around the world as well as fine German wines.
🕒 Daily 11am–midnight (Jan, Feb evenings only)
🍴 Main courses from €12.90, glass of wine from €4.30

DESSAU-WÖRLITZ

KORNHAUS
Kornahausstrasse 146, 06846 Dessau
Tel 0340 640 4141
Combine culture with refreshment when you visit this restaurant, in one of Dessau's key Modernist buildings. The panoramic restaurant, with a striking glazed rotunda and view of the Elbe, was built by Bauhaus architect Carl Fieger in 1930. Brave souls should try

the huge *Eisbein Franz Fürst Franz* (pork knuckle) or the less daunting *Räucherwurst* (smoked sausage).
🕒 Daily 11.30am–11pm/midnight
🍴 Main courses from €8.50

DRESDEN

CAFÉ ZUR FRAUENKIRCHE
An der Frauenkirche 7, 01067 Dresden
Tel 0351 498 9836
www.restaurant-dresden.de
This Franco-German café claims that it is *the* place in Dresden to see and be seen throughout the day. It has an enviable location at the foot of the newly rebuilt Frauenkirche, and makes a fine place to take a break from sightseeing, from breakfast to late at night, whether you stop for a meal, a snack, a coffee, a beer or a cocktail. Credit cards are not accepted.
🕒 9am–2am
🍴 Main courses from €9, glass of wine from €4
🚋 Tram 1, 2, 4, 49 to Neumarkt; tram 3, 7, 9, 12 to Pirnaischer Platz

CAROUSSEL
Rähnitzgasse 19, 01097 Dresden
Tel 0351 80030
www.buelow-residenz.de
This elegant establishment belongs to the Bülow Residenz, one of Dresden's most sophisticated small hotels. The hotel has five stars, and its restaurant has gathered a wealth of commendations, including one from a former German president. A number of intimate side rooms lead off the main restaurant. The tempting dishes are a satisfying blend of German and Mediterranean cuisine, prepared with an inventive

use of seasonings. The quality of the food and the place's reputation make reservations essential.
🕒 Tue–Sat noon–2, 6.30–late
🍴 Set-price menus from €60
🚋 Tram 4, 8, 9, 49 to Neustädter Markt

COSELPALAIS
An der Frauenkirche 12, 01067 Dresden
Tel 0351 496 2444
www.restaurant-dresden.de
With a view of Dresden's great Frauenkirche, the rebuilt Coselpalais of 1765 is one of the city's finest baroque mansions, its interior adorned with mirrors and tasteful furnishings. The restaurant serves meticulously prepared French and Italian dishes, as well as local cuisine such as pheasant breast in a ham

wrapping. The 18th-century atmosphere is enhanced by appropriate music, played live on Saturday evenings and also on Sunday mornings. Select your own home-made delicacy from the pâtisserie counter of the Grand Café.
🕒 Daily 10am–1am
🍴 €50 for 2 people, reservations essential
🚋 Tram 3, 7, 9, 49 to Synagoge

ITALIENISCHES DÖRFCHEN

Theaterplatz 3, 01067
Dresden
Tel 0351 498160
www.italienisches-doerfchen.de

The Italienisches Dörfchen (Italian Village), erected in the 18th century to house the workers who were building the nearby Hofkirche, has evolved into a complex of eating places with a spacious

terrace overlooking the River Elbe. It has something of the Mediterranean about it, with a café-cum-pâtisserie and restaurants serving a choice of Italian dishes (in the Bellotto) or Saxon dishes (in the Kurfürstenzimmer).

🍽 Daily from 10am
🍴 Set-price menus from €18
🚊 Tram 4, 8, 49 to Theaterplatz

PATTIS

Merbitzer Strasse 53, 01157 Dresden
Tel 0351 42550
www.pattis.net

The Pattis family were among the pioneers of contemporary cuisine in post-1989 eastern Germany and have been rewarded with numerous commendations. The restaurant in their hotel in Dresden's western suburb of Briesnitz has two sections of equal attractiveness: The Gourmet is the place to go for a serious feast, while the Vitalis is for those seeking something lighter. The Gourmet has the Saxon Court Menu, a challenging seven-course affair of great sophistication, served on Meissen porcelain. The offerings of the Vitalis, equally tasty, could be enjoyed on an everyday basis. The restaurant is non-smoking.

🍽 6pm–midnight
🍴 The Gourmet: Saxon Court Menu €79, wine from €50. Vitalis: Main courses from €15, three-course set-price menu €30
🚌 Bus 94 to Merbitzer Strasse

SÄCHSISCH-BÖHMISCHES BIERHAUS 'ALTMARKTKELLER'

Altmarkt 4, 01067
Dresden
Tel 0351 481 8130
www.altmarktkeller-dresden.de

This atmospheric cellar establishment lies deep beneath the rebuilt Altmarkt (Old Market Place), its vaults held up by massive stone pillars. When it comes to food and drink, much is made of the long-standing relationship between Saxony and Bohemia, now part of the Czech Republic. There's draught beer from Prague as well as from nearby Radeberg, both ideal for drinking with hearty dishes such as roast goose or suckling pig. For a musical accompaniment to your meal, come on Friday or Saturday evening, when Czech brass bands or jazz ensembles play live.

🍽 11am–midnight
🍴 Dish of the day and a beer €6.99
🚊 Tram 1, 2, 4, 49 to Altmarkt

VILLA MARIE

Fährgässchen 1, 01309
Dresden
Tel 0351 311 1186
www.villa-marie.com

In an idyllic riverbank setting close to the 'Blue Wonder' bridge over the Elbe, this stylish restaurant in an Italianate villa serves creative cuisine made from fresh ingredients, with fine wines to match. There is a laid-back atmosphere, helped along by the varied clientele of young people, artists, politicians and business people. It's a wonderful place to dine outside in the summer months.

🍽 11.30am–1am
🍴 Menu from €56 for 2 people
🚊 Tram 6, 12 to Schillerplatz

EISENACH

THÜRINGER HOF

Karlsplatz 11, 99817
Eisenach
Tel 03691 280
www.steigenberger.de

Right in the old town of Eisenach is the Thüringer Hof, a long-established and sensitively modernised hotel with an excellent bistro-style restaurant overlooking the Karlsplatz. Here you have a choice of traditional Thuringian cuisine or European and Asian

delicacies. In the Leander-Bar Bistro, the show kitchen serves Mediterranean specialities.

🍽 From 11.30am
🍴 Main courses €12–€26

DER ZWINGER

Wartburgallee 2, 99817
Eisenach
Tel 03691 88890

Occupying the vaulted cellars of the old Kaiserhof hotel, Zwinger is one of the most venerable establishments in this town. Great attention has been paid to the interior design, and the restaurant has a fine range of Thuringian dishes and a choice of beers from the world-renowned Paulaner brewery in Munich.

🍽 Mon–Sat 12.30–11pm, Sun noon–10pm
🍴 Main courses from €6, Wine €3 per glass

ERFURT

ALBOTH'S

Futterstrasse 15, 99084
Erfurt
Tel 0361 568 8207

This is probably the best restaurant in Erfurt, with an original interior and a limited number of tables. The finest French- and Italian-inspired

dishes, as well as regional specialties, are prepared under the supervision of a master chef. There is also a well-chosen wine list.

🍽 Tue–Sat evenings. Closed Sun, Mon and three weeks in Jul and Aug
🍴 Set-price menus €26–€60, Wine €28

GÖRLITZ

SCHNEIDER STUBE
Romantik Hotel Tuchmacher,
Peterstrasse 8, 02826 Görlitz
Tel 03581 47310
www.tuchmacher.de
The intimate Tailor's Den restaurant, in the 16th-century Romantik Hotel Tuchmacher, has impeccable service and a carefully

constructed menu listing Silesian dishes and international cuisine. Begin your meal with a slice of rabbit brawn, and continue with saddle of venision or the chef's special version of *Silesian Himmelreich*, accompanied by wines from the restaurant's princely supplier, Schloss Prossnitz.
🕒 Mon 6–10pm, Tue–Sun 11.30–3pm, 6–10pm
🍷 Three course menu €54 for 2, glass of wine €6

HALLE

WEINKONTOR
Robert-Franz-Ring 21, 06108 Halle
Tel 0345 200 3351

This converted brick warehouse near Moritzburg is a fine place in which to try wines from the little-known Saale-Unstrut region (and elsewhere).
🕒 Daily 6pm–late
🍷 D €30, Wine €10

LEIPZIG

APELS GARTEN
Kolonnadenstrasse 2, 04109
Leipzig
Tel 0341 960 7777
www.apels-garten.de
The sombre interior of this long-established restaurant, within walking distance of downtown Leipzig, still has something of the atmosphere of GDR days, but it's a cheerful and friendly place, with prompt service and an excellent choice of traditional local dishes. *Leipziger Allerlei*

(▷ 357) features on the menu, as do game, fish, tasty pork dishes and delicious desserts. There is outside eating in summer, and children under 10 dine free of charge. There is also a good selection of Saxon, German and international wines.
🕒 Mon–Sat 11am–midnight, Sun 11pm–3pm
🍷 Set-price menu €17.50, Wine €16
🚋 Tram 9 to Thomaskirche

BAYERISCHER BAHNHOF
Bayerischer Platz 1, 04103
Leipzig
Tel 0341 124 5760
Leipzig is home to a very special beer, the top-fermented *Gose*, so called because it originally came from the town of Goslar in the Harz mountains. The old Bavarian Station, a rare survivor from the earliest days of train travel, has been converted into a pub/restaurant, and is a fun place to sample *Gose*, whether you take it straight or with a shot of fruit syrup or spirits such as cherry brandy.
🕒 From 11am
🍷 Varies
🚋 Tram 16 to Bayerischer Platz

AUERBACHS KELLER
Mädlerpassage, Grimmaische
Strasse 2–4,
04109 Leipzig
Tel 0341 216100
www.auerbachs-keller-leipzig.de
This vaulted basement establishment, just off Leipzig's most prestigious arcade, is one of the city's best-known sights, not least because it was the setting for a famous scene in Goethe's *Faust*. Visitors and townsfolk both appreciate the restaurant's hearty, carefully prepared food and its bustling atmosphere. Try something satisfyingly Saxon, like stuffed venison roulade with red cabbage and mushrooms.
🕒 Daily 11.30am–midnight
🍷 Main courses €14, glass of wine €4
🚋 Tram 9 to Thomaskirche; tram 4, 7, 9, 10, 11, 12, 15, 16 to Augustusplatz

CAFÉ GRUNDMANN
August-Bebel-Strasse 2, 04275
Leipzig
Tel 0341 222 8962
The closure of the long-established Café Günther brought heartache to many Leipzigers, but their pain ended when it reopened with this new name, its art deco grandeur carefully restored. Now catering for a varied clientele, the café has a select range of drinks, including fine wines, together with Italian, Spanish and French cuisine. Credit cards are not accepted.
🕒 Mon–Fri 10am–1am, Sat–Sun 2pm–1am
🍷 Light meals from €6
🚋 89 to Schenkendorfstrasse

EATING

CAFÉ KANDLER

Thomaskirchhof 11, 04109
Leipzig
Tel 0341 213 2181
www.cafe-kandler.de

The Café Kandler is an intimate establishment on two floors linked by a spiral staircase, and has a fine view over the square in front of the city's famous Thomaskirche. It has an excellent range of teas as well as coffee. This is one of the places to try a *Leipziger Lerche*, a marzipan and strawberry jam

confection invented to replace the real lark pies that were once a part of the city's cuisine. Alternatively, there's the equally delicious *Bachtaler* (Bach dollar), an unusual praline souvenir that is the Leipzig equivalent of Salzburg's *Mozartkugel*.

🕐 Tue–Sat 9am–10pm, Sun–Mon 9am–8pm
🍽 Varies
🚋 Tram 9 to Thomaskirche

GOSENSCHENKE

Menekestrasse 5, 04155
Leipzig
Tel 0341 566 2360
www.gosenschenke.de

Now one of Leipzig's most interesting inner suburbs, Gohlis was a village in the 18th century and still has its own picturesque little castle, the Gohlisches Schlösschen. It is also home to the Gosenschenke, the only surviving traditional pub serving the Leipzig thirst-quencher of choice, *Gose* beer. You can enjoy your tipple in the rustic cellar or in the 500-seater beer garden. Food is also available.

🕐 5.30pm–1am
🍽 D from €32 per person
🚋 Tram 12 to Fritz-Seeger-Strasse

LANDGASTHOF PODELWITZ

Wiederitzscher Strasse 2–5, 04519
Podelwitz
Tel 034294 8240

This friendly country inn on the northern outskirts of Leipzig was one of the first of a wave of gastronomic establishments to open after 1989, and for years it had little competition. Those days have gone, but people still head out of the city to enjoy substantial meals here (such as goulash of wild boar), served in a variety of settings including a conservatory. Podelwitz is a popular side trip with people visiting the new trade-fair grounds, and is not far from the international airport. Credit cards are not accepted.

🕐 Mon–Fri 4–11, Sat–Sun 11–11
🍽 Main courses from €10

RATSKELLER DER STADT LEIPZIG

Lotterstrasse 1, 04109
Leipzig
Tel 0341 123 4567
www.ratskeller-leipzig.de

Like all good German town halls, Leipzig's Neues Rathaus has a *Ratskeller* (town hall cellar), whose job it is to serve food and drink of which the lord mayor can be proud. The building itself is a colossal edifice with a 110m (361ft) tower. Up to 700 diners can be

served here in a variety of rooms, each of which has its own distinctive ambience. They include the *Ratskeller* itself, seating up to 200, a sophisticated wine restaurant, a 'clubroom' with leather armchairs, the rustic *Alte Wache* and others. At the entrance, look for the sculpture of the taxpayer being fleeced by a councillor.

🕐 Mon–Sat 11–11, Sun 11–3
🍽 Main courses from €8, glass of wine €3.30
🚋 Tram 2, 8, 9 to Neues Rathaus

STADTPFEIFFER

Augustusplatz 8, 04109
Leipzig
Tel 0341 217 8920
www.stadtpfeiffer.de

Popular among concert-goers and with a deservedly high reputation among all Leipzigers is the Stadtpfeiffer restaurant, within the walls of the city's world-renowned Gewandhaus concert hall (▷ 165). The inspiring seven-course menu could be considered the gastronomic equivalent of Beethoven's Ninth, but other dishes are more chamber music in style.

🕐 Jan–end Nov Mon–Sat 6–midnight; Dec daily 6–midnight
🍽 Seven-course meal €95
🚋 Tram 4, 7, 8, 10, 11, 12, 15, 16 to Augustusplatz

ZUM ARABISCHEN COFFE BAUM

Kleine Fleischergasse 4, 04109
Leipzig
Tel 0341 961 0061
www.coffe-baum.de

Leipzig's coffee houses have long been famous. This is one of the most venerable, beautifully restored and covering several floors, with a pair of restaurants as well as delightful rooms serving excellent coffee. In addition, there is a fascinating coffee museum. Don't miss the splendid motif of an indolent Turk with Cupid and coffee bush above the entrance.

🕐 Cafés: 10–6. Restaurants: 10am–midnight
🍽 Set-price menus from €17
🚋 Tram 9 to Thomaskirche

MEISSEN

VINCENZ RICHTER

An der Frauenkirche 12, 01662
Meissen
Tel 03521 453285
www.vincenz-richter.de

This 16th-century timber-framed building is one of the sights of old Meissen and has been a refined wine tavern since 1873. A meal or wine-tasting hereis an essential part of any discriminating visitor's trip to Meissen. Wines come from the owners' nearby vineyards, while the menu includes sophisticated versions of traditional Saxon dishes such as *Sauerbraten* of wild boar, in which the meat is braised.

Reservations are advisable as the restaurant is very popular.

🕐 Tue–Fri from 4pm, Sat–Sun from noon

🍽 Three-course set-price menus from €21, wine-tasting from €11.50 (four local varieties)

MORITZBURG

RESTAURANT LAUBENHÖHE

Köhlerstrasse 77, 01689 Weinböhla
Tel 035242 36186
www.laubenhoehe.de

Founded in 1900, this establishment on the Moritzburg side of the small town of Weinböhla has been run since 1977 by one of eastern Germany's leading catering families. Now the owners, they have completely modernized it in tasteful country-house style, and pride themselves on their friendly service and their unpretentious but delicious dishes, such as pigeon terrine and saddle of venison. The menu is changed according to availability and freshness of ingredients. The wine list includes bottles from many countries and there is a good choice of open wines, available by the glass.

🕐 Tue–Sun noon–3, 6–midnight

🍽 Set-price menus from €16

NAUMBURG

WEINGUT LÜTZKENDORF

Saalberge 31, 06628 Bad Kösen
Tel 034463 61000
www.weingut.luetzkendorf.de

This model estate is near the little spa town of Bad Kösen, 7km (4.5 miles) upstream from Naumburg, and produces some of the finest wines of the picturesque Saale-Unstrut region. Call in advance for a tasting beneath the vine-covered pergola on the summer terrace. Credit cards are not accepted.

🕐 Visits by appointment only

🍽 Wine-tasting (eight wines) with bread and cheese €13, cold meal (small side orders only) €6.50

POTSDAM

KRONGUT BORNSTEDT

Ribbeckstrasse 6/7, 14469 Potsdam
Tel 0180 576 6488
www.krongut-bornstedt.de

Within easy walking distance of Schloss Sanssouci, the Crown Estate of Bornstedt is a beautifully restored Italianate complex of buildings laid out for King Friedrich Wilhelm IV in the mid-19th century. There are two cafés here (one in the royal bakery), plus a brick-vaulted beer hall serving Brandenburg brews, as well as quality boutiques and crafts-people (glass-blowers, hatters, medallion-makers and so on) at work. The courtyard setting is very pleasant, enhanced by views of the nearby lake.

🕐 Daily from 10am

🍽 Two-course meal €15, glass of wine (beer hall) €3.50

🚋 Tram 92 to Kirschallee terminus

MAISON CHARLOTTE

Mittelstrasse 20, 14467 Potsdam
Tel 0331 200 0536

Potsdam's *Holländisches Viertel* (Dutch Quarter) is the place to head for a great selection of pubs, bars and restaurants, none of which is more agreeable than the Maison Charlotte. It has a cheerful bistro atmosphere

and friendly service, with a mixed clientele from all age groups. The menu lists French dishes made from good German ingredients. The restaurant is very popular, so reservations are essential.

🕐 Daily noon–11pm

🍽 Two-course meal €20, glass of wine €3.50

🚋 Tram 90, 92, 95 to Nauener Tor

SPECKERS GASTSTÄTTE ZUR RATSWAAGE

Am Neuen Markt 10, 14467 Potsdam
Tel 0331 280 4311

This establishment, in one of Potsdam's most atmospheric old squares, gained a reputation as the city's finest place to eat soon after it opened. Nowadays, there is more competition, but the old Weigh House still produces fine German regional cuisine with an international touch. Signature dishes include breast of chicken from the Uckermark served with apricot compote, roast rabbit accompanied by black pudding, and rarities such as fig tartare. The service is attentive and there is an extensive wine list. Reservation is recommended.

🕐 Tue–Sat noon–3, 6–late

🍽 Set-price menu €30–€65

🚋 Tram 90, 92, 93, 96 to Alter Markt

VILLA KELLERMANN

Mangerstrasse 34–36, 14467 Potsdam
Tel 0331 291572
www.villa-kellermann.de

This elegant Italian restaurant enjoys a privileged location on the banks of the Heiligen See, with superb views across the lake to the Marble Palace. You could hardly invent a more romantic setting for a leisurely meal as twilight falls over the water. The grand villa has an illustrious past as a royal guest house for eminent visitors to the Prussian court. It owes its name to the writer Bernhardt Kellermann (1879–1951) and its refined appearance to its present owners, who fought more than 30 court cases to rescue it from destruction by vandals. The menu consists of superior Italian fish, meat and pasta dishes.

🕐 Tue–Sun noon–midnight, Mon 6pm–midnight (closed in winter)

🍽 Main courses from €16, glass of wine €8

🚋 Tram 93 to Mangerstrasse

QUEDLINBURG

WEINSTUBE
Romantik Hotel am Brühl,
Billungstrasse 11, 06484
Quedlinburg
Tel 03946 96180
www.hotelambruehl.de

In a stylishly furnished and
decorated listed building
beneath Quedlinburg's citadel
is the Wine Cellar, a sophisticated restaurant belonging to
one of this lovely town's best
hotels. In summer, there is
outdoor dining in the attractive
courtyard.
🕓 Evenings only
🍴 Set-price menus from €24, snacks
€7.50–€14.50, Wine (from Saale-
Unstrut region) €26

SPREEWALD

ZUM GRÜNEN STRAND
DER SPREE
Dorfstrasse 53, 15910 Schlepzig
Tel 035472 6620
In the depths of the green and
watery world of the Spreewald
north of the town of Lübben,
this country inn in the village
of Schlepzig has won a reputation for fish, game and other
dishes served in a refined
ambience. It has its own
brewery, which offers a tasting
tour at a very reasonable price,
and there are fruit brandies to
sample as well. House specials
from the River Spree include

Wels catfish and zander (pike-
perch), or you could try Omas
Grützwurst (grandma's grits
sausage) with Sorbian

sauerkraut. There's a veranda
and a terrace overlooking the
surrounding countryside.
🕓 Daily noon–10
🍴 Main courses from €14, three-
course set-price menu €22.30

WEIMAR

ALT WEIMAR
Prellerstrasse 2, 99423 Weimar
Tel 03643 86190
www.alt-weimar.de
This 150-year-old building was
the home of Rudolf Steiner
(1861–1925), the founder
of anthroposophy, and it
was here that he edited the
collected works of poet and
dramatist Johann Wolfgang
von Goethe (1749–1832), his
great inspiration. In 1909 the

building was turned into a
wine bar and became the
haunt of artists, actors and
musicians. More recently it has
been renovated by a contemporary architect, and is now
an exquisite small hotel with
lovely Jugendstil and Bauhaus
touches. There is a wine bar,
plus a bistro with a cosmopolitan wine list, refined versions
of Thuringian cuisine and
Tuscan dishes.
🕓 Daily 11am–late
🍴 L €35, D €50, Wine €14

CAFÉ RESIDENZ
Grüner Markt 4, 99423 Weimar
Tel 03643 59408
www.residenz-cafe.de
This stylish café in the middle
of town is more than 160 years
old. Thanks to its friendly
atmosphere, it attracts a mixed
clientele of students, locals
and visitors. Come here for
excellent breakfasts, snacks,
cakes or full meals, which you
can have with a choice from
the full range of alcoholic and
non-alcoholic drinks.
🕓 Mon–Fri 8am–1am, Sat–Sun
from 8am
🍴 Starters from €3, meals from €10,
desserts from €3, Wine €13

ZUM ZWIEBEL
Teichgasse 6, 99423 Weimar
Tel 03643 502375
www.zum-zwiebel.de
Zum Zwiebel is a traditional
downtown establishment
whose rustic atmosphere and
furnishings are complemented
by hearty meals cooked
following recipes 'from
Grandma's times'. Typical
Thuringian dishes include
game and poultry with
dumplings to mop up the rich
gravy, plus the inevitable
mouthwatering sausages and
home-made apple strudel.
The Grillplatte, comprising
sausages, pork and turkey, and
served with woodland mushrooms and roast potatoes, is a
real challenge. Beer is served
from the barrel and the wines
come from all over, including
the nearby Saale-Unstrut
region.
🕓 Mon–Fri 11.30am–1am, Sat–Sun
11am–1am
🍴 Menu €14.50

WITTENBERG

BRAUHAUS WITTENBERG
Markt 6, 06886
Lutherstadt Wittenberg
Tel 03491 4331 3039
www.brauhaus-wittenberg.de
Built around a courtyard, this
atmospheric 16th-century
brewery once belonged to

Christian Beyer, mayor of
Wittenberg and a friend of
Protestant reformer Martin
Luther (1483–1546). The
central feature of its main
restaurant is the brewery itself,
whose gleaming copper vats
produce not just ordinary
Pilsner but also special brews
such as 'Cuckoo'. Satisfy your
hunger with typical Germanic
dishes such as Grillhaxe
(grilled leg of pork or lamb) or
home-smoked eel and trout.
🕓 Daily 6am–11pm
🍴 Set-price menu from €15.50

EATING

MUNICH

In Munich, people like to eat early and it is not unusual to find older Munich residents having lunch as early as 11.15am. As hotel breakfast buffets are substantial, you may not be hungry enough for an early lunch. In this case, choose one of the many bars, cafés and restaurants that serve full meals or even breakfast right into the afternoon. Non-smokers should be aware that bars, cafés and many mid-range restaurants do not have a designated non-smoking area.

Bavarian food, usually accompanied by a beer, is hearty and heavy and is almost always based on meat. Munich has a strong affinity with Italy, which means the city has plenty of Italian restaurants. Locals share the Italians' love of dining alfresco—at the first hint of sunshine, chairs and tables are swiftly moved outside to terraces, courtyards and gardens. In recent years, the number of Thai, Japanese, Mexican and tapas restaurants in the city has also grown.

PRICES

The prices given are for a two-course lunch (L) and a three-course dinner (D) for two people, without drinks. The wine price is for the least expensive bottle.

ANNA'S BISTRO

Westenriederstrasse 35, 80331 München (Altstadt)
Tel 089 2423 1873
As an antidote to all those heavy Bavarian dishes, go light at this organic, vegetarian café upstairs from the organic food store Basic (▷ 275). Main courses start at €6.50, or you can help yourself to the cous-cous, hummus and olives at the salad bar—although don't get too carried away because these items are sold by weight. There are delicious fresh juices or bottles of organic beer to go with your meal. Credit cards are not accepted.
🕐 Mon–Fri 9–8, Sat 8.30–6
🍴 €14 (for 2)
Ⓜ Marienplatz
🚊 Marienplatz, Isartor

AUGUSTINER

Neuhauserstrasse 27, 80331 München (Altstadt)
Tel 089 2318 3257
www.augustiner-restaurant.com
This beer hall and restaurant belongs to the Augustiner brewery and dates from the 14th century. Here 200 members of staff cater for up to 1,500 people. Try Bavarian

top-sellers such as suckling pig roasted in dark beer and served with dumplings, meatloaf, boiled beef with potato salad or sausages. Vegetarians steer clear!
🕐 Beerhall: Daily 9am–midnight. Restaurant: Daily 10am–midnight
🍴 L €34, D €42, Wine €12
Ⓜ Karlsplatz, Marienplatz
🚊 Karlsplatz, Marienplatz

AYINGERS

Platzl 1a, 80331 München (Altstadt)
Tel 089 2370 3665
www.platzl.de
Enjoy Bavarian food and six different draught beers from the Aying family brewery (the family which owns the Platzl Hotel and the Pfistermühle restaurant next door; ▷ 366). Sit outside in the square or in the snug wood-panelled bar. The set-price lunch menu costs €8 and gives you the option of a Bavarian dish such as fried duck with blue cabbage and potato dumplings, or a lighter dish such as grilled chicken breast with vegetable rice.
🕐 Daily 11am–1am
🍴 L €26, D €36, Wine €20
Ⓜ Marienplatz
🚊 Marienplatz

BARISTA

Kardinal-Faulhaberstrasse 11, 80333 München (Altstadt)
Tel 089 2080 2180
This cocktail bar and restaurant is in the fashionable Fünf Höfe covered shopping area in the middle of town. The menu is short, with light dishes such as breast of duck with raspberry vinegar and swordfish served with peppers and sautéed potatoes. The three-course set-price dinner menu, which you can eat on the terrace in summer, is particularly good value at €26.50. Credit cards are not accepted.
🕐 Mon–Sat 10am–1am, Sun 3pm–1am

🍴 L €50, D €62, Wine €22
Ⓜ Odeonsplatz, Marienplatz
🚊 Marienplatz

BENJARONG

Falckenbergstrasse 7, 80539 München (Altstadt)
Tel 089 291 3055
The exotic decor and furniture stay on the right side of kitsch in this fabulous Thai restaurant. Eat in the main room, with its plush red seats and teak tables, or in a separate room with low tables and cushions on the floor. Dishes to try include chicken satay, fishcakes, spicy chicken soup with coconut milk and fried duck with pineapple and mushrooms.
🕐 Mon–Fri noon–2.30, 6–11.30, Sat–Sun 6–11.30
🍴 L €44, D €56, Wine €15
Ⓜ Marienplatz
🚊 Marienplatz

BISTRO TERRINE

Amalienstrasse 89, 80799 München (Schwabing)
Tel 089 281780
www.bistro-terrine.de
For an alternative to hearty Bavarian dishes, try this Parisian bistro in the heart of Schwabing, which has one Michelin star. For starters, try asparagus in a vinaigrette, rabbit with oyster mushrooms or salmon with leeks and rocket (arugula). Main courses include meat (venison with cabbage) and fish (plaice with spinach in a chervil sauce) dishes. Classic French desserts include crêpes and crème brûlée. They have a non-smoking section.
🕐 Tue–Fri noon–3, 6.30–1, Mon, Sat 6.30–1. Closed Sun
🍴 L €60, D €76, Wine €18
Ⓜ Universität
🚌 Bus 53 to Universität

BODEGA DALÍ

Tengstrasse 6, 80799
München (Maxvorstadt)
Tel 089 2777 9696

This *bodega* (wine cellar) is in an atmospheric vault where you can enjoy Spanish food and a great selection of full-bodied Riojas by the glass or bottle. Dishes go beyond the usual tapas—there's tuna fish salad with tomatoes, paella and robust stews with tuna, potatoes and stuffed peppers (capsicums) or ham, cabbage, potatoes, peppers and beans.

🕐 Daily 5pm–midnight
🍴 D €38, Wine €14
Ⓜ Josephsplatz
🚌 Bus 53 to Josephsplatz

CAFÉ AM BEETHOVENPLATZ

Goethestrasse 51, 80336
München (Hauptbahnhof)
Tel 089 5440 4348

It's hard to describe this café, which dates from 1899. With its high-ceilinged rooms and chandeliers, it's like a Viennese coffee house during the day, while at night it becomes a restaurant serving international food (main dishes €8–€15). It's also a music bar, with classical, jazz or blues bands playing live almost every night.

🕐 Daily 9am–1am
🍴 L €13, D €26, Wine €11
Ⓜ Goetheplatz

CAFÉ PUCK

Türkenstrasse 33, 80799
München (Schwabing)
Tel 089 280 2280
www.cafepuck.de

If you're visiting one of the Pinakothek galleries nearby, this bar/café is handy for lunch or coffee and cake. The huge breakfast menu is ideal for very late risers, and is available dur-

ing weekdays until 6pm and on Sundays and holidays until 8pm. Alternatively, choose from salads (€7 or €8), burgers (€10) or pasta dishes (€6 or

€7), or have an ice cream with cream for €2.60 or a milkshake for €3. The lounge music leads to a laid-back atmosphere, although the smokiness may not appeal to all. Happy hour is from 9pm to 1am, when cocktails are €4.50. Credit cards are not accepted.

🕐 Daily 9am–1am (food until 11.45pm)
🍴 L €18, D €25, Wine €12.80
Ⓜ Universität
🚌 Bus 53, tram 27

CAFÉ STÖR

Rosenheimerstrasse 1, 81667
München (Haidhausen)
Tel 089 482222

If you've been to the Gasteig or Deutsches Museum and would like to eat in a place with a bit of atmosphere, then this café/bar in the art nouveau Müller'schen Volksbad bathhouse is ideal. It's like being in a covered courtyard, with conservatory-style furniture, red leather sofas to sink into and tables made from the workings of old-fashioned wrought-iron sewing machines. The café specializes in large salads, while a typical dish of the day is pasta with courgette (zucchini) and salmon. There's a long drinks menu with wine, champagne and expensive cocktails, and the café serves warm cakes until 11.30pm. Credit cards are not accepted.

🕐 Daily 10am–1am
🍴 L from €6.30 per person, soups from €3.80, D from €13.80
🚌 Tram 18 to Deutsches Museum

CAFÉ VOILÀ

Wörthstrasse 5, 81669
München (Haidhausen)
Tel 089 489 1654

This friendly bar and café has long opening hours and is the sort of place where you can order food in the middle of the afternoon and the staff are happy to oblige. The breakfast menu is long, soups cost about €4, main dishes are between €7 and €12 and there is a set-price lunch menu for €7. You'll find it hard to resist the cake cabinet and the generous happy hours (5–8pm and 11pm–1am), when cocktails are just €4.60. There's a selection of magazines and an internet kiosk.

🕐 Daily 7am–1am (food until 12.30am)
🍴 L €17, D €20, Wine €3.50 a glass
🚌 Tram 15, 19, 25 to Wörthstrasse

CAFFÈ FLORIAN

Hohenzollernstrasse 11, 80801
München (Schwabing)
Tel 089 336639

This is arguably Schwabing's best-known café. It has a real Italian feel to it, with a little espresso bar at the front, and is a great place for coffee and cake or a filling plate of pasta. The menu changes every day and there are lunch specials for about €7. Meat and fish courses are between €9 and €16. The Coccodrillo bar is downstairs (▷ 276).

🕐 Sun–Thu 9am–1am, Fri–Sat 9am–3am
🍴 L €15, D €25
Ⓜ Giselastrasse, Münchner Freiheit
🚌 Tram 12, 27 to Kurfürstenplatz; bus 23

COMERCIAL BAR ENOTECA

Theatinerstrasse 16, 80333
München (Altstadt)
Tel 089 2070 0266

Run by an Italian family, this bar in the Fünf Höfe shopping area is a great place for a mid-shop cappuccino or lunch, with Italian dishes costing between €5 and €9. The

padded leather wall seats are set quite high, so those who are a bit short in the leg should choose one of the seats outside instead, under the giant metal sculpture of a globe.

🕐 Mon–Sat 9am–midnight, Sun noon–8
🍴 L and D €5–€10 per dish, Wine €10
Ⓜ Marienplatz
🚌 Tram 19
Ⓢ Marienplatz

CONTI BISTRO

Max-Josephstrasse 5, 80333
München (Altstadt)
Tel 089 5517 8684
www.conti-bistro.de

You have a choice of dining experiences here: The ground floor is light and airy, with changing collections of modern art on the walls, while downstairs in the basement you'll find yourself in an alpine chalet with wooden floor, walls and ceiling. Dishes include mushroom and truffle ravioli with grilled courgette (zucchini), and grilled chicken breast with pesto and polenta.

🕐 Mon–Fri 11.30am–1am
🍽 L €46, D €58, Wine €18
Ⓜ Odeonsplatz
🚋 Tram 27

CONVIVA

Hildegardstrasse 1, 80539
München (Altstadt)
Tel 089 2333 6977

There's a fresh, contemporary feel to this restaurant, which is reflected in some of its light Italian-influenced dishes. Try ricotta cheese flan with balsamic vinegar to start, and follow it with saffron risotto with white fish. There's a daily three-course set-price lunch menu at €15. The only credit card accepted is EC-card.

🕐 Mon–Sat 11am–1am, Sun 5pm–1am
🍽 L €34, D €47, Wine €12
🚋 Tram 19
🚇 Isartor

DA CAPO

Hildegardstrasse 9, 80539
München (Altstadt)
Tel 089 223715

This is another reasonably priced, central restaurant run by an Italian family. Dishes are simple and tasty—spaghetti with mussels, tortelloni with cream and ham, veal *schnitzel* in a lemon sauce and different types of steak.

🕐 Mon–Sat 11.30–2.30, 6–midnight
🍽 L €50, D €62, Wine €20
🚋 Tram 19
🚇 Isartor

DALLMAYR

Dienerstrasse 14–15, 80331
München (Altstadt)
Tel 089 213 5100
www.dallmayr.de

This historic restaurant is the place to come for a first-class breakfast, lunch or afternoon tea in refined surroundings. Start with quail salad with marinated pumpkin, and follow it with braised pork in sherry vinegar accompanied by chervil and parmesan biscuits. Before leaving, browse the fabulous delicatessen on the ground floor to take some of the Dallmayr experience home with you (▷ 274).

🕐 Breakfast Mon–Sat 8am–11am; lunch and cakes Mon–Wed 11.30–6.30, Thu–Fri 11.30–7, Sat 9–3
🍽 L €76, Wine €25
Ⓜ Marienplatz
🚇 Marienplatz

DUKATZ IM LITERATURHAUS

Salvatorplatz 1, 80333
München (Altstadt)
Tel 089 291 9600
www.dukatz.de

Dukatz has a high vaulted ceiling and glass front, giving a feeling of space, and is frequented by the city's smart set. It's a good place for a coffee if you are out shopping in Theatinerstrasse and the Fünf Höfe. The menu includes main dishes (€13–€22) such as roast lamb with couscous and venison with celery purée and cranberries. Credit cards are not accepted.

🕐 Mon–Sat noon–2.30pm, 6.30–10.30pm
🍽 L €32, D €50, Wine €22
Ⓜ Odeonsplatz
🚋 Tram 19 to Theatinerstrasse

FRAUNHOFER

Fraunhoferstrasse 9, 80469
München (Isarvorstadt)
Tel 089 266460

This traditional tavern comes with its own heavy wooden tables. The relaxed atmosphere makes it a great place to dine on hearty Bavarian meat dishes. After a meal, watch a performance at the little theatre in the inner courtyard here or a film at the on-site arthouse cinema. Credit cards are not accepted.

🕐 Daily 4.30–midnight
🍽 D €40, Wine €15
Ⓜ Fraunhoferstrasse

GLOCKENSPIEL CAFÉ

Marienplatz 28/5th floor, 80331
München (Altstadt)
Tel 089 264256

Squeeze into the tiny elevator (accessed from Rosenstrasse) and head up to the fifth floor for a drink or a meal with a view of Marienplatz. Sit inside or on the terrace. Glockenspiel is a café, bar and restaurant.

🕐 Mon–Sat 10am–1am, Sun 10–7 (meals are served until 7pm)
🍽 L €18, D €24, Wine €15
Ⓜ Marienplatz
🚌 Bus 52
🚇 Marienplatz

HACKERHAUS

Sendlingerstrasse 14, 80331
München (Altstadt)
Tel 089 260 5026
www.hackerhaus.de

Although it seats many diners, this traditional restaurant retains an intimate atmosphere. The building dates from 1738 and has a beautiful inte-

rior, with vaulted ceilings and rich lighting. Tables in the lovely courtyard at the back fill up quickly—the area is heated in the winter and is covered when it rains. Choose from dishes such as liver-dumpling soup, roast pork and eight different types of sausage.

🕐 Daily 9am–midnight
🍽 L €30, D €38, Wine €11
Ⓜ Sendlinger Tor, Marienplatz
🚇 Marienplatz

HOFBRÄUHAUS

Platzl 9, 80331 München (Altstadt)
Tel 089 2901 3610
www.hofbraeuhaus.de

You're more likely to come here for the beer, atmosphere, singing and oompah bands than for the cuisine. However, it's always good to have something hearty to eat with your beer, so order a sausage with your next drink.

🕔 Daily 9am–midnight
🍴 L and D €10, Wine €14.50
Ⓜ Marienplatz
🚆 Marienplatz

LA FAMIGLIA

Tal 41, 80331 München (Altstadt)
Tel 089 2280 7523
www.torbraeu.de

La Famiglia, next to Hotel Torbräu (▷ 398), is owned by an Italian family and serves Tuscan cuisine. Try quail breast in balsamic vinegar with grilled artichokes, and follow this with home-made tagliatelle with asparagus or veal fillet with mushrooms and roast potatoes. Finish with an espresso and a grappa.

🕔 Mon–Sun 11.30am–12.30am
🍴 L €38, D €53, Wine €15
🚆 Isartor

LAST SUPPER

Fürstenstrasse 9, 80333, München (Schwabing)
Tel 089 2880 8809
www.lastsupper.de

If you are looking for Mediterranean food in Bavarian surroundings, then Last Supper may be for you. Try rocket (arugula) salad with tomatoes and parmesan, and follow it with chicken with potato cakes and a mushroom sauce, or suckling pig with artichoke ravioli and sausage. Credit cards are not accepted.

🕔 Tue–Sun 7pm–1am
🍴 D €48, Wine €16
Ⓜ Odeonsplatz

MÖVENPICK

Lenbachplatz 8, 80333 München (Altstadt)
Tel 089 545 9490
www.moevenpick.com

Mövenpick is a Munich legend for its vast Sunday brunch buffet, served 10.30–2. It's an amazing place for breakfast too, which is available from 8 until 11 and is half-price for

children. Under the same roof you'll also find the restaurant Venecia, the cocktail bar Sir Hyke's Place, another restaurant called Grappa's and a traditional English-style cigar lounge. Cake lovers will be in paradise when they see the vast and tempting selection on display.

🕔 Mon–Fri 8am–midnight, Sun 9am–midnight
🍴 Breakfast €12.10 per person (half-price for children aged 6–14), Sun brunch €29.20 per person
Ⓜ Karlplatz Stachus
🚆 Karlplatz Stachus

MÜNCHNER KARTOFFELHAUS

Hochbrückenstrasse 3, 80331 München (Altstadt)
Tel 089 296331

Those on a low-carbohydrate diet will want to avoid this restaurant, although everyone else will enjoy the potatoes (Kartoffeln) that are the central ingredient in every dish here. Choose from potatoes with shrimp and mushrooms, with spinach baked in a creamy cheese sauce or with herring in a sour cream sauce with beetroot. There is another branch of this restaurant in the Schwabing district. All credit cards except Diner's Club are accepted.

🕔 Mon–Sat noon–1am, Sun 5.30pm–1am
🍴 L and D €48, Wine €13
Ⓜ Marienplatz, Isartor
🚆 Marienplatz, Isartor

NEWS BAR

Amalienstrasse 55, 80799 München (Maxvorstadt)
Tel 089 281787

This popular bar and café is in the heart of the university district of Schwabing. It's a good place for a coffee or a

meal at any time of day—they serve Bavarian dishes as well as salads, omelettes, pasta and vegetarian options. There's a decent selection of magazines and newspapers in various languages, so you can catch up on events over a cup of coffee.

🕔 Daily 7.30am–2am
🍴 L €2.50–€9.50 per dish, Wine €4 per glass
Ⓜ Universität

PFISTERMÜHLE

Pfisterstrasse 4, 80331 München (Altstadt)
Tel 089 2370 3865
www.platzl.de

Pfistermühle is an elegant restaurant in a historic setting—it's in the vaults of a 16th-century former mill, right in the heart of town near Marienplatz and the Hofbräuhaus. The food is high-quality Bavarian fare, and there's an excellent selection of wines, as well as draught beer from the Aying family brewery (the Aying family owns this restaurant, the brewery and the beautiful Platzl Hotel nearby, ▷ 399). In summer, dine outside in the little beer garden.

🕔 Mon–Sat 11.30am–1am
🍴 L €36, D €50, Wine €20
Ⓜ Marienplatz
🚆 Marienplatz

EATING

PRINZ MYSHKIN

Hackenstrasse 2, 80331
München (Altstadt)
Tel 089 265596
www.prinzmyshkin.com

This vegetarian restaurant is welcome after all those Bavarian dishes. The building is a 450-year-old brewery with a high, white, vaulted ceiling that gives the place a monastic feel. You'll still feel virtuous even after tucking into dishes like spinach gnocchi, Indian curries, sushi, tofu stroganoff and pasta filled with pumpkin and tomatoes. There are also dairy- and egg-free dishes. To drink, there are fresh juices and wines by the glass.

🕐 Daily 11am–12.30am
🍴 L €30, D €42, Wine €12.60
🚇 Sendlinger Tor, Marienplatz
🚊 Marienplatz

RATSKELLER

Marienplatz 8, 80331
München (Altstadt)
Tel 089 219 9890
www.ratskeller.com

This vast traditional restaurant (seating 1,200) underneath the Rathaus has lots of booths and quiet corners where you can enjoy an intimate meal. In summer, it's a particularly pleasant place to eat—the cellar is 10°C (18°F) cooler

than at street level and there's a garden that soon fills up. The food is Bavarian and Franconian, and as well as beer, there are wines from the Juliusspital Würzburg vineyards.

🕐 Daily 10am–midnight
🍴 L €20, D €35, Wine €14
🚇 Marienplatz
🚊 Marienplatz

RESTAURANT AM CHINESISCHEN TURM

Englischer Garten 3, 80538
München (Schwabing)
Tel 089 3838 7315
www.chinaturm.de

The setting here at the Chinese Tower in the Englischer Garten is beautiful, and there is a dining room inside as well as plenty of seats outside. Expect soups, salads, Bavarian dishes, fish and some vegetarian options too. The *apfelstrudel* is hard to resist.

🕐 Mon–Sun 10am–midnight
🍴 L €32, D €42, Wine €12
🚇 Universität

RISTORANTE ALBARONE

Stollbergstrasse 22, 80539
München (Altstadt)
Tel 089 2916 8687

The fresh, light dining room at this Italian restaurant leads to a lovely garden where you can imagine you are enjoying your meal in Italy. Expect Italian dishes with a twist, such as

pheasant ravioli with sheep's milk cheese and slices of wild boar with a fig *confit*. There's a three-course set-price lunch for €24 and a five-course set-price dinner at €45.

🕐 Mon–Fri noon–2.30, 6.30–11, Sat 6.30–11
🍴 L €63, D €77, Wine €20
🚇 Marienplatz
🚊 Marienplatz

RIVA

Tal 44, 80331 München (Altstadt)
Tel 089 220240
www.rivabar.com

It's difficult to find a really good pizza outside Italy, but this bar and pizzeria does pretty well. The pizzas, cooked in a wood-fired oven, range from the traditional margharita to ginger or curried chicken varieties.

🕐 Mon–Sat 8am–1am, Sun 10am–1am
🍴 L €32, D €42, Wine €15
🚇 Isartor

SCHLOSSCAFÉ IM PALMENHAUS

Schlosspark, Nymphenburg Eingang 43, 80638 München (Neuhausen)
Tel 089 175309
www.palmenhaus.de

The *schloss* in the name refers to the Palace of Nymphenburg, where you'll find this elegant café in a huge old glasshouse. It's an atmospheric place for a coffee after visiting the palace, or stop for lunch—particularly recommended are the pork in a cream sauce with vegetables from the royal garden, and ricotta ravioli with tomatoes and pancetta.

🕐 Apr–end Oct daily 10–7; Nov–end Mar daily 10–5. Closed Mon in Dec–end Feb
🚊 Tram 17, bus 41 to Schloss Nymphenburg; tram 16 to Romanplatz (less convenient)

SPATENHAUS AN DER OPER

Residenzstrasse 12, 80333
München (Altstadt)
Tel 089 290 7060
www.kuffler.de

Come here for high-quality Bavarian food served in pleasant surroundings by staff dressed in traditional costume. The ground-floor dining room is the place to eat Bavarian food, while upstairs they serve

what is described international cuisine. Expect Bavarian specials such as *Wiener schnitzel*, *Schweinebraten* (crispy pork in a dark beer sauce) and boiled beef, as well as fish and more unexpected dishes such as coconut curry soup.

🕐 Daily 9.30am–midnight
🍴 L €48, D €62, Wine €19.50
🚇 Marienplatz, Odeonsplatz
🚊 Tram 19
🚊 Marienplatz

STADTCAFÉ

St.-Jakobs-Platz 1, 80331
München (Altstadt)
Tel 089 266949

This friendly café/bar in the Stadtmuseum is good for a late breakfast or an early lunch. International newspapers are provided to read over breakfast (€3.50–€6.50), a coffee (€2.50 for a cappuccino) or a glass of wine (€3.40). There's no official menu—dishes are written on a chalkboard on the wall. In summer, sit outside in the pleasant courtyard. Credit cards are not accepted.

🕐 Sun–Thu 11am–midnight, Fri–Sat 11am–1am
🍴 Daily menu, from €7 a person
🚇 Marienplatz, Sendlinger Tor
🚌 Bus 52, 56 to Blumenstrasse
🚊 Marienplatz

VILLANIS CAFÉ

Kreuzstrasse 3b, 80331
München (Asamhof)
Tel 089 260 7972
www.villanis.com

This traditional-style café is popular with Munich's gay community.

🕐 Mon–Sat 10am–1am, Sun 11am–1am
🍴 Soup €3, curry sausage and chips €4.90, coffee and muffin to go €2.80
🚇 Sendlinger Tor

VINAIOLO

Steinstrasse 42, 81667
München (Haidhausen)
Tel 089 4895 0356
www.vinaiolo.de

The interior includes old pharmacy cabinets that are used to store the restaurant's wine collection. The cooking is high-quality northern Italian (Vinaiolo has one Michelin star). Starters include white asparagus with Parmesan and Parma ham. Pasta dishes are kept to a minimum, but there are robust dishes such as roast perch with aubergine (eggplant) and pepper (capsicum).

🕐 Tue–Sun noon–3, 6.30–1am, Mon 6.30pm–1am
🍴 L €64, D €77, Wine €20
🚇 Rosenheimerplatz, Max-Weber-Platz
🚊 Tram 19

WEINHAUS NEUNER

Herzogspitalstrasse 8, 80331
München (Altstadt)
Tel 089 260 3954
www.weinhaus-neuner.de

You can expect a high standard of cooking and service here.

The restaurant lives up to its name (Wine House) with a huge list of wines, particularly from Germany and Austria. The cuisine leans towards Italy and France, with starters such as rocket (arugula) salad with ham and Parmesan, and veal cannelloni with spinach and tomato. Main courses include duck in a cognac and pepper (capsicum) sauce, and roast rabbit with a chervil and mustard sauce.

🕐 Mon–Sat 11.30–3, 5.30–midnight.
🍴 L €50, D €64, Wine €20
🚇 Karlsplatz Stachus
🚊 Karlsplatz Stachus

YUM

Utzschneiderstrasse 6, 80469
München (Altstadt)
Tel 089 2323 0660
www.yum-thai.de

This successful Thai restaurant has a stylish interior, a cocktail list and delicious food. Start with mushroom and shrimp

soup, and follow it with a stir-fry, such as pad krapow (meat or smoked tofu, mixed vegetables and oyster sauce). Credit cards are not accepted.

🕐 Daily 6pm–11.30pm
🍴 D €38, Wine €15
🚇 Marienplatz
🚊 Tram 17, 18
🚊 Marienplatz

ZUM ALTEN MARKT

Dreifaltigkeitsplatz 3
(am Viktualienmarkt), 80331
München (Altstadt)
Tel 089 299995
www.zumaltenmarkt.de

Stepping into this Bavarian restaurant is like walking into a mountain chalet—the wood panelling and furniture give the small dining room an intimate feel. The menu changes every month, and the Bavarian dishes are good quality. As well as meat, there are plenty of regional fish dishes. In winter, Christmas decorations cover the ceiling. In summer sit outside in the pleasant courtyard. The only credit card accepted here is the EC-card.

🕐 Mon–Sat 11am–midnight (in winter the kitchen closes 3pm–6pm)
🍴 L €45, D €57, Wine €11
🚇 Marienplatz, Isartor
🚊 Marienplatz, Isartor

ZUM FRANZISKANER

Perusastasse 5, 80333,
München (Altstadt)
Tel 089 231 8120
www.zumfranziskaner.de

In this traditional Bavarian restaurant, dating back to the 14th century, each room has a different name. Dine in the Student Room, King Ludwig Room, Fox Room or the unappealingly named Cell. The meat is supplied by the restaurant's own butcher. Try the suckling pig roasted in dark beer and served with that most Bavarian of accompaniments—potato dumplings and sauerkraut. Credit cards are not accepted.

🕐 Daily 9am–midnight
🍴 L €36, D €46, Wine €16
🚇 Marienplatz
🚊 Isartor, Marienplatz

ZUM SPÖCKMEIER

Rosenstrasse 9, 80331
München (Altstadt)
Tel 089 26888
www.zum-spoeckmeier.de

You're right by the Marienplatz here, and when the Glockenspiel strikes at 11am people start coming in for lunch. This is a large traditional restaurant, and has been around for more than 500 years. Expect the hearty Bavarian dishes for which Munich is famous. Credit cards are not accepted.

🕐 Daily 9am–midnight
🍴 L €30, D €38, Wine €13
🚇 Marienplatz
🚊 Marienplatz

SOUTHERN GERMANY

Cuisine from Baden-Württemberg ranges from the wonderful fresh fish netted in Bodensee (Lake Constance) to *Schwarzwälder Kirschtorte* (Black Forest gateau), an irresistible creation of chocolate cake, cream and black cherries. Meat dishes use mainly pork, but you will also find some excellent beef. The Schwarzwald (Black Forest) is famous for its ham. In autumn and winter, game—including venison—is used to create imaginative dishes across the region. Potatoes in particular feature prominently—usually fried, mashed or roasted—as does *sauerkraut*. A variation of *sauerkraut* is *Blaukraut*, or *Rotkohl*, made using red cabbage. And instead of potatoes you may be served *Spätzle*, a type of chewy home-made pasta.

Bavaria, in the east of the region, is renowned for its sausages, and even has specialized *Wurstküchen* (sausage kitchens), some of which have gained Michelin ratings. The sausages here are served with sweet or spicy mustard and either *sauerkraut* or potato salad. Each region has its own special sausage, including the small, thin *bratwurst* that is grilled in *Wurstküchen* in Nürnberg (Nuremberg) and Regensburg. In Bavaria, potatoes are often replaced with dumplings. Asparagus is also popular in season.

PRICES

The prices given are for a two-course lunch (L) and a three-course dinner (D) for two people, without drinks. The wine price is for the least expensive bottle.

ANSBACH

LA RUSTIKA

Waldstrasse 2, 91522 Ansbach
Tel 0981 95430

This restaurant is renowned for its steak and fish menu. The wood panels, rustic tables and benches give you the impression you are sitting in a log cabin. The restaurant uses only prime Argentinian beef, and the steaks in particular are delicious.
🕐 Mon–Sat 5am–11pm, Sun 11am–10pm
🍴 L €18, D €24, Wine €13

AUGSBURG

BISTRO 3M

Maximilianstrasse 40, 86150 Augsburg
Tel 0821 50360
www.august-steigenberger.de
This is *the* place to find good French and Mediterranean cuisine. Bistro 3M is in the Steigenberger hotel (▷ 400) and serves a good range of evening meals; you can also have a baguette at lunchtime, or morning coffee and pastries. The intimate restaurant has very good service.
🕐 Wed–Sat 9am–1am, Sun–Tue 9am–midnight
🍴 L €35, D €55, Wine €24

DIE ECKE

Elias-Holl-Platz 2, 86150 Augsburg
Tel 0821 51 06 00
www.restaurantdieecke.de
This popular restaurant is in a pretty square in the heart of Augsburg. The wonderful

display of modern art helps to give it a relaxed bistro atmosphere. The food is excellent and includes classic Swabian and Bavarian dishes. Try the game served with *Spätzle*.
🕐 Daily 11.30am–2.30pm, 5.30pm–1am
🍴 L €32, D €45, Wine €20

BAD AIBLING

ROMANTIK HOTEL LINDNER

Marienplatz 5, 83043 Bad Aibling
Tel 08061 90630
Hotel Lindner is in a fairy-tale setting—the former Bavarian castle of Prantshausen. The restaurant offers a wonderful blend of Mediterranean and Bavarian cuisine. Special dishes include a Viennese *schnitzel* with cranberries, spinach and ricotta ravioli with a ragout of tomatoes, and home-made cakes.
🕐 Daily 7am–11pm
🍴 L €40, D €48, Wine €21

BADEN-BADEN

KURHAUS

Kaiserallee 1, 76530 Baden-Baden
Tel 07221 907100
The beautiful Kurhaus spa building, with its stately rooms, casino, underground parking and restaurant, is the hub of Baden-Baden's social scene. This is a special place for a light lunch or coffee, but whatever you choose don't miss the Black Forest gateau, which has to be the best in the region. It's worth waiting for a table if you have the time. There's a very good tourist office in the same building, which is an ideal place to browse if you do have to wait.
🕐 Daily 10am–midnight
🍴 L €22.50, D €30, Wine €7.90

BAMBERG

BRAUEREIGASTSTÄTTE KLOSTERBRÄU

Obere Mühlbrücke 1–3, 96049 Bamberg
Tel 0951 52265
www.klosterbraeu.de
This restaurant is in Bamberg's oldest brewery. Many of the dishes are cooked using the brewery's own beer—try the *Bierhaxe* (knuckle of veal or pork cooked with beer) or Franconian *Kummelbraten* (hot sliced pork with a crispy skin seasoned with caraway seeds). The brewery produces excellent beers to accompany your meal, and also makes schnapps. Credit cards are not accepted.
🕐 May–end Oct Mon–Thu, Sat 11–11, Sun, Fri 10am–late. Closed Nov–end Apr
🍴 L €14, D €15, Beer €2.30 (0.5 litre)
🚌 Centre

BRUDERMÜHLE

Schranne 1, 96049, Bamberg
Tel 0951 955220
www.brudermuehle.de
Close to the river in the middle of Bamberg's historic old town, this former mill has been developed into an attractive hotel (▷ 400) with an excellent restaurant. Eat in the intimate restaurant or on the pretty veranda, and you'll have a wide choice of Franconian dishes to choose from. Spring is a particularly good time to eat here, when there's fresh carp and trout, lamb, asparagus and strawberries on the menu. In autumn and winter, the game dishes are good.
🕐 Daily 10am–midnight
🍴 L €40, D €50, Wine €19
🚌 Centre

EATING

BAYREUTH

GOLDENER LÖWE
Kulmbacher Strasse 30, 95444
Bayreuth
Tel 0921 746060

Where better to enjoy a meal than in a restaurant next to a brewery? Not only is the beer brewed on site, but the sausages and *schnitzel* are also made here. This is the ideal venue for lunch, after which you can tour the brewery next door. Credit cards are not accepted.

Ⓖ Mon–Sat 11.30am–2pm, 5.30–10.30pm, Sun 11.30am–2.30pm
Ⓤ L and D €15

COBURG

GOLDENE TRAUBE
Am Victoriabrunnen 2, 96450
Coburg
Tel 09561 8760
www.romantikhotels.com/coburg

This superb hotel-restaurant (▷ 400) specializes in both regional and international cuisine; in season, the fish dishes in particular are very good. If you prefer something more informal, the hotel also has a wine tavern, the comfortable Weinstubla.

Ⓖ Mon–Sat noon–2.30pm, 6–10.30pm, Sun 1–10pm
Ⓤ L €36, D €52, Wine €19

DINKELSBÜHL

BRAUEREIGASTSTÄTTE ZUM WILDEN MANN
Wornitzstrasse 1, 91550
Dinkelsbühl
Tel 09851 552525
www.wilder-mann-dinkelsbuehl.de

In the restaurant here you will find a choice of excellent Franconian and international cuisine, plus a large selection of wines to accompany your meal. The *Braustube*, with its tiled floor and dark timber cladding, has a very rustic feel and a pub atmosphere; it serves Franconian-Bavarian fare as well as local wines and beers. The beer garden, where you can enjoy a good meal and a cool beer, is the place to be on a fine day.

Ⓖ Thu–Tue 10.30am–2pm, 6–10pm
Ⓤ L €15, D €25, Wine €14

EBERBACH

CAFÉ VIKTORIA
Friedrichstrasse 5–9, 69412
Eberbach
Tel 06271 2018

Although this superb café in Eberbach can get very busy, it's somewhere you just have to visit. Sit out on the terrace overlooked by a giant mural of Queen Victoria and enjoy live piano music as you sample the culinary delights. The café's signature dish is Viktoria gateau, which was created in 1962 by Heinrich Strohauer at a royal dinner and became so famous that it is now shipped throughout the world in special packaging. Credit cards are not accepted.

Ⓖ Daily 6am–6.30pm
Ⓤ L €14, D €20, Wine €4 per glass

ESSLINGEN

CAFÉ AM RATHAUS
Rathausplatz 8, 73728
Esslingen
Tel 0711 354411

This pretty little café is next to the old town hall in Esslingen, which is near Stuttgart. It's a lovely place to sit outside in the cobbled square and watch the world go by. The café has a great selection of mouthwatering cakes and pastries, plus a good-value lunch menu that is especially worth trying on weekends. Credit cards are not accepted.

Ⓖ Mon–Fri 9–6, Sat 8.30am–10pm, Sun 10–6.30
Ⓤ Cakes €3, pastries €4

FÜSSEN

SCHLOSSGASTHOF ZUM HECHTEN
Ritterstrasse 6, 87629 Füssen
Tel 08362 91600
www.hotel-hechten.com

The popular restaurant on the first floor of this hotel has a wonderful choice of Bavarian dishes to suit all tastes and appetites. If you are looking for a lighter meal, try the self-service buffet on the ground floor, where there's a choice of reasonably priced salads and hot dishes.

Ⓖ Thu–Tue 11.30–2, 5–9
Ⓤ L €25, D €35, Wine €14.40

FREIBURG

ZUM ROTEN BÄREN
Oberlinden 12, 79098
Freiburg
Tel 0761 387870
www.roter-baeren.de

The historic Red Bear is housed in one of the oldest buildings in Freiburg and is the oldest inn in Germany. The chef here prepares an excellent selection of seasonal dishes using fresh local produce, including fish, game and wild mushrooms. Many tables are placed in individual booths, and together with the soft lighting this creates a relaxed atmosphere. Be sure to take a guided tour through the cellars of this historic building before you leave. Reservations are recommended.

Ⓖ Mon–Sat noon–2.30pm, 6.30–11.30pm
Ⓤ L €60, D €80, Wine €19

GARMISCH-PARTENKIRCHEN

GASTHOF FRAUNDORFER
Ludwigstrasse 24, 82467
Garmisch-Partenkirchen
Tel 08821 2176

This homey inn has been run by the same family for nearly 200 years (▷ 401). Everyone is made to feel welcome here, and every night except Tuesday there's Bavarian accordion music, *Schuhplattler* (Bavarian folk dancing), yodelling and singing. The restaurant has a marvellous atmosphere and the knotty pine fittings give it a rustic feel. One of the wooden tables is a *Stammtisch*, the exclusive territory of a group of regulars and around which each person always sits in the same place. Home-made

Bavarian dishes accompanied by good German beer and wine are served by traditionally dressed waitresses. This is the place to go if you want a lively night out.

🕓 Thu–Mon 7am–1am, Wed 5pm–1am

🍴 L €18, D €20, Wine €14

RIESSERSEE

Riess 6, 82467 Garmisch-Partenkirchen
Tel 08821 95440

The café-restaurant Riessersee is on a lakeside high above the towns of Garmisch and Partenkirchen. The peace and tranquillity here seem far from the hustle and bustle of the towns below, both of which are within walking distance if you wish to tackle the climb. The restaurant, with its open beams and tiled floors, has a very rustic feel, and there are stunning views from the lakeside terrace. The menu includes a variety of fish and game dishes, and there are home-made cakes and pastries to enjoy with your coffee. Credit cards are not accepted.

🕓 7.30am–9pm

🍴 L €24, D €30, Wine €16

SPECIAL IN GARMISCH-PARTENKIRCHEN

GIPFELSTUBE

Zugspitze, 82475
Garmisch-Partenkirchen
Tel 08821 921291

This is Germany's highest restaurant, on the peak of the Zugspitze, Germany's highest mountain at 2,962m (9,715ft). To get here, first take the rack railway to the Sonn-Alpin restaurant, then the glacier railway. The restaurant serves a selection of Bavarian dishes, such as fresh pretzels with *Weisswurst* (white sausage) and *Leberkäse* (baked meatloaf made with minced meat, eggs and spices). The food apart, the journey up the mountain and the breathtaking views from the terrace into Germany, Austria, Switzerland and Liechtenstein make for an unforgettable experience.

HEIDELBERG
KULTURBRAUEREI

Leyergasse 6, 69117
Heidelberg
Tel 06221 502980
www.heidelberger-kulturbrauerei.de

The food and beer at the Kulturbrauerei are both excellent. There's a choice of traditional dining rooms—the

Braustube, Brauhaus, Scheffelstube and *Empore*—all of which have plenty of atmosphere and character. The *Biergarten* is also a nice place to sit on a fine day to enjoy a traditional meal chosen from the comprehensive menu. Try to take a tour of the brewery itself, as it is very informative and will give you a good insight into the beer-making process. Credit cards are not accepted.

🕓 Daily 11am–1am

🍴 L €36, D €55, Wine €24

RESTAURANT SCHLOSSWEINSTUBE

Schlosshof, 69117, Heidelberg
Tel 06221 97970

In the historic castle courtyard above the city, a choice of excellent food made from fresh seasonal ingredients is served in wonderful surroundings. Highly recommended is the duck, stuffed with apples and herbs and basted to create a crispy skin. Ducks are cooked fresh to order, and the smell that emanates from the castle ovens will set your mouth watering. Depending on the season and success of the local hunters, there's also a variety of other game to choose from. In addition, the wine list is extensive and includes many labels from the Bergstrasse region.

🕓 Thu–Tue 6pm–midnight

🍴 L €60, D €85, Wine €23.50

SIMPLICISSIMUS

Ingrimstrasse 16, 69117
Heidelberg
Tel 06221 183336
www.restaurant-simplicissimus.de

This popular restaurant, in Heidelberg's historic quarter, has a great choice of food cooked in the French tradition. There's an excellent range of wines from prestigious vineyards and producers as well as bottles in the middle price range. The fillet of beef with wild mushrooms is particularly popular. In summer, try to get a table in the small courtyard.

🕓 Wed–Mon 6pm–11pm

🍴 L €38, D €68, Wine €22

HOHENSCHWANGAU
SCHLOSSHOTEL LISL

Neuschwansteinstrasse 1–3, 87645
Hohenschwangau
Tel 08362 8870
www.hohenschwangau.de

The restaurant-café Lisl is in the middle of the village between the fairy-tale castles of Neuschwanstein and Hohenschwangau. If it's a fine day you can sit out on the sun terrace with your coffee and enjoy the magnificent views. Inside, there's a spacious café with elegant white basket-weave furniture and a comfortable restaurant serving both regional and international cuisine. Both have large picture windows, so you can watch the hustle and bustle outside as visitors flock to the royal palaces.

🕓 Daily 7am–10am, 11am–9pm. Closed 19–26 December

🍴 L €30, D €40, Wine €22

KARLSRUHE
OBERLÄNDER WEINSTUBE

Akademiestrasse 7, 76133
Karlsruhe
Tel 0721 25066

This intimate wine bar is the oldest in town. It specializes in both French and regional cooking, producing such dishes as lamb with chanterelle mushrooms and pigeon with celeriac purée. There's also a choice of delicious sorbets and an attractive courtyard where you can enjoy your meal on a fine day.

🕓 Tue–Sat 11.45am–2pm, 6–9.30pm

🍴 L €80, D €120, Wine €25

LADENBURG

FODY'S FÄHRHAUS

Neckarstrasse 62, 68526
Ladenburg
Tel 06203 938383
www.fodys.com
Part of a chain of restaurants
already popular in Mannheim
and Heppenheim, this new
branch of Fody's is a big hit.
The restaurant has a large
terrace and beer garden, and
lies 15km (10 miles) north of
Heidelberg. The interior has a
Mediterranean theme, which
creates a wonderfully warm
and lively atmosphere. The
menu includes a huge choice
of soups, salads, regional
and international dishes and
drinks. Look out for the 'Eat as
much as you like' buffet, which
is great value.

🕐 Mon–Sat 11am–2am, Sun
9am–2am

🍴 L €15, D €25, Wine €18

LANDSHUT

FÜRSTENZIMMER

Fürstenhof, Stethaimer Strasse 3,
84034 Landshut
Tel 0871 92550
André Greul is the chef at this
hotel restaurant, and he cooks
fine international and organic
regional dishes such as duck
sausage and honey-glazed
suckling pig. This is an ideal
spot for a candlelit dinner.
Less formal, and with a rustic
Bavarian atmosphere, is the
Herzogstueberl restaurant,
which also serves regional and
international dishes.

🕐 Mon–Sat noon–2pm, 6.30–10.30pm

🍴 L €40, D €90, Wine €23

LINDAU

ZUM SÜNFZEN

Maximilianstrasse 1, 88131,
Lindau (Bodensee)
Tel 08382 5865
This is a popular restaurant,
and the food is exceptional.
The fish dishes use catches
from Lake Constance, while
the game is from the owners'
own hunting grounds and the
meat from their own butchery.
There's a range of Allgau
Bavarian food and international dishes too. It's advisable
to book in advance.

🕐 Daily 9.30am–midnight

🍴 L €30, D €40, Wine €13.90

MANNHEIM

DREHRESTAURANT SKYLINE

Hans-Reschke-Ufer 2, 68165 Mannheim
Tel 0621 419292
You will have magnificent
views over the entire region
when you dine in this revolving
restaurant in the Skyline Tower,
125m (410ft) above the city.
The menu is varied, with
a wide choice of regional
cuisine, à la carte dishes and
buffet meals. The grilled
perch on dill mustard sauce
with fresh spinach is highly
recommended, as is the
grilled chicken leg stuffed with
tomatoes, mushrooms, herbs
and cheese.

🕐 Daily 10am–midnight. Closed Feb

🍴 L €40, D €70, Wine €22

EICHBAUM BRAUHAUS

Käfertalerstrasse 168, 68167 Mannheim
Tel 0621 35385
This excellent café/restaurant
in Mannheim's largest brewery
is an ideal refreshment stop at
any time of the day, for breakfast, morning coffee, a quick
lunch or an informal dinner.
The restaurant is roomy and
light, with traditional furnishings, lovely beamed ceilings
and carved wooden chairs. The
food is very good and there's a
wide choice of menus; try the
home-made *Spätzle*, North
Sea crab on the kitchen's
own-baked brown bread,
Norwegian herring matured in
red wine, Argentinian rump
steaks or Nürnberg *bratwurst*.

🕐 Daily 9am–midnight

🍴 Breakfast from €3 per person, main
dish and salad €5 per person

MEERSBURG

HOTEL RESIDENZ AM SEE

Uferpromenade 11, 88709 Meersburg
Tel 07532 80040
www.romantikhotels.com/meersburg
The setting is beautiful for this
hotel restaurant, in the picturesque town of Meersburg. The
hotel is surrounded by historic
buildings and vineyards on
three sides and overlooks Lake
Constance, so it's a perfect
place to stop for a meal or
even just a coffee. The menu
has a wide choice of regional
dishes, including excellent fish
from the lake, local vegetables
and wines.

🕐 Wed–Mon noon–2pm,
5.30–9.30pm

🍴 L €60, D €120, Wine €13.90

MOSBACH

CAFÉ GRAMLICH

Hauptstrasse 88, 74821 Mosbach
Tel 06261 2389
www.cafe-gramlich.de
The selection of home-made
cakes and pastries here is
exceptional, making it a great
place to enjoy an indulgent
break. Every type of cake imaginable is on display, so making
a choice is a hard decision; if
you really can't decide, try the
Swiss cheesecake. The breads
here are equally good, as the
owners believe in baking
quality bread rather than
great quantities.

🕐 Wed–Sun 10am–9pm

NECKARGERACH

GRÜNER BAUM

Neckarstrasse 13, 69437 Neckargerach
Tel 06263 706
This hotel is owned and run
by a Greek family (▷ 402),
and in the restaurant you will
find an amazing selection of
freshly prepared Greek dishes
alongside popular local dishes.
The salads in particular are
exceptional, whether ordered
as a meal or just as a side
dish. The restaurant's interior
is typically Greek in its design
and has a casual style. Credit
cards are not accepted.

🕐 Mar–end Aug daily 11.30–2pm,
5–11pm; Sep–end Feb Mon–Sat
5pm–11pm, Sun 11.30am–2pm,
5–11pm

🍴 L and D €25, Wine €11.50

NÜRNBERG

BRATWURSTHÄUSLE

Rathaus-Platz 1, 90403 Nürnberg
Tel 0911 227695
The Bratwursthäusle is
the place to try the famous
bratwurst (grilled sausages).
Here, the traditional Nürnberg
sausages are made fresh every
day in the factory below the
restaurant, then are taken
upstairs to be grilled over
beechwood and served on
pewter plates with horse-
radish, *sauerkraut* and potato
salad. The grills are in the
middle of the restaurant and
form the focal point, as chefs
and waitresses scurry around
to meet the vast demand.
This place is popular and
gets very busy at lunchtimes
and on weekends.

🕐 Mon–Sat 10am–10.30pm

🍴 L and D from €5.50 per person,
Wine €3.50 a glass

EISCAFÉ ROMA

Plobenhofstrasse 1, 90403
Nürnberg
Tel 0911 202 9160

This Italian café has been a popular meeting place for more than 50 years, and has a terrace that overlooks the river. The Italian food is exceptional, especially the pasta and pizzas, but there's also a choice of fresh fish and meat dishes on the menu. There's a wonderful range of coffees, as well as legendary ice creams and cakes.

🕐 Daily 11–11
🍴 L and D €20, Wine €3 a glass

GASTHAUS ROTTNER

Winterstrasse 15–17, 90431
Grossreuth, Nürnberg
Tel 0911 658480

The attractive black-and-white timber-framed former farmhouse that is now the Gasthaus Rottner is in the small village of Grossreuth on the outskirts of Nürnberg. The restaurant is welcoming, with traditional but innovative fare that is always adapted to include fresh seasonal and regional produce. The menu includes such dishes as tomato bread, herb pancakes, smoked venison and some amazing salads. In summer, ask for a table in the restaurant garden so that you can enjoy your dinner in the shade of the old lime trees (▷ 403).

🕐 Mon–Fri 10am–11pm, Sat 10am–noon
🍴 L and D €35–€50, Wine €21

OBERAMMERGAU

PARKHOTEL SONNENHOF

Konig-Ludwig-Strasse 12, 82487
Oberammergau
Tel 08822 9130
www.parkhotel-sonnenhof.de

This spacious hotel restaurant is typically Bavarian in style. The chef specializes in both regional and international cuisine, so the menu has a wide choice. Although the restaurant is large, it has plenty of character—many of the tables are tucked away in intimate corners. There is a good range of wines and beers, mainly from the wineries of Württemberg and the breweries of Ingolstadt.

🕐 Daily 6.45am–9pm
🍴 L and D €30, Wine €14

RESTAURANT ZUR TINI

Dorfstrasse 7, 82487
Oberammergau
Tel 08822 7152

This is a superb little restaurant in the heart of Oberammergau, where you can sit outside in the pedestrian area on a fine day and watch the world go by. The restaurant specializes

in light Bavarian meals and snacks. Credit cards are not accepted.

🕐 Thu–Tue 10am–2.30pm, 5.30–midnight
🍴 L and D €30, Wine €4.20 per glass

OBERSTDORF

BACCHUS STUBEN

Freibergstrasse 4, 87561 Oberstdorf
Tel 08322 4787

This is a family-run restaurant serving fabulous traditional food. Seasonal dishes use fresh regional produce, including brown trout, zander (pike-perch), salmon, asparagus, game and meat. The portions are large, but there are scaled-down versions for children. The views of the mountains from the sun terrace are exceptional. Credit cards are not accepted.

🕐 Tue–Sun 11.30am–2pm, 5.30–8.30pm
🍴 L €20, D €40, Wine €17

PASSAU

KAISERIN SISSI

Im Hotel Wilder Mann, Am Rathausplatz, 94032, Passau
Tel 0851 35075
www.wilder-mann.com

The gourmet restaurant Kaiserin Sissi, in the Wilder Mann hotel, is very exclusive and serves exquisite food. The chef uses regional produce and during the festival weeks will adopt a theme for the set meals. During the daytime, the rooftop café-restaurant is the ideal setting for coffee and cakes or lunch. The rich and famous stay at the Wilder

Mann, so you never know who may be sitting at the table next to you or wandering around the hotel. Be sure to visit the Passau Glass Museum on the ground floor.

🕐 Feb Thu–Sun from 6pm, Sun also 11.30am–2pm; Mar–end Jan Mon–Sat from 6pm, Sun 11.30am–2pm and from 6pm
🍴 L €46, D €92, Wine €18

RAVENSBURG

HOTEL OBERTOR

Marktstrasse 67, 88212 Ravensburg
Tel 0751 36670

This historic hotel dates back more than 700 years (▷ 403), and has a restaurant serving typically Swabian food, creatively presented using fresh seasonal produce. The wood-panelled dining room has beamed ceilings and beautiful objects—look for the special carved wooden lamp-shade holders that hang low over each table. History is everywhere around you at the Obertor, with its vaulted cellars and wooden ceilings—so much so that you feel that time stands still here.

🕐 Mon, Wed–Sat 5pm–midnight

REGENSBURG

ORPHEE

Untere Bachgasse 8, 93047
Regensburg
Tel 0941 596020

Once the largest brewery in the German Oberfalz region, it was converted by a Hungarian Gypsy baron to a French-style café and wine bar, and no major changes have been made in the restaurant since 1896. The café was established to allow people to meet and enjoy a coffee or sit and read a newspaper in comfort; today, it is still an ideal place to relax and soak up the atmosphere, with its old wooden floor and antique furnishings. The menu has everything from pastries, baguettes, soups and crêpes to three-course meals.

🕐 Daily 8am–1am
🍴 L €23, D €45, Wine €12

HISTORISCHE WURSTKUCHL

Thundorferstrasse 3, 93047 Regensburg
Tel 0941 466210
www.wurstkuchl.de

This restaurant is beside the Danube, and on a fine day it's great to sit outside here enjoying a plate of home-made sausages and *sauerkraut* with a cool beer. The sausages are made fresh on the premises every day, and the cabbage for the

sauerkraut is fermented in the cellar vats. The method of grilling the sausages over charcoal until crisp has been used from the 12th century. Try to find a table in the original small kitchen, because the atmosphere here is wonderful. If that's not possible, there's a large modern dining room across the road on the ground floor of the Salt Barn, one of Germany's largest historic warehouses. Credit cards are not accepted.

🕐 Daily 8am–1pm
🍴 Sausages from €2.50

PRINZESS CONFISERIE

Rathausplatz 2, 93047 Regensburg
Tel 0941 595310
www.prinzess.de

The Prinzess Confiserie is the oldest café and chocolate manufacturing house in Germany. When you enter the shop on the ground floor, you are greeted with an amazing selection of home-made cakes, pastries and chocolates, the latter with exotic names such as *Kussmund* (kissing lips), *Liebeszauber* (magic love), *Toller Romer* (great Roman) and *Romerinnen* (ladies of Rome). The intimate seating

areas on the upper floors have marble tables and comfortable armchairs.

🕐 Mon–Sat 9.15am–6.30pm, Sun 11am–6.30pm

VITUS CAFÉ UND RESTAURANT

Hinter der Grieb 8, 93047 Regensburg
Tel 0941 52646

This attractive restaurant and café is housed in a former chapel. The large arched doorways and windows, and pale decorations and fittings, make it feel nice and airy. Tables are well spaced, allowing plenty of room to admire the architecture in this historic building. It's a very popular place for morning coffee and mouth-watering pastries. Credit cards are not accepted.

🕐 Daily 9am–11pm
🍴 L €20, D €30, Wine €14

ROTHENBURG OB DER TAUBER

HOTEL RESTAURANT SCHRANNE

Schrannenplatz 6, 91542 Rothenburg ob der Tauber
Tel 09861 95500

A family-run hotel restaurant specializing in Franconian cuisine; the meat dishes are particularly good, using produce from the Schranne's own butchery. The large restaurant is very light and spacious, with lovely pine floors and panelling. The staff are very friendly and are always ready to help you with the menu or to recommend dishes. There's a good selection of local wines and beer to accompany your meal.

🕐 Mon–Sun 11am–9.30pm
🍴 L €15, D €20, Wine €12

ZUR HÖLL

Burggasse 8, 91541, Rothenburg ob der Tauber
Tel 09861 4229

Zur Höll literally means 'to hell', and you're certain of a warm welcome at this medieval tavern! The house is the oldest and one of the most beautiful in Rothenburg, and serves fine regional dishes as well as one of the best selections of Franconian wines in Germany. The small dinner menu complements the wines perfectly. Some of the tables are tucked away in secluded alcoves to

create a wonderfully intimate, old-fashioned atmosphere.

🕐 Daily 5pm–1am
🍴 L €16, D €25, Wine €18

SCHWÄBISCH HALL

CAFÉ ILGE

An der Rittersbrücke, 74523 Schwäbisch Hall
Tel 0791 71684

This popular first-floor café is ideal for a relaxing coffee or beer. It has a friendly atmosphere, and wonderful views from the two terraces that overlook the River Kocher and the ancient wooden bridge across it. There's a good choice of snacks and pastries to enjoy with your drink, but as it's a popular venue with locals it does get busy, especially during the evenings.

🕐 Sun–Thu 11am–1am, Fri, Sat 11am–2am
🍴 Snacks from €3 per person, Wine from €3.50 a glass

SPEYER

RESTAURANT BACKMULDE

Karmeliter Strasse 11–13, 67346 Speyer
Tel 06232 71577

In Speyer, south of Mannheim, this popular restaurant is a good place to sample regional dishes and wines. The dim lights and small rooms create an intimate atmosphere, and the waiters are helpful and give very good service. Try the leg of goose and, when in season, the salads of fresh greens picked from the owner's garden.

🕐 Tue–Sat 11.30am–2.30pm, 7–11.30pm
🍴 L €50, D €80, Wine €23

STUTTGART

EMPORE

Dorotheenstrasse 4, 70173 Stuttgart
Tel 0711 245979

This lively Italian restaurant is on the second floor above the busy market hall in the middle of Stuttgart. It is perfect for a pasta lunch, a cappuccino or a bowl of delicious Italian ice cream.

🕐 Mon–Fri 9am–10pm, Sat 9am–6pm
🍴 L €30, D €40, Wine €15.80

EATING

KACHELOFEN

Eberhardstrasse 10, 80173
Stuttgart
Tel 0711 24 23 78

A traditional restaurant,
specializing in Swabian dishes,
in the middle of Stuttgart, is
very popular with locals. It's
always busy, and the atmosphere is informal and jovial
as waitresses squeeze
between the closely spaced
tables to serve the excellent

food and wine. Each table
has a small flag to indicate
the nationality of the diner,
so look around and see where
everyone comes from.
Ⓒ Mon–Sat 5pm–1am
🍴 L €12, D €20, Wine €16.50

WEINSTUBE ZUR KISTE

Kanalstrasse 2, 70182 Stuttgart
Tel 0711 24 40 02

This quaint little restaurant,
close to the Bohnenviertel
(Bean Quarter), is the oldest in
Stuttgart and probably its best-
known and most popular wine
tavern. It's a superb place to
experience traditional Swabian
dishes and regional wines, but
it does get very busy and loud.
Ⓒ Mon–Fri 5–midnight, Sat
11.30–3.30, 6–midnight
🍴 L and D from €10, Wine €4.50 a
glass

TÜBINGEN

FORELLE RESTAURANT

Kronenstrasse 8, 72072 Tübingen
Tel 07071 240 94

In the middle of the old city,
this little restaurant specializes
in Swabian dishes. The lunch
menu is good value and the
small interior is welcoming
with a relaxing old-fashioned
atmosphere. The game dishes,
roasted duck liver and trout are
all highly recommended.
Ⓒ Daily 11.30am–10pm
🍴 L €15, D €25, Wine €17

RESTAURANT MAUGANESCHTLE

Hotel Am Schloss, Burgsteige 18, 72072
Tübingen
Tel 07071 929 40

This beautiful hotel restaurant
is in a historic part of town.
Maultaschen, a ravioli-like
stuffed pasta, is Tübingen's
local dish and you can choose
from 28 types of *Maultaschen*,
as well as many other excellent dishes. If you like fish, try
the zander (pike-perch), which
is available in season. The terrace overlooks the river and is
a wonderful place to sit on a
fine day.
Ⓒ Daily 11.30am–2pm, 6–10pm.
Closed Mon–Tue Oct–end Mar
🍴 L €20, D €40, Wine €15

VOLKACH

GASTSTUBE

Hotel zur Schwane, Haupstrasse 12,
97332 Volkach
Tel 09381 806 60

To the east of Würzburg in
Volkach is the comfortable
Hotel zur Schwane, which is
furnished with many interesting antiques and the Gaststube
has a traditional tiled fireplace.
The chef specializes in
Franconian cuisine. The
cobbled courtyard is great in
the summer months, and
as the hotel has its own vineyard there's a fine selection of
wine to choose from.
Ⓒ Daily noon–2pm, 6.30–9.30pm.
Closed Mon lunch
🍴 L €40, D €60, Wine €18

WEINHEIM

SCHLOSSPARK RESTAURANT

Obertorstrasse 9, 69469 Weinheim
Tel 06201 995 50

Beautifully located in the
wing of an historic building, in
parkland surrounded by exotic
trees, manicured lawns, bright
flowerbeds and overlooking a
lake with dancing fountains,
this restaurant is the perfect
place to enjoy a meal. The chef
uses fresh seasonal produce to
provide a varied menu that will
suit all tastes; in spring, the
lamb and zander (pike-perch)
are especially good. It's a very
popular restaurant, so advance
booking is advisable (Tuesday
is the quietest day). Enjoy a
walk through the park before
or after your meal.
Ⓒ Daily 10am–midnight
🍴 L €20, D €40, Wine €13.50

WÜRZBURG

WÜRZBURGER RATSKELLER

Langgasse 1, 97070
Würzburg
Tel 0931 130 21

This is an elegant restaurant
in the vaulted basement of
the town hall. The towered
building is as impressive on
the inside as it is from the
outside, as room after room
sprawls across the basement
floors, each with its own
distinctive style and ambience.
The menu has both local
dishes and international
cuisine, all wonderfully
prepared and presented.
This is a special place to go for
a special meal.
Ⓒ Daily 10am–midnight
🍴 L and D from €12 per person,
Wine €10

ZUM STACHEL

Gressengasse 1, 97070
Würzburg
Tel 0931 527 70

A classy restaurant in a
historic building in the middle
of Würzburg's Old Town. The
woodwork is highly polished,
the lights are dim and tables
are tucked away in alcoves,
creating a relaxing, unhurried
atmosphere. The beautiful
terrace garden is wonderful
on a fine summer's day. The
restaurant is very popular with
local business people and gets
busy at lunchtimes on weekdays. The menu has a variety
of Franconian dishes, and the
seasonal fish specials, such as
zander (pike-perch) and carp,
are exceptional.
Ⓒ Mon–Tue 5pm–1am, Wed–Sat
11am–1am
🍴 L from €10, D €90, Wine €17.60

STAYING IN GERMANY

Accommodation options in Germany range from luxury designer hotels with a sauna and spa to basic farm-stay rooms with clean sheets and hot and cold running water. Hotels tend to be better value in Germany than in the UK or the US, except in areas such as the Rhine and Mosel in peak season and in cities during trade fairs. You may be pleasantly surprised at the amount of luxury €150 will buy for two people.

Accommodation ranges from a simple Gasthof *(gueshouse) to rooms with a view at Schlosshotel Lisl*

HOTELS

Most hotels in Germany are assigned a star rating from one to five, and prices usually reflect this. However, bear in mind that higher prices are not necessarily a guarantee of quality: A hotel that claims three stars may be quite threadbare, while another hotel that has only one or two stars might be comfortable, clean and perfectly functional. For this reason, it's always a good idea to ask to see a room before booking, or, if you're making a reservation online, to look at any pictures you can find. This is less of a problem with four- and five-star hotels, which are equivalent to their counterparts in the UK or US in terms of standards and amenities.

Budget accommodation (around €115 or less per room) is relatively easy to find—even in downtown areas—if you're prepared to look around, although during trade fairs prices can double or even triple. Double rooms are better value than singles: It's quite possible, for example, to find a comfortable double with private bathroom in the heart of a major city for as little as €85. Visitors with more to spend will be spoiled for choice, particularly in the bigger towns. Most hotels include a buffet breakfast in the room price, and all but the cheapest rooms will have a television with at least one or two satellite channels in English (such as CNN).

PENSIONS

Pensions tend to be small, privately run inns (with a restaurant) or hotels (without a restaurant), offering simple rooms and basic amenities. They're usually found outside the town or downtown city area, and charge prices that reflect their no-nonsense nature (around

€40 to €60 for a single and €60 to €85 for a double). They are usually great value but it helps if you have your own transportation.

FARM STAYS

Staying on a farm is one of the best ways to experience rural Germany, but, as with pensions, it's not practical for those without their own transportation. Home stays and farm stays can be arranged by local tourist information offices, sometimes for a small fee (this is never more than a euro or two). Such accommodation tends not to be starred, and quality ranges from rustic but serviceable to downright luxurious.

HOSTELS

The Germans are mad about hostels and hostelling, so it's hardly surprisingly that there are more than 600 DJH (Deutsches Jugendherbergswerk or German Youth Hostel Association) hostels dotted across the country, not to mention hundreds more independent ones. Facilities are generally good, but some hostels require visitors to vacate the building during the day, and others have a curfew (although this is usually sensibly late, particularly in large cities). Expect to pay anything from €20 to €35 for a bed in a shared room with breakfast, plus €4 to €6 for bedding if you need some. For reservations and further information, log onto www.djh-ris.de, which has an English version.

CAMPING

As with many pensions, most campsites in Germany are well away from downtown city areas, and the majority are of the RV/caravan sort, so you'll usually need to make your own way there. Most are open only from April to the end of September, although some of the bigger ones are open year-round. Campers are often charged per tent, per person and per car, so the final price does add up, but it's still the least expensive option as far as accommodation goes. A comprehensive list of German campsites can be found at www.camping-club.de.

SELF-CATERING

Renting a room or an apartment for a few days is popular with holidaying Germans, and there's no reason why overseas visitors can't get in on the act too. Again, quality varies from the simple to the sublime, but because the rent is shared between two or more people, it can be great value. For this reason, rented accommodation is ideal for families, particularly as it also offers a lot more privacy and flexibility. Local tourist offices can advise you on the options, or you can visit www.germany-tourism.co.uk.

FINDING A ROOM

Rooms can be booked in advance through most local tourism information websites (see Sight entries for details) or through the hotel finder at www.germany-tourism.co.uk. The best place to start your search once you're in situ is at the local tourist office, which may offer a room-finding service for a nominal fee (usually €2 to €3). If the tourist office is closed, there's often a noticeboard outside with a list of nearby hotels and—if you're lucky—a map. If not, just take a stroll round the middle of town.

It is always best to reserve ahead, particularly in the peak season, when many resort and downtown city hotels will be close to capacity. Check-out time is usually 11am or noon, although most hotels will be happy to store your luggage free of charge until later in the afternoon. In the chart below, (R) indicates that this is the number for reservations.

ROOM RATES

Rates vary considerably according to the season and whether or not there is a trade fair in town. For this reason, if you're planning on staying in one of the major commercial hubs such as Düsseldorf or Frankfurt, it's a good idea to find out from the local tourist office when the major trade fairs are taking place and try to avoid those dates.

Hotels often quote their most expensive rate, so a little perseverance might elicit a better deal. By law, they must display a list of prices in every room, so you'll know you're not being ripped off. Extra beds can usually be added for a small charge (ideal for families with young children).

MAJOR HOTEL CHAINS

Name	Description	Contact number and website
Best Western	The world's largest hotel chain, offering four-star accommodation close to city downtown areas.	0180 221 2588 www.bestwestern.com
Crowne Plaza	Part of the Inter-Continental group, with quality four-star hotels in Germany's big cities.	0800 181 5131 www.crowne-plaza.com
Dorint	Stylish and luxurious four-star spa hotels and resorts at locations throughout Germany.	0180 226 2524 (R) www.dorint.de
Ibis	Comfortable, great-value rooms in two- and three-star French-owned hotels, usually near city downtown areas.	06995 307595 (R) www.ibishotel.com
Hilton	US-based chain providing quality four-star accommodation, usually in central locations. (Note: international phone rates outside US.)	+1-800/774-1500 www.hilton.de
Holiday Inn	Part of the Inter-Continental group, offering four-star accommodation in main cities.	0800 181 5131 (R) www.holiday-inn.com
Inter-Continental	High-end, luxury hotel chain providing four- and five-star accommodation in cities.	0800 185 3955 www.intercontinental.com
Maritim	A German-based chain offering central four-star accommodation in 33 German cities.	01802 312121 (R) www.maritim.com
Marriott	A global group with luxury hotel and resort accommodation in more than 20 German cities.	0800 185 4422 (R) www.marriott.com
Mövenpick	Elegant and exclusive top-end hotels and resorts in 13 German cities. Swiss owned.	0800 849 9999 (R) www.moevenpick.com
Novotel	Part of the Accor group, offering slightly classier versions of the Ibis hotels.	06995 307595 (R) www.novotel.com
Park Plaza	Modern, stylish designer hotels providing four-star accommodation in six German cities.	0800 200 0129 (R) www.parkplaza.com
Radisson SAS	Part of the same group as Park Plaza, Radisson SAS provides accommodation in a series of large, stylish hotels in numerous cities across the world.	0800 181 4442 (R) www.radisson.com
Ramada	Part of the Marriott group, Ramada hotels provide four-star quality and service at affordable prices; they are centrally located in more than 40 different German cities.	0800 181 9098 (R) www.ramadahotels.com
Sheraton	Mid- to high-end four- and five-star accommodation in 24 towns and cities across Germany.	1-888-625-5144 (R) www.sheraton.com
Sofitel	The pinnacle of the Accor empire, offering luxury facilities in some splendid buildings.	06995 307595 (R) www.sofitel.com

STAYING

NORTHERN GERMANY

With no mountains worth speaking of, northern Germany's scenery complements the Alpine views of the south with plenty of coastline and the charms of its venerable towns. The region's accommodation options reflect this, with a large quantity and a variable quality of lodgings at the coast—luxury hotels, plain but welcoming rooms in converted houses, B&Bs, caravan parks and more. In the Vier Jahreszeiten, Hamburg has what is considered to be one of the top hotels in the country. The city also has plenty of accommodation in all price categories, catering to business and vacation visitors. The picture is similar in cities like Bremen, Hannover and Lübeck. Formerly in East Germany, Mecklenburg-Vorpommern's hotel stock is enormously varied. It ranges from Stalin-era monstrosities and down-at-heel old properties, to convivial lodgings run by a new breed of entrepreneurs, restored imperial-era jewels, and all points between. The good news is that higher standards are being established, particularly at the coast and in the old Hanseatic towns, as building and rebuilding continue apace.

PRICES AND SYMBOLS

Prices are per night for two people sharing a double room. The prices include breakfast unless otherwise stated, but check when you make your reservation. Note that rates vary widely throughout the year.
For a key to the symbols, ▷ 2.

BREMEN

HOTEL BUTHMANN

Löningstrasse 29, 28195 Bremen
Tel 0421 326397
www.hotel-buthmann.de
Although it is short on amenities, this small hotel in a renovated townhouse compensates with reasonable rates, a friendly welcome and the personal touch from its long-time family owners. The location's not bad either: a

quiet side street southeast of the Hauptbahnhof, off Rembertiring, on the edge of the Altstadt. The guest rooms are clean and comfortable rather than stylish. Since there are plenty of repeat guests, it's best to reserve in advance.
💶 €69–75
🛏 10
🚇 1, 4, 5, 10

PARK HOTEL BREMEN

Im Bürgerpark, 28209 Bremen
Tel 0421 34080
www.park-hotel-bremen.de
This hotel has a grandiose 19th-century style, but it actually dates from the 1950s. There's a small lake, the Hollersee, and the 19th-century park makes a quiet retreat. The public spaces are graceful, and the large, elegant rooms are fully equipped. There are several restaurants as well as the Meierei im Bürgerpark (▷ 342).
💶 €230–325
🛏 177
🍴
🐕
🚇 5, 6

CELLE

SPECIAL IN CELLE

FÜRSTENHOF CELLE

Hannoverschestrasse 55–56, 29221 Celle
Tel 05141 2010
www.fuerstenhof.de
Since you're visiting a town where the main attraction is the fantastical ducal seat of the house of Brunswick and Lüneburg (▷ 71), you may as well pamper yourself by staying at this well-bred establishment. The bed-rooms of the 17th-century salmon-hued mansion, south of the castle, are a shade less distinguished than the antiques-encrusted public spaces, but they have views of the gardens. Relax in the indoor pool. The restaurant, Entenfang, has a Michelin star.
💶 €179–240
🛏 63
🍴
🏊 Indoor 🐕

GOSLAR

KAISERWORTH

Markt 3, 38640 Goslar
Tel 05321 7090
www.kaiserworth.de
In a small town with plenty of visitor accommodation, this hotel stands out, not least for its location on the main square, where it occupies the Gothic Tailors' and Weavers' Guild Hall (1494). It easily combines traditional looks and

service in its public spaces with modern facilities in the guest rooms. Front rooms look onto the Markt—some have a view of the mechanical figures accompanying the glocken-spiel on the Kämmereige-bäude (▷ 71). Additional assets include the fine Die Worth restaurant, a bar, wine bar and a summertime out-door café terrace.
💶 €101–171
🛏 66
🍴

HAMBURG

AUSSEN ALSTER

Schmilinskystrasse 11, 20099 Hamburg
Tel 040 241557
www.aussen-alster.de
In the St.-Georg district on the southeastern shore of the Aussen Alster, this boutique hotel in a dazzlingly white, beautifully renovated 19th-century mansion has earned plaudits for personal care and

attention to detail. Despite being close to the heart of a busy city, the ambience is that of a sophisticated country villa, a feeling enhanced by the courtyard garden. Hidden in the cellar is an exquisite Mediterranean and Italian

restaurant. The hotel has bicycles for its guests, and its own sailboat.

🛏 €129–155
🛌 27
🍴 ❢
🚇 Lohmühlenstrasse

HAFEN HAMBURG

Seewartenstrasse 9, 20459 Hamburg
Tel 040 311130
www.hotel-hamburg.de

Set back from the domes and spires of the Landungsbrücke, the hotel is built around a 19th-century seaman's residence. It is ideal if location, comforts and facilities are important, but not if you are looking for tradition. Try

to get a harbour view. The restaurant has a maritime theme and a terrace overlooks the harbour.

🛏 €90–200
🛌 355
🍴
❢ ❢
🚇 Landungsbrücke

VIER JAHRESZEITEN

Neuer Jungfernstieg 9–14, 20354 Hamburg
Tel 040 34940
www.hjv.de

The superb Vier Jahreszeiten (Four Seasons) has appeared in a number of films, and is renowned in Germany. The public spaces are all but dripping in antiques, and guest rooms are individually styled, with more antiques, de-luxe beds and other fittings. With all this, fine restaurants and the years of tradition since 1897, you may still decide that the view of the Binnenalster, from many of the rooms, is the hotel's best feature.

🛏 €158–340, excluding breakfast
🛌 156
🍴
❢ ❢
🚇 Hauptbahnhof

HAMELN

HOTEL ZUR KRONE

Osterstrasse 30, 31785 Hameln
Tel 05151 9070
www.hotelzurkrone.de

This hotel, behind a half-timbered façade near the top of the bustling main street, is ideal for exploring. Close by is the Rattenfängerhaus (Pied Piper's House), and at the far

end of Osterstrasse are the main sites associated with the fairy-tale. Most rooms have a comfortable, modern style but some have exposed wooden beams and more stylish fittings. The restaurant serves Continental and German dishes, and in summer there's a café terrace on the street.

🛏 €87–158
🛌 32
🍴

HANNOVER

AGENDA 21 HAUS

Wülferoder Strasse 62–72, 30539 Hannover-Kronsberg
Tel 0511 563580
www.agenda21-haus.de

On the city's southeastern fringe, this futuristic lodging is way out on the cutting edge of hotel design. A complex of small buildings, the rooms and public spaces have plenty of cool touches but don't sacrifice comfort and good taste. The surrounding commercial district is not exactly loaded with atmosphere, but Agenda 21 is near the *autobahn*—and, anyway, is an attraction itself.

🛏 €60–100
🛌 21
🚇 Kronsberg

GEORGENHOF

Herrenhäuser Kirchweg 20, 30167 Hannover
Tel 0511 702244
www.telehotel.de/georgenhof_hannover

The hotel is in the northwest of the city within easy walking distance of the Herrenhäuser Gärten complex. In the style of a country villa, it is in a relaxing setting in its own park. The comfortable rooms are taste-fully decorated. Stern's restaurant is highly regarded, and the terrace beside a pond is a big draw in good weather.

🛏 €123–143
🛌 14
🍴
🚇 Georgengarten

LÜBECK

KAISERHOF

Kronsforder Allee 11–13, 23560 Lübeck
Tel 0451 703301
www.kaiserhof-luebeck.de

On a busy street just outside the ring canal, two graceful mansions have been renovated, modernized and umbilically joined to create a fine hotel that retains their original character. Rooms are individual and pleasant in a pastel, chintzy way. There's a lounge, bar, attractive terrace overlooking the garden and a heated indoor pool. Try to get a room in the main hotel.

🛏 €100–135
🛌 60
❢
🏊 Indoor ❢
🅿
🚌 2, 7, 10, 16, 32

RINGHOTEL JENSEN

An der Obertrave 4–5, 23552 Lübeck
Tel 0451 702490
www.ringhotel-jensen.de
In a modernized gabled town-house across the canal from the Holstentor, the Jensen is well placed for exploring. The large, comfortable rooms over-look the canal at the front and gardens at the rear. The highly regarded seafood restaurant, the Yachtzimmer, is a deluxe interpretation of a Hanseatic cog ship's 'tween-decks.

€85–108
42
1, 3, 11

ROSTOCK

HOTEL VERDI

Wollenweberstrasse 28, 18055
Rostock
Tel 0381 252240
www.hotel-verdi.de
This hotel, in a baroque house, is close to the Petrikirche. The family owners offer a friendly welcome and a commitment to comfort and value. The low-

on-frills modern rooms are comfortable and clean. Some are small apartments with a kitchen. You can rent bicycles.
€74–84
10

RÜGEN

STEIGENBERGER RESORT HOTEL RÜGEN

Neddesitz 4, 18551 Sagard-Rügen
Tel 038302 95
www.ruegen-steigenberger.de
This all-inclusive resort, in the Nationalpark Jasmund, is a self-contained world. Visit the beach (6km/4 miles away) by hopping on the shuttle. The focal point is a restored villa, with rooms and chalets around it.
€66–130
145 rooms, 155 holiday chalets
Indoor and outdoor

SCHLESWIG

STRANDHALLE

Strandweg 2, 24837 Schleswig
Tel 04621 9090
www.hotel-strandhalle.de
A small hotel that is ideal for a visit to the Schlei on the Baltic. What it lacks in style, it makes up for with friendly charm. Everything is bright and cheer-ful. The neat little rooms are furnished in a modest modern style, and front rooms look over the waterfront. There's a small indoor pool and rowing boats to rent. The restaurant specializes in seafood.
€93–115
25
Indoor

SCHWERIN

NIEDERLÄNDISCHER HOF

Karl-Marx-Strasse 12–13,
19055 Schwerin
Tel 0385 591100
www.niederlaendischer-hof.de
The hotel, dating back to 1901, is on the west bank of the Pfaffenteich, a small inland lake between the Old Town and Hauptbahnhof. Oceans of marble define the bathrooms in the luxurious rooms. Relax in front of the fireplace in the stately library-lounge. The restaurant has a reputation for its modern take on Mecklenburg cuisine.
€129–139
33
Reservations only

RINGHOTEL ARTE SCHWERIN

Dorfstrasse 6, 19061
Schwerin-Krebsförden
Tel 0385 63450
www.ringhotel-arte.de
A 19th-century country inn that has been modernized but hasn't lost all of its traditional character. The hotel is close to the Ostorfer See and handy for the outer ring road. Guest rooms are comfortable. The Fontane restaurant serves seasonal and regional cuisine.
€89–129
40

SYLT

HOTEL MIRAMAR

Friedrichstrasse 43, 25890
Westerland-Sylt
Tel 04651 8550
www.hotel-miramar.de
This island of calm is on the western edge of Westerland. The hotel has been owned by one family since 1903 and tradition and family pride are much in evidence. The large guest rooms are modern and there is a seafood restaurant and a heated pool.
€165–360
93
Indoor

WISMAR

CHEZ FASAN

Bademutterstrasse 19/20a,
23966 Wismar
Tel 03841 213425
www.pension-chez-fasan.de
Townhouses on a quiet street north of the Markt make up this family-owned pension. There is a characterful restau-rant, with a tile-roofed bar, and

guest rooms are modern and comfortable (some are in annexes). There is a garden.
€50–60
25

STEIGENBERGER HOTEL STADT HAMBURG WISMAR

Am Markt 24, 23966 Wismar
Tel 03841 2390
www.wismar.steigenberger.de
In an unbeatable position on the central square, the Stadt Hamburg has become ever more exclusive. Guest rooms have every modern comfort and there's a restaurant and, in the 14th-century cellar, a bar.
€286
104

STAYING

WESTERN GERMANY

There's no shortage of places to stay to suit all tastes and budgets in western Germany. Chain hotels offer modern, air-conditioned rooms at affordable prices. However, if you're prepared to be a little adventurous, you can find a more traditional, family-run hotel in the same price range. Even the more classy hotels tend to be less expensive than in the UK and the US—a superior double room in Münster's superb Hotel Kaiserhof, for example (▷ 383), costs as little as €100 per night. Breakfast—usually a buffet of cereals, cold meats and cheeses—is almost always included in the price (but check with the hotel), but parking may not be. In bigger towns and cities, parking can add from €5 to €15 a night to your bill. Cologne, Düsseldorf and Frankfurt are popular venues for international trade fairs, and when these are in town, hotel prices can triple. Check in advance with the local tourist office to find out when such events are taking place.

PRICES AND SYMBOLS

Prices are per night for two people sharing a double room. The prices include breakfast unless otherwise stated, but check when you make your reservation. Note that rates vary widely throughout the year.
For a key to the symbols, ▷ 2.

AACHEN

HOTEL BENELUX
Franzstrasse 21–23, 52064 Aachen
Tel 0241 400030
www.hotel-benelux.de
This immaculate designer hotel is just a few minutes' walk south of the cathedral. As well as an elegant restaurant and bar, it has a fitness room and roof garden. The rooms have contemporary furniture and original art. Awarded three stars, this hotel offers quality service and amenities. Package deals that include a visit to Carolus Thermen (▷ 252) are available for €120 per double room.
€97–133
33
Chinese and Mongolian

DÜSSELDORF

BEST WESTERN HOTEL SAVOY
Oststrasse 128, 40210 Düsseldorf
Tel 0211 388380
www.savoy.bestwestern.de
The renovated Savoy has a striking neoclassical façade and is between Düsseldorf's main train station and the Königsallee shopping precinct (▷ 252). Its young, English-speaking staff are friendly and helpful, and its immaculate rooms (all with private bathroom) are decorated with dark wooden furniture, pale yellow walls and crisp white linen. In the basement is a small health suite.

€100–150
114 (48 non smoking)
Daily 5pm–midnight
Indoor pool, sauna, solarium
Oststrasse

BONN

SPECIAL IN BONN
HOTEL MOZART
Mozartstrasse 1, 53115 Bonn
Tel 0228 659071
www.hotel-mozart-bonn.de
In a stunning townhouse a short walk west of the main train station, this hotel has bags of charm, thanks to its antique furniture and sumptuous wallpaper and carpets. The bright, lofty rooms have

sparkling renovated bathrooms. The welcoming owners speak good English.
€60–99
39 (4 non smoking)
Small private garage beneath hotel, €5 per night
Hauptbahnhof

ESSEN

HOTEL ESSENER HOF
Teichstrasse 2, 45127 Essen
Tel 0201 24250
www.essener-hof.com
A palatial hotel, opposite the main train station, that has been in the Bosse family since its foundation in 1883. It's

arranged around a quiet courtyard, and all the rooms have muted tones with tasteful, contemporary furniture. The snug restaurant serves a wide choice of beers and freshly cooked meals. The Moonlight Express Bar is laid out like an art deco railway carriage.
€135–180
130 rooms, 3 apartments
Hauptbahnhof

FRANKFURT-AM-MAIN

HOTEL MIRAMAR
Berliner Strasse 31, 60311 Frankfurt-am-Main
Tel 069 920 3970
www.miramar-frankfurt.de
The Miramar is within walking distance of the city's 'museum embankment', its central shopping precinct and its famous Sachsenhausen district. The four-star hotel is small but its rooms are comfortable.
€110–140 (prices double during trade fairs)
39
Nearby underground parking area, €18 per 24 hours
Römerberg

STAYING

KOBLENZ

HOTEL BRENNER

Rizzastrasse 20–22, 56068
Koblenz
Tel 0261 915780
www.hotel-brenner.de

The unprepossessing façade of this hotel belies its beautifully restored rococo interior, characterized by elaborately gilded furniture, delicately painted floral wall panels and crisp white linen. Owner Michaela Dietz speaks excellent English and is friendly, welcoming and very helpful. Most rooms are light, airy and spacious and are excellent value. It's just south of the Friedrich-Ebert-Ring, 10 minutes' walk from the heart of downtown Koblenz.

🛏 €71–92
ⓘ 24

HOTEL MERCURE

Julius Weleger Strasse 6, 56068
Koblenz
Tel 0261 1360
www.mercure.de

The imposing, ultramodern Mercure is a few minutes' walk from the middle of Koblenz

and Deutsches Eck (▷ 106). Cheerful rooms with all modern conveniences are complemented by a functional lobby bar and a small fitness room. The riverside location makes up for what the hotel lacks in charm and tradition.

🛏 €60–140
ⓘ 168
🍴
🇻 Sauna and gym

KÖLN

CITYCLASS HOTEL CAPRICE

Auf dem Rothenberg 7–9, 50667 Köln
Tel 0221 920540
www.cityclass.de

Despite its rather bland exterior, the Caprice offers understated luxury in the heart of Cologne's Altstadt. All rooms are simply but stylishly furnished, and have gleaming bathrooms, cable TV and a well-stocked mini-bar. There's a health area with a whirlpool, sauna and Jacuzzi. Try for a room overlooking the Eisenmarkt.

🛏 €60–100
ⓘ 53
🇻 Sauna, whirlpool and Jacuzzi
🚌 Bus/tram to Heumarkt

SPECIAL IN KÖLN

DAS KLEINE STAPELHÄUSCHEN

Fischmarkt 1–3, 50667 Köln
Tel 0221 257 7862
www.koeln-altstadt.de/
stapelhaeuschen

One of Köln's oldest and most romantic hotels. In the heart of the old town, it's full of wood-panelled walls, antique furniture and creaking floorboards. Many of the rooms have beamed ceilings, some come with enormous old baths, and one has the remains of a wooden wheel, up in the rafters, once part of a pulley system that hoisted goods up from the market below. The friendly owners run an intimate restaurant on the first floor, serving traditional dishes, such as pork knuckle with sauerkraut and potato.

🛏 €65–141
ⓘ 60 beds
🍴
🚌 Bus/tram to Heumarkt

MAINZ

HOTEL CENTRAL EDEN

Bahnhofplatz 8, 55116 Mainz
Tel 06131 2760
www.goldentulip.com

With an imposing neoclassical façade, this is a family-run hotel opposite the main train station. The reception hall, dining room and bar have brass fittings, marble pilasters

and polished mahogany furniture. The lofty, simply furnished rooms feel airy and spacious, as do the bathrooms, many of which have an old-fashioned bathtub. Breakfast is served in the beautifully restored 19th-century breakfast room, and the ground floor restaurant serves local and international dishes.

🛏 €105–150
ⓘ 60
🍴 🇻

RHEINTAL

BELLEVUE RHEINHOTEL

Rheinallee 41, 56154 Boppard
Tel 06742 1020
www.bellevue-boppard.de

The whitewashed Bellevue, with its steeply pitched gabled roof and first-floor balconies, has been looking after guests since 1887. One of the most elegant and inviting hotels on the Rhine, the rooms range from old-fashioned opulence to modern simplicity, as do its two restaurants (one with live piano music) and its wood-panelled bar. There's also a wine cellar for tastings and a new health spa with sauna, steam room and swimming pool.

🛏 €100–150, suite €204
ⓘ 92
🏊 Indoor 🇻 Sauna, steam bath and fitness room
🍴 Two restaurants 🇻 🇻
🚉 Boppard

MÜNSTER

HOTEL KAISERHOF
Bahnhofstrasse 14, 48143 Münster

Tel 0251 41780
www.kaiserhof-muenster.de
Opposite the city's main train station, the Hotel Kaiserhof makes for a memorable stay. Owners Peter and Anne Cremer have combined their unerring eye for design with meticulous attention to detail. The result is calming tones, clean lines and stylish contemporary design features.
€98–123
108
Sauna

SAABRÜCKEN
HOTEL AM TRILLER
Trillerweg 57, 66117 Saarbrücken
Tel 0681 580000
www.hotel-am-triller.de
This hotel is unique in Germany. The reception area isn't remarkable, but the rooms are: Many of them are themed, with design elements chosen to reflect (for example) the seasons, night sky or sea. More unusual are the art rooms, each dedicated to a European master. In addition to a copy of the artist's most famous work, these rooms also have a coffee-table book on the relevant artist. The highlight has to be the Moulin Rouge Suite (€270 per night), which is painted a dark, seductive red and has six different light settings and a large, luxury bathroom.
From €140
110 (60 non-smoking)
Sauna, solarium and gym

SOEST
HOTEL RESTAURANT 'IM WILDEN MANN'
Markt 11, 59494 Soest
Tel 02921 15071
www.im-wilden-mann.de
If it's tradition you're after, you can't go wrong with this half-timbered hotel in the heart of Soest. Some rooms are beamed, and they all have a rustic, romantic feel. The restaurant is equally atmospheric and serves traditional Westphalian dishes (such as

bratwurst with savoy cabbage and fried potatoes), plus snacks, cakes, coffees and cocktails. The themed menu changes every few weeks, and might offer anything from stewed reindeer (during 'Scandinavian Week') to Breton sole (during 'French Week').
€78–85
12

SPEYER
HOTEL AM TECHNIK MUSEUM
Am Technik Museum 1, 67346 Speyer
Tel 06232 67100
www.speyer.de
Although it doesn't look much more than a whitewashed concrete building from the outside, this hotel is surprisingly well appointed. The refurbished rooms are clean and comfortable, the young, helpful members of staff all speak excellent English, and the hotel is just a short walk from the middle of town, the cathedral and the Technology Museum. It is ideal for families, or for those on a budget.
From €75
108

HOTEL DOMHOF
Im Bauhof 3, 67346 Speyer
Tel 06232 13290
www.domhof.de
Almost next door to the beer hall of the same name (▷ 350), this is the most attractive hotel in Speyer thanks to its cobbled court-yard, summer terrace and medieval details. All the rooms are individual, and many have antique furniture and shutters on the windows. They also include modern amenities such as cable television, phone lines with internet access and mini-bars. The Domhof is close to the cathedral and Maximilianstrasse, but because it's so tucked away, it could easily be in the middle of nowhere. The combination of a room in the hotel with a meal at the Domhof Hausbrauerei is certainly hard to beat.
€106–122
50

TRIER
HOTEL PARK PLAZA TRIER
Nikolaus-Koch-Platz 1, 54290 Trier
Tel 0651 99930
www.parkplaza-trier.de
In the heart of Trier, this is a contemporary, stylish hotel. Clean lines and warm tones characterize the beautifully designed rooms, each of which has a replica of a Roman object unearthed in

the city. This Roman theme is continued in the carpets and prints that line the hotel corridors. The fourth floor has a sauna and steam room.
€116–126, excluding breakfast
148
Sauna and steam room

STAYING

BERLIN

The steadily increasing number of visitors to Berlin has brought with it rapid growth and investment in the city's hotel industry, mainly in the four- and five-star market. Good-quality mid-range and budget hotels tend to book up fast. There is an excellent selection of hostels, some with better facilities than some budget hotels. Most of the four- and five-star hotels, business hotels and chain hotels are concentrated around Mitte, the Kurfürstendamm and Savignyplatz, but you can get some good deals farther out. Berlin's public transportation system is efficient and extensive, so unless you are beyond the limits of the city and the S-Bahn you are unlikely to be more than a half-hour's journey away from anything you want to see. Budget hotels and hostels tend to be tucked away on side streets and require a bit of searching out, but they are never far from public transportation links.

The average price of a hotel room in Berlin is lower than in many other major European cities. Most hotels have a breakfast buffet, which can be a simple spread of *Kaffee und Schrippen* (coffee and rolls) with cheese and cold meats, or a bountiful feast of smoked meats, smoked salmon, muesli, fresh fruit and even cake. Breakfast is often not included in the price of a room in luxury and mid-range hotels, but is included in budget hotels and hostels. Some business hotels have less expensive weekend rates and discounts for longer stays. You can book hotels through the website www.berlin-tourist-information.de.

PRICES AND SYMBOLS

Prices are per night for two people sharing a double room. The prices include breakfast unless otherwise stated, but check when you make your reservation. Note that rates vary widely throughout the year.
For a key to the symbols, ▷ 2.

ALAMEDA-BERLIN

Michaelkirchstrasse 15, 10179 Berlin (Mitte)
Tel 030 3086 8330
www.alameda.de
Relax after sightseeing in this rooftop haven in the heart of the city. The light, spacious rooms, which take up a top-floor conversion, have sloping ceilings, arched windows, balconies and great views. The Alameda-Berlin is within walking distance of all the major sights around Mitte and close to regular transportation links. Internet access is provided.
🛏 €80–154
🛌 17
🚇 Jannowitzbrücke, Heinrich-Heine-Strasse
🚌 265, 240

ALEXANDER PLAZA

Rosentrasse 1, 10178 Berlin (Mitte)
Tel 030 240010
www.alexander-plaza.com
This is one of the few good mid-range hotels in the area of Hackescher Markt, so reserve in advance. You'll get an excellent standard of service and an impressive range of facilities, including a guest room that is modern and functional, with a stylish bathroom suite. The hotel has two restaurants: the

SPECIAL IN BERLIN
ADLON
Unter den Linden 77, 10117 Berlin (Mitte)
Tel 030 22 61 11 11
www.hotel-adlon.de
The original Hotel Adlon was opened in 1907 at a ceremony attended by Kaiser Wilhelm II.

It was one of the most luxurious hotels in the world. In May 1945 a fire demolished part of the hotel and in 1984 it was torn down. The current building, equally luxurious, opened in 1997. Its Gourmet Restaurant Lorenz Adlon (▷ 353) is one of the best in the city.
🛏 €290–600
🛌 337 (128 non-smoking)
🍴
🏊 🔲 Indoor 📺
🚇 Unter den Linden
🚌 100

à la carte Wintergarten Restaurant and the Lounge, which serves lighter meals and snacks. Bicycles can be rented.
🛏 €160–190
🛌 92 (16 non-smoking)
🍴
🏊 Indoor 📺
🅿 €15 per day
🚇 Alexanderplatz, Hackescher Markt
🚌 100, 157, 348

ANDECHSER HOF

Ackerstrasse 115, 10115 Berlin (Mitte)
Tel 030 2809 7844
www.andechserhof.de
The rooms at this affordable hotel near Alexanderplatz and Hakescker Markt are a little dated, but they are clean and spacious. Double and single rooms have a shower, toilet, fridge and television, and suites also have a kitchenette. Restaurant Kürbis serves traditional Austrian cuisine and a great selection of German beers and Austrian wines. The breakfast buffet has plenty to fill you up for the day, including Austrian treats and organic and healthy options.
🛏 €70–90
🛌 40
🍴
🚇 Nordbahnhof, Rosenthaler Platz
🚌 Bus 147, 328; tram 6, 8, 50

APARTMENTHAUS AGON AM ALEXANDERPLATZ

Mollstrasse 4, 10178 Berlin (Mitte)
Tel 030 275 7270
www.agon-alexanderplatz.de
This monolithic 1960s-style building is near Museumsinsel, the Berliner Dom and the Fernsehturm. Inside, the guest rooms are functional and have everything you will need

STAYING

for a comfortable stay, including bath or shower and toilet, television, fax and internet line. The suites also have a small kitchenette.

€69–139
150
P
Alexanderplatz
100, 142, 200, 257, 340

ARTEMISIA–DAS FRAUENHOTEL

Brandenburgische Strasse 18, 10707 Berlin (Wilmersdorf)
Tel 030 873 8905
www.frauenhotel-berlin.de
This was the first hotel in Germany to cater exclusively for women and it still accepts only female guests. It lies within easy reach of the Kurfürstendamm. It is on the third, fourth and fifth floors of a renovated building accessed by an elevator. Changing exhibitions of paintings by female artists decorate the rooms and halls. Two of the modern, light and bright rooms have shared bathroom facilities, but the rest have their own shower and toilet.
During the summer you can have breakfast outside on the sun deck.

€82–104
12
P
Konstanzer Strasse
101, 109, 104

ART OTEL BERLIN MITTE

Wallstrasse 70–73, 10179 Berlin (Mitte)
Tel 030 240620
www.artotel.de
Primary shades and contemporary design leave a lasting impression at this ultramodern art hotel in Mitte, which attracts both business guests and independent visitors. The modern art on display throughout the hotel is by the German artist Georg Baselitz (1933–), who also has works in the Deutsche Guggenheim

in Berlin and the Museum of Modern Art in New York. Choose from a red, green, blue or purple room, all with modern furnishings, television, internet lines and a sparkling white bathroom. The suites also have a kitchenette, are spacious and have plenty of storage. The Factory Restaurant, in the covered courtyard and decorated with pop art, serves international cuisine; its breakfast buffet is open throughout the morning, and includes bacon, mushrooms, eggs, cold meats, cheeses, smoked salmon, fresh breads, fresh fruit, yoghurts, muesli and a cake of the day.

€130–260
109
🍴
🔊
Märkisches Museum, Jannowitzbrücke
240, 256

ARTIST RIVERSIDE HOTEL AND SPA

Friedrichstrasse 106, 10117 Berlin (Mitte)
Tel 030 284900
www.tolles-hotel.de
All the rooms in this small, romantic artists' hotel on the bank of the River Spree have been individually designed and beautifully decorated with antique furnishings, mirrors and chandeliers. The honeymoon suite—not just for

newlyweds—has a waterbed, a whirlpool bath and a fantastic view over the river. The hotel gives discount rates to creative guests such as artists, film production companies and designers.

€100–200
28
Day spa
Friedrichstrasse
Bus 100, 157, TXL, tram: 1, 6, 13, 50

BERLINER CITY-PENSION

Proskauer Strasse 13, 10247 Berlin (Friedrichshain)
Tel 030 4208 1615
www.berliner-city-pension.de
The rooms in this renovated budget hotel, close to Mitte and Alexander Platz, are very clean, airy and light, and have high ceilings and large windows. The furnishings are a little sparse, but they are practical and the odd plant is scattered around for company. Rooms come with a shower and toilet, or you can take one that is less expensive and share facilities.

€40–52, excluding breakfast
22
Frankfurter Allee, Storkower Strasse, Samariterstrasse, Frankfurter Tor
Tram 21

BOARDING HOUSE MITTE

Mulackstrasse 1, 10119 Berlin (Mitte)
Tel 030 2838 8488
www.boarding-house-berlin.de
These modern apartments are ideal for those planning a longer stay in the capital. They are within easy reach of all the major attractions in the historical heart of the city, and there are plenty of restaurants, cafés and bars nearby. Choose from studios, apartments with separate living and sleeping areas, or maisonettes spread over two floors. All have a fully equipped kitchen with dishwasher and fridge, plus a living area with television, video recorder, telephone and internet access. Apartments are cleaned once a week; there is a shopping, ironing and washing-up service and bicycle and video rental are available. A daily breakfast of coffee, tea and pastries is also included.

€87–135
Hackescher Markt, Rosa-Luxemburg-Platz, Weinmeisterstrasse
Bus 100; tram 1, 2, 3, 15

BOULEVARD

Kurfürstendamm 12, 10719
Berlin (Charlottenburg)
Tel 030 884250
www.berlin.the-hotels.com/best-
western-boulevard.htm

This Best Western hotel offers
excellent service, clean and
spacious rooms and a
convenient location—just off
the Kurfürstendamm and close
to the action, making it great
value for money. The hotel's
main selling point is its rooftop
café terrace, a great spot for
relaxing and admiring the view
on a summer's evening.

€157–168
57

Zoologischer Garten,
Kurfürstendamm
109, 129, 219

CIRCUS

Weinbergsweg 1a, 10119
Berlin (Mitte)
Tel 030 2839 1433
www.circus-berlin.de

Choose from a dormitory bed
or a two- or four-bedroom
apartment with private
bathroom at this popular,
well-maintained hostel close
to the sights, restaurants and

nightlife of Mitte. Some rooms
even have a rooftop terrace
and their own kitchen. The
rooms are clean, functional
and bright. There is another
Circus hotel in Mitte, at
Rosa-Luxemburg-Strasse 39.

Dormitories €15–20, doubles
€48–75, excluding breakfast
180 beds
Rosenthaler Platz

CITY HOSTEL BERLIN

Meininger Strasse 10, 10823 Berlin
(Schöneberg)
Tel 030 666 36100
www.meininger-hostels.de

You don't have to rough it if
you are on a budget in Berlin.
City Hostels are the best-value
modern and stylish hostels in
the city. The one-, two-, three-,
four- and five-bed rooms or
dormitories have, bright,
co-ordinated furnishings and
are very clean. All rooms have
their own shower and toilet.
An all-you-can-eat breakfast is
included in the price; there is a
bar, internet access and table
football. Weekly film screenings are put on for guests. The
staff at the 24-hour reception
desk are very friendly and
knowledgeable, and there is
no curfew. There are two other
City Hostels in Berlin, in
Tiergarten at Hallesches Ufer
30 and at Tempelhofer Ufer 10.

Dormitories €12.50–26, double
room €23–49
48 rooms

Rathaus Schöneberg

CROWNE PLAZA HOTEL

Nürnberger Strasse 65, 10787
Berlin (Schöneberg)
Tel 030 210070
www.berlin-citycentre.crowneplaza.com
/bercc/index.shtml

Rooms here have cable
television, a video recorder,
telephone, internet and fax
line, voicemail and a mini-bar.
The restaurant, Wilson's, serves
international and regional
cuisine, and one of the best
breakfast buffets in the city.
The snug on-site pub, Pinte,
serves local and regional
dishes such as *Boulette* (Berlin
meatballs), as well as German
beer on tap. Kemmons Bar has
an extensive cocktail menu, or
you can relax in the Lobby
Lounge. Garage and outdoor
parking are available for a fee.

€195–355
423

Indoor

Zoologischer Garten
100, 119, 129, 146, 185

DERAG GROSSER KURFÜRST

Neue Rosstrasse 111–112, 10179
Berlin (Mitte)
Tel 030 2460 0900
www.deraghotels.de

Choose from a stylish room, a
fully furnished apartment with
kitchenette, or an exclusive
suite at this modern four-star
hotel on the river, close to
Museumsinsel. All have a
bathroom, internet access and
satellite television. Restaurant
Fischerinsel has a terrace.
Bicycle rental is available.

€175–240
53

Märkisches Museum,
Jannowitzbrücke
147

DORINT AM GENDARMENMARKT

Charlottenstrasse 50–52, 10117
Berlin (Mitte)
Tel 030 203750
www.dorint.de/berlin-gendarmenmarkt

The rooms in this exclusive
hotel are contemporary in
style, with an emphasis on
dark marble and frosted glass.
Extra touches include a pull-
cord lullaby music box built
into every headboard.
Don't miss the views of the
Gendarmenmarkt from
the fifth floor. The glitzy

Delphinium function room is
often used for film award
ceremonies. The 1920s café-
restaurant was transported
from Vienna piece by piece;
its traditional Austrian and
international menu attracts
politicians and diplomats from
the nearby government district.

€245–300
92

Stadtmitte, Französische Strasse
100, 148, 157

GENDARM

Charlottenstrasse 61, 10117
Berlin (Mitte)
Tel 030 206 0660
www.hotel-gendarm-berlin.de

If you want to be close to the Gendarmenmarkt, the most beautiful square in Berlin, this four-star hotel is a good-value option. It may be a little chintzy for modern tastes, but co-ordinating blue-, white- and yellow-striped classic fabrics give the rooms a regal edge, and the white bathrooms are clean and functional. You can rent bicycles here.

€119–199
30
Sauna and solarium
Stadtmitte

GRAND HOTEL ESPLANADE

Lützowufer 15, 10785 Berlin
(Tiergarten)
Tel 030 254780
www.esplanade.de

This is an exclusive choice for those who want the comforts and services of a luxury hotel. The suites and rooms are stylishly decorated with contemporary furnishings. The hotel has a huge reception area with a water wall where Restaurant Piazza serves Mediterranean food in bright, open surroundings. The gourmet Harlekin restaurant is very popular. There are two bars: Harry's New York Bar, one of the best in Berlin, attracts a chic crowd; and the Eck-Kneipe, a traditional Berlin pub, has a great selection of German beers.

€195–305
386
Indoor
P
Nollerndorfplatz
100, 129, 187, 341, X9

GRAND HYATT

Marlene-Dietrich-Platz 2, 10785
Berlin (Tiergarten)
Tel 030 2553 1234
www.berlin.grand.hyatt.com

José Raphael Moneo, the Pritzker Prize-winning Spanish architect, designed this luxury hotel, which was built in the late 1990s. It is opposite the casino, musical theatre and Imax cinema, and has played a key part in the redevelopment of Potsdamer Platz. There are two restaurants—the intimate

Tizian Italian Restaurant and Lounge and the Vox Restaurant, where the chefs prepare meals in full view of diners. The Club Olympus Fitness Centre and Spa is on the roof.

€230–350
344
Indoor
Potsdamer Platz
148, 341, 348, 129

HILTON

Mohrenstrasse 30, 10117 Berlin (Mitte)
Tel 030 2023 4255
www.hilton.de

Next to Stadtmitte U-Bahn station and overlooking the historic Gendarmenmarkt square, this popular hotel oozes stylish elegance. Art nouveau touches, dark wood,

stained glass, classic lighting and a waterfall surrounded by tropical palms create a lasting impression in the marble atrium. The waterfall is flanked by two wide staircases, leading up to the dining areas and guest rooms. This is one of the few hotels in the heart of Berlin to have an indoor pool, and it also has good fitness facilities. All rooms have internet access and television.

€199–325
589
Indoor
P
Stadtmitte

HONIGMOND GARDEN HOTEL

Invalidenstrasse 122, 10115
Berlin (Mitte)
Tel 030 2844 5577
www.honigmond-berlin.de

The main attraction of this small family hotel in the heart of the Scheunenviertel is its beautiful garden and intimate surroundings. Here, you can sit outside during the summer

under the umbrellas and palms. The owners provide excellent service, and also run a smaller, less expensive hotel above their restaurant and café on nearby Tieckstrasse.

€109–159
9 (all non-smoking)
Nordbahnhof
Tram 8, 50

HOTEL MIT-MENSCH

Ehrlichstrasse 48, 10318
Berlin (Mitte)
Tel 030 509 6930
www.mit-mensch.com

This hotel has been designed to accommodate people with disabilities. Information is provided in Braille, seven of the 15 modern and function-ally furnished rooms are wheelchair-accessible and all have a television and telephone. The bathrooms are also fully adapted for wheel-chair users, with a movable shower stool and handles on the shower and around the toilet. The comfortable common room has internet access and there is also a games room. A shuttle service operates to and from the airport or train station and sightseeing tours are in buses adapted for wheelchairs.

€72–93
15
P
Karlshorst
Bus 196, tram 21

STAYING

HOTEL AM ZOO

Kurfürstendamm 25, 10719 Berlin
(Charlottenburg)
Tel 030 884370
www.hotel-am-zoo.de
This building dates back to the
turn of the 20th century. Some
rooms have a great view of the
Kurfürstendamm shopping and
entertainment district, but all
are quiet and comfortable,
with telephone, fax line, radio,
television, safe, mini-bar and
hairdryer. The hotel also has
conference rooms. The parking
areas can be accessed through
the hotel.

€174–255
136

Zoologischer Garten,
Kurfürstendamm
119, 129, 149, 219, X9

INTERMEZZO—HOTEL FÜR FRAUEN

Gertrud-Kolmar-Strasse 5, 10117
Berlin (Mitte)
Tel 030 2248 9096
www.hotelintermezzo.de
This small, down-to-earth bed-
and-breakfast is for women
only, and is a short walk from
Friedrichstrasse and Unter den
Linden. The rooms are simply
furnished with pine beds,
tables and chairs, and each
has a shower room.

€68–78, excluding breakfast
17
Potsdamer Platz, Mohrenstrasse
200, 348, TXL

KÜNSTLERHEIM LUISE

Luisenstrasse 19, 10117
Berlin (Mitte)
Tel 030 284480
www.kuenstlerheim-luise.de
Different well-known artists
have designed each room in
this hotel for art buffs. The
hotel was built in 1825 as
a city palace, and is only a
few minutes' walk from
Friedrichstrasse, Unter den
Linden and the Brandenburger
Tor. The lobby is filled with
sculptures, the large hall is
often used for exhibitions
and events, and philosophical
maxims decorate the main
stairwell. The restaurant,
Wein Guy, serves up ambitious
and creative German cuisine
and has an excellent selection
of fine wines.

€124–135
32

Friedrichstrasse
Bus 147, TXL; tram 1, 50

LETTE'M SLEEP HOSTEL

Lettestrasse 7, 10437 Berlin
(Prenzlauer Berg)
Tel 030 4473 3623
www.backpackers.de
This relaxed backpacker hostel
in Prenzlauer Berg attracts a
friendly crowd of guests.
Coffee, tea and internet access
are all free, and a 10 per cent
discount is given to those who
stay more than four nights.
In addition, there is a beer
garden in the summer, a
basketball court and table
tennis. All rooms have hand
basins, and you are guaranteed to get a hot shower at any
time of the day. There is no
curfew, and the multilingual
staff (on hand 24 hours) are
pleased to volunteer local
knowledge and help you get
your bearings in the capital.

Dormitories €15–19, double room
€22–33
46 beds, 10 rooms
Prenzlauer Allee, Schönhauser Allee

MEINEKE ARTE

Meinekestrasse 10, 10719 Berlin
(Charlottenburg)
Tel 030 889 2120
The staff are extremely friendly
at this wonderfully quirky and
relaxed old hotel filled with
modern collages and paintings
by Austrian artist Günter
Ecllinger. The original elevator
was built in 1899 and is still
running. The spacious rooms
in the restored building have
high ceilings and are decorated in an odd mixture of old

and new. There are bigger
family rooms, as well as off-
street parking. The hotel is
very quiet despite being just
off the Kurfürstendamm. It is a
particularly popular choice
around the time of the Berlin

MADISON

Potsdamerstrasse 3, 10785 Berlin
(Tiergarten)
Tel 030 5900 50000
www.madison-berlin.de
A waterfall cascading behind
frosted glass greets you as
you walk into this contemporary hotel. The grey,
brown and black minimalist
furnishings and marble-
topped tables in the bar are
lifted by slowly changing
red, blue, yellow and green
lighting. The rooms sit
around a quadrangle, with
balconies overlooking the
bamboo garden and the
conservatory that houses the
renowned restaurant Facil
(▷ 353). Each suite has
dark green fabrics, cherry
wood and furniture by US

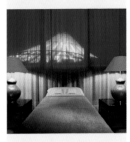

designer Donghia. The hotel
prides itself on its discreet,
quality service—for example,
your cleaner will arrange a
meeting when you arrive to
discuss your requirements
and the best time to clean
your room. This personal
approach makes the hotel
popular with celebrities. The
health suite has a full-time
masseur and the gym has
the latest equipment and a
great view over the rooftops
of Potsdamer Platz.

€190–515
166

Potsdamer Platz
100

Love Parade (▷ 265), when
you will need to book ahead.

€140–169
60

Kurfürstendamm
109, 119, 129, 204, 219, 249

STAYING

MONDIAL

Kurfürstendamm 47, 10707 Berlin
(Charlottenburg)
Tel 030 884110
www.hotel-mondial.com

Mirrors, plush red leather
chairs, chandeliers and glass
coffee tables give an air of
sophistication to the lobby of
this four-star hotel, off the
Kurfürstendamm. The large,
elegant guest rooms have a
contemporary feel, while the
restaurant is reasonably priced
and serves traditional German
cuisine, international dishes
and bistro fare. This is one of
the few hotels in the heart of
the city that cater to wheelchair users: All public areas
are accessible, and some bedrooms are designed to assist
visitors who have a disability.

🛏 €140–245
ⓘ 75
🍴
🏊 Indoor 🛗
🚇 Savignyplatz, Adenauerplatz,
Uhlandstrasse
🚌 109, 110, 119, 129, 219

NH BERLIN-MITTE

Leipziger Strasse 106–111,
10117 Berlin (Mitte)
Tel 030 203760
www.nh-hotels.com

The four-star NH Berlin-Mitte
is close to all the major sights
of Mitte. The rooms in this
business hotel are tastefully
decorated, and have large
bathrooms, satellite television

and internet connection. You
can admire the view of the
city from the roof terrace. The
restaurant serves international,
local and seasonal dishes and
has a well-stocked wine cellar.

🛏 €149–259
ⓘ 392
🍴
🔲 🛗
🅿
🚇 Potsdamer Platz, Stadtmitte
🚌 100, 108, TXL

PALACE BERLIN

Budapester Strasse 45, 10787 Berlin
(Charlottenburg)
Tel 030 25020
www.palace.de

Built in the late 1960s, the
Palace Berlin is close to
amenities and public transportation. No two rooms

are the same: You can choose
between an emerald-green
twin-bedded room, a
burgundy-red deluxe double
or a blue and gold corner
suite with a bathroom in
marble or granite. There are
two restaurants and a bar,
plus a health suite.

🛏 €200–335
ⓘ 282
🔲 🏊 Indoor 🛗
🚇 Zoologischer Garten,
Kurfürstendamm
🚌 100, 119, 129, 219

PARK INN

Alexanderplatz, 10178 Berlin (Mitte)
Tel 030 23890
www.parkinn.com

This towering hotel on
Alexanderplatz is a city
landmark. Owned by the Park
Inn group, the functional
business hotel is the largest
such establishment in the
heart of the city. All the rooms
have internet access, and there
are three restaurants, two
bars, a beer garden and the
Panorama Salon on the 37th
floor, with a casino and views
across Berlin.

🛏 €89–185
ⓘ 1,006 rooms, plus 12 suites
🍴 🛗
🔲 🛗
🅿
🚇 Alexanderplatz
🚌 148

PEGASUS HOSTEL

Strasse der Pariser Kommune 35, 10243
Berlin (Friedrichshain)
Tel 030 297 7360
www.pegasushostel.de

This hostel has a lot on offer:
a garden, excellent cooking
facilities, apartments and the
choice of private or shared
showers. Formerly a school
founded in 1903, it has a
beautiful courtyard, where you
can relax or enjoy a barbeque.
Rooms are bright, comfortable
and quiet. The members of
staff are very friendly and are
happy to answer questions
about Berlin and throw in a
few insider tips. The hostel is
close to bus and tram links.

🛏 €23–40, excluding breakfast
ⓘ 25
🚇 Ostbahnhof, Weberwiese
🚌 340

PENSION SAVOY

Meinekestrasse 4, 10719 Berlin
(Charlottenburg)
Tel 030 8847 1610
www.hotel-pension-savoy

The Pension Savoy is in
the west of the city off the
Kurfürstendamm, and is only
a short walk away from the
famous KaDeWe department
store (▷ 259). It is also within
walking distance of the Kaiser
Wilhelm Gedächtniskirche and
the city's zoo and aquarium,
and is right beside a U-Bahn
and S-Bahn station and a bus
stop, making it an ideal base
from which to explore the city.
An impressive entrance hall
with baroque-style columns
and a marble floor greets you
as you enter this friendly
guesthouse. The furnishings
have a predominantly floral
theme and the rooms are
clean and comfortable. Each
of the 20 guest rooms has
modern amenities such as
cable television, telephone,
hairdryer and safety deposit
box, as well as a bathroom
with bath or shower. Bicycles
are available to rent.

🛏 €105–149
ⓘ 15
🅿

🚇 Kurfürstendamm, Zoologischer Garten

🚌 109, 119, 129, 219

PROPELLER ISLAND CITY LODGE

Albrecht-Achilles-Strasse 58,
10709 Berlin (Mitte)
Tel 030 891 9016
www.propeller-island.de

The owner of this fantastic hotel, artist Lars Stroschen, has designed every room according to a different theme. Stay in the futuristic Space Cube; The Table, where you climb up to your table-top bed; Upside Down, with furniture stuck on the ceiling, or Grandma's, a reconstruction of a traditional wooden house. Symbol Zimmer (Symbol Room) is painted white and covered in different black symbols; although it is eye-catching and busy in the extreme, it may actually give you nightmares! All the furnishings are original hand-made pieces and some rooms also contain sound sculptures. This really is a unique guest-house and staying here is an experience you are unlikely to forget.

💶 €79–180 (per person; each extra person in a room costs €15 extra per night)

🛏 18

🚇 Charlottenburg, Adenauer Platz

🚌 110, 119, 129

SWISSÔTEL KURFÜRSTENDAMM

Augsburger Strasse 44,
10789 Berlin (Charlottenburg)
Tel 030 220100
www.swissotel.de

The Swissôtel is great for business visitors or for those planning a luxury weekend in the capital. Everything runs like clockwork and it is clear that a

great deal of attention is paid to every detail. The friendly staff are eager to please and

you are guaranteed to receive impeccable service during your stay. The minimalist, oriental-style wood-and-glass interior is clean and contemporary, while sculptures and paintings by the Austrian artist Luepertz (1941–) decorate the corridors and foyers. Guest are welcome to use the fitness suite, with its gym, sauna, solarium and monsoon showers. Rooms between the seventh and tenth floors have good views of the Kaiser Wilhelm Gedächtniskirche and the Tiergarten (▷ 148–149), with the Reichstag, Berliner Dom and Alexanderplatz in the distance. The suites are very spacious, and have internet and email access integrated into the digital television units. The hotel's Restaurant 44 serves a mixture of classic European and Asian cuisine, as well as a few experimental combinations.

💶 €180–270

🛏 316

🍴

🔲 🔳

🚇 Zoologischer Garten

🚌 X9, 119, 129, 149, 219

TRANSIT LOFT

Greifswalder Strasse 219,
10405 Berlin (Prenzlauer Berg)
Tel 030 4849 3773
www.hotel-transit.de

A factory in the 19th century, this modern yellow-brick building with a glass tower at the front has recently been converted into a budget hotel. It is near Kollwitzplatz, and

close to, but not on top of, the restaurants, cafés, pubs, bars, cinema and cabaret venues of Prenzlauer Berg. The hotel's five floors are filled with bright, clean and functional furnish-ings, and all the rooms have their own shower and toilet. The staff are very friendly and helpful, and are happy to

accommodate the needs of groups and families with children. Breakfast is included and parking is available.

💶 €69–72

🛏 47

🅿

🚇 Alexanderplatz

🚋 Tram 2, 3, 4

UNTER DEN LINDEN

Unter den Linden 14,
10177, Berlin (Mitte)
Tel 030 238110
www.hotel-unter-den-linden.de

This affordable, functional hotel is in a prime location on Unter den Linden, close to all

the major sights in Mitte and the shops, restaurants and bars of Friedrichstrasse. The rooms are neutral and functional in design, and all have their own bathroom with shower or bath and toilet. The hotel caters for both business visitors and holidaymakers, and all rooms have internet access. There is ample undercover parking.

💶 €86–163

🛏 331

🅿

🚇 Friedrichstrasse

🚌 100, 147, 157, 348

STAYING

EASTERN GERMANY

The process of modernizing and adding to the run-down hotel infrastructure of the GDR is now more-or-less complete, and the range and standard of accommodation here are now much the same as in the rest of Germany. Among the outstanding finds in the area are the Crown Prince Wilhem's mock-Tudor country house near the lakeside in Potsdam, Weimar's venerable Hotel Elephant and the baroque palace in Dresden that now houses the Kempinski. Elsewhere, it can be a real delight to find a small hotel that seems to capture the spirit of your destination. Such an experience awaits you in establishments like the Tuchmacher Renaissance town mansion in Görlitz or the Theophano in Quedlinburg, lovingly stitched together out of several ancient timber-framed houses by an enterprising family.

PRICES AND SYMBOLS
Prices are per night for two people sharing a double room. The prices include breakfast unless otherwise stated, but check when you make your reservation. Note that rates vary widely throughout the year.
For a key to the symbols, ▷ 2.

BAUTZEN

SPREE-HOTEL
An den Steinbrüchen 9, 02625 Bautzen
Tel 03591 21300
www.spreehotel.de
This convenient, modern, four-star hotel enjoys a quiet location on the banks of a reservoir. It is only a few minutes' drive from town, and has pleasant, functional rooms, a restaurant with regional cuisine and a café-bar.
€72–82
81

TRADITIONSHOTEL 'GOLDENER ADLER'
Hauptmarkt 4, 02625 Bautzen
Tel 035 914 8660
www.goldeneradler.de
With its flower-bedecked façade and steep dormer-pierced roof, this 450-year-old, four-star hotel has all the character you'd expect. But while the granite vaults of the wine cellar evoke the past, the bedrooms are fully up to date. Saxon and international dishes are served in the restaurant.
€97–120
30

COLDITZ

CAMPINGPLATZ
Am Waldbad 5, 04680 Colditz
Tel 034381 43122, 034381 40313
www.colditz.de/camping
Halfway between Dresden and Leipzig, Colditz is well situated for exploring central Saxony.

The campsite has an enviable location on the edge of the castle's former game park, near the town's heated outdoor swimming pool. There are plenty of facilities, plus chalets and caravans for rent.
Bungalow (for 5): €26
5 bungalows
Bistro

DESSAU-WÖRLITZ

LANDHAUS WÖRLITZER HOF
Markt 96, 06786 Wörlitz
Tel 034905 4110
www.woerlitzer-hof.de
Absorb the delights of the Dessau-Wörlitz region by basing yourself at this attractive country hotel, right by the Schlossgarten in Wörlitz. The hotel's restaurant serves local dishes and stages themed

evenings; complete meals here start at €19, with bottles of wine from €18.
€97–132
33 standard rooms, 14 superior suites

DRESDEN

HOTEL MARTHA HOSPIZ
Nieritzstrasse 11, 01097 Dresden
Tel 0351 81760
www.marthahospiz.dresden.vch.de
This mid-range hotel belongs to the reliable Christian Hoteliers chain. The dignified 100-year-old building occupies a quiet position in Dresden's attractive Neustadt. The 15-minute walk to the heart of the city on the far bank of the Elbe is an experience in itself. Saxon dishes are served in the rustic Zum Kartoffelkeller restaurant.
€102–118
50
Tram 4, 8, 49 to Palaisplatz

HOTEL SCHLOSS ECKBERG
Bautzner Strasse 134, 01099 Dresden
Tel 0351 80990
www.schloss-eckberg.de
Completed in 1861 on the heights overlooking the Elbe, this wonderful neo-Gothic stronghold has been transformed into one of Dresden's outstanding hotels. The castle has few rooms, but these are the ones to choose—for their clever combination of modern and antique furnishings, and for the river view. The extension has rooms with views over the castle's parkland. There is an excellent restaurant and a cellar with Saxon wines.
Castle: €235–298; Kavaliershaus (extension): €135–180
Castle: 17 rooms/suites; Kavaliershaus: 67 rooms/suites
Tram 11 to Schloss Albrechtsberg

STAYING

IBIS

Prager Strasse, 01069 Dresden
Tel 0351 485 6442
www.ibishotels.com
The three high-rises on Prager Strasse shopping esplanade (the Bastei, the Lilienstein and the Königstein) may look bleak, but they offer convenience and comfort. The location is central, but quiet. The Bastei is slightly more expensive.

🖐 €65–74
ⓘ 306
🔣
🅿 Unsupervised
🚋 Tram 3, 7, 8, 9, 10, 11 to Hauptbahnhof Nord

KEMPINSKI HOTEL TASCHENBERGPALAIS DRESDEN

Taschenberg 3, 01067 Dresden
Tel 0351 49120
www.kempinski-dresden.de
This superb palace, built for Augustus the Strong (1670–1733), has been rebuilt with exquisite taste and converted into a luxurious hotel.
🖐 From €285
ⓘ 214 (including 32 luxury suites)
🔣 🏊 Indoor
🅿 Garage
🚋 Tram 1, 2, 4, 6, 8, 11, 12, 49 to Postplatz

MERCURE NEWA DRESDEN

St. Petersburgerstrasse 34, 01069 Dresden
Tel 0351 48140
www.mercure.com
This skyscraper overlooking the Prager Strasse shopping mall

dates from GDR times, but its interior has been transformed with generous public areas and tasteful bedrooms.
🖐 €135–165
ⓘ 319 (169 non-smoking)
🔣
🅿 Garage
🚋 Tram 3, 7, 8, 9, 10, 11 to Hauptbahnhof Nord

EISENACH

BERGHOTEL

An der Göpelskuppe 1, 99817 Eisenach
Tel 03691 22660
www.berghotel-eisenach.de
The comfortable, small and friendly Berghotel has a fabulous position high above the town, just below the Burschenschaftsdenkmal

(Fraternities Memorial). From here you have views over the foothills of the Thuringian Forest to Wartburg castle.
🖐 €85–125
ⓘ 16
🅿

HOTEL AUF DER WARTBURG

99817 Eisenach
Tel 03691 7970
www.wartburghotel.de
This luxury hotel nestles just below the walls of Wartburg castle, with some stunning

views to the Thuringian Forest. Rooms are snug and the service is refined. The restaurant serves Thuringian fare.
🖐 €200–320
ⓘ 35
🅿 🍴

ERFURT

HOTEL UND GASTHOF NIKOLAI

Augustinerstrasse 30, 99084 Erfurt
Tel 0361 598170
www.hotel-nikolai-erfurt.com

Attractively decorated and stylish, this historic building is in the heart of old Erfurt, not far from the famous Krämerbrücke. It has a romantic atmosphere, friendly staff on reception, a brasserie, a small restaurant and an outdoor terrace.
🖐 €84–90 (€110 suite)
ⓘ 17 rooms, 1 suite
🍴
🅿

FREIBERG

HOTEL ALEKTO

Am Bahnhof 3, 09599 Freiberg
Tel 03731 7940
www.alekto.de
In this old mining and industrial town, why not stay in a former factory? The Alekto once turned out cutlery, but the art nouveau building close to the train station is now a hotel with plenty of facilities. There is a bar and a restaurant with meals at very reasonable prices.
🖐 €70–90
ⓘ 52
🍴 🔣
🅿

GÖRLITZ

ROMANTIK HOTEL TUCHMACHER

Peterstrasse 8, 02826 Görlitz
Tel 03581 47310
www.tuchmacher.de
One of the Romantik group of individually run hotels, the Tuchmacher occupies one of the finest buildings in Görlitz, a Renaissance town mansion built in 1528 for the then mayor, the immensely rich Franz Schneider. Carefully restored, the building has

STAYING

period details, including late-Gothic vaulting otherwise found only in Prague. The restaurant serves refined versions of the cuisine of Silesia.

€109–125

42

GOTHA

HOTEL AM SCHLOSSPARK

Lindenauallee 20, Gotha 99867
Tel 03621 4420
www.hotel-am-schlosspark.de
Just above the old town and with direct access to spacious parkland, this four-star hotel

has friendly service and comfortable, contemporary rooms. There is a choice of two restaurants, and the use of a Roman-style spa is included in the price of the room.

€72

95

HALLE

MARTHA HAUS

Adam-Kuckhoff-Strasse 5–8, 06108 Halle
Tel 0345 51080
www.marthahaus.halle.vch.de
A member of the reliable VCH (Christian Hotels Association) chain, the Martha Haus is a carefully modernized baroque mansion in a quiet side street in the middle of the city.

€95

24

HARZ-ILSENBURG

LANDHAUS ZU DEN ROTEN FORELLEN

Marktplatz 2, 38871 Ilsenburg
Tel 039452 9393
Ilsenburg is one of the smaller resorts of the Harz, and this country hotel in one of its most attractive buildings offers a luxurious, peaceful stay on the edge of the mountains. Rooms either face onto the mountains or overlook a little lake. Every comfort is provided, and after hiking in the hills you will be glad to relax in the sauna or in the lavish pool area. The hotel also has a gourmet restaurant and its own pâtisserie.

€170

52

Indoor

HARZ-WERNIGERODE

TRAVEL CHARME HOTEL GOTHISCHES HAUS

Marktplatz 2, 38855 Wernigerode
Tel 03943 6750
www.tc-hotels.de
To stay here is like stepping back in time: The venerable 15th-century timber-framed building overlooks the main square in the most attractive town in the Harz, right next

door to one of Germany's most picturesque medieval town halls. The rooms have been beautifully restored and furnished. There is a fully equipped spa with a range of beauty treatments, plus a piano bar, wine cellar and restaurant.

From €168

116

JENA

SCHWARZER BÄR

Lutherplatz 2, 07743 Jena
Tel 03641 4060
www.schwarzer-baer-jena.de
The names of those who have lodged within these walls range from Protestant reformer Martin Luther (1483–1546) and dramatist Johann Wolfgang von Goethe (1749–1832) to the celebrities and politicians of today. The hotel's restaurant prides itself on its cusine and its range of wines (including rarities from around Jena) and beers.

€50–90

66

Garage

LEIPZIG

AM RATSHOLZ

Anton-Zickmantel-Strasse 44, 04249 Leipzig
Tel 0341 494 4500
www.am-ratsholz-leipzig.de
This attractive hotel is on a direct tram route to the downtown area. Fresh, light furnishings contribute to the welcoming atmosphere. There is a choice of rooms, or stay in one of the apartments, which have kitchenettes. There is also a family-style restaurant.

€69, excluding breakfast

113

Tram 3 to Kunzestrasse or Huttenstrasse

BEST WESTERN PREMIER VICTOR'S RESIDENZ-HOTEL

Georgiring 13, 04103 Leipzig
Tel 0341 68660
www.victors-leipzig.bestwestern.de
Close to the middle of the city, this comprehensively renovated four-star establishment offers its guests every comfort, plus a choice of places to eat—including a beer garden.

€110–190

101 (42 non-smoking)

Hauptbahnhof

HOTEL FÜRSTENHOF LEIPZIG

Tröndlinring 8, 04105 Leipzig
Tel 0341 1400
An extremely luxurious,
central hotel that occupies
an 18th-century house. The
Serpentine Salon is a princely

setting for formal dining.
Other special features of the
hotel include a lavish,
Mediterranean-style pool
and a wine cellar.
🏷 €150–305
🛏 92
🍽 🍷
♿ 🏊 Indoor
🅿
🚇 Hauptbahnhof

LINDNER HOTEL LEIPZIG

Hans-Driesch-Strasse 27, 04179 Leipzig
Tel 0341 44780
www.lindner.de
This four-star establishment is
on the edge of the Auenwald,
the meadowland that is a

feature of Leipzig. Peace is one
of the hotel's draws, its distinctive architecture another. It is
particularly popular with business people, and has a choice
of rooms and suites, or apartments for longer stays. The Am
Wasserschloss serves
Mediterranean-style meals.
🏷 €86–130
🛏 200
🍽
🍷
🚇 S-Bahn to Leutzsch (10-minute
walk)

MAGDEBURG

HERRENKRUG PARKHOTEL

Herrenkrug 3, 39114 Magdeburg
Tel 0391 85080
www.herrenkrug.de
The English-style park here is a
lovely setting for this complex,

which features *Jugendstil*
interiors as well as modern
extensions. Most of the
spacious, comfortable bedrooms overlook the park.
Sample fine cuisine in the airy
19th-century dining room, in
the winter garden or in the
beer garden.
🏷 €78–164
🛏 147
🍽
🏊 Indoor
🅿
🚊 Tram 6

RESIDENZ JOOP

Jean-Burger-Strasse 16, 39112
Magdeburg
Tel 0391 62620
www.residenzjoop.de
In a quiet, leafy district, this
100-year-old villa is within
walking distance of downtown
has been turned into a stylish
hotel by the descendants of its
original resident, Magdeburg's
Swedish consul. A *hotel garni*
(it has no restaurant, but
serves drinks and snacks), it
has regularly been voted into
Germany's top ten in this class
of hotel.
🏷 €82–154
🛏 25
🅿 Garage
🚊 Am Fuchsberg/Erich-Wenert-Strasse
🚊 Tram 3, 9

MEISSEN

MERCURE GRAND HOTEL MEISSEN

Hafenstrasse 27–31, 01662 Meissen
Tel 03521 72250
www.accorhotels.com/mecure_grand_
hotel_meissen.htm
This opulent villa on the Elbe
was restored in 1993 to create
a luxury hotel. You'll find peace

and quiet among the mature
trees, yet it is only a short walk
from the town. There is a shuttle service to Dresden airport.
🏷 From €66, excluding breakfast
(€13 per person)
🛏 97
🅿

POTSDAM

RELEXA SCHLOSS CECILIENHOF

Neuer Garten, 14469 Potsdam
Tel 0331 37050
An English-style manor in a
wonderful lakeside setting. The
reason this exclusive hotel is
not a five-star establishment is
that its status as a listed (protected) building does not
allow air-conditioning.
🏷 €150–175
🛏 41
🅿
🚊 Cecilienhof

STEIGENBERGER MAXX

Allee nach Sanssouci 1, 14471 Potsdam
Tel 0331 90910
www.potsdam.maxx-hotels.de
This hotel is just outside one of
the gates to Sanssouci Park.
Facilities include bicycle rental
and a complimentary pass for
bus, tram and train services in
Potsdam and Berlin.
🏷 €130–150
🛏 135
🅿 Underground garage
🚊 Tram 96/X98; bus 606/605

SÄCHSISCHE SCHWEIZ

BERGHOF LICHTENHAIN

Am Anger 3, 01855 Lichtenhain
Tel 035971 56512
www.berghof.li
A modest timber-built hotel in
an area of sandstone rock
formations and forest, popular
with hikers and climbers. The
main building has a modern
annexe. There is a terrace with
fine views, plus a restaurant.
🏷 €46–60
🛏 27
🍽
🅿

STAYING

ROMANTIK HOTEL DEUTSCHES HAUS

Niedere Burgstrasse 1, 01796 Pirna
Tel 03501 443440
www.romantikhotels.com/pirna
A fine old gabled Renaissance building in a quiet, central position, which has a barrel-vaulted cellar, an elegant first-floor salon and individually styled rooms.
€86–98
40
P

HOTEL FORSTHAUS

Kirnitzschtalstrasse 5, 01814
Bad Schandau
Tel 035022 5840
www.weka-touristik.de/hotels/forsthaus
The valley of the crystal-clear River Kirnitzsch is one of the prettiest parts of Saxon Switzerland, and the lovingly restored timber-framed Forest House Hotel has won awards for enhancing the surroundings. The comfortable rooms are individually furnished.
€27–40, excluding breakfast
29

P

QUEDLINBURG

ROMANTIK HOTEL THEOPHANO

Markt 13/14, 06484 Quedlinburg
Tel 03946 96300
www.hoteltheophano.de
A lovely half-timbered,

steep-roofed hotel with comfortable individually furnished rooms, some with four-poster beds. Breakfast is served in the café leading onto the square; the cellar restaurant serves fine food.
€98–120
22

P

SPREEWALD
SCHLOSSHOTEL LÜBBENAU

Schlossbezirk 6, 03222 Lübbenau
Tel 03542 8730
www.schloss-luebbenau.de

This neoclassical mansion sits in an English-style park and has comfortable, tastefully furnished rooms and apartments.
€104–134
46

P

SPREEWALDHOTEL LEIPE

Leipes Dorfstrasse 29, 03222
Lübbenau/Ortsteil Leipe
Tel 03542 2234
www.hotels-im-Spreewald.de
Get away from the crowds by staying at this small, modernized hotel. The restaurant serves local dishes. Boats and bicycles are available for guests.
€62–95
21

P

WEIMAR
DORINT SOFITEL AM GOETHEPARK

Beethovenplatz 1–2, 99423 Weimar
Tel 03643 8720
www.dorint.com
This five-star, central hotel combines contemporary comfort with classic features.

€115–264, excluding breakfast (€16)
143

P

HOTEL ELEPHANT

Markt 19, 99423 Weimar
Tel 03643 8020
www.arabellasheraton.com
On Weimar's market place, this hotel has welcomed guests for more than 300 years. The opulent bedrooms and public spaces have art nouveau furnishings and contemporary art. Dine

in the Michelin-starred Anna Amalia restaurant or the cellar restaurant.
€121–245
99

P

ROMANTIK-HOTEL DOROTHEENHOF

Dorotheenhof 1, 99247 Weimar
Tel 03643 4590; 03643 45 92 00
www.romantikhotels.com/weimar
This carefully restored manor house has an idyllic setting among trees and there's a summer terrace and a herb garden.
€102–150
60

Outdoor
P

WITTENBERG
HOTEL UND GESTÜT FALKENHOF

Zum Reiterhof 1, 14823 Niemegk-Neuendorf
Tel 033843 6450
www.hotel-gestuet-falkenhof.de
A country house hotel set in an estate. Among the spacious rooms are some with four-poster beds. The restaurant is a lovely setting for meals featuring produce from the estate.
€77–98
52

P

STAYING

MUNICH

There are more than 40,000 hotel beds in Munich, and by the time the soccer World Cup comes to the city in 2006 there will be several thousand more. If you are visiting in low season (November to March) you will probably be spoiled for choice—unless a large trade fair is taking place. *Oktoberfest* is a busy time, so you will need to reserve somewhere as much as a year in advance. The best advice is to reserve ahead whatever time of year you plan to visit. Munich has its share of well-known hotel chains, but there are still many that are family-owned, and almost all of the hotels listed here fall into this category. Smaller privately owned hotels sometimes do not have any rooms designated as non-smoking, so check when you book. Air-conditioning is not standard in Munich hotels, particularly those in historic buildings, and a few may not have an elevator. A large breakfast buffet is normally included in the price in mid-range hotels. Some smaller hotels and pensions do not accept credit cards—Diner's Club is the least widely accepted.

ACANTHUS

An der Hauptfeuerwache 14, 80331 München (Altstadt)
Tel 089 231880
www.acanthushotel.de
Carola and Jörg Günther want you to relax at the hotel they have run for 14 years, and they provide books in different languages plus a generous

breakfast served until late to help you do just that. Rooms have a phone, mini-bar and television, and are decorated in either an English-floral style with antique furniture or in pastel shades with modern furniture. They accept most credit cards but not Diner's Club.
🛏 €90–105
🛌 36
🅿 Underground garage
Ⓢ Sendlinger Tor

ADMIRAL

Kohlstrasse 9, 80469 München (Isarvorstadt)
Tel 089 216350; 089 293674
www.hotel-admiral.de
The rooms in this four-star hotel, close to the River Isar and the Deutsches Museum, are extremely comfortable— chocolates on the pillow and a basket of fruit await your arrival. All rooms also have internet access, a television, telephone, desk and hairdryer.
🛏 €150–230
🛌 33 (8 non-smoking)
🅿
🅿 Parking spaces for €12 per day, public parking area nearby
Ⓢ Fraunhoferstrasse

AM SIEGESTOR

Akademiestrasse 5, 80799 München (Schwabing)
Tel 089 399550
www.hotel-siegestor.de
This pension, opposite the university's art school, has a wonderful old-fashioned Parisian-style elevator, one of only two of its kind in Munich.

The English-speaking owner, friendly Frau Clauss, is proud of the building, which dates from 1879. Guest rooms don't have a private bathroom (some have a basin). No credit cards are accepted.
🛏 €55–65
🛌 20
Ⓢ Universität

CARLTON

Fürstenstrasse 12, 80333 München (Schwabing)
Tel 089 282061
www.carlton-garni.de
This is a comfortable four-star hotel at the edge of the student area and near the Pinakothek galleries. All rooms have telephone, television, mini-bar and hairdryer. The breakfast here is a bit special,

with salmon and champagne as well as the usual cereals, meats and cheeses.
🛏 €112–178
🛌 49 (one non-smoking floor)
Ⓢ Odeonsplatz

CORTIINA

Ledererstrasse 8, 80331 München (Altstadt)
Tel 089 242 2490
www.cortiina.com
Cortiina is the type of boutique hotel you would expect to find in one of the world's style capitals, such as London or New York. Rooms are minimal-ist, and everything is made using the highest-quality materials, from the stone tiles in the bathroom to the oak parquet floors. The hotel does a wonderful English afternoon tea on weekends in the colder months (think cakes and cucumber sandwiches), and the breakfast is more Italian than Bavarian, with cappuc-cino and light pastries.

STAYING

🛏 €186 (studio €206)
🚪 33 (3 non-smoking floors)
🅿
♿
Ⓜ Marienplatz
🚋 Marienplatz, Isartor

CVJM JUGENDGÄSTEHAUS
Landwehrstrasse 13, 80336
München (Hauptbahnhof)
Tel 089 552 1410; 089 550 4282
www.cvjm-muenchen.org/hotel
You don't have to be young to
stay at this youth hostel, which
is near the main train station
and Karlsplatz. The rooms
are simple and very clean,
although none has a private
bathroom. However, considering that a filling breakfast is
included in the price, it's an
excellent budget option,
particularly for families or
friends travelling together. If
you are over the age of 26
you have to pay a 16 per cent
surcharge, and the only credit
cards they accept are Visa
and MasterCard.
🛏 €27.97–29.05 per person per night
(€25.80–26.80 if you are under 26)
🚪 85 beds (all non-smoking)
Ⓜ Karlsplatz, Hauptbahnhof,
Sendlinger Tor
Ⓜ Karlsplatz, Hauptbahnhof

HOTEL AM
VIKTUALIENMARKT
Utzschneiderstrasse 14, 80469
München (Isarvorstadt)
Tel 089 231 1090
www.hotel-am-viktualienmarkt.com/de
Its position behind the
Viktualienmarkt is this family-
run hotel's main advantage; its
main disadvantage is that
although it is on four floors
there is no elevator, which may
put off less able visitors. Guest
rooms (with two, three or four
beds) are comfortable and
have internet access, television
and telephone. Generous
breakfasts are served in the
pretty breakfast room on the
ground floor. Make sure
you don't trip over Fritz, the
friendly black cat. The hotel
accepts most credit cards, but
not American Express.
🛏 €83–110
🚪 27 (2 non-smoking floors)
🚋 Tram 17, 18

HOTEL APOLLO
Mittererstrasse 7, 80336 München
(Hauptbahnhof)
Tel 089 539531
www.apollohotel.de
Rooms in this three-star hotel
are quiet considering the
location is so close to the
Hauptbahnhof. They each have

a safe, television, telephone,
mini-bar and hairdryer, and
about 25 also have a balcony.
There is a little bar, which is
open in the evenings.
🛏 €84–175
🚪 74 (18 non-smoking)
🅿
🅿 Covered parking area €6 per night
Ⓜ Hauptbahnhof
🚋 Hauptbahnhof

HOTEL BAYERISCHER HOF
Promenadeplatz 2–6, 80333
München (Altstadt)
Tel 089 21200
www.bayerischerhof.de
The Volkhardt family has run
this five-star hotel since 1897.
You're in absolute luxury here
and could enjoy a day without
even leaving the building, as
there are three restaurants,
several bars, designer
boutiques, a beauty and hair
salon, a rooftop pool, a sauna
and steam bath, a gym and
a sun terrace. Rooms have

21st-century technology in the
form of internet access and
even PlayStations.
🛏 €243–403
🚪 337 rooms and 58 suites
(half non-smoking)

🍴
🅿
🔆 🏊 Outdoor 🛁
Ⓜ Karlsplatz, Marienplatz
🚋 Tram 19

HOTEL DACHS
Amalienstrasse 12, 80333
München (Schwabing)
Tel 089 286 9480
www.hoteldachs.de
You're five minutes away from
the Englischer Garten in this
quiet hotel. There are rooms
with one, two or three beds,
all with a television and
phone and most with a
private bathroom.
🛏 €77–130
🚪 50
🅿 Parking spaces €8 per day, lockable
garage €12
Ⓜ Odeonsplatz
🚋 Bus 55 to Ludwigstrasse

HOTEL EXQUISIT
Pettenkoferstrasse 3, 80336
München (Altstadt)
Tel 089 551 9900
www.hotel-exquisit.com
This is a very comfortable four-
star hotel in a great location
near Sendlinger Tor, with a
sauna and solarium, and a
restaurant that serves breakfast, brunch on the weekends

and lunch from Monday to
Friday. In addition to the
regular singles and doubles,
there are suites, a maisonette
and a room that is fully
accessible to wheelchairs.
🛏 €160–205
🚪 50 (10 non-smoking)
🍴
🛁 Sauna, solarium
🅿 Private garage €11 per day
Ⓜ Sendlinger Tor

HOTEL GÄSTEHAUS ENGLISCHER GARTEN

Liebergesellstrasse 8, 80802
München (Schwabing)
Tel 089 383 9410
www.hotelenglishgarden.de
It would be difficult to find a place to stay with more charm than this 200-year-old converted watermill right by the Englischer Garten. There are only 12 rooms (six with bathroom and six without), so you'll need to book early. For

families, there are 17 furnished apartments in a more modern building opposite. In summer, you can have breakfast in the garden, where you'll find it hard to believe you're in the middle of a city.

💶 €68–118, excluding breakfast (€9)
🛏 12 rooms, 17 apartments
Ⓜ Münchner Freiheit

HOTEL ST. PAUL

St.-Paul-Strasse 7, 80336
München (Theresienwiese)
Tel 089 5440 7800
www.hotel-stpaul.de
Ideally situated for reaching the *Oktoberfest* ground, the Hotel St. Paul has rooms with television, telephone, a safe and internet access. There are two breakfast rooms (one non-smoking) and you can eat outside in the little courtyard in summer. The hotel accepts all credit cards except Diner's Club.

💶 €92–168
🛏 40 (20 non-smoking)
Ⓜ Theresienwiese

HOTEL SAVOY

Amalienstrasse 25, 80333
München (Schwabing)
Tel 089 287870
www.renner-hotel-ag.de
The Savoy is one of four hotels owned by the Renner family; Carlton (▷ 396) is one of the others. Rooms have a television, minibar and phone,

although note that some have been redecorated more recently than others. There are two breakfast rooms, one of which is non-smoking. The hotel accepts most credit cards, except for Diner's Club.

💶 €107–186
🛏 74 (10 non-smoking)
Ⓜ Odeonsplatz

HOTEL SCHLICKER

Tal 8, 80331 München (Altstadt)
089 242 8870
www.hotel-schlicker.de
You're in a central location here, near Marienplatz, though the noise is reduced as rooms that face onto the busy Tal have double-glazed windows.

There are different grades of room, which are priced accordingly, including suites, triple rooms and a split-level maisonette. In summer you can have breakfast outside in the little garden.

💶 Rooms €115–200
🛏 69 rooms, 2 suites
🅿 Private spaces €10 per night
Ⓜ Marienplatz
🚊 Marienplatz

HOTEL SEIBEL

Theresienhöhe 9, 80339
München (Theresienwiese)
Tel 089 540 1420
www.seibel-hotels-munich.de
The three-star Hotel Seibel is owned by the same family as Pension Seibel (▷ 399), but is not as central because it is on the other side of the Theresienwiese. Rooms are large, with heavy wooden Bavarian-style furniture, radio, cable television and telephone. There is also a sauna where you can relax after a hard day's sightseeing.

💶 €79–189
🛏 65 (30 non-smoking)
🧖 Sauna
Ⓜ Schwanthalerhöhe, Theresienwiese

HOTEL TORBRÄU

Tal 41, 80331 München (Altstadt)
Tel 089 2423 4234
www.torbraeu.de
Manager Manfred Fritsch proudly tells guests that this historic hotel was founded in 1490, before Christopher Columbus set sail for America. It has been in the same family for more than 100 years, and was renovated in 2004 and 2005. There are two types of double room, standard and deluxe; both are very comfortable, with modern furniture, and some have views of Frauenkirche. Unusually for a hotel in a historic building, all rooms are air-conditioned. There's also a café, which serves lunch until 2pm and cakes from 2pm onwards, while the Italian restaurant La Famiglia (▷ 366) is next door.

💶 €170–210
🛏 92 rooms (60 non-smoking) and 3 suites
🖥
♨
🚊 Isartor

HOTEL UHLAND GARNI

Uhlandstrasse 1, 80336
München (Theresienwiese)
Tel 089 543350
www.hotel-uhland.de
This friendly hotel has been in the same family for 50 years and is near the *Oktoberfest* ground. The rooms are large and have a mini-bar, hairdryer, internet access, cable television and telephone, and one even has a waterbed. There's a small lounge where

STAYING

you can help yourself to a coffee, and where you can surf the internet and receive emails on your own Uhland email address.

💶 €70–174)
🛏 27 (9 non-smoking)
🅿 Off-street parking
Ⓜ Theresienwiese
🚌 Bus 58

PENSION GEIGER
Steinheilstrasse 1, 80333 München (Maxvorstadt)
Tel 089 521556
www.pensiongeiger.de
This bright but basic pension is close to the Pinakothek galleries. There are rooms with or without a shower, and rooms with three beds. Only six rooms have a television, so if you would like one in your room you will need to request this from the friendly owner when you make your reservation. No credit cards are accepted.

💶 €55–60
🛏 17
Ⓜ Theresienstrasse

PENSION SEIBEL
Reichenbachstrasse 8, 80469 München (Isarvorstadt)
Tel 089 231 9180
www.seibel-hotel-munich.de
This wonderful pension has bags of charm thanks to manager Ludwig Buchwieser's warm welcome and the traditional Bavarian decoration (heavy wooden furniture and tiled floors) in the bedrooms and breakfast room. It also has a great location, just behind the Viktualienmarkt. All but two rooms have their own private bathroom, and at the top of the building are three apartments, which sleep four to six people, and have two bedrooms and a kitchenette each. There are lower rates if you book early and if you stay in low-season (November to March).

SPECIAL IN MUNICH
PLATZL HOTEL
Sparkassenstrasse 10, 80331 München (Altstadt)
Tel 089 237030
www.platzl.de
You could only be more central than this four-star Bavarian-style hotel if you were in the Marienplatz itself. The hotel has been in the same family for 50 years and feels truly Bavarian, from the traditional costumes of the reception staff to the wooden furniture and tiled floors of the bar, reception and Pfistermühle restaurant, in the 16th-century vaults. The comfort-

able rooms are decorated in blue and yellow, and are quiet thanks to double glazing. The hotel's pièce de résistance is the Moroccan-themed Maurischer Kiosk, which opened in 2004—it has a mini gym, sauna, Jacuzzi, steam room with underfloor heating and a floor mosaic incorporating real gold. The state-of-the-art showers have to be experienced to be believed.

💶 Rooms €157–242, suite €360
🛏 166 rooms (65 non-smoking) and 1 suite
🍴 🛋
🍸
Ⓜ Marienplatz
🚌 Bus 52 to Marienplatz
Ⓢ Marienplatz

SPLENDID DOLLMANN
Thierschstrasse 49, 80538 München (Lehel)
Tel 089 23 80 80
www.splendid-dollmann.de
The Hotel Splendid used to be on Maximilianstrasse but moved across the road to its present location a few years ago. It has the atmosphere of an exclusive members club, and as a result is popular with actors and those working in the media. Rooms are elegantly decorated and there are also suites, rooms with extra large beds and an apartment with kitchen. There's an elegant sitting room, the perfect place for afternoon tea.

💶 €130–170, excluding breakfast (€10.50)
🛏 33
Ⓜ Lehel
🚌 Tram 19 to Maxmonument; tram 17 to Lehel

YOUTH HOSTEL MUNICH-NEUHAUSEN
Wendl-Dietrichstrasse 20, 80634 München (Neuhausen)
Tel 089 131156
www.djh.de/jugendherbergen/muench enneuhausen
Slightly outside the middle of town in the fashionable district of Neuhausen, this youth hostel is great value considering that a hearty breakfast is included in the price. The hostel is open 24 hours a day and there is an upper age limit of 26.

💶 €23.05–29.80
🛏 388 beds (2-, 4- and 6-bed rooms, plus a large dormitory)
Ⓜ Rotkreuzplatz, then a 5-minute walk

💶 Rooms €89–155, apartments €165 (€280 during the *Oktoberfest* and large trade fairs)
🛏 20 (12 non-smoking)
🚌 Tram 17 or 18

STAYING

SOUTHERN GERMANY

Accommodation in southern Germany ranges from historic buildings that have been converted into grand hotels to traditional *Gästehäuser* (guesthouses) in the Bavarian Alps. The major chains are represented in the cities, but rooms can be expensive and extras such as parking soon add up. There are many privately run small hotels in towns and villages that offer tidy rooms and excellent facilities at reasonable prices.

Many hotels have restaurants, and sometimes the price includes meals. *Halbpension* includes breakfast and dinner or lunch, while *Vollpension* includes lunch or dinner too. *Garni* hotels serve breakfast only. Bed-and-breakfast Pensions are good value but many lack private bathrooms and rooms vary in quality—always ask to see a room before you check in. The chalet-type *Gasthaus* offers spacious and well-furnished rooms and some will have a balcony. In some resorts, particularly health spas, a *Kurtaxe* is levied. In return, guests get a *Kurkarte*, entitling them to free or reduced fares on public transportation and entry to many attractions.

PRICES AND SYMBOLS

Prices are per night for two people sharing a double room. The prices include breakfast unless otherwise stated, but check when you make your reservation. Note that rates vary widely throughout the year.
For a key to the symbols, ▷ 2.

AMORBACH

DER SCHAFHOF HOTEL

Otterbachtal, 63916 Amorbach
Tel 09373 97330
www.schafhof.de

This hotel is in beautiful countryside next to a working farm. The main building dates from 1721 and originally belonged to the estate of the Amorbach Benedictine abbey. The hotel, now owned by the Ullrich family, has comfortable guest rooms, some with beamed ceilings, in both the main building and the barn. Relax in front of a blazing log fire in the delightful lounge. There are some lovely walks around the farm.

€130–170
22
Sauna, solarium and spa treatments

AUGSBURG

STEIGENBERGER DREI MOHREN HOTEL

Maximilianstrasse 40, 86150 Augsburg
Tel 0821 50360
www.augsburg.steigenberger.de

In a historic building in the heart of Augsburg, this hotel offers luxury and comfort. In 1730 King Friedrich Wilhelm I of Prussia stayed here. All the rooms are well appointed, with cable and pay television, mini-bar, telephone and hairdryer. They overlook either the traffic-restricted Maximilianstrasse or the glass-roofed tea salon, which has been beautifully restored.

€163–183 (weekend rate €150)
99 (plus 6 suites)
Indoor/outdoor

BAD AIBLING

ROMANTIK HOTEL LINDNER

Marienplatz 5, 83043 Bad Aibling
Tel 08061 90630
www.romantikhotels.com/bad-aibling

This hotel is in the fairy-tale setting of the former Bavarian castle of Prantshausen, near Rosenheim. You feel history at every turn when you wander through the wood-panelled hallways and rooms. The large, elegant bedrooms are well furnished and there's an excellent restaurant (▷ 369). The quiet location makes the hotel an ideal base for walking and bicycling (bicycles are available free for guests' use).

€120–160
26

BADEN-BADEN

HOTEL AM MARKT

Marktplatz 18, 76530 Baden-Baden
Tel 07221 27040
www.hotel-am-markt-baden.de

In this opulent town, this is an excellent, less expensive option. It is ideally located, tucked away in a quiet cobbled square close to the Old Town and Romerplatz. The attractive dining room, with its Windsor chairs and small tables, is open only to hotel guests. The guest rooms on the first two floors are spacious, with high ceilings, but not all rooms have a private bathroom.

€58–80 (*Kurtaxe* €2.80 per person)
12

BAMBERG

HOTEL BRUDERMÜHLE

Schranne 1, 96049 Bamberg
Tel 0951 955220
www.brudermuehle.de

Close to the river in the middle of Bamberg's historic old town, this 14th-century former mill has been developed into an attractive hotel. The public rooms of the three-floor building, with its shuttered windows and steeply pitched red roof, are furnished with antiques. The guest rooms are in the original mill and in a house across the street. Try to book in advance and ask for a room overlooking the river or the stream and waterfall. (▷ 369 for details of the hotel's restaurant.)

€108–125
20, plus 3 apartments (all non-smoking)

COBURG

HOTEL GOLDENE TRAUBE

Am Victoriabrunnen 2, 96450 Coburg
Tel 09561 8760
www.romantikhotels.com/coburg.de

This is an ideal base for exploring Coburg and its Veste fortress. The Goldene Traube has a history dating back to 1756, and the restaurant-cum-wine tavern is lively and has good service (▷ 370). The hotel's guest rooms are comfortable and decorated in warm pastel shades; all have a private bathroom. Each room also has a television, telephone and hairdryer.

€107–139
72

STAYING

DINKELSBÜHL

GOLDNER HIRSCH

Weinmarkt 6, 91550 Dinkelsbühl
Tel 09851 2347
www.wunderle.claranet.de

The foundation walls of this house date back to the 14th century and are among the oldest in Dinkelsbühl. The guest rooms are modern and spacious, with satellite television and private bathroom. Breakfasts are exceptional, with delicious home-made jam, fresh rolls and typical German fare. The restaurant is known for its fish dishes.

€58–64

14

ESSLINGEN-BERKHEIM

HOTEL LINDE

Ruiter Strasse 2, 73734
Esslingen-Berkheim
Tel 0711 345305
www.linde-berkheim.de

This welcoming, family-run hotel is in a small village near the autobahn leading into Stuttgart. The guest rooms are more like small apartments— spacious and comfortably furnished with armchairs, a table and a desk. They have a bathroom, mini-bar, satellite television, radio, telephone and hairdryer. The hotel has a wonderful indoor swimming pool plus a sauna, solarium and fitness suite.

€85–117

86

Indoor

FREIBURG

ZUM ROTEN BÄREN

Oberlinden 12, 79098 Freiburg
Tel 0761 387870; 0761 387 8717

Zum Roten Baren is the oldest inn in Germany. The Romanesque house was transformed in later years into a magnificent baroque building, and the historic hotel has retained many of these architectural features. Most of the guest rooms have their own character, and all have a shower or bath, satellite television, mini-bar and internet access. Try to arrange a guided tour of the inn's cellars. There is a restaurant (▷ 370).

€93–138

25

Indoor

GARMISCH-PARTENKIRCHEN

GASTHOF FRAUNDORFER

Ludwigstrasse 24, 82467
Garmisch-Partenkirchen
Tel 08821 9270
www.gasthof-fraundorfer.de

This traditional hotel in the historic part of Partenkirchen has been run by the Fraundorfer family since 1820. Its façade is decorated with fabulous murals and bright window boxes, and the rustic interiors are typically Bavarian. The guest rooms vary in size and the furnishings range from traditional in the main house to whimsically modern in the much quieter Gästehaus

Barbara, just behind the hotel. Some rooms have a balcony and all have a bathroom, television and telephone. Other hotel facilities include a sauna, steam room and solarium. Every night except Tuesday, there's a Bavarian evening in the bar-restaurant (▷ 370), with music and *schuhplattler* (Bavarian dancing).

€78–110

30

Sauna, steam room and solarium

LANDIDYLL HOTEL LEINER

Wildenauerstrasse 20, 82467
Garmisch-Partenkirchen
Tel 08821 95280
www.landidyll.de/leiner

The hotel, in a quiet area of Partenkirchen near the Olympic ski stadium, makes an ideal base for exploring this region. The rooms are comfortable and have a bathroom, telephone, television and radio. Hotel facilities include a sun terrace, lounge, indoor pool, sauna, solarium and large garden. It's a short walk to the entrance of the Partnachklamm (Partnach Gorge), or through the park to the heart of Garmisch.

€53–96

50

Indoor Sauna and solarium

RENAISSANCE RIESSERSEE

Am Riess 5, 82467
Garmisch-Partenkirchen
Tel 08821 7580
www.renaissance-riessersee-hotel.de

The Riessersee is on a beautiful lakeside high above Garmisch and Partenkirchen, yet is still within walking distance of the two towns. The rooms and apartments are well appointed, and have stunning views of the lake and mountains. You can swim in the summer or just relax and enjoy the scenery. The hotel has a restaurant (▷ 371).

€160–206

155

Indoor

HEIDELBERG

MOLKENKUR HOTEL

Klingenteichstrasse 31, 69117
Heidelberg
Tel 06221 654080
www.molkenkur.de

This beautifully located hotel is in peaceful surroundings with views of the Neckartal, yet just a five-minute drive from Heidelberg's Old Town. The rooms are spacious and comfortably furnished, and all have a private bathroom, telephone, laptop connection, television and free mineral water. They also have large picture windows leading onto balconies with amazing views.

€79, excluding breakfast

20

ZUM RITTER ST. GEORG

Hauptstrasse 178, 69117 Heidelberg
Tel 06221 1350
www.ritter-heidelberg.de

This hotel is in one of the most popular parts of town in the pedestrianized Hauptstrasse. The stately façade of this Renaissance building dates from 1592, and its architectural beauty and elegance make it the finest historical, and most artistically valuable townhouse in Heidelberg. Many of the guest rooms have been renovated and provide comfortable accommodation with good facilities. If you don't want to be in a room overlooking the busy Hauptstrasse, request a quieter room in the new wing at the rear of the hotel.

€141–171
39

KONSTANZ

PARKHOTEL AM SEE

Seestrasse 25a, 78464
Konstanz
Tel 07531 8990
www.parkhotel-am-see.de

The Parkhotel is an elegant villa-style house in a quiet traffic-free area alongside Bodensee (Lake Constance). Surrounded by beautiful, wooded gardens and with direct access to the lakeside promenade, this is the ideal spot for visitors to downtown Konstanz, which is just a 10-minute walk away. The modern guest rooms are comfortable and well furnished, with good facilities. All the rooms have a balcony or terrace, but for the best views request a balcony room facing the lake.

€102–195
39

LINDAU

HOTEL LINDAUER HOF

Seepromenade, 88131
Lindau
Tel 08382 4064
www.lindauer-hof.de

This former granary store dating from the 17th century is beautifully located directly on the harbourfront and has commanding views across Lake Constance. The smart, modern furnishings have been carefully chosen by the owners

HOHENSCHWANGAU

SCHLOSSHOTEL LISL

Neuschwansteinstrasse 1–3, 87643
Hohenschwangau
Tel 08362 930830
www.lisl.de

The Schlosshotel Lisl makes an ideal base for visiting the castles of Neuschwanstein and Hohenschwangau. From many of the rooms you get unobstructed views up to

one or both of the castles, which are particularly impressive at night when you can see them dramatically lit against a night sky long after the crowds of day visitors have departed. The hotel dates back more than 100 years to when it housed castle workers. Today, the stylish furnishings and spacious guest rooms make this the perfect place to enjoy a relaxing stay.

€110
35

Indoor

to give a warm welcoming feeling to the public rooms and a restful one to the guest rooms. Some guest rooms have lovely panelled pine ceilings and a separate sitting room with views across the lake, while others have their own terrace overlooking the harbour.

€138–158
32

Indoor

MANNHEIM

DORINT KONGRESS HOTEL

Friedrichsring 6, 68161
Mannheim
Tel 0621 12510
www.dorint.de/mannheim

This is a modern hotel conveniently located in downtown Mannheim. The guest rooms are decorated in pastel shades to give a gentle ambience, and are furnished with a table, desk and chairs. They all have private bathrooms, cable television, mini-bar and hairdryer. Parking is available for guests in the basement garage, and hotel facilities include a swimming pool, fitness suite, sauna and solarium.

€98–220
287

Indoor
Basement garage

MEERSBURG

GASTHOF ZUM BÄREN

Marktplatz 11, 88709 Meersburg
Tel 07532 43220
www.baeren-meersburg.de

In the heart of Meersburg, this 15th-century inn has been owned by the same family for five generations. The guest rooms are furnished with an interesting mixture of old painted furniture and country pine pieces, along with some antique touches, and some have beautifully carved wooden ceilings and daintily patterned wallpapers. All the rooms are homey, very comfortable and have a private bathroom, television and telephone.

€76–102
20

Indoor/outdoor

NECKARGERACH

HOTEL GRÜNER BAUM

Neckarstrasse 13, 69437 Neckargerach
Tel 06263 706
www.gruenerbaum-neckargerach.de

This pretty little hotel in the quiet village of Neckargerach is run by the Greek Papadopoulos family, and you can be assured of a very warm welcome. The guest rooms are basic but comfortable, with a bathroom and a television. It's best to book in advance and request a room with a balcony, from where you will have stunning views of the

STAYING

Minneburg or the river Neckar. (▷ 372 for details of the hotel's restaurant.)

🏷 €60
🛏 14
🍴
🆂 🏊 Indoor/outdoor 🐾
🅿

NÜRNBERG

BURGHOTEL STAMMHAUS
Schildgasse 14–16, 90403 Nürnberg
Tel 0911 203040
Don't be put off by the small external appearance of this hotel, because inside the facilities are adequate and its location in the middle of the Old Town makes it ideal for visitors. The rooms are small but reasonably priced, and are well equipped with television, radio, mini-bar and private bathroom. The terrace behind the hotel is the ideal setting for breakfast, and there's a small swimming pool.

🏷 €62–89
🛏 22
🆂 🏊 Indoor 🐾
🅿

GASTHAUS ROTTNER
Winterstrasse 15, 90431, Grossreuth, Nürnberg
Tel 0911 658480
www.rottner-hotel.de
This black-and-white half-timbered building is wonderfully located just 7km (4.3 miles) from Nürnberg in the village of Grossreuth. The spacious rooms are beautifully furnished and decorated in pastel shades. All the guest rooms have a bathroom, television, telephone and hairdryer. Views are over well-manicured gardens and a terrace, which are great spots for enjoying a meal or a stroll. (▷ 373 for details of the hotel's restaurant.)

🏷 €140–155
🛏 38
🍴
🅿

OBERAMMERGAU

PARKHOTEL SONNENHOF
Konig-Ludwig-Strasse 12, 82487 Oberammergau
Tel 08822 9130; 08822 3047
www.parkhotel-sonnenhof.de
This hotel is in a quiet area away from the hustle and bustle of Oberammergau's visitor attractions, yet it is still within walking distance of the

SPECIAL IN OBERAMMERGAU

PENSION NEU
Passionswiese 3, 82487 Oberammergau
Tel 08822 6328
www.oberammergau.de
Here you can stay in the traditional Bavarian family home of an Oberammergau woodcarver and watch him at work in his studio. The house is ideally located near the middle of town and the Passionsspielhaus, has its own private parking and all the rooms are tastefully designed and have private bathrooms. Guests can use the large living room, along with the Bavarian-style dining area and traditional Bavarian tiled oven. The Neu family are very welcoming and speak English.

🏷 €22–26
🛏 6 (4 double, 2 single)

middle of town. The modern guest rooms are spacious and light, with large windows leading out onto a balcony. Room facilities include satellite television, radio/CD player, hairdryer, telephone, safe and mini-bar, and the hotel has a restaurant (▷ 373), plus a swimming pool, sauna, steam room and beauty salon.

🏷 €62–89
🛏 61 (non-smoking)
🍴 🖥 🏊
🆂 🏊 🐾 Sauna, steam room and beauty salon
🅿

RAVENSBURG

HOTEL OBERTOR
Marktstrasse 67, 88212 Ravensburg
Tel 0751 36670
www.hotelobertor.de
There's more than 700 years of history at the Obertor, so walking through the building is like a journey through time. The foundations date back to the 13th century, and during later centuries extra floors were added. Evidence of this can be seen in some of the guest rooms on the first and second floors, which have carved wooden ceilings dating from the 17th and 18th centuries, features that are unique to Ravensburg. The rooms are modern and comfortable, with satellite television and telephone. Hotel facilities include a sauna and whirlpool. (▷ 373 for details of the hotel's restaurant.)

🏷 €47.50–95
🛏 55 (2 apartments)
🍴 🖥 🏊
🆂 🏊 Indoor 🐾 Sauna and whirlpool
🅿

REGENSBURG

HOTEL BISCHOFSHOF
Krauterermarkt 3, 93047 Regensburg
Tel 0941 58460
www.hotel-bischofshof.de
This is a historic hotel close to the Porta Praetoria, the northern gate of the former Roman camp of Casta Regina, and St. Peter's Cathedral. Emperors and kings have stayed in the Bischofshof during many

Reichstag meetings held in Regensburg. The rooms are quiet and face either the courtyard or the cathedral. Each is individually decorated and equipped with television, telephone, hairdryer, mini-bar and radio.

🏷 €122–135
🛏 55
🍴 🖥 🏊
🅿

STAYING

ORPHEE

Untere Bachgasse 8, 93047 Regensburg
Tel 0941 59 60 20
www.hotel-orphee.de
This hotel in a former brewery appears to have been caught in a time warp, as you wander around three floors of nooks and crannies. Even the French-style café and wine bar on the ground floor seems to have hardly changed since the late 19th century (▷ 373). Guest rooms are furnished in nostalgic style, including old Italian furniture, hand-crafted Turkish tiles and even washstands abandoned by hairdressing salons long ago.

€77–116
15

ROTHENBURG OB DER TAUBER

SPECIAL IN
ROTHENBURG OB DER
TAUBER

HOTEL SCHRANNE

Schrannenplatz 7, 91541 Rothenburg ob der Tauber
Tel 09861 95500
www.schranne.rothenburg.de
This family-run hotel is fronted by a large cobbled square within the medieval town. The comfortable rooms are modern, spacious and tastefully furnished. They have bathrooms and are well equipped. There's a

garden restaurant, and the breakfast and dining rooms are excellent (▷ 374). It makes an ideal base for enjoying this historic town.

€64–98
100 beds

SCHÖNAU AM KÖNIGSSEE

ALPENHOTEL ZECHMEISTERLEHEN

Wahlstrasse 35, 83471 Schönau am Königssee
Tel 08652 9450
www.zechmeisterlehen.de
This delightful resort is amid Alpine meadows and is conveniently located for visiting Berchtesgaden, Königssee and Salzburg—just a 30-minute drive away. Guest rooms are spacious and well appointed, with lovely views from the balconies across open meadows dotted with Alpine flowers and chalets to the distant mountains. The facilities include children's play areas, pools and a spa.

€52–116
14
Indoor and outdoor

SCHWANGAU-HORN

HOTEL CAFÉ HELMERHOF

Frauenbergstrasse 9, 87645 Schwangau-Horn
Tel 08362 8069
www.helmerhof.de
The Helmerhof is conveniently located for visiting the castles of Neuschwanstein, Hohenschwangau and Linderhof, as well as the Wieskirche. The spacious rooms have private bathrooms and are well appointed, with a sofa, balcony or terrace, radio alarm clock, telephone, cable television and safe. You can also stay in one of the hotel's fully fitted apartments, each of which has a private kitchen. Hotel facilities include a sauna, whirlpool and solarium, plus the use of a washing machine and tumble dryer if required.

€38–40
20
Sauna, whirlpool and solarium

STUTTGART

HOTEL TRAUBE

Brabandgasse 2, 0599 Stuttgart-Plieningen
Tel 0711 458920
www.romantik-hotel-traube.com
If you are visiting Stuttgart and want to stay outside the city, the Hotel Traube is ideal. The small inn is on a quiet square off the main street of the suburb of Plieningen, yet is close to Stuttgart airport and the Mercedes factory, and just a 20-minute drive from the middle of the city. The hosts describe their house as being comfortable, elegant and rustic, and it is indeed all of these things. The guest rooms are attractive, with traditional furnishings and comfortable beds.

€105–195
25

PARKHOTEL AM RUNDFUNK

Villastrasse 21, 70190 Stuttgart
Tel 0711 28010
www.parkhotel-stuttgart.de
The Parkhotel is just on the edge of the city but within easy reach of its heart, and overlooks a park. The guest rooms are spacious and have large windows, and they come well equipped with satellite television, radio, mini-bar, sofa, telephone and hairdryer. Some of the rooms have superb views of the Villa Berg and the park, so it's advisable to book in advance and request one of these.

€102–160
75
Outdoor

WÜRZBURG

MARITIM HOTEL

Pleichertorstrasse 5, 97070 Würzburg
Tel 0931 30530
www.maritim.de
The Maritim is a modern hotel in an excellent location overlooking the River Main. The comfortable guest rooms are well furnished, with a table, desk and chairs, and the pastel shades give them a restful ambience that makes for a relaxing stay. The rooms have private bathrooms, cable television, a mini-bar and hairdryer, while the hotel's facilities include a swimming pool and a fitness suite.

€122–269
287 (195 non-smoking)
Indoor

STAYING

Planning

BEFORE YOU GO

CLIMATE AND WHEN TO GO

Generally speaking, Germany enjoys a mild climate, with average temperatures reaching around 20°C (68°F) in July and August and dropping to around 0°C (32°F) in December and January. Average rainfall is also fairly seasonal, with most regions receiving up to 120mm (4.75in) a month in the height of summer and less than 20mm (0.75in) in the depths of winter. Having said that, however, the weather in Germany is also very changeable, not just from year to year, but also from month to month, week to week and even day to day. Similarly, good weather in, say, western Germany is no guarantee of similar weather in the north, south or east of the country. This can make packing something of a lottery, but so long as you're prepared for cold

WEATHER STATIONS

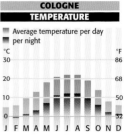

Be prepared for extreme weather in the mountains

snaps in the winter and the odd day of rain in the summer you can't go far wrong (see 'What to Take', opposite).

In cold winters, snow is not uncommon, particularly in the south and southeast, where higher altitudes and a more continental climate contribute to a greater variation in seasonal temperatures. Western Germany tends to experience milder winters, while northern Germany usually feels a few degrees cooler than you might expect thanks to bracing winds blowing in off the North Sea. In warm summers, meanwhile,

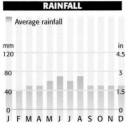

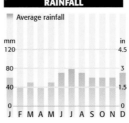

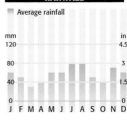

PLANNING

temperatures in June and July have been known to reach a little above 30°C (90°F), with the weather often remaining relatively warm and dry until well into September.

The most reliable months for a visit in terms of weather are May to September, although some areas, such as the Rhine and the Mosel, are probably best avoided in July and August, when the tourist tide is at its height. For those who are interested in winter sports, the ski slopes and cross-country trails in the Alps and the Black Mountains are generally open from December to March inclusive, while the slopes of the Rothaargebirge mountains further north (▷ 111) enjoy a much shorter season.

WEATHER REPORTS

For up-to-date information in English on the weather forecast for Germany, log onto the website of your local

meteorological office, such as www.met-office.gov.uk, or your local news network, such as www.bbc.co.uk or www.cnn.com. Other specialist weather websites include www.weather.com and www.weatheronline.com. Germany's official tourist information website, www.germany-tourism.de,

In the summer, it's usually warm enough to sit outside

provides brief information on the current weather in all of the country's major cities. For those who can follow even a little German, most national and local television networks provide regular forecasts, which should give you an idea of what to expect once you're there.

WHAT TO TAKE

Avoid packing too much, as anything you forget can invariably be bought almost anywhere in Germany. Having said that, however, be sure to pack enough clothes to cope with the sort of weather you can expect at the time of year you're planning to visit.

● Germans tend to dress quite casually, and jeans and training shoes are acceptable almost everywhere (with the exception of some nightclubs, golf courses and so on). A tie is generally required only for casinos and business meetings. Visitors to cathedrals and other sights of religious importance should dress appropriately. If in doubt, dress as the locals dress.

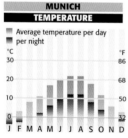

MUNICH
TEMPERATURE

Average temperature per day
per night

°C / °F
30 / 86
20 / 68
10 / 50
0 / 32

J F M A M J J A S O N D

RAINFALL

Average rainfall

mm / in
120 / 4.5
80 / 3
40 / 1.5
0 / 0

J F M A M J J A S O N D

TIMES ZONES

Germany is on Central European Time (CET), which is one hour ahead of Greenwich Mean Time (GMT). Daylight saving, when the clocks go forward an hour, runs from the last Sunday in March to the last Sunday in October. Compared to Germany, the time in other major cities is as follows:

CITY	TIME DIFFERENCE
Auckland	+11 hours
Dublin	-1 hour
London	-1 hour
Los Angeles	-9 hours
New York	-6 hours
Perth	+7 hours
Sydney	+9 hours
Toronto	-6 hours
Vancouver	-9 hours
Seattle	-9 hours

PLANNING

- Light, waterproof jackets and/or umbrellas are useful back-ups at any time of year, while warm coats, hats and gloves will almost certainly be required in the winter months.
- Whether you're planning on trekking in the mountains or just wandering around the cities, be sure to pack a pair of sturdy, comfortable shoes.
- Electricity sockets in Germany require the standard, two-pin plugs that are used across most of mainland Europe, so visitors from the UK and the US will need to bring a travel adaptor for use with laptops and other electrical devices. Some appliances from the US may also need a transformer (check the user's manuals for details).
- If you are on any prescribed medication, take enough to last for your entire visit. Many medicines—including some that are only available on prescription in other countries—can be obtained over the counter in a pharmacy (*Apotheke*; ▷ 413).
- It's a good idea to make photocopies of all important documents (passport, driver's licence and so on) and to keep these separate from the originals. It's also a good idea to make a note of emergency phone numbers (such as those required for cancelling stolen credit cards), the serial numbers of traveller's cheques and the registration numbers of expensive items like computers, in case you need to report a loss or theft to police.

PASSPORTS AND VISAS
- All visitors to Germany must carry a valid passport or, in the case of EU nationals, a national identification card.
- EU visitors do not require a visa for entry into Germany, although for stays of more than 90 days either a residence permit or a work permit will need to be applied for.
- Visitors from Australia, Canada, New Zealand and the US require a visa only for stays exceeding 90 days. The same goes for visitors from around 40 other countries.
- Visitors from other countries require a three-month tourist visa, which can be obtained from local German embassies or consulates. Fees vary depending on the country, and you may need to provide proof of having sufficient funds for your stay.

Visiting from another EU country
The amounts shown below are in line with other EU countries. There is no limit on the amount of foreign currency or euros that you can bring into Germany. Tax-paid goods for personal use (such as video cameras) can be brought in from other EU countries without customs charges being incurred. Guidance levels for tax-paid goods bought in the EU are as follows:

- 3200 cigarettes or
- 400 cigarillos or
- 200 cigars or
- 3kg of smoking tobacco

- 10 litres of spirits or
- 20 litres of fortified wine (such as port or sherry) or
- 90 litres of wine (of which only 60 litres can be sparkling wine) or
- 110 litres of beer

Visiting Germany from outside the EU
You are entitled to these allowances only if you travel with the goods and do not plan to sell them. Check the latest position with the customs department in your home country.

- 200 cigarettes or
- 100 cigarillos or
- 50 cigars or
- 250g of smoking tobacco

- 1 litre of spirits or strong liqueurs
- 2 litres of still table wine or 2 litres of fortified wine, sparkling wine or other liqueurs
- 50cc of perfume
- 250cc/ml of eau de toilette

Make sure you know how much wine you can take home

- The situation can change at short notice, so check with the German embassy in your home country before you travel.

TRAVEL INSURANCE
- In addition to covering the loss or theft of money and belongings, make sure your travel insurance covers repatriation in the event of an emergency.
- If you're planning to take part in any sports or adventurous activities, you should ensure you are covered for these.
- Report losses or thefts to the police as soon as possible (check individual insurance policies to see if there is a specified time limit), and be sure to obtain a signed and dated copy of your statement, as many insurance companies won't pay you any money without one.

HEALTH INSURANCE
- British visitors are advised to fill in an E111 form before leaving the UK. This entitles you to reciprocal healthcare in any EU country. The forms can be obtained from any post office in the UK. Without this form, you may be charged private rates, and your insurance company may not refund costs that you could have avoided with a completed E111. Note that from the end of 2004, you will need a new E111, even if you already hold one. During 2005, all new E111s will be replaced with a European Health Insurance Card (EHIC). Even with an E111 or EHIC, private insurance is still recommended.
- For those visiting Germany from outside the EU, private health insurance is strongly recommended.

PRACTICALITIES

ELECTRICITY
The power supply in Germany is 220V AC. Sockets take plugs with two round pins, so if you're planning on using your own electrical appliances such as hairdryers, laptops or radios, bring a travel adaptor with you (they don't cost very much and are sold at most international airports). Visitors from the US (where the power supply is 110V) should also bring a transformer from home, as these are harder to find in Germany.

LAUNDRY
All the major cities and many of the smaller towns in Germany have coin-operated laundrettes, or *Waschsalon*. Campsites often have their own washing facilities, and many hotels also offer a laundry service, although this is usually charged per item and so can get quite expensive when you start throwing in socks, underwear, T-shirts and the like.

MEASUREMENTS
The metric system is used throughout Germany. Distances and speed limits are given in kilometres and kph, fuel is sold by the litre, and food is sold by the gram or kilogram.

PUBLIC TOILETS
Finding a public toilet (*öffentliche Toilette*) in Germany isn't usually a problem, particularly in major towns and cities. Toilets in bars, restaurants and department stores are generally free, although it's impolite to use them without buying anything or asking first.

There are also public toilets at most train stations, bus stations and shopping malls, but there's often a charge for using them (from 25c to 50c). If there's an attendant on duty, it's polite to tip him or her around 25–50c, but only if the toilet is clean. Major train stations, bus stations and international airports may also have shower facilities.

Public toilets range from basic to space-age

SMOKING
Cafés and restaurants with non-smoking sections are the exception rather than the rule in Germany. For non-smokers, one way round this is to eat outside (when it's warm enough). Another option is to eat when restaurants aren't too busy (i.e. late morning or early afternoon for lunch, and early evening for dinner).

LOCAL WAYS
If you're hoping to practise your language skills, be aware that there are two forms of 'you' in German: the informal '*du*' and the more polite '*Sie*.' In general, you should always use *Sie* unless invited to do otherwise. Children, who are generally addressed as *du* by adults, are the only exception to this rule. Similarly, females should be addressed as *Frau* (Mrs) rather than *Fräulein* (Miss), and doctors should be addressed as *Herr Doktor*. Most Germans will be fairly forgiving if you get this sort of thing wrong, but they'll invariably warm to you more quickly if they can see you're making an effort to get it right.

When being introduced to Germans (by friends, for example), expect to shake hands with the men and sometimes to kiss the women on both cheeks—take your lead from the

CONVERSATION CHART		
FROM	**TO**	**MULTIPLY BY**
Inches	Centimetres	2.54
Centimetres	Inches	0.3937
Feet	Metres	0.3048
Metres	Feet	3.2810
Yards	Metres	0.9144
Metres	Yards	1.0940
Miles	Kilometres	1.6090
Kilometres	Miles	0.6214
Acres	Hectares	0.4047
Hectares	Acres	2.4710
Gallons	Litres	4.5460
Litres	Gallons	0.2200
Ounces	Grams	28.35
Grams	Ounces	0.0353
Pounds	Grams	453.6
Grams	Pounds	0.0022
Pounds	Kilograms	0.4536
Kilograms	Pounds	2.205
Tons	Tonnes	1.0160
Tonnes	Tons	0.9842

CLOTHING SIZES
Clothing sizes in Germany are in metric. Use the chart below to convert the size you use at home.

UK	Metric	USA	
36	46	36	
38	48	38	
40	50	40	SUITS
42	52	42	
44	54	44	
46	56	46	
48	58	48	
7	41	8	
7.5	42	8.5	
8.5	43	9.5	SHOES
9.5	44	10.5	
10.5	45	11.5	
11	46	12	
14.5	37	14.5	
15	38	15	
15.5	39/40	15.5	SHIRTS
16	41	16	
16.5	42	16.5	
17	43	17	
8	36	6	
10	38	8	
12	40	10	DRESSES
14	42	12	
16	44	14	
18	46	16	
20	46	18	
4.5	37.5	6	
5	38	6.5	
5.5	38.5	7	SHOES
6	39	7.5	
6.5	40	8	
7	41	8.5	

PLANNING

people you are being introduced to. If you're invited to someone's house for lunch or dinner, it's usually considered polite to take a small gift such as a bunch of flowers or a bottle of wine, as a thank you.

Another thing to bear in mind about Germans is that they take a fairly relaxed view of nudity. It's not uncommon to see naked women in adverts or on the covers of mainstream magazines, and many beaches and spa baths encourage nude bathing.

CHILDREN
Germany is very child-friendly, and family days out are commonplace throughout the country. There are numerous theme parks geared towards younger children (▷ 244), and most museums, theatres and zoos offer substantial discounts for younger visitors (although the age limit seems to vary considerably). Many hotels and guest houses also offer reduced rates for children, and public transportation is free for children under four and half-price for under-twelves.

Informal restaurants, bistros and cafés generally welcome children of all ages, particularly during the day or early in the evening, but if you do want to leave them behind, many hotels offer a babysitting service. Similarly, most tourist offices keep up-to-date lists of recommended babysitters and details of (usually very good) childcare facilities.

Car-rental companies can supply child safety seats for a nominal fee, but these must be reserved in advance. Finally, all manner of baby foods, milks, nappies

Some museums organize children's activities

(diapers) and other infant essentials can be found in most German supermarkets.

VISITORS WITH A DISABILITY
Germany is quite a wheelchair-friendly country, although other disabilities (such as blindness) tend to be less well catered for. Many museums, theatres and cinemas, plus train and bus stations, are wheelchair accessible, as are autobahn rest stops. Most trains and U-Bahns are also wheelchair accessible, and trams and buses are slowly catching up. The government agency responsible for assisting people with a disability publishes a number of useful leaflets on places and hotels with suitable facilities. For further details, write to Hilfe für Behinderte (Help for the Disabled), Kirchfeldstrasse 149, 40215 Düsseldorf.

Holiday Care in the UK has information on accessibility for visitors with disabilities (7th Floor, Sunley House, 4 Bedford Park, Croydon, Surrey CR0 2AP, tel 0845 124 9971, www.holidaycare. org.uk). In the US, SATH (Society for Accessible Travel and Hospitality) has lots of tips for visitors with visual impairment or reduced mobility (www.sath.org). Mobility International

Some U-Bahn and S-Bahn stations have wheelchair access—look for the symbol

(www.miusa.com) also offers disability advice (▷ 68).

PLACES OF WORSHIP
The two main religions in Germany are Catholicism and Protestantism, although there are also sizeable Muslim and Jewish communities—plus dozens of other religions—all over the country. The south of Germany is predominantly Catholic while the north and east are predominantly Protestant, although there are pockets of Catholicism in the far north. Religious tolerance is preached and (to a large extent) practised throughout Germany, and although religion is no longer as important as it was, say, 20 or 30 years ago, it still plays a large part in many people's lives. Most tourist offices (▷ 419) have information on local places of worship and service times, as do the places themselves.

Remember to dress appropriately when visiting places of worship.

There are plenty of places to worship in Germany

PLANNING

MONEY MATTERS

THE EURO

Since January 2002, Germany's currency has been the euro (indicated by the symbol €), which at the time of writing it shares with 11 other EU countries (Austria, Belgium, Finland, France, Greece, Italy, Luxembourg, the Netherlands, Portugal, the Republic of Ireland and Spain). All euro coins have one side dedicated to their country of origin, while all euro notes are identical across the euro zone. Both coins and notes can be used in any of the countries listed above, regardless of where they were minted.

BEFORE YOU GO

It's a good idea to take a combination of cash, traveller's cheques and credit cards when travelling to Germany, so that you don't have to rely on any one means of paying for things in the event of an emergency. Change a small amount of cash before you go or when you get to the airport—enough to cover you for a day or two.

Traveller's cheques are a safe bet for the rest of your money, but make a note of the serial numbers and keep these in a safe place, separate from the cheques themselves.

Also check with your credit or debit card company whether you can withdraw money from ATMs (cashpoints); the exchange rate is usually quite good, although you may have to pay a fixed fee each time you withdraw money, so it makes sense not to take it out in dribs and drabs. Make a note of the number you need to call if your card is stolen. Internationally recognized credit cards, in particular MasterCard and Visa, are accepted at major hotels, fuel stations, large shops and supermarkets, but it's always a good idea to check in advance in smaller hotels, restaurants and shops, as they may prefer cash.

EXCHANGE RATES

The exchange rate for the euro is subject to daily fluctuations. At the time of writing, €1 was worth approximately £0.69, US$1.23, or CDN$1.65.

BANKS

There are plenty of banks throughout Germany, and most will exchange foreign currency. International airports and many bigger cities also have currency exchanges.

BANKNOTES AND COINS

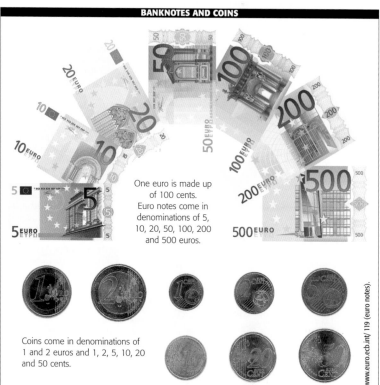

One euro is made up of 100 cents.
Euro notes come in denominations of 5, 10, 20, 50, 100, 200 and 500 euros.

Coins come in denominations of 1 and 2 euros and 1, 2, 5, 10, 20 and 50 cents.

www.euro.ecb.int/ 119 (euro notes).

PLANNING

ATMS

Automatic teller machines (ATMs, or cashpoints) are widespread throughout Germany, and can be found in all but the smallest towns and villages. Cards with a Maestro, Cirrus, Delta or Plus logo can be used to withdraw cash and pay for goods and services all over the country. Many credit and debit cards are now allocated a four-digit security number that can be used instead of a signature. If you don't have a security number, you may need to show another form of ID, such as a passport or driver's licence, when paying for goods over the counter.

POST OFFICES

Post offices (*Postämter*) are normally found in the middle of towns and cities and are often at or near the train station. *Poste restante* letters and parcels can be sent to any German post office: Simply mark the item '*postlagernd—bitte halten*', and then write your surname in capitals followed by the address of the post office. You will usually be asked to show some ID, such as a passport or driver's licence, when collecting it. Officially, post offices will only hang on to uncollected mail for two weeks, so it's a good idea to plan any advance correspondence carefully. Mail posted in Germany usually reaches the UK in three to four days, the US in four to five days and Australia or Asia in about a week.

EXCHANGING MONEY

Banks and currency exchanges (*Wechselstuben*) invariably charge a flat fee or a commission

ATMs often have instructions in various languages

(typically €3 for amounts under €100, or 1 per cent—with a minimum charge of €5—for amounts above €100). Currency exchanges offer reasonable rates, and can be found at all international airports and main train stations throughout Germany. Money can also be changed at some of the bigger post offices in major towns and cities. Traveller's cheques can be changed in banks, currency exchanges and post offices, but they aren't usually accepted as payment in shops, restaurants and hotels.

WIRING MONEY

Money can be wired from home, but it's very expensive (as much as 10 per cent commission is charged for small amounts) and so is best avoided if at all possible. If you find yourself short of money, Western Union (www.westernunion.com) and MoneyGram (www.moneygram.com) can arrange instant cash transfers through many of Germany's major main street banks.

TAX REFUNDS

VAT, or sales tax, is called *Mehrwertsteuer* (MwSt) in Germany, and currently stands at 16 per cent. Non-EU citizens can reclaim this tax (minus any administrative fees) when they leave the EU. Not all shops stock the necessary tax-free shopping cheques, so if you're planning on buying anything expensive, it's worth double checking this beforehand. (This facility is often indicated by a sign in the window saying 'tax-free for tourists' in English.) Participating shops will issue a cheque for the amount to be refunded, which can then be cashed at a VAT cash refund office (found at all international airports and harbours). The cheque, along with the receipt, must be stamped by customs when you leave the country, and strictly speaking you're not allowed to use tax-free goods until you've left the EU. Alternatively, tax can also be reclaimed through the Global Refund Tax Free Shopping Service, which is offered by major retailers all over the world. For more details, log onto www.globalrefund.com.

DISCOUNTS

Children, students and senior citizens can get substantial discounts for many services and attractions in Germany, from public transportation to museum admissions. With this in mind, it's always a good idea to carry some proof of age or status, such as a passport, International Student Identity Card (ISIC) or International Youth Travel Card (IYTC). You can get an ISIC from your student union or from CTS. Contact www.ctstravelusa.com in the US or www.ctstravel.co.uk in the UK. An ISIC costs US$10 or £7; an IYTC costs US$10 or £6.

Don't forget to tip the barmaid

TIPPING

At restaurants, bistros and cafes, the service charge is always included in the bill, so tipping is not compulsory, although most people will round up the bill, perhaps adding 5 to 10 per cent. For other services, the following are rough guidelines:

Bar service	Change
Tour guide	Optional
Hairdresser	5–10 per cent
Taxi driver	5–10 per cent
Chambermaid	€3–€6

10 EVERYDAY ITEMS AND HOW MUCH THEY COST	
Cup of tea or coffee	€1–€2
Bottle of water	80c–€1
Glass of wine	€2–€4
Glass of beer	€2–€3
Daily paper	60c–€1
Camera film	€4.50–€6
20 cigarettes	€3.50–€4
Sandwich	€2.50–€4
Ice cream	€1–1.50
Litre (0.26 US gallons) of petrol	€1.20

HEALTH

Germany's national health service works alongside the private sector, and hospitals and clinics are of a very high standard. Visitors from EU countries can claim free medical treatment, provided they have filled out an E111 form (▷ 408 and below for details). However, private health insurance is still recommended—and essential for visitors from non-EU countries.

BEFORE YOU GO
● No inoculations are required for visiting Germany, although it's a good idea to make sure your tetanus protection is up to date (boosters are required every 10 years).
● If you are on any medication and think you might need a repeat prescription while you're away, ask for it well before you travel, and keep the packaging and/or the prescription in case you run out or lose your medication while you're in Germany.
● If you are planning to stay in Germany for a month or more, it may also be a good idea to have a full dental and medical check-up before you go.

WHAT TO TAKE
Although Germany hasn't got a reputation for scorching summers, the sun can still be quite fierce, so it's important to take plenty of high-SPF suncream, particularly if you're travelling with children. A basic first-aid kit is also useful. This could include:
● After-sun to soothe sore, sunburned skin.
● Wet wipes for cleaning and refreshment.
● Antihistamine cream for insect stings or bites.
● Antihistamine pills if you suffer from hay fever.
● Antiseptic cream, spray or wipes for cuts and grazes.
● Fabric plasters (Band Aids).
● Motion sickness remedies, if this is likely to be a problem.
● Painkillers such as paracetamol (acetominophen) for colds, and ibuprofen for muscular aches and pains.

IF YOU NEED TREATMENT
The quality of healthcare in Germany is comparable to that

If you need a pharmacist, look for this distinctive sign

of the UK, US and Canada. Germany has an agreement with other EU countries that entitles all EU citizens to free reciprocal healthcare, including emergency hospital treatment. However, to take advantage of this, UK residents must fill out an E111 form (available from most post offices) and have it checked and stamped by the post office prior to departure. Note that, even if you already have a completed E111, you will need to obtain a new one. During 2005, E111s are being phased out and replaced with a European Health Insurance Card (EHIC), which will be sent automatically to holders of new E111s. The EHIC will serve the same purpose as the E111, but it's worth noting that this should not be seen as an alternative to adequate travel insurance, as (for example) reciprocal healthcare will not cover the costs of repatriation in the event of an emergency, or the cost of travel plans that have to be curtailed as a result of illness. Nor does form E111 cover private treatment.

US visitors should check that their existing travel/health insurance is valid in Germany.

EMERGENCY TREATMENT
In the event of an emergency, go to the casualty department (Emergency Room) of the nearest hospital; for most minor ailments, visit a pharmacy (*Apotheke*) or a doctor (see below).

FINDING A DOCTOR
If you need a doctor (*Doktor*), ask at your hotel or your nearest pharmacy, who will be able to find one who is on call.

FINDING A HOSPITAL
Public hospitals are listed in the phone book under *Krankenhäuser*, although most hotels and guest houses should be able to point you in the right direction if required.

PHARMACIES
Pharmacies (*Apotheken*) can be found in every town and almost every village in Germany. They are more common than they are in the UK or US, although in Germany they generally stock pharmaceuticals, toiletries and cosmetics, which are also available at a *Drogerie*.

German pharmacists are highly trained and can offer excellent over-the-counter advice; as such they're usually the first port of call for minor ailments, or if you're not sure whether or not you need to see a doctor. Generally speaking, you should be able to find someone who speaks at least some English to help you decide.

If you think you might need a repeat prescription while you're away, ask your doctor for the chemical name (rather than the brand name) of the drug before you travel, as it may be marketed under a different name in Germany. In larger towns, a rota system ensures that there is always at least one pharmacy open 24 hours a day—which one it is on any given night is displayed in other pharmacy windows in the area.

WATER
It is completely safe to drink the tap water in Germany, although mineral water (*Mineralwasser*) is also widely available. It's sold *mit Kohlensäure* (carbonated) or *still* (still).

SUMMER AND WINTER HAZARDS
If you find yourself in the middle of a summer heatwave, take adequate precautions against sunburn and dehydration. Wear light, loose-fitting clothing and cover all exposed areas with high-SPF suncream. Drink at least two litres (4 pints) of water or other non-diuretic drinks a day (diuretic drinks such as tea and coffee actually contribute to dehydration by making you want

PLANNING

to go to the toilet), and avoid doing anything too strenuous in the heat of the midday sun, particularly if you've got any children in tow.

In winter, it's important to stay wrapped up, especially if you're planning on doing any skiing, trekking or mountaineering. Wear lots of thin layers rather than one thick one, carry a warm hat and gloves and take a waterproof jacket in case of wet weather.

DENTAL TREATMENT

Dental treatment is expensive in Germany, so if you're having any problems with your teeth it makes sense to get them looked at before you leave. It's also a good idea to make sure your travel or medical insurance covers the cost of emergency dental care. If you need a dentist (*Zahnarzt*), again your hotel will be able to help, or ask at the pharmacy.

OPTICIANS

If you wear glasses or contact lenses, take spares with you, and have a copy of your prescription handy in case you break or lose them. If you're going for a few weeks and don't want to carry lots of contact lens solution with you, it's easy enough to resupply at any *Apotheke* (pharmacy). Opticians (*Optiker*) are listed in the phone book.

COMMON AILMENTS

The two most common ailments you're likely to suffer from in Germany are diarrhoea (from eating unfamiliar foods) and dehydration (from not drinking enough on hot days or during periods of prolonged activity). The former is unlikely to last more than a day or two, while the latter is easily treated with plenty of sugary drinks (water alone often isn't enough), or, in severe cases, a rehydration solution.

ALTERNATIVE MEDICINE

There is a long tradition of alternative medicine, or *Heilpraxis*, in Germany, particularly at spa resorts and towns. For a list of practitioners, including osteopaths, chiropractors, homoeopaths and acupuncturists, look up 'Heilpraktiker' in the local phone book.

HEALTHY FLYING

● Visitors to Germany from as far as the US, Australia or New Zealand may be concerned about the effect of long-haul flights on their health. The most widely publicized concern is Deep Vein Thrombosis, or DVT. Misleadingly called 'economy class syndrome', DVT is the forming of a blood clot in the body's deep veins, particularly in the legs. The clot can move around the bloodstream and could be fatal.

● Those most at risk include the elderly, pregnant women and those using the contraceptive pill, smokers and the overweight. If you are at increased risk of DVT see your doctor before departing. Flying increases the likelihood of DVT because passengers are often seated in a cramped position for long periods of time and may become dehydrated.

To minimize risk:
Drink water (not alcohol)
Don't stay immobile for hours at a time
Stretch and exercise your legs periodically
Do wear elastic flight socks, which support veins and reduce the chances of a clot forming

EXERCISES

1 ANKLE ROTATIONS	2 CALF STRETCHES	3 KNEE LIFTS

Lift feet off the floor. Draw a circle with the toes, moving one foot clockwise and the other counterclockwise

Start with heel on the floor and point foot upward as high as you can. Then lift heels high keeping balls of feet on the floor

Lift leg with knee bent while contracting your thigh muscle. Then straighten leg pressing foot flat to the floor

Other health hazards for flyers are airborne diseases and bugs spread by the plane's air-conditioning system. These are largely unavoidable but if you have a serious medical condition seek advice from a doctor before flying.

SUNBURN INDEX
SKIN TYPE

Index	Fair, burns	Fair, tans	Brown skin	Black skin
1/2	Low	Low	Low	Low
3/4	Medium	Low	Low	Low
5	High	Medium	Low	Low
6	Very high	Medium	Medium	Low
7	Very high	High	Medium	Medium
8	Very high	High	Medium	Medium
9	Very high	High	Medium	Medium
10	Very high	High	High	Medium

Low risk: The sun is not likely to harm you, but you should still use sun cream.
Medium risk: Do not stay in direct sunlight for more than 1–2 hours.
High risk: You could burn in 30–60 minutes. Avoid direct sunlight, cover up and use sunscreen of SPF 15+.
Very high risk: You could burn in 20–30 minutes. Avoid direct sunlight, cover up and use sunscreen of SPF 15+.

FINDING HELP

EMERGENCY NUMBERS

**Ambulance
(Krankenwagen)**
112

**Fire Brigade
(Fuerwehr)**
112

Police (Polizei)
110

**Roadside Rescue (ADAC—
Allgemeiner Deutscher
Automobil-Club)**
01802 22 22 22

CONTACTING YOUR EMBASSY IN BERLIN

If you lose your passport or are arrested, contact your embassy at the address below:

Australia	Wallstrasse 76–79, 10179 Berlin	tel 030 880 08 80
Canada	Friedrichstrasse 95, 10117 Berlin	tel 030 20 31 20
New Zealand	Friedrichstrasse 60, 10117 Berlin	tel 030 20 62 10
Republic of Ireland	Friedrichstrasse 200, 10117 Berlin	tel 030 22 07 20
UK	Willhelmstrasse 70–71, 10117 Berlin	tel 030 20 45 70
US	Neustädtische Kirchstrasse 4–5, 10117 Berlin	tel 030 830 50

If you have any concerns about your safety while you're in Germany, talk in the first instance to an English-speaking member of staff at your hotel or at your nearest tourist office, as they will almost certainly be able to advise you on where to go for help.

PERSONAL SECURITY

Germany is quite a safe country and crimes committed against visitors are rare, although some of the larger cities inevitably have areas that are best avoided (these are usually away from the main tourist areas, so shouldn't really present a problem). There are, however, some sensible precautions that are worth taking wherever you are:

● Never carry more cash with you than you need, and keep all valuable and irreplaceable items in your hotel room or, better still, in a hotel safety deposit box. Note down credit card and traveller's cheque numbers and keep them in a safe place.

● Carry bags and cameras slung diagonally across your chest rather than over one shoulder, and position them under one arm in

This SmartCar helps the police to negotiate streets of historic towns...

busy places. Backpacks might seem like a good idea, but when they're worn using both straps it's almost impossible to keep an eye on them. If you must use a backpack, make sure that the zips are either lockable (i.e. with a miniature padlock) or hard to access. Again, if you're at all concerned about busy crowds, turn the backpack round and wear it on your front where you can see it.

● In public places, keep belongings close by: Try to get out of the habit of leaving wallets, mobile phones, sunglasses and the like on tables, as this just increases the chances of them being stolen or forgotten. In busy eateries, particularly outside, make sure bags are securely closed, and put a chair leg through a strap to dissuade would-be thieves.

● Be wary of anyone who appears to invade your personal space, particularly if they bump into you. Avoid keeping wallets and other valuables in back pockets, where they're easy to get to. Similarly, never leave luggage or valuables on display in a parked car—in fact, even maps and other travel paraphernalia are a giveaway to a potential thief, so try to keep everything hidden whenever you're away from your car for any length of time.

● At night, stick to brightly lit, main streets whenever possible and avoid quiet areas.

LOST PROPERTY

If you lose money or valuables, inform the police and, depending on the small print of your policy, your travel insurance company as

...while this larger car has more of a presence in the cities

PLANNING

soon as possible (to be covered, lost or stolen belongings often have to be reported within 24 hours). Similarly, if your traveller's cheques are lost or stolen, notify the issuing company and tell them the serial numbers of the missing cheques (for this reason, it's also a good idea to keep a note of their telephone number and the serial numbers of the cheques you have spent).

LOSS OF PASSPORT
● Always keep a note of your passport number, and make a photocopy of the page that carries your details. Store both of these separately from your passport in case it is stolen.
● If you're really organized, you could also scan the relevant page of your passport and email it to

an account that's accessible from any computer, such as at www.hotmail.com.
● Finally, if you do lose your passport or have it stolen, report it to the police as soon as possible, and contact your nearest embassy or consulate for assistance (▷ 415).

CONTACTING YOUR EMBASSY OR CONSULATE
Many countries are represented by an embassy in Berlin, and may also operate consulates in other major cities. In addition to the main embassies in Berlin, for example, there are British, American and Canadian consulates in Düsseldorf, Hamburg, Stuttgart and Munich, and British and Australian consulates in Frankfurt.

EMERGENCIES
In an emergency, phone 110 for the police and 112 for the fire or ambulance services. The latter number can be phoned from anywhere in the EU for any type of emergency. It's worth emphasizing, however, that 110 is an emergency number only, and should not be used for non-urgent calls, such as reporting a theft. Thefts should be reported to your nearest police station, where you should be able to find someone who speaks at least a little English. You will need to show some form of photo ID when reporting a theft. Many insurance companies won't pay out for lost or stolen goods without a police report, so for expensive items it's worth the trouble.

COMMUNICATION

USEFUL TELEPHONE NUMBERS
Directory enquiries (national) **11833**
Directory enquiries (international) **11834**
Directory enquiries (English-speaking) **11837**

INTERNATIONAL DIALLING CODES	
To call home from Germany, dial the international access code (00) followed by the country code:	
Australia	61
Canada	1
New Zealand	64
Republic of Ireland	353
UK	44
US	1

AREA CODES WITHIN GERMANY	
Berlin	030
Bonn	0228
Dresden	0351
Düsseldorf	0211
Frankfurt	069
Hamburg	040
Köln (Cologne)	0221
Leipzig	0341
München (Munich)	089
Stuttgart	0711

With internet cafés springing up all over Germany and with email access now available in many hotels, keeping in touch while you're away has never been easier. Many mobile phones can be used all over Europe, although call charges can be expensive, and mobile companies also charge a fair whack for receiving a call from home. Text messages are one way of keeping costs down, but if you're planning on phoning home a lot, it may be worth investing in a prepaid phone card (▷ 417).

Now there's no excuse not to call home

TELEPHONES
As you'd expect, the telephone system in Germany is fast, efficient and relatively inexpensive. The country code for Germany is 49, and the main phone company is Deutsche

Telecom. To call the UK from Germany, dial 00 44, then drop the first 0 from the area code before dialling the rest of the number. To call the US, simply prefix the area code and number with 001. To call Germany from

abroad, dial the relevant international access code (i.e. 00 from the UK and 001 from the US) and the country code, followed by the local area code without the zero, and then the number.

Using your mobile phone while abroad can be expensive—check the rates with your supplier before leaving home

PUBLIC TELEPHONES

Most pay phones in Germany accept only phone cards (*Telefonkarte*), which can be bought at tourist or post offices, fuel stations, newspaper kiosks and elsewhere. International calls can be made from all pay phones except for those marked '*National*'. Phone calls can also be made from main post offices, where the connection will be made for you; you pay after the call has been completed. If you're using a phone card to call abroad, shop around for the best rates (these are usually printed on the back of the cards), as these vary from company to company. Similarly, avoid using the phone in your hotel room for external calls, as this could well work out to be up to four times more expensive than using a pay phone. If you must call from your room, get the person at the other end to call you back, as they'll only be charged their standard national or international rate.

The number for directory enquiries is 11833 for domestic numbers, 11834 for foreign numbers and 11837 for English-language enquiries. Call rates from private phones are lower after 6pm and at weekends, but public phones cost the same no matter what time you call.

MOBILE PHONES

Check with your mobile supplier to see if your phone will work in Germany, and to find out what the charges will be to make and receive calls and text messages. Most phones bought in the UK are dual band, and should work all over Europe. For visitors from North America, only tri-band phones will work in Europe. Again, if you're unsure whether your phone is dual band or tri-band, check with your supplier. Don't forget to take a phone charger and a plug adaptor in case the batteries run low.

POSTAL SERVICES

Mail boxes in Germany are bright yellow and can be found outside and inside main post offices. Stamps (*Briefmarken*) can be bought from the post office counter or from stamp machines near the entrance—it's usually clear on these which stamps are required for postcards and/or letters abroad. In areas popular with visitors, some souvenir shops may also sell

Look for the bright yellow mailboxes

POSTAGE RATES FOR LETTERS UP TO 20G	
Within Germany	55c
To western Europe	55c
To eastern Europe	55c
To Australia	€1.55
To America	€1.55
To Africa	€1.55
To Asia	€1.55

stamps, but don't count on it. The postal service in Germany is generally quite quick: Letters sent within Germany usually arrive the following day, while letters to the rest of Europe may take three to four days. Letters sent to North America, Australia or Asia should take around a week, although they can take longer.

INTERNET ACCESS

There are plenty of internet cafés dotted all over Germany, so you shouldn't have any problem finding one in most major cities. Many hotels also offer internet access, either via a high-speed ISDN line in each room, or from a computer at or near reception. Expect to pay anything from €1 to €2 for every half-hour, depending on where you are.

OPENING TIMES AND TICKETS

Museum opening times vary— check the Sights section for details

ADMISSION CHARGES

Most visitor attractions in Germany charge an admission fee, and these can start to add up if you're paying for a whole family. To encourage you to visit more places, some cities sell welcome cards, which entitle you to significant discounts in museums, as well as free public transportation. If you're planning on packing it in, these cards are definitely worth the initial outlay. (See the individual site entries for details.)

Some museums offer free or reduced price entry on a certain day or after a certain time—again, check individual entries for details, or ask at your nearest tourist information office.

YOUTH AND STUDENT DISCOUNTS

Full-time (but not part-time) students can buy an international student identity card, or ISIC, which provides proof of student status as well as entitling users to a wide range of reductions on everything from air fares to CDs. Under-27s can buy the International Youth Travel Card, which offers similar benefits, although at most attractions discounts are available only for full-time students or children aged 18 or under.

OPENING TIMES

Germany's traditionally strict shopping laws have been relaxed considerably in recent years, which means that shops can now stay open until 8pm from Monday to Saturday, although that's not to say they actually do so. For the most part, only bakeries are open on Sunday and even they may open up for only a few hours during the morning.

Banks

Banks tend to open from 8.30 or 9 and close at 4 (6 on Thursdays). Some smaller places may close for an hour or two at lunchtime. Banks are closed at weekends, although currency exchanges (particularly those at airports and train stations) may stay open from 6am to 10pm, seven days a week.

Bars, Restaurants and Cafés

Eateries and bars are generally open all day, although some live-music venues may open in the evening only. Bars tend to stay open until at least 1 or 2am, while many restaurants and cafés will close at midnight and will stop serving food at 10 or 11pm. Cafés usually open at 8 or 9am, while restaurants open for lunch at 11 or 11.30. In smaller towns and villages, particularly in the winter, restaurants may serve food only between noon and 2pm and then again after 5 or 6.

Churches

Churches have sporadic opening hours, but most of them—particularly the more famous churches and cathedrals—are open for at least a few hours every morning and a few hours every afternoon, six or even seven days a week. There is rarely, if ever, a charge for entry and most publish a leaflet or fact sheet in English as well as German.

Museums

Museum opening hours vary, but they're generally from 9 or 10 until 5 or 6, with or without a one-hour break for lunch between 1 and 2. Many of the bigger art galleries, particularly in major cities, are open late (7 or 8) one evening a week. Most are closed for one day each week, usually Mondays.

Tourist Information Offices

Tourist information offices also keep sporadic opening hours, but most of them are open from around 9 to 5 on weekdays and 10 to 1 on Saturdays. In the high season (April to September) they may also be open on Sundays, and in major cities they will often stay open seven days a week (and occasionally well into the evening).

Offices

Standard business hours in Germany vary greatly, but are generally from 9 to 5 or 5.30. Government offices may close earlier, at 4 from Monday to Thursday, and as early as 1 on Fridays.

Shops

Shops in Germany tend to be open from 9 to 5 or 6 on weekdays and 9 to 4 or 5 on Saturdays. In smaller towns and villages, particularly in the winter, shops may close at 1 or 2 on Saturdays. Larger shops, such as department stores and supermarkets, may stay open later on weekdays and on Saturdays (i.e. until 7 or 8), while fuel stations are often open until 9 or 10pm, if not later.

PLANNING

TOURIST OFFICES

Almost every town and village in Germany has a tourist information office, and the staff invariably speak at least some English. In larger towns and cities, staff members are likely to be pretty fluent, so getting hold of advice and information on your destination should never be a problem. Similarly, almost every tourist office has at least some printed information in English, even if it's just a map and a town guide; in bigger cities there's almost as much information available in English as there is in German.

Many tourist information offices also operate an accommodation booking service, where you tell them your budget and the sort of place you're looking for, and they phone around to book a room for you. The service is free in many places, but even when there's a charge it's unlikely to be more than a euro or two. Even if you're not looking for somewhere to stay, tourist information offices make a great first point of contact when you've just arrived in a region or city. Many tourist information offices run a variety of guided tours, and although these might sound a bit tacky and touristy, a few hours in the company of a local expert will make the world of difference to how much enjoyment you get out of your stay.

The tourist information offices will help you find all the best places to see

TOURIST INFORMATION OFFICES IN GERMANY

Below are the contacts details for tourist information offices in Germany's main towns:

Berlin	Europa-Center, Budapester Strasse 45, 10787 Berlin	tel 030 250025
Bonn	Windeckstrasse 1, 53103 Bonn	tel 0228 775000
Dresden	Postfach 120952, 01010 Dresden	tel 0351 491920
Frankfurt am Main	Hauptbahnhof, 60329 Frankfurt am Main	tel 069 2123 8800
Hamburg	Hauptbahnhof (Kirchenallee), Hamburg	tel 040 3005 1201
Köln (Cologne)	Unter Fettenhennen 19, 50667 Köln	tel 0221 2213 0400
Leipzig	Richard-Wagner-Strasse 1, 04109 Leipzig	tel 0341 7104260
München (Munich)	Marienplatz, 80331 München	tel 089 2339 6500
Stuttgart	Königstrasse 1a, Stuttgart	tel 0711 2228240

GERMAN TOURIST BOARD OFFICES ABROAD

Australia (also New Zealand)	G.P.O. Box 1461, Sydney, NSW 2001	tel 02 8296 0488
Canada	480 University Avenue, Suite 1410, Toronto, Ontario, M5G 1V2	tel 416/968 1685
UK (also Republic of Ireland)	P.O. Box 2695, London, W1A 3TN	tel 020 7317 0908
US	P.O. Box 59594, Chicago, IL 60659-9594	tel 773/539-6303
	8484 Wilshire Boulevard, Suite 440, Beverly Hills, CA 90211	tel 323/655-6085
	122 E. 42nd Street, 52nd Floor, New York, NY 10168-0072	tel 212/661-7200

PLANNING

MEDIA, BOOKS, MAPS AND FILMS

TELEVISION

The two biggest state-run television networks in Germany are ARD (usually channel 1) and ZDF (usually channel 2), but there are a few smaller networks, most of them regional. There are also dozens of cable channels, which usually require a satellite dish. Most mid-range hotels get all of these channels plus either CNN or Sky News, and many also get other English-language channels such as Eurosport and BBC World.

RADIO

In terms of its content, German radio peddles the same sort of stuff that you'll find anywhere in Europe, America, Australia or Asia. Mainstream pop and rock dominate the airwaves, with classics and oldies coming a close second and classical music a distant third. Adverts are hard to escape, and many shows feature as much chat as music, so if your German's not up to much, finding a consistently good music channel can be a frustrating experience. If you're desperate to hear some English-speaking broadcasters there are a number of options: The BBC World Service can be found at various wavelengths on both AM and FM (depending on where you are in the country), while BFBS (British Forces Broadcasting Service) airs music, news and chat across much of western Germany. The American Armed Forces Radio and Television Service, meanwhile, broadcasts throughout the day in the south of the country.

NEWSPAPERS AND MAGAZINES

The leading quality national dailies in Germany are the conservative *Frankfurter Allgemeine Zeitung* and the more liberal *Süddeutsche Zeitung* (both based in Munich). Less high brow are *Die Welt* and the sensationalist tabloid *Bild*, the two main dailies of the right-wing Springer group. Also popular are weekly news magazines such as *Der Spiegel* and *Focus*, and women's weeklies such as *Brigitte*, which usually feature in-depth investigative reports alongside more light-hearted

NEWSPAPERS AND NEWS MAGAZINES
Bild Zeitung
Germany's most widely read daily, with a circulation of around 5 million. Tabloid sensationalism with a conservative slant.
Focus
Similar to Der Spiegel (see below) but with a more modern, eye-catching layout. Not unlike Time or Newsweek in the US.
Frankfurter Allgemeine Zeitung
National daily. One of Germany's most prestigious papers, with conservative views.
Der Spiegel
A highly respected weekly news magazine with a reputation for hard-hitting investigative journalism that's often highly critical of the incumbent government.
Die Zeit
A respected weekly with social democratic leanings and around half a million readers.

articles. English-language papers that can usually be found in the major cities include the *International Herald Tribune* (based in Paris), the *Financial Times* (based in London) and the *Wall Street Journal* (based in New York). *Time* and *Newsweek* are also widely available at airports, main train stations and large bookstores. Most towns and cities also have their own dailies or weeklies, plus one or more listings magazines, which may or may not be available in English.

BOOKS

It's perhaps inevitable that some of the best writing on Germany focuses not on vineyards and olive groves, as seems to be the case for France and Spain, but on its history. Arguably the best novel ever written about World War I is Erich Maria Remarque's *All Quiet on the Western Front* (1929), which says more about the futility of war than anything written before or since. *The Rise and Fall of the Third Reich* (1960), written by journalist William L. Shirer, remains required reading for anyone interested in World War II, as does A.J.P. Taylor's *The Origins of the Second World War* (1961). *The Longest Day* (1959), by Cornelius Ryan, is a graphic account of the D-Day landings and was made into a successful

Bookshops abound in Germany, but you will also find German-based novels at home

Hollywood film in 1962 by Daryl F. Zanuck. *Escape from Sobibor* (1982), by Richard Rashke, and *Schindler's Ark* (also 1982), by Thomas Keneally, both provide harrowing accounts of life in Nazi concentration camps. One of the most recent books to come out of this period is the highly recommended *My Wounded Heart* (2004) by Martin Doerry, based on letters smuggled out of Breitenau and Auschwitz concentration camps by the author's grandmother.

Less serious but no less intriguing is *Fatherland* (1992) by Robert Harris, a thriller that imagines Europe as it might have been had Hitler won the war. For similarly gripping fiction, John le Carré's *The Spy Who Came in from the Cold* (1963) has a fantastic finale set at Checkpoint Charlie along the Berlin Wall. For a more light-hearted read, try to

PLANNING

get hold of a copy of *A Tramp Abroad* (1880) by Mark Twain, which includes two chapters on Germany and a hilarious postscript entitled 'The Awful German Language'.

MAPS AND OTHER PUBLICATIONS

The Automobile Association in the UK publishes the *Big Road Atlas Germany*, which highlights scenic sites and routes, and which also has detailed maps of all major towns and cities. For a more general overview, the AA's 1:800,000 double-side map of the whole of Germany is great for planning your trip and getting your bearings. A smaller scale atlas of Germany can be found on pages 428–443 of this book. If you don't get a chance to buy a map before you go, road maps and atlases in Germany are usually of a very high standard and can be bought at most major bookshops and fuel stations.

Tourist offices have detailed maps of cities and nearby attractions. In addition, there are maps of the following cities in this book: Berlin (▷ 120–121), Hamburg (▷ 79), Köln (Cologne; ▷ 103), Dresden (▷ 157) and München (Munich; ▷ 178–179). There is also a U-Bahn map of Berlin on page 53. A regional map is on page 7, an airport and port map on page 48, a map showing main road networks on page 56 and a map showing main rail networks on page 60. All of the drives in this book are also accompanied by a simplified map, as are the walks in Berlin and Munich.

Maps for Hikers

Specially designed tourist maps showing footpaths and bicycle routes in popular destinations are widely available throughout Germany (look for *Wanderkarte* or *Sonderkarte*).

For a complete list of available maps, contact Stanfords at 12–14 Long Acre, London, WC2E 9LP (tel 020 7836 1321), or log onto their website at www.stanfords.co.uk. Also try www.mapstore.com and www.mapsworldwide.com.

FILMS

A seminal film on World War I is Lewis Milestone's classic *All Quiet on the Western Front*, based on Erich Maria Remarque's novel of the same name (▷ 420). It was made in 1930, but has lost none of its meaning and power in the intervening years. Another

The movies are popular in Germany and often dubbed into German

German-language film that beats any subsequent Hollywood blockbuster is Wolfgang Petersen's *Das Boot* (*The Boat*; 1981), based on Lothar-Günther Buchheim's book of the same name. In this exciting and disturbingly realistic film, the fear and claustrophobia of living on a German U-boat is brought vividly to life.

Locally filmed World War II movies that are hard to beat include Steven Spielberg's *Schindler's List* (1993) and *Saving Private Ryan* (1998), which despite their Hollywood pedigree and occasional sentimentality deal unflinchingly with the horrors of war. Less harrowing but certainly no less moving is Roberto Benigni's *Life is Beautiful* (1998), a bittersweet comedy set in a Nazi concentration camp; if this film doesn't make you cry, nothing will.

Equally entertaining but much more light-hearted is Wolfgang Becker's *Good-bye Lenin!* (2003), which hilariously documents a young man's attempts to keep the fall of Communism and the collapse of the Berlin Wall from his stalwart socialist mother (▷ 23).

SPECIALIST MAP SHOPS	
UK	
National Map Centre	22–24 Caxton Street, London SW1H 0QU (tel 020 7222 2466), www.mapsnmc.co.uk
Stanfords	12–14 Long Acre, London WC2E 9LP (tel 020 7836 1321), www.stanfords.co.uk
US	
The Complete Traveler	199 Madison Avenue, New York, NY 10022 (tel 212/685-9007)
Map Link, Inc.	30 S La Patera Lane, Unit 5, Santa Barbara, CA 93117 (tel 805/692-6777), www.maplink.com

TREKKING AND CLIMBING GUIDEBOOKS
Bourne, Grant and Kröner-Bourne, Sabine, *Walking in the Bavarian Alps*, Cicerone Press, Milnthorpe, UK (1997)
Castle, Alan, *Walking the River Rhine Trail*, Cicerone Press, Milnthorpe, UK (1999)
McLachlan, Gordon, *Germany's Romantic Road*, Cicerone Press, Milnthorpe, UK (1997)
Speakman, Fleur and Speakman, Colin, *Walking in the Black Forest*, Cicerone Press, Milnthorpe, UK (1990)
Speakman, Fleur and Speakman, Colin, *Walking in the Harz Mountains*, Cicerone Press, Milnthorpe, UK (1994)

USEFUL WEBSITES

GENERAL TOURIST INFORMATION
www.germany-info.org
German Embassy site, with an emphasis on politics, business and cultural affairs.
www.germany-tourism.co.uk
A superb website providing comprehensive information on all things German.

BACKPACKERS
www.backpackers.com
An excellent site for backpackers or those travelling on a budget.

DOCUMENTATION
www.fco.gov.uk
Up-to-the minute advice from the British Foreign Office about getting help abroad.
www.travel.state.gov
The website of the US Department of State Bureau of Consular Affairs.

DRIVING
www.aaa.com
No information on driving abroad, but you can order your International Driving Permit here.
www.adac.de
Website of Germany's equivalent of the AA in the UK and the AAA in the US. German only.
www.tank.rast.de
Provides a list of autobahn service stations, including those with facilities for travellers with disabilities.
www.theaa.com
Up-to-date advice and information from the UK's leading motoring organization, plus a route planner to help you map out your itinerary in advance.

FESTIVALS
www.germany-tourism.co.uk
The official website of the German Tourist Board in the UK provides comprehensive information on festivals and events throughout the country.

FOOD AND DRINK
www.gaultmillau.de
Although only in German, this website is easy to navigate: Click on *Unsere Besten* for a list of recommended restaurants, which have been graded out of 20. There are links to those with their own websites.

www.schlemmer-atlas.de
Although not as easy for non-German speakers to navigate as the above, you can search for restaurants regionally by clicking on the home page's map.
www.varta-guide.de
As well as listing selected hotels in Germany (see hotels below), this website provides information in German on the pick of the country's restaurants.

HEALTH
www.cdc.gov
Website of the Center for Disease Control, the US's leading authority on health and travel abroad.
www.doh.gov.uk/traveladvice
Travel-specific information from the UK's Department of Health.
www.who.int
The official website of the World Health Organization.

HOTELS
www.bed-and-breakfast.de
Provides a list of bed-and-breakfast options across Germany for those on a budget.
www.hotelguide.de
Features a selection of around 10,000 hotels in Germany, from pensions to palaces.
www.hotellerie.de and www.hrs.de
On-line booking for hotels across Germany, in English (the latter is also available in 28 other languages).
www.varta-guide.de
A guide recommending hotels throughout Germany to suit all tastes and budgets.

MUSEUMS
www.icom.org
The International Council of Museums website. Listings and virtual tours of some of the world's most famous museums, including a handful in Germany.
www.europeanmuseumguide.com
An excellent online directory providing information on the best museums in Europe.

VISITORS WITH A DISABILITY
www.access-able.com
A US-based website for people with a disability.
www.dircsa.org.au
An Australia-based website.
www.dpa.org.nz
A New Zealand-based website.
www.radar.org.uk
A UK-based website offering advice and information to people with a disability.
www.tourismforall.org.uk
Another UK-based organization dedicated to improving access to visitor attractions.

WEATHER
www.weatheronline.com and www.weather.com
Comprehensive worldwide weather forecasts.
www.met-office.gov.uk
UK-based site offering one- and five-day forecasts for countries throughout Europe.

WORKING HOLIDAYS
www.travelalternatives.org
Information on working holidays all over the world.

You can do much of the research for your trip on the internet

PLANNING

GERMAN WORDS AND PHRASES

There is one official standard German language, *Hochdeutsch* (High German), which is taught in school and which everyone in the country should be able to understand. However, regional dialects, with strong local accents, are widely spoken in many areas. The words and phrases that follow are High German, and the guide below should help you with the pronunciation.

Vowels:

a	short as in hand, or long as in father
e	short as in bet, or long as in day
i	short as in fit
o	short as in lost, or long as in coach
u	long as in boot
ä	short as in wet, or long as in wait
ö	long as in fur
ü	long as in blue

Vowels are always short after a double consonants, and long when followed by 'h'

Dipthongs:

ai	as in mine	ie	as in tree
ei	as in spy	eu	as in boy
au	as in how	äu	as in boy

Consonants:

b is like **p** }
d is like **t** } at the end of a word or syllable
g is like **k** }
ch is either a throaty sound, like the Scottish lo**ch**, after a, o, u and au, or an exaggerated **h** sound after i, e ä, ö, eu, and ie
j is like **y** in **y**acht
s is either like **z** in **z**ip when the first letter of the word, or like **s** in bu**s** if it goes before a consonant
sch is like **sh** in **sh**ut
sp and st are pronounced **shp** and **sht**
v is like **f** in **f**it when the first letter of the word
w is like **v** in **v**ery

°CONVERSATION

What is the time?
Wie spät ist es?

I don't speak German
Ich spreche kein Deutsch

Do you speak English?
Sprechen Sie Englisch?

I don't understand
Ich verstehe nicht

Please repeat that
Wiederholen Sie das, bitte

Please speak more slowly
Sprechen Sie bitte langsamer

Write that down for me please
Schreiben Sie das bitte auf

Please spell that
Buchstabieren Sie das, bitte

My name is...
Ich heisse...

What's your name?
Wie heissen Sie?

Hello, pleased to meet you
Guten Tag, freut mich

This is my friend
Das ist mein Freund/meine Freundin

This is my wife/husband/daughter/son
Das ist meine Frau/mein Mann/meine Tochter/mein Sohn

Where do you live?
Wo wohnen Sie?

I'm from …
Ich komme aus ...

Good morning/afternoon
Guten Morgen/Tag

Good evening/night
Guten Abend/gute Nacht

Goodbye
Auf Wiedersehen

How are you?
Wie geht es Ihnen?

Fine, thank you
Sehr gut

MONEY

Is there a bank/currency exchange office nearby?
Ist hier in der Nähe eine Bank/Wechselstube?

I'd like to change sterling/dollars into euros
Ich möchte Pfund/Dollars in Euro tauschen

Can I use my credit card to withdraw cash?
Kann ich mit meiner Kreditkarte Geld abheben?

USEFUL WORDS

yes **ja**	thank you **danke**	where **wo**	when **wann**	why **warum**
no **nein**	you're welcome **bitte schön**	here **hier**	now **jetzt**	who **wer**
please **bitte**	excuse me! **entschuldigung**	there **dort**	later **später**	may I/can I **darf ich/kann ich**

IN TROUBLE

Help
Hilfe

Stop, thief
Haltet den Dieb

Can you help me, please?
Können sie mir bitte helfen?

Call the fire brigade/police/an ambulance
Rufen sie die Feuerwehr/ Polizei/einen Krankenwagen

Where is the police station?
Wo ist das Polizeirevier?

I need to see a doctor/dentist
Ich muss zum Arzt/Zahnarzt gehen

Please direct me to the hospital
Wie komme ich zum Krankenhaus?

I have lost my passport/ wallet/purse
Ich habe meinen Pass/meine Brieftasche/Handtasche

I have been robbed
Ich bin bestohlen worden

Is there a lost property office?
Gibt es hier ein Fundbüro?

I am allergic to …
Ich bin allergisch gegen …

I have a heart condition
Ich habe ein Herzleiden

COLOURS

black **schwarz**	purple **dunkellila**
blue **blau**	red **rot**
brown **braun**	turquoise **türkis**
green **grün**	yellow **gelp**
grey **grau**	white **weiss**
orange **orange**	light **hell**
pink **rosa**	dark **dunkel**

NUMBERS

0 **null**	7 **sieben**	14 **vierzehn**	21 **einundzwanzig**	90 **neunzig**
1 **eins**	8 **acht**	15 **fünfzehn**	30 **dreissig**	100 **hundert**
2 **zwei**	9 **neun**	16 **sechsehn**	40 **vierzig**	1000 **tausend**
3 **drei**	10 **zehn**	17 **siebzehn**	50 **fünfzig**	million **million**
4 **vier**	11 **elf**	18 **achtzehn**	60 **sechzig**	quarter **viertel**
5 **fünf**	12 **zwölf**	19 **neunzehn**	70 **siebzig**	half **hälfte**
6 **sechs**	13 **dreizehn**	20 **zwanzig**	80 **achtzig**	three quarters **dreiviertel**

SHOPPING

Could you help me, please?
Können Sie mir helfen, bitte?

I'm looking for …
Ich möchte …

When does the shop open/close?
Wann macht das Geschäft auf/zu?

I'm just looking, thank you
Ich sehe mich nur um, danke

Do you have anything less expensive/smaller/larger?
Haben Sie etwas Billigeres/ Kleineres/Grösseres?

How much is this?
Was kostet das?

Can you gift wrap this please?
Können Sie das bitte als Geschenk einpacken?

Do you accept credit cards?
Nehmen Sie Kreditkarten?

I'd like a kilo of …
Ich möchte ein Kilo …

I'd like ….grams please
Ich möchte … Gramm bitte

Do you have shoes to match this?
Haben Sie dazu passende Schuhe?

My American/English size is …
Meine amerikanische/ englische Grösse ist …

This is the right size
Das ist die richtige Grösse

This doesn't suit me
Das steht mir nicht

Do you have this in …?
Haben Sie das in …?

Should this be dry cleaned
Sollte das chemisch gereinigt werden?

I'll take this
Ich nehme das

ON THE ROAD

Can you direct me to…?
Wie komme ich zum/zur/nach …?

How many kilometres to…?
Wie viele Kilometer nach/ bis …?

Is this the way to…?
Ist dies der Weg nach …?

Excuse me, I think I am lost
Entschuldigen Sie, ich glaube ich habe mich verlaufen/ verfahren

What is the quickest route to…?
Was ist der schnellste Weg nach …?

Go straight on
Gehen Sie geradeaus

Turn left
Biegen Sie links ab

Turn right
Biegen Sie rechts ab

Head north/south
Gehen/Fahren Sie nach Norden/Süden

Cross over
Gehen/Fahren Sie über

Traffic lights
Die Ampel

Roundabout
Der Kreisverkehr

Intersection
Die Kreuzung

Corner
Die Ecke

Tunnel
Der Tunnel

One way
Einbahn

No parking
Parken verboten

Restricted parking
Beschränktes Parken

Pedestrian zone
Fußgängerzone

GETTING AROUND BY PUBLIC TRANSPORTATION

Where is the train/bus station?
Wo ist der Bahnhof/ Busbahnhof?

Does this train/bus go to …?
Fährt dieser Zug/Bus nach …?

Does this train/bus stop at …?
Hält dieser Zug/Bus in …?

Where are we?
Wo sind wir?

Do I have to get off here?
Muss ich hier aussteigen?

Where can I buy a ticket?
Wo kann ich eine Fahrkarte kaufen?

Please can I have a single/return ticket to …
Einmal einfach/hin und zurück nach … bitte

I would like a standard/first class ticket to…
Ich möchte eine Fahrkarte zweiter/erster Klasse nach …

Do you have a subway/bus map?
Haben Sie einen U-Bahn/ Busplan?

Where is the timetable?
Wo ist der Fahrplan?

Where is the information desk?
Wo ist die Auskunft?

Where can I find a taxi?
Wo bekomme ich ein Taxi?

Please take me to …
Fahren Sie mich bitte zum/zur/nach …

How much is the journey?
Was kostet die Fahrt?

Please turn on the meter
Stellen Sie bitte das Taxameter an

I'd like to get out here please
Ich möchte hier aussteigen

TOURIST INFORMATION

Where is the tourist information office/desk, please?
Wo ist die Touristeninformation, bitte?

Do you have a city map?
Haben Sie einen Stadtplan?

Where is the museum?
Wo ist das Museum?

Can you give me some information about…?
Können Sie mir etwas Information über … geben?

What are the main places of interest here?
Was sind hier die Hauptsehenswürdigkeiten?

Please could you point them out on the map
Können Sie sie mir bitte auf der Karte zeigen

What sights/hotels/restaurants can you recommend?
Welche Sehenswürdigkeiten/Hotels/ Restaurants können sie empfehlen?

Is there an English-speaking guide?
Gibt es einen Führer, der Englisch spricht?

Are there organized excursions?
Gibt es organisierte Ausflüge?

Can we make reservations here?
Können wir hier buchen?

Is there a discount for senior citizens/students?
Gibt es eine Ermässigung fewr Senioren/ Studenten?

Do you have a brochure in English?
Haben sie eine Broschüre auf Englisch?

TIMES/DAYS/MONTHS

Monday **Montag**	Friday **Freitag**	February **Februar**	June **Juni**	October **Oktober**	Yesterday **Gestern**
Tuesday **Dienstag**	Saturday **Samstag**	March **März**	July **Juli**	November **November**	Tomorrow **Morgen**
Wednesday **Mittwoch**	Sunday **Sonntag**	April **April**	August **August**	December **Dezember**	Day **Der Tag**
Thursday **Donnerstag**	January **Januar**	May **Mai**	September **September**	Today **Heute**	Week **Woche**

RESTAURANTS

Waiter/waitress
Kellner/Kellnerin

I'd like to reserve a table for … people at …
Ich möchte einen Tisch für … Personen um … reservieren

A table for …, please
Einen Tisch für … bitte

We have/haven't booked
Wir haben/haben nicht reserviert

Could we sit there?
Können wir dort sitzen?

Are there tables outside?
Gibt es draußen Tische?

We'd like something to drink
Wir möchten etwas zu trinken

Could we see the menu/wine list
Wier hätten gern die Speisekarte/Weinkarte

Do you have a menu/wine list in English?
Haben Sie eine Speisekarte/Weinkarte auf Englisch?

Is there a dish of the day?
Gibt es ein Tagesgericht?

What do you recommend?
Was empfehlen Sie?

I can't eat wheat/sugar/salt/pork/beef/dairy
Ich vertrage keinen Weizen/Zucker/kein Salz/Schweinefleisch/Rindfleisch/keine Milchprodukte

I am a vegetarian
Ich bin Vegetarier

I'd like…
Ich möchte …

Could we have some salt and pepper?
Könnten wir etwas Pfeffer und Salz haben

May I have an ashtray?
Kann ich einen Aschenbecher haben?

This is not what I ordered
Das habe ich nicht bestellt

The food is cold
Das Essen ist kalt

The meat is too rare/overcooked
Das Fleisch ist zu roh/verbraten

Can I have the bill, please?
Wir möchten zahlen, bitte

The bill is not right
Die Rechnung stimmt nicht

I'd like to speak to the manager, please
Ich möchte mit dem Geschäftsführer sprechen

The food was excellent
Das Essen war ausgezeichnet

HOTELS

Do you have a room?
Haben Sie ein Zimmer frei?

I have made a reservation for … nights
Ich habe ein Zimmer für … Nächte bestellt

How much per night?
Was kostet es pro Nacht?

Is the room air-conditioned/heated?
Hat das Zimmer eine Klimaanlage/Heizung?

Is there a lift in the hotel?
Hat das Hotel einen Fahrstuhl?

Do you have room service?
Haben Sie Zimmerservice?

When is breakfast served?
Wann gibt es Frühstück?

I need an alarm call at...
Ich möchte um … geweckt werden

May I have my room key?
Kann ich meinen Schlüssel haben?

Will you look after my luggage until I leave?
Kann ich bis zu meiner Abreise mein Gepäck hier lassen?

Where can I park my car?
Wo kann ich meinen Wagen parken?

Could I have another room?
Könnte ich ein anderes Zimmer haben?

I am leaving this morning
Ich reise heute Morgen ab

Please can I pay my bill?
Kann ich bitte meine Rechnung bezahlen?

Thank you for your hospitality
Vielen Dank für Ihre Gastfreundschaft

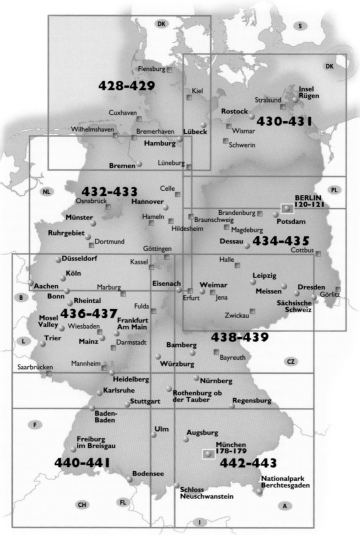

Toll motorway (Turnpike)

Motorway (Expressway)

Motorway junction with and without number

National road

Regional road

Railway

International boundary

Administrative region boundary

Built-up area

■ City / Town

National park

● Featured place of interest

✈ Airport

621
▲ Height in metres

– – Port / Ferry route

Mountain pass

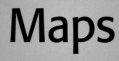

Maps

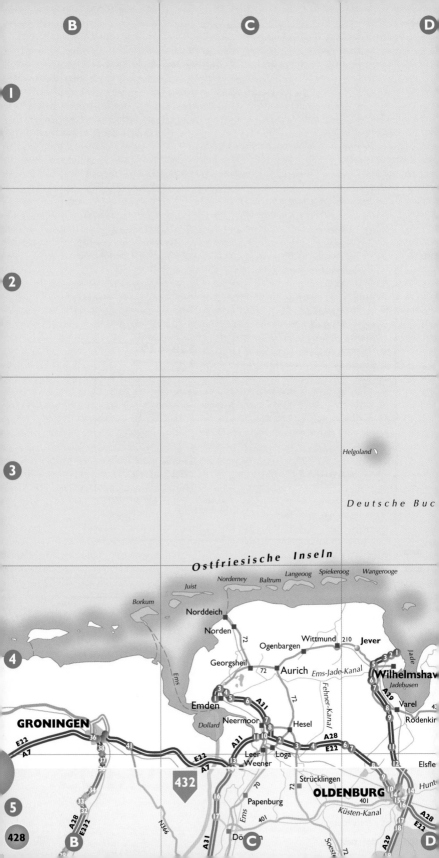

Helgoland

Deutsche Buc

Ostfriesische Inseln

Norderney   Langeoog   Spiekeroog   Wangerooge
Juist   Baltrum

Borkum

Norddeich

Norden

72

Ogenbargen   Wittmund   210   Jever

Georgsheil

72   Aurich   Ems-Jade-Kanal

Wilhelmshav

Ems

Jadebusen

Emden

A31

Varel

Dollard   Neermoor

Hesel

Rodenkir

GRONINGEN

72

A28

Elsfle

E22

A7   E22   A7

Leer   Loga

Weener

432

Strücklingen

Hunt

Papenburg   OLDENBURG

Küsten-Kanal

A28

E22

Ems   401

A29

2

Kap Arkona

Naturpark

Nationalpark
Jasmund

Hiddensee

Sassnitz

**Insel
Rügen**

3

E22/E251

Ostseebäder

96

E22

Stralsund

Samtens
Putbus

Löbnitz

Rügen

96

Reinberg

Greifswalder
Bodden

Abtshagen

E251

Grimmen

Greifswald

Zinnowitz

Poggendorf

194

109

111

Wolgast

Koserow

Usedom

Gnoien

Trebel

Loitz

Naturpark

Bansin
Heringsdorf

Dargun

110

Demmin

Jarmen

Usedom

Ziethen

Ahlbeck

KLENBURG-

Peene

Anklam

Stettiner
Haff

3

4

kow
erow

Kummerower
See

94

Golchen

Malchin

Tollense

E65

chiner

Reuterstadt
Stavenhagen

Altentreptow

Friedland

109

Uckermünder

3

Ferdinandshof

Randow

Heide

P O M M E R N

104

KI Plasten

A20

Varren

192

Tollense
See

Neubrandenburg

Pasewalk

SZCZECIN

Penzlin

104

Woldegk

104

PL

96

E251

s
e
e

**Müritz-
Nationalpark**

Möllenbeck

Naturpark

198

Göritz

A20

10

5

Neustrelitz

Feldberger

3

E65

irow

Wesenberg

Müritz

Nationalpark

Üecker

Prenzlau

A11

E28

A6

E28

10

Ravensbrück

Landschaft

198

Nationalpark

4

E65

Fürstenberg

Naturpark

109

Hassleben

Gramzow

3

96

Mittenwalde

Unteres

166

Uckermärkische

Milmersdorf

8

Odertal

Dannenwalde

Seen

Biosphärenreservat

Schwedt

Gransee

2

132

6

eur-
ppin

Alt Ruppin

B R A N D E N B U R G

Schorfheide-

Angermünde

Herzberg

Gross
Schönebeck

Lowenberg

Chorin

435

Liebenwalde

Naturpark

A11

Eberswalde

23

Finow

24

Oranienburg

E28

Bad Freienwalde

Barnim

167

E26

Biesenthal

Wriezen

Oder

Herzberg

25

30 31 32 33

Naturpark
Märkische
Schweiz

431

A111

34

Bernau

auen

A10

E55

Tegel

BERLIN

Oder
bruch

Spandau

J

BE LIN

Marxwald

K

132

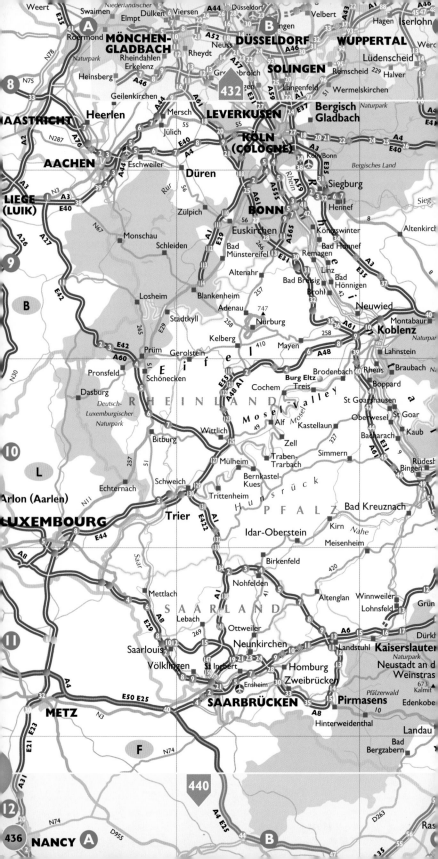

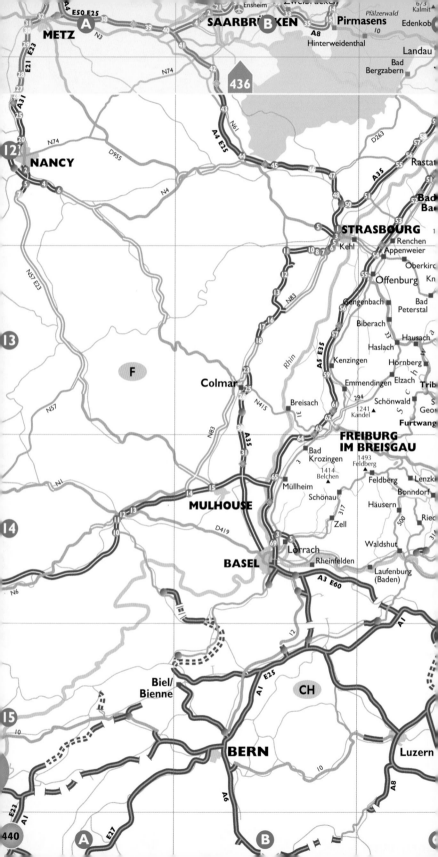

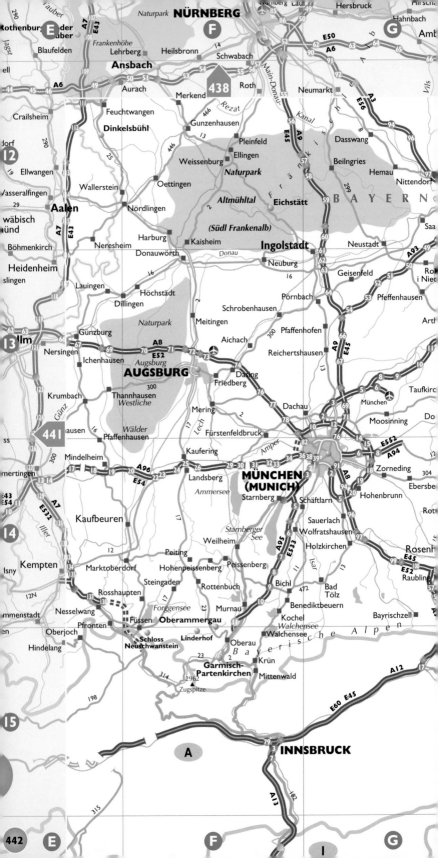

Dessau	434 H7	Emmendingen	440 B13

450 INDEX

452 INDEX

N

ACKNOWLEDGMENTS

Abbreviations for the credits are as follows:
AA = AA World Travel Library, t (top), b (bottom), c (centre), l (left), r (right), bg (background)

UNDERSTANDING GERMANY

4 AA/Jonathan Smith; 5cl AA/M. Jourdan; 5c AA/P. Bennett; 5cr AA/A. Kouprianoff ;6cl AA/S. McBride; 6c AA/T. Souter; 6cr AA/T. Souter; 6b AA/T. Souter; 8tl AA/P. Bennett; 8tr AA/D. Traverso; 8ctr AA/A. Kouprianoff; 8ctr AA/A. Kouprianoff; 8ctr AA/A. Kouprianoff; 8cbr AA/A. Kouprianoff; 8br AA/Jonathan Smith; 9tl AA/Jonathan Smith; 9ctl AA/P. Bennett; 9cl AA/M. Jourdan; 9cr AA/AS; 9cbl AA/M. Jourdan; 9bl AA/M. Jourdan; 10tr AA/T. Souter; 10ctr AA/T. Souter; 10cl AA/T. Souter; 10cr AA/A. Kouprianoff; 10cbr AA/M. Jourdan; 10bl AA/AS; 10br AA/A. Kouprianoff

LIVING GERMANY

11 AA/T. Souter; 12/13bg ©. 2001 Tourismus + Congress GmbH Frankfurt am Main; 12cl © Reuters/CORBIS; 12tc Rex Features Ltd; 12cr AA/M. Jourdan; 12bl AA/M. Jourdan; 13tl ©. 2001 Tourismus + Congress GmbH Frankfurt am Main; 13tr AA/M. Jourdan; 13cl AA/A. Kouprianoff; 14/15bg © 2001 Tourismus + Congress GmbH Frankfurt am Main; 14tl AA/T. Souter; 14tc AA/A. Kouprianoff; 14tr AA/T. Souter; 14ctl AA/P. Bennett; 14cl AA/T. Souter; 14b Rex Features Ltd; 15tl AA/T. Souter; 15c AA/T. Souter; 16/17bg AA/Jonathan Smith; 16tl AA/S. McBride; 16c © 2001 Tourismus + Congress GmbH Frankfurt am Main; 16cl AA/T. Souter; 16/17 © Reuters/CORBIS; 17c Rex Features Ltd., 17tr © 2001 Tourismus + Congress GmbH Frankfurt am Main; 18/19bg AA/S. McBride; 18tl AA/C. Sawyer; 18tc AA/D. Traverso; 18tr AA/T. Souter; 18bl AA/P. Bennett; 19t AA/S. McBride; 19cl AA/M. Jourdan; 19c AA/C. Sawyer; 19cr AA/M. Jourdan; 20/21bg AA/A. Kouprianoff; 20tl Junghaus Watches; 20tc Siemens Press Picture; 20tr Bosch Appliances; 20cl Daimler Chrysler Media Services; 20cr Bosch Appliances; 20bl Siemens Press Picture; 21tl Beiersdorf Corporate Images; 21tr Rex Features Ltd; 21cl Siemens Press Picture; 22/3t AA/P. Bennett; 22/3bg AA/P. Bennett; 22/3t AA/P. Bennett; 22tl AA/T. Souter; 22tr AA/P. Bennett; 22br AA/Jonathan Smith; 22/3c Rex Features Ltd; 23tl AA/P. Bennett; 23tr AA/Jonathan Smith; 24bg AA/P. Bennett; 24tl AA/A. Kouprianoff; 24c AA/P. Bennett; 24ctl AA/S. McBride; 24cr Rex Features Ltd; 24cbl © Joe McDonald/CORBIS

THE STORY OF GERMANY

25 AA/Jonathan Smith; 26/7bg AA; 26ctl AKG Images/Erich Lessing; 26cbl AA/A. Kouprianoff; 26bl AKG Images; 26cr © Archivo Iconografico/CORBIS; 26/7 AA/A. Kouprianoff; 27cl AA; 27c AA; 27br AA/A. Baker; 28/9bg AA/P. Bennett; 28c AA/P. Bennett; 28bl AA/P. Bennett; 28br AA/P. Bennett; 29ctl AA; 29cbl AKG Images; 29cr AKG Images; 29br AA/D. Traverso; 30/1bg AA; 30cl AKG Images; 30bl AKG Images; 30/1 Mary Evans Picture Library; 31ctc AA; 31cbc AA/A. Kouprianoff; 31cl AA; 31br Mary Evans Picture Library; 32/3 AA/Jonathan Smith; 32/3bg AA/Jonathan Smith; 32c AKG Images; 32cr AA; 32bl AA/A. Kouprianoff; 33cl AKG Images; 33clc AA/P. Bennett; 33c AA/P. Bennett; 33bl AKG Images; 33br © 2002 Tourismus + Congress GmbH Frankfurt am Main; 34/35bg AA; 34bl AA/C. Sawyer; 34cr AKG London; 34/35 AKG London;

35cl &clc AA/A. Kouprianoff; 35rc AA; 35br AA/P. Bennett; 36/7bg Mary Evans Picture Library; 36c Mary Evans Picture Library; 36bl AKG Images; 36br AA/C. Sawyer; 36/7 AKG Images; 37cl AKG Images; 37br AKG Images; 38/9bg Illustrated London News; 38ctr AA/M. Jourdan; 38c Illustrated London News; 38cbr AKG Images; 38bl Illustrated London News; 38/9 AKG Images; 39cl Illustrated London News; 39c AKG Images; 39br Mary Evans Picture Library; 40/41bg AA/C. Sawyer; 40c AKG Images; 40bl AKG Images; 40/41 AKG Images; 41cl Illustrated London News; 41c AKG Images; 41bc AA/T. Souter; 41br AKG Images; 42/43bg AA/T. Souter; 42c AA/D. Traverso; 42bl AA/T. Souter; 42/43b © David Turnley/CORBIS; 43cl AA/T. Souter; 43c AKG Images; 43c AKG Images; 43bl AA/S. McBride; 43br AKG Images; 44bg AA/Jonathan Smith; 44cl AA/T. Souter; 44cr © Reuters/CORBIS; 44bl AKG Images; 44br AA/S. McBride

ON THE MOVE

45 AA/S. McBride; 46t © 2001 Tourismus + Congress GmbH Frankfurt am Main; 47 © 2001 Tourismus + Congress GmbH Frankfurt am Main; 48t © 2001 Tourismus + Congress GmbH Frankfurt am Main; 49t © 2001 Tourismus + Congress GmbH Frankfurt am Main; 49c AA/T. Souter; 50t © 2001 Tourismus + Congress GmbH Frankfurt am Main; 50c AA/M. Jourdan; 50b AA/P. Bennett; 51t AA/S. McBride; 51c AA/T. Souter; 51b AA/S. McBride; 52t AA/S. McBride; 52c and 52b AA/Jonathan Smith; 53 AA/S. McBride; 54t AA/M. Jourdan; 54c AA/T. Souter; 54b AA/M. Jourdan; 55t AA/M. Jourdan; 55c AA/P. Bennett; 56t AA/M. Jourdan; 56b AA/P. Bennett; 57 AA/M. Jourdan; 58t AA/M. Jourdan; 58/59 AA/T. Souter; 58c AA/M. Jourdan; 59t AA/M. Jourdan; 61t AA/S. McBride; 61c AA/A. Kouprianoff; 62t AA/S. McBride; 62c AA/M. Trelawney.; 62b AA/T. Souter; 63t AA/T. Souter; 63c and 63b AA/M. Jourdan; 64t Air Berlin; 64bl AA/T. Souter; 64br © 2001 Tourismus + Congress GmbH Frankfurt am Main; 65t Air Berlin; 65ct Lufthansa; 65c AA/T. Souter; 66t AA/P. Bennett; 66c AA/T. Souter; 67t AA/P. Bennett; 67cl AA/P. Bennett; 67cr AA/P. Bennett; 68t AA/N. Setchfield; 68b AA/N. Lancaster

THE SIGHTS

69 AA/S. McBride; 70/71bg AA/S. McBride; 71tl AA/D. Traverso; 71tcl AA/D. Traverso; 71tr AA/P. Bennett; 72t AA/P. Bennett; 72c AA/P. Bennett; 72cr AA/P. Bennett; 72b AA/P. Bennett; 73cr AA/P. Bennett; 73br AA/P. Bennett; 74tl AA/A. Kouprianoff; 74tc AA/D. Traverso; 74tr AA/A. Kouprianoff; 74b AA/D. Traverso; 75tl AA/A. Kouprianoff; 75tr AA/D. Traverso; 76–81 AA/P. Bennett; 82–83 AA/A. Kouprianoff; 84–87 AA/P. Bennett; 88tl AA/D. Traverso; 88tc AA/P. Bennett; 88tr AA/P. Bennett; 88b AA/P. Bennett; 89tl AA/P. Bennett; 89tr AA/D. Traverso; 90 AA/P. Bennett; 91 AA/D. Traverso; 92tl AA/D. Traverso; 92tr AA/P. Bennett; 94–97 AA/A. Kouprianoff; 98–99 © 2001 Tourismus + Congress GmbH Frankfurt am Main; 100 AA/A. Kouprianoff; 101t AA/A. Kouprianoff; 100/101c AA/A. Kouprianoff; 101c AA/A. Hemmisen; 101cr AA/A. Hemmisen; 102cl AA; 102cr AA/A. Kouprianoff; 102b AA/A. Kouprianoff;

103bl AA/PE; 103br AA/A. Kouprianoff; 104 AA/A. Kouprianoff; 105t AA/A. Hemmisen; 105b AA/A. Kouprianoff; 106tl AA/D. Traverso; 106tc AA/A. Kouprianoff; 106tr AA/A. Kouprianoff; 107t AA/A. Kouprianoff; 107cr AA/A. Baker; 108t and 108cl AA/A. Kouprianoff; 108c AA/A. Baker; 108cr AA/A. Kouprianoff; 109tl AA/A. Kouprianoff; 109cr AA/A. Baker; 110tl AA/A. Kouprianoff; 110tr AA/D. Traverso; 111tl AA/A. Kouprianoff; 111c AA/A. Baker; 111tr AA/A. Kouprianoff; 112/117 AA/A. Kouprianoff; 118tl AA/A. Kouprianoff; 118tr AA/A. Baker; 122tl AA/T. Souter; 122tc AA/T. Souter; 122tr AA/S. McBride; 122b AA/Jonathan Smith; 123l AA/S. McBride; 123r AA/S. McBride; 124t AA/Jonathan Smith; 124cl AA/ T. Souter; 125t AA/S. McBride; 125cr AA/C. Sawyer; 126 AA/A. Baker; 127tl AA/S. McBride; 127tc AA/T. Souter; 127tr AA/C. Sawyer; 128tl AA/A. Baker; 128tr AA/Jonathan Smith; 129tl AA/A. Baker; 129tr AA/C. Sawyer; 129b AA/D. Traverso; 130 AA/Jonathan Smith; 131t AA/S. McBride; 131cl AA/Jonathan Smith; 131c AA/Jonathan Smith; 131cr *The Dance* or *Iris*, 1719–20 by Jean Antoine Watteau, Gemaldegalerie, Berlin/Giraudon/Bridgeman Art Library; 132 AA/Jonathan Smith; 133tl *Portrait of a Young Woman in a Pinned Hat*, c.1435 by Rogier van der Weyden, Gemaldegalerie, Berlin/Bridgeman Art Library; 133tr *Head of Christ*, c.1648 by Rembrandt Harmensz van Rijn, Gemaldegalerie, Berlin/Bridgeman Art Library; 134t *Portrait of the Merchant George Gisze*, 1532 by Hans Holbein the Younger, Gemaldegalerie, Berlin/Bridgeman Art Library; 134c *Portrait of Cornelius Anslo and his Wife* (detail), 1641 by Rembrandt Harmensz van Rijn, Gemaldegalerie, Berlin/Bridgeman Art Library; 134b AA/S. McBride; 136tl AA/R. Strange; 136tc AA/S. McBride; 136tr AA/T. Souter; 137t AA/A. Baker; 137cr AA/Jonathan Smith; 138t AA/Jonathan Smith; 138cl AA/Jonathan Smith; 138cr AA/S. McBride; 139 AA/Jonathan Smith; 140 AA/Jonathan Smith; 141tr AA/Jonathan Smith; 141b AA/T. Souter; 142tl AA/Jonathan Smith; 142b AKG Images; 143 AA/Jonathan Smith; 144t AA/S. McBride; 144cl AA/Jonathan Smith; 145 AA/S. McBride; 146t AA/T. Souter; 146cl AA/C. Sawyer; 146c AA/A. Baker; 146cr AA/S. McBride; 146b AA/Jonathan Smith; 147 AA/Jonathan Smith; 148t AA/A. Baker; 148cl and 148c AA/Jonathan Smith; 148cr AA/T. Souter; 149tr AA/T. Souter; 149b AA/Jonathan Smith; 150tl and 150c AA/C. Sawyer; 150tr AA/Jonathan Smith; 152–159 AA/P. Bennett; 160t AA/A. Kouprianoff; 160cl AA/A. Kouprianoff; 161tl AA/P. Bennett; 161tc AA/D. Traverso; 161tr AA/D. Traverso; 162–163 AA/P. Bennett; 164 AA/D. Traverso; 165–166 AA/P. Bennett; 167tl AA/A. Kouprianoff; 167tc AA/D. Traverso; 167tr AA/P. Bennett; 167b AA/P. Bennett; 168t, cl & c AA/S. McBride; 168–169 AA/S. McBride; 169c AA/S. McBride; 169cr AA/Jonathan Smith; 169b AA/S. McBride; 170tl AA/Jonathan Smith; 170b AA/S. McBride; 171 AA/S. McBride; 172tl AA/S. McBride; 172/173 AA/S. McBride; 172b AA/Jonathan Smith; 173cr AA/S. McBride; 173b AA/Jonathan Smith; 174–176 AA/P. Bennett; 180t AA/M. Jourdan; 180cl AA/A. Baker; 180cr AA/M. Jourdan; 181 AA/M. Jourdan; 182t *Two Children Eating a Melon and Grapes*, 1645–46, by Bartolome Esteban Murillo, Alte Pinakothek, Munich/Bridgeman Art Library; 182cl *Lamentation of Christ*, c. 1490 by Sandro Botticelli, Alte Pinakothek, Munich/Bridgeman Art Library; 182c *Self-Portrait at the age of 28*, 1500 by Albrecht Dürer, Alte Pinakothek, Munich/Bridgeman Art Library; 182cr AA/C. Sawyer; 183tr *Two Satyrs* (detail) by Peter Paul Rubens, Alte Pinakothek, Munich/Bridgeman Art Library; 183b *Adoration of the Magi* by Hans Holbein the Elder, Alte Pinakothek, Munich/Bridgeman Art Library; 184tl AA/T. Souter; 184tc AA/C. Sawyer; 184tr AA/T. Souter; 184b AA/C. Sawyer; 185tl AA/C. Sawyer; 185tr AA/M. Jourdan; 186–190 AA/M. Jourdan; 191cl AA/M. Jourdan; 191b Courtesy of the Deutsches Museum, Munich; 192t AA/T. Souter; 192cl AA/M. Jourdan; 193t AA/AB; 193cr AA/T. Souter; 194tl AA/C. Sawyer; 194r AA/M. Jourdan; 194c AA/T. Souter; 195tl AA/T. Souter; 195tr AA/M. Jourdan; 196–197 AA/C. Sawyer; 198 AA/T. Souter; 199 AA/M. Jourdan; 200t AA/M. Jourdan; 200cl AA/C. Sawyer; 200c and 200cr AA/M. Jourdan; 201b AA/M. Jourdan; 202tl AA/M. Jourdan; 202tr AA/T. Souter; 202b AA/M. Jourdan; 204tl AA/A. Baker; 204tr AA/T. Souter; 205 AA/A. Baker; 206 AA/M. Jourdan; 207 AA/A. Baker; 208–209 AA/T. Souter; 210t AA/M. Jourdan; 210cl AA/A. Baker; 210c AA/M. Jourdan; 210cr AA/A. Baker; 211 AA/M. Jourdan; 212 AA/A. Baker; 213–215 AA/M. Jourdan; 216tl AA/M. Jourdan; 216c AA/M. Jourdan; 216tr AA/T. Souter; 217 AA/A. Baker; 218t AA/M. Jourdan; 218cl AA/M. Jourdan; 218c AA/M. Jourdan; 218cr AA/A. Baker; 219c AA/M. Jourdan; 219bl AA/M. Jourdan; 219br AA/M. Jourdan; 220tl AA/M.Jourdan; 220tc AA/M. Jourdan; 220tr AA/A. Baker; 221 AA/A. Baker; 222 AA/M. Jourdan; 223b AA/A. Baker; 223cl AA/M. Jourdan; 224t AA/T. Souter; 224c AA/T. Souter; 224cl AA/T. Souter; 224cr AA/T. Souter; 224b AA/T. Souter; 225 AA/M. Jourdan; 226–227 AA/T. Souter; 228–229 AA/M. Jourdan; 230tl AA/A. Baker; 230tc AA/A. Baker; 230tr and 230b AA/M. Jourdan; 231 AA/M. Jourdan; 232 AA/T. Souter

WHAT TO DO

233 AA/M. Jourdan; 234/235t AA/S. McBride; 234 AA/S. McBride; 236/37t AA/T. Souter; 236 AA/Jonathan Smith; 236/7c AA/P. Bennett; 238t AA/T Souter; 238c AA/S. McBride; 239t Carlton Kosmetik; 239c AA/M. Jourdan; 240c AA/T. Souter; 240/1t AA/M. Jourdan; 241 AA/T. Souter; 242t AA/M. Jourdan; 242c AA/P. Bennett; 243t AA/T. Souter; 243c AA/P. Bennett; 244t AA/D. Traverso; 244l AA/M. Jourdan; 244r AA/M. Jourdan; 245t AA/T. Souter; 245 AA/T. Souter; 246/7t; AA/P. Bennett; 246 AA/P. Bennett; 247 AA/P. Bennett; 248/9 AA/P. Bennett; 248 AA/P. Bennett; 249 AA/D. Traverso; 250t AA/P. Bennett; 250 AA/P. Bennett; 251t AA/A. Baker; 251 AA/A. Kouprianoff; 252/3t AA/A. Baker; 252 AA/A. Kouprianoff; 253 AA/A. Kouprianoff; 254/5t AA/A. Baker; 254 © 2000 Tourismus + Congress GmbH Frankfurt am Main; 255 Digitalvision; 256/7t AA/A. Baker; 256 Image 100; 257 AA/A. Kouprianoff; 258t AA/A. Baker; 258 AA/A. Kouprianoff; 259t AA/T. Souter; 259 AA/S. McBride; 260/1t AA/T. Souter; 260 AA/Jonathan Smith; 261 AA/Jonathan Smith;

262/3t AA/T. Souter; 262 AA/S. McBride; 263 AA/N. Lancaster; 264/5t AA/T. Souter; 264 AA/T. Souter; 265 AA/Jonathan Smith; 266/7t AA/P. Bennett; 266 AA/P. Bennett; 267 AA/P. Bennett; 268/9 AA/P. Bennett; 268 AA/P. Bennett; 267 AA/P. Bennett; 270/1t AA/P. Bennett; 270 Brand X Pictures; 271 AA/D. Traverso; 272t AA/P. Bennett; 272 AA/P. Bennett; 273t AA/T. Souter; 273 AA/M. Jourdan; 274/5t AA/T. Souter; 274 AA/A. Baker; 275 AA/M. Jourdan; 276/7t AA/T. Souter; 276 AA/T. Souter; 277 AA/T. Souter; 278/9t AA/T. Souter; 278 AA/M. Jourdan; 279 AA/C. Sawyer; 280/1t AA/T. Souter; 280 AA/M. Jourdan; 281 Photodisc; 282/3t AA/T. Souter; 282 AA/A. Baker; 283 AA/A. Baker; 284/5t AA/T. Souter; 284 AA/M. Jourdan; 285 AA/M. Jourdan; 286t AA/T. Souter; 286 AA/M. Jourdan

OUT AND ABOUT

287 AA/M.Trelawney; 289–291 AA/P. Bennett; 292t AA/A. Kouprianoff; 292b AA/D. Traverso; 293–297 AA/A. Kouprianoff; 298 AA/S. McBride; 299 AA/C. Sawyer; 300–303 AA/P. Bennett; 304 AA/D. Traverso; 305–307 AA/P. Bennett; 308 AA/D. Traverso; 309 AA/P. Bennett; 310 AA/PD; 311t AA/T. Souter; 311c AA/C. Sawyer; 311b AA/T. Souter; 312 AA/T. Souter; 313 AA/M. Jourdan; 314–316 AA/A. Baker; 317 AA/A. Baker; 318t AA/M. Jourdan; 318cl AA/A. Baker; 318cr AA/T. Souter; 319 AA/M. Jourdan; 320–321 AA/M. Jourdan; 322–323 AA/A. Baker; 324t AA/A. Baker; 324b AA/M. Jourdan; 325 AA/M. Jourdan; 326 AA/A. Baker; 327t AA/A. Baker; 327b AA/M. Jourdan; 328t AA/A. Baker; 328b AA/M. Jourdan; 329–334 AA/M. Jourdan; 335 Mike Holzemer/Burgenreich; 336tl AA/P. Bennett; 336tc AA/M. Jourdan; 336tr AA/P. Bennett; 337 AA/Jonathan Smith

EATING

338 AA/T. Souter; 339cl AA/M. Jourdan; 339c AA/M. Jourdan; 339cr AA/T. Souter; 340cl AA/T. Souter; 340c AA/M. Jourdan; 340cr AA/P. Enticknap; 341cr AA/T. Souter; 341bl AA/P. Bennett; 342bl AA/P. Bennett; 342br AA/P. Bennett; 343r A. Kouprianoff; 344 AA/A. Kouprianoff; 345br AA/P. Bennett; 346–351 AA/A. Kouprianoff; 352br AA/N. Lancaster; 353r Hotel Adlon, Berlin; 355c AA/N. Lancaster; 356l AA/N. Lancaster; 357–360 AA/P. Bennett; 361b AA/Jonathan Smith;

361tl AA/P. Bennett; 362tl AA/P. Bennett; 362bl AA/P. Bennett; 362c AA/P. Bennett; 362r AA/P. Bennett; 363bl Augustiner; 364bl AA/M. Jourdan; 364br AA/M. Jourdan; 365tr AA/M. Jourdan; 365br Hackerhaus; 366bl AA/M. Jourdan; 366c AA/M. Jourdan; 366tr AA/M. Jourdan; 366bl Ratskeller; 367c AA/M. Jourdan; 367r AA/M. Jourdan; 368c AA/M. Jourdan; 368tr Zum Alten Markt; 370 Gasthof Frauendorfer; 371 AA/M. Jourdan; 373 Restaurant Zur Trini; 374 AA/M. Jourdan; 375 AA/M. Jourdan

STAYING

376cl AA/M. Jourdan; 376c AA/A. Kouprianoff; 376cr AA/M. Jourdan; 378bl AA/P. Bennett; 378cr AA/P. Bennett; 379tl AA/P. Bennett; 379bl AA/P. Bennett; 379c AA/A. Kouprianoff; 380l AA/P. Bennett; 380r AA/P. Bennett; 381/3 AA/A. Kouprianoff; 384l Hotel Adlon, Berlin; 384br AA/Jonathan Smith; 385–386 AA/Jonathan Smith; 387br AA/N. Lancaster; 387tc AA/Jonathan Smith; 387c Hilton, Berlin; 388tr AA/Jonathan Smith; 388cr Madison, Berlin; 388bc Meinecke Arte, Berlin; 389 AA/Jonathan. Smith; 390bl Swissotel, Berlin; 390c AA/Jonathan Smith; 390r AA/Jonathan Smith; 391 AA/P. Bennett; 392tc AA/A. Kouprianoff; 392tl AA/P. Bennett; 392bl AA/P. Bennett; 392bc AA/A. Kouprianoff; 392tr AA/P. Bennett; 393–395 AA/P. Bennett; 396cl Acanthus Hotel, Munchen; 396c AA/M. Jourdan; 396cr Carlton, Munchen; 397tc Hotel Apollo, Munchen; 397bc AA/M. Jourdan; 397cr AA/M. Jourdan; 398tl AA/M. Jourdan; 398tc Hotel Savoy, Munchen; 398bc Hotel Schlicker, Munchen; 399 AA/M. Jourdan; 401cr Gasthof Frauendorfer; 402c AA/M. Jourdan; 403c Parkhotel Sonnenhof; 403br AA/M. Jourdan; 404 Hotel Schranne

PLANNING

405 AA/Jonathan Smith; 406–407 AA/M. Jourdan; 408 AA/T. Souter; 409 AA/N. Lancaster; 410t AA/T. Souter; 410 AA/M. Jourdan; 412t AA/P. Bennett; 412b AA/T. Souter; 413 AA/M. Jourdan; 415t AA/P. Bennett; 415b AA/K. Gould; 416 AA/T. Souter; 417 AA/P. Bennett; 417tr AA/M. Jourdan; 417b AA/P. Bennett; 418 AA/M. Jourdan; 419l AA/M. Jourdan; 419r AA/P. Bennett; 420 AA/P. Bennett; 421 AA/T. Souter; 422 Photodisc

Project editor
Kathy Gould

Interior design
David Austin, Glyn Barlow, Kate Harling, Bob Johnson,
Nick Otway, Carole Philp, Keith Russell

Additional design work
The Company of Designers, Katherine Mead, Nautilus Design, Jo Tapper

Picture research
Kathy Lockley

Cover design
Tigist Getachew

Internal repro work
Susan Crowhurst, Ian Little, Michael Moody

Production
Lyn Kirby, Helen Sweeney

Mapping
Maps produced by the Cartography Department of AA Publishing

Main contributors
Margaret Campbell, Mike Ivory, Paul Grogan, Nicola Lancaster, Isla Love,
George McDonald, Derek Mackenzie-Hook

Copy editor
Susi Bailey, Audrey Horne

See It Germay ISBN 1-4000-1512-X

Published in the United States by Fodor's Travel Publications and simultaneously in Canada by
Random House of Canada Limited, Toronto. Published in the United Kingdom by AA Publishing.

Fodor's is a registered trademark of Random House, Inc., and and Fodor's See It
is a trademark of Random House, Inc.
Fodor's Travel Publications is a division of Fodor's LLC.

Colour separation by Keenes
Printed and bound by Leo, China

Special Sales: Fodor's Travel Publications are available at special discounts for bulk purchases for
sales promotions or premiums. Special editions, including personalized covers, excerpts of existing
guides, and corporate imprints, can be created in large quantities for special needs. For more
information, contact your local bookseller or write to Special Marketing, Fodor's Travel Publications,
1745 Broadway, New York, NY 10019. Inquiries from Canada should be directed to your local Canadian
bookseller or sent to Random House of Canada, Ltd., Marketing Department,
2775 Matheson Blvd. East, Mississauga, Ontario L4W 4P7.

A01610
Maps in this title produced from mapping © Mairs Geographischer Verlag / Falk Verlag, D-73751
Ostfildern, Germany.

Relief map images supplied by Mountain High Maps® Copyright © 1993 Digital Wisdom, Inc
Weather chart statistics supplied by Weatherbase © Copyright 2004 Canty and Associates, LLC
Communicarta assistance with distance/time charts gratefully acknowledged.

Important note: Time inevitably brings changes, so always confirm prices, travel facts,
and other perishable information when it matters. Although Fodor's cannot accept
responsibility for errors, you can use this guide in the confidence that we have taken
every care to ensure its accuracy.

Fodor's Key to the Guides

AMERICA'S **GUIDEBOOK LEADER** PUBLISHES GUIDES FOR **EVERY KIND OF TRAVELER**. CHECK OUT OUR MANY SERIES AND FIND YOUR **PERFECT MATCH**.

FODOR'S GOLD GUIDES

America's favorite travel-guide series offers the most detailed insider reviews of hotels, restaurants, and attractions in all price ranges, plus great background information, smart tips, and useful maps.

COMPASS AMERICAN GUIDES

Stunning guides from top local writers and photographers, with gorgeous photos, literary excerpts, and colorful anecdotes. A must-have for culture mavens, history buffs, and new residents.

FODOR'S CITYPACKS

Concise city coverage in a guide plus a foldout map. The right choice for urban travelers who want everything under one cover.

FODOR'S WHERE TO WEEKEND

A fresh take on weekending, this series identifies the best places to escape outside the city and details loads of rejuvenating activities as well as cool places to stay, great restaurants, and practical information.

FODOR'S AROUND THE CITY WITH KIDS

Up to 68 great ideas for family days, recommended by resident parents. Perfect for exploring in your own backyard or on the road.

FODOR'S TRAVEL HISTORIC AMERICA

For travelers who want to experience history firsthand, this series gives in-depth coverage of historic sights, plus nearby restaurants and hotels. Themes include the Thirteen Colonies, the Old West, and the Lewis and Clark Trail.

FODOR'S FLASHMAPS

Every resident's map guide, with 60 easy-to-follow maps of public transit, parks, museums, zip codes, and more.

FODOR'S LANGUAGES FOR TRAVELERS

Practice the local language before you hit the road. Available in phrase books, cassette sets, and CD sets.

THE COLLECTED TRAVELER

These collections of the best published essays and articles on various European destinations will give you a feel for the culture, cuisine, and way of life.

FODOR'S HOW TO GUIDES

Get tips from the pros on planning the perfect trip. Learn how to pack, fly hassle-free, plan a honeymoon or cruise, stay healthy on the road, and travel with your baby.

KAREN BROWN'S GUIDES

Engaging guides—many with easy-to-follow inn-to-inn itineraries—to the most charming inns and B&Bs in the U.S.A. and Europe.

OTHER GREAT TITLES FROM FODOR'S

Baseball Vacations, The Complete Guide to the National Parks, Family Vacations, Golf Digest's Places to Play, Great American Drives of the East, Great American Drives of the West, Great American Vacations, Healthy Escapes, National Parks of the West, Skiing USA.

Dear Traveler

From buying a plane ticket to booking a room and seeing the sights, a trip goes much more smoothly when you have a good travel guide. Dozens of writers, editors, designers, and cartographers have worked hard to make the book you hold in your hands a good one. Was it everything you expected? Were our descriptions accurate? Were our recommendations on target? And did you find our tips and practical advice helpful? Your ideas and experiences matter to us. If we have missed or misstated something, we'd love to hear about it. Fill out our survey at www.fodors.com/books/feedback/, or e-mail us at seeit@fodors.com. Or you can snail mail to the See It Editor at Fodor's, 1745 Broadway, New York, New York 10019. We'll look forward to hearing from you.

Tim Jarrell
Publisher